ROUTLEDGE HANDBOOK ON MIDDLE EASTERN DIASPORAS

Bringing together different strands of research on Middle Eastern diasporas, the *Routledge Handbook on Middle Eastern Diasporas* sheds light on diverse approaches to investigating diaspora groups in different national contexts.

Asking how diasporans forge connections and means of belonging, the analyses provided turn the reader's gaze to the multiple forms of belonging to both peoples and places. Rather than seeing diasporans as marginalised groups of people longing to return to a homeland, analyses in this volume demonstrate that Middle East diasporas, like other diasporas and citizens alike, are people who respond to major social change and transformations. Those we count as Middle Eastern diasporas, both in the region and beyond, contribute to transnational social spaces, and new forms of cultural expressions. Chapters included cover how diasporas have been formed, the ways that diasporans make and remake homes, the expressive terrains where diasporas are contested, how class, livelihoods and mobility inflect diasporic practices, the emergence of diasporic sensibilities and, finally, scholarship that draws our attention to the plurilocality of Middle Eastern diasporas.

Offering a rich compilation of case studies, this book will appeal to students of Middle Eastern Studies, International Relations, and Sociology, as well as being of interest to policymakers, government departments, and NGOs.

Dalia Abdelhady is Associate Professor in the Department of Sociology at Lund University, Sweden. Her work features the application of postcolonial analysis to the sociology of migration. Following a comparative perspective, her work focuses on the meeting point between individual immigrants (and their communities) and institutions in receiving countries (such as schools, labour markets, media and political policies). In addition to a number of journal articles and book chapters, she is the author of *The Lebanese Diaspora: The Arab Immigrant Experiences in Montreal, New York and Paris* (2011), and co-editor of *Refugees and the Violence of Welfare Bureaucracies in Northern Europe* (2020).

Ramy Aly is Assistant Professor of Anthropology at the American University in Cairo, Egypt. Ramy's first monograph *Becoming Arab in London: Performativity and the Undoing of Identity* was published in 2015. The book is the first ethnographic account of gender, race and class practices among British-born and -raised Arabs in London and attempts to provide an account of the everyday experiences of Arabness in the British capital. Ramy's research interests and publications engage with the anthropology of ethnicity, migration and diaspora; anthropology and media studies; cultural studies; and youth cultures.

'This volume offers an impressive range of theoretically up-to-date studies of Middle Eastern diasporas both in the region and internationally that are particularly valuable in building on recent insights in the field of diaspora studies and applying them creatively to different communities in a time of increasing transnational movement and connection.'

Anthony Gorman, *Senior Lecturer in Islamic and Middle Eastern Studies, University of Edinburgh, editor of* Cultural Entanglements in the Pre-Independence Arab World

'This is an excellent collection that showcases the richness of an anthropological approach to diasporic existence that never loses sight of people's experiences. The individual chapters do justice to the diasporic communities they are investigating, and the book as a whole through its excellent curation manages the difficult task of giving a holistic sense of the multiple diasporic processes of departure and arrival that mark the Middle East.'

Ghassan Hage, *Professor of Anthropology and Development Studies, Melbourne University, author of* The Diasporic Condition

'This groundbreaking volume is a *tour de force*, offering the single most comprehensive and transdisciplinary examination of Middle Eastern diasporas in the world today. Focusing on diasporic processes and sensibilities—or the multiple identifications and belongings of diasporans both within and well beyond the Middle Eastern region—this volume deconstructs controlling images and highlights instead the agency, creativity, dynamism, and global consciousness of those living in a wide range of diasporic settings. Historians, anthropologists, and political scientists of the Middle East will find this volume to be an invaluable resource, as will those interested in migration, globalization, and political activism.'

Marcia C. Inhorn, *William K. Lanman, Jr. Professor of Anthropology and International Affairs, Yale University, author of* Cosmopolitan Conceptions

ROUTLEDGE HANDBOOK ON MIDDLE EASTERN DIASPORAS

Edited by Dalia Abdelhady and Ramy Aly

LONDON AND NEW YORK

Cover image: Dreamstime

First published 2023
by Routledge
4 Park Square, Milton Park, Abingdon, Oxon OX14 4RN

and by Routledge
605 Third Avenue, New York, NY 10158

Routledge is an imprint of the Taylor & Francis Group, an informa business

© 2023 selection and editorial matter, Dalia Abdelhady and Ramy Aly; individual chapters, the contributors

The right of Dalia Abdelhady and Ramy Aly to be identified as the authors of the editorial material, and of the authors for their individual chapters, has been asserted in accordance with sections 77 and 78 of the Copyright, Designs and Patents Act 1988.

All rights reserved. No part of this book may be reprinted or reproduced or utilised in any form or by any electronic, mechanical, or other means, now known or hereafter invented, including photocopying and recording, or in any information storage or retrieval system, without permission in writing from the publishers.

Trademark notice: Product or corporate names may be trademarks or registered trademarks, and are used only for identification and explanation without intent to infringe.

British Library Cataloguing-in-Publication Data
A catalogue record for this book is available from the British Library

Library of Congress Cataloging-in-Publication Data
A catalog record has been requested for this book

ISBN: 978-0-367-21792-1 (hbk)
ISBN: 978-1-032-30440-3 (pbk)
ISBN: 978-0-429-26610-2 (ebk)

DOI: 10.4324/9780429266102

Typeset in Bembo
by Newgen Publishing UK

To Noot and Ryan, our diasporic children

CONTENTS

List of figures   xi
Notes on contributors   xii
Acknowledgements   xix

1 Coming to and coming from the Middle East: the unfolding of diaspora   1
   Dalia Abdelhady and Ramy Aly

PART I
Forming diasporas   21

2 To be denied a homeland: British Mandate policy and the making of the Palestinian diaspora in Chile   23
   Nadim Bawalsa

3 The AKP government in Turkey and diaspora-making: lobbying, public diplomacy and the erasure of difference   39
   Bengi Bezirgan-Tanış

4 Critical events and the formation of a Coptic diaspora in North America between Al-Khanka and Al-Zāwiya Al-Hamrā   52
   Michael Akladios

5 Opportunities here and there: digital diasporas and the Iranian American election moment   66
   Hajar Yazdiha

6   The limits of diaspora: double vulnerabilities among Eritreans in
    Saudi Arabia   78
    Nicole Hirt and Abdulkader Saleh Mohammad

PART II
Making and remaking homes   89

7   The lifecycle of Amazigh diaspora activism in Europe: from institutional
    pioneers to the new ethnicities of the postmodern age   91
    Ángela Suárez-Collado

8   The diasporic Amazigh movement in France: articulating indigeneity   104
    Jonathan Harris

9   Valorising some and marginalising others: the diasporic field in the
    making of Lebanon   117
    Paul Tabar and Wahib Maalouf

10 Transnational networks in Tunisia's democratisation: Diaspora activism
    in France and Italy   130
    Alessandra Bonci

11 Secularism, sectarianism and the transnational connectivity of the
    Lebanese diaspora in Senegal   143
    Mara A. Leichtman

PART III
Expressive terrains of contestation   157

12 The semantics and substance of contesting Turkishness in
    the diaspora   159
    Pinar Dinc

13 De-orientalising queer Iranian diasporic identities   171
    Farhang Rouhani

14 Queering diaspora through visual art: contesting the double binds of
    homonationalism   181
    Andrew Gayed

15 Post-*tarab* identities in diaspora: a sonic imaginary of Arab Canada 197
    Jillian Fulton-Melanson

16 Resisting marginalisation, renegotiating gender: intersectional narratives of diaspora experiences 209
Dalia Abdelhady

17 Creativity as a contested site of identity-making: careers, gender and diaspora for Sydney's Lebanese Australians 221
Sherene Idriss

PART IV
Class, livelihood and mobility 235

18 Exploring the creative Israeli diaspora: reading class and profession in the diaspora 237
Nir Cohen and Steven J. Gold

19 Making middle-class lives: diaspora and belonging among Pakistanis in Dubai 250
Gennaro Errichiello

20 Diasporic before the move: China's Hui Muslims' trade and ties with Iran and Muslimness 262
Man Xu

21 A diasporic balancing act: Syrian entrepreneurs in Turkey, Egypt and Jordan 274
Ching-An Chang

22 Diaspora Syrians and humanitarian aid in the Syrian civil war 286
Shawn Teresa Flanigan

PART V
Diasporic sensibilities 301

23 Return migration and repatriation: myths and realities in the interwar Syrian *mahjar* 303
Stacy D. Fahrenthold

24 The emergence of diasporic sensibilities among Iraqis in London 316
Zainab Saleh

25 Healed pasts, multiple belongings and multifocal engagements: a Danish-Palestinian diaspora tour 328
Nina Gren

26 Idioms of care: ageing and connectivity among older Turkish
    migrants in Sweden   341
    Öncel Naldemirci

27 The Egyptian Muslim Brotherhood in Turkey after the 2013
    coup: organisational renewal and renegotiation in the diaspora   351
    Lucia Ardovini

PART VI
Plurilocal diasporas, rethinking *mahjar*   365

28 The Hadrami diaspora: a plurilocal *mahjar*   367
    Iain Walker

29 Hadrami connections with the Malay world: creole histories,
    transcultural Islam and racialisation   383
    Sumit K. Mandal

30 Towards a new mode of reading Muslim diaspora writing: Muslimness
    and the homing desire in Abu-Jaber's *Crescent* and Shafak's *The Saint of
    Incipient Insanities*   394
    Neriman Kuyucu

31 The Armenian Middle East: boundaries, pathways and horizons   405
    Sossie Kasbarian

32 Negotiating placemaking: public-private spaces and Hinduism
    in Oman   420
    Sandhya Rao Mehta

Index   *433*

FIGURES

14.1	*Be My Guest.*	185
14.2	*Be My Guest.* Detail of chair.	185
14.3	*Be My Guest.* Detail of pattern.	186
14.4	*Be My Guest.* Detail of Oud Player.	187
14.5	*There Are No Homosexuals in Iran.* Inkjet print.	189
14.6	*There Are No Homosexuals in Iran.* Inkjet print.	190
14.7	*There Are No Homosexuals in Iran.* Inkjet print.	191
14.8	Still image from video *Torn*.	192

CONTRIBUTORS

Dalia Abdelhady is Associate Professor in the Department of Sociology at Lund University, Sweden. Her work features the application of postcolonial analysis to the sociology of migration. Following a comparative perspective, her work focuses on the meeting point between individual immigrants (and their communities) and institutions in receiving countries (such as schools, labour markets, media and political policies). In addition to a number of journal articles and book chapters, she is the author of *The Lebanese Diaspora: The Arab Immigrant Experiences in Montreal, New York and Paris* (New York University Press, 2011), and co-editor of *Refugees and the Violence of Welfare Bureaucracies in Northern Europe* (Manchester University Press, 2020).

Michael Akladios earned his PhD in history from York University, Canada. Michael Akladios is a Sessional Lecturer in the Department of Historical Studies at the University of Toronto. He is also the Founder and Executive Director of Egypt Migrations, an archival and community outreach non-profit organization affiliated with the Clara Thomas Archives at York University and the Orfalea Center at UC Santa Barbara.

Ramy Aly is Assistant Professor of Anthropology at the American University in Cairo, Egypt. Ramy's first monograph, *Becoming Arab in London: Performativity and the Undoing of Identity* was published in 2015 with Pluto Press as part of their celebrated 'Anthropology, Culture and Society Series'. The book is the first ethnographic account of gender, race and class practices among British-born and raised Arabs in London and attempts to provide an account of the everyday experiences of Arabness in the British capital. Ramy's research interests and publications engage with the anthropology of ethnicity, migration and diaspora; anthropology and media studies; cultural studies and youth cultures.

Lucia Ardovini is a Postdoctoral Research Fellow in the MENA Programme at The Swedish Institute of International Affairs. Her research focuses on current trajectories of Islamist movements across the MENA region, with a special focus on the Egyptian Muslim Brotherhood. In particular, she traces the movement's restructuring process following the 2013 coup, examining its repercussions on ideology, identity, and organisational structures. She is the author of *Surviving Repression: The Egyptian Muslim Brotherhood after the 2013 Coup* (Manchester University Press, 2021).

Notes on contributors

Nadim Bawalsa is Commissioning Editor at Al-Shabaka: The Palestinian Policy Network, USA. He received a joint doctorate in History and Middle Eastern & Islamic Studies from New York University in 2017. His forthcoming book explores the formation of a Palestinian diaspora community in interwar Latin America. Specifically, he examines transnational political activism among Palestinian migrants in the interwar period as they struggled to secure their rights to Palestinian citizenship.

Bengi Bezirgan-Tanış is an Assistant Professor in the Department of Sociology at the Nişantaşı University, Turkey. She completed her PhD in Sociology at the London School of Economics and Political Science in 2015. Previously she received her Master's degree in Sociology from the Middle East Technical University. Her research interests include nationalism and national identity, race and ethnicity, minority and diaspora communities and the sociology of memory.

Alessandra Bonci is a PhD Candidate in Political Science at Laval University, Canada. She is currently working on a dissertation on Islamic fundamentalism and Salafism in Tunisia from a gender perspective based on two years of fieldwork in Tunis (2019–2020). She is interested in gender studies and politics in Tunisia and the MENA region. She has written a number of articles and book chapters on Tunisia and the Maghreb as generally construed.

Ching-An Chang is an Assistant Professor in the Department of Arabic Language and Culture at the National Chengchi University in Taiwan (R.O.C). His research focuses on migration/refugee-related issues in the Middle East. He is currently working on a project on 'Non-poor refugees: The impact of the economic elite refugees on host countries – Syrian refugee business community in Turkey, Egypt, and Jordan', which is funded by the MOST Young Scholar Fellowship from the Ministry of Science and Technology in Taiwan.

Nir Cohen is a Senior Lecturer in the Department of Geography and Environment at Bar Ilan University, Israel. His research interests include relations between states and diasporas, the politics of migration and citizenship, and urban social geographies in Israel. His work on policies towards skilled migrants, stratified citizenship and socio-spatial relations in Israeli cities has appeared in such journals as *IJURR*, *Cities, Population, Space and Place*, *Environment and Planning D*, *Social and Cultural Geography* and *Geoforum*. In spring 2018, he was Visiting Fellow of Jewish Migration at The Parkes Institute for Jewish/Non-Jewish Relations at the University of Southampton, UK. In 2019, he was Visiting Professor for Urban Studies at TU Vienna, Austria. He is currently co-editing a book for Routledge on cities and care.

Pinar Dinc is a Researcher in the Department of Physical Geography and Ecosystem Science and an Affiliated Researcher at the Centre for Advanced Middle Eastern Studies, Lund University, Sweden. She received her PhD in Political Science from the London School of Economics. Following a Marie Curie Individual Fellowship at CMES with the Fighting Insurgency Ruining Environment project, she is currently leading the 'Turkey Beyond Borders: Critical Voices, New Perspectives' project, which is funded by the Swedish Institute in Istanbul.

Gennaro Errichiello teaches at SOAS in London and works for the Office for National Statistics, UK. He holds an MA in Global Migration from Swansea University, and a PhD in Social Sciences from Loughborough University. He has carried out extensive ethnographic research on Muslims in Italy, the United Kingdom and the Gulf countries. He has published articles in peer-reviewed journals and presented the results of his research at many international conferences. His research interests revolve around the sociology of the Muslim world, migration studies, South-South migration, highly-skilled migrants, migrant associations, ethnicity, nationalism, belonging, (mis)recognition, class and gender.

Stacy D. Fahrenthold is Associate Professor of History at the University of California Davis, USA. She is the author of *Between the Ottomans and the Entente: The First World War in the Syrian and Lebanese Diaspora, 1908–1925* (Oxford University Press, 2019), and currently serves as co-editor for *Mashriq & Mahjar: Journal of Middle Eastern and North African Migration Studies*.

Shawn Teresa Flanigan is a Professor in the School of Public Affairs at San Diego State University, USA. She received her PhD in Public Administration and Policy from the University at Albany State University of New York. Her research focuses on service-seeking behaviour by lower-income populations, minorities, and other marginalised and vulnerable groups (such as migrants). She also examines the ways in which health and human services needs are met by nonprofit/non-state organisations and public programs.

Jillian Fulton-Melanson is a PhD candidate in Social Anthropology at York University, Canada, trained in ethnomusicology and music performance. Her research is located in Morocco, the Arab world, and its diaspora communities in Canada, and focuses on identity politics, nationalism and transnationalism, violence, and subaltern queer collectives. Sonically, it is located within EDM (noise, industrial, techno, house) and traditional music from the SWANA region. Outside of academia, she actively performs at underground electronic music events and collaborates with Arabic folk musicians.

Andrew Gayed is Assistant Professor of Art History and Visual Culture at the Ontario College of Art and Design University in Toronto, Canada. An Egyptian-Canadian art historian, he has an academic background in diasporic art, queer visual culture, and Middle Eastern art histories. Before joining OCADU, Gayed was the Visiting Scholar at NYU's Center for the Study of Gender and Sexuality, where he researched the artistic practices of the queer diaspora. Gayed's research is located in art history, gender studies, and critical race theory.

Steven J. Gold is Professor in the Department of Sociology at Michigan State University, USA. His scholarly interests include international migration, ethnic economies, ethnic community development, qualitative field methods and visual sociology. He is the author, co-author or co-editor of nine books including *The Israeli Diaspora* (Routledge/University of Washington Press, 2002) which won the Thomas and Znaniecki Award from the American Sociological Association's International Migration Section for the best book on international migration in 2003. The chair of 22 PhD dissertations and author of over 100 journal articles and book chapters, Gold received the Charles Horton Cooley Award for Distinguished Scholarship in Sociology from the Michigan Sociology Association in 2007 and the Distinguished Career Award from the American Sociological Association, International Migration Section, in 2019.

Nina Gren is a Senior Lecturer in Social Anthropology in the Department of Sociology, Lund University, Sweden. Her research focuses on refugees and politics. She is interested in resilience in conflict situations, collective memory, gender and diasporic relations. She has fieldwork experience from the Palestinian territories and from Denmark and Sweden. Currently, she is conducting research on 'Occupied Intimacies', which focuses on family relations in situations of political conflict and military occupation. She is the author of *Occupied Lives: Maintaining Integrity in a Palestinian Refugee Camp in the West Bank* (The American University in Cairo Press, 2015).

Jonathan Harris is a political geographer with a regional focus on France and North Africa, whose work focuses on the intersection of culture, power and space in the context of migration and diaspora. Also a professional teacher, he is currently a Research Fellow at the Centre for Research in Educational Underachievement, Stranmillis University College, Belfast, Northern Ireland.

Nicole Hirt is a political scientist focusing on the Horn of Africa, specifically on Eritrea, Ethiopia and Djibouti. She was a Professor at the University of Asmara, Eritrea, and has conducted several research projects in Eritrea. Her current research interests include transnational governance and diaspora communities, the role of remittances in authoritarian political systems, and the persistence of authoritarian rule. She is also interested in the dynamics of European migration policies. Hirt is a Research Fellow at the GIGA German Institute of Global and Area Studies in Hamburg, Germany. She has published in *African Affairs*, *The Journal of Modern African Studies* and *Globalizations*.

Sherene Idriss is a Postdoctoral Research Fellow at the Alfred Deakin Institute for Citizenship and Globalisation, Deakin University, Australia. Her current research examines the intersections between labour, community, gender and race among migrant young women. She is the author of *Young Migrant Identities: Creativity and Masculinity* (Routledge, 2018).

Sossie Kasbarian is a Senior Lecturer in Politics at the University of Stirling, Scotland. She earned her doctorate from the School of Oriental and African Studies (SOAS), University of London. She has been a Postdoctoral Research Fellow at the University of Edinburgh and has taught at SOAS, the Graduate Institute of International and Development Studies, Geneva, the University of Lancaster, England, and the American University in Cairo, Egypt. She is co-editor of *Diaspora: A Journal of Transnational Studies*. Her research interests and publications broadly span diaspora studies, contemporary Middle East politics and society, nationalism and ethnicity, transnational political activism, and refugee, displacement and migration studies. She is the co-editor (with Anthony Gorman) of *Diasporas of the Modern Middle East: Contextualising Community* (Edinburgh University Press, 2015). She is the author of the forthcoming book, *Diasporizing the Modern Middle East: Armenian Remnants, Resilience and Reconfigurations*.

Neriman Kuyucu is currently a writing instructor in the Department of Academic Writing at Koç University, Turkey. Born and raised in Istanbul, Turkey, she has developed a passion for interdisciplinary approaches to literature. She holds a PhD in contemporary Anglophone literature from the University of Missouri where she worked on the notions of Muslimness in contemporary literary imaginations. Her research focuses on transnationalism, diaspora studies, and world literatures.

Mara A. Leichtman is Associate Professor of Anthropology at Michigan State University, USA, and a 2020–2021 Luce/ACLS Fellow in religion, journalism and international affairs. She is the author of *Shi'i Cosmopolitanisms in Africa: Lebanese Migration and Religious Conversion in Senegal* (Indiana University Press, 2015). She co-edited *New Perspectives on Islam in Senegal: Conversion, Migration, Wealth, Power, and Femininity* (Palgrave Macmillan, 2009);

'The Shi'a of Lebanon: New Approaches to Modern History, Contemporary Politics, and Religion' (*Die Welt des Islams*, 2019); and 'Muslim Cosmopolitanism: Movement, Identity, and Contemporary Reconfigurations' (*City and Society*, 2012). As a 2016–2017 Fulbright Scholar at the American University of Kuwait, she launched a new project on Gulf Islamic humanitarianism in Africa.

Wahib Maalouf holds an MA in migration studies from the Lebanese American University. He recently co-authored *Migration and the Formation of Political Elite in Lebanon* (Arab Center for Research and Policy Studies). He previously worked as a researcher at the Center for Behavioral Research at the American University of Beirut and authored a biography of the Lebanese MP Abdallah al-Hajj, a populist politician who played a role in the popular mobilisation in the early 1950s (Dar Annahar, 2007). He is interested in the relationships between diaspora, nation-building and the intellectual/cultural production related to the homeland.

Sumit K. Mandal is Associate Professor in the School of Politics, History and International Relations at the University of Nottingham, Malaysia. He is the author of *Becoming Arab: Creole Histories and Modern Identity in the Malay World* (Cambridge University Press, 2017). As a historian, he is interested in the transregional architecture of Asian societies. His research focuses primarily on Muslim societies in the Malay world – in relation to the Indian Ocean – as well as contemporary Indonesia, Malaysia and Singapore.

Abdulkader Saleh Mohammad is a retired Professor of Sociology and worked at the Universities of Sebha, Libya, and Asmara, Eritrea. He was a Visiting Professor and Senior Research Fellow at the University of Oslo, Norway, and Oslo University College, and a Senior Advisor to International Law and Policy Institute (ILPI) in Oslo, and an Associate Researcher for GIGA Hamburg. His particular expertise includes rural and pastoral community development in the Horn of Africa, political sociology, ethno-social identities, traditional mediation systems, transnational governance and diasporas. He has published in *Globalizations* and *The Journal of Modern African Studies* and is the author of *The Saho of Eritrea: Ethnic Identity and National Consciousness* (LIT Verlag Münster, 2013).

Öncel Naldemirci is a Lecturer in the Department of Social Work, Umeå University, Sweden. He completed his PhD in Sociology at the University of Gothenburg, Sweden. His research interests include the sociology of health, emotions and migration. His publications have appeared in peer-reviewed academic journals, such as *Sociology of Health and Illness*, and *Health and Health Expectations*. He is also a translator from French to Turkish.

Sandhya Rao Mehta is an Associate Professor of World Literature in the Department of English Language and Literature at Sultan Qaboos University, Oman. She has published widely in the areas of diaspora studies, EFL and critical thinking. She is the editor of *Language and Literature in a Glocal World* (Springer, 2018), *Exploring Gender in the Literature of the Indian Diaspora* (Cambridge Scholars Publishing 2014), *and Language Studies: Stretching the Boundaries* (Cambridge Scholars Publishing, 2012). She is presently working on a collected anthology entitled *Language and Identity in the Arab World* and a book entitled *Oman-India ties: Across Sea and Space*.

Farhang Rouhani is Professor of Geography at the University of Mary Washington, USA, where he teaches courses in human geography, geopolitics, migration, the Middle East, queer space and social justice. His research focuses on the intersections of anarchist social theory, queer spatialities and diasporic politics.

Zainab Saleh is an Assistant Professor of Anthropology at Haverford College, USA. Her research focuses on memory, nostalgia, belonging, war, and violence in Iraq and the Iraqi diaspora. She is the author of *Return to Ruin: Iraqi Narratives of Exile and Nostalgia* (Stanford University Press, 2021). Currently, she is working on a book project entitled, *Uprooted Memories: Citizenship, Denaturalization, and Deportation in Iraq*, which focuses on the deportation of Iraqi Jews, Iraqis of Iranian origin and communists throughout the twentieth century. Her work also has appeared in *American Anthropologist, Arab Studies Journal, Anthropology News*, and the Costs of War project with Brown University.

Ángela Suárez-Collado is an Assistant Professor in the Political Science and Public Administration Department at the University of Salamanca, Spain. She holds a BA in Political Science and Sociology from the University of Granada, an MA in International Mediterranean Studies and a PhD in Arab and Islamic Studies from the Autonomous University of Madrid. She was a Postdoctoral Fellow at the Käte Hamburger Kolleg-Centre for Global Cooperation Research, Germany. She has been a visiting researcher at Georgetown University, Oxford University, the College of Europe in Brugges and the Centre Jacques Berque pour le Développement des Sciences Humaines et Sociales au Maroc. She has participated in various research projects conducted by different national and international institutions. Her research focuses on social movements and local politics in North Africa and Moroccan migration in Europe.

Paul Tabar is the Director of the Institute for Migration Studies and a Professor of Sociology/Anthropology at the Lebanese American University, Lebanon. Recently, he published *Migration and the Formation of Political Elite in Lebanon* (Arab Center for Research and Policy Studies, 2021) and *Arab Communities in Australia* (Arab Centre for Arab Unity Studies, 2013). He is also the primary author of *On Being Lebanese in Australia: Identity, Racism and the Ethnic Field* (Institute for Migration Studies, LAU, 2010), and is a co-author of *Bin Laden in the Suburbs: Criminalizing the Arab Other* (Institute of Criminology, 2004). He is currently working on two projects: one on migrant habitus focusing on second-generation Lebanese Australians as a case study, and the other on social inequalities in Lebanon using a Bourdieusian perspective. He is the author of many articles on Lebanese and Arab migrants in international journals.

Iain Walker is currently a Senior Research Fellow at the Max Planck Institute for Social Anthropology in Halle, Germany. He holds a PhD in anthropology from the University of Sydney, where he wrote his thesis on mimesis and social change on the Comorian Island of Ngazidja. His research interests encompass questions of identity and belonging, whether among migrants, diasporans or people who do not move, and over the past two decades he has worked on the Hadrami diaspora in various locations in the western Indian Ocean while maintaining his long-term research interests in the Comoros. His most recent book is *Islands in a Cosmopolitan Sea: A History of the Comoros* (Oxford University Press, 2019).

Man Xu is a PhD candidate in Sociology at the University of Toronto, Canada. Her general research interests include issues related to migration in the Global South, transnationalism, globalisation and identity formation. Her doctoral research examines the participation of Chinese Muslims in small commodity trade businesses in Yiwu, China.

Notes on contributors

Hajar Yazdiha is an Assistant Professor of Sociology at the University of Southern California, USA, and faculty affiliate of the Equity Research Institute. She received her PhD in Sociology from the University of North Carolina, Chapel Hill. Her research examines the mechanisms underlying the politics of inclusion and exclusion at the intersection of immigration, race and ethnicity, and social movements.

ACKNOWLEDGEMENTS

We would like to thank our colleagues at the Department of Sociology at Lund University and the Department of Sociology, Anthropology and Egyptology at The American University in Cairo, for their consistent support, solidarity and encouragement. The Centre for Advanced Middle Eastern Studies at Lund University provided valuable support at different stages of organising and finalising this volume, for which we are grateful.

We thank James Root for providing valuable editorial assistance, and the editors at Routledge for seeing through the project. Special thanks are due to the chapter authors for being patient with us while producing this volume at a time when we have all struggled with uncertainty and the strains of life during the pandemic. Our families and friends have provided tremendous support that has made the completion of this project possible. Perhaps more than ever before the bonds of reliance and interdependence with family, friends, colleagues and interlocutors are so precious and appreciated.

1
COMING TO AND COMING FROM THE MIDDLE EAST

The unfolding of diaspora

Dalia Abdelhady and Ramy Aly

Diaspora transmits legacies and possibilities that are sometimes antagonistic: it can cite dislocation and destruction, on the one hand, fluidity and new ways of articulating self and collectivity, on the other. The notion of diasporic dispersal still implicates us in a sense that something undesirable has happened, a kind of aberration to the natural order and certainty of people living undisturbed in their places of arboreal origin. In its original articulation, diaspora is associated with experiences of forced dislocation, trauma and exile. This original articulation dominated academic analyses through the twentieth century and remains relevant to our attempts to understand the historical experiences of Africans, Jews, Armenians and Palestinians, all prominent examples of diasporic formations stemming from colonialism, slavery, genocide and occupation. In Arabic, one of the Middle East's many languages, this might be understood as *al-shatat*, which stands not only for dispersion but equally dismemberment and fragmentation. In this sense, diaspora is about the destruction of particular lifeworlds and their transportation to new settings. These experiences are not confined to the past, they continue to unravel for an ever-growing litany of people who have been forced to flee neo-colonial wars, authoritarianism, religious and ethnic persecution, civil war, economic collapse and state failure. In this book, we revisit the notion of diaspora, relocating it within general experiences of human movement, globalisation and articulations of self, collectivity and otherness. This opening chapter reflects on the diaspora literature and sheds light on the contributions offered by this collection to the study of diasporas in general and those associated with the Middle East in particular. Since it is impossible to cover all diasporic groups connected to the Middle East in either the edited volume or the introductory chapter, our analysis focuses on themes instead of groups. In so doing, we hope that these themes can provide a new point of departure for further analyses of the rich array of experiences and contexts beyond the volume itself.

When one thinks of Middle Eastern diasporas, understandably, the political and social conflicts that characterise much research on the region and its people come to the fore of our expectations, explanations and concerns for casuistry. Palestinians, Iraqis, Syrians, Assyrians, Eritreans, Imazighen, Egyptian Copts and Kurds, to name but a few, have all fallen foul of 'the Middle East', as a region that has been constructed politically, geographically and geo-strategically by both colonial powers and local elites in equal measure. As a result, associating these groups with conflict, marginalisation and persecution at home and abroad is a dominant strand in the literature, often veering towards essentialising these groups as much as the region itself. In this opening chapter to the volume, we highlight the ways diaspora, as an analytical tool, can motivate analyses of immigrant communities and immigrant subjectivities and include generations that have not experienced migration per se and yet maintain diasporic subjectivities. In this way, we hope to go beyond essentialising tendencies and draw attention to the non-territorialised ways of understanding identification and belonging. To that end, we reflect on the developments within diaspora studies as a field of inquiry and connect these to the study of Middle East diasporas in particular.

Initially, diaspora was associated with sinister and brutal experiences and conceived of as a normative concept (see, for example, Chaliand and Rageau, 1995). In the broader diaspora literature, however, the 1990s offered a decade in which scholars began to take an interest in diasporas beyond experiences of trauma and exile (for example, as in the writings of Safran, 1991; Sheffer, 1997; Van Hear, 1998; Vertovec and Cohen, 1999). For these authors, among others, ties to the homeland were of added importance. The homeland provided the basis of collective memory and ethno-communal solidarity and consciousness. Alienation from host societies followed and was at the time considered the other side of the same forced dispersion coin of longing for the homeland (Safran, 1991; Vertovec and Cohen, 1999).

Historically, there has been a focus on connections between homeland and host society, which has often been taken up within analyses of transnational spaces. The analysis of diaspora has often underlined a triadic relationship between *the* diaspora community, *the* host society and *the* homeland. This three-way conception of diaspora communities, with ostensibly clear collective identities related to places of origin, places of residence and a scattered community to which migrants are assumed to belong, continues to shape much of the analyses of diaspora. Middle Eastern groups that formed diasporas outside the region have often been approached through the triadic lens. Early studies by Humphrey (1998), Hanafi (1999), Naficy (2001) and Kaya (2002) employed the triadic approach to the study of Lebanese, Palestinian, Iranian and Turkish diasporas, respectively. This period notably saw the emergence of a focus on women in the work of Rothenberg (1999) and Moallem (2000), who provided an important gendered perspective on the Palestinian and Iranian diasporas, respectively.

The turn of the twenty-first century ushered in the processual turn in thinking around diaspora, which challenged the static modes of belonging that had become so customary in analyses centred on the triadic spheres of interaction. Instead of scrutinising being in and belonging to a diaspora, Butler (2001) suggests that we approach the homeland, host society and diaspora communities as dimensions that serve as analytical categories. As a category of analysis, diaspora becomes a way of investigating migrant communities not as homogeneous entities that are out there, but as entities that are constantly negotiated and contested, that exclude as much as include. In a decisive article entitled 'The "Diaspora" Diaspora', Brubaker (2005) emphasises the study of diaspora as a process, something that people claim and practice. This approach encourages the study of diaspora from within, as well as from a migrant-centred perspective (see Tölölyan, 2007).

The processual turn inspired a surge in the study of Middle Eastern diasporas which problematised diasporas instead of taking their coherence for granted. Peteet's (2007) work on the Palestinian diaspora, Gualtieri's (2009) on the Syrian diaspora, Hage's (2005) on the Lebanese diaspora, and Gold's (2002) on the Israeli diaspora, are notable among the many earlier examples of the processual turn in Middle East diaspora studies. This diverse body of literature has as a common theme: the interrogation of the formation of diaspora and the drawing of attention to the ways that people activate, express or mobilise diasporic identifications.

Even with a growing corpus of research on various Middle Eastern diasporas, the field is still relatively new and there remains an urgent need to produce accounts that recognise the expansive ways in which life is made meaningful by diasporans. In curating this volume, we found ourselves asking *who* and *where* are Middle Eastern diasporas? *Where* are Middle Eastern diasporas leads us first to assert that the Middle East is not simply a point of departure but equally a destination of arrival. While this may seem commonsensical, it is often assumed that when we are studying Middle Eastern diasporas, we are studying diasporic settings external to the region. As many of the chapters in this volume attest, the Middle East is a diasporic space. If diaspora is about modes of belonging, ideas and expressions of home, these apply as much to the diasporas *in* the Middle East as they apply to diasporas *of* the Middle East. In a formative volume, Anthony Gorman and Sossie Kasbarian (2015) contextualise the study of Middle East diasporas and emphasise the commonalities between diaspora communities outside the region with those who reside in it. In this volume, we invite readers to apprehend the relationships between diaspora communities within and outside the region. Indeed, we stress that these relationships and linkages reflect the world in which we live, one that is connected in complex, uneven and unprecedented ways and, in turn, produces diasporic sensibilities. We argue that diasporic sensibilities, the sense of multiple identifications and belongings, should no longer be seen as an exceptional experience of the physically displaced and mobile. The diasporic aspects of the lives and practices of certain groups are divided into those who have migrated and those who have stayed in place, yet the interrelationship between is inflected and informed by the dynamics of diaspora. Thus, we invite readers to think of the way in which life as, say, an Imazighen, a Hui, a Kurd or a Copt is implicated in a web of diasporic connections and modes of deterritorialisation, even in the absence of the individual experience of physical displacement and in turn can redefine one's sense of self and belonging outside national boundaries.

The fact that most of the countries in the region provide few if any avenues to citizenship for migrants has not precluded people from making homes in the region, notwithstanding the reality that 'home' is not always the serene refugee many imagine it to be. The reality for many is that the Middle East is a place in which they dwell and make lives even if it is less hospitable than it could be. From temporariness and precarity, through to the challenges faced by refugees, indigenous people and religious and ethnic minorities, diasporas in the Middle East can and do face discrimination, hardship and an absence of basic political, economic and social rights. In this regard, diasporas in the Middle East share a fate with the millions of Middle Easterners ostensibly privileged with citizenship. Meanings, belongings, relationships, homes and identities are imagined and expressed nonetheless, making it incumbent upon us to appreciate and account for the complexity of the region and the lives lived in and through it.

With regards to diasporas of the Middle East, the metanarrative of the problematic 'Middle East' exporting an unending torrent of people to deliverance in settings less tumultuous and more accommodating is a familiar one, as is the notion that those dispersed from the region are culturally problematic in their new settings, resistant to assimilation and integration, religiously intemperate, socially conservative and whose children are afflicted with identity crises. A stereotypical and normative understanding of diaspora can provide support for these assumptions, as they rely on a traditional connection to the homeland and assumptions about the nature of integration in a new setting. However, many of the accounts in this collection provide evidence to the contrary. Asking how diasporans forge connections and means of belonging, the narratives we present here shift our gaze to the multiple forms of belonging to both peoples and places.

Rather than seeing diasporans as marginalised groups who long to return to a homeland, the analyses in this volume demonstrate that Middle East diasporans, like other diasporas and citizens alike, are people who respond to major social change and transformations. Those we count as Middle Eastern diasporans, both in the region and beyond, contribute to transnational social spaces and new forms of cultural expression. A more expansive and nuanced notion of diaspora allows us to appreciate the complex lives of diasporans. Identification and belonging are not static, they are developed, added to and reorientated throughout a lifetime, expressed through the arts, music, film and literature, as well as active political engagement and involvement in various societies. The study of diaspora allows for an analysis of experiences of fragmentation, homelessness, injustice and displacement as productive conditions that can create subversive identities and non-traditional communities. Such we believe is the promise and potential of diaspora as a terrain of experience, which is well demonstrated by many chapters in this volume.

Middle East diaspora studies

The rich literature on Middle Eastern diasporas is hard to summarise, given the diverse communities and approaches employed within it. Nonetheless, it is useful to mark out some of the most prominent approaches or analytical strands to Middle Eastern diasporas to make sense of the state of the art. These strands or general research approaches also reflect much of the writing within diaspora studies as a general field of inquiry. Given that the field of diaspora studies is inter-disciplinary and transdisciplinary, these general approaches are not always reflective of disciplinary boundaries, even if at times they are influenced by specific disciplinary conventions and concerns.

The foundational writings of William Safran, Robin Cohen and Khachig Tölölyan were heavily influenced by the triadic relationships and underscored connections between diaspora communities and the homeland in general, paying specific attention to political conflict at home. A large body of literature explores diasporic ethno-political organisations in host societies and engagement with and influence of the homeland. On the one hand, political conflicts involving the homeland affect those in the diaspora as part of the larger configuration of international political dynamics (see, for example, Howell and Shryock, 2003). On the other hand, *the* diaspora is often portrayed as situated in between social, political and economic dynamics traversing the homeland and the host nation. This relationship has been explored well from a historical perspective (see, for example, Aboud, 2002; Fahrenthold, 2019). The study of diasporic ethno-political mobilisation and activism provides a rich source of contemporary analyses (see, for example, Mojab and Gorman, 2007; Karam, 2008; Wald, 2009; Baser, 2015; Asal and Ayres, 2018, Wilcock, 2018; Cohen and Yefet, 2021). Particular historic moments and events that lead to the mobilisation of those in the diaspora attract significant academic and public attention. Uprisings like the Green Movement in Iran in 2009 and those that spanned the region in late 2010 and continue today have involved increased mobilisation and engagement among those in the diaspora, which is reflected in a growing body of literature (see, for example, Beaugrand and Geisser, 2016; Moss, 2016, 2020; Koinova, 2018; Müller-Funk, 2020).

Situating the diaspora community in between the homeland and the host society is also reflected in a second strand of Middle Eastern diaspora analyses, one in which cultural production takes centre-stage. These reflect a strong connection between diaspora studies and cultural studies with a particular emphasis on diasporic sensibilities, consciousness and cultural expression. Building upon the work of Edward Said, James Clifford, Homi Bhabha, and Arjun Appadurai, diasporic cultural analysis is a realm in which multiple identifications and belongings can be explored. For example, Zahia Smail Salhi and Ian Richard Netton (2006) and Layla Al Maleh (2009) provide two edited volumes that focus on the literature of the Arab diaspora and present it as a bridge between host societies and countries of origin, with diasporic novels, poetry and autobiography providing the medium (see also, Civantos, 2006; Karim, 2006; Hout, 2011; Motlagh, 2011; Bayeh, 2015).

Film has also been an important area of cultural expression for investigating diasporic sensibilities and belonging (see Gadassik, 2011), as has music (see Mansour and Sabry, 2019). A more general approach to cultural expression is taken by Evelyn Alsultany and Ella Shohat (2013), who focus on diasporic cultural production and consumption in *Between the Middle East and the Americas* to demonstrate how identity, nation and geography are contested. In this volume, the same mediums and concerns are taken up by several authors whereby cultural politics and concerns with identity and culture are sites of struggles in which the self and the other are made intelligible within the context of transnational cultural flows.

The two strands of literature outlined above approach diaspora as the in-between space characteristic of the study of hyphenated identities and ethnic communities within multicultural contexts. In this understanding, diaspora offers a position to understand the processes of othering faced by migrants and ethnic minorities *in* and *of* the Middle East, and the reactions of diasporans to such othering through mechanisms of translation, bridging and affirmations of ethnic identification. Inspired by the writings of Stuart Hall and Paul Gilroy in particular, another articulation of diaspora emphasises the ways that 'diaspora identities are ... constantly producing and reproducing themselves anew, through transformation and difference' (Hall, 1990, p. 235). This view allows us to analyse communities and identities beyond the traditional frames of nationality and ethnicity. For example, in their writings about the literary representations of the Iranian diaspora, Babak Elahi and Persis Karim (2011) observe a move away from analyses of exilic and immigrant narratives to a more global diasporic consciousness. In our view, these assertions and observations resonate clearly in the diasporic experiences of the Middle East more broadly and are characteristic of the third analytical thread in the field.

Instead of treating 'states' and 'societies' as discrete entities, this approach to diaspora emphasises the dynamism and contemporaneousness of diasporans and diaspora communities. Importantly, it does not ignore the role played by nation-states as institutions shaping and disciplining bodies and framing and delineating identities. In lieu of privileging the nation-state, however, emphasising a global diaspora consciousness allows us to analyse the connections and movements between local identities and experiences and global transformations. In both of our formative works, *The Lebanese Diaspora* (Abdelhady, 2011) and *Becoming Arab in London* (Aly, 2015), the interplay of the local and the global were important to understanding diasporic subjectivities. In Dalia Abdelhady's account, ethnic and national identifications and differences were less significant for diasporans who frame their experiences with migration, displacement and ambivalence within global narratives. In Ramy Aly's work on Arabness in London, the structures of formal multiculturalism and symbols of difference in Britain, on the one hand, and the economy of meaning about the Arab world, on the other, led many young British-born or raised Arabs to express their sense of belonging in ways that were neither straightforwardly British nor Arab, while always being framed by others through these markers. Both studies point to the need to understand identification and belonging not only as multiple but also as simultaneously local and global.

More recently, Griet Steel (2021) provides an analysis of global narratives and networks as she investigates online communities among Sudanese women in both Sudan and the diaspora and demonstrates the emergence of a global community that extends beyond national boundaries, while also disrupting the binary between migrants and non-migrants. While not necessarily new phenomena, the globalisation of media, capital and culture are connected to 'the rise of new and complex identities and identity narratives that collide and collude in unprecedented ways' (Ndhlovu, 2016, p. 30). Thus, global narratives and dynamics provide a framework within which diaspora identities and experiences can be analysed beyond the allure of methodological nationalism and in ways that emphasise diaspora as a space of creative and disruptive narratives of self and community. Writing generally about Muslims in Europe, and, more specifically, those with ancestry related to Turkey and Morocco, Riva Kastoryano (2018, p. 65) explains that:

> In an "imagined global diaspora" where individuals and groups and transnational communities are connected in global networks, the traditional diaspora loses its territorial bases in which home is an imagined place to express precisely "co-responsibility" without a territorial reference as "home".

The notion of co-responsibility provides a springboard for conceptualising the attachments and affinities that resonate with the diasporic experiences portrayed in this volume.

Curating this volume has been part of our sense of co-responsibility to tell a story of Middle East diasporas. As co-editors of the volume, we are also part of the diasporas that we study, and the academic analyses have direct resonance with our lives. Despite having almost three decades of researching diaspora between the two of us, the process of working on this volume has shown us the potential for Middle Eastern diaspora scholarship to be a nexus of transdisciplinary engagement. The scholars who have contributed to this assemblage come from a broad spectrum of disciplinary backgrounds, such as Anthropology and Sociology, Art history, Ethnomusicology, Political Science, Film and Cultural Studies. For all of them, *diaspora* remains a challenging experience to engage with; what is diasporic about diasporans is never obvious and, as a living concept, it unfolds in ways that require we revisit our paradigms and assumptions. That mode of engagement is far from being a straightforward intellectual or practical endeavour. As scholars, we speak of transdisciplinarity with great enthusiasm while we struggle to listen to each other and accept that we speak different languages. We have felt both challenged and privileged to have had the opportunity to engage with each author and debate, discuss and tease out how their research engagements tell a story about diaspora as an experience and a notion. That is perhaps the best way to think about this volume and the way it is arranged. It tells a complex and unfolding diasporic story. The act of unfolding offers a poignant analogy, when we unfold something, we pull back the creases that have been made for it to fit inside or around something else. In asserting that diaspora is an unfolding story we hope to offer opportunities for open-ended readings of rich and complex lives and places, stories that are about the fading of one way of life and the creation of new ones.

We have chosen to step away from organising this story chronologically, geographically, nationally or based on the disciplinary traditions through which they have been produced. Rather we have arranged this volume based on how different places and experiences resonate, connect and contrast with the chapters that follow and those that precede. The result is a particular sort of movement whereby the sections move from the ways in which diasporas have been formed, to the ways that diasporans make and remake homes, to the expressive terrains where diasporas are contested, to how class, livelihoods and mobility inflect diasporic practices, to the emergence of diasporic sensibilities and, finally, to scholarship that draws our attention to the plurilocality of this vast human *mahjar*.

Part I Forming diasporas

Moving away from experiences of trauma poses a question about the formation of diasporas. If experiences of persecution and forced displacement are not among the core features of diasporas, then what differentiates diaspora communities from other forms of migration and movement? Several analyses in this volume turn our attention to the important role played by the state in providing the conditions for forming diasporas. The state is a notoriously complex entity in terms of the way we can apprehend it (Abrams, 2006). Within the diaspora literature, it occupies a central role in the triadic formulation, and it is safe to say that in many instances the failures of states and homogenising nation-building projects have been prominent factors in diasporic experiences.

The state's denial of the right to belong to a homeland is perhaps the most extreme in the experience of members of the Palestinian diaspora. In Chapter 2 on the Palestinian diaspora in Chile, Nadim Bawalsa documents some of the effects of the British Mandate's Order-in-Council on Palestinian Citizenship that took effect in 1925, through which British authorities denied Palestinian citizenship to tens of thousands of Palestinian migrants throughout the interwar period. The Order effectively rendered Palestinian migrants stateless, with no legal representation or claim to Palestine. Bawalsa argues that through their transnational activism in this new world order, Palestinian migrants developed into a political and national collective, distinct from their Syrian and Lebanese counterparts with whom they migrated from Greater Syria before the First World War as Ottoman Syrians. Bawalsa, therefore, posits that exclusionary British Mandate citizenship legislation was a critical component in the Palestinian migrant community's formation into a diaspora, one that persists, to this day, to be defined by an ongoing exclusion from a historic homeland.

In Bengi Bezirgan-Tanış' account in Chapter 3, the role of the Turkish state and the Justice and Development Party (AKP) in particular is brought to the fore. Bezirgan-Tanış shows how Turkish diasporas have gone from being seen as remittance émigrés to being recognised and instrumentalised by the Turkish state. In that regard, the politics of the homeland has found institutionalised avenues for its expression and propagation in the lives and organisations of the diaspora. One of the most pernicious aspects of that process has been how Turkishness has been made to stand for ethnically Turkic and Sunni Muslims only. The Armenians, Kurds, Assyrians and Alevis of Turkey and their diasporas are thus seen as seditious and threatening others who must be combatted not only at home but also in and through the diaspora.

Relationships to the homeland are also a product of strategic action on the part of home states. As several chapters in this volume describe, nation-states often reach out to their diasporas, but in many cases, members of these diasporas do not identify with the nation-state (see also, Gamlen, 2019). Diaspora formation can thus result from hostile relations between immigrants and governments in their homeland. In Chapter 4, Michael Akladios provides an analysis of the formation of the Coptic diaspora in North America vis-à-vis the Egyptian state. During the early waves of migration from Egypt to North America, Egyptian migrants in general and especially the Copts among them were courted to provide remittances and become active partners in Egypt's development efforts. Sectarian violence in Cairo in the 1970s and 1980s and the inadequacy of the response provided by the Egyptian state triggered the politicisation of the Coptic diaspora in North America. In Akladios' analysis, a social and cultural presence in the United States and Canada facilitated the ability of Coptic activists to respond to Coptic activism in Egypt. Diaspora activism and critique of the Egyptian state rendered Egyptian Copts abroad an enemy of the state that required control in the diaspora.

Along similar lines, in Chapter 5, Hajar Yazdiha argues that the 2009 Green Movement, which took place as a response to political suppression in Iran, motivated the public display of identification and mobilisation among Iranians in the United States. Analysing the 2009 protests as a global movement, Yazdiha shows that it drew the children of Iranian immigrants, who were otherwise not politically active, into forming a digital diaspora to participate in collective action. Digital mobilisation allowed the second-generation Iranian Americans to mobilise to challenge political oppression in Iran and social marginalisation in the US. The analysis draws on the role played by new technologies that inform forms of belonging that are not limited by national borders. Additionally, the analysis also reverses traditional understandings of diaspora involvement in homeland politics, with both Akladios and Yazdiha showing that mobilisation in the homeland informs mobilisation in the diaspora.

The analysis offered in Chapter 6 by Nicole Hirt and Abdulkader Saleh Mohammad of the Eritrean diaspora in Saudi Arabia highlights the role of the home and host states in determining diasporic experience. Eritreans are simultaneously subjected to the coercive activities of their home government and limitations on their agency by immigration policies of the Arab Gulf States. The double bind that Eritreans in the Gulf experience reflects their lack of belonging to both their home and host states, which in turn suggests that their diasporic experiences are structured by experiences of simultaneous exclusion and a struggle for survival. Many have fled Eritrea as refugees seeking asylum and yet no such recognition is possible for those whose migratory journey brings them to locations in the Gulf. Having no chance of acquiring political asylum or naturalisation, Eritreans in the Gulf are considered labour migrants who ultimately become dependent on temporary work visas. The inability to secure permanent settlement outside Eritrea for those residing in Saudi Arabia leads to their dependence on the very state institutions that they escaped from. The result is not only that they are subject to surveillance and diaspora taxation by the Eritrean authorities but equally that their lives are marked by permanent precarity and dependence on the goodwill of their employers and the constant threat of deportation and the exacting of ever-increasing costs of visa fines and renewal in Saudi Arabia.

While all chapters in Part I highlight diaspora formation as a result of political oppression and the denial of rights, they also demonstrate that diaspora formation is a process of active mobilisation and a desire to resist state aggression. While the confrontation may not result in the lifting of state oppression, it provides an important foundation for diaspora mobilisation in various spheres of interaction and expression.

Part II Making and remaking homes

Processual analyses of diaspora continue to focus on the triadic spheres shaping the diaspora while replacing static understandings of identities and communities with more open-ended approaches to analyses. Understandably, the relationship to the homeland continues to occupy a central position within analyses of diaspora. For many scholars, 'a rhetoric of restoration and return' that relates to the homeland (Tölölyan, 2007) provides an important feature of diaspora communities. At the same time, the connection between diasporas and their homeland has been forced open as attention began to focus on how members of the diaspora define home and forge a connection to it (Abdelhady, 2008). Describing this shift, Cohen and Fischer (2019, p. 6) hold that 'homeland as a concrete entity with some historical geographical reference point has given way to "home", "homemaking" and other looser forms of connection and belonging to natal communities and places.'

Looser forms of connections to the homeland are demonstrated in the experiences of indigenous groups who are involved in organised attempts at homemaking. For Clifford (1994), connections to the homeland and the desire to return differentiate diasporas from indigenous ethnic groups. While recognising these differences, contemporary scholarship on indigeneity in this volume draws our attention to connections between diaspora, indigeneity and home-making. In Chapter 7 on the lifecycle of Amazigh diaspora activism in Europe, Ángela Suárez-Collado demonstrates how Moroccan Amazigh activism in Madrid in the mid to late twentieth century was central to the forging of Amazigh identity more broadly by contributing to the reconstruction of the Amazigh language through the recovery and collection of oral tradition and the promotion of literary activity, as well as by elaborating the ideological corpus of Amazigh activism in the Rif. In Suárez-Collado's account, home-making activities were not focused on a place of origin, but more on a general claim to the recognition of difference. Suárez-Collado's account also alludes to a synchronous relationship between Amazigh activism in Catalonia and the region's long-standing claims to autonomy within Spain in the early 2000s. Comparing the activism of Amazigh groups in Catalonia with similar groups in the Netherlands, Suárez-Collado's analysis points to the importance of geographic location and state policies in providing opportunities for diasporic articulations, which we discuss later in the Introduction.

In Chapter 8, Jonathan Harris' work on Amazigh activism in France points to an emergent Indigenous diaspora whose discourse and politics have wide-ranging and sometimes unexpected effects. Harris argues that the discourse and politics of indigeneity have been led by the diaspora and are only very recently emerging in the Amazigh movement 'at home' in North Africa. Harris' analysis reflects the role of the diaspora as an enduring space of political and cultural innovation for the Amazigh movement. These relationships are neither linear nor straightforward and can expose tensions between those in the diaspora and those in the homeland while equally manifesting points of convergence. In Harris' analysis, a global discourse of indigeneity facilitates the articulation of diasporic claims for recognition and difference.

The two chapters on the Amazigh diaspora point to an approach to home and homelands that is more fluid and open-ended. Paul Tabar and Wahib Maalouf's Chapter 9 on the role of the Lebanese diaspora in nation-state building at the end of the French mandate period demonstrates the sometimes contradictory and competing imaginations of the homeland among different diasporic groups that are often based on different political goals and interests. The analysis of the particular historical moment shows that diasporas do more than connect to or re-construct a homeland, they can create it. Following this line of argument, homemaking should be understood as a process that no longer reflects a desire to resurrect and restore a home, but more a re/invention and re/articulation of self, identity and nation.

Instead of taking the connection to the homeland as a reality, some chapters interrogate the ways that connection is created, maintained but sometimes unpredictably mutable. These chapters demonstrate that the process of connecting to the homeland is not as unambiguous as some of the classical analyses claimed. The comparative analysis of the Tunisian diaspora following the 2011 revolution, provided in Chapter 10 by Alessandra Bonci, also shows that a desire to be an agent of positive social change in the homeland can result in disappointment and frustrations instead of fulfilment. Bonci's narrative shows that the fragmentation that results from disappointing experiences with homeland politics leads members of the Tunisian diaspora to redefine their political interests and identities in non-national ways.

Mara Leichtman's narrative of the experience of the Lebanese diaspora in Chapter 11 demonstrates a more regressive transformation as a result of involvement in homeland politics. As Leichtman explains, the Lebanese in Senegal have formulated a group identity around secular identities and managed to avoid replicating the sectarian divide characteristic of Lebanese society. However, the 2006 war with Israel created pressures to resurrect religious divisions as Shi'i Islam became equated with Lebanese nationalism. In this process, homeland politics strengthened transnational connections to the homeland but weakened the diasporic, secular and cosmopolitan identity of the Lebanese in Senegal. Leichtman's account is particularly important in light of traditional assumptions that transnational connections between homeland and host society are building blocks for diaspora communities (see, for example, Levitt, 2001). Leichtman shows that transnationalism can have negative implications for diaspora communities; while Bonci argues that abandoning transnational ambitions may lead to a rejuvenation in diasporic identification.

Part III Expressive terrains of contestation

The critique of methodological nationalism warns against conflating territory, identity and belonging (Wimmer and Glick Schiller, 2002). Diaspora as a framework facilitates the study of belonging in complex and often multi-layered ways. The previous sections identified several chapters that question the identification of members of the diaspora with the nation-states that are seen as their places of origin. The chapters in Part III centre the analysis on the fluidity of diaspora experiences, highlighting that besides the common predicament of crossing multiple societies and cultures, immigrants share experiences of simultaneous inclusion and exclusion vis-à-vis their national, ethnic, diasporic and host communities.

The inability of '*the* diaspora' to bring together all migrants from a nation-state is most evident in Pinar Dinc's analysis of the semantics of defining Turkey's many diasporas in Chapter 12. In a chapter that picks up where Bezirgan-Tanış leaves off, Dinc's chapter is based on an understanding of the hyphenated identity 'Euro-Turks' as insufficient in defining diverse diasporic communities that are connected to Turkey. Dinc proposes the label of *Türkiyeli* as an alternative to the hyphenated identity Euro-Turks, arguing that it would allow people and observers of Turkey to acknowledge and emphasise the heterogeneity of Turkey's diasporas in Europe. In doing so, the analysis shows that the *Türkiyeli* identity was already introduced by Turkey's leftist diaspora groups in Europe from the late 1960s, but has since been contested by Turkey's different diaspora groups, on the one hand, and lost in translation when converted into other languages (i.e. English, French or German), on the other.

A queer analytic lens to diaspora communities adds to our understanding of the complexities of diaspora experiences. In Chapter 13, Farhang Rouhani applies a queer lens to the textual analysis of the film *Appropriate Behavior*, which delves into the representation of queer Iranian American experiences in Brooklyn. Rouhani's analysis interrogates the classed and racialised experience of 'Iranianness' in the United States and points to articulations of new identifications and communities among queer Iranians as expressed in the film. The creative arts provide avenues for expressing various sentiments associated with diaspora experiences such as loss, loneliness, fragmentation and nostalgia, often articulated by diaspora artists (Abdelhady, 2011). Simultaneously, diasporic artistic expression also provides interventions that demand recognition, and articulate new identities and communities (ibid.). This is well demonstrated in Andrew Gayed's work in Chapter 14 on the art of the queer Middle Eastern diaspora, which draws our attention to the tensions of being queer and Middle Eastern in the diaspora. Gayed suggests that a very particular diaspora consciousness emerges as a result, one that grapples with conflicting processes of identification in which the art that emerges offers critiques that move beyond the clichés of sexual oppression in the Middle East versus sexual acceptance in the 'West' beyond it.

Alternative articulations of identity and belonging in diaspora communities are also taken up by Jillian Fulton-Melanson in Chapter 15, who provides an analysis of underground electronic dance music in Canada that is produced and performed by Arab DJs and musicians. In Fulton-Melanson's analysis, the counter-public artistic space provides a unique avenue for community building and a response to 'othering' in the diaspora. Building on the belief that music enables the formation of bonds between individuals, the analysis shows that the emerging diaspora space is not devoid of tensions over definitions of self, other and community, but rather one in which new articulations can be performed and experimented with.

Taken together, the chapters in Part III show that processes of exclusion (based on race, ethnicity, sexuality and gender) are challenged by diaspora experiences that articulate new spaces of belonging and cultural citizenship. These interventions open up new diasporic terrains where language, art, film and music are disruptive of particular modes of normativity. The gendered body is no less significant a site for these disruptive gestures. In Chapter 16 on the gendered geographies of power, Dalia Abdelhady illustrates how the narratives of Lebanese immigrants show how migration provides opportunities for both men and women to question hegemonic social structures (such as those imposed by class, gender and nation) and to more broadly entertain alternative understandings of gendered lives and social relationships. Her approach to gendered geographies of power highlights how diaspora subjects renegotiate gendered positions and norms and traverse power hierarchies in multiple societies, providing a fitting prelude to the work of Sherene Idriss in Chapter 17 on Lebanese-Australians in Sydney and their gendered and racialised experiences of career-making in creative industries. Idriss shows how these experiences can disrupt attachments to a Lebanese-Australian community and ideas of masculinity and femininity. Furthermore, Idriss draws our attention to the performativity of ethnicity, particularly within predominantly white-dominated and middle-class spaces offering a niche pathway into a highly competitive sector. In this context, the creativity sector becomes a contested site of identity-making where stereotypes are redressed and traditional and gendered routes of social mobility for young Lebanese-Australian people are challenged.

Part IV Class, livelihood and mobility

Several chapters in this book point to the dynamic interplay between diaspora and class, which we understand as concerning class and livelihood defined broadly. In an important turn-of-the-century volume on life and livelihoods in a globalising world, Karen Fog Olwig and Ninna Nyberg Sørensen emphasise the importance of examining 'livelihood as practised, and conceived, by specific social actors in particular ethnographic and historical contexts, and the local, regional and more distant spheres of activity that these livelihoods imply' (2001, p. 4). Among the most helpful elaborations of livelihoods is Norman Long's (2000), where livelihood 'best expresses the idea of individuals and groups striving to make a living, attempting to meet their various consumption and economic necessities, coping with uncertainties, responding to new opportunities, and choosing between different value positions' (in Fog Olwig and Nyberg Sørensen, 2001: 4).

In a recent contribution to the literature on diaspora and class, Van Hear (2019) draws attention to the importance of class positions and the ways they shape diaspora experiences. In particular, Van Hear calls analyses of diaspora to take into 'consideration of the material conditions that shape socio-economic standing (which) has been neglected in favour of concern with cultural factors that shape identity and identity politics' (ibid., p. 135). In this volume, concerns with class and livelihoods seem to be inextricably linked to concerns and expressions of culture. New ways of conceptualising class and livelihood have emerged, such as entrepreneurship and creative economies, and these have found resonance in diaspora scholarship in turn.

The emergence of a globalised creative sector has led to the need for a nuanced reading of the groups that are hailed and come to constitute what Nir Cohen and Steven Gold describe in Chapter 18 as a 'creative diaspora' in this volume. The emergence of Israel's creative diaspora reflects a class/profession-based group with distinct characteristics. Highly skilled and educated, often having been trained vocationally and/or academically at institutions outside Israel, Israeli creatives are disproportionately concentrated in global cities/regions and are inclined towards working and socialising with other creatives – Israeli or not. Since many of them were doing well *prior* to emigration, most attributed their relocation to a mixed set of both pecuniary and non-pecuniary – mostly professional and cultural – reasons. Among these are limited opportunities in Israel in some sectors, a passion for exploring new cultural terrains, the desire for less stressful everyday social environments, and disillusionment with the social and political impasse between liberals and hard-liners, on the one hand, and vis-à-vis the Palestinians, on the other. As with many chapters, Cohen and Gold show that new waves of migrants are not simply subsumed within existing diasporic terrains. Indeed, diasporic terrains seem to be constantly broadening in the sense that many creatives already have diasporic connections and relationships that facilitate their mobility.

Connections to diasporic terrains and their impact on physical mobility among diasporans are also taken up by Gennaro Errichiello in Chapter 19, who provides an analysis of middle-class Pakistanis in Dubai. Errichiello's analysis illustrates how diaspora emerges as a strategic resource, whereby middle-class migrants tend to preserve their Pakistani identity and background in such a way as to construct their sense of belonging within and beyond ethnic boundaries. In the Gulf states, where migration is characterised by temporariness, it emerges that Pakistanis' temporary status does not impede them from forging attachments within diasporic communities, particularly when they use their transnational connections and networks in other countries to move and relocate themselves and their businesses somewhere else.

Studying Chinese immigrants in Iran, in Chapter 20, Man Xu shows that class differences among members of the group motivate a diasporic consciousness among those who face exclusion and marginalisation within the community. Xu focuses on Hui Muslims who are engaged in transnational activities between China and Iran and describes circular and open-ended movement instead of the often-stressed unidirectional relocation of diaspora formation. Xu argues that as they search for opportunities for socio-economic mobility, Hui Muslims become diasporic even before they migrate to Iran. Experiences with migration allow Hui people to acquire cross-cultural competency and complicate their sense of belonging. After returning to China, Hui people forge new diasporic connections and community imaginations through participation in global trade. Xu's analysis moves beyond the theorisation of diaspora as connected to cross-border travel and conceptualises diasporic disposition primarily as a way of being and understanding the world that can be embodied by experiences of people on the move as well as the prospective and returned migrant. Embeddedness in global trade and narratives, as Xu shows, facilitate such dynamics.

The role of diasporic formation in search of livelihood is further elucidated in Ching-An Chang's analysis of Syrian diaspora entrepreneurs in countries neighbouring Syria, in Chapter 21. Chang investigates the business practices of Syrian entrepreneurs and shows that their business activities are being conducted in a transnational context between homeland and host societies. Diasporic Syrian entrepreneurs in Chang's study adapt some of their ways of conducting business to local forms. Nevertheless, adaption to local customs and rules does not detach them from their identity as Syrian entrepreneurs. Similar to Israeli creatives and middle-class Pakistanis in Dubai, at times, diasporic Syrian entrepreneurs rely on the diasporic terrain for the successful relocation of their business from Syria to neighbouring countries.

Following on from Chang's account of Syrian business practices and entrepreneurial journeys that have come about as the result of the violent conflict and authoritarianism in Syria, in Chapter 22, Shawn Teresa Flanigan draws our attention to philanthropy as a meaningful diasporic practice among both new migrants and more established diasporans, many of whom have never lived in Syria at all. Flanigan sees diaspora philanthropy in terms of the broader literature on the role of diasporas in economic development and humanitarian aid. Diaspora philanthropy is often subsumed under a broader understanding of remittances, yet philanthropic remittances reflect a socio-political, identitarian, moral and development economy that warrants disaggregation and specific attention.

Part V Diasporic sensibilities

The chapters in this book investigate diaspora as a process of forging attachments and connections to places, peoples and ideas. Almost all entries provide analyses of diaspora from the perspective of the lived experience of the migrants themselves. Even chapters that focus on state-diaspora relations or collective social movements are simultaneously attentive to the standpoint of the migrant activists. From the vantage point of the migrants' lived experience, the different analyses explain the ways diaspora offers an arena through which we can understand the connections between the local, transnational, regional and global. As the different contributions indicate, the idea of diaspora is understood as more contingent, more fluid, more open to negotiations between the relevant social actors (Cohen and Fisher 2019; see also Amelina and Barglowski, 2019). These experiences of contingency, fluidity and negotiations are easily overlooked when the focus is on a triadic relationship between homeland, host society and diaspora community, even more so when the focus is on experiences of integration or discrimination – two key fields of investigation within migration studies.

In Chapter 23 on myths and realities of return and repatriation in the interwar Syrian *mahjar*, Stacy Fahrenthold notes that the concept of return is intoxicating for scholars for several reasons. The idea that migrants return home creates opportunities to reclaim them from the hegemony of the bordered nation-state. For diaspora theorists, 'return' can constitute a rebuttal to the field's preoccupations with exile and loss. Fahrenthold argues that migrants return home all the time, temporarily as tourists or permanently as repatriates. In examining the interwar Syrian, Lebanese and Palestinian diasporas, her chapter considers return migration along three planes: (1) as a scholarly problem; (2) as a diasporic mythology; and (3) as a reality for thousands of emigrants who returned from the American *mahjar*.

In Zainab Saleh's Chapter 24 on the emergence of diasporic sensibilities among Iraqis in London, we find an elaboration of the process through which different generations of Iraqis have transitioned and transformed from exilic and transnational communities in the 1980s and 1990s, respectively, into diasporic communities after 2003. Before 2003, Iraqis in London experienced exile as a condition of enforced absence but hoped that return would be possible once the conditions of expulsion were changed. While regime change in Iraq in 2003 opened the national space for Iraqis abroad for visits and cultural exchange, it also foreclosed the possibility of permanent return due to escalating violence and instability. This status quo engendered diasporic sensibilities among young Iraqis who cultivated attachments to multiple places, pushed the boundaries of what it meant to be both British and Iraqi, and formed new notions of subjectivity and *home*, informed by hybridity, linkages and temporality.

The increasing level of complexity concerning diasporic consciousness and praxis is also to be found in the work of Nina Gren in Chapter 25, whose ethnographic engagement with Danish-Palestinians focuses on a diaspora tour to the Palestinian homeland. Gren presents the diaspora tour as a ritualised homecoming and a response to the losses Palestinians have experienced since their dispossession and flight, which (re)creates community and relationships with Palestine and its people. For many young people undertaking these journeys, the diaspora tour involves a transformation of their sense of belonging and also of emotional states. One significant part of this change happens during visits to ancestral villages in today's Israel. Another vital part takes place in the accumulation and acquisition of 'Palestinian objects'. After the tour, many of the travellers get involved in outreach work for Palestine and also engage in Danish public life more fully through voluntary work. In the narratives of Danish-Palestinians, the tour becomes a rebirth of sorts and points to the transformative potential of diasporic practices, their meaningfulness, and the complexities and ambivalences of belongings in the present world.

While Gren and Saleh's chapters focus on the diasporic subjectivities of those who have been born and raised in Denmark and Britain, respectively, Öncel Naldemirci's Chapter 26 draws our attention to the process of ageing in the diaspora for the pioneering generation of Turkish migrants in Sweden. In this instance, idioms of care in old age help us to appreciate how diaspora is experienced temporally. Turkish migrants' experience of being away from home, *gurbet*, their longing, *gurbetlik*, and their ideals of care take on specific meaning as they anticipate growing old in the diaspora. Having once lost caring relations, ageing in the diaspora can nourish and reinforce a quest for a diasporic community in older age. This quest and desire for care and community can be seen as one response to the unknown future and the fear of solitude, abandonment and isolation in old age. Ageing in the diaspora coincides with working out different possibilities of connectivity, care needs and caring relations.

What the four different contributions show is that the 'myth of return', which was once considered a defining feature of diasporas, is no longer meaningful, even as a rhetorical device. Instead, moving back and forth is attainable even if not always practised. Importantly, the four authors demonstrate how 'being at home' is no longer pursued 'over there'. Fahrenthold demonstrates that movement between homes is not unidirectional but more like a pendulum, where back and forth is part of life. Gren illustrates how the homeland tour for Palestinians can trigger an interest in active engagement with Danish society. Saleh also shows that multiple visits to Iraq can lead to a rearticulation of someone's sense of Iraqiness and sometimes strengthen their Britishness. Likewise, Naldemirci demonstrates that, despite fears of solitude and abandonment in old age, Turkish diasporans choose to live in the diaspora and seek ways of making the diaspora into the caring home they long for rather than simply a place from which they seek to flee back to the homeland.

The process of settling and rebuilding abroad is also developed by Lucia Ardovini in Chapter 27, who looks at the experiences of members of the Muslim Brotherhood who have relocated to Istanbul in the wake of the 2013 coup in Egypt and how they have embarked on a process of reconsidering the terms of their belonging to the movement. Focusing on the personal narratives of Brotherhood members in Istanbul, Ardovini looks at diasporic identification to better understand how core principles such as 'listen and obey', isolationism and hierarchical structures are challenged by a growing number of members in the diaspora and thus, she argues, generating the potential for organisational renewal.

Part VI Plurilocal diasporas, rethinking *mahjar*

In the literature on Middle Eastern diasporas, the term *mahjar* is closely, if not exclusively, associated with migration from the Levant to North and South America in the mid-to-late nineteenth century. In Chapter 28, Iain Walker invites us to reconsider the meanings and potential of the term by using it to describe the plurilocality of the Hadrami diaspora. Plurilocality and *mahjar*, more broadly defined, offer an openness whereby we might understand Middle Eastern diasporans as being socially emplaced in particular times and places, but equally as being plurilocal, connected to others in intimate ways, constantly producing and reproducing complex modes of identification and practice that do not fit neatly into the assumptions about race, ethnicity, nation, regionalism, subregionalism or religion. The Hadrami *mahjar* is presented to us as a case in point. As Walker illustrates, Hadramis have been emigrating to various destinations around the Indian Ocean from East Africa to Southeast Asia for centuries. Hadramis have been particularly adept at integrating into these new contexts largely because few women emigrated from the *Hadramaut*. Hadrami men married local women and their children have come to hold plural identities, belonging in the land of their birth but maintaining affective and often practical links with the homeland, returning for family visits, education or retirement. Walker argues that the Hadrami *mahjar* has endured through time and space and yet retains a coherent, truly global identity that today extends beyond the Indian Ocean world.

Notably, while focusing on the Hadramis of the Malay World, in Chapter 29, Sumit Mandal offers a slightly different reading of the Hadrami experience. Mandal reads the Hadramis as an Arab diaspora in Southeast Asia whose transcultural network challenges the bounded understandings of identity that have dominated with the rise of nation-states as a unit of analysis. Instead, Mandal emphasises the transcultural and creole history and culture of the Hadramis in Indonesia, Malaysia and Singapore. Mandal's account is set against the backdrop of discourses in the Malay world that link conservatism and Salafism with the 'Arabisation' of these national cultures. Hadramis, as Arabs, have been associated with the flow of an orthodox Islam from west to east that has transformed the region from tolerant to intolerant understandings of the faith. Yet, Mandal argues that Hadrami Arabness in the Malay world has weathered the racialised politics of colonial and post-colonial Indonesia, Malaysia and Singapore, expressing itself in new ways in the present. To illustrate this, Mandal engages with the contemporary performance of *selawat*, or songs of praise to the Prophet, by preachers of Hadrami origin, which suggests that Hadramis, as Arabs, help to bridge the Malay world, but also advocate an Islam that is transcultural.

The discourses that tie Hadrami Arabness to conservatism and radicalism in the Malay world are not a million miles away from similar discourses in the West. In Chapter 30. Neriman Kuyucu's literary analysis of Abu-Jaber's *Cresecent* (2003) and Shafak's *The Saint of Incipient Insanities* (2004) foregrounds the debate on Muslim identities in the West and the assumptions about Islamist extremism, the flux of refugees, and the incompatibility of Islam with Western democratic principles. These have been so amplified in the decades after 9/11 that Muslimness, as represented and articulated by Muslims themselves, is continually set aside by their stereotypical representations in the mainstream media as violent, radical and oppressed. By examining the intersection of Muslimness and the complex politics of homing desires as depicted in Shafak's and Abu-Jaber's novels, Kuyucu seeks to explore the possibilities of a new conceptual framework, *Muslim diaspora space*, as a lens for reading Muslim narratives in which diverse characters interact among themselves and relate to the larger society, suggesting a Muslimness that is both transcultural and translocal.

Walker's, Mandal's and Kuyucu's works advocate plurilocality and transculturalism in the way that diasporas from the Middle East ought to be understood. This is similarly advocated by Sossie Kasbarian and Sandhya Rao Mehta in their chapters on the Armenians and the Hindus of the Middle East. In Middle East studies, diaspora groups within the region have traditionally been studied as ethnoreligious minorities (such as Jews, Circassians and Armenians). 'The Ottoman millet system and its modern-day forms in most Middle Eastern states have been a pivotal factor in perpetuating the idea of "preserving" distinct, static (potentially reified and essentialist) identities' (Kasbarian, Chapter 31). Yet Rao Mehta's and Kasbarian's accounts show that diasporas groups within the region should not be excluded from the same nuance and fluidity just because they are in the Middle East.

In her chapter on the Armenian experience in the Middle East, Kasbarian exposes the limitations of the triadic model by advocating an approach to the Armenians spread throughout the Middle East and beyond as a transnational people, rooted at home and routed through multiple orientations and connections. Her framework considers the Armenian diaspora in the region through differentiated experiences, recognising the intrinsic fluidity of diaspora both as concept and practice, and the Middle East as a site that is living and vibrant. As Kasbarian puts it:

> It is perhaps most fruitful to view the Middle East with the familiarity and intimacy of a domestic home – characterised by farewells and reunions, departures and arrivals, dilapidations and renovations. It is a site of permanence as well as fluidity, where Armenian communities are rooted and invested, as well as unsettled and routed elsewhere.

In Chapter 32, Sandhya Rao Mehta draws our attention to the experiences of the Hindus of the Gulf region and the Sultanate of Oman in particular, to which little attention has been paid in the Middle Eastern diaspora literature. Rao Mehta calls upon readers to recognise but also to look beyond the framework of understanding the experience of religious minorities only in so far as they pertain to the absence of formal political and religious rights in the region. This challenging invitation does not ignore the grave human cost of the ethnoreligious and political disadvantages experienced by Hindus in the region but rather asks us to read it alongside the negotiated approaches and strategies employed by Hindus in Oman. As Rao Mehta explains, Hinduism is based in large measure on highly public, participatory and performative rituals; how then have Hindus been able to practise Hinduism for over four hundred years in a publicly Muslim setting like Oman? In her account, Rao Mehta shows how Hindus have strategically used the historical mercantile relations established and maintained by Hindu merchants with the ruling families of Oman to foster both formal and informal rights of religious observance, by participating in transnational networks and imaginatively repurposing private spaces as spaces of public ritual practice. This nuanced and delicate balancing act is reflected and contrasted with other diasporic settings that are assumed to offer Hindus unproblematic religious freedom and adds to emerging studies on diaspora and transnational mobilities, de-essentialising the binary relations of the state with religious minorities in this part of the world.

The rich and complex accounts in this volume defy and resist any sort of linear or conventional arrangement by group, nationality, religion, ethnicity or discipline. Rather, the volume reflects the expansive relationships and experiences that contemporary diaspora scholarship engages with. We hope that this volume will go some way towards addressing the relative absence of cross- and inter-group diasporic analysis and push back against the tendency to think of the Middle East as a defined area with a fixed geography, fixed groups and knowable culture(s), or diaspora as a fixed set of ideas and theories. In placing the diasporic themes of formations, homes, livelihoods, expressions, sensibilities and plurilocality before categories and classifications, we are hopeful that readers will see the connections, complexity and openness that raise productive questions about diaspora as a lived experience that continually challenges disciplinary orthodoxies, engenders human empathy and leaves much to be studied and understood.

References

Abdelhady, D. (2008) 'Representing the homeland: Lebanese diasporic notions of home and return in a global context', *Cultural Dynamics*, 20(1), pp. 53–72.

Abdelhady, D. (2011) *The Lebanese Diaspora: The Arab Immigrant Experience in Montreal, New York and Paris*. New York: New York University Press.

Aboud, B. (2002) 'The Arab diaspora: immigration history and the narratives of presence, Australia, Canada and the USA', in Hage, G. (ed.) *Arab Australians Today: Citizenship and Belonging*. Victoria: Melbourne University Press, pp. 63–91.

Abrams, P. (2006) 'Notes on the difficulty of studying the state', in Sharma, A. and Gupta, A. (eds) *The Anthropology of the State: A Reader*. Oxford: Blackwell Publishing, pp. 112–130.

Abu-Jaber, D. (2003) *Crescent: A Novel*. New York: W. W. Norton & Company.

Al Maleh, L. (2009) *Arab Voices in the Diaspora: Critical Perspectives on Anglophone Arab Literature*. Amsterdam: Brill.

Alsultany, E. and Shohat, E. (2013) *Between the Middle East and the Americas: The Cultural Politics of Diaspora*. Ann Arbor, MI: The University of Michigan Press.

Aly, R. (2015) *Becoming Arab in London: Performativity and the Undoing of Identity*. London: Pluto Press.

Amelina, A. and Barglowski, K. (2019) 'Key methodological tools for diaspora studies: combining the transnational and intersectional approaches', in Cohen, R. and Fischer, C. (eds) *The Routledge Handbook of Diaspora Studies*. London: Routledge, pp. 31–39.

Asal, V. and Ayres, R.W. (2018) 'Attention getters: diaspora support for ethno-political organizations in the Middle East', *Studies in Conflict and Terrorism*, 41(1), pp. 24–38.

Baser, B. (2015) *Diasporas and Homeland Conflicts: A Comparative Perspective*. Farnham: Ashgate Publishers.

Bayeh, J. (2015) *The Literature of the Lebanese Diaspora: Representations of Place and Transnational Identity*. London: I.B. Tauris.

Beaugrand, C. and Geisser, V. (2016) 'Social mobilization and political participation in the diaspora during the "Arab Spring"', *Journal of Immigrant and Refugee Studies*, 14(3), pp. 239–243.

Brubaker, R. (2005) 'The "diaspora" diaspora', *Ethnic and Racial Studies*, 28(1), pp. 1–19.

Butler, K. (2001) 'Defining diaspora, refining a discourse', *Diaspora: A Journal of Transnational Studies*, 10(2), pp. 189–219.

Chaliand, G. and Rageau, J-P. (1995) *The Penguin Atlas of Diasporas*. New York: Viking Penguin.

Civantos, C. (2006) *Between Argentines and Arabs: Argentine Orientalism, Arab Immigrants and the Writing of Identity*. Albany, NY: State University of New York Press.

Clifford, J. (1994) 'Diasporas', *Cultural Anthropology*, 9(3), pp. 302–338.

Cohen, R. and Fischer, C. (2019) 'Diaspora studies: an introduction', in Cohen, R. and Fischer, C. (eds) *The Routledge Handbook of Diaspora Studies*. London: Routledge, pp. 1–10.

Cohen, R.A. and Yefet, B. (2021) 'The Iranian diaspora and the homeland: redefining the role of a centre', *Journal of Ethnic and Migration Studies*, 47(3), pp. 686–702.

Elahi, B. and Karim, P.M. (2011) 'Introduction: Iranian diaspora', *Comparative Studies of South Asia, Africa and the Middle East*, 31(2), pp. 381–387.

Fahrenthold, S. (2019) *Between the Ottoman and the Entente: The First World War in the Syrian and Lebanese Diaspora, 1908–1925*. Oxford: Oxford University Press.

Fog Olwig, K. and Nyberg Sørensen, N. (2001) *Work and Migration: Life and Livelihoods in a Globalizing World*. London: Taylor and Francis Group.

Gadassik, A. (2011) 'A national filmmaker without a home: home and displacement in the films of Amir Naderi', *Comparative Studies of South Asia, Africa and the Middle East*, 31(2), pp. 474–486.

Gamlen, A. (2019) 'Why engage diasporas?' in Cohen, R. and Fischer, C. (eds) *The Routledge Handbook of Diaspora Studies*. London: Routledge, pp. 302–310.

Gold, S. (2002) *The Israeli Diaspora*. London: Routledge.

Gorman, A. and Kasbarian, S. (2015) *Diasporas of the Modern Middle East: Contextualising Community*. Edinburgh: Edinburgh University Press.

Gualtieri, S. (2009) *Between Arab and White: Race and Ethnicity in the Early Syrian American Diaspora*. Berkeley, CA: University of California Press.

Hage, G. (2005) 'A not so multi-sited ethnography of a not so imagined community', *Anthropological Theory*, 5(4), pp. 463–475.

Hall, S. (1990) 'Cultural identity and diaspora', in Rutherford, J. (ed.) *Identity, Community, Culture, Difference*. London: Lawrence and Wishart, pp. 222–237.

Hanafi, S. (1999) 'Between Arab and French agendas: defining the Palestinian diaspora and the image of the other', in Shami, S. and Herrera, L. (eds) *Between Field and Text: Emerging Voices in Egyptian Social Science*. Cairo: The American University in Cairo Press, pp. 139–159.

Hout, S. (2011) 'Cultural hybridity, trauma, and memory in diasporic anglophone Lebanese fiction', *Journal of Postcolonial Writing*, 47(3), pp. 330–342.

Howell, S. and Shryock, A. (2003) 'Cracking down on diaspora: Arab Detroit and America's "War on Terror"', *Anthropological Quarterly* 76(3), pp. 443–462.

Humphrey, M. (1998) *Islam, Multiculturalism, and Transnationalism, from the Lebanese Diaspora*. Oxford: Centre for Lebanese Studies and I.B. Tauris.

Karam, J.T. (2008) *Another Arabesque: Syrian Lebanese Ethnicity in Neoliberal Brazil*. Philadelphia, PA: Temple University Press.

Karim, P.M. (2006) *Let Me Tell You Where I've Been: New Writing by Women of the Iranian Diaspora*. Fayetteville, AR: University of Arkansas Press.

Kastoryano, R. (2018) 'Transnational politics of integration and an "imagined global diaspora"', in Fossum, J.E., Kastoryano, R. and Siim, B. (eds) *Diversity and Contestations over Nationalism in Europe and Canada*. London: Palgrave, pp. 63–87.

Kaya, A. (2002) 'Aesthetics of diaspora: contemporary minstrels in Turkish Berlin', *Journal of Ethnic and Migration Studies*, 28(1), pp. 43–62.

Koinova, M. (2018) 'Diaspora mobilisation for conflict and post-conflict reconstruction: contextual and comparative dimensions', *Journal of Ethnic and Migration Studies*, 44(8), pp. 1251–1269.

Levitt, P. (2001) *The Transnational Villager*. Berkeley, CA: University of California Press.

Long, N. (2000) 'Exploring local/global transformations: A view from anthropology', in Arce, A. and Long, N. (eds) *Anthropology, Development and Modernities: Exploring Discourses, Counter-tendencies and Violence*. London: Routledge, pp. 184–201.

Mansour, N. and Sabry, T. (2019) 'Introduction: reading popular music in the Arab region and the diaspora', *Middle East Journal of Culture and Communication*, 12(1), pp. 3–6.

Moallem, M. (2000) 'Iranian immigrants, exiles and refugees: from national to transnational contexts', *Comparative Studies of South Asia, Africa and the Middle East*, 20(1), pp. 161–164.

Mojab, S. and Gorman, R. (2007) 'Dispersed nationalism: war, diaspora and Kurdish women's organizing', *Journal of Middle East Women's Studies*, 3(1), pp. 58–85.

Moss, D. (2016) 'Transnational repression, diaspora mobilization, and the case of the Arab Spring', *Social Problems*, 63(4), pp. 480–498.

Moss, D. (2020) 'Voice after exit: explaining diaspora mobilization for the Arab Spring', *Social Forces*, 98(4), 1669–1694.

Motlagh, A. (2011) 'Autobiography and authority in the writings of the Iranian diaspora', *Comparative Studies of South Asia, Africa and the Middle East*, 31(2), pp. 411–424.

Müller-Funk, L. (2020) 'Fluid identities, diaspora youth activists and the (post-)Arab Spring: how narratives of belonging can change over time', *Journal of Ethnic and Migration Studies*, 46(6), pp. 1112–1128.

Naficy, H. (2001) *An Accented Cinema: Exilic and Diasporic Filmmaking*. Princeton, NJ: Princeton University Press.

Ndhlovu, F. (2016) 'A decolonial critique of diaspora identity theories and the notion of superdiversity', *Diaspora Studies*, 9(1), pp. 28–40.

Peteet, J. (2007) 'Problematizing a Palestinian diaspora', *International Journal of Middle East Studies*, 39(4): 627–646.

Rothenberg, C.E. (1999) 'Proximity and distance: Palestinian women's social lives in diaspora', *Diaspora: A Journal of Transnational Studies*, 8(1), pp. 23–50.

Safran, W. (1991) 'Diasporas in modern societies: myths of homeland and return'. *Diaspora: A Journal of Transnational Studies*, 1(1), pp. 83–99.

Salhi, Z.S. and Netton, I.R. (2006) *The Arab Diaspora: Voices of an Anguished Scream*. London: Routledge.

Shafak, E. (2004) *The Saint of Incipient Insanities*. New York: Farrar, Straus and Giroux.

Sheffer, G. (1997) 'Middle Eastern diaspora: introduction and readings', *Middle East Review of International Affairs*, 1(2). Available at: https://ciaotest.cc.columbia.edu/olj/meria/meria797_sheffer.html (accessed 9 September 2021).

Steel, G. (2021) 'Going global-going digital: diasporic networks and female online entrepreneurship in Khartoum, Sudan', *Geoform*, 120, pp. 22–29.

Tölölyan, K. (2007) 'The contemporary discourse of diaspora studies', *Comparative Studies of South Asia, Africa and the Middle East*, 27(3), pp. 647–655.

Van Hear, N. (1998) *New Diasporas: The Mass Exodus, Dispersal and Regrouping of Migrant Communities*. Seattle, WA: University of Washington Press.

Van Hear, N. (2019) 'Diaspora and class, class and diaspora', in Cohen, R. and Fischer, C. (eds) *The Routledge Handbook of Diaspora Studies*. London: Routledge, pp. 129–137.

Vertovec, S. and Cohen, R. (1999) *Migration, Diasporas and Transnationalism*. Northampton: Elgar.

Wald, K.D. (2009) 'The diaspora project of Arab Americans: assessing the magnitude and determinants of politicized ethnic identity', *Ethnic and Racial Studies*, 32(8), pp. 1304–1324.

Wilcock, C. (2018) 'Mobilising towards and imagining homelands: diaspora formation among UK Sudanese', *Journal of Ethnic and Migration Studies*, 44(3), pp. 363–381.

Wimmer, A. and Glick Schiller, N. (2002) 'Methodological nationalism and beyond: nation-state building, migration and the social sciences', *Global Networks*, 2(4), pp. 301–334.

PART I
Forming diasporas

2
TO BE DENIED A HOMELAND

British Mandate policy and the making of the Palestinian diaspora in Chile

Nadim Bawalsa

'Pay attention and wake up, Palestinians!' Philip Badran, a journalist in Lima, Peru, wrote these words in an article published on 26 December 1925 in *al-Watan* (The Homeland),[1] an Arabic newspaper based in Santiago de Chile. Badran, a Lebanese migrant in Peru, was calling on Palestinians to appeal the British authorities' rejection of their applications for Palestinian citizenship following the promulgation of the Palestinian Citizenship Order-in-Council in July 1925. The legislation was designed as part of the British Mandate for Palestine, which was officially enacted in September 1923 and under which Palestine was entrusted to Britain by the League of Nations, following the collapse of the Ottoman Empire at the end of the First World War in 1918.[2] In the eastern Mediterranean, Britain held mandates over Palestine, Transjordan and Iraq, while France received mandates over Syria and Lebanon. These mandates remained in place until the 1940s.

Unlike its other mandated territories, Britain had also promised the Zionists to see to the establishment in Palestine of a 'national home for the Jewish people' three years prior. On 2 November 1917, the British Foreign Secretary, Arthur Balfour, wrote this promise in a letter to Walter Rothschild, a prominent Jewish financier, who was asked to relay the message to the Zionist Federation of Great Britain and Ireland. The letter, known as the Balfour Declaration, was fundamental to the British Mandate in Palestine, and the primary reason for Palestinian opposition to British rule throughout the interwar period. As part of the declaration, Britain also promised to facilitate the acquisition by Jews of Palestinian citizenship. Article 7 of the text of Britain's Mandate over Palestine stated:

> The Administration of Palestine shall be responsible for enacting a nationality law. There shall be included in this law provisions framed so as to facilitate the acquisition of Palestinian citizenship by Jews who take up their permanent residence in Palestine.

To implement this policy, British authorities facilitated the yearly in-migration of tens of thousands of Jews to Palestine. In *A Survey of Palestine*, prepared between December 1945 and January 1946 for the Anglo-American Committee of Inquiry, the Government of Palestine indicated that in 1925 alone, the year of the promulgation of the citizenship law, of a total of 34,641 immigrants, 33,801 were Jews (Shaw, 1946, p. 185). These immigrants applied for Palestinian citizenship and most received it, and due to what British authorities considered to be Palestine's limited economic absorptive capacity, non-Jewish applicants for Palestinian citizenship were regularly denied. This included applications from thousands of Palestinian migrants who had left Palestine as subjects of the Ottoman Empire before the war, many of whom had settled across Latin America, effectively barring them from their rights to Palestinian citizenship and nationality.[3]

The story of Palestinian migrants' struggle to secure their rights to Palestinian citizenship from British authorities throughout the interwar period is central to the narrative of their formation into a diaspora. Today, Chile is home to the largest number of descendants of Palestinian migrants outside of the Arab world. Exact figures vary, but approximately 500,000 descendants of Palestinians are scattered throughout the long and narrow country. The history of this diaspora community, both as part of a larger collective of Arabic-speaking migrants from Greater Syria – the region which today comprises Syria, Lebanon, Jordan, Palestine and Israel – and as a distinct diaspora, sheds light on the processes of migration and settlement of Palestinian migrants since they first arrived in the latter half of the nineteenth century and through the interwar period. It also indicates the importance of examining Palestine's unique status as a mandated territory in a transnational context. That is, how did Britain's lopsided rule over Palestine during the mandate years impact Palestinian migrants throughout the Americas? How did their exclusion from Palestinian citizenship contribute to their formation into a distinct diaspora community?

Situating Palestinians in pre- and post-Ottoman migration history

While Lebanese Christians formed the largest number of Arab Ottoman migrants around the turn of the twentieth century, a significant number of Palestinians were also on the move. As Philip Hitti put it in 1924, 'all portions of Syria and Palestine contributed to the westward-flowing stream' (2005, p. 48), even, he adds, Bethlehem and Nazareth, relatively small towns compared to Damascus, Beirut or Aleppo. Yet until recently, the stories of Palestinian migrants have remained largely untold. The disparity in information regarding the Palestinian constituents of Arab outmigration in the late nineteenth and early twentieth centuries is primarily due to how immigration records were kept in Latin America at the time. As Ottoman subjects carrying Ottoman travel documents, most migrants who arrived in the years before 1918 were indiscriminately registered as Turks, Syrians or Arabs (*turcos*, *sirios* or *arabes*) in Latin American registries upon arrival; their specific origins were thus obscured.

It is generally agreed that approximately 600,000 persons emigrated from Greater Syria to both North and South America between 1860 and 1920 (Karpat, 1985, p. 185). The Ottoman provinces of Greater Syria at the turn of the twentieth century included the Vilayets of Aleppo, Beirut, Syria and Deir az-Zor, and the Mutasarrifate of Jerusalem. Inhabitants of these provinces were collectively referred to as Syrians. A reasonable estimate of the combined populations of these provinces, based on Ottoman census records from 1885, 1897 and 1900, is approximately 1.8 million around the turn of the century. In the United States alone, Alixa Naff (2002) points out, the Department of Commerce and Labor estimated that between 1899 and 1907, 41,404 Arabs from different locales in Greater Syria were admitted to the country. By 1910, she adds, 'the figure swelled to 56,909, a veritable exodus from the homeland' (ibid., p. 5).[4] The movement westward for these small communities across Greater Syria was certainly significant, and different historians have for decades singled out Lebanese and Syrian diaspora communities for historical analysis. It is worthwhile, then, to question the continued dearth of scholarly material regarding the case of Palestinian migrants who amounted to approximately 10,000 by the start of the First World War and over 40,000 by 1936 (Baeza, 2010, p. 97).

Estimates of Palestinian migrants are not entirely absent. A French consular report published in 1907 put the number of Palestinian migrants to the United States at 4,000 persons during ten years (Karpat, 1985, p. 180). Data from the American Consul in Jerusalem of 1914 placed emigration from the Mutasarrifate of Jerusalem at 3,000 in 1913, of which the majority were young men (Issawi, 1966, p. 272). Established in 1872 during Ottoman rule, the Mutasarrifate of Jerusalem was an administrative demarcation that designated the city of Jerusalem and a swathe of territory that stretched west from the city to the Mediterranean coast, south to the Naqab desert and east across the Jordan River, and included Jerusalem, Bethlehem, Bi'r al-Sabi', Gaza, Jaffa and Hebron. Along with the Sanjaks of Nablus and Acre to the north, these three districts were collectively referred to as Southern Syria or Palestine. According to Ottoman census records, the population of Palestine was approximately 600,000 in 1900. Half of the migrants from these districts brought their families over afterwards, mostly to Argentina, Brazil, Chile, Honduras, Mexico and El Salvador (Qafisheh, 2008, p. 104). In Chile, Palestinian migrants amounted to 56 per cent of the total number of Arab Ottomans within the country between 1905 and 1914 alone (Saffie and Agar, 2012, p. 65).

As for other Latin American countries, Roberto Marin-Guzman (2012) and Manzar Foroohar (2012) demonstrate that the proportions of Palestinian migrants in Nicaragua, El Salvador, Costa Rica and Honduras were relatively high, with Honduras receiving the most. Marin-Guzman shows that up to 1955, when the numbers were tallied, Honduras was overwhelmingly the most common destination for these early migrants with 255 registered family names, followed by El Salvador (199), Nicaragua (25), Guatemala (23) and Costa Rica (2) (Marin-Guzman, 2012, p. 27). In other words, notwithstanding unreliable and often muddled migration registers, historians have been able to determine that by the time of the establishment of the British Mandate in Palestine, there was a sizeable population of Palestinian migrants residing abroad who only possessed Ottoman travel papers and who were registered as *turcos*, *sirios* or *arabes* in Latin American registries.

Several factors contributed to the migration of Palestinians from their homes starting in the latter half of the nineteenth century. As with other migrant communities throughout the Mediterranean basin, the potential for economic success in the Americas attracted many Palestinians. In addition, political, social and economic instability in the Ottoman Empire around the turn of the century made it easier for them to take the difficult decision to pack up their lives and make the long and arduous journey west. The story of the Saade family offers an example of the experiences that characterised the narrative of Palestinian migration before the First World War. The Saade family first emigrated in 1906 from Bethlehem to Kyiv, in the Russian Empire, seeking financial betterment. The Saades were Orthodox Christians, and Abdullah, the patriarch of the family, earned a living selling 'Holy Land' items such as rosaries, incense and olive wood. The family first chose Kyiv due to their Orthodox Christian connection and drawn in part to Tsar Nicolas II's support of the Russian Orthodox Church that 'ensured a large market for religious articles from the Holy Land' (Kenny, 2008, p. 8).

Kathy Kenny, Abdullah's great-granddaughter, explained that her family lived relatively comfortably in Kyiv, making periodic return trips to Palestine to collect more merchandise and tend to their properties in Bethlehem. In 1914, they were forced to return permanently to Bethlehem with Russia's entry into the First World War. Katrina, Kenny's grandmother, described to her granddaughter their family's struggle leaving Kyiv and resettling in Palestine in 1914:[5]

> There were a lot of problems. They [Russians] started killing people. My family went to a priest who made some papers to allow them to escape. They had a lot of money – paper money. They were hoping that the money would regain its value, but they lost every cent … When we returned to Palestine, we had a hard time surviving. My father had a lot of land. He was forced to sell to provide for the family. There were a lot of mouths to feed. The land helped them survive.
>
> *(Kenny, 2008, p. 9)*

Yet conditions in Palestine were also dire, particularly with the Ottoman participation in the war on the side of the Central Powers and the economic pressures that swept through Greater Syria (ibid., p. 8).[6] In 1914, within months of their return to Bethlehem from Kyiv, 14-year-old Katrina Saade was betrothed to a Palestinian Christian, Jamil (Emilio) Kabande, who had settled successfully with his family in Mexico earlier that decade. Accompanied by her sister and future brother-in-law, she travelled halfway across the world to marry 18-year-old Emilio. Apart from a short visit she made back to Palestine in the 1930s, Katrina spent the rest of her life in Mexico and, later, California.

The story indicates what was arguably one of the most compelling reasons why Palestinians and other residents of the Arabic-speaking Eastern Mediterranean chose to immigrate. As Karpat describes, successful migrants 'represented a strong argument in favor of bold initiative and enterprise on the part of their fellow Ottomans' (1985, p. 179). Those who heard their stories of success were attracted to seek wealth and stability in the Americas. Starting in the last decades of the nineteenth century, therefore, thousands left Greater Syria each month in the hopes of improving their socio-economic standing and securing more stable lives for themselves and their families. Briefly, as Saliba (1983, p. 39) put it, 'emigration became popular' for many in the region, and it set in motion a way of life that influenced the ways that Ottoman Arab subjects ensured their livelihoods and self-identified.

But why Chile?

Emilio Dabed, a Chilean of Palestinian origin, has reflected on this question.[7] In the preface to his dissertation, he stops to wonder what would have motivated his great-grandfather, a Palestinian merchant from the town of Beit Jala in Palestine, to choose Illapel, Chile, as a final destination for settlement and permanent residence. The town of Illapel is home to approximately 30,000 residents and is nestled in the western foothills of the Andes, 300 kilometres north of Chile's capital. The trip by car to Illapel from Santiago is strenuous even today; the hills rise dramatically a few kilometres inland from the flatter coastal terrain, and the single road that leads into the mountains narrows and snakes upwards for another 40 kilometres before briefly plateauing and plummeting again towards Illapel.

Following his doctoral research in Beit Jala, Dabed believes he managed to solve the mystery of why his ancestors chose Illapel when they arrived in Chile in the 1890s. The landscape and climate they arrived to in Illapel would have reminded them of the Palestine they had left behind. As Dabed describes it:

> I remember that from the age of twelve onward I started speculating about the reasons that brought my family from Beit Jala, Palestine, to my village, in Chile.

> They went from Beit Jala to Haifa; from Haifa on boat to Marseille and then to Le Havre in France; from Le Havre on boat again to Buenos Aires; and from Argentina, on donkey backs through the Andes mountain chain, to Chile, and subsequently, to Illapel. At the time, I advanced all kinds of metaphysical and material reasons for this journey and I am sure that all of them are part of the final explanation. Yet, I had to wait to know Beit Jala in order to understand that immigrants, wherever they go, try in one way or another and more often than not to reproduce the world that they know. I was in awe to discover that Beit Jala and Illapel were in many ways – geographically, topographically, climatically, economically and socially – almost one and the same place.
>
> *(Dabed, 2012, p. 23)*

Indeed, the hills that surround Illapel bear a striking resemblance to those of Beit Jala and its hinterlands. Frequent droughts, mild winters and sunny, dry summers also characterise this mountainous enclave, much like most of Palestine's towns and villages inland from its humid coastline. In a word, Chile felt most like home. Furthermore, Illapel's geographic isolation within the foothills of the towering Andes would have appealed to early migrants seeking less competitive markets to sell their goods; Buenos Aires and São Paulo were already flooded with migrants and merchants, and Santiago and Valparaiso (Chile's main city centres), while relatively less boisterous, were but a few hundred kilometres away. The chances of success were thus promising. Indeed, as Cecilia Baeza explains, the prevalence of Syrian and Lebanese migrants in the richest commercial zones of Latin America, namely São Paulo, Buenos Aires and the Mexico-US border region, motivated many Palestinians to invest in 'intermediary economical development zones like Chile, Peru, Bolivia, and Central America' (2010, p. 81).[8] The choice to settle in less competitive markets, Baeza continues, was a way for these Palestinians to avoid what she terms 'suicidal concurrence' with their Syrian and Lebanese neighbours. In other words, for the benefit of the greater Arabic-speaking migrant community, Palestinians chose less economically developed destinations to avoid potentially cut-throat competition with other Arab migrants, or *paisanos* (countrymen), as they were wont to call each other.

As Dabed's description of his ancestors' arrival in Chile suggests, the voyage through the Andes from Argentina to Chile was not easy. Saffie and Agar (2012, p. 64) describe what travellers would have gone through to arrive in Chile by way of the Andes. After disembarking at Buenos Aires, migrants took a train westward to the town of Mendoza at the edge of the Argentine Andes. From there, the harrowing journey began:

> [The journey] began in Mendoza, Argentina, in the foothills of the Andes, where the adventurers had to wait for the weather to settle down before crossing the mountains. Then they undertook the journey on mules, challenging for about four days dangerous cliffs and the cold Andean mountain range in order to reach the city of Los Andes on Chilean soil. Only in 1908 did the railroad come to the mountain range of Puente del Inca and in 1912, to the station of Las Cuevas, and down to the Chilean station, Caracoles. From there, the passengers continued on mules to Juncal, where they boarded the Chilean Trans-Andean train.

Once safely on the western side of the Andes, migrants were rewarded with a terrain and climate that resembled Palestine's, and a burgeoning economy that welcomed their business. As an interesting example of the dynamic between Chile's hazardous entryways and its Arabic-speaking migrants, the Santiago-based Arabic newspaper, *al-Watan*, printed a story on 8

October 1927 in which two fictionalised Palestinian characters, Abu Azar (AA) and Abu Elias (AE), sit and chat upon the latter's arrival in Santiago:

AA: Where have you been all these long years and why haven't I gotten news from you?
AE: ... I went back to the homeland and I was thinking about living out the rest of this life there, but after staying there seven months, I was shocked 70 times over! So, I travelled to Brazil, and two years later I moved to Argentina, and today I came to Chile because they told me that its climate and lifestyle are like our homeland ...
AA: You did good coming here. Chile is stunning in its values, rich in its nature, attractive in its lifestyle, and healthy in its regions.

This anecdote represented the appeal of Chile to migrants of different generations. That is, in the story, Abu Elias' wife had just died, and his children had all been married off. Living out the remainder of his years in politically and economically volatile Palestine, or economically competitive Brazil and Argentina, was far less appealing than the more relaxed lifestyle he could enjoy in Chile, a country that reminded him of home.

According to Saffie and Agar (2012), in 1941, 2,994 Arab families were registered in Chile. This included approximately 15,000 people 'of whom 85% were immigrants and 15% were their first offspring born on Chilean soil. Half of them were of Palestinian origin' (ibid., p. 65). They further estimate that 18 per cent of all Arab migrants in Chile came from Beit Jala and that 17 per cent were from Bethlehem. Moreover, Myriam Olguin and Patricia Peña (1990, p. 82) estimate that between 1900 and 1930, 36 per cent of Palestinians who arrived in Chile came from Beit Jala, and 35 per cent from Bethlehem. Indeed, the proportion of migrants from Bethlehem and Beit Jala was also high in other parts of Latin America, with 90 per cent of Palestinians in Central American countries coming from Bethlehem, while Peru mostly received Palestinians from Beit Jala (Baeza, 2010, p. 81).[9] The remainder would have come from Jerusalem, Ramallah, Beit Safafa, Beit Sahour and other neighbouring towns and villages. Beit Sahouris, for example, accounted for nearly 6 per cent of Chile's Palestinian migrant community between 1900 and 1930 (Olguin and Peña, 1990, p. 82).

As explained through the Dabed family story, the smaller and more insular the town of settlement, the better the chances of economic success and of recreating a community of endogamous Bethlehemites, Bajjaalis and so on.[10] In Chile, these villages and towns included Illapel, La Calera and Ovalle to the north of Santiago, and Concepción, Chillan and Los Angeles to the south. According to Saffie and Agar, this type of 'chain migration' was common to Arab migrants, and they estimate that by 1940, 62 per cent of the total Arab population of Chile was settled in towns and villages outside of the major urban centres. Likewise, they continue, only 36 per cent of Palestinian families chose Santiago as their place of work and residence (Saffie and Agar, 2012, p. 66). Notwithstanding, Santiago and Valparaiso remained the hubs of the Chilean Arabic printing press, the Arab community's different associations and clubs, and of European consulates to which migrants needed to go to receive permits to travel back to Palestine.

While Palestinians in Chile came to dominate large sectors of Chile's economy, including banking, manufacturing and textiles throughout the latter half of the twentieth century, they had humbler beginnings upon arrival to Chile. Like many Arabic-speaking migrants across the Americas, Palestinians in Chile first took to peddling 'Holy Land' goods including olive wood, oils and other Christian souvenirs they carried with them from Palestine. Within a few years of arriving, however, most found the means to travel less and to sell a variety of daily necessities locally, door to door. These vendors were known as '*falte*' due to the phrase they would yell repeatedly in broken Spanish while roaming the streets, '*¿hay algo que le falte?*' or, 'Is there something you need?' (ibid., p. 66). These items included 'scarves, socks, mirrors, pins, spools of thread, soap, buttons and combs', and by the time the first Arabic-speaking peddlers set up shop in Santiago in 1910, they had visited virtually every settled part of Chile (Olguin and Peña, 1990, p. 82). Some have pointed out that Arabic-speaking peddlers exposed many remote regions of Chile to modern, urban sensibilities through their travels across the country (Allel, 1937, p. 35).

These accomplishments, coupled with a hard work ethic and, for the most part, respect for local customs and laws, earned these migrants relatively good reputations, though discrimination was not absent either. Arabic newspapers in 1920s Chile urged Arabic-speaking shop owners to reduce corruption in their trades. Specifically, these merchants were known to swindle customers and compete with other shop owners in different neighbourhoods. For example, Arab merchants were notorious for staying open until late in the evenings and on Sundays and holidays, which left their neighbouring merchants disgruntled and complaining to the Chilean authorities. Arabic newspapers thus frequently compelled their readers to be more respectful of local customs by closing down their shops before dinnertime and always on Sundays and holidays. In the exchange between Abu Azar and Abu Elias, for example, *al-Watan* reported a conversation in which the characters complained of the impropriety of members of their immigrant community (*jaaliya*) who refuse to abide by local customs:

AA: ... I have begun thinking about an issue that has surprised me often when it comes to our community in Santiago. They keep their stores open until 9PM, while in Brazil they close up at 6PM and go have dinner with their families ...

AE: Until 9PM only? [They stay open] until 10! Until midnight! They stay open on Sundays and on holidays, and if they could connect the night with the day, they wouldn't say no. Frankly, if they stopped work on church holidays, the scourge of the country would be relieved. But they do not abide by the sanctity of the national holidays to such an extent that they are not aware of the indignation of the Chilean countrymen. They have started openly holding [Arabs] in contempt. What would you say if you knew that many of our community's merchants stay working until 11 at night, and on Sundays and holidays until 1 and 2 in the afternoon?

AA: Jeez! Stop, stop! You've torn up my heart.

But, as Saffie and Agar point out, many of these workers would have lived in dwellings attached to their stores, either in the back or upstairs, and so, in these tight quarters, it is small wonder that many migrants lived modestly, spending little and working around the clock to make ends meet (2012, p. 66).

From simple street vendors to modest shop owners, Arabic-speaking migrants in Chile managed to enter virtually every sector of the country's economy fairly quickly. Within 15 years, Saffie and Agar show, entrepeneurs of Middle Eastern origin owned 80 per cent of Chile's textile and spinning mills. In 1937, the Palestinian Yarur family, which today is one of the wealthiest in the country, built the country's most advanced spinning mill, introducing Chile's textile exports to regional markets. Other business ventures started by Palestinians in Chile included those in the agriculture, livestock, mining and pharmaceutical sectors, and by 1941, Middle Eastern-owned industries employed between 9,000 and 10,000 workers at a time of high unemployment and an economic crisis depressing the economy since the 1930s (Saffie and Agar, 2012, p. 70). As Marco Allel (1937, p. 69) put it, 'Members of Arab families, from their arrival to Chile, played an important role in business development; and in this country, it was in need of a strong push.'

Middle Eastern migrants in Chile were mimicking the entrepreneurial practices of their Arabic-speaking compatriots in neighbouring countries. In keeping with the ethos of greater cooperation in the diaspora, Palestinian, Syrian and Lebanese migrants worked together to spread their successful businesses and cultural and social initiatives to every corner of the continent. The early Arabic-speaking migrants in Brazil and Argentina, for example, established the first sports clubs, colleges and schools as early as 1912 in São Paulo and Buenos Aires (Baeza, 2010, p. 80). These communities also established political organisations devoted to nationalist causes that concerned the homeland and the diaspora. Indeed, Stacy Fahrenthold (2019) shows how Syrian and Lebanese migrants across the Americas, and specifically in the United States, Brazil and Argentina, played important roles in supporting and subverting homeland politics during the 1908 Young Turk Revolution, the First World War and the French mandates over Syria and Lebanon.[11] Chile would see similar developments starting in the 1920s and 1930s. For example, Palestinian migrants in Santiago established the Palestinian Sports Club (*Club Deportivo Palestino*) in 1920, and it remains one of Chile's most prominent football clubs to this day.[12] Similarly, in 1924, they established *La Sociedad Juventud Palestina*, which worked to protect the rights of Palestinian migrants within Chile, including keeping them abreast of developments back home. Settlement in Chile, therefore, was beneficial not only for the large number of Palestinians there but also for the larger Arab community in the diaspora.

Becoming Palestinos-Chilenos

When British Mandate authorities began rejecting Palestinian migrants' applications for citizenship in late 1925, Palestinian migrants across Latin America were part of an expanding migrant community that worked actively to defend its members. A close reading of two Santiago-based Arabic newspapers printed in the 1920s, *al-Watan* and *al-Sharq* (The East),[13] suggests that Arabic-speaking migrants in Chile actively connected with other Arabic-speaking communities regionally and transnationally to demand rights for Palestinians throughout Britain's Mandate for Palestine. This activism played a critical role in this community's formation into a diaspora – or, as Rogers Brubaker (2005) puts it, the process through which groups of migrants and their descendants come to see and speak about themselves in terms of groups or collectives. When it came to Chile's Palestinian migrants, the struggle to secure a legal means to return to Palestine – and to preserve rights to landed properties, working permits and inheritance in Palestine – became a formative component of the story of their development into a distinct diaspora community during the interwar period.

Chile's Arabic periodicals

In 1912, an Arab Orthodox priest, Paul Jury, founded *al-Murchid* (The Guide), Chile's first Arabic newspaper. Jorge Hirmas, a Palestinian migrant from Bethlehem, funded this newspaper, which, according to Saffie and Agar, sought to create an 'Arabic publication in the country to advertise the business community and to discuss events and news on the homeland from [the migrants'] perspective' (2012, p. 65). Several Arabic periodicals followed: *al-'Awaatif* (Sentiments) and *al-Muneer* (The Torch) in 1916, *ash-Shabeebah* (The Youth) in 1918, and *al-Watan* in 1920, Chile's longest-running Arabic newspaper. Founded by Issa Khalil Daccarett, a Palestinian migrant, *al-Watan* circulated for nine years, during which time it began printing in Spanish, attracting a larger readership that spanned the continent. *Al-Sharq* was founded in 1927. On August 5, 1928, its editors wrote: 'We saw to naming the newspaper *al-Sharq* out of respect for and pride in our beloved East: the source of the soul, of poetic, philosophical, and human inspiration, and the place of values and the land of civility.'[14]

In Chile, *al-Watan*'s and *al-Sharq*'s editors circulated information that strengthened meaningful and durable connections between the homeland, the diaspora and the local. These three spheres appeared regularly and often sequentially in these periodicals. For example, in many of its issues, *al-Sharq* had separate sections titled 'Homeland News', 'Letters from the Diaspora' and 'Local News'. This contributed to the creation of interconnected networks of communication between local, regional and transnational Arabic-speaking *jaaliyaat* (communities). Consequently, these networks strengthened the scattered *jaaliyaat*'s connectedness and 'groupness', as Rogers Brubaker terms it, around, among other things, calls for social and economic success in the diaspora, for preserving connections with the homeland, and for defending their political rights (2005, p. 13).

Prior to the European mandates, newspapers generally addressed their readers as Arabs and Syrians, particularly when calling for collective action to rectify the pejorative '*turco*' misnomer, a despised slur used against Middle Eastern migrants in Latin America starting in the late nineteenth century. But as the mandate years progressed and new nationalities emerged throughout Greater Syria in the 1920s and 1930s, Chilean newspapers began differentiating between the Lebanese, Syrian and Palestinian experiences under French and British rule. Therefore, when it came to Palestine and its unique experience with British and Zionist forces, the newspapers' coverage of specifically Palestinian developments reflected and contributed to a growing sense of commonality among Palestinian migrants who began seeing themselves increasingly as Palestinians and no longer only as Arabs or Syrians.

In the interwar years, the struggle to secure Palestinian migrants' rights to Palestinian citizenship and nationality following the 1925 Palestinian Citizenship Order-in-Council became a cause for collective action in the Arabic-speaking diaspora, certainly since it implied Palestinians' loss of legal and consular representation in the *mahjar*. Different groups and organisations formed to directly address it, including *El Club Deportivo Palestino* (the Palestinian Sports Club), *El Club Sirio-Palestino* (the Syrian-Palestinian Club) and *La Sociedad Juventud Palestina* (the Palestinian Youth Society). *La Sociedad Juventud Palestina* formed in 1924 with the following objectives: 'The mutual protection of Palestinian residents in the Chilean territory as well as the moral and intellectual advancement of its members.'[15] These groups, among others, offered Chile's Arabic-speaking *jaaliya* opportunities to support their compatriots in Palestine regardless of their new political and legal designations as Syrians, Lebanese or Palestinians.

Indeed, *al-Watan* notified its readers of the issue of Palestinian representation before the promulgation of the ordinance in July 1925. On 11 February 1925, it printed a letter from Philip Badran in Lima. In the letter, Badran addressed *jaaliyatna*, 'our community', which, he elaborated, included Lebanese, Syrians and Palestinians. Subsequently, he described a problem which he said concerned *jaaliyatna*: Palestinians' political and legal representation following Britain's new policies. Evidently, Palestinian members of the Peruvian *jaaliya* had gone to the British consulate in Lima to ask for help in resolving a conflict between Palestinian merchants and the Peruvian police which involved the murder of a Palestinian merchant. Badran explained that they were told by the British consul that nothing could be done for them:

> As for our notables in this town, they have taken this matter very seriously, but … the English consul replied to them that there is nothing he can do since issues relating to Palestinians are the direct concern of the Colonial Office, and not of England's

ambassadors and consuls who do not have the official power or legitimate agency to protect Palestinian migrants. Furthermore, the state of Peru does not grant the right of protection to Palestinians, nor does it recognise England as their representative since they do not carry official or legal documents to that effect.

Briefly, English agencies do not consider Palestinians to be English citizens, and therefore, it cannot defend them, protect them, or interfere in their matters. This is what the representative of the British consulate said.

Badran was alarmed that the Palestinian community in Peru could not seek justice for the killing of one of its members. His plea, subsequently, was for action on the part of the sizeable Chilean Palestinian *jaaliya*:

> Our *jaaliya* here awaits Palestinians in Chile to expose this tragedy and the position of the British consul to the British embassy there so they can inform them of their opinions on this matter ... They will know that as it stands, they have no international representative, consulate, or agency to turn to during hard times or for their commercial needs, especially when it comes to travelling outside these countries and obtaining the legal documents required of every mobile migrant and traveller ... I have been asked to take charge of the duty of the editor-in-chief of this newspaper and reach out to the chivalrous Palestinians and Arabs to remedy this ... defect.

Though Badran was not Palestinian, he considered the issue of Palestinian migrants' rights to legal recourse and representation a concern for all Arabic speakers in Latin America. Indeed, in reaching out to Chile's Palestinian *and* Arab community from Peru, and in printing his words, Badran and *al-Watan*'s editors enhanced the connectedness among Palestinians throughout Latin America. In turn, they contributed to building networks of solidarity and groupness among Arabic-speaking *jaaliyaat* that supported their Palestinian counterparts and loved their *watan*.

By the promulgation of the 1925 Palestinian Citizenship Order-in-Council in July of that year, therefore, Chile's Arabic newspapers were speaking of immigration and nationality in the context of Palestinians alone. On 26 December 1925, six months after the promulgation of the citizenship ordinance, *al-Watan* printed another letter from Badran in Lima in which he urged Palestinians to reject being referred to as Ottomans since it implied their ineligibility for Palestinian citizenship under the new citizenship ordinance. Badran insisted this was part of a plot to give Palestine to the Zionists, and he described its deleterious consequences for Palestinians:

> The gravest plague and most evil illness threatening the existence and future of the Palestinian migrant is the phrase 'An Ottoman resident of Palestine' which the current Government of Palestine writes in the passports of Palestinians; in other words, in the documents required of every traveller and migrant, and especially of the migrants, to get by and establish financial and moral futures for themselves abroad.
>
> This phrase makes the true Palestinian a foreign Ottoman in Palestine, thereby costing him his British Palestinian citizenship rights which afford him British protection like every British citizen. The law provides for this. Therefore, the Palestinian carrying that document containing that corrupt 'phrase' becomes an Ottoman Turk. The British consul therefore does not acknowledge his right to protection, nor to his Palestinianness. The Palestinian is therefore deprived of British protection, of his

nationalism, and of his nation as well ... [Palestinians] are forbidden from returning to their birthplaces and to the country of their fathers and grandfathers.

Badran was referencing Jerusalem's and London's refusal to acknowledge Palestinian migrants' claims to Palestinian citizenship since they had left Palestine when it was under Ottoman rule. British authorities often replied to Palestinian migrants that they were considered Ottomans and recommended they apply for Turkish citizenship.[16] As previously mentioned, Badran instructed Palestinians to 'pay attention and wake up':

> To prevent this danger, every Palestinian migrant must refuse under any circumstance to have that expression placed on his [passport]. Instead, he must insist that he is a Palestinian, son of Palestine, with Palestinian forefathers, and that he is not an Ottoman because the Ottoman state withdrew from Palestine and Syria years ago ... . [Palestinians] have the right to return to their nation as nationals and not as foreign Ottomans. Pay attention and wake up, Palestinians!

Badran was adamant that Palestinians needed to react and resist being identified as Ottoman Turks by British authorities. *Al-Watan*'s editors propagated the reality that the issue of Palestinian citizenship was critical and needed to be dealt with separately and urgently.

The debates surrounding citizenship and nationality intensified in 1927 following a slew of rejections of applications for citizenship by Palestinian migrants. Chile's Arabic newspapers thus began printing more strongly worded reactions. On 29 January 1927, *al-Sharq* printed an article on the issue of nationality. Salvador Sackel, a contributor to the newspaper, authored 'El Concepto de Nacionalidad' (the concept of nationality), in Spanish. Sackel described his philosophy on nationality and the importance of what he called '*el sentimiento patrio*' (the patriotic sentiment). This sentiment, he began, is born in every man, and it develops as an affection towards the defence of freedom. He explained: 'This laudable sentiment, based on deep affection and caused by that which is closest to the individual, becomes something familiar to the inner self when contemplated daily over time.' And as the patriotic sentiment becomes a matter of second nature to man, Sackel proceeded, he must guard it as he would his own home, fighting for it when it is endangered. 'It is a primary duty of sustaining deep down our undying ideal of freedom,' Sackel declared, 'which is the sublime communion of the soul. And when we meet this most sacred duty of all duties, only then can we be proud of having rights.' For Sackel, inborn nationality was congruous with achieving freedom, and 'Only a citizen who has duties and civic rights is worthy to be called man! Others are vile slaves!' The issue of Palestinian citizenship was so acute, it incited philosophical sermons in the pages of *al-Sharq*. Indeed, Sackel linked inborn patriotism with nationality, freedom and civic duty. True rights, he believed, were only achieved with nationality.

Chile's Arabic newspapers also gave Palestinians their own forums for deliberating solutions to the loss of their nationality. To do so, they addressed Palestinian members of the *jaaliya* directly. On 19 November 1927, for example, *al-Watan* published a call to Palestinian migrants urging them to take action against losing their rights to Palestinian nationality by registering for a committee that was established that year to defend their national rights:

> Are you Palestinian?
>
> If you are a real Palestinian, concerned for the wellbeing of your nation upon which your dignity rests – and he without dignity does not have a life – if you

are this Palestinian, then hurry to register for the Committee for the Defence of Palestinian National Rights which defends your nation and your nationality against the colonising ghoul.

Newspaper editors solicited their readers' support for multinational groups and organisations that emerged in the *mahjar* throughout the interwar period. Earlier that year on 22 January, for example, *al-Sharq* reported that La Sociedad Juventud Palestina held a public hearing and invited 'all members of the Palestinian community' in Santiago to discuss the crisis of Palestinian nationality. The purpose of the hearing was to collect 'financial and moral support from every national who has enthusiasm and patriotism and who desires that the English government recognises their Palestinian nationality and forbids the Zionist greed that prevails in our homeland.' The committee accepted donations from Palestinians in 'all parts of this Republic'.

Chile's Arabic newspapers also printed articles about the crisis of citizenship that were authored by Palestinians in Palestine. On 20 August 1927, *al-Watan* printed a letter from Khalil Murqus, secretary of the Committee for the Defence of the Rights of Palestinians in Foreign Countries, which was formed in Beit Jala earlier in 1927. In the letter, Murqus reiterated the seriousness of the citizenship crisis:

> The Palestine citizenship law has been issued, with all its injustices and inequities that fall on our sons and brothers in the diaspora, as well as the financial and moral damages that ensue. … We have received your letters filled with complaints about this law which has hit the core of our hearts, and your voices have been heard on the pages of the newspapers yelling at the Mandate Government, appealing to the sons of the nation to join them in protesting this injustice … which makes them in their diaspora as sheep without a shepherd, and a savoury bite for every greedy lawmaker, for if it passes, it will make Palestinians' souls and stores, which are the mainstays of Palestine and its wealth, susceptible to treachery and loss. It will also deprive them of international laws, which protect them from injustice and uphold their matters before other nations.

Murqus proceeded to add his voice and the voices of Palestinians throughout Palestine in protesting the legislation:

> We are with you in voicing your demands, standing as one with our brothers in Jerusalem, Jaffa, Haifa, Bethlehem, Ramallah, Nazareth, Hebron, and elsewhere in Palestine, unified in protest against the Mandatory Government about this unjust law, demanding of it to amend it or to add to it an article which defends our brothers. The same applies to our brothers in all diasporas … And our voices will raise and our protests will continue until the highest level of protest, doing anything and everything we can for the sake of obtaining our desired rights, whether with the local government in Palestine, the supreme references in London, or the League of Nations.

Finally, he asked for the financial support of Palestinians abroad to contribute to the defence of their nationality, the purpose for which his committee had been formed:

> Considering what this lively project will require in hardships and expenses, we write to you this letter begging for your devotion, and enlivening your motivation to gather the necessary money and send it to us as soon as possible so we may go forward.

> Money is the basis of winning these projects and their success. Therefore, we will have carried out our duties to our sons and nation.

Migrants' remittances were central to sustaining Palestine's economy, and also to the operation of its national movement. The Committee for the Defence of the Rights of Palestinians in Foreign Countries, which linked the *mahjar* with the *watan*, also needed the support of Palestinian migrants to carry out its duties.

Arabic newspaper editors in Santiago even reprinted the calls for political action and support from Palestinians throughout the *mahjar*, which they received from Palestinian newspapers in Palestine. These publications kept Palestinians across the world connected to the greater Palestinian national cause promoted by nationalist newspapers in Palestine – namely, *Filastin* – and they had the added effect of constructing shared experiences among Palestinians in the *watan* and throughout the *mahjar*. On 8 April 1928, for example, *al-Watan* reprinted an article that appeared in *Filastin* from a Palestinian residing in El Salvador. Nakhla al-Da'da' addressed his *kitaab maftouh* (open book) to 'God Almighty', suggesting that the tone of the community's frustration with Britain's citizenship policies had reached new levels since Britain was unrelenting with its rejections.

He began by asserting, unequivocally, that he and those on whose behalf he was addressing his letter are Palestinians and from Palestine: 'Oh, Lord / You have willed it and thus created us as Palestinians in the land of Palestine, in the birthplace of the Revelation and religions, of prophets and protectors.' He proceeded to describe the long history of oppressive colonisation they had endured as Palestinians which culminated with the Ottomans. This dramatic opening set the tone for al-Da'da's discussion about the difficulties Palestinians in El Salvador were facing as a result of Britain's unjust policies:

> [The] government of El Salvador has issued a new law ... and imposed it on every migrant that he must present citizenship papers, notarised by the government of his nation, or else he would be prohibited from work in El Salvador. This came as a direct blow to Palestinians as it ceased upon the remainder of their hopes and rendered them homeless without a nation or citizenship.

Al-Da'da' reassured the Lord that he and Palestinians in El Salvador had also sought to remedy this situation through diplomacy. Indeed, he explained that the Palestinians of El Salvador even formed a delegation to meet with the British representative, to no avail:

> The delegation petitioned him and sent him a telegraph requesting a time to meet, but the representative refused to meet the delegation and provided the following strange reply through his scribe: 'The consul says to you that Britain has only colonised the land of Palestine, but it has nothing to do with its people'!!!
> The delegation did not succeed in meeting the consul face to face since the consul refused, so it then requested from the consul to broadcast his reply to the community, but his reply on the following day was the text of the unjust Palestinian Citizenship Order-in-Council, and nothing less!

He then pleaded with the Lord for answers:

> The Republic of El Salvador does not want to consider us its subjects ...

So, tell us, oh God, what we should do and to whom we should go. We have become sheep without a shepherd, a pasture for wolves, and the coveted of the oppressors! Shall we commit suicide and die, and bid farewell to our country, its nationality and its people???

Al-Da'da' was desperate, a feeling that resonated with Palestinian communities across Latin America whose connections to Palestine were being threatened. And the fact that *al-Watan* received al-Da'da's open book to the Lord from *Filastin* indicates that for these newspapers' editors, the crisis of Palestinian citizenship was a thoroughly transnational issue that impacted Palestine, as well. Throughout the interwar period, Palestinians worldwide thus grew increasingly interconnected through their shared struggle. Diaspora periodicals reinforced these bonds.

Chile's Palestinian diaspora story

The proliferation of national identifiers in the Middle East into Lebanese, Syrian and Palestinian categories in the interwar period was accompanied by the simultaneous circulation of rhetoric among Arabic-speaking *jaaliyaat* in Latin America about a shared struggle for transnational recognition and representation as a migrant collective newly made up of multiple nationalities, each facing myriad obstacles. The emerging diaspora community of Palestinians experienced the most difficulty when it came to transnational recognition and representation as a political collective. That is, the exclusionary measures put in place by British Mandate authorities in the aftermath of 1925 Palestinian Citizenship Order-in-Council left thousands of Palestinian migrants vulnerable to permanent material losses and legal complications.

This new reality spurred a transnational campaign to raise awareness among those who identified as Palestinians and their allies throughout the *mahjar* about the importance of fighting for nationality and citizenship. Chile's Arabic newspapers were platforms for circulating such information, and for urging their readers to action. This, in turn, contributed to forging diaspora connections and to fostering local, regional and transnational solidarity around a cause that was considered to be shared and worthy of immediate action. In a concerted campaign that combined Chile's Palestinian community with Palestinians throughout the Americas and in the *watan*, Chile's Arabic newspapers continually urged readers to demand redress, rights and citizenship as Palestinians. They also called on all members of the *jaaliya* to support Palestinians in their struggle.

In significant ways, this is a key component in the narrative of the Palestinian migrant community's formation into a diaspora. And to this day, Palestinos-Chilenos, like many others in the Palestinian diaspora, feel unified and empowered by an ongoing and shared experience of distance from a homeland that continues to hold symbolic and material significance for their collective.

Notes

1 *Al-Watan* newspaper (11 February 1925, 29 December 1925, 20 August 1927, 8 October 1927, 19 November 1927, 8 April 1928) [periodical entries] held at: Biblioteca Nacional de Chile, Santiago, Chile. Microfilm section.
2 The ousting of the Ottomans from Arab lands ushered in the age of European mandates, which were established as temporary trusteeships by the newly created League of Nations to guide former Ottoman subjects towards national self-determination. As laid out in Article 22 of the Covenant of the League of Nations, this was based on the assumption among European powers that

> Certain communities formerly belonging to the Turkish Empire have reached a stage of development where their existence as independent nations can be provisionally recognised subject to the rendering of administrative advice and assistance by a Mandatory until such time as they are able to stand alone.

Article 22 was signed in 1919 and came into effect in January 1920.
3 See Bawalsa (2017) and Banko (2016) for in-depth investigations into the citizenship legislation and how it was used to deny citizenship to thousands of Palestinian migrants.
4 For a thorough history of the settlement and assimilation of Syrians in the United States, see Naff (1985).
5 Katrina Saade, as quoted by her granddaughter, Kathy Kenny. Kenny collected this information from audiotapes that her aunt, Mary (Farhat) Bond, Katrina's youngest daughter, and her husband Henry Bond had recorded in Wyoming during the mid-1970s. Katrina Saade, who was 6 when her family first left Palestine in 1906, also corresponded with different family members in letters throughout her travels that spanned over 20 years. For more information about Katrina Saade and her letters, see Bawalsa (2011).
6 As an example, cotton and silk from Syria and Lebanon were the most affected crops in the region due to global competition from the Far East, and by the First World War, production of both had 'practically ceased', as Saliba (1983, p. 34) points out. Khater (2013) has estimated that in 1890, silk accounted for 50 per cent of the GDP of Mount Lebanon.
7 Emilio Dabed was the director of the International Law and Human Rights Program at al-Quds/Bard College in Jerusalem between 2011 and 2015. During 2015–2016, he was awarded the Palestine and Law Fellowship at Columbia University and was an adjunct professor in the Columbia University Law School. He received his doctorate in Political Sciences from Institut de Sciences Politiques in Aix-en-Provence, France.
8 All translations from Arabic, French and Spanish are provided by the author. All emphases appear in the original sources.
9 It is not known why Palestinians from Bethlehem and Beit Jala specifically were leaving at a higher rate. Historians seem to agree that, since endogamy within the extended family or religious community was a preferred form of socialisation, the existence of a growing population of Bethelehemites and Bajjaalis in Chile would have ensured a steady outflow of migrants from those towns in Palestine.
10 Endogamy was a central component of socialisation across many communities in the Mediterranean, including the Middle East.
11 In the opening pages to the book, Fahrenthold (2019) includes a list of the different political organisations that were formed throughout the Lebanese and Syrian diaspora.
12 See Baeza (2010) for more information about the different organisations, sports clubs and committees devoted to different Middle Eastern national and cultural collectives that emerged in Chile, Honduras and Brazil in the first two decades of the twentieth century.
13 *Al-Sharq* newspaper (22 January 1927, 29 January 1927, 5 August 1928) [periodical entries] held at: Biblioteca Nacional de Chile, Santiago, Chile. Microfilm section.
14 All translations from Arabic and Spanish to English of periodical entries from *al-Sharq* newspaper were conducted by the author. All emphases appear in the original sources.
15 'Estatutos: Sociedad Juventud Palestina', 26 May 1924, in the periodicals of the Biblioteca Nacional de Chile, Santiago, Chile. Translated from Spanish by the author.
16 See Bawalsa (2017) for more information about the reasons British authorities gave for rejecting Palestinian migrants' applications for citizenship.

References

Allel, M. (1937) *Las industrias de las colectividades de habla Arabe in Chile*. Santiago, Chile: Syrian- Palestinian Business Association.
Baeza, C. (2010) *Les Palestiniens d'Amérique Latine et la cause Palestinienne: Chile, Brésil, Honduras, 1920–2010*. Paris: Institut de Sciences Politiques.
Banko, L. (2016) *The Invention of Palestinian Citizenship, 1918–1947*. Edinburgh: Edinburgh University Press.
Bawalsa, N. (2011) 'Trouble with the in-laws: family letters between Palestine and the Americas, 1925–1939', *Jerusalem Quarterly*, 47, pp. 6–27.

Bawalsa, N. (2017) 'Legislating exclusion: Palestinian migrants and interwar citizenship', *Journal of Palestine Studies*, 46(2), pp. 44–59.Brubaker, R. (2005) 'The "diaspora" diaspora', *Ethnic and Racial Studies*, 28(1), pp. 1–19.

Dabed, E. (2012) *A Constitution for a Non-State: The False Hopes of the Palestinian Constitutional Process, 1988–2007*. Paris: Institut de Sciences Politiques.

Fahrenthold, S. (2019) *Between the Ottomans and the Entente: The First World War in the Syrian and Lebanese Diaspora, 1908–1925*. Oxford: Oxford University Press.

Foroohar, M. (2012) 'Palestinian diaspora in Central America – a story of hardship and success', in Raheb, V. (ed.) *Latin American with Palestinian Roots*. Bethlehem: Diyar Publishers, pp. 45–62.

Hitti, P. (2005) *The Syrians in America*. Piscataway, NJ: Gorgias Press.

Issawi, C. (1966) 'Migration from and to Syria, 1860–1914', in Issawi, C. (ed.) *The Economic History of the Middle East, 1800–1914*. Chicago: University of Chicago Press, pp. 269–273.

Karpat, K. (1985) 'The Ottoman emigration to America, 1860–1914', *International Journal of Middle East Studies*, 17(2), pp. 175–209.

Kenny, K. (2008) 'The power of place: Katrina in five worlds', *Jerusalem Quarterly*, 35, pp. 5–30.

Khater, A. (2013) 'Little Syria, NYC: history and advocacy', presentation at CUNY University, New York, 20 May.

Marin-Guzman, R. (2012) 'Political participation and economic success of the Palestinians of Christian origin in Central America', in Raheb, V. (ed.) *Latin American with Palestinian Roots*. Bethlehem: Diyar Publishers, pp. 25–44.

Naff, A. (1985) *Becoming American: The Early Arab Immigrant Experience*, Carbondale, IL: Southern Illinois University Press.

Naff, A. (2002) 'New York: the mother colony', in Benson, K., Kayal, P., and Museum of the City of New York (eds) *A Community of Many Worlds: Arab Americans in New York City*. Syracuse, NY: Syracuse University Press, pp. 3–10.

Olguin, M. and Peña, P. (1990) *La inmigración Arabe en Chile*. Santiago: Instituto Chileno Arabe de Cultura.

Qafisheh, M. (2008) *The International Law Foundations of Palestinian Nationality: A Legal Examination of Nationality in Palestine Under Britain's Rule*. Boston: Martinus Nijhoff Publishers.

Saffie, N. and Agar, L. (2012) 'A century of Palestinian immigration to Chile: a successful integration', in Raheb, V. (ed.) *Latin American with Palestinian Roots*. Bethlehem: Diyar Publishers, pp. 63–82.

Saliba, N. (1983) 'Emigration from Syria', in Abraham, S. and Abraham, N. (eds) *Arabs in the New World*. Detroit: Wayne State University, pp. 31–43.

Shaw, W. (1946) *A Survey of Palestine; Prepared in December 1945 and January 1946 for the Information of the Anglo-American Committee of Inquiry*. Available at Berman Jewish Policy Archive: www.bjpa.org/content/upload/bjpa/a_su/A%20SURVEY%20OF%20PALESTINE%20DEC%201945-JAN%201946%20VOL%20I.pdf

3
THE AKP GOVERNMENT IN TURKEY AND DIASPORA-MAKING

Lobbying, public diplomacy and the erasure of difference

Bengi Bezirgan-Tanış

Introduction

Nation-states reshape their approaches to diaspora politics in response to the ongoing debates concerning citizenship rights, the visibility of religious and ethnic identities and different claims of immigrant communities. Equally, the shifting nature of official approaches and policy priorities concerning diasporas are a reflection of the ways in which diaspora politics now plays a crucial role in national and international politics. The literature on the relationship between diaspora communities and their homelands is mainly based on two strands of research: (1) the distinction between diasporas as actors in homeland politics; and (2) as objects of state policies (Adamson, 2019). The former highlights the effects of diasporas on the politics of their homeland governments. Several researchers have identified diasporas as actively shaping homeland politics and their effects on processes of democratisation, economic development and foreign policy (ibid., p. 213). The second strand of scholarship points out how sending states implement policies and establish institutions to reach out to their diaspora populations abroad. Highlighting how diasporas are relevant to state policy, this body of scholarship concentrates on state-diaspora engagement, diaspora integration and diaspora-building policies, as well as the nature of citizenship and de-territorialised political practices such as the voting rights of citizens abroad (ibid., p. 214).

Drawing on these two strands of research, this chapter addresses the concept of diaspora as a field of competing stances or a category of practice (Brubaker, 2005) and views diaspora politics as 'a form of transnational political engagement structured around a particularistic identity category (such as a national, ethnic, religious, or sectarian identity)' (Adamson, 2019, p. 215). The strategies of diaspora engagement adopted by the Turkish state indicate that the Turkish and Armenian diaspora communities are regarded as significant transnational actors and, as such, have become objects of state policies that cast them not as 'victims of conflicts and/or passive recipients of the politics of homeland and host country' but rather as active and influential political actors (Baser and Toivanen, 2018, p. 345). While the Justice and Development Party government (hereafter AKP) in power uses the category of the diaspora for political purposes by advocating the transformation of Turkish guest workers and emigrants into a diasporic community, efforts on the part of members of the Armenian diaspora for recognition of the Armenian genocide are treated as a political threat that undermines a particular perception of Turkish state interests. Since the 2000s, the diaspora engagement policies of the Turkish state vis-à-vis the Turkish diaspora (e.g. in Germany or France) and the Armenian diaspora (e.g. in France or the United States) have influenced the process of state-sponsored diaspora-building in Turkey, which has reduced the possibilities of a Turkish diaspora to a Sunni, Muslim and ethnically Turkic rubric.

With this dynamic in mind, this chapter explores how the AKP, in the guise of the Turkish state, positions itself in relation to these two diaspora communities, adopting selective diaspora management policies that pit an imagined and acceptable Turkish diaspora against the Armenian diaspora. More specifically, I concentrate on the questions of how the Turkish state manages, moulds, supports and engages Turkish citizens abroad to actively counter the genocide recognition claims of the Armenian diaspora. The attempts of the Turkish state to rely upon the political potential of the Turkish diaspora as a counterforce against the Armenian diaspora depend on three types of diaspora engagement policies. Following Gamlen (2006, pp. 5–6), who adopted Foucault's (1982) understanding of the exercise of power, I highlight how the Turkish state's diaspora engagement policies include capacity-building policies, extending rights to the diaspora and extracting obligations from the diaspora. In so doing, I first turn to the processes through which this state-sponsored diaspora has been created in the context of the debates on transnationalism and diaspora politics.

Situating the Turkish community in the diaspora-making project

The emigration of Turkish citizens from Turkey to Europe that began in the 1960s was considered first and foremost in terms of their economic role but has since been transformed into a political issue over the years. Approximately 20 years after the start of the guest-worker system, a transition from temporary to permanent migration through family reunification and formation took place (Bilgili and Siegel, 2010, p. 21). The permanent settlement of Turkish citizens brought about changes in the Turkish state's 'expectations and its obligations towards its citizens' (ibid., p. 22). The increasing heterogeneity of the Turkish diaspora, which came to include refugees and asylum seekers from politically active ethnic or religious minority groups in Turkey (İçduygu and Kirişci, 2009), resulted initially in a heterogeneous set of relationships between the state and the different diasporic groups (Bilgili and Siegel, 2010, p. 22). However, over time, the ethnic and religious diversification among Turkish immigrants has been actively ignored in the strategies employed by the AKP government that assert and emphasise a Sunni Muslim and ethnically Turkic diaspora. The attempt to build a diaspora focused on Sunni Muslim Turks residing abroad reflects the domestic agenda of the AKP, which has sought to homogenise Turkishness and promote Turkey's image as a regional and global power. In the process, Kurds, Alevis, Armenians, non-Muslim Turks and their organisations have been marginalised and framed as groups hostile to a purified Sunni Turkishness. In turn, Sunni Turks in the diaspora have come to be seen as a kind of human resource both domestically and transnationally and have been ascribed the roles of lobbyists and agents of public diplomacy. Thus, diaspora policies reflect and produce 'acceptable citizens' both at home and abroad (Mencutek and Baser, 2018, p. 88).

The government's adoption of the term diaspora to describe Turks abroad emerges as one of the strategic moves of the official nomenclature of statecraft. Before the era of AKP rule in Turkey, Turks abroad were 'never referred to as a "diaspora" by the Turkish state' (Ünver, 2013, p. 183). The transformation from guest workers and emigrants to the diaspora, from the state's viewpoint, represents how Turkey as a 'strategically selective state encourages certain forms of transnational participation while trying to selectively manage what migrants can and cannot do' (Mügge, 2012, p. 33). By using the concept of the diaspora to mean Sunni Turks abroad exclusively, the state seeks to co-opt this community for a decidedly political end. While the state recognises the transnational existence and participation of the Turkish community abroad, which is henceforth seen as part of the nation, it seeks to ensure that this community acts in line with the state's national political goals as it is imagined as a homogeneous entity. By 'extending extraterritorial cultural and citizenship rights for Turkish migrants and their descendants in various countries of residence', Turkey's diaspora engagement policies attempt 'to mobilise the Turkish diaspora holistic approach including social, economic and political agendas' (Baser, 2017, pp. 222, 230). Consequently, Sunni Muslim Turks in the diaspora have come to be seen as bearers of the national interest, representatives of soft power, and a bulwark against external national threats towards the Turkish state.

Following the period of the AKP's ascension to power in 2002, the state's ties to Turkish communities abroad have strengthened and its engagement policies towards citizens living overseas have become more visible (Ünver, 2013; Arkilic, 2016; Köşer-Akçapar and Bayraktar-Aksel, 2017). The AKP government has progressively implemented 'global nation policies' that 'encourage migrants to stay abroad but stay in touch', rather than adopting 'homeland policies' that seek to 'create institutions aimed at orienting migrants towards return' (Østergaard-Nielsen, 2003a, p. 766). The support provided by the Turkish state for its citizens residing overseas is conditional, based on an assessment of what 'these populations can offer the homeland state' (Waterbury, 2010, p. 135). For example, in the run-up to the first general elections in which Turks in Europe were able to vote in 2015, President Erdoğan delivered a speech to Turkish immigrants living in Karlsruhe, Germany, in which he elicited their active involvement in the work of statecraft. After describing 'voting as a privilege and an opportunity', he addressed his audience as follows:

> Why shouldn't my brothers who are currently in this hall take part in state parliaments? Why shouldn't they take part in the federal parliament? Why shouldn't they take part in the European Parliament? You are the national voice, so we need this. This is not the voice of those who stand up in the European Parliament and keep silent about the Armenian issue but the voice of those who strike an attitude in the issue. That's how I see you guys.
>
> *(Presidency of the Republic of Turkey, 2015)*[1]

As this excerpt suggests, the Turkish diaspora is seen by the AKP government as one of the sources of both national and transnational political action. It additionally discloses how the government seeks to make this community a campaign partner in general elections in the homeland and to make them participate in a common cause with the state regarding the issue of genocide denial in the host states. This approach creates the Turkish nation-state beyond the boundaries of the homeland by marshalling the diaspora against a perceived existential common goal such as recognition of the Armenian genocide. In 2016, as reported by the Turkish state-run news agency, around 10,000 Turkish immigrants rallied in Berlin to protest the parliamentary proposal to call the events of the 1915 genocide. The largest organisations of

Turkish immigrants in Germany, including the Turkish Community in Berlin and the Union of European Turkish Democrats, joined together against this 'smear campaign' against Turks and described this resolution as a one-sided Armenian motion (Şimşek, 2016). Following this protest and the adoption of the resolution by the Parliament of the Federal Republic of Germany, the Ministry of Foreign Affairs of Turkey issued a press release that drew attention to the issues of 'Turcophobia and Islamophobia' by recalling Germany's record of past crimes against humanity and described this decision as 'an attempt to assimilate Turks and Germans of Turkish origin' and 'to alienate them from their own history and self-identity' (Republic of Turkey Ministry of Foreign Affairs, 2016).[2]

The AKP's political instrumentalisation of the diaspora casts the Turkish diaspora as an overtly political category of practice, its loyalty to the homeland and thus its ability 'to mobilize energies' (Brubaker, 2005, p. 13) against the Armenian genocide allegations then becomes a measure of its legitimacy. From the perspective of AKP, what makes the Turkish community abroad a diasporic community is their Sunni Muslim identity as well as their Turkishness. What then makes this group distinct from Armenians and Kurds is the extent to which Sunni Turks reproduce the state's ambivalence towards the Armenian and Kurdish causes. The Islamic component of Turkish national identity has come to take precedence over the ethnic. Indeed, the notion of the Turkish nation has come to be closely connected with the Muslim nation, i.e. the ummah, the global community of Muslims (Tziarras, 2019, p. 3), which underwrites ethnic particularism in favour of an ostensibly colour-blind Islam. Turkey's diaspora engagement policies towards Turkish communities are thus based on 'a new view of the nation, which is compatible with multiple Muslim identities' but exclusionary of other forms of collectivity (Aydın, 2014, p. 13). The emphasis on multiple religious identities has been accompanied by 'the propagation of Muslim nationalism that is not based primarily on race and language but is oriented towards a historic Turkish and Ottoman identity' (ibid., p. 11). The AKP has sought to consolidate bonds with Muslim communities abroad as part of the government's commitment 'to revive historical ties with previously Ottoman territories' (Baser, 2017, p. 230). Thus, while excluding Kurds, Armenians, Assyrians and Alevis, 'the Turkish government effectively broadened its diaspora to include Azerbaijani, Kyrgyz, Kazakh, Uzbek and Turkmen groups as external members' as the Turkish nation is conceived to consist of Turkish citizens, relatives and kin groups (ibid., p. 231). Recognising that these groups have 'common historical and cultural heritage', the Turkish government's diaspora policy concentrating on Turks in Europe is closely tied with 'a foreign policy that aims to intensify relations to Muslims in the Balkans and the Caucasus and to Turkic peoples' (Aydın, 2014, p. 12). Official estimates put the number of Turkish citizens in the diaspora at around 6 million citizens, a figure that is then significantly inflated to 200 million when kin and related communities are counted (Yurtnaç, 2012). From this point of view, in terms of contemporary political usage, the term Turkish diaspora encapsulating only Sunni Muslim Turks in Europe fails to 'capture many of the political and cultural activities of the Alevi, Yazidi, Assyrian or – more controversially – Muslim "diasporas" in Europe and elsewhere' (Adamson, 2019, p. 212).

Moreover, the notion of de-territorialised nation-states becomes significant as it incorporates citizens living 'physically dispersed within the boundaries of many other states, but who remain socially, politically, culturally and often economically part of the nation-state of their ancestors' (Basch, Glick Schiller, and Szanton Blanc, 1994, p. 9). The Turkish case exemplifies a de-territorialised nation-state in which the political leadership perceives the Sunni Muslim Turkish community abroad as part of both the nation and the state. This also leads Turkey as a sending state to engage in ' "re-territorializing" (Louie, 2000) their overseas citizens by launching policies that reincorporate them not only in the nation but also in the national economy and political life of their country of origin' (Østergaard-Nielsen, 2003b, p. 21). In other words, the Turkish state's diaspora policies involve both processes of de-territorialisation and re-territorialisation.

Furthermore, the Turkish state's objective to create its own diaspora and to open up a political space for its members signifies 'a transnationally dispersed collectivity that distinguishes itself by clear self-imagination as community' (Sökefeld, 2006, p. 267). The crucial aspect for the formation of an imagined transnational community is obviously 'an idea of shared identity, of common belonging to that group' (ibid.). Nevertheless, the critical questions here are how individuals identify themselves as members of a transnational community (ibid., p. 271) and how the state reinforces such self-identification of its citizens. To answer these questions, both Sökefeld (2006, p. 267) and Bauböck (2010, p. 300) underline that diasporas are invented through 'discursive constructions of imaginations of community' and 'discourses about transnational belonging to a political community'. According to a report published by the Center for American Progress in 2020, 'most in the Europe-based Turkish diaspora continue to identify themselves first and foremost as Turks rather than as full members of the societies they inhabit' (Hoffman, Makovsky, and Werz, 2020, pp. 1–2). This finding is also substantiated by the result that the interaction of the Turkish diaspora with developments and politics in Turkey is far greater than with their current countries of residence (ibid., p. 2). These results demonstrate the limitations of the AKP government-led policy promoting the integration of Turks in Europe and encouraging their political involvement in the European host states.

Official narratives play a particular role in creating such a discursive sphere in which diaspora communities are defined and their actions are intended to be managed. Turkey's efforts to reach out to its citizens abroad and the identification of the Turkish populations abroad as a diaspora thus demonstrate that 'the politics of transborder membership is in the first instance a politics of identification' (Brubaker and Kim, 2011, p. 24). Based on this argument, the Turkish population as a transborder population is first 'identified and construed as "belonging" to the state' and then 'they can become the object of state policies' (ibid.). This is also connected to how the Turkish state exercises symbolic power 'to name, identify, define, and demarcate; to classify and categorize; to specify authoritatively who is who, and what is what; and thereby to help "make and unmake groups"' (ibid.). When viewed from this perspective, the formation of the Turkish diaspora in Europe is not straightforwardly an outcome of migration movements. Rather, 'the rise of a diasporic imagination of the community' is prompted by specific 'events and developments' (Sökefeld, 2006, p. 271) that take place both in the homeland and host-state politics. In this regard, the ongoing conflict between the Turkish state and the Armenian diaspora, and in particular, efforts to recognise the Armenian genocide, have fuelled the making of a state-sponsored Turkish diaspora.

The thorn of the Armenian genocide

The Armenian diaspora, described as a classic (Smith, 2010) or victim (Cohen, 1997) diaspora, strives for the recognition of the Armenian genocide of 1915. The Turkish state, as the heir of the Ottoman Empire, still refuses to acknowledge the atrocities committed against Armenians as a genocide. While the issue of political recognition of the killings of Armenians as genocide is an integral part of the identity of the Armenian diaspora (Herzig and Kurkchiyan, 2005), the Turkish state continues to reduce these massacres to an allegation. On the website of the Ministry of Foreign Affairs, we find the following formulation: 'We do not describe the 1915 events as a "genocide", and we do not accept this term while referring to these tragic events.' The official narrative underlines that the killing of Armenians was the unforeseen result of the 1915 Relocation Law while also claiming that the death toll has been exaggerated by the radical factions of the Armenian diaspora.³ Although this approach admits that there were 'some' losses, it also claims that these deaths are not sufficient to call what happened in 1915 a genocide. The involvement of the Armenian diaspora in raising awareness of the genocide unsettles this official standpoint, which appears to be the reason for denouncing the Armenian genocide activists as distorting historical facts.

Armenian genocide recognition and reparations demands might be regarded as one of the central themes in Turkey's diaspora engagement policies. The refusal to recognise the genocide continues to reveal itself in the Turkish government's efforts 'to engage "its diaspora" in activities such as demonstrations and lobbying against Armenian Genocide resolutions abroad' (Adamson, 2019, p. 226). This government-led approach also reinforces the 'disagreements between Turkish and Armenian diaspora members over how to interpret and understand the events of 1915' (ibid., pp. 227–228). Genocide denial has repeatedly led conservative Turkish diaspora organisations to act collectively in their countries of residence. In 2012, the French Senate's passing of a bill criminalising denial of genocide caused the largest ever collective demonstration of the Turkish diaspora in France, in which 35,000 people gathered in Paris. According to one of the organisers, this protest was 'organized thanks to the Turkish state's endeavours to stymie the influence of Armenian lobby groups in France' (Arkilic, 2020, p. 11). Similarly, on the centenary of the 1915 massacre, following German President Gauck's use of the term genocide, a protest march against genocide allegations was organised in Berlin and the largest Turkish diaspora organisations, including the Turkish-Islamic Union for Religious Affairs, the Turkish Community in Berlin and the Union of European Turkish Democrats, called on their members to join the rally (Anadolu Agency, 2015).⁴

There are three sets of 'others' for Turkish national identity: (1) the non-Muslims (the Jews, Armenians and Greeks); (2) non-Turkish Muslims (Kurds, Arabs and Alevis); and (3) any groups that are critical of the Ottoman past (Kadıoğlu, 2007, pp. 286–289). These remain relevant as it undermines attempts by the modern Turkish state to distance itself from inconvenient parts of the historical heritage of the Ottoman Empire. The denial policies of the Turkish state in this regard have shown historical continuity and have been always at the centre of Turkish diplomatic statecraft. However, the particular political strategies and discourses with which the AKP government seeks to deal with the atrocities against the Armenian community and discredit the claims of the Armenian diaspora are distinct from those of previous governments. In addition to well-established official national narratives and diplomatic positions that have denied the genocide since 1915, the AKP government portrays the massacres against the Armenians as one of the inevitable vagaries of war, in a sense, a kind of unintended collateral damage. For instance, when, in 2014, then Prime Minister Erdoğan offered condolences to the grandchildren of Armenians who lost their lives in the massacres, he said, 'Millions of people of all religions and ethnicities lost their lives in the First World War' and described the war incidents as 'our shared pain' (Letsch, 2014).⁵ This apology represented an important change in the state's long-standing official denial policy since it was the first time that 'the suffering of the Armenians was recognised publicly and officially at the highest bureaucratic level' (Aybak, 2016, p. 134). However, the official rhetoric of 'common pain' has become 'an integral part of the government's diplomatic strategy'. This type of discourse, in fact, 'trivializes and normalizes the Armenian trauma as the inevitable outcome of a great geopolitical catastrophe', which is signified by 'the banality of non-apology' (ibid.). Similarly, in his letter to the Armenian Patriarch of Turkey in 2020, Erdoğan again underlined the harsh conditions of the First World War which caused the loss of Ottoman Armenians (Presidency of the Republic of Turkey, 2020).⁶ These statements indicate how the unique sufferings of the Armenian community are presented as just one of the ordinary outcomes of the inhumane circumstances of war. The attempt to cluster the Armenian sufferings with those of all Ottoman citizens at that time also results in equalising and relativising the Armenian sufferings. More importantly, it is an effort to disguise the genocidal nature of this anguish since only the Armenians were sent away from their ancestral lands (Göçek, 2014, p. 3). This attitude also overlooks the fact that the forced expulsion of Armenians from the lands in which they had lived for centuries and their dispersal to various parts of the world were the principal reason for the formation of the Armenian diaspora.

The apparatus of diaspora-making

Under AKP rule, diaspora engagement strategies have gone from the intentional reframing of Turkish immigrants as a diasporic community to the establishment of the new coordinative mechanisms, such as the creation of the 'Presidency for Turks Abroad and Relative Communities' (thereafter YTB) in 2010. This has been followed by assigning roles and obligations to the Turks abroad. A good example of how this apparatus is articulated can be found in the quarterly journal *Artı 90* (Plus 90), published by the YTB, which gave generous coverage to then Prime Minister Erdoğan's views on the Turks abroad:

> My brothers and sisters living abroad should know this well: They are not alone anymore. Behind them, there's the power of the Republic of Turkey...Be sure of that, now with a strong economy, with an active foreign policy and with having a say in its region and world, the Republic of Turkey is behind you. You should aim for more just like in your own country. From the moment you decide to stay here, settle down, buy a house and start a business, you are a part of this place. You should definitely not have the slightest problem with integration. When you keep your unity, cooperation and solidarity strong, you will be the strongest, most influential and dynamic society in Europe.
>
> *(Altınok, 2013, pp. 6–7)*[7]

This emphasis on strengthening ties between the homeland and the diaspora is the founding purpose of YTB, with its mantra that 'Wherever we have a citizen, kin or relative, there we are.' More importantly, as a pro-regime scholar argues, YTB seeks 'to transform this potential into an organized diaspora like that of Israel and Armenia', with the construction of a global diaspora community indicating the political strategy of the AKP government to represent Muslims around the world and strengthen the political philosophy of democratic Islam (Ekşi, 2019, p. 189). Since diaspora policies and lobbying in this context are regarded as significant means to 'gain a leverage in international relations, especially in the Islamic world', the Sunni Muslim Turkish diaspora community is expected to 'serve as a lobby group and as a bulwark against the pseudo-genocide drafts of some countries that might damage the image of Turkey' (ibid.). YTB declares the three main objectives of Turkey's diaspora policy as 'maintaining ties of Turkish citizens living abroad with the homeland, preserving the native language, culture and identity of Turkish citizens abroad and strengthening social status of Turkish citizens living abroad'.[8] However, this state-sponsored institution operates in line with 'Turkey's deliberate selective empowerment of diaspora actors' (Arkilic, 2020, p. 18). While most conservative Turkish diaspora organisations in France and Germany 'have received the lion's share of YTB support', Alevi and Kurdish diaspora groups are largely excluded from financial or moral support from the government and stigmatised by 'the development of a biased diaspora engagement policy' (ibid., pp. 10, 16).

The Yunus Emre Institute (*Yunus Emre Enstitüsü*; YEE) was established as a public foundation in 2007 to promote the Turkish language, history, culture and art abroad, with cultural centres in different parts of the world including many countries in Europe, the United States, Russia and South Africa. The mission of YEE is proclaimed 'to enhance Turkey's recognition, credibility and prestige in the international arena'.[9] The President of YEE explicitly declares that the essential mission of the institution is 'to create communities that are related and close to Turkey'. More remarkably, he highlights the fact that the goal of the organisation is 'to act as a soft-power flag-bearer of Turkish culture' and to introduce it to other nations 'in accordance with Turkey's strategic goals' (Ünal, 2017).[10] While these institutions operate for the extension of rights to the Turkish diaspora as well as the members of kin and related communities, they bring their historical, cultural and religious connectedness to the forefront to form an understanding of a broader extraterritorial Turkish nation. For the protection and dissemination of Turkish culture abroad, 'certain *selected* cultural elements, particularly language and religion' are employed 'as a means of appealing to the defined cultural heritages to be utilized in strengthening societal and political ties' (Kaya and Tecmen, 2011, p. 17, emphasis in original). Both YTB and YEE are thus assigned duties of building and consolidating these societal and political ties between kin and related communities abroad and in the homeland. Through this network of cultural centres and institutes, the Turkish state aspires to promote an '"official national identity" toward "domestic" populations abroad, constructed as "friendly" to the state' (Ragazzi, 2009, p. 386). These state-sanctioned organisations are also instrumentalised to achieve political, economic, cultural and ideological ends and to enable (trans-) 'national diaspora' to act as representatives and defenders of the current government. To frustrate the international efforts of the Armenian diaspora for genocide recognition, the diaspora politics of Turkey constructs 'friendly communities' and enables them to stand against 'enemy emigrants' (ibid., p. 390).

Considered as the Diaspora Ministry, the YTB intends 'to organize Turkish lobbying activities around the world' since the Turkish lobby was believed to be 'weaker compared to the Armenian and Jewish lobbies' and hence a stronger Turkish diaspora is needed 'to counter Armenian genocide recognition claims in other states' parliaments' (Baser, 2019, p. 208). The passage of the Armenian bill by the Swedish Parliament in 2010 (Baser, 2014) and the draft bill criminalising the denial of the Armenian genocide voted on by the French Senate in 2012 (Okyay, 2015) led to nationalist reactions and protests in Turkey and among Turkish migrant populations in Europe. The statement of the then-Minister of Customs and Trade illustrates this point as follows:

> The existence of a strong interaction will increase the economic and social efficiency of our country all over the world. On the other hand, a strong Turkish diaspora will make an important contribution to the political power of our country all over the world. The formation of such a diaspora will pave the way for presenting the historical facts, of which we as Turkey is legitimate and right in many issues, to the world public opinion accurately. The so-called Armenian Draft Bill adopted by the French Parliament further increased the importance of this diaspora.
>
> *(Habertürk, 2011)*[11]

In a similar vein, the President of the Union of Chambers and Commodity Exchanges of Turkey and the then-Minister of Economy addressed the Turkish diaspora at the World Turkish Entrepreneurs Congress and stated:

> The time has come for Turkey and the Turkish Diaspora to come together around shared global goals. We have always approached such concepts as lobbying and Diaspora with doubt. We have identified these things as foreign powers acting against us in our country. We weren't aware of our own Diaspora. Now, as the Turkish Diaspora, we declare 'We are here!'
>
> We have high expectations of you: You will, without becoming assimilated, without forgetting your language and your religion, become citizens of the country you live in, take part in the politics and trade of that country and be able to call to account and vote in that country.
>
> *(The Union of Chambers and Commodity Exchanges of Turkey, 2011)*[12]

The members of the Turkish diaspora, perceived as actors in the political realm, are encouraged 'to behave in a concerted way to make homeland-oriented claims' (Koinova, 2015, p. 501). More importantly, 'based on the premise that emigrants owe loyalty to a legitimate sovereign' (ibid., p. 22), the AKP government, with its discourses and institutions, seeks to create awareness in the diaspora community that it must act together against a common goal and thus expects its members' loyalty to the homeland. From the state's perspective, the lobbying power of the diaspora and its potential to challenge Armenian genocide claims are regarded as ways of demanding obligations from the Turkish diaspora. In other words, being a counterforce to the allegations of the Armenian diaspora affirms the loyalty of Turks abroad to the homeland and in turn becomes the basis on which they are given privileges, rights and benefits. However, even before the AKP government, the statements of national assembly deputies also reveal how the notion of a Turkish lobby in Europe has become the conscious instrumental use of Turkish citizens abroad for political ends (Østergaard-Nielsen, 2003b, p. 90):

> Turks abroad could serve to counter the information campaigns of dissident Turkish and Kurdish movements abroad as well as other 'anti-Turkish' groups including the Armenian and Greek lobbies in Europe and the US.
>
> *(Interview by Østergaard-Nielsen with National Assembly Deputy for DSP, 20 October 2000, Ankara)*

> Turkish citizens abroad should mobilize firstly to defend their own rights and secondly to: Be a kind of public relations for Turkey, and if possible, a lobby for their own country. This should be one of the tasks of a more efficient diplomacy– to mobilize the people abroad.
>
> *(ibid.)*

This continuity in the state tradition concerning nurturing nationalist sentiments in Turks abroad also prompts 'long-distance nationalism' (Anderson, 1998), which in turn determines the relationship between the diaspora community and the homeland. There is an expectation of the Turkish diaspora that it needs to struggle against the Armenian lobbies in Europe and the United States along with the Turkish state. Within this framework, the mobilisation of the Turkish diaspora does not simply refer to an 'engagement with homeland politics from afar', it also comes to mean an engagement with 'host country actors to pursue a certain agenda in relation to their homeland' (Mencutek and Baser, 2018, p. 89). When viewed from this perspective, long-distance nationalism provides 'a justification for governments to reconfigure themselves as transnational nation-states' (Mügge, 2012, p. 341). Turkey, in particular, 'acts on its exiled population by way of language, religion and dual nationality' and 'tries to reinforce as much as possible the loyalty of its nationals' (Bruneau, 2010, p. 44). Long-distance nationalism enables the Turkish state to reach out to its target population by creating a sense of national unity and solidarity, similar to many forms of nationalism. From the standpoint of Alevis, Kurds and political opponents, state-sponsored institutions and policies in Germany and Sweden are considered 'as part of a state effort to strengthen ties with religiously conservative Turks, or even only with supporters of the current government' (Mencutek and Baser, 2018, p. 95). In this regard, the ethnic, religious and political others of Turkish nationalism again become evident in selective diaspora engagement policies stimulated by long-distance nationalism. From the state's perspective, transnational institutions serve a specific purpose that opens up a space for the lobbying activities of the Turkish diaspora in opposition to the Armenian lobbies. In short, ethnic and religious lobbying of the Turkish diaspora as an accepted form of transnational participation and its limits for political manoeuvres for genocide denial are included in the diaspora engagement policies of the Turkish state.

Conclusion

This chapter focuses on the question of how the Turkish state positions itself concerning the Turkish and Armenian diasporas and how it uses particular strategies and discourses to engage with these communities. By addressing the recent changes during the AKP government, I demonstrate how diaspora engagement policies have resulted in the construction of the Turkish population abroad as a diaspora community. The creation process of the Turkish diaspora by the Turkish state is also notable in unmasking the continuity of the state tradition in terms of the prioritisation of the demands and rights of Sunni Muslim Turkish communities. This indicates how state policies towards the Turkish diaspora are consistently fundamental to the re-definition of a particular Turkish national identity. In addition, the strong presence of the Armenian diaspora and its lobbying efforts for genocide recognition in different countries have also increased the importance given to the duties of the Turkish population abroad. This is also one of the underlying reasons for the state-led diaspora-making project, with the endeavour correspondingly revealing itself in the attempt to locate the Turkish diaspora as a powerful rival to the Armenian diaspora. The enduring controversy between the Turkish state and the Armenian diaspora concerning the genocide denial has been transformed into a new site of political contestation between two diaspora communities. The launch of state-sanctioned institutions, at this juncture, both extends the rights of the Turkish diaspora and assigns to it the role of being the representative of the Turkish state abroad to refute the allegations of the Armenian diaspora. The institutionalisation of diaspora politics targeting the Turkish diaspora has thus become a state strategy that focuses on diaspora-making against the Armenian diaspora.

Notes

1 See Presidency of the Republic of Turkey (2015).
2 See Republic of Turkey Ministry of Foreign Affairs (2016).
3 See Republic of Turkey Ministry of Foreign Affairs (n.d.).
4 See Anadolu Agency (2015).
5 See Letsch (2014).
6 See Presidency of the Republic of Turkey (2020).
7 See Altınok (2013).
8 See Presidency for Turks Abroad and Related Communities (n.d.) 'General Information'.
9 See Yunus Emre Institute (n.d.) 'Vision-Mission'.

10 See Ünal (2017).
11 See Habertürk (2011).
12 See the Union of Chambers and Commodity Exchanges of Turkey (2011).

References

Adamson, F. (2019) 'Sending states and the making of intra-diasporic politics: Turkey and its diaspora(s)', *International Migration Review*, 53(1), pp. 210–236.

Altınok, M. (2013) 'Artı 90 Özel', *Artı 90*, (5), pp. 6–15. Available at: https://ytbweb1.blob.core.windows.net/files/resimler/dergiler_pdf/arti-05.pdf (accessed 30 November 2020).

Anadolu Agency (2015) 'Turkish community protests German parliament's motion on 1915 events', 25 April [online]. Available at: www.aa.com.tr/en/world/turkish-community-protests-german-parliaments-motion-on-1915-events/53762 (accessed 6 December 2020).

Anderson, B. (1998) *The Spectre of Comparisons: Nationalism, Southeast Asia and the World*. London: Verso.

Arkilic, Z.A. (2020) 'Empowering a fragmented diaspora: Turkish immigrant organizations' perceptions of and responses to Turkey's diaspora engagement policy', *Mediterranean Politics*, doi:10.1080/13629395.2020.1822058

Arkilic, Z.A. (2016) 'Between the homeland and host states: Turkey's diaspora policies and immigrant political participation in France and Germany', Unpublished PhD thesis. The University of Texas. Available at: https://repositories.lib.utexas.edu/bitstream/handle/2152/61482/ARKILIC-DISSERTATION-2016.pdf?sequence=1 (accessed 3 July 2020).

Aybak, T. (2016) 'Geopolitics of denial: Turkish state's 'Armenian problem', *Journal of Balkan and Near Eastern Studies*, 18(2), pp. 125–144.

Aydın, Y. (2014) 'The new Turkish diaspora policy: its aims, their limits, and the challenges for associations of people of Turkish origin and decision-makers in Germany', SWP Research Paper 10/2014, Berlin: Stiftung Wissenschaft und Politik. Available at: www.swp-berlin.org/fileadmin/contents/products/research_papers/2014_RP10_adn.pdf (accessed 25 June 2020).

Basch, L., Glick Schiller, N. and Szanton Blanc, C. (1994) *Nations Unbound: Transnational Projects, Postcolonial Predicaments and Deterritorialized Nation-States*. London: Routledge.

Baser, B. (2014) 'The awakening of a latent diaspora: the political mobilization of first and second generation Turkish migrants in Sweden', *Ethnopolitics*, 13(4), pp. 355–376.

Baser, B. (2017) 'Turkey's ever-evolving attitude-shift towards engagement with diaspora', in Weinar, A. (ed.) *Emigration and Diaspora Policies in the Age of Mobility*. Cham: Springer, pp. 221–238.

Baser, B. (2019) 'Governing Turkey's diaspora(s) and the limits of diaspora diplomacy', in Özerdem, A. and Whiting, M. (eds) *The Routledge Handbook of Turkish Politics*, New York: Routledge, pp. 202–213.

Baser, B. and Toivanen, M. (2018) 'Diasporas building peace: reflections from the experience of Middle Eastern diasporas', in Cohen, R. and Fischer, C. (eds). *Routledge Handbook of Diaspora Studies*. London: Routledge, pp. 345–353.Bauböck, R. (2010) 'Cold constellations and hot identities: political theory questions about transnationalism and diaspora', in Bauböck, R. and Faist, T. (eds) *Diaspora and Transnationalism: Concepts, Theories and Methods*. Amsterdam: Amsterdam University Press, pp. 295–321.

Bilgili, Ö. and Siegel, M. (2010) 'Understanding the changing role of the Turkish diaspora', UNU-MERIT Working Paper Series, 2011/039, Maastricht: Maastrich Graduate School of Governance.

Brubaker, R. (2005) 'The "diaspora" diaspora', *Ethnic and Racial Studies*, 28 (1), pp. 1–19.

Brubaker, R. and Kim, J. (2011) 'Transborder membership politics in Germany and Korea', *European Journal of Sociology*, 52(1), pp. 21–75.

Bruneau, M. (2010) 'Diasporas, transnational spaces and communities', in Bauböck, R. and Faist, T. (eds) *Diaspora and Transnationalism: Concepts, Theories and Methods*. Amsterdam: Amsterdam University Press, pp. 35–49.

Cohen, R. (1997) *Global Diasporas: An Introduction*. London: Routledge.

Ekşi, M. (2019) 'Public diplomacy and soft power in recent Turkish foreign policy', in Doğan, N. and Sözen, A. (eds) *Turkish Foreign Policy*, I. Eskişehir: Anadolu University Press. Available at: https://ets.anadolu.edu.tr/storage/nfs/ULI351U/ebook/ULI351U-19V1S1-7-0-1-SV1-ebook.pdf (accessed 5 February 2021).

Foucault, M. (1982) 'The subject and power', in Dreyfus, H.L. and Rabinow, P. (eds) *Michel Foucault: Beyond Structuralism and Hermeneutics*. Sussex: The Harvester Press Limited, pp. 208–226.

Gamlen, A. (2006) 'Diaspora engagement policies: what are they, and what kinds of states use them?', Centre on Migration, Policy and Society Working Paper 06-32, Oxford: University of Oxford.

Available at: www.compas.ox.ac.uk/wp-content/uploads/WP-2006-032-Gamlen_Diaspora_Enga gement_Policies.pdf (accessed 5 May 2020).

Göçek, F.M. (2014) 'Turkish Prime Minister Erdogan's non-apologies to the Armenians and Kurds'. Available at: www.e-ir.info/2014/07/07/turkish-prime-minister-erdogans-non-apologies-to-the-armenians-and-kurds/ (accessed 13 May 2020).

Habertürk (2011) 'Türk diasporası ciddi destek sağlar', 28 November [online]. Available at: www.habert urk.com/dunya/haber/701055-turk-diasporasi-ciddi-destek-saglar (accessed 10 November 2020).

Herzig, E. and Kurkchiyan, M. (2005) *The Armenians: Past and Present in the Making of National Identity*. London: Routledge.

Hoffman, M., Makovsky, M. and Werz, M. (2020) 'The Turkish diaspora in Europe: integration, migration and politics', Center for American Progress. Available at: www.americanprogress.org/issues/secur ity/reports/2020/12/10/491951/turkish-diaspora-europe/ (accessed 16 December 2020).

İçduygu, A. and Kirişci, K. (2009) *Land of Diverse Migrations: Challenges of Emigration and Immigration in Turkey*. Istanbul: Istanbul Bilgi University Press.

Kadıoğlu, A. (2007) 'Denationalization of citizenship? The Turkish experience', *Citizenship Studies*, 11(3), pp. 283–299.

Kaya, A. and Tecmen, A. (2011) 'The role of common cultural heritage in external promotion of modern Turkey: Yunus Emre Cultural Centres', European Institute Working Paper No. 4. EU/4/2011, Istanbul: Istanbul Bilgi University Press.

Koinova, M. (2015) 'Sustained vs. episodic mobilization among conflict-generated diasporas', *International Political Science Review*, 37(4), pp. 500–516.

Köşer-Akçapar, S. and Bayraktar-Aksel, D. (2017) 'Public diplomacy through diaspora engagement: the case of Turkey', *Perceptions*, 22(4), pp. 135–160.

Letsch, C. (2014) 'Turkish PM offers condolences over 1915 Armenian massacre', The Guardian, 23 April [online]. Available at: www.theguardian.com/world/2014/apr/23/turkey-erdogan-condolen ces-armenian-massacre (accessed 4 December 2020).

Mencutek, Z.S. and Baser, B. (2018) 'Mobilizing diasporas: insights from Turkey's attempts to reach Turkish citizens abroad', *Journal of Balkan and Near Eastern Studies*, 20(1), pp. 86–105.

Mügge, L. (2012) 'Managing transnationalism: continuity and change in Turkish state Policy', *International Migration*, 50(1), pp. 20–38.

Okyay, A.S. (2015) 'Diaspora-making as a state-led project Turkey's expansive diaspora strategy and its implications for emigrant and kin populations', Unpublished PhD thesis, European University Institute. Available at: http://cadmus.eui.eu/handle/1814/38044 (accessed 10 January 2020).

Østergaard-Nielsen, E. (2003a) 'The politics of migrants' transnational political practices', *International Migration Review*, 37(3), pp. 760–786.

Østergaard-Nielsen, E. (2003b) 'International migration and sending countries: key issues and themes', in Østergaard-Nielsen, E. (ed.) *International Migration and Sending Countries: Perceptions, Policies and Transnational Relations*. New York: Palgrave Macmillan, pp. 3–31.

Presidency for Turks Abroad and Related Communities (n.d.) 'General information'. Available at: www. ytb.gov.tr/en/abroad-citizens/general-information-2 (accessed 20 September 2019).

Presidency of the Republic of Turkey (2015) 'Almanya "Karlsruhe Buluşması" and Yaptıkları Konuşma', 10 May [online]. Available at: www.tccb.gov.tr/konusmalar/353/32131/almanya-karlsruhe-bulusmasi nda-yaptiklari-konusma (accessed 5 December 2020).

Presidency of the Republic of Turkey (2020) 'The letter President Recep Tayyip Erdoğan sent to Armenian Patriarch of Turkey, Reverend Sahak Maşalyan', 24 April [online]. Available at: www.tccb.gov.tr/en/ speeches-statements/558/119167/the-letter-president-recep-tayyip-erdogan-sent-to-armenian-patria rch-of-turkey-reverend-sahak-masalyan (accessed 2 August 2020).

Ragazzi, F. (2009) 'Governing diasporas', *International Political Sociology*, 3, pp. 378–397.

Republic of Turkey Ministry of Foreign Affairs (2016) 'No. 125, 2 June 2016, press release regarding the resolution by the Parliament of the Federal Republic of Germany of 2 June 2016 on the events of 1915'. 2 June [online]. Available at: www.mfa.gov.tr/no_-125_-2-june-2016_-press-release-regard ing-the-resolution-by-the-parliament-of-the-federal-republic-of-germany-of-2-june-2016-on-the-events-of-1915.en.mfa (accessed 6 December 2020).

Republic of Turkey Ministry of Foreign Affairs (n.d.) 'Frequently asked questions'. Available at: www.mfa. gov.tr/questions.en.mfa (accessed 6 December 2020).

Şimşek, A. (2016) 'Germany: Turks protest one-sided Armenian motion', Anadolu Agency, 1 June [online]. Available at: www.aa.com.tr/en/europe/germany-turks-protest-one-sided-armenian-mot ion/582623 (accessed 6 December 2020).

Smith, A.D. (2010) 'Diasporas and homelands in history: the case of the classic diasporas' in Gal, A., Leoussi, A.S. and Smith, A.D (eds) *The Call of the Homeland: Diaspora Nationalisms, Past and Present.* Leiden: Brill, pp. 3–25.

Sökefeld, M. (2006) 'Mobilizing in transnational space: a social movement approach to the formation of diaspora', *Global Networks,* 6 (3), pp. 265–284.

Tziarras, Z. (2019) 'Kinship and diasporas in Turkish foreign policy–an introduction', in Hatay, M. and Tziarras, Z. (eds) *Kinship and Diasporas in Turkish Foreign Policy: Examples from Europe, the Middle East and the Eastern Mediterranean.* Oslo: Peace Research Institute Oslo, pp. 1–10.

Ünal, Ali (2017) 'Yunus Emre Institute Head Ateş: As an element of soft power, our aim is to introduce Turkey, its culture to the world', Daily Sabah, 24 July [online]. Available at: www.dailysabah.com/diplomacy/2017/07/24/yunus-emre-institute-head-ates-as-an-element-of-soft-power-our-aim-is-to-introduce-turkey-its-culture-to-the-world (accessed 15 October 2019).

Union of Chambers and Commodity Exchanges of Turkey (2011) 'Turkish entrepreneurs from four corners of the world together to make dreams into goals and goals into reality', 18 November [online]. Available at: www.tobb.org.tr/Sayfalar/Eng/Detay.php?rid=1047&lst=MansetListesi (accessed 10 November 2020).

Ünver, O.C. (2013) 'Changing diaspora politics of Turkey and public diplomacy', *Turkish Policy Quarterly,* 12(1), pp. 181–189. Waterbury, M. (2010) 'Bridging the divide: towards a comparative framework for understanding kin state and migrant-sending state diaspora politics', in Bauböck, R. and Faist, T. (eds) *Diaspora and Transnationalism: Concepts, Theories and Methods.* Amsterdam: Amsterdam University Press, pp. 131–148.

Yunus Emre Institute 'Vision-Mission'. Available at: www.yee.org.tr/en/corporate/vision-mission (accessed 21 September 2019).

Yurtnaç, K. (2012) 'Turkey's new horizon: Turks abroad and related communities', Sam Papers No. 3. Istanbul: Center for Strategic Research. Available at: http://sam.gov.tr/wp-content/uploads/2012/10/SAM_paper_ing_03.pdf (accessed 10 December 2020).

4
CRITICAL EVENTS AND THE FORMATION OF A COPTIC DIASPORA IN NORTH AMERICA BETWEEN AL-KHANKA AND AL-ZĀWIYA AL-HAMRĀ

Michael Akladios

On 6 November 1972, unknown assailants set fire to the offices of the headquarters of the Holy Bible Society in al-Khanka, Qalyubia, because Coptic villagers were using part of the building as an unlicensed church. On 12 November, Pope Shenouda III (r. 1971–2012) ordered an entourage of priests and bishops to visit the village (12 miles northeast of Cairo) and celebrate mass. Following a public procession that day, local Muslims staged demonstrations, shots were fired in the crowd and half a dozen Coptic homes were set ablaze during the ensuing violence. President Anwar Sadat (1970–1981) initiated a parliamentary investigation led by Jamal al-Utayfi, Deputy Speaker of the Egyptian House of Representatives. The al-Utayfi Committee's final report recommended clarifying government procedures for licensing church construction and issuing permits, recommendations that were never followed through (*Arab-West Report*, 1972). Instead, Sadat denounced the Church's actions as a challenge to his authority and government officials accused foreign agents of fomenting troubles (Heikal, 1983, pp. 162–164). No charges were made against the perpetrators in al-Khanka.

The violence that erupted in November galvanised a number of immigrant Copts across central Canada and the northeastern United States to develop politically engaged diasporic organisations. In the following years, tensions mounted between President Sadat and Pope Shenouda with successive acts of violence, including reported attacks in Alexandria, Minya, Asyut and Samaloot (Naguib, 1996, p. 11). In 1977, the government introduced draft legislation to the People's Assembly for the application of Islamic law (Shari'a) and stiffer punishment for apostasy (Farah, 1986). Coptic diasporic activists responded to these developments using their transnational press to counter the Egyptian state's dismissal of sectarian violence and challenge hegemonic interpretations of Sadat as a peacemaker. Consequently, Coptic émigrés (*Aqbāt al-mahjar*) became villains in the pages of the Egyptian daily newspapers *Al Ahrām* and *Akhbar Al-Yom* (Iskander, 2012, p. 41).

This chapter charts the historical trajectory of emigration from Egypt to North American cities and the formation of a Coptic diaspora from a comparative and transnational perspective. Focusing on the Coptic diaspora in Canada and the United States between two critical events, al-Khanka in 1972 and al-Zāwiya al-Hamrā in 1981, I investigate Coptic immigrants' social, cultural and political associational life. In so doing, I map out the origins and transnational entanglements of Coptic diasporic activism and centre the relationship between immigrants, the Coptic Orthodox Church and the Egyptian state. As Perin (1993) observed, immigrant history is not simply an extension of the history of the immigrants' country of origin, nor does it begin at the border of the country of adoption. Organisations that mobilised a politicised diasporic identity responded to activism in the homeland, carrying their own distinct worldviews and cultural practices and engaging North American political authorities to support their cause. The material motivations, emotional dilemmas and advocacy of diasporic activists tied them to Egypt while living fully in Canada and the United States. Political mobilisation aided their self-understanding as a diaspora, a global community interested in affecting political change in Egypt.

Coptic migrants have navigated their enduring ties with the homeland in new contexts across multiple geographies. While many middle-class Copts in Egypt chose to emigrate in response to economic precarity and religious oppression in their country of origin, they were nevertheless connected to the homeland spiritually through activities organised by the Coptic Church and through sending remittances. At the same time, immigration and debates about acculturation in North America affected Copts' social, cultural and political activities. A critical event, such as al-Khanka, mobilised a politicised diasporic identity, which transformed what it meant to be a Copt and Egyptian in the *mahjar* (see Sökefeld, 2006 for a discussion of the role of critical events). By highlighting the different forms of organisational lives that existed among Coptic immigrants in North America, my analysis shows that diasporic political involvement is one among multiple options that immigrants may choose to pursue. More importantly, my analysis shows that the process of building a diaspora among Coptic immigrants is one that is fraught with mixed emotions towards the homeland.

A Coptic diaspora emerged well after the establishment of the first, and largest, immigrant communities in central Canada and the northeastern United States. As Martin Sökefeld (2006) has argued, the formation of diasporas can be considered 'as a special case of ethnicity' (p. 266). Like the Kashmiri diaspora in the UK or the Alevi diaspora in Germany, members of settled immigrant groups may perceive themselves as a diaspora after an event that destabilised their homeland (ibid.). Based on archival research, family collections and oral histories with first-generation Coptic immigrants in North America, I show that certain Copts mobilised following a critical event in al-Khanka that was instrumental in the formation of a diasporic identity. My analysis charts the responses of immigrant activists to shifting homeland politics and the intentional formation of a diasporic identity, a form of politicised ethnicity with a home-oriented gaze (Pastor, 2017; Fahrenthold, 2019). As transnationals unbounded by the limits on political protest in Egypt, diasporic activists acted intentionally to support their communities and often argued that 'if émigrés don't raise their voice, who will?' (Karas and Karas, 1985).

The chapter proceeds as follows. I start by highlighting some of the key features of academic scholarship on the Copts and the Coptic diaspora. Then, I describe the emigration context in post-1952 Egypt and the legal context in North America that shaped the pattern of migration. The next section charts the associational life for early Egyptian immigrants and highlights the cosmopolitan aspirations of the social and cultural activities they engaged in. The argument then focuses on the relationship between the Egyptian state and the Coptic diaspora, and the following section describes the shift from an amicable relationship to a more tenuous one instigated by the al-Khanka event. The historical narrative spans the two critical events, al-Khanka in 1972 and al-Zāwiya al-Hamrā in 1981, as a period of mobilisation among Copts both in Egypt and in the diaspora. If al-Khanka instigated Coptic mobilisation, al-Zāwiya al-Hamrā was responsible for its surge. That surge was short-lived, however, as the state responded by forcing the Coptic Pope into hermitage and manipulating the institutional structure of the Church. The chapter concludes by highlighting the multipolar activism that characterised the period under investigation and explaining its eventual decline as a result of political suppression in the homeland.

Defining a Coptic diaspora: Egyptian history in a global perspective

Despite being the largest Christian demographic minority in the Middle East, Copts are often ignored within Middle East studies, and their experiences are framed through notions of a *dhimmī*, second-class minority population that is marginal to Egyptian national history (Sedra, 2014). Coptic populations are 'left to' Coptic scholars and the topic of Eastern Christianity has long been the domain of scholars of ecclesiastical history and theology. Aside from a few valued contributions by Heather Sharkey (2008) and Paul Sedra (2011), much of the scholarship in Coptic studies privilege late antiquity research while modern Copts are often framed as passive victims of sectarian persecution (Kamil, 2002; Hasan, 2003). Recent interdisciplinary literature in the fields of anthropology, ethnomusicology and political science have contributed to correcting that imbalance, bringing needed attention to the study of modern Copts' legal, ideological and faith-based practices in Egypt (Shenoda, 2012; Mahmood, 2016; Ramzy, 2017). Yet religion remains the prism for studying the Copts in Egypt (Heo, 2018, p. 14). Consequently, a constant and monolithic stereotypical characterisation dominates, in which one understands a Copt by understanding their Church and spiritual experience.

This framing persists in the few studies of Coptic immigrants in North America. Two dichotomous representations prevail in the existing scholarship. First, most Coptic immigrants are characterised as having reconstituted their religious practices with seemingly little interaction in their host societies (Botros, 2006; Dickinson, 2008). Second, a numerical minority of activists are judged to be assimilated immigrants and framed as a marginal group that is antithetical to the majority's assumed 'acquiescence' to Church authority and the Egyptian state (Rowe, 2001, p. 87). Indeed, scholarly attention on the Coptic diaspora has almost exclusively focused on activists' engagement with Western politicians in the US context since the 1980s (Marzouki, 2016). Adopting an assimilationist approach, scholars such as Haddad and Donovan (2013, p. 211) have cast diasporic activists as a threat 'molded by the trends of neoconservativism and Islamophobia in America', with relative disregard for societal norms and the interests of co-religionists in Egypt.

Copts are not simply passively accepting the authority of the Church and state in Egypt or assimilated diasporic dissidents hampering disputes with the Egyptian state. Bosmat Yefet (2016, p. 1218) recently called for a comparative study to direct attention away from disparaging diasporic activists and to instead explore the relationships that exist between the Coptic diaspora and the homeland. This chapter proposes that the Coptic immigrant experience has been marked by both integration in North American cities and enduring material and emotional ties to Egypt, which motivated the activism of diasporic organisations. Rather than a one-way process of assimilation, Coptic integration in Toronto, Montreal, and the New York and New Jersey area occurred in multiple ways that best preserved their ethno-religious particularity (Barber and Watson, 2015). At one level, Copts in North America maintained connections with the clerical hierarchy in Egypt to unite immigrant families and finance the purchase of churches. On another level, cultural organisations were formed to bring together diverse immigrant groups from Egypt, including Coptic and Muslim Egyptians, Greeks, Armenians and Jews. In this context, celebrations of ethnic particularity in homes, social clubs and concert halls became a continuation of their cosmopolitan lives before emigration (Akladios, 2020b). In the midst of these levels of social and cultural interactions, the Coptic diaspora emerged with a specific political orientation.

In using the term 'diaspora', I insist that it is neither a neutral substitute for population movements nor a natural consequence of engagement with homeland concerns. Often used interchangeably with 'migration' in past scholarship, I ask: when and in what context is diaspora a useful category of analysis for the study of Coptic migrants? By tracing the intentional formation of diasporic organisations in a comparative perspective, this chapter shows that diaspora is most fruitfully employed when it describes activism that is multipolar – operating in networks of ideological and material exchange across more than two geographies. In that process, Coptic activists worked in Canada, the United States and Egypt to gather social, political and financial capital to enact change in the homeland. Building on studies by historians of Irish immigration, Donald Akenson (1995) and Kevin Kenny (2013), I frame diaspora as a shared understanding and sense of responsibility that does not emerge latently. Rather, it is a politicised form of ethnic identity that is produced and maintained by certain immigrants in positions of power.

International migration in post-revolution Egypt

As Egypt contended with anxieties occasioned by modernity and urbanisation in the mid-twentieth century and grappled with issues surrounding independence, identity and Islamic revival, a wave of antipathy towards any group considered 'foreign' or 'other' spread through society, prompting many to emigrate. Until the Free Officers revolution of 1952, Egypt was a receiving society that welcomed and benefited from international immigration. After the revolution, anti-colonial sentiment engendered discriminatory attitudes towards foreign nationals, which forced out the descendants of early Greek, Italian, Jewish, Armenian, Syrian and Lebanese groups (Tsourapas, 2018). Fears of political and religious persecution mounted during Nasserite 'Egyptianisation', a term used in both Egyptian political discourse and foreign government documents to define Nasser's nationalisation of businesses and industry. This prejudice eventually extended to one of the last remaining minorities: the Coptic Orthodox. Middle-class, urban and university-educated Copts chose to leave, motivated by discriminatory hiring practices and fears of economic precarity, lured by expanding post-secondary education and employment opportunities in North American cities (Akladios, 2020b).

Egypt's population more than doubled between the end of the Second World War and the mid-1980s, from 20 to 50 million. The 1947 census reported approximately one-and-a-half million Copts, the absolute majority of whom lived in Upper Egyptian Governorates (Wassef, 1978, p. 42). By November 1976, the census reported a total of 2,315,560 Copts, or 6.31 per cent of the total population of Egypt. Low census figures, however, were strongly contested by the Church and Coptic sources, who spoke of much higher numbers between 12 and 15 per cent. Discrepancies were attributed to wilful deceit by bigoted government officials or accidental recording of Christians with names that 'pass' for Muslim. Urban Coptic populations were better represented in Cairo than in any other Egyptian city, as owners of businesses, medical professionals and tradesmen (Pennington, 1982, p. 158).

Emigration from Egypt coincided with changes to Canadian and US immigration policies. The Canadian government began to accept more immigrants from Egypt following the

1956 Suez Crisis (Akladios 2020a, pp. 142–144) but maintained strict guidelines for accepting Westernised affluent professionals because it did not want to set a precedent that would open the gates more broadly to immigration from the Middle East (Smith, 1956). In this process, emigration from Egypt to North America was guided by class and ethnic hierarchies: Greeks and Italians were at the top, Armenian and Jewish immigrants were tolerated, Westernised Catholic and Protestant Christians became acceptable as the previous categories declined, and Orthodox Copts and Muslims were the last to be accepted (Akladios, 2020a).

Foreign nationals leaving Egypt presented both Canada and the United States with an opportunity to take in qualified immigrants – bank officials, accountants, import-export specialists, insurance and sales representatives and administrators – and maintain their quotas when the number of Greeks, Italians, Jews and others of adequate qualifications were dwindling in Europe (Department of Citizenship and Immigration, 1962). Both the quality of immigrants and the number of applications surprised and delighted Western officials. The expansion of Canada's immigration programme in Egypt facilitated the movement of Coptic professionals and young families (Immigration Operations Division, 1962, p. 1). The United States maintained a strict quota system and mostly male Coptic immigrants arrived through connections to American industry or Cold War scholarships. Graduate students were accepted to the Educational Council for Foreign Medical Graduates (ECFMG), prominent universities invited lecturers, and Bishop Samuel (general bishop of Public, Ecumenical, and Social Services) used his contacts in the World Council of Churches and at Princeton University to facilitate this movement (Boulos, 2006).

Coptic immigrants who settled in North American cities reflect the changing composition, orientation and dynamics of international Egyptian migration following the Second World War. Already urbanised, they entered Canada and the United States at a somewhat higher socio-economic level than European immigrants, who were mostly landless labourers or peasants (Gans, 2017). Drawing on hundreds of immigrant letters and 44 oral histories with Egyptian immigrants, I discovered that many Copts emigrated to build financial security and stability, and decisions to relocate abroad were rarely unidirectional. Doctors and university professors arrived with job offers in hand, having completed graduate degrees in Switzerland, France or the United Kingdom. Newly established universities and opportunities in medicine, engineering, architecture and teaching attracted single graduate students and some young families. Once settled, Copts in Toronto, Montreal, or the New York and New Jersey area gathered for social activities in rented halls and immigrants' homes. They often worshipped in Greek or Syrian Orthodox churches until arrangements were made to celebrate mass according to the Coptic Orthodox rite (Akladios, 2020a).

The emigration of Coptic and Muslim Egyptians rose dramatically after Egypt's defeat in the 1967 war with Israel (*Naksa*). In part, this was influenced by the introduction of less restrictive immigration policies in Canada and the United States. Canada eliminated overt racial discrimination in the lead-up to the 1967 Points System (Kelley and Trebilcock, 1998), while the United States introduced the 1965 Hart-Celler Immigration Act, which inaugurated more equitable procedures and prioritised family reunification (Gerber, 2011). Simultaneously, the Egyptian government increasingly viewed emigration as a trade in manpower for foreign currency. Egypt opened a Migration Department in 1968, which was jointly administered by the Egyptian ministries of Foreign Affairs, Labour, and Youth. The collaboration of these separate ministries reflects the concern of the Egyptian government at the time with finding a solution for unemployed graduates (Ministry of UAR Foreign Affairs, 1969, p. 3).

Less restrictive immigration policies and economic self-interest on the part of the Egyptian, Canadian and US governments ensured that Egyptians became the fastest-growing Arabic group in North America (Abu-Laban, 1980, pp. 64–67). After the mid-1970s, the growing involvement of Egyptian embassy officials, settled immigrants and Coptic churches in North American cities changed the demographic character of Coptic immigrant communities. Immigrant families increasingly appealed for sponsorship and family reunification, leading to an increase of new arrivals with less education and cultural resources at their disposal. From a few dozen immigrants in the 1950s, the population of Orthodox Copts grew to several thousand by the 1970s. Although no concrete figures exist, recent studies estimate the number of Copts in Canada and the United States at between 400,000 and 900,000 by the late-1990s (Takla et al., 1997; Khalil, 1999; Elsässer, 2014).

The cosmopolitan aspirations of early immigrant associations

Once dominantly Syro-Lebanese, the character of Middle Eastern immigrant associations in Canada and the United States changed following the Second World War. The influx of new immigrants from Egypt, Iraq and Jordan, among others, meant greater diversity and demand for a larger and more unifying identity. By 1960, Arab Friendship Societies with chapters in Toronto, London, Ottawa, Detroit and New York included a cross-section of groups, but membership lists were dominated by Palestinian, Lebanese and Syrian immigrants (Peters, 1960). Following Israel's victory over the Arab states in the 1967 war, a distinctly politicised Arab immigrant associational life emerged. The activism of Arab associations was marked by a deeply held belief among its advocates in Arab nationalism and the defence of Arab sovereignty against Zionist aggression (ibid.). The pro-Nasser pan-Arab nationalism of Arab associational politics was generally less attractive to new immigrants seeking to meet immediate needs. Egyptians, regardless of religious affiliation, rarely registered for these associations.

Notwithstanding the lack of common political trajectories, social activities such as film screenings and folklore performances attracted many Arabic speakers. Interlocutors fondly recalled occasional Coptic participation in joint cultural commemoration activities, such as a performance of the play *Hasan, Morcos, and Cohen* in Toronto in 1971. Written by Najīb Rīhānī (a Coptic actor who is considered the father of Egyptian comedy, d.1949), the plot follows three co-owners of a supermarket – a Muslim, a Christian and a Jew – and their scheme to rob their luckless employee after he came into a large inheritance. The story culminates in the main protagonists reconciling with each other after falling out over money and reaffirming their brotherhood. The play was first performed in Egypt in 1943 and reflects the multicultural and inter-religious make-up of Egyptian society at the time (Abou Saif, 1973). The play is an example of explicit celebrations of Egypt's cosmopolitan past, where diversity and peaceful coexistence were valued, which often united Arabic immigrants.

Egyptians created their own organisations and social and cultural associations developed along both religious and ethnic lines. The Canadian Coptic Association in Montreal and the Coptic Association of America in New York were founded in 1963. They were intended to unite dispersed urban professionals through cultural activities, finance the building of churches and request the sending of a priest from Egypt. As more Muslim Egyptian professionals immigrated in the 1970s, they joined interethnic mosques and founded secular initiatives such as the Nile Egyptian Cultural Centre (est. 1973) in Montreal. The Centre offered Arabic courses for several years as well as a range of social and recreational activities (Wassef, 1978, pp. 188–191). Coptic, Muslim and Jewish Egyptian immigrants founded *La Cercle Franco-Egyptien* (The Franco-Egyptian Club) in 1976 with the support of *Le Centre Francophone de Toronto* (The Francophone Centre of Toronto). A concert was held that year to provide what one pamphlet called a 'Franco-Italo-Hispano-Egyptienne' ambience. It was renamed the Egyptian Canadian

Club in 1979, a staunchly non-religious and non-political initiative (The Egyptian Canadian Club/Cercle des Canadiens d'Egypte/el Nadi el Masri el Kanadi, 1996).

Industrious immigrants from Egypt organised cultural events, imported Egyptian periodicals and established Arabic record labels to create a transnational space and provide new immigrants with a place to belong. Coptic associations developed mutual aid services, hosted lectures to promote French or English language education, made donations of food and medicine to Upper Egyptian villages and called on the patriarchate to send liturgical supplies. Egyptian secular organisations hosted film screenings and music performances, particularly popular were the films of acclaimed director Youssef Chahine and the songs of Um Kalthoum. Newspapers were sold in churches and social clubs across the continent, such as the semi-official Egyptian newspaper *Al Ahrām* and the Coptic *Watani*. Salah Allam began his *Arabic Record Club* (ARC) journal in 1974, two years after arriving in Montreal. The only Egyptian publication in Canada until that point, by December 1975, it had an average total distribution of 2,600 copies (Wassef, 1978, p. 194). Columns reflected on contemporary debates, including changes to immigration policies, daily adaptation in manners and dress codes and homeland politics. The editorial board was comprised of Muslims and Copts living in Canada, the United States and Egypt.

The *Naksa* galvanised the leaders of Arab associations in North America to engage in a form of long-distance pan-Arab nationalism. Similarly, the violence in al-Khanka and escalating sectarian tensions in Egypt motivated certain Copts to mobilise a diasporic identity after 1972. The politics of Coptic activism generally involved a dedicated numerical minority with different goals than those of church-affiliated and cultural organisations, or the pan-Arab nationalist associations. Coptic activists focused almost exclusively on defending Coptic rights in Egypt and a broader narrative of Christian persecution in the Middle East. Their activities were to inspire a mobilisation of diasporic identification and change the relationship between the Egyptian state and Coptic immigrants in North America, which I describe in the next section.

From a promising frontier to a seditious diaspora

The Egyptian state and the Coptic Church had not always seen emigrants as dangerous. Following the investiture of Gamal Abdul Nasser in 1956, the state conceived of emigration as an unpatriotic act and continued to do so until the mid-1960s. Nasser's financial support of anti-imperialist protests across Africa slowly exhausted the Egyptian economy and, in the years leading to the June 1967 war, the state began to enquire after emigrant nationals and demand that they send back remittances. This need for foreign currency grew markedly following the war. The state sought to re-establish ties with its nationals abroad and dual citizenship was granted for the first time (External Affairs, 1967, p. 1). As Fahrenthold (2019) argued for the Syrians and Lebanese during the First World War, for a time, Egyptian nationals abroad represented an overseas frontier, a source of economic development and a useful population to be groomed and reclaimed through diplomacy. The Migration Department established under Nasser in 1968 and the reopening of the Egyptian consulate in Montreal in 1972 by Sadat were manifestations of that mission.

Unlike his predecessor, Anwar Sadat eventually rejected all Soviet influence and sought to restructure the Egyptian economy with US aid. Part of this process was a turn to immigrants as not only a source of income through remittances but as affluent expatriates who could invest in Egypt's private businesses and public industry. The Church supported the nation in the lead-up to economic liberalisation (*Infitah*) policies and immigrants were told that they had a role to play by the Church hierarchy during a pastoral trip by Archbishop Antonius and Bishop Samuel in August 1971. In reports of the visit in *Watani*, Egypt's largest Coptic newspaper, and the *Monthly Message*, the continent-wide church bulletin, the theme of immigrants' continued responsibility to support the Church and the nation was at the forefront (*Monthly Message*, 1971a; Sidhom, 1971). The reports detailed successive meetings with religious leaders in Canada and the United States and pledges to support prospective émigrés. The bishops charted a path for Coptic immigrants to make a good impression on their host societies and repay Egypt for defending their interests.

Immigrant Copts from across central Canada and the northeastern United States gathered in Toronto to meet the bishops. In Bishop Samuel's sermon following the liturgy, the immigrant was asked to become an 'ambassador' to the West because 'as life in North America offers you technological and material gain, you should offer up your heritage and the spirit of your Church in exchange' (Acting Pontiff, 1971). Intertwining both sacred and secular cultures, it was argued that since the Coptic Orthodox Church prioritised the well-being of its adherents, the immigrant had a duty to both integrate into the host society and return to Egypt with knowledge and finances as loyal Copts and Egyptians. To facilitate this renewed economic relationship between the immigrant and the homeland, the Church offered to take a more proactive role in supplying immigrants with news to dispel fears of sectarian tensions in Egypt and to keep them better informed of investment opportunities (*Monthly Message*, 1971b).

This change of course during the *Infitah* years did not last long. The events in al-Khanka had repercussions among immigrant Copts. Aware of the tepid government response to the violence, Shawki Karas and his wife Leila created the American Coptic Association (ACA) to denounce Sadat's political ambitions in Egypt and raise awareness about discrimination against Copts among US policymakers (Karas, 1985). Through their contacts in New Jersey, they secured an office in 1972 and gathered a group of Coptic professionals, including engineers, entrepreneurs and teachers, which ushered in the emergence of a diasporic community of activists. The Canadian Coptic Association (CCA), which was established earlier by lawyer Selim Naguib, his wife Nadia Naguib, and chemist Alfonse Kelada, and focused on religious and cultural initiatives, was also driven to action by the events in al-Khanka. Leaders of the two associations became acquainted because of their mutual efforts and were motivated by their experiences in Egypt.

Each activist I interviewed communicated their own bitter experience with verbal abuse, job discrimination or Egypt's secret police (Akladios, 2020a). Shawki and Leila Karas had immigrated to New Jersey as part of a student exchange mission in 1959 with their two children. In 1967, they moved to New Haven, CT, when Shawki Karas secured a position as a professor of mathematics at the Southern Connecticut University. Originally from the province of Sohag in southern Egypt, the couple experienced verbal abuse and the preferential treatment Muslim graduate students received on university campuses. The al-Khanka events triggered harsh memories of discrimination, and their presence in North America facilitated the activists' ability to organise, away from the constraints on political organisation in Egypt.

Coptic diasporic activism engaged the Egyptian context. As Nadia Naguib eulogised following her husband's death, the 'trio Copts in diaspora' of Selim Naguib, Alfonse Kelada and Shawki Karas conceived of themselves as inheritors of the liberal and secular ideals of midcentury Coptic nationalists (Naguib, 2015, p. 7). Members of the ACA and the CCA found inspiration in Michael Zugheib's 1950 *Farriq Tasud* (Divide and Rule), in which the author detailed instances of personal conflicts and property damage and called on Muslims to 'refrain from persecuting the Christian Copts'. Selim Naguib called the book 'vigorous and courageous … intended to be an indictment against the discrimination and under-representation suffered by the Copts, systematically reduced to the status of second-class citizens' (Naguib, 1996, pp. 65–66).

Diasporic activists were attuned, pragmatic and aware of the consequences of the positions they took as the Egyptian government used strategies to monitor and intimidate diasporic populations. Reflecting on the risks involved in taking a stand, Nadia Naguib described the dilemma: 'Do you speak out or have the ability to go home again?' This anxiety was prominent in the memories of diasporic activists who maintained ties to the homeland but faced the prospect of never returning to Egypt. Interlocutors confided that Egyptian officials often photographed protesters during rallies and their pictures were circulated by officials and on display at Egyptian embassies in Washington and Ottawa. Nevertheless, in response to escalating violence in Egypt, their calls grew louder and their publications and opinion pieces in mainstream North American media outlets intensified with every visit of Sadat to the United States. Members of the American and Canadian Coptic Associations lobbied state authorities and staged protests in Ottawa, in Washington and at the United Nations headquarters in New York (ibid., p. 68).

Immigrant academics and professionals documented sectarian violence in Egypt and mobilised their cosmopolitan heritage and defended Coptic rights through appeals to universal human rights. They hoped to garner the support of North American political and religious authorities to their cause. *The Copts: Christians of Egypt* magazine began in 1974 as the chief news organ of the American and Canadian Coptic Associations. Featuring articles and case reports on the Coptic situation by immigrants and correspondents in Egypt, the magazine often included a vivid narration of events and listed the date, time, location and circumstances surrounding attacks against churches (Anon, 1981). Articles included excerpts from Sadat's speeches to the People's Assembly and summarised changes in Egyptian state policy. Appealing to the UN Declaration of Human Rights, the magazine provided detailed analyses on specific human rights violations by the Egyptian government. Including international news articles depicting human rights violations against Middle East Christians more broadly, *The Copts* emphasised Islamist fundamentalism as a global threat. Coverage was equally divided between English and Arabic, designed for both Western audiences and those Coptic immigrants who could advocate on behalf of their co-religionists.

Diasporic Copts did not act in a vacuum but responded to activism taking place in the homeland. In Egypt, the clergy and community council met in December 1976 at a conference demanding fair and equal rights for Copts under the law. In February 1977, the Holy Synod presented a joint statement denouncing the implementation of Shari'a in civil law and in August, the Bishopric of Assiut presented a memorandum documenting various attacks on Coptic churches, criticising police inaction and contesting forced conversion of Christians (Naguib, 1996, pp. 66–67). Diasporic Coptic activists responded to the actions initiated by the Church and community in Egypt. Clergy and lay Coptic activists from Egypt joined the ACA and CCA in denouncing sectarian violence at conferences in New Jersey in May 1978, and in Montreal in December 1978 and October 1979. In the following years, sister associations were founded by a network of diasporic activists pursuing complementary initiatives in Germany under economist Youssef Farag, in France, under law professor Magdi Zaki, and, in Australia, under lawyer Ramses Ghabrawy (ibid., pp. 71–72).

Initial reactions from the Egyptian government triggered hope among diasporic activists. According to Shawki Karas (1985), diaspora organisations united with Church leaders and public intellectuals in Egypt to successfully place enough pressure on the Egyptian government to withdraw the proposal for the application of Shari'a in cases of apostasy (pp. 131–132). However, editorials, public demonstrations and meetings with North American authorities during Sadat's official visits with President Jimmy Carter resulted in the former publicly criticising ACA and CCA leaders. Nadia Naguib recalled that in one of his speeches Sadat derided 'the failed lawyer in Montreal' in reference to Selim's opposition. On other occasions, Sadat acknowledged the growing voice of diasporic activists and their threat to his international image (Sadat, 1981). According to Nadia Naguib, Shawki Karas and Selim Naguib were roused by Sadat's recognition of their activism. Diasporic activists pragmatically capitalised on their unique position. Sadat's political ambitions were a perfect target since his good reputation was vital for ensuring that Egypt continued to receive international aid and investment during its liberalisation project.

Unable to restrain political activists, Sadat's government relied on the state-controlled Egyptian media and newspapers to defame *Aqbāt al-mahjar*, claiming immigrants were inherently less loyal to Egypt for choosing to leave. *Akhbar Al-Yom*, one of the largest dailies, frequently characterised *Aqbāt al-mahjar* as 'fanatics', 'extremists', and unpatriotic zealots (Sa'dah 1980, p. 8). This oppositional force in the *mahjar* was framed in Egypt as an ideological threat and a party to foreign influences seeking to destabilise Egyptian society and its economy (Elsässer, 2014, p. 83). Correspondingly, immigrant churches began to denounce the activists, and bishops were dispatched by the patriarch to calm Copts in North America.

In June 1981, violence between Muslims and Copts erupted in Cairo's al-Zāwiya al-Hamrā and left approximately 17 people dead and 54 injured. The Egyptian press downplayed the violence and damage to property as the actions of crazed individuals (ibid., p. 84). The diasporic press, on the other hand, repeatedly demonstrated state complicity in hate crimes against Coptic Christians. The violence in al-Zāwiya al-Hamrā, another critical event, mobilised more immigrants to join the political cause. Interlocutors confided that during the sermons of bishops in Jersey City, Queens and Brooklyn, responses ranged from dismissive scoffs to accusations of government collusion, and Sunday school leaders escorted the protesters from church grounds. Fearing further agitation, the patriarch wrote letters urging obedience to Church authority and bishops repeated their message of calm in parishes across Toronto and Montreal (Pope Shenouda, [1981] 1986).

In anticipation of Sadat's scheduled talks in the United States, diasporic activists and Church leaders used the American press to debate who represents the Copts and their shared consciousness of an Egyptian national identity (see Anderson, 1991). In August 1981, priests across Canada and the United States bought a full-page advertisement in *The New York Times*, stating that the Coptic community was praying 'for the success of his [Sadat's] peace mission for the Middle East' (*The New York Times*, 1981a, p. B3). Diasporic organisations, for their part, purchased a full-page advertisement in the *Washington Post* that accused the Egyptian President of lacking 'courage in handling the systematic assaults launched by Muslim fanatics against the Christians of Egypt', and called on him to put an end to 'state-sponsored fundamentalism' (*The Washington Post*, 1981, p. A20). Clergy in Canada and the United States bought a full-page advertisement in *The New York Times* to deny that these diasporic organisations spoke for Coptic immigrants and included a message from Pope Shenouda in which he stressed that 'The Coptic Orthodox Church … strongly objects to the behavior, writings, and harassment by this organization against our nation.' 'The Copts are united', the statement added, 'with their Moslem brothers for the security, peace, welfare, and progress of Egypt' (*The New York Times*, 1981b, p. A12). Sadat was not appeased. Vocal opposition in the *mahjar* heightened tensions between immigrants, the Church and the Egyptian state.

In an unprecedented move in September 1981, Sadat revoked the presidential decree approving Shenouda as pope and supported the creation of a council of five bishops to lead the Church in his absence, tasking them with resolving the unrest that he accused the pope of fomenting domestically and abroad (Elsässer, 2014, p. 84). Pope Shenouda was forced into hermitage in St. Bishoy Monastery, Wadi Natrun Valley, as part of a country-wide crackdown that included the imprisonment of approximately 1,500 religious leaders, politicians and journalists. Diasporic political activists denied the council's authority and depicted its member bishops as conspirators with the state (Karas, 1985, p. 195). On 6 October 1981, Anwar Sadat and Bishop Samuel (who had been appointed head of the council) were assassinated in Cairo by Islamist army officers belonging to *Al-Gama'a Al-Islamiya*. Following his investiture, President Hosni Mubarak did not release Pope Shenouda and Bishop Gregorius succeeded Samuel as the head of the council of five bishops. New diasporic magazines emerged in opposition to the actions of both the Egyptian government and the Church council, such as New Jersey-based immigrant Rudolph Yanni's *Al Rasala* (Yanni, 1982).

Seeking to preserve its intermediary position and seeing an opportunity for renewed peaceable relations with the state against a common Islamist threat, the Church had little choice but to frame activists as dangerous. In a 1985 interview, Shawki Karas expressed his frustration with the Church's public discrediting of ACA activities. Karas framed the Coptic situation in Egypt as a matter of citizenship and insisted that it was the duty of all faithful and patriotic immigrant Copts to denounce 'religious suppression, injustice, and discrimination'. For Karas, the state was responsible for the 'cleavage' between Christians and Muslims. When the interviewer challenged Karas: 'they [the Egyptian government] say that you [ACA] degrade Egypt's reputation and are traitors', he replied: 'if exposing the actions of the Egyptian government [is] degrading Egypt, then why does the Egyptian government continue to act in such a manner?' Egypt's Copts, he maintained, were maligned and it was the responsibility of the state to serve and protect all its citizens equally (Karas and Karas, 1985).

After his release on 3 January 1985, Pope Shenouda opted for an alliance with President Hosni Mubarak. A more amenable Pope Shenouda emerged from the monastery and his relationship with Mubarak promised 'the community's allegiance in return for concessions such as church permits and security' (Ramzy, 2017, p. 383). Clerical influence grew with mass ordinations, and legitimacy within Coptic immigrant communities was increasingly only possible with the clergy's oversight and approval. The Church strengthened its control over activities in the *mahjar*, which continues to shape the internal and external dynamics affecting the Coptic diaspora at present.

Conclusion

This chapter charted a path for understanding the diversity of social, cultural and political associational activities and their place in relations between Coptic immigrants, the Orthodox Church and the Egyptian state. Following arrival in North American cities, Copts sought acculturation in multiple ways that best preserved their ethno-religious particularity. Middle-class professionals arrived in Canada and the United States with skills and material resources that were valued in their host societies and social and cultural organisations were formed to celebrate Copts' sacred and cosmopolitan origins. After 1972, a Coptic diaspora emerged when a number of immigrant Copts responded intentionally to the violence in al-Khanka at a particularly precarious moment in Egyptian international relations. Diasporic political involvement was one among multiple options that immigrants chose to pursue.

By virtue of their mobility and transnational lives, immigrant Copts engaged with local, national and international contexts. Operating in networks of ideological and material exchange, Coptic activists worked in Canada, the United States and Egypt to gather social, political and financial capital to enact change in the homeland. Diasporic activism affected how the Egyptian state and the Coptic Orthodox Church perceived immigrants. Up to the early 1970s, Egypt saw them as a population to be reclaimed and groomed for economic development. Afterwards,

Aqbāt al-mahjar became a threat to the national cause, no longer partners in it. This agitation was inflamed by the al-Zāwiya al-Hamrā episode, which mobilised more immigrants to join the political cause. Coptic activism in-between and across borders undermined a state narrative of national unity in Egypt. Eventually, political suppression and a renewal of peaceable relations between the Church and state in Egypt peripheralised the role of diasporic organisations.

The motivations and activities of Coptic activists are central to our understanding of the multipolar character of diaspora formations. Activists carried ideas about the importance of defending Coptic rights with them to their countries of adoption, marshalled those ideas in reaction to a critical event in the homeland and lived transnationally, seeking to enact change in Egypt while working, studying and raising families in North American cities. Diasporic organisations maintained material and emotional ties to clergy and Coptic activists in Egypt, while also appealing to North American political authorities to support their cause. Despite the Egyptian authorities' attempts to monitor, intimidate and harass diasporic activists, the latter capitalised on their unique position abroad to defend Coptic rights beyond the limits to political organisation in Egypt. The diasporic nationalism that developed unfolded within a unique context of intolerance, fear and anxiety. The Coptic immigrant experience is as much about 'routes' as it is about 'roots'.

Acknowledgements

The author thanks Roberto Perin, Paul Sedra, Miray Philips and the editors of this volume for their comments and suggestions on earlier versions of the chapter. This research was supported by the Social Sciences and Humanities Research Council of Canada.

References

Abou-Saif, L. (1973) 'Najib Al-Rihani: from buffoonery to social comedy', *Journal of Arabic Literature*, 4, pp. 1–17.
Abu-Laban, B. (1980) *An Olive Branch on the Family Tree: The Arabs in Canada*. Toronto: McClelland and Stewart.
Akenson, D. (1995) 'The historiography of English-speaking Canada and the concept of diaspora: a skeptical appreciation', *Canadian Historical Review*, 76(3), pp. 377–409.
Akladios, M. (2020a) 'Ordinary Copts: ecumenism, activism, and belonging in North American cities, 1954–1992', PhD thesis. Toronto: York University.
Akladios, M. (2020b) 'Heteroglossia: interpretation and the experiences of Coptic immigrants from Egypt in North America, 1955–1975', Histoire sociale / *Social History*, 53(109), pp. 627–650.
Anderson, B.R. (1991) *Imagined Communities: Reflections on the Origin and Spread of Nationalism*. London: Verso.
Anon (1981) 'Churches which were burned or smashed', *The Copts: Christians of Egypt*, 8(3): 3.
Arab-West Report (1972) 'Report by Dr Jamal al-Utayfi on the al-Khanka sectarian events'. Translated and published by *Arab-West Report*, 4 January 2009. Available at: www.arabwestreport.info/en/year-2009/week-13/2-report-dr-jamal-al-%E2%80%98utayfi-al-khankah-sectarian-events.
Barber, M. and Watson, M. (2015) *Invisible Immigrants: The English in Canada since 1945*. Winnipeg: University of Manitoba Press.
Botros, G. (2006) 'Religious identity as an historical narrative: Coptic Orthodox immigrant churches and the representation of history', *Journal of Historical Sociology*, 19(2), pp. 174–201.
Boulos, S. (2006) *The History of the Early Coptic Community in the USA (1955–1970)*. New Jersey: self-published.
Department of Citizenship and Immigration (1962) 'Movement of immigrants from the United Arab Republic', Deputy Minister to Director of Immigration, 14 June. [Letter] Held at: Ottawa: Library and Archives Canada, R223-80-9E, RG26-A-1-C, vol. 168, file 3-25-11-42, 1947–1967.
Dickinson, E. (2008) *Copts in Michigan*. East Lansing, MI: Michigan State University Press.

Elsässer, S. (2014) *The Coptic Question in the Mubarak Era*. Oxford: Oxford University Press.

External Affairs (1967) 'UAR foreign currency control', Canadian Embassy in Cairo to Under-Secretary of State for External Affairs, 20 January. [Dispatch] Held at: Ottawa: Library and Archives Canada, R1206-135-3-E, RG76-B-1-C, vol. 989, file 5850-3-642, 1965–1975, 1–2.

Fahrenthold, S.D. (2019) *Between the Ottomans and the Entente: The First World War in the Syrian and Lebanese Diaspora, 1908–1925*. Oxford: Oxford University Press.

Farah, N. (1986) *Religious Strife in Egypt: Crisis and Ideological Conflict in the Seventies*. New York: Gordon and Breach Publications.

Gans, H. (2017) 'Another look at symbolic ethnicity', *Ethnic and Racial Studies*, 40(9), pp. 1410–1417.

Gerber, D. (2011) *American Immigration: A Very Short Introduction*. Oxford: Oxford University Press.

Haddad, Y. and Donovan, J. (2013) 'Good Copt, bad Copt: competing narratives on Coptic identity in Egypt and the United States', *Studies in World Christianity*, 19(3), pp. 208–232.

Hasan, S.S. (2003) *Christians Versus Muslims in Modern Egypt: The Century-Long Struggle for Coptic Equality*. Oxford: Oxford University Press.

Heikal, M. (1983) *Autumn of Fury: The Assassination of Sadat*. London: Andre Deutsch.

Heo, A. (2018) *The Political Lives of Saints: Christian-Muslim Mediation in Egypt*. Berkeley, CA: University of California Press.

Immigration Operations Division (1962) 'Immigration from U.A.R. 1962', Immigration attaché in Cairo C. Coutu to Chief, 21 May. [Report] Held at: Ottawa: Library and Archives Canada, R1206-130-4-E, RG76-I-B, vol. 801.1, file 547-5-538, 1948–1962, 1–2.

Iskander, Elizabeth. (2012) *Sectarian Conflict in Egypt: Coptic Media, Identity and Representation*. New York: Routledge.

Kamil, J. (2002) *Christianity in the Land of the Pharaohs: The Coptic Orthodox Church*. New York: Routledge.

Karas, S. (1985) *The Copts since the Arab Invasion: Strangers in Their Land*. New Jersey: The American, Canadian, and Australian Coptic Associations.

Karas, S. and Karas, L. (1985) 'Interviewed by Khalil, E., New Haven, CT', [video recording, 1 hr]. Held at: Khalil, E. private collection, California.

Kelley, N. and Trebilcock, M.J. (1998) *The Making of the Mosaic: A History of Canadian Immigration Policy*. Toronto: University of Toronto Press.

Kenny, K. (2013) *Diaspora: A Very Short Introduction*. Oxford: Oxford University Press.

Khalil, M. (1999) *Aqbāt al-mahjar: dirasah maydaniyah hawla humum al-watan wa al-muwatinah* [Immigrant Copts, a field study on the concerns of the citizens]. Cairo: Dar al-Khayyal.

Mahmood, S. (2016) *Religious Difference in a Secular Age: A Minority Report*. Princeton, NJ: Princeton University Press.

Marzouki, N. (2016) 'The U.S. Coptic diaspora and the limit of polarization', *Journal of Immigrant & Refugee Studies*, 14(3), pp. 261–276.

Ministry of UAR Foreign Affairs (1969) 'Emigration, June 1969. Meeting between Canadian Ambassador Carter and Abdul Aziz Gamil, Director of Immigration Department', [Report] Held at: Ottawa: Library and Archives Canada, R1206-135-3-E, RG76-B-1-C, vol. 989, file 5850-3-642, 1965–1975, 1–5.

Monthly Message (1971a) 'Acting Pontiff and Bishop Samuel Visit Congregation in North America', September, 1–2. Held at: Ottawa: Library and Archives Canada, MG55.9-No22, 1963–1971.

Monthly Message (1971b) Special Issue, November, 1. Held at: Ottawa: Library and Archives Canada, MG55.9-No22, 1963–1971.

Naguib, N. (2015) *The Coptic Awakening: Dr. Selim Naguib (1933–2014)*. Montreal: self-published.

Naguib, S. (1996) *Les Coptes dans L'Égypte d'aujourd'hui: Angoisses et espoirs d'une minorité aux Abois* [The Copts in Egypt today: fears and hopes of a desperate minority]. Brussels: Solidarité-Orient.

Pastor, C. (2017) *The Mexican Mahjar: Transnational Maronites, Jews, and Arabs Under the French Mandate*. Austin, TX: University of Texas Press.

Pennington, J.D. (1982) 'The Copts in modern Egypt', *Middle Eastern Studies*, 18(2), pp. 158–179.

Perin, R. (1993) 'National histories and ethnic history in Canada', *Cahiers de Recherche Sociologique*, 20, pp. 113–128.

Peters, J. (1960) 'Press release to *Toronto Star*', 6 November. [Letter] Held at: Ottawa: Library and Archives Canada, MG30 D201, vol. 1, file 17, 1.

Peters, J. (1968) 'The Canadian Arab Federation', *The Arab Dawn*, 1(1), October. [Newsletter] Held at: Ottawa: Library and Archives Canada, MG30 D201, vol. 2, file 18, 2.

Pope Shenouda ([1981] 1986) 'Our dear children', 4 August. [Letter] In al-Masry, I.H.,. *Bishop Samuel of Public and Social Services*. Cairo: Mehaba Bookstore, 1986, p. 69.

Ramzy, C. (2017) 'Singing heaven on earth: Coptic counter-publics and popular song at Egyptian mulid festivals', *International Journal of Middle East Studies*, 49(3), pp. 375–394.

Rowe, P. (2001) 'Four guys and a fax machine? Diasporas, new information technologies, and the internationalization of religion in Egypt', *Journal of Church and State*, 43(1), pp. 81–92.

Sa'dah, I. (1980) 'Copts in the United States', Akhbar Al-Yom, 12 April, 8.

Sadat, A. (1981) 'Interview ', Le Figaro, 26 September, 1.

Sedra, P. (2011) *From Mission to Modernity: Evangelicals, Reformers, and Education in Nineteenth Century Egypt*. London: I.B. Tauris.

Sedra, P. (2014) 'Copts and the millet partnership: the intra-communal dynamics behind Egyptian sectarianism', *Journal of Law and Religion*, 29(3), pp. 491–509.

Sharkey, H. (2008) *American Evangelicals in Egypt: Missionary Encounters in an Age of Empire*. Princeton, NJ: Princeton University Press.

Shenoda, A. (2012) 'The politics of faith: on faith, skepticism, and miracles among Coptic Christians in Egypt', *Ethnos: Journal of Anthropology*, 77(4), pp. 477–495.

Sidhom, A. (1971) 'Visit of Archbishop Antonius and Bishop Samuel to North America', *Watani*, 22 August, 2.

Smith, A. (1956) 'Ambassador in Cairo to Smith CES, Director of Immigration Branch', 26 May. [Letter] Held at: Ottawa: Library and Archives Canada, R1206-130-4-E, RG76-I-B, vol. 821, file 552-1-540, 1952–1958.

Sökefeld, M. (2006) 'Mobilizing in transnational space: a social movement approach to the formation of diaspora', *Global Networks*, 6(3), pp. 265–284.

Takla, H.N., Mikhil, M.N. and Moussa, M.R. (1997) 'Egyptian Copts', in Levinson, D. and Ember, M. (eds) *American Immigrant Cultures: Builders of a Nation*, vol. 1. New York: Macmillan Reference USA, pp. 244–247.

The Egyptian Canadian Club/*Cercle des Canadiens d'Egypte*/*el Nadi el Masri el Kanadi* (1996) [Pamphlet]. Held at: Clara Thomas Archives and Special Collections, Coptic Canadian History Project collection. Toronto: self-published, non-paginated.

The New York Times (1981a) 'Welcome President Sadat to the United States of America', 3 August, B3.

The New York Times (1981b) 'The Christian Orthodox Church', 8 August, A12.

The Washington Post (1981) 'Open letter to President Sadat of Egypt', 5 August, A20.

Tsourapas, G. (2018) *The Politics of Migration in Modern Egypt: Strategies for Regime Survival in Autocracies*. Cambridge: Cambridge University Press.

Wassef, N.H. (1978) 'The Egyptians in Montreal: a new colour in the Canadian ethnic mosaic', MA thesis. McGill University.

Yanni, R. (1982) 'Open letter to President Hosni Mubarak', *Al Rasala*, 1(1), pp. 1–2.

Yefet, Bosmat. (2016) 'The Coptic diaspora and the status of the Coptic minority in Egypt', *Journal of Ethnic and Migration Studies*, (43)7, pp. 1205–1221.

5
OPPORTUNITIES HERE AND THERE

Digital diasporas and the Iranian American election moment

Hajar Yazdiha

On June 12, 2009, Iranian President Mahmoud Ahmadinejad ran for re-election against three challengers. Leading among them was Mir-Hossein Mousavi, a 'reformist' challenger favoured by those eager for a less fiery president who might ease tensions with the United States. The next morning, news agencies reported Ahmadinejad the victor with an overwhelming 62 per cent of the counted votes, compared to 34 per cent for Mousavi (Worth and Fathi, 2009). Protests erupted across Iran and in over 90 cities around the world activating the furthest reaches of the Iranian diaspora, many decrying the unexpected election results as allegedly fraudulent. Newspapers called it the 'biggest unrest since the 1979 revolution' (Al Jazeera, 2009). So began the Green Movement, initially the colour of Mousavi's campaign, evolving into a symbol of collective unity against President Ahmadinejad and the Iranian government.

Six thousand miles away, in my studio apartment in New York City, I began receiving urgent Facebook messages from Iranian Americans to come and join the protests. This was new. As a German-born Iranian American growing up in a mostly white community on the East Coast, I did not know many Iranian Americans. After all, beyond the concentrated clusters of Iranians in places like 'Tehrangeles' (Los Angeles), Iranian Americans are spatially diffuse (Mahdi, 1998). The 2008 Public Affairs Alliance of Iranian Americans (PAAIA) suggested as much when they reported that only one in five Iranian Americans indicated that they interact mostly with other Iranian Americans outside of work (PAAIA, 2008). However, after the results of the Iranian election were publicised through mainstream media that summer of 2009, I immediately began receiving mass emails, Facebook messages and text messages encouraging me to join groups of fellow Iranian Americans and attend protests in New York City to 'support our people'. My digital life was filled with discussions of Iran and 'the homeland', international news articles, blog posts, and activist accounts from the ground in Iran. Suddenly Iranian Americans were everywhere, visible in numbers, seemingly coalescing overnight. Iranian American activists identified me as a member of their movement by my ethnicity, signalled by my Iranian name, a digital call to connect across national borders to the Iranian diaspora by going out to the streets of New York City in protest.

How did these global politics activate digital diasporas – 'diasporas organized on the internet' (Brinkerhoff, 2009) – drawing diffuse second-generation Iranian Americans into the streets in protest? How did Iranian Americans understand these protests as a political opportunity to challenge conditions both *there* (Iran) and *here* (the United States)? As a generation removed from the homeland and raised in the United States, second-generation Iranian Americans' prominent role in these protests offers a particularly interesting case study. Examining second-generation Iranian Americans' understandings of their participation in the New York City protests, this chapter explores how global politics, distributed quickly through digital diasporas, shape second-generation Iranians' connections to the diaspora, actions for constituting these connections, and how these diasporic identities become their own strategic modes of belonging.

Drawing on theories of diaspora, this chapter shows how second-generation identities are not only made through negotiations of homeland and hostland. Instead, global politics can stimulate digital diasporic networks and spur action that challenges the limits of national identity, generating opportunities for conceptions of belonging that transcend the nation. In this instance, against the backdrop of rising, global anti-Muslim hostility and a political context categorising Iran as a member of the 'Axis of Evil', second-generation Iranians came together online, then in the streets, to perform solidarity and collectivism with Iranians across the world. Yet this performed solidarity also generated an opportunity to redefine the way Iranians were imagined and understood in the United States, innovating new forms of inclusion in both 'Iranianess' globally and 'Americaness' at home.

Global politics, diasporic identity formation and digital diasporas

For Middle Eastern diasporas, historically embedded Orientalism that pits a 'good, civilised, rational West' against an 'evil, backwards, threatening East' (Said, 1979) has long shaped the experiences and identity conflicts of Middle Eastern immigrants. Dual loyalty is particularly difficult in times of national conflict between host and sending countries when global tensions can generate tightened sanctions on immigrants. Global events like the Iranian Hostage Crisis and the terrorist attacks of September 11, 2001, exacerbate Orientalist constructions of Middle Eastern Americans as terrorists, shifting the identity options available to immigrants (Bozorgmehr and Douglas, 2011; Maghbouleh, 2017; Karam, 2020). What results is a persistent sense of interstitiality, of placelessness, of belonging neither 'here' nor 'there' (Shams, 2020).

Yet in the face of constraining national boundaries, racialised repression and societal exclusion, immigrants also innovate and engage in 'creative adaptations and strategic maneuvering' (Abdelhady, 2011). Through formations of diasporic identity, immigrants deploy new identities that transcend national borders (Portes and Zhou, 1993; Zhou, 1997; Ajrouch, 2004; Peek, 2005; Kasinitz, 2008; Rumbaut, 2008; Bakalian and Bozorgmehr, 2009). For example, in reaction to post-9/11 discrimination, many second-generation Muslim Americans claimed, rather than obscured, their Muslim religious identity as the most salient source of personal and social identity, simultaneously connecting to Muslim communities across ethnic boundaries and across borders (Peek, 2005). A transnational framework would understand this process as activation of existing cultural networks, family and religious ties, carried forward across borders (Haller and Landolt, 2005). Yet the evidence suggests a more creative process at play.

The diaspora framework better explains this dynamic, malleable, and relational process (Abdelhady, 2006; 2011). Diasporic identification is not only about reconstructing homeland culture, it also entails *inventing* homeland culture (Abdelhady, 2008). The continual negotiations of inclusion and exclusion across spaces and places generate layered and hybrid conceptions of belonging and, importantly, the *creation* of identities that are not only shaped by 'here' and 'there' but also 'elsewhere' (Shams, 2020). As Tahseen Shams describes, immigrants 'both produce and experience the interconnectedness of societies' (2020, p. 2). Understanding this recursive relationship illuminates how immigrants and their children do not merely move between fixed national identities of homeland and hostland. Rather, they innovate identities to generate diasporic spaces of belonging that transcend the limits of national borders and their bounded modes of inclusion (Abdelhady, 2008; 2011; Aly, 2014; Shams, 2020). Through diasporic spaces, 'migrants forge their sense of identity and their community ... as something that is at once new and familiar – a bricolage constructed of cultural elements from both the homeland and the receiving nation' (Kivisto, 2001, p. 568), transgressing boundaries and enabling new, political forms of existence (Yazdiha, 2010). For the second generation, the sites and products of these identity negotiations often vary significantly from those experienced by their immigrant parents. Where diaspora is in many ways embodied for immigrants as a homeland inscribed in their memory (Abdelhady, 2008), for the second generation, a diasporic identity is not given.

Yet digital diasporas are an emergent space in which even children of immigrants who have never visited their ancestral homeland can be drawn into diasporic networks (Brinkerhoff, 2009; Alinejad, 2013; Marlowe, Bartley and Collins, 2017). For many migrants with internet access, these digital diasporas are a feature of everyday life where new technologies spur connection not only with one's own family members in the homeland, but also distant diaspora members all over the globe (Brinkerhoff, 2009; Alonso and Oiarzabal, 2010; Mandaville and Brinkerhoff, 2010; Andersson, 2019). Through digital diasporas, information flows quickly across vast spaces and places, where social media like Twitter and Facebook offer near-immediate news from the ground without the filter or censorship of state media (Brinkerhoff, 2009; Turner and Berckmoes, 2020). Studies find that even international news broadcasters – like BBC Arabic and BBC Persian – are central to the shape and activity of digital diasporas as they generate far-reaching audiences following news from the homeland (Gillespie, Mackay and Anderson, 2010). These digital diasporas generate spaces where immigrants and their children can bypass the limited boundaries of nation that may exclude them and find belonging, connection and identity online (Mandaville and Brinkerhoff, 2010; Dubinsky, 2020; Ponzanesi, 2020). Laura Candidatu and colleagues expand theories of digital diaspora to conceptualise these spaces not as fixed *things* but rather as dynamic and relational processes, as 'mutually constituted here and there, through bodies and data, across borders and networks, online and offline, by users and platforms, through material, symbolic, and emotional practices that are all reflective of intersecting power relations' (Candidatu, Leurs and Ponzanesi, 2019, p. 39). This conceptualisation helps us understand how digital diasporas are both continually shaped by action offline and are *shaping* action offline.

When larger social forces, the configurations of conditions here and elsewhere, are particularly intensified, these digital diasporas light up, generating or transforming diasporic connections and collective action. Studies show how global politics and impactful events in the homeland can mobilise immigrants to act collectively in their receiving countries, shaping collective action through evaluations of potential repression and backlash both here and there (Brinkerhoff, 2009; Moss, 2016; Dubinsky, 2020). These patterns also show children of immigrants, second and third generations, claiming identification with the diaspora and leading collective action to draw public attention to the atrocities 'over there' (Wayland, 2004; Lundy, 2011; Hess and Korf, 2014; Rivera-Salgado, 2014; Moss, 2016; 2020; Alinejad, 2017; Guarnizo, Chaudhary and Sørensen, 2019). Critically, this collective action directed toward homeland politics can also serve a dual purpose: challenging the identity conflicts and societal exclusion of the hostland (Brinkerhoff, 2009; Dubinsky, 2020).

In this chapter, I show that as second-generation Iranian Americans were activated through digital diasporas in the wake of the Iranian election, their resulting collective action was not only directed toward challenging the government back in Iran. As participants explained, the election protests also offered an opportunity to challenge the stigmatisation of Iranians in the United States. Performing Iranian diasporic identity on their own terms, shaping these identities digitally then mobilising them to the streets, would counter racialised, Orientalist conceptions of Iranians and limited conceptions of belonging as circumscribed by the nation.

As social movement studies show, the advent of a perceived political opportunity can explain the emergence of collective action (McAdam, 1982; Gamson and Meyer, 1996; Meyer and Staggenborg, 1996). In mobilising individuals towards this collective action, generating a unified collective identity is critical for coordinating a cohesive, political effort. Yet the construction of collective identity can be the political goal itself, strategically deployed to generate a new public understanding of members of the group (Bernstein, 1997). Groups facing a stigmatised identity, whether LGBTQ communities or immigrant rights activists, may deploy strategies specifically to reshape and reconstruct a new collective identity (Taylor and Whittier, 1992; Simon and Klandermans, 2001; Bernstein and De la Cruz, 2009). While seemingly instrumentalist, on the contrary, this approach shows that reshaping collective identity is as much about strategically challenging societal exclusion as it is about activating social bonds, forging new and solidary collectives, imagining alternative forms of belonging (Yuval-Davis, 2007; Klandermans, 2014). The emergence of information and communication technologies has enabled digital diasporas to arise in dynamic and creative ways that are particularly valuable to second-generation immigrants, negotiating the limits of identity and questions about who they are and where they belong (Brinkerhoff, 2009; Alinejad, 2017; Dubinsky, 2020; Turner and Berckmoes, 2020).

Joining these theoretical streams from diaspora studies, digital diasporas and social movement studies, the argument is laid out as follows: for second-generation Iranian immigrants, a global event stemming from the homeland draws young Iranians into digital diasporas where collective action takes shape. This collective action offers second-generation Iranians a dual political opportunity to mobilise, both regarding conditions 'there' and conditions 'here', drawing a loosely organised second generation into a diasporic digital space. Through this space, the second generation constructs a collective diasporic identity on their own terms that blends cultural elements of homeland, hostland and elsewhere. Through this diasporic identity, the second generation both challenges the conditions 'over there' and the dominant, exclusionary societal narrative about the group 'at home', contesting popular notions about who they are and where they belong.

Sketching the Iranian American diaspora

The United States is the largest site of the Iranian diaspora, with nearly one million Iranians, roughly 45 per cent of whom are classified as second generation or children of immigrants (Bozorgmehr and Douglas, 2011). Iranians in the United States largely arrived either as students before the Iranian Revolution or as visitors or exiles during and after the revolution. As a result, the combination of well-educated students and elite exiles makes for a highly educated, secular immigrant group with high concentrations in professional occupations (ibid.). Like other Middle Eastern and 'Muslim-appearing' groups, this socioeconomic status has not shielded Iranians from increased hostility and discrimination. The National Security Entry-Exit Registration System (NSEERS) government initiative to monitor and prevent terrorism singled out Iranians as a group subject to surveillance, and, in 2002, President Bush declared Iran part of the 'Axis of Evil' (ibid.). Mobasher (2012) argues that the culmination of the Iranian Revolution, the 1979 hostage crisis, and the rise of anti-Islamic religious sentiments in the

United States have caused an 'identity crisis' among Iranians in America. In contrast, Naficy (1993) describes how Iranians have resisted stigmatised images through hybrid exile cultures. In this process, exiles, meaning those who are banished or who escaped out of fear, maintain the familiar symbols of ethnic identity within the confines of American mainstream culture, while also expressing resistance or opposition to subordination by the host country.

Despite their experiences of discrimination analogous to other Middle Eastern and Muslim groups, Iranians have long distinguished themselves from other 'Brown' people through collective narratives, bound in a legal designation as White, about their whiteness as the original 'Aryans' (Maghbouleh, 2017). It has not been uncommon for some Iranian Americans to Anglicise their names, lighten their hair and undertake plastic surgery to remould 'ethnic' noses. At the same time, many Iranians have retained 'safe', symbolic aspects of Iranian ethnicity like food and music, referring to themselves as 'Persian' to elicit images of an ancient, romanticised Persian Empire, disassociating their identities from the Islamic Republic of Iran (Tehranian, 2008; Maghbouleh, 2010). Through periods of heightened anti-Iranian sentiment, this integration of sending and receiving cultures was a survival tactic as much as a negotiation of cultures. Since the 1990s and the rise of the Internet, Iranian Americans have been active in online spaces with a rich network of diasporic blogs and digital media (Naficy, 1993; Alinejad, 2017). Iranian women, for example, have used digital spaces like blogs and diasporic websites to organise diasporic members around women's issues (Nasirpour, 2016).

Meanwhile, the children of Iranian immigrants have navigated contradictions of identity and politics from a young age, between the 'Aryan myth' passed down by their parents that Iranians are not racialised minorities and their daily experiences of discrimination that tell them they are seen as 'Others' in their own homeland (Maghbouleh, 2017). Meanwhile, this second generation has grown up in the digital age where the growth of social media like Twitter and Facebook allows for immediate flows of culture, information, news and politics, accessibility to spaces beyond the nation that complicate ideas of 'home' (Alinejad, 2013). In this space of fraught identity, the 2009 Iranian election posed a powerful political opportunity for second-generation Iranians to tap into and embody the digital diasporas at their fingertips. They would organise these catalysed connections online to action offline, telling the world 'who they were', both claiming their solidarity with Iranian diasporas to challenge the Iranian government and transcending stifling identity boundaries in the United States.

Analysing second-generation Iranian Americans' mobilisation

To examine second-generation Iranian Americans' mobilisation around the Iranian election, I analyse 20 in-depth interviews with participants gathered through a snowball sample of second-generation Iranian Americans living in New York City who participated in the protests. I gained access to participants through two Iranian American acquaintances, limiting myself only to second-generation Iranian Americans who lived in one of the five boroughs of New York City. Focusing on interviews with second-generation Iranian Americans in New York City rather than large-scale surveys allows me to examine the complex motivations and perceptions of protest and identity in depth. Of the respondents, 16 resided in Manhattan and four in Brooklyn. Twelve of my respondents are women and eight men. All participants were between the ages of 26 and 35, all were employed full-time in a range of professions, from IT consulting to magazine publishing, and all had internet access. Due to the busy schedules of young professionals living in fast-paced New York City, it was difficult to secure lengthy interviews with every participant and interviews ranged from 45 minutes during a lunch break to two hours after work. The purpose of these interviews was to elicit open articulations of their experience of being Iranian American, their perceptions of identity, their uses of digital media, and to understand what motivated their participation in collective action. Pseudonyms are used to protect participants' anonymity.

The duality of political opportunities and diasporic identities

Before making sense of participants' motivations to protest, I wanted to understand participants' attachments to Iranian identity and their embeddedness in an Iranian diaspora, online and offline. Participants largely cited their Iranian identity as 'very important' to who they were, where their family traditions were central to their sense of what it meant to be Iranian. For example, Layla, a financial analyst in her late twenties, described how her family had instilled 'pride in being Persian' and she 'carries this on' through cooking, as she can 'cook polo like my mom'. Others mentioned 'Persia's rich history' and how they grew up with 'Persian pride', or referred to their family's relationship to other Iranian families, which instils 'a reminder' of who they are. However, when asked about how many of their friends are Iranian American, how often they speak to family in Iran, and how often they visit Iran, respondents had more varied attachments. Some participants made annual trips to Iran with their families. Arash, a doctor in his early thirties, described his summers in Iran as a kid, lessening in frequency in adulthood. Others, like me, had never even been to Iran. Parvin, a freelance graphic designer living in Brooklyn, described how she knew Iranian Americans who returned to Iran every summer, but that 'it didn't make much sense for us, since our family is spread out all over'. She explained how her mother's and father's siblings had also left during the Iranian Revolution, landing in Canada, Germany and the United States. Most participants were engaged with extended family through the internet, whether by email or WhatsApp, but fewer were actively connected to digital diaspora beyond their family members.

There was also notable homogeneity among respondents in their secularism and family background as children of exiles. Most respondents described how their parents left Iran because of their dissatisfaction with the government, so unsurprisingly these second-generation youth were more likely to have been raised with negative attitudes towards homeland politics. 'I remember being, like, five and my parents yelling about the [Iranian] government at the dinner table,' Layla recalled, describing how she had long understood that her parents had a contentious relationship with their homeland. However, the seeming invisibility of Iranian Americans in the civic sphere until the 2009 protests suggests that there were additional social forces that caused the second generation to construct a collective in that particular moment, to mobilise then when they had not done so before. Though there had been a significant wave of Muslim coalition-building after 9/11 that some Iranians had readily participated in (Bakalian and Bozorgmehr, 2009), specific political mobilisation around Iranian identity and homeland politics was far less common.

Yet participants described how it was very much this anti-'Brown' fervour, of coming of age during the post-9/11 'War on Terror', that shaped their perceptions of the limits of national inclusion. Growing anti-Muslim sentiment had made their non-White identity unavoidably salient, but while it was clear where they did *not* belong, it was less clear where Iranian Americans *did* fit in. Kamran, a doctor in his mid-thirties, hailing from Long Island, described a common sentiment of navigating the contradictory space between legal categorisation as White and social reality, explaining:

My mom is telling me, '*Azizam*, you're White', and I'm in school where kids are like, 'Yo, Saddam [Hussein]' and it's pretty clear to everyone I am not White, but I'm not

Black, right? I'm not Asian, right? Like, what am I? What box is that? So every chance I got, I'd check off 'Other.'

Participants described a growing sense of injustice over the treatment of Muslim and Middle Eastern immigrants in the United States and around the world that preceded the 2009 Iranian election. They described being unjustly discriminated against at airports, pulled aside for extra security screenings. Participants' experiences were comparable to those found by the PAAIA survey, which showed that nearly half of Iranian Americans surveyed had experienced or personally knew another Iranian American who experienced discrimination because of their ethnicity or country of origin. The most common types of discrimination reported were airport security, social discrimination, employment or business discrimination, racial profiling and discrimination by immigration officials.

Some participants lamented being unfairly grouped with terrorists by the media and the publics, and they expressed a desire to prove their belonging to the United States. When asked about their perception of how American society views Iran, many participants specifically mentioned their anger over President Bush's grouping of Iran with the 'Axis of Evil' after 9/11. Nima, a mid-thirties business manager who grew up in Southern California, became animated as he leaned forward, eyes flashing, and said, 'Where do people get off acting like we're these backwards people? I am an American through and through and I don't agree with what goes down over there either!' Sara, an editorial assistant also originally from Southern California, said of the post-9/11 era and the War on Terror, 'People would expect me to be, like, this expert in Muslim women, like, "Why do they make women cover their faces, why do they do this and that?", and, like, I grew up *here*, why the hell would *I* know?' Yet where these respondents described the hypervisibility of 'being Brown' in a time where Iranians were subsumed under a larger umbrella category, this experience was distinct from being identified as specifically Iranian. As Nima explained, 'I could have been Iraqi or Afghani or whatever, people act like "we're all the same."'

And then came that pivotal moment in June 2009. The widely-publicised Iranian election and the powerful uprising in its wake brought not only the Iranian government but also its people into the global spotlight. News, images and reports from regular Iranians on the ground flowed quickly through digital spaces, activating digital diasporas and, importantly, creating new ones. In interviews, second-generation Iranian Americans described the strange sense of sudden visibility in everyday life, both online and offline. Dynamic conversations about Iranian politics that had once been confined to their family dinner tables were taking place in public view among non-Iranians, on the news, on social media, blogs, websites and the radio. Ali, an IT consultant in his late twenties, raised in the suburbs of northern California, described his initial bafflement over his White friends' sudden interest in his country of origin. 'Suddenly they want to talk about it, like, "You were there last summer, right? What was it like?" and I'm like, "You never cared that I was Iranian before…"' He went on to describe his initial wariness of their interest, as it stirred feelings of being the 'kid with the funny name' in elementary school. 'I wasn't about to go back there and have them make me out to be this foreigner again, you know?' he explained. Farimah, a stockbroker in her late twenties raised in the white suburbs of Ohio, described a similarly spontaneous feeling of visibility, describing, 'Like, overnight, I had my [White] friends texting me like, "Hey, are you following the news? What the hell is going on over there?" It made me feel weird.' When I probed her to explain why, she said, 'It's not that I'm not proud to be Iranian but, like, I grew up here, so don't act like I'm suddenly this Iran expert.' She, and other second-generation Iranians who had long grappled with feelings of invisibility and placelessness, described the perception of sudden conspicuousness and initial feelings of unease at being identified as not just a general 'Brown person' but rather, specifically Iranian. As Sara put simply, 'Suddenly they're looking at me like, "Wait, *you're* Iranian, right?"'

However, participants described how the sense of sudden visibility shifted from vulnerability to opportunity as they followed the news and discussion unfolding on social media and saw an emergent frame about an inspiring movement of young, cosmopolitan Iranians. Babak – a med student in his late twenties – explained, 'It wasn't like the usual story of "Oh, this horrible backwards country," it was like, "Hey, look at these cool young people, who look like you, fighting their effed-up government."' As second-generation Iranian Americans saw the media and publics online portraying an Iranian identity they related to, one that ran counter to the Orientalist ascriptions so many of them had grown up negotiating, there was a growing sense of political opportunity. They began organising online, growing digital diasporas within the United States and beyond. The global moment drew second-generation Iranians into a diasporic identity that would both draw them towards Iranians all over the world and away from the deeply felt exclusion at home in the United States. Participants shared rich stories detailing with remarkable comparability the desire to show fellow Americans who Iranians 'really were'. To perform this diasporic Iranian identity, they would organise online, then take to the streets.

(Re)constructing and performing diasporic identity through protest

The calls to protest landed in inboxes, Facebook messages and texts all across the world, including New York City, as diffuse Iranians constituted a mobilising digital diaspora. Most protest participants I interviewed reported learning about the protests through emails and Facebook messages. The most cited organisation was a nonprofit organisation called Where's My Vote, founded in 2009 by Iranian Americans in Los Angeles to follow the Iranian election and organise protests but eventually expanded to cover worldwide political election issues. From June through July of 2009, Iranian Americans in New York City, including myself, received regular Facebook messages from Where's My Vote calling for collective action. I had not signed up for this group, but as Babak hypothesised in our interview, 'They probably search for Iranian names who live in the city.' The use of social media to organise protest tapped into networks of young, internet-savvy Iranian Americans. The calls to action generated a bricolage diasporic identity deploying solidarity with the Iranian people while challenging Orientalist conceptions of 'backwards' Iranians by playing up cosmopolitan values resonant to Western publics.

First, the digital calls to action generated a sense of collectivity through diasporic connections across borders, drawing second-generation Iranians towards identification with the Iranian diaspora by advocating that Iranian Americans had a duty to support 'our people back home'. Second, calls to protest were framed through a cosmopolitan discourse of freedom and democracy, challenging Orientalist conceptions of Iran as backward, barbaric and autocratic. One call to protest listed reasons to take action including, 'Freedom of assembly, freedom of expression, and freedom of press as guaranteed by the Iranian constitution and Iran's obligations under international covenants it has signed' (via Facebook, 7/13/09). Connoting democracy and constitutional norms, these frames strategically elicited cultural resonance with values familiar to Western publics. Third, calls to action emphasised the importance of *performing* this collective diasporic identity offline with the use of symbolic posters and clothing to show support and unanimity. Digital calls to action emphasised the importance of wearing green to simultaneously exhibit solidarity and resistance. One Facebook event page said, 'To show our grief for our fallen friends and countrymen, wearing black with a green headband/wristband is recommended' (via Facebook, 7/10/09). Another suggested, 'Please join us at any time between 4–5:30, wearing green and/or black, to show the world the Iranian Freedom Seekers are heard and seen everywhere!' (via Facebook, 7/13/09).

Understanding the world's eyes were on Iranians, Iranian diasporas who had joined together online to organise action took to the streets of New York City dressed in green and black, hands raised in solidarity, proudly performing an intergenerational diaspora. Faced with their interstitiality as 'Others' in the United States, second-generation Iranians were drawn into diasporic identity, crafting and performing an Iranian identity on their own terms that challenged not only the Iranian government in their parents' homeland but also their exclusion in the country they called home. This diasporic identity would transcend national boundaries, challenging what Western publics understood as 'backward Iranians', creating a new space of belonging. In interviews, second-generation Iranian Americans described that following these calls to protest online, they were being drawn in by the growing conviction that their participation would both show their support for Iranians 'back home' and also challenge Western stigma towards Iranians. Reconstructing diasporic identity was a dual process by which the second generation described joining an Iranian identity to generate solidarity and belonging across borders and challenge exclusion within borders, specifically by disassociating from a stigmatised Iranian identity. All participants articulated how the global moment offered an opening, an opportunity, to 'show' a new characterisation of Iranian identity. Where the 'Persian pride' so many articulated had been limited to the domains of family, now Iranians – 'not this insane, embarrassing president [Ahmadenijad] but the *beautiful Iranian people*', in Layla's words – were on the world's stage. Daniel, a business consultant with an MBA in his early thirties, raised on Long Island and living in Manhattan, explained:

> I felt like I had to protest to show the world that we're not these backwards Muslim people who are, like, living in some small village without plumbing. We don't agree with what goes on over there … I was so happy I had my American friends coming up to me saying, 'Oh, it's terrible what's happening there, but it's cool that the people are protesting and Tweeting about it.' Like, the protests showed people that Iranians are progressive and they thought, 'Oh, they're like us.'

Daniel's comments, like some other participants, drew distinctions between the young, cosmopolitan, 'progressive' Iranians he was proud to associate with and conservative, rural Iranians – understood to be the populist base that turned out to vote for Ahmadenijad. The distinctions at times reproduced – at most, Orientalist, and at least, classist – ideas about the right way to portray Iranian identity to the world. Yet, at the core, the impulse was the same among participants. Where Orientalist conceptions, sedimented over time in the popular imagination, had long characterised Iranians as what participants described as 'barbaric', 'backward' and of an 'oppressive culture', diasporic identity organised digitally would shape action offline by challenging exclusion 'here' and politics 'there' by drawing together Iranians everywhere.

Conclusion

In the wake of the 2009 Iranian election and with the Iranian people on the global stage, a dual opportunity emerged for Iranian Americans to counter politics in Iran and the United States. Second-generation Iranians, coming of age in a post-9/11 era that simultaneously rendered them hypervisible as generic 'Brown threats' and invisible as hard-to-categorise non-Whites, constituted a digital diaspora. Having long concealed aspects of their societally stigmatised Iranian identity to mitigate discrimination, second-generation Iranians described their motivation to strategically claim and proudly perform diasporic Iranian identity across borders. Mobilising diaspora networks online, they would show their fellow Americans and the world a new face of Iranian identity offline, to challenge the stifling boundaries of being Iranian in America. They would forge the interconnectivity of Iranians across borders as evidence of a cosmopolitan Iranian people, young and politically engaged, committed to the same values and freedoms as Western publics.

Joining theories of diaspora with social movement theories, this framework offers insights beyond the case of the Iranian diaspora, helping examine more generally how the children of non-White immigrants growing up in the digital age perceive, negotiate and react to unsettled questions of identity and belonging in a globalised world. Faced with the provisional limits of national inclusion at home, the children of immigrants turn outward, to the 'elsewheres', towards new conceptions of belonging beyond borders. Crafting 'roots' anew, they may use global politics as openings for constituting digital diasporas to reconstruct diasporic identities in strategic ways that generate new collectivities. We can also examine these digital diasporas as their own generative spaces that not only respond to global events but also shape them, inspiring new forms of collective action and contentious politics. Understanding the ways that diaspora is made and remade relationally, online and offline, constrained and enabled against the larger structural forces that shape the identity options available to immigrant groups, we can better understand the ways that diasporas reshape societies, reimagine their limits and spur social change.

References

Abdelhady, D. (2006) 'Beyond home/host networks: forms of solidarity among Lebanese immigrants in a global era', *Identities*, 13, pp. 427–453. https://doi.org/10.1080/10702890600839595

Abdelhady, D. (2008) 'Representing the homeland: Lebanese diasporic notions of home and return in a global context', *Cultural Dynamics*, 20, pp. 53–72. https://doi.org/10.1177/0921374007088055

Abdelhady, D. (2011) *The Lebanese Diaspora: The Arab Immigrant Experience in Montreal, New York, and Paris*. New York : New York University Press.Ajrouch, K.J. (2004) 'Gender, race, and symbolic boundaries: contested spaces of identity among Arab American adolescents', *Sociological Perspectives*, 47, pp. 371–391. https://doi.org/10.1525/sop.2004.47.4.371

Alinejad, D. (2013) 'Locating home in a "digital age": an ethnographic case study of second-generation Iranian Americans in LA and their use of internet media', *Iranian Studies*, 46, pp. 95-113. https://doi.org/10.1080/00210862.2012.743309

Alinejad, D. (2017) *The Internet ad Formations of Iranian American-Ness: Next Generation Diaspora*. Cham: Springer.

Al Jazeera (2009) 'Poll results prompt Iran protests', 14 June. Available at: www.aljazeera.com/news/2009/6/14/poll-results-prompt-iran-protests (accessed 31 January 2021).Alonso, A. and Oiarzabal, P. (2010) *Diasporas in the New Media Age: Identity, Politics, and Community*. Reno, NV: University of Nevada Press.

Aly, R.M.K. (2014) *Becoming Arab in London: Performativity and the Undoing of Identity*. London: Pluto Press.

Andersson, K. (2019) 'Digital diasporas: an overview of the research areas of migration and new media through a narrative literature review', *Human Technologies*, 15, pp. 142–180.

Bakalian, A. and Bozorgmehr, M. (2009) *Backlash 9/11: Middle Eastern and Muslim Americans Respond*. Berkeley, CA: University of California Press.

Bernstein, M. (1997) 'Celebration and suppression: the strategic uses of identity by the lesbian and gay movement', *American Journal of Sociology* 103, pp. 531–565. https://doi.org/10.1086/231250

Bernstein, M. and De la Cruz, M. (2009) '"What are you?": Explaining identity as a goal of the multiracial hapa movement', *Social Problems*, 56, pp. 722–745. https://doi.org/10.1525/sp.2009.56.4.722

Bozorgmehr, M. and Douglas, D. (2011) 'Success(ion): second-generation Iranian Americans', *Iranian Studies*, 44, pp. 3–24. https://doi.org/10.1080/00210862.2011.524047

Brinkerhoff, J.M. (2009) *Digital Diasporas: Identity and Transnational Engagement*. Cambridge: Cambridge University Press.

Candidatu, L., Leurs, K., and Ponzanesi, S. (2019) 'Digital diasporas: beyond the buzzword', in Retis, J. and Tsagarousianou, R. (eds) *The Handbook of Diasporas, Media, and Culture*. Chichester: John Wiley & Sons, Ltd, pp. 31–47. https://doi.org/10.1002/9781119236771.ch3

Dubinsky, I. (2020) 'Digital diaspora: Eritrean asylum seekers' cyberactivism in Israel', *African Diaspora*, 12, pp. 89–116. https://doi.org/10.1163/18725465-bja10002

Gamson, W.A. and Meyer, D.S. (1996) 'Framing political opportunity', in Zald, M., McAdam, D., and McCarthy, J. (eds) *Comparative Perspectives on Social Movements: Political Opportunities, Mobilizing Structures, and Cultural Framings*. Cambridge: Cambridge University Press, pp. 275–290.

Gillespie, M., Mackay, H., and Andersson, M. (2010) 'Mapping digital diasporas @ BBC World Service: users and uses of the Persian and Arabic websites', *Middle East Journal of Culture and Communication*, 3, pp. 256–278. https://doi.org/10.1163/187398610X510047

Guarnizo, L.E., Chaudhary, A.R., and Sørensen, N.N. (2019) 'Migrants' transnational political engagement in Spain and Italy', *Migration Studies*, 7, pp. 281–322. https://doi.org/10.1093/migration/mnx061

Haller, W. and Landolt, P. (2005) 'The transnational dimensions of identity formation: adult children of immigrants in Miami', *Ethnic and Racial Studies*, 28(6), pp. 1182–1214. https://doi.org/10.1080/01419870500224554

Hess, M. and Korf, B. (2014) 'Tamil diaspora and the political spaces of second-generation activism in Switzerland', *Global Networks* 14, pp. 419–437. https://doi.org/10.1111/glob.12052

Karam, R.A. (2020) 'Becoming American by becoming Muslim: strategic assimilation among second-generation Muslim American parents', *Ethnic and Racial Studies*, 43(2), pp. 1–20. https://doi.org/10.1080/01419870.2019.1578396

Kasinitz, P. (2008) 'Becoming American, becoming minority, getting ahead: the role of racial and ethnic status in the upward mobility of the children of immigrants', *The Annals of the American Academy of Political and Social Science*, 620, pp. 253–269. https://doi.org/10.1177/0002716208322880

Kivisto, P. (2001) 'Theorizing transnational immigration: a critical review of current efforts', *Ethnic and Racial Studies*, 24(4), pp. 549–577. https://doi.org/10.1080/01419870120049789

Klandermans, P.G. (2014) 'Identity politics and politicized identities: identity processes and the dynamics of protest', *Political Psychology*, 35, pp. 1–22. https://doi.org/10.1111/pops.12167

Lundy, G. (2011) 'Transnationalism in the aftermath of the Haiti earthquake: reinforcing ties and second-generation identity', *Journal of Black Studies*, 42, pp. 203–224.

Maghbouleh, N. (2010) '"Inherited nostalgia" among second-generation Iranian Americans: a case study at a Southern California University', *Journal of Intercultural Studies*, 31, pp. 199–218. https://doi.org/10.1080/07256861003606382

Maghbouleh, N. (2017) *The Limits of Whiteness: Iranian Americans and the Everyday Politics of Race*. Palo Alto. CA: Stanford University Press.Mahdi, A.A. (1998) 'Ethnic identity among second-generation Iranians in the United States', *Iranian Studies*, 31, pp. 77–95.

Mandaville, P. and Brinkerhoff, J.M. (2010) 'Digital diasporas: identity and transnational engagement', *Perspectives on Politics*, 8, pp. 394–395. http://dx.doi.org.libproxy2.usc.edu/10.1017/S153759270999257X

Marlowe, J.M., Bartley, A., and Collins, F. (2017) 'Digital belongings: the intersections of social cohesion, connectivity and digital media', *Ethnicities*, 17, pp. 85–102. https://doi.org/10.1177/1468796816654174

McAdam, D. (1982) *Political Process and the Development of Black Insurgency, 1930–1970*. Chicago: University of Chicago Press.

Meyer, D.S. and Staggenborg, S. (1996) 'Movements, countermovements, and the structure of political opportunity', *American Journal of Sociology*, 101, pp. 1628–1660.

Mobasher, M.M. (2012) *Iranians in Texas: Migration, Politics, and Ethnic Identity*. Austin, TX: University of Texas Press.

Moss, D.M. (2016) 'Transnational repression, diaspora mobilization, and the case of the Arab Spring', *Social Problems*, 63, pp. 480–498. https://doi.org/10.1093/socpro/spw019

Moss, D.M. (2020) 'Voice after exit: explaining diaspora mobilization for the Arab Spring', *Social Forces*, 98, pp. 1669–1694. https://doi.org/10.1093/sf/soz070

Naficy, H. (1993) *The Making of Exile Cultures: Iranian Television in Los Angeles*. Minneapolis, MN: University of Minnesota Press.

Nasirpour, S. (2016) 'Iranian women and the politics of diasporic websites in the digital age', *Anthropology of the Middle East*, 11, pp. 76–90. https://doi.org/10.3167/ame.2016.110206

PAAIA (Public Affairs of Alliance of Iranian Americans) (2008) 'National Survey of Iranian Americans'. Available at: https://paaia.org/CMS/Data/Sites/1/PDFs/survey_of_iranian_americans_final_report_dec_102008.pdf.

Peek, L. (2005) 'Becoming Muslim: the development of a religious identity', *Sociology of Religion*, 66, pp. 215–242. https://doi.org/10.2307/4153097

Ponzanesi, S. (2020) 'Digital diasporas: postcoloniality, media and affect', *Interventions*, 22, pp. 977–993. https://doi.org/10.1080/1369801X.2020.1718537

Portes, A. and Zhou, M. (1993) 'The new second generation: segmented assimilation and its variants', *The Annals of the American Academy of Political and Social Science*, 530, pp. 74–96.

Rivera-Salgado, G. (2014) 'Transnational indigenous communities: the intellectual legacy of Michael Kearney', *Latin American Perspectives*, 41, pp. 26–46. https://doi.org/10.1177/0094582X13518753

Rumbaut, R.G. (2008) 'Reaping what you sow: immigration, youth, and reactive ethnicity', *Applied Developmental Science*, 12, pp. 108–111. https://doi.org/10.1080/10888690801997341

Said, E.W. (1979) *Orientalism*. New York: Vintage Books.

Shams, T. (2020) *Here, There, and Elsewhere: The Making of Immigrant Identities in a Globalized World*. Palo Alto, CA: Stanford University Press.

Simon, B. and Klandermans, B. (2001) 'Politicized collective identity: asocial psychological analysis', *American Psychologist*, 56, pp. 319–331. https://doi.org/10.1037/0003-066X.56.4.319

Taylor, V. and Whittier, N.E. (1992) 'Collective identity in social movement communities: Lesbian feminist mobilization', in Morris, A.D. and Mueller, C.M. (eds) *Frontiers in Social Movement Theory*. New Haven, CT: Yale University Press, pp. 104–129.

Tehranian, J. (2008) *Whitewashed: America's Invisible Middle Eastern Minority*. New York: New York University Press.

Turner, S. and Berckmoes, L. (2020) 'Reticent digital diasporas in times of crisis: the shifting emotion work of the Burundian diaspora', *African Diaspora*, 12, pp. 38–63. https://doi.org/10.1163/18725465-01201001

Wayland, S. (2004) 'Ethnonationalist networks and transnational opportunities: The Sri Lankan Tamil diaspora', *Review of International Studies*, 30, pp. 405–426.

Worth, R.F. and Fathi, N. (2009) 'Both sides claim victory in presidential election in Iran', *The New York Times*. Available at: www.nytimes.com/2009/06/13/world/middleeast/13iran.html (accessed 14 October 2019).

Yazdiha, H. (2010) 'Conceptualizing hybridity: deconstructing boundaries through the hybrid', *Formations: The Graduate Center Journal of Social Research*, 1, pp. 31–38.

Yuval-Davis, N. (2007) 'Intersectionality, citizenship and contemporary politics of belonging', *Critical Review of International Social and Political Philosophy*, 10, pp. 561–574. https://doi.org/10.1080/13698230701660220

Zhou, M. (1997) 'Segmented assimilation: issues, controversies, and recent research on the new second generation', *International Migration Review*, 31, pp. 975–1008.

6
THE LIMITS OF DIASPORA
Double vulnerabilities among Eritreans in Saudi Arabia

Nicole Hirt and Abdulkader Saleh Mohammad

Introduction

This chapter explores the ways diaspora Eritreans are simultaneously subjected to the coercive activities of their home government and limitations on their agency by the immigration policies of the Arab Gulf states, based on a case study of Eritreans in Saudi Arabia. State policies in both home and host countries intertwine to define the diasporic experiences of Eritreans in the Gulf Cooperation Council (GCC) and limit political expression. We examine how the restrictive labour and residence laws of the GCC states contribute to the dependency of Eritrean nationals on the benevolence of their own government or have forced them to seek protection in third countries after being deported from Saudi Arabia. The double bind that Eritreans in the GCC experience defines their lack of belonging to both their homeland and the host society, which constitutes their diasporic experiences as simultaneous exclusion and struggle for survival. Our work is informed by empirical data collected by the second author, who has been in permanent contact with diaspora Eritreans living in several Arab countries, including Saudi Arabia, over decades. These data are complemented by 20 narrative interviews conducted between 2016 and 2020 with Eritreans who are currently living, or have stayed for extended periods, in the Gulf region. Additional information was obtained from numerous personal conversations in Eritrea's capital Asmara with Eritreans with work experience in Saudi Arabia. Our informants have different educational backgrounds (from university degrees to persons without formal qualifications) and more than half of the sample is female.

Eritrea has been under the rule of its unelected President Isaias Afewerki, head of the People's Front for Democracy and Justice (PFDJ), since de facto independence from Ethiopia in 1991. Due to continuous armed conflicts and political oppression, Eritrea has turned into a diasporic country with at least half of its population living abroad.[1] Flight and outmigration started during the mid-1950s and intensified during the time of the country's struggle for independence from Ethiopia (1961–1991). Emigration decreased in the early years of independence, but a mass exodus began when the government introduced an open-ended national service in 2002, shortly after a devastating border war between Eritrea and Ethiopia from 1998 to 2000. As a result of the mandatory national service, all Eritreans of productive age must serve as recruits in military or civil functions for a meagre wage, which has been described as a systematic form of forced labour (COIE, 2016). People in the service are prevented from making a living by earning an income and supporting their extended families (Kibreab, 2017). This has caused an ongoing mass exodus from the country. Today there is an established diaspora, which was initially constituted by the former refugees of the independence struggle. During the past two decades, they have been joined by hundreds of thousands of refugees from the current regime, who have varying legal statuses and orientations towards the homeland. Members of the diaspora live dispersed across the globe with a strong homeland orientation and a distinctive Eritrean identity (for a definition of the term diaspora, see IOM, 2020). For Eritreans in the GCC, their diasporic experiences are defined by a tenuous relationship with the homeland government and the institutions on which they are dependent and by whom they are exploited, as this chapter demonstrates.

It is a little-known fact that over one million diaspora Eritreans reside and work in Arab countries, due to the academic focus on Eritrean communities in democratic environments (Koser, 2003; Redeker Hepner, 2008; Tecle, 2012). Research on Eritreans in the GCC is limited and we know very little about their views regarding the homeland regime and its demands. Currently, labour migration from Asia to the GCC countries increasingly attracts well-deserved international media attention. However, few observers have described the plight of Ethiopian, Eritrean and other East African migrants, most of whom work in low-paid jobs as domestic workers in private homes, cattle herders at isolated farms, and unskilled labourers at remote construction sites (Thiollet, 2007; Pessoa, Harkness and Gardner, 2014).

This chapter focuses on the largest member state of the GCC, Saudi Arabia. Saudi Arabia's labour market has attracted Eritreans for decades, and more than one hundred thousand Eritrean nationals live in the Saudi Kingdom today (Thiollet, 2007, p. 8). All Eritreans who left Eritrea since independence are usually considered refugees. Leaving Eritrea is only allowed after obtaining an exit visa, which is hardly ever granted, particularly for those in the national service age (18–60 for men, and 18–27 for women). Leaving the country illegally is considered treason, and so temporary migration is not an option for Eritreans. Eritreans in Sudan and countries in the Global North thus enjoy refugee status because they need protection from their home country's autocratic government. Countries of the GCC are not party to the Geneva Convention on Refugees and therefore do not allow permanent settlement for groups who would otherwise be granted protection status. As such, Eritreans in the Gulf states have no chance of acquiring political asylum or naturalisation and are considered labour migrants who are dependent on temporary work visas. The inability to secure permanent settlement outside Eritrea for those residing in the GCC leads to their dependence on the very state institutions that they escaped from by migrating. The State of Eritrea maintains diplomatic missions in all countries with a sizeable diaspora population, including the Gulf states. Consulates, embassies and cultural associations (*mahbere-koms*) serve as tools to control Eritreans abroad (Koser, 2003; Redeker Hepner, 2008; Hirt and Mohammad, 2018a; Tsourapas, 2020). The lack of political and social rights in the GCC countries and the lack of legal protection make it easier to have a firm grip on their lives than in countries where they can settle permanently.

Instead of prosecuting Eritrean migrants in the GCC as traitors who deserted the national service, the regime cultivates their dependence on state institutions to maintain the docility and political support of the diaspora. The Eritrean regime levies a 2 per cent diaspora tax and relies on Eritreans abroad to support their relatives at home. Paying the diaspora tax enables Eritreans abroad to enjoy a number of government services, such as obtaining birth and marriage certificates, among which the extension of passport services is of primary importance to those living in the GCC. The levy is highly controversial among diaspora Eritreans, who are split between supporters and opponents of President Isaias' rule (Hirt 2015; Hirt and Mohammad

2018), but the government employs different strategies to secure financial flows from all diaspora communities, irrespective of their political stance. Our analysis shows that the diaspora contributes decisively to the stability of the Eritrean regime, which employs different strategies, such as coercion, intimidation and manipulation of patriotic feelings to make diaspora Eritreans pay either voluntarily or under duress (see Gerschewski, 2013). Consequently, these very same mechanisms that contribute to the stability of the regime also shape diasporic experiences in the form of feelings of persecution and alienation connected to the homeland government. At the same time, the diaspora community takes form through forging ties with other co-nationals for economic survival, political mobilisation, or attempts to join the diaspora in locations outside the GCC.

The chapter proceeds as follows: First, we illustrate the origins of the Eritrean diaspora communities in Saudi Arabia. We then highlight the reasons for the current mass exodus from the country. This is followed by an analysis of the impact of the GCC states' restrictive labour laws and the transnational control exercised by the Eritrean government on Eritrean diaspora communities. In the conclusion, we highlight that repressive political environments in host countries favour transnational control and restrict the possibility of political engagement.

Dynamics of mass exodus over history

Eritrea was an Italian colony from 1890 to 1941, when it came under British military administration. In 1952, the UN federated the country with Ethiopia and, in 1962, Emperor Haile Selassie annexed Eritrea. Eritrean Muslims witnessed exclusion and marginalisation under Ethiopian occupation (Miran, 2005), and, in 1961, exiled Muslim politicians and students founded the Eritrean Liberation Front (ELF), which launched an independence struggle that lasted for 30 years. The Eritrean People's Liberation Front (EPLF) established itself as a rival movement to the ELF in the mid-1970s and ousted the ELF from the field in 1982 during a civil war (Connell, 1997). It established transnational mass organisations to spread its ideology and to mobilise refugees to support the struggle financially (Koser, 2003; Redeker Hepner, 2008). The Ethiopian regime's atrocities caused a mass exodus, and Muslim-dominated Eritrean diasporas emerged in Sudan, Egypt, Saudi Arabia and other Arab countries, while Eritrean refugees with Christian backgrounds tried to reach Europe or North America to claim asylum. In 1994, almost 600,000 Eritreans were officially registered as refugees in Sudan with a high number of unrecorded cases (Kibreab, 1996).

There is a sizeable diaspora community of roughly 150,000 Eritreans who settled in Saudi Arabia and the other Gulf states.[2] During the independence struggle, many Arab countries, including Saudi Arabia, sympathised with the ELF. Although they refrained from signing the 1951 Geneva Refugee Convention,

> the Gulf countries and Saudi Arabia, in particular, supported the Eritrean guerrillas from the 1960s to the 1990s on an ideological basis and allowed Eritrean refugees to enter and settle in the oil-rich countries using migration politics as an asylum policy by proxy.
>
> *(Thiollet, 2011, p. 113)*

The ELF was even temporarily granted the status of *kafyl* (personal sponsor) for Eritreans working in Saudi Arabia. Residence permits could be obtained free of charge upon presentation of an ELF letter recognising the applicant as an Eritrean (ibid., pp. 113–114). This generous policy facilitated the establishment of the Eritrean diaspora community. However, the

ELF arranged almost exclusively work contracts for female domestic workers, because young men were supposed to participate in the armed struggle.

After de facto independence in 1991, the EPLF, renamed PFDJ in 1994, took over the government and opened embassies in countries with a significant diaspora population, including most Arab countries. The new government introduced a 2 per cent diaspora tax, and paying the levy became a precondition for government services, such as the renewal of passports and the acquisition of property inside Eritrea. After independence, those Eritreans who lived as refugees in Sudan, many of them ELF supporters, could no longer trust in the support of the UNHCR and were not welcomed as returnees by the EPLF-led Eritrean government. Accordingly, their only option was to migrate to the GCC states.

Political oppression intensified in the years following independence (Mekonnen and Tronvoll, 2014). In 2002, an institutionalised system of forced labour was introduced by the government which reflects systematic societal militarisation (Kibreab, 2009; Hirt and Mohammad, 2013) whereby the country has been turned into a state-controlled command economy, justified by the lingering conflict with Ethiopia. Additionally, internal criticism of the government is crushed by oppression (Mekonnen and Tronvoll, 2014; COIE, 2016), and life under military surveillance prevents people from protesting. As a result, hundreds of thousands of Eritreans have fled the country since 2002, despite shoot-to-kill orders at the borders. Most of them remain in the neighbouring countries; the UNHCR counted about 173,000 registered Eritrean refugees in Ethiopia in 2020, and 140,000 in Sudan. Sudan also hosts approximately one and a half million second- and third-generation diaspora Eritreans. We do not know how many Eritreans have moved to the Arab Peninsula in recent years to join the migrant labour force, but the Eritrean embassy in Sudan has sold thousands of passports to Eritrean refugees to enable them to work in the GCC states (Wikileaks, 2009).

Most female Eritreans who reside in GCC states, including Saudi Arabia, are employed as domestic workers, while their male counterparts often work in the service sector or as truck and taxi drivers. A minority of Eritreans, most of them low-skilled rural migrants who enter Saudi Arabia illegally through Yemen, are forced to work as animal herders in the remote areas of Jazan, Abha and Asir because they lack the financial resources to find a *kafyl*. These migrant workers are subject to overtime work, degrading living conditions and severe limitations on their personal freedom. They often do not receive a regular monetary salary and can be deported at will if their work is no longer needed.[3]

The precarious life of Eritrean workers in the Gulf states

As migrant workers, Eritreans in the GCC are restricted by conditions imposed by their regimes in their homeland and the receiving states. As their residence status depends on a work contract, which is only issued for holders of valid passports, Eritreans are vulnerable vis-à-vis the institutions of their homeland, since Eritrean diplomatic missions can exert pressure on the migrants to comply with the demands of the government as a precondition to the necessary documents being issued (Hirt, 2015; Hirt and Mohammad 2018a; 2018b; Mohammad, 2021). As temporary migrant workers, they are also vulnerable vis-à-vis the institutions of their host societies.

The labour laws of the GCC member states are based on the *kafala* system, which is a government policy to exert total control over the temporary labour migrants. This form of sponsorship implies that every migrant worker needs a sponsor (*kafyl*) to be permitted to stay and work in a GCC country. The *kafyl* may work either as an individual or act as the head of a company or agency (Pessoa, Harkness and Gardner, 2014; Froilan and Naufal, 2016). This system has been persistently criticised by human rights organisations for facilitating conditions amounting to forced labour, at times approaching slave-like work conditions. In early 2021, Saudi Arabia overhauled its *kafala* system allowing workers to change jobs more easily (Al Arabiya, 2021), but the practical effects of these reforms are yet to be seen. Given that our interlocutors have experienced the stricter forms of *kafala* systems for many years, the ways the old restrictions shape their diasporic experiences will likely persist into the future.

Under the old system, workers could not change their employer and the *kafyl* could prevent workers from leaving the country or terminate the worker's employment contract, which left them facing deportation (Murray, 2012). Such was the fate of a number of our interlocutors. Many female Eritrean domestic workers in Jeddah pointed out that their fate was entirely dependent on the goodwill of their employers, who at any time could threaten to terminate their contract. If they failed to comply with their contracts and left their workplace without permission, they were obliged to pay the cost of deportation. This left them in a desperate situation because, while they would be fined by the Saudi authorities for the travel expenses, they owed money to their relatives, who had paid for their ticket and visa-associated fees, as well as debts to the recruitment agency. Pande (2013) observed similar dilemmas in her study on domestic workers in Lebanon.

Despite this dire situation, many Eritreans experience the support of others in the diaspora that provides slim opportunities for pursuing life elsewhere. For example, Sofia,[4] who was deported forcefully from Saudi Arabia to Sudan in 2018 and later managed to move to Egypt, explains the increasingly challenging living conditions in Saudi Arabia and the new regulations regarding residency requirements, which imply additional taxes for all family members. Surviving the hard conditions in Saudi Arabia, and later the ability to move to Egypt, were facilitated by fellow Eritreans:

> I came to Jeddah in the mid-1970s at the age of 18. My mother worked in the cereal market of Asmara and encouraged me to travel to Saudi Arabia on a pilgrimage visa, and she borrowed money to cover my travel expenses. After ten years I married and became the mother of five children. Yet, my husband passed away and I had to become the breadwinner for my children. Fortunately, some Eritrean neighbour families supported me and took care of my children while I worked. Eventually, I sent my elder son to work as a cleaner in a garage, and later he became a taxi driver, which enabled us to survive in Saudi Arabia's deteriorating economic situation. In 2016, the Saudi authorities required from us additional residency fees amounting to 100 Riyal (around 27 USD) per month for each person registered in the family residency permit including underage children. We decided to pay the fee for my taxi driver son only, and I was deported to Port Sudan with my other children. Later we managed to travel further to Cairo and registered ourselves at the UNHCR with the aim to continue our journey.

In 2016, the Saudi authorities increased fees, requiring that migrant workers pay 100 riyals per month for each dependent family member registered on their residency permit, including children. If workers failed to pay this fee, amounting to hundreds of riyals per month, their residency would not be renewed and they would lose their legal right to reside and work in Saudi Arabia. However, they would not be allowed to leave the Kingdom until their debts with additional fines are paid off (Cole, 2020).

Eritreans in the GCC are particularly vulnerable because the Eritrean government does not protect the right of its citizens (Hirt and Mohammad, 2018b). Eritreans who face deportation due to a lack of appropriate papers often ask the local authorities to send them either to Sudan or to Ethiopia, and sometimes to Egypt or even Uganda, because upon their return to Eritrea they risk punishment for national service evasion and subsequent recruitment into the national army. Others want their children to be spared the national service. For the majority that stay in the GCC, their precarious conditions are amplified as a result of the activities of transnational Eritrean state institutions, which we explain in the next section.

Exploiting the diaspora in the GCC

Eritreans who fled from their repressive home regime to the Gulf states are not only subjected to the widespread abuse of migrant workers in the Gulf states but also exploited by their own repressive government. Their temporary status and their reliance on their sponsors for residency and work permits ensure their subordination in their host societies. Additionally, they have limited agency to organise politically and resist the demands made by the Eritrean government due to their insecure status; thus, they are forced to satisfy the demands of their sponsors as well as those of the Eritrean embassies and consulates.

All Eritreans abroad are supposed to pay the 2 per cent diaspora tax, which has been collected by 'using extortion, threats of violence, fraud and other illicit means' according to the UN Security Council (2011, pp. 3–4), and to make additional donations. In the GCC states, the government has even stronger control mechanisms due to the dependence of the Eritrean migrant workers on consular services. The UN Security Council report from 2012 states that in Saudi Arabia, 'Eritreans must visit their Embassy every other year and pay taxes, or they will not legally be able to remain in the Kingdom' (UNSC, 2012, p. 53). The relationship between the government and its diasporic communities is maintained by a network of transnational organisations, including diplomatic missions and community centres that function to control the diaspora. Furthermore, members of the Eritrean diaspora are obliged to remit funds to their relatives at home, who are deprived of income-earning opportunities due to national service requirements. This social obligation increases their docile position vis-à-vis the labour market conditions in the GCC and the dictates of their homeland institutions.

Authoritarian regimes tend to stabilise their rule by applying a mix of strategies to ensure legitimation, repression and co-optation among members of the diaspora. According to Gerschewski (2013, pp. 22–25), these 'three pillars' are achieved through ideological indoctrination (legitimation), oppression and/or violence (repression), and tying important political and social actors to the regime elite (co-optation). The Eritrean regime uses its transnational structures to control diaspora communities. Its cultural organisations operate under the umbrella of the diplomatic missions in Riyadh and Jeddah in Saudi Arabia (and other cities around the GCC). These community centres function as hubs of political pro-government mobilisation, facilitating social control and collecting donations from Eritrean nationals on the occasion of seminars, cultural events and festivals related to Independence Day, the Beginning of the Armed Struggle, Martyrs Day and other national holidays (Koser, 2003; Redeker Hepner, 2008; Hirt, 2015). This means that in the few locations where social get-togethers for Eritrean diaspora communities in the GCC can take place, the long arm of the Eritrean regime is always present.

The effects of legitimation are observed among regime supporters in the diaspora. A substantial part of the diaspora supports the regime, despite its notorious human rights violations and takes pride in paying their dues to the government (Hirt, 2015). In the GCC, legitimation may be seen as a weak or unnecessary strategy given the dependence of Eritreans on the goodwill of their homeland's institutions to maintain their residency and ability to earn income.

As such, for Eritreans in the Gulf states, the regime relies on suppression and co-optation in extracting economic and political support, which we demonstrate below.

Despite their precarious position and dependence on the institutions of the homeland and the host society for their survival, a growing number of Eritreans abroad oppose the regime because of its failed economic policies, its strategy of societal militarisation and its increasing political repression. Regime opponents belong either to established opposition groups, among them supporters of the former ELF and EPLF dissidents, or to civil society groups that emerged in the wake of the Arab uprisings and lobby for human rights, protection of refugees and regime change in Eritrea (Mohammad and Tronvoll, 2015). None of these political and civic opposition groups can be openly active in the repressive environments of the GCC countries, which do not permit any form of political organisation among expatriate communities.[5] Despite the restricted transnational political space, most opposition parties have representatives in the GCC states, who meet periodically at private salons under the pretext of social and cultural entertainment, which also includes fundraising events. These limited spaces are also monitored by the diplomatic missions, despite their clandestine nature.

In addition to the presence of opposition parties, there are private meetings of Eritrean anti-regime activists that may be less known, but also continue to take place within the purview of the Eritrean state institutions. For example, Mohammed, who studied computer science in India and has been working as a computer technician in Jeddah since 1988, states that he has attended numerous meetings of diverse political opposition organisations. Mohammed's activism favours one organisation in particular, the Lowlanders League (LL), which is a political movement that strives for the rights of the Eritrean lowland population, most of whom are Muslims. Mohammed understands his affiliation to the LL is known to the Eritrean security organs, and as a result, he participates in various activities to assert his loyalty to the Eritrean state to ensure his ability to renew his passport among other services that he depends on. He explains:

> I've been trying to keep in touch with PFDJ representatives and I have never missed the cultural meetings organised by the local *mahbere-kom*. I even acted as a local collector of the 2 per cent diaspora tax in the Jeddah neighbourhood where I live.

Mohammed's example shows that his political opposition also constitutes an added pressure and increased financial burden; he needs to keep good personal relations with the Eritrean government's agents to compensate for his engagement with the opposition. Like any Eritrean in the GCC, he must pay the tax and make regular donations to secure his residence permit, which depends on his Eritrean passport. In addition, the opposition group that has his sympathy demands financial contributions for NGOs that provide social services in Sudanese refugee settlements.

Both the embassy in Riyadh and the consulate in Jeddah host community centres (so-called *mahbere-koms*) that serve as meeting points for Eritreans and offer some entertainment, such as bingo and card games. However, these community centres are also used for political seminars, in which Eritrean nationals are updated on the conditions in the homeland from the state's perspective (these are called 'objective' by the state institutions organising them). During these events, Eritrean migrants are expected to donate to various reconstruction and social welfare programmes at home (see, for example, Shabait, 2015). Those who fail to show up regularly at their local *mahbere-kom* raise the suspicion of the authorities. For example, Osman, an informant from Jeddah who returned to Eritrea's capital Asmara to visit his family, was warned by the local community officials in his neighbourhood. It had come to their knowledge that he had failed to attend the *mahbere-kom* in Jeddah regularly, and they advised him to attend the activities more frequently to avoid repercussions for his family in Asmara.

The National Union of Eritrean Women (NUEW), designed as a control organ, is also active in Saudi Arabia and operates in a fashion similar to the *mahbere-koms*. Hayat, an Eritrean woman married to an Eritrean migrant worker who raised her children in Jeddah before she moved to Germany in 2015, explained the pressure she felt from both Eritrean and Saudi authorities:

> Members of NUEW told me to join them and to attend their meetings, but I declined with the excuse of having small children to watch. In addition, as a woman in Saudi Arabia you cannot take a bus, you are obliged to travel by taxi, which is very expensive. You need to show your residence papers wherever you go.

For Eritreans in the GCC with young children like Hayat, their loyalty to the government is a condition for their ability to access middle and secondary education in schools that are run by the Eritrean government. The Saudi government does not grant education beyond the primary level to the children of migrant workers, and accordingly, the migrant communities must establish their own schools. The control of these schools by the Eritrean government makes them part of the mechanisms whereby suppression and co-optation are exerted on members of the diaspora. For Hayat, these limited prospects she saw for her own and her children's future in Saudi Arabia prompted her to risk taking a dangerous journey by boat to Europe for the chance to start a new life in Germany.

Conclusion

This chapter portrays the double bind of a group of diaspora Eritreans whose living conditions have rarely been investigated by scholars of diaspora studies. Based on Gerschewski's assumption that authoritarian regime stability rests on three pillars, we argue that the Eritrean government can extract considerable funds from its citizens abroad by applying mechanisms based on legitimation, repression and co-optation. Members of the Eritrean diaspora communities in Saudi Arabia and the GCC are exploited more generally by their employers and find themselves in disadvantaged positions in the domestic labour markets. At the same time, their homeland government relies on the diaspora's moral obligation to support their relatives at home and builds on it to extract loyalty and economic and political support for the regime. In Eritrea, the government does not provide any social welfare services, and Eritreans of a productive age are trapped in the national service, unable to sustain their families. As a result, those in the diaspora are deliberately held responsible to send substantial private remittances to guarantee the survival of their extended families. Hence, Eritreans residing in the GCC are under multiple pressures not only from the side of the repressive *kafala* system but also from their own government and their relatives at home, who expect financial support from them in order to survive.

Eritrean migrants in the GCC provide economic support to their oppressive state in the form of the diaspora tax. Additionally, by supporting their family members in Eritrea, they ease the pressure on the state to deliver social welfare services or even allow the large segment of the population of productive age to seek employment opportunities. As a result, the oppression of the diaspora stabilises the regime and is of significant importance for regime survival. To control its emigrant population, the Eritrean regime has developed surveillance systems disguised under a number of mechanisms. Some citizens are co-opted by social services, such as education, through expatriate schools. Most are forced to pay the diaspora tax that is imposed by the regime to keep their legal residence status, which depends on a valid passport issued by the homeland authorities. Cultural community centres also work to maintain frequent acts of loyalty and keep members of the diaspora under surveillance and control. When these mechanisms do not work as they should, threats to family members in Eritrea are implemented. As a result, the connection between Eritrean migrant workers in the GCC and their homeland regime is one of dependency and oppression, which emphatically shapes their belonging to the diaspora as a community that shares experiences of marginalisation and exploitation.

Eritreans in the Gulf states also suffer from the non-democratic environments of their respective host countries, whose authoritarian governments do not permit any open political activity, whether regarding labour rights or opposition to the home government. The recent economic deterioration in Saudi Arabia has forced Eritrean families to live separately because workers are forced to send their families to Sudan, Ethiopia, Egypt or Turkey to avoid paying the ever-increasing residency fees, and because living expenses in these countries are lower compared to Saudi Arabia.

Few Eritreans who are forced to live under such circumstances will find the passion and energy to engage in clandestine political movements to improve the situation in their homeland. Those who are motivated to participate in organisations that oppose the regime find themselves increasing their financial burdens and forced to perform acts of loyalty to the regime to protect their status as migrant workers. They live their lives sandwiched between the demands of an autocratic home regime and an authoritarian host, with no possibility of having their voices heard.

Notes

1 The number of Eritreans at home and in exile can only be estimated. According to the government, Eritrea's population stood at 3.5 million in 2010 according to the last Population and Health Survey (State of Eritrea, 2014, p. 15). During the independence struggle, around one million Eritreans left their country (World Bank, 1991, p. ii) and most have since stayed abroad and started families. According to the European Asylum Support Office (2015, p. 1), almost 90,000 Eritreans applied for asylum in Europe from 2014 to 2015 alone. Some 175,000 Eritreans live as refugees in Ethiopia, and Sudan hosts more than 100,000 registered Eritrean refugees. The United States, Canada, Australia and many Arab states host large Eritrean diaspora communities.
2 Saudi authorities conceal the nationality breakdown of the foreign workforce in their country (De Bel-Air, 2014, p. 5). Thiollet (2007, p. 8) states that the number of Eritreans in Saudi Arabia was more than 100,000 according to the Eritrean Embassy, but was most likely higher.
3 Information derived from decade-long observations by Abdulkader Saleh Mohammad, who interviewed large numbers of relatives and acquaintances who have been working in various regions of Saudi-Arabia, including the Jazan area. See also International Labor Organization (2013).
4 All the names in this chapter have been changed to protect the identities of our informants.
5 Freedom House (2020) ranks Qatar and Saudi Arabia as 'not free'. Available at: https://freedomhouse.org/sites/default/files/2020-02/FIW_2020_REPORT_BOOKLET_Final.pdf.

References

Al Arabiya (2021) 'All the changes to Saudi Arabia's Kafala system'. Available at: https://english.alarabiya.net/News/gulf/2021/03/14/All-the-changes-to-Saudi-Arabia-s-kafala-sponsorship-system (accessed 17 April 2021).
Cole, G. (2020) 'Forced departures from Saudi Arabia: new displacement dynamics and challenges of protection', blog. Research and Evidence Facility, EU Emergency Trust Fund for Africa. Available at https://blogs.soas.ac.uk/ref-hornresearch/2020/04/16/forced-departures-saudi-arabia/ (accessed 15 May 2020).

COIE (UN Commission of Inquiry on Human Rights in Eritrea) (2016) 'Report on human rights in Eritrea'. A/HRC/32/47. Available at: https://documents-dds-ny.un.org/doc/UNDOC/GEN/G16/093/42/PDF/G1609342.pdf?OpenElement (accessed 15 May 2021).
Connell, D. (1997) *Against All Odds. A Chronicle of the Eritrean Revolution*. Lawrenceville, Asmara: Red Sea Press.
De Be-Air, F. (2014) 'Demography, migration and labour market in Saudi Arabia',GLMM, Explanatory note, 1/2014, Migration Policy Centre. Available a: https://cadmus.eui.eu/bitstream/handle/1814/32151/GLMM%20ExpNote_01-2014.pdf?sequence=1&isAllowed=y (accessed 1 April 2022).
European Asylum Support Office (2015) ,'Press Release: Eritrea in Focus', PR 11/2015, Available at: www.easo.europa.eu/sites/default/files/public/Press-release-Eritrea.pdf (accessed 22 May 2021).
Freedom House (2020) 'Freedom in the World, 2020'. Available at: https://freedomhouse.org/sites/default/files/2020-02/FIW_2020_REPORT_BOOKLET_Final.pdf/ (accessed 22 May 2021).
Froilan, M.T. and Naufal, G. (2016) 'Asymmetric information under the Kafala Sponsorship System: impacts on foreign domestic workers' income and employment status in the GCC countries', *International Migration*,, 54(5), pp. 77–90.
Gerschewski, J. (2013) 'The three pillars of stability: legitimacy, repression, and co-optation in autocratic regimes', *Democratization* 20(1), pp. 13–38.
Hirt, N. (2015) 'The Eritrean diaspora and its impact on regime stability: responses to UN Sanctions', *African Affairs*, 114(454), pp. 115–135.
Hirt, N. and Mohammad, A.S. (2013) '"Dreams don't come true in Eritrea": anomie and family disintegration due to the structural militarisation of society', *Journal of Modern African Studies*, 51(1), pp. 139–168.
Hirt, N. and Mohammad, A.S. (2018a) 'By way of patriotism, coercion or instrumentalization: How the Eritrean regime makes use of the diaspora to stabilise its rule', *Globalizations*, 15(2), pp. 232–247.
Hirt N. and Mohammad A.S. (2018b) 'The lack of political space of the Eritrean diaspora in the Arab Gulf and Sudan: torn between and autocratic home and authoritarian hosts', *Mashriq & Mahjar Journal of Middle East and North African Migration Studies, NC State University*, 5(1), pp. 101–126.
International Labor Organization (2013) 'Tricked and trapped: human trafficking in the Middle East'. Available at: www.ilo.org/beirut/publications/WCMS_211214/lang--en/index.htm (accessed 15 June 2020).
International Organisation for Migration (2020) 'Migration data portal, diasporas'. Available at: https://migrationdataportal.org/themes/diasporas#definition (accessed 18 December 2020).
Kibreab, G. (1996) *Ready and Willing… But Still Waiting. Eritrean Refugees in Sudan and the Dilemma of Return*. Uppsala: Life and Peace Institute.
Kibreab, G. (2009) 'Forced labour in Eritrea', *Journal of Modern African Studies*, 47(1), pp. 41-72.
Kibreab, G. (2017) *The Eritrean National Service: Servitude for the "Common Good" and the Youth Exodus*. Cambridge: Cambridge University Press.
Koser, K. (2003) 'Mobilizing new African diasporas: an Eritrean case study', in Koser, K. (ed.) *New African Diasporas*. London, Routledge, pp. 111–123.
Mekonnen, D.R. and Tronvoll, K. (2014) *The African Garrison State: Human Rights and Development in Eritrea*. Woodbridge: James Currey.
Miran, J. (2005) 'A historical overview of Islam in Eritrea', *Die Welt des Islams*, 45(2), pp. 177–215.
Mohammad, A.S. (2021) 'The resurgence of religious and ethnic identities among Eritrean refugees: a response to the government's nationalist ideology', *Africa Spectrum*, 41(2), pp. 249–271.
Mohammad, A.S. and Tronvoll K. (2015) *Eritrean Opposition Parties and Civic Organisations*. Oslo: NOREF Expert Analysis.Murray, H.E. (2012) 'Hope for reform springs eternal: how the sponsorship system, domestic laws and traditional customs fail to protect migrant domestic workers in GCC countries', *Cornell International Law Journal*, 45, pp. 461–485.
Pande, A. (2013) '"The paper you have in your hand is my freedom". Migrant domestic work and the sponsorship (Kafala) system in Lebanon', *International Migration Review*, 47(2), pp. 414–441.
Pessoa, S, Harkness, L., and Gardner, A. (2014) 'Ethiopian labor migrants and the "free visa" system in Qatar', *Human Organization*, 73, pp. 205–213.
Redeker Hepner, T. (2008) 'Transnational governance and the centralization of state power in Eritrea and exile', *Ethnic and Racial Studies*, 31(3), pp. 476–502.
Shabait (2015) 'Eritrean nationals in Jeddah commemorate Martyrs Day'. Available at: https://shabait.com/2015/06/19/eritrean-nationals-in-jeddah-commemorate-martyrs-day/ (accessed 17 May 2020).

State of Eritrea (2014) 'Health Development Millennium Goals Report'. Available at: www.er.undp.org/content/eritrea/en/home/library/mdg/eritrea-health-mdgs-report-2014.html (accessed 16 June 2020).

Tecle, S. (2012) 'The paradoxes of state-led transnationalism: Capturing continuity, change and rupture in the Eritrean transnational field'. MA thesis. York University, Toronto.

Thiollet, H. (2007) 'Refugees and migrants from Eritrea to the Arab world: the cases of Sudan, Yemen and Saudi Arabia 1991–2007', Forced Migration & Refugee Studies Program. The American University in Cairo, Cairo, 23–25 October.

Thiollet, H. (2011) 'Migration as diplomacy: labor migrants, refugees, and Arab regional politics in the oil-rich countries', *International Labor and Working Class History*, 79, pp. 103–121.

Tsourapas, G. (2020) 'Global autocracies. Strategies of transnational repression, legitimation, and co-optation in world politics', *International Studies Review*, 23(3), pp. 616–644.

UNSC (United Nations Security Council) (2011) 'Resolution 2023 (2011)', S/RES/2023, New York, 5 December 2011, pp. 3–4.

UNSC (United Nations Security Council) (2012) 'Letter dated 11 July 2012 from the Chair of the Security Council Committee pursuant to resolutions 751 (1992) and 1907 (2009) concerning Somalia and Eritrea addressed to the President of the Security Council', UN Report S/2012/545.

Wikileaks (2009) 'Public Library of US Diplomacy', cable dated 5 May 2009. Available at: www.wikileaks.org/plusd/cables/09ASMARA146a.html (accessed 18 May 2020).

World Bank (1991) 'Eritrea: options and strategies for growth', World Bank Report No. 12930-ER: Washington, DC: World Bank.

PART II
Making and remaking homes

7
THE LIFECYCLE OF AMAZIGH DIASPORA ACTIVISM IN EUROPE

From institutional pioneers to the new ethnicities of the postmodern age

Ángela Suárez-Collado

The Amazigh people is an indigenous people of North Africa distributed unequally across the region. Although there are no official statistics, it is estimated that *Imazighen* make up between 40 and 60 per cent of the population in Morocco, 20–30 per cent in Algeria, up to 10 per cent in Libya, 1 per cent in Tunisia, and in Egypt are thought to number around 20,000 people in the Siwa Oasis. In total, approximately 20 million people live in *Tamazgha*, the name used by Amazigh activists to describe the territory of the Imazighen, which extends from the Siwa Oasis in Egypt to the Atlantic Ocean, encompassing a great part of the Sahel and the Canary Islands. Despite its demographic significance or perhaps because of it, Amazigh culture and identity have been systematically undermined and suppressed against the backdrop of Arabisation and Islamisation in the postcolonial period in Northern Africa. As a result, Amazigh cultural and political activism emerged in response in the Maghreb region.

Outside North Africa, the Amazigh diaspora is concentrated mainly in France, the Netherlands, Germany, Belgium, Spain, Italy and Scandinavia and is estimated to stand at around 2.5 million people,[1] but European Amazigh Associations themselves put the number at 3.5 million people.[2] Amazigh people have tended to be counted as 'Moroccan' or 'Algerian' (national), or 'Muslims' (religious), and even as 'Arab' in some contexts. This fluctuation in the numbers reflects problems with the classification and categorisation of groups that contest and fall outside the neat categories of statehood for institutions in Europe's receiving countries tasked with knowing and managing immigrant populations. The statistical invisibility of the Amazigh in Europe has been one of the driving forces behind many of the campaigns of Amazigh activists to promote the well-being and recognition of the community in their host countries while also extending support to the homeland, and indeed to other members of the diaspora in other countries. These modes of diaspora activism do not necessarily operate separately; indeed, as I shall go on to demonstrate, they often overlap and reinforce each other (Østergaard-Nielsen, 2003; Quinsaat, 2013).

Amazigh activism in Europe has experienced different shifts and phases, thus one of the aims of this chapter is to consider the trajectories and developments in Amazigh diaspora organisation in Europe over the last 50 years and the impact that these have had on the recognition of its cause. As such, I focus on Moroccan Amazigh communities in Spain and the Netherlands, two countries where Amazigh activism has been prominent and where associations have been composed of people who originate from the Rif region of Northern Morocco. It is necessary to point out that Spain and the Netherlands differ in their colonial connections with Morocco, have had dissimilar migratory histories, and their policies towards the immigrant population have evolved differently over time. Nonetheless, there is much to be learned from comparing and contrasting Amazigh activism and life in these settings.

In this chapter, I apply social movement theories to explain the dynamics of diaspora activism in Spain and the Netherlands. To do so, I look at the specific historical contexts and changes in the structure of opportunities for diaspora activism in host countries and home countries, paying particular attention to the institutional sphere. Furthermore, I center on the changes within the diaspora community organisations themselves from a social, generational and ideological standpoint, and, finally, I examine the evolution of activists' careers, with a focus on the impact of individual leadership and their biographical availability to the institutions they have helped to form in the diaspora. This study focuses mostly on formal organisations, which often play an important role in providing a framework for providing services, spaces for the expression of identities, and arenas for the formulation of social and political grievances. I draw on field research in Spain and the Netherlands from 2013 to 2017 when I conducted interviews with first-, second- and third-generation Amazigh activists as well as state representatives. Before turning to these insights, I first outline how the conceptualisation of 'diaspora' in the case of the Amazigh communities in Europe has been understood and provide a general overview of the migratory history of Imazighen.

The Amazigh diaspora in Europe

I use the term diaspora to refer to groups of people who share a sense of origin, who are scattered between two or more destinations and who establish multiple connections and exchanges between the homeland, the host country and the larger diaspora community (Van Hear, Pieke and Vertovec, 2004). The interactions between the three spheres (the homeland, the host society and the diaspora) play an important role in the configuration of diasporas and their political activism. In this regard, the orientation towards a homeland, real or imagined, represents a source of values, identities and loyalties. Moreover, host societies influence the specific concerns, processes of claim-making and the different strategies adopted by diaspora activists, based on the participatory channels available in each country (Ireland, 1994; Kastoryano, 1996; Guiraudon, 2004). Thus, the models of political inclusion in each state constitute the dominant frame of reference for immigrant social movements (Guiraudon, 2004), shaping political activity and organisational structures. The simultaneous embeddedness of migrants in more than one society gives rise to multi-layered and multi-sited arenas, including not only the home and host countries, but other sites around the world that connect migrants to their co-nationals and coreligionists (Levitt and Jaworsky, 2007, p. 131), and at times provide opportunities for articulating non-traditional forms of belonging and identification (Abdelhady, 2011).

Amazigh emigration developed in various waves over the twentieth century. In the case of Morocco, migratory movements began to take shape in the 1960s when guest worker agreements between Morocco and different European countries facilitated departure from three particular Amazigh areas: the eastern part of the Rif, the southwestern Sous region, and the southeastern oases of the High Atlas (de Haas, 2007). Even though this out-migration was initially conceived as temporary, it became more permanent in the 1970s. By then, Amazigh communities in North Africa had been subject to cultural assimilation and marginalisation within the newly independent Arab states. In contrast, those who were living abroad found a different context in which they enjoyed greater political freedoms and a new global discourse on minority language, cultural rights and indigeneity (Bengio and Maddy-Weitzman, 2013).

Besides labour and family reunification migration in the 1980s, many Moroccan Amazigh activists sought refuge in Europe as a result of their politics. These activists promoted the establishment of Amazigh organisations in the early 1990s, together with successive groups of university students (Van Heelsum, 2003; Suárez-Collado, 2018). The following decades brought about further diversification within the migrant communities as Amazigh unskilled workers migrated to southern Europe due to the high demand for lower-wage labour (de Haas, 2007). Consequently, these different migration waves diversified the communities in the Netherlands and Spain over time, which impacted their types of activism.

Amazigh activism in Spain: regional strongholds and the waxing and waning of diasporic organisation

Amazigh diaspora activism in Spain dates back to the 1970s and has been influenced by the political opportunity structure offered by Spain and the role of student elites within the community itself. The nascent Amazigh movement in Spain took hold in the last throes of Francoism (1939–1975) and the first years of democratic transition (1975–1978), which promoted the emergence of a new cultural and political atmosphere and the strengthening of different social movements, including regionalist and nationalist activism. Amazigh university students in Spain participated in this transformative momentum by trying to foster a similar environment back in their home region through the creation of an association called *Intilaka Atakafia* in 1978. Kais, currently a university professor in Morocco and at that time an undergraduate student in Madrid, recalls:

> It was 1977 and we were sitting in the Café Manila at Gran Vía Street. In Spain, at that time, there was a real effervescence: avant-garde theatre, protest music, Victor Jara ... and we wondered, why not do that there? That summer, when we returned to the Rif to spend our vacations, we got together, prepared the project [the Amazigh Association] and launched it.

While these pioneers joined Madrid's new political and cultural life, their actions were focused on furthering the Amazigh question in the homeland. In fact, *Intilaka Atakafia* came to become a model for the Moroccan Amazigh movement. In this regard, the role of diasporic activists was extremely influential in forging Amazigh identity more broadly by contributing to the reconstruction of the Amazigh language, through the recovery and collection of oral tradition and the promotion of literary activity, as well as the elaboration of the ideological corpus of Amazigh activism in the Rif. The initiatives taken up by the so-called Madrid Working Group included the elaboration of a repertoire of studies on Amazigh writing, the adoption of an alphabet and the creation of grammar rules and transcription, which constituted one of the first attempts to standardise the language, used by the association in the Rif. However, this involvement in Amazigh diaspora activism was limited to a small university elite, so once those Amazigh students returned to their home region upon completion of their degrees, activities for promoting Amazigh culture in Madrid disappeared. Yakhlef, who arrived in Madrid a decade later to pursue a PhD in Amazigh linguistics, explains:

> Despite the fact that there were Riffians in Spain since the 1960s, nobody thought of creating an Amazigh association [in Spain] until the 1990s. The people who came to Spain had no intention of undertaking social, cultural or political actions on the issue. There were individual illusions [for promoting Amazigh activism] within the student community, but they were only a few.

The lack of engagement of the majority of the Amazigh diaspora in activism associated with culture and identity is not uncommon among immigrant groups during the early stages of their settlement in a new context (Penninx and Schrover, 2001). An initial settling-down period is required before diasporic modes of organisation can take place at the domestic and international levels. As Bruneau (1995) suggests, the so-called proletarian diasporas, those built on the labour from which the host country's economy benefits, need to acquire the necessary means to establish their religious, cultural or socio-political networks. In this vein, the initial phases of Amazigh immigration and community activism focused on improving their legal position and living conditions as immigrants rather than Amazigh identity per se.

From the beginning of the 1990s, the Amazigh movement took hold in Algeria as well as in Morocco as a consequence of a marginal political openness. Both states became more tolerant towards the creation of Amazigh organisations, which facilitated the flourishing of associations. In the case of Morocco, this openness had included measures aimed at normalising the situation of the Amazigh language in the country's public life. Additionally, transnational advocacy that culminated in the Amazigh World Congress (AWC), whose first general assembly was held in Tafira in Spain in 1997, gave the movement a global outlook and platform (Suárez-Collado, 2013). This dynamism impacted the Amazigh diaspora in Spain, and it motivated its political activism to no longer focus solely on the homeland.

The drafting process of the Statute of the Autonomous City of Melilla (1995), a Spanish enclave located on the Northern African coast, highlighted the existence of an Amazigh population in Spain and is one of the defining moments for Amazigh activism. In the years leading to its approval, the inclusion of Tamazight as the co-official and mother language of the Muslims of Melilla was controversial, sparking local debate and contestation as various political and social constituencies aired their differing perspectives on the matter. The arguments in favour drew on studies and reports that identified school failure among the Muslim population and linked such failure to the lack of institutional attention to the mother language. The statute was approved in March 1995 and, although ultimately it only recognised Melilla's 'cultural and linguistic plurality', it served to consolidate an advocacy network for the Amazigh cause at local and national levels (ibid.). Particularly noteworthy were the ties that were built at this time with political parties, such as the Socialist Party, which promoted the inclusion of the Amazigh language in the inventory of European languages issued by the European Parliament's Committee on Culture in 1996, as well as certain nationalist parties, like the Basque Nationalist Party (PNV), Convergència i Unió (CiU) and the Republican Left of Catalonia (ERC), which became major political and economic supporters of Amazigh activism at both the local and international levels (ibid.).

The relations with these political parties and the expansion of Amazigh activism in Spain were promoted by a new generation of diaspora members who were already engaged with the Amazigh cause. These new immigrants brought with them their previous knowledge and skills in organising and mobilising (ibid.), which led to the flourishing of organisations such as the Collective of Documentation and Amazigh Studies (1992) in Granada, the Amazigh Cultural Association in Bilbao (1994) and the Tamazight Cultural Association in Granada (1995). Personal networks were also an important means of recruitment and the associations became spaces of sustained activism around ideas of homeland, community and identity. Thus, associations became centres of ritual expression and they were responsible for organising both the celebrations of important events for the Amazigh population, such as the *Yennayer* festival (Amazigh New Year) and *Tafsut n'Imazighen* (The Amazigh Spring) as well as demonstrations, meetings, debates and conferences on Amazigh historical events and heroes.

The strengthening of Amazigh activism continued into the 2000s and extended to different parts of Spain using different organisational structures, which included coordinating platforms like Agraw Amazigh Assembly of Catalonia, women's associations, such as Tamettur and Timazighin, and mixed organisations like the Association of Friendship between Imazighen and Catalans in Badalona, Catalonia. This expansion was fostered by new generations of activists who continued to arrive in Spain and helped to reinforce transnational relations, including co-development projects and regular meetings between Amazigh activists in the Rif and in Spain.

In this period of expansion, Amazigh activism in Spain was increasingly influenced by local political developments. Amazigh organisations in Catalonia and the Basque Country developed closer relationships with local authorities and institutions, at times, receiving public political support for their cause (ibid.). In Catalonia, Amazigh activism achieved unprecedented recognition in the form of Resolution 1197/VI of the Parliament of Catalonia on 6 March 2002, which was the first official expression of support made by a foreign parliament for Amazigh cultural and linguistic demands in and outside North Africa.[3] Later, when the Republican Left of Catalonia Party (ERC) was part of the regional government from 2003–2010, further institutionalisation of Amazigh activism took place. Amazigh groups received political and economic support and different public authorities recognised Imazighen's particularism within the immigrant communities, leading to the teaching of the Amazigh language in some Catalan schools, covering Tamazight in the local media, and publishing policy documentation on integration in Catalan and Tamazight. The Catalan Observatory of the Amazigh Language (OCLA) was established in 2005, and, in 2010, the Casa Amaziga of Catalunya was recognised by the regional government as the official representative body of the Imazighen in Catalonia (ibid.).

The favourable political environment allowed associations to establish collaborative relationships with many different local entities, ranging from educational institutions and research centres to city councils, different regional ministries and local NGOs. These collaborations encouraged Amazigh associations in Catalonia to follow a different line of activism than the rest of the Imazighen communities in the diaspora. In this regard, associations and activists promoted strong identification with Catalonia within the Amazigh communities in and outside of North Africa. Actions such as the teaching of Tamazight were used as an example of the commitment of local institutions to the cause and served to legitimise attempts to make Catalonia the centre of Amazigh activism in Europe, through initiatives such as the creation of a Riffian European Council in Catalonia and moving the headquarters of the AWC from Paris to Barcelona. On the other hand, a symbiosis in the narratives and patterns of representation crystallised from the mid-2000s among Amazigh activists in Catalonia, including a sort of 'ethno-territorial mimesis'[4] with Catalonian politics in their discourse towards the homeland's politics, and other symbolic issues, like renaming the *Yennayer*, which had always been considered a cultural event, as 'The National Day of the Imazighen'. It is no coincidence that Amazigh activism flourished in the Basque region and Catalonia. The federalist and separatist movements in these Spanish regions seemed to have looked favourably upon the Amazigh cause as representing similar claims to their own vis-à-vis the centralising powers of the nation-state.

These various institutional gains were short-lived as the global financial crisis in 2008 brought many of these initiatives to a halt. In the Basque Country, the requirements for access to funding became more stringent and the flagship association of the region, AZRAF, was forced to stop its activity for more than two years. In Madrid, financing for Amazigh organisations disappeared. In Catalonia, the economic crisis was coupled with the end of the coalition government that included ERC in 2010, and budget cuts paralysed initiatives such as the OCLA and the teaching of Tamazight in schools. Cuts in local government financing led to efforts to self-finance many of the activities on the part of Amazigh organisations, furthering their dependence on the personal resources of the members but also constraining the scope of what they could do (ibid.).

In addition to the scaling back of these activities in Catalonia, the process of electing representatives for the Casa Amaziga generated several power struggles within the community, to the point that collaboration between associations, which had previously worked together, became impossible after the election. Furthermore, as the Amazigh community had become more diverse with the arrival of new members over the previous decade, collaboration between members of the different generations also became more difficult. For activists from the second generation, the ideological past of the first generation of activists, who had been connected to the pan-Arabist left before their involvement in Amazigh activism, became a point of contention and an obstacle to collaboration. This situation became evident in Madrid between the associations created by those who had experienced Moroccan universities in the 1980s, still controlled by the Marxist-Leninist movement, and those who had done so in the mid-to-late 1990s, when Moroccan campuses were divided between a marginal left-wing, a dominant Islamism and an emerging Amazigh movement. The new generations could not forgive their predecessors for their past association with the pan-Arabist left, which denied the existence of cultural and structural discrimination towards the Amazigh (Suárez-Collado, 2013). As Cohen (1996) demonstrates, these kinds of inter-generational diasporic conflicts are not uncommon; intra-diaspora frictions tend to arise as new waves of migrants meet people of previous waves who preserve bygone traditions or who left with greatly differing political views under different circumstances (Vertovec, 2005).

Moreover, another feature of the recent period of Amazigh activism in Spain has been the waning of certain activist careers of individuals who had previously led and energised the cause in Spain. Regardless of the region of settlement, most associations are made up of a group of between four and ten members on whom community activism depends. Although a large part of the community identifies itself as Amazigh, the associations and the organisation of activities have excessively depended on the involvement of specific individual actors and, consequently, on their biographical availability. Biographical availability refers to the absence of personal constraints that may make it more difficult to be involved in a social movement (McAdam, 1986). Getting a job, emigrating to a new country, getting married or becoming a parent are situations that may affect activist careers and preclude investment in the cause. Thus, while Amazigh born or raised in Spain have shown an interest in the Amazigh cause, they often express feeling disconnected from the problems and controversies that older members of the diaspora bring to the movement. These young people have embraced Amazigh identity as a means for personal self-definition in their own time but have found books and online platforms more rewarding than formal organisations. The lack of engagement of younger generations in the organisational life of the diaspora has threatened the survival of some of the organisations, since older and often founding members have started to feel more constrained by their personal circumstances. As Abdelatif, who was involved in Amazigh activism in the 1990s in Morocco and from the early 2000s in Spain, explains:

> We have not succeeded in involving the young people who come to the Amazigh New Year celebration. It happened to us and to other European associations before ... When the association has only a few active members, each one with a personal life to take care of, and there is no generational replacement in the association, then it is a sure death.

Even if the associations have lost the economic capacity and human resources to mobilise, critical events have been triggers in reuniting the community again in demonstrations, rallies and talks, often in reaction to episodes of repression in the Amazigh territories or against grassroots activists in the homeland, particularly since the anti-authoritarian revolts from 2010 onwards. Nevertheless, the transnational involvement of the diaspora has decreased, as well as the activism of the Amazigh diaspora in Spain, which has been reduced to a local phenomenon situated in specific cities, or at best at a regional level, and is to be found mostly on the Internet. Thus, as with so many subcultures and modes of commonality, the Internet has offered new ways to maintain the circulation of information among diaspora members (Suárez-Collado, 2018). Beyond the online sphere, the Amazigh diaspora in Spain remains fragmented by the existence of different local specificities and generational differences that have been consolidated over the past two decades. Similar to other cases (Khosravi, 2018), the Amazigh experience in Spain suggests that diasporas are certainly not homogeneous units but rather a set of historically situated experiences, practices and circumstances. This observation can also be applied to the Dutch case, in which the evolution of politics and community dynamics have also influenced the pathways of diaspora activism.

The Amazigh diaspora activism in the Netherlands: caught between host and home countries policies

Amazigh migrants arrived in the Netherlands between the mid-1960s and the mid-1970s as guest workers reluctant to become involved in politics due to their perceived temporary status. Local institutions in the Netherlands, as well as the Moroccan state, saw the guest worker arrangement as short-term. In this vein, Morocco fostered the creation of *Amicales des travailleurs et commerçants Marocains à l'étranger* aimed at attracting remittances, discouraging the integration of Moroccans into European societies, and controlling their political activities abroad (Brand, 2006). The dominance of the associative field by the *Amicales* during the first years of settlement played a significant role in stalling the organisation of the Amazigh in many diaspora settings.

This situation changed with the 1973 oil crisis, which ushered in a new period of immigration to the Netherlands. Despite the increase in the country's unemployment rate and the suspension of formal recruitment through the guest worker system, many Moroccan labour migrants decided not to return to their homeland (Entzinger, 2014). Migration flows from Morocco increased through family reunification and illegal labour migration during the 1970s and 1980s, which coincided with extensive regularisation of immigrants by the Dutch government, with the Moroccans being one of the most favoured groups (Engbersen, Snel and van Meeteren, 2013). This situation caused the Moroccan community to grow significantly in number, and to generate new organisational needs focused on immigration status and living conditions. Alternative associations to the *Amicales* emerged to defend the social and labour rights of the Moroccan immigrants. These associations did not have specific interests in Amazigh ethnic or cultural claims, although most of the Moroccan community settled in the country was Amazigh (Van Heelsum, 2003). Similar to their co-ethnic migrant workers in Spain, identity issues were kept in the background during the early stages of immigration, with survival concerns dominating the sphere of immigrants' demands (Penninx and Schrover, 2001).

Likewise, local institutions did not recognise any particularism within the Moroccan immigrant community at that time, despite the new state multiculturalist discourse (Entzinger 2006), embodied in the so-called 'Minorities Policy', launched in 1979 with the aim of helping immigrants' integrate while retaining their own identity (Entzinger, 2014). In response to the minoritisation discourse, newcomers started to define themselves in terms of their ethnic origins, and specific group-oriented provisions and institutions were created in areas such as education, health care, social work, broadcasting and culture (ibid., p. 696). Local and national consultative councils were also set up to facilitate the participation of the 'ethnic minorities' in the political decision-making process (Bousetta, 1997, p. 220; Entzinger, 2014, p. 696). Notwithstanding these institutionalised forms of recognition, the Moroccan Imazighen were seen with little nuance and were considered to be 'Arabs' like the rest of Moroccans. Accordingly, Ahmed, a poet and activist who arrived in the country more than 25 years ago, said to me:

> During the seventies and eighties, Dutch people knew nothing about the Amazigh question. All Dutch organisations and institutions demanded Arabic translators because they did not know that there were Imazighen in Morocco. They thought that Morocco was only Arab and Muslim, so all those who came from Morocco were Arabs and Muslims.

This situation persisted until the 1990s. However, similar to the change observed in Spain, Amazigh activism in the Netherlands strengthened in parallel to the transformations experienced in the homeland in the early 1990s and at the transnational level with the creation of the AWC. This global expansion and the emergence of a new structure of political opportunity in the Netherlands favoured the spread of Amazigh associations in the country.

By the late 1980s, the Minorities Policy began to show its deficits in different fields, including the existence of ethnic enclaves and housing segregation, as well as low levels of immigrant integration in terms of educational attainment and labour market incorporation (Vasta, 2007, p. 717). In this regard, the 'Education in their Own Language and Culture' programme (OETC) started to reveal significant weaknesses. The programme aimed at ensuring immigrants' native language and culture instruction in primary schools, but language acquisition as planned by the OETC was problematic, particularly in the case of Moroccan Amazigh children who were forced to learn standard Arabic – a language they did not speak at home (Rietveld-van Wingerden, Westerman and ter Avest, 2009). As was also the experience in Spain, shortcomings in public policy concerning immigration management raised the Amazigh question and attracted the attention of the Dutch authorities. The Committee for Non-Indigenous Pupils in Education (CALO), created in 1991, reported the need to take into account cases of home and standard language divergence and defended parents' right to decide on the foreign language used to support their children learning (Ruiter, Spotti and Grande, 2012, p. 43). Following these recommendations, a new integration policy was introduced in 1994 that emphasised the individual over the group approach and the responsibility of immigrant groups to preserve their culture (Entzinger, 2014). Accordingly, the OETC was replaced by the 'Law on Education in Allochthonous Languages' (OALT) programme, obliging municipalities to offer language education to immigrant groups based on parents' demands. This process of policy change, initiated by the late 1980s, encouraged the Imazighen to organise around their language demands, as Mohamed, a journalist based in the country for 30 years and founder of one of the first associations, explained:

> There was a big lack of attention [in immigrant associations] to the world of Amazigh culture, and we thought we were responsible for that. We could not lose our identity and we decided to start organising meetings, seminars, debates, and we created the Bades Cultural Association in 1990.

The Bades Cultural Association in Roosendaal was among the first Amazigh associations created in the Netherlands, along with the Izaouran Association (1990) in Amsterdam, the Adrar Association (1991) in Niejmejen and the Syphax Association (1993) in Utrecht. These organisations were built up by a small group of two to five people on whom all the responsibilities of management and organisation of activities rested. At the same time, new waves of Amazigh immigrants and the diversity within the community were important assets in the constitution of the new Amazigh associations, as many of the newcomers had already taken part in the above-mentioned raising of Amazigh activism in Morocco (Van Amersfoort and Van Heelsum, 2007). Bringing their previous experience in their homeland to the host society, they contributed to the strengthening of the Amazigh cause, as Mohammed, who was born in the Rif and arrived in 1998 after family reunification, remembered:

> When I got here, it was very difficult because I arrived when I was 14. I had been very active at home in demonstrations and student strikes, and when I came here, besides language problems, I felt I was missing something. I did not feel right being represented by organisations that were here, especially in what concerns our cultural identity. Then I thought: why not create a group to defend human rights, especially Amazigh rights? We started working mainly with music and created a group called *Imtla*, which means something like diaspora.

By the end of the 1990s, Amazigh associations had managed to become an important part of the cultural lives of the Amazigh community, as they were responsible for organising poetry and music festivals, debates, conferences, demonstrations and other activities, such as Amazigh language teaching and private tutoring classes for students. Some of these organisations began working with educational authorities to develop teaching material for Amazigh language courses, which were introduced in the Dutch system for foreign pupils in 1998 (ibid.). They also tried to respond to the emerging needs of the community, for instance with the creation of electronic dictionaries for translation between Riffian Amazigh and other European languages (ibid.). At that point, Amazigh associations in the country had developed a close relationship with local institutions to strengthen their position as a particular group within the immigrant community. Moreover, collaborations between the associations also expanded, as well as with other organisations in the homeland and the Amazigh diaspora in neighbouring countries, mainly Belgium. Amazigh activists, musicians and artists who went from the Netherlands to other countries to attend meetings and festivals organised by other organisations in Europe played an important role in building connections between Amazigh organisations across borders.

The level of activity of Amazigh associations continued to be intense over the first half of the 2000s. Various factors led to the weakening of the movement; to begin with, public debates on immigration and multiculturalism questioned the integration of Muslim immigrants in the Netherlands. As multiculturalism could no longer be considered a satisfactory model for managing immigration, different measures were introduced from 2003 that aimed at establishing mandatory integration requirements while rolling back public services that supported minority cultural identities (Entzinger, 2014). Consequently, programmes such as the OALT language policy and the use of allochthonous languages in the media were abolished, affecting the normalisation of Tamazight as a language of immigration in the Netherlands. This new situation meant that the Amazigh language and culture received less support and funding from local institutions, leaving their continuity dependent on finding alternative sources and on individual leadership. The scarcity of local support led some associations to turn to institutions in Morocco, where the state's attitude towards the Amazigh had changed in the early 2000s with the introduction of Tamazight education in schools, the creation of official institutions like the Royal Institute of Amazigh Culture (IRCAM) and the later official recognition of the Amazigh language and identity in the 2011 Constitution. These new policies on the part of the Moroccan state meant that some diaspora associations explored partnerships with state institutions such as the Moroccan embassies and consulates, the IRCAM or the Council of the Moroccan Community Abroad (CCME). However, the wide spectrum of political attitudes towards the Moroccan state by Imazighen in the diaspora has meant that while some have explored a rapprochement, they have concurrently opened themselves up to criticism and boycotts by Imazighen who consider them to be collaborators who have compromised Amazigh freedom and independence.

Beyond these collaborative channels and with limited support from local institutions, Amazigh diaspora associations and projects have depended on self-financing and the economic and personal resourcefulness of activists, as is the case of the Internet-based Amazigh TV and the website of the newspaper *Amazigh Times*. These circumstances have conditioned the continuation of Amazigh activism in the Netherlands, as well as other important factors also present in the Spanish case, such as the existing disunity among the members of the diaspora (Karrouche, 2013), and biographical ruptures in the careers of activist leaders as Mohammed pointed out: 'I'm not active any more. I hardly participate because I'm busy with other things now, with the kids, work, my wife…'

These challenges have made it difficult for Amazigh activism in the Netherlands to maintain continuity, which in turn has discouraged previously committed activists, as illustrated by Najjar, a 40-year-old professor of Dutch and activist in different associations located in the southern province of North Brabant:

> Associations are not like they used to be. They used to do a lot of activities and many different events. But now people are not so involved in organising anything. I think people are tired, because it [Amazigh activism] has not gone any further. In the past, people were very curious about what was organised, but now any association brings together no more than thirty or forty people in the room. There is less interest because there is no evolution in this domain [Amazigh activism], no progress. Also, there are funding problems and no stable resources, and there is no strategic vision either in the medium or long term. It cannot continue because there are no stages to reach and there are not professionalised associations.

The challenges of Amazigh activism in the Netherlands have mirrored those in Spain, where online content and networks now dominate, particularly for those born in the Netherlands. As Van Heelsum and Van Amersfoort (2007) have observed, this is connected to the negative coverage of Moroccans in the Dutch media, which has spurred interest in Amazigh identity and 'Berber', which is portrayed somewhat more romantically than 'Moroccan' and attracts a less negative attitude from the general public in the Netherlands (Brouwer, 2006; Suárez-Collado, 2016).

Although Amazigh activism has not ceased, it has undergone profound changes. As some of my interlocutors confirmed, there has been a significant decline in the number of attendees at association activities and in active involvement in diaspora organisations in recent years. Thus, besides exceptional episodes of mobilisation or repression in Morocco, such as the February 20th Movement (2011–2012) or the *Hirak* movement in the Rif (2016–2017), the presence of Amazigh activism through formal organisations in the Dutch public sphere has diminished considerably.

Conclusion

Amazigh diaspora activism in both Spain and the Netherlands suggests that diasporas constitute a complex interplay of spaces, boundaries and dynamics. They are not a monolithic phenomenon, but a permanent source of plurality; neither should they be considered static, but rather seen as in a state of permanent change. This complexity and the changing nature of diasporas have an impact on their patterns of social and political mobilisation, as I have tried to demonstrate, in the opportunities and obstacles to diasporic organisation that emanate from specific configurations, in which both structure (historical and political conditions) and agency (the personal conditions and practices of social actors) play a role in the shaping of diaspora activism. In both Spain and the Netherlands, Amazigh activism has progressively fragmented because of differences in integration regimes and ideological and generational differences within the group. This fragmentation has affected the continuity of collective action based on formal community organisations and has given way to new forms of activism and identity expression, which might be unrecognisable to the early pioneers of Amazigh activism in Europe.

Notes

1 See 'François Alfonsi, député européen, crée un "groupe d'amitié" avec le peuple berbère - amazigh', Réseau Citoyen des Associations Franco-Berbères, 20 April 2010. Available at: www.cbf.fr/news/82 (accessed 15 June 2010).
2 *Déclaration du Congrès Mondial Amazigh à l'occasion du Forum permanant des peuples autochtones*, New York, 18–24 May 2009.
3 In this resolution, the Government of Spain is urged to demand respect for Imazighen's rights in its bilateral negotiations with North African governments. Likewise, Catalonia is declared a political and cultural home for the Amazigh population, and it states the intention to promote the teaching of Tamazight in schools and university education.
4 This is to imitate the model of the state-region relationship, powers, institutions and symbols previously adopted by others (Moreno, 1997).

References

Abdelhady, D. (2011) *The Lebanese Diaspora: The Arab Immigrant Experience in Montreal, New York and Paris*. New York: New York University Press.
Bengio, O. and Maddy-Weitzman, B. (2013) 'Mobilised diasporas: Kurdish and Berber movements in comparative perspective', *Kurdish Studies*, 1(1), pp. 65–90.
Bousetta, H. (1997) 'Citizenship and political participation in France and the Netherlands: reflections on two local cases', *Journal of Ethnic and Migration Studies*, 23(2), pp. 215–231. doi: 10.1080/1369183x.1997.9976587
Brand, L.A. (2006) *Citizens Abroad: Emigration and the State in the Middle East and North Africa*. Cambridge: Cambridge University Press. doi: 10.1017/cbo9780511491498
Brouwer, L. (2006) 'Dutch Moroccan websites: a transnational imagery?' *Journal of Ethnic and Migration Studies*, 32(7), pp. 1153–1168. doi: 10.1080/13691830600821869

Bruneau. M. (1995) *Diasporas*. Montpellier: GIP Reclus.
Cohen, R. (1996) 'Diasporas and the nation-state: from victims to challengers', *International Affairs*, 72(3), pp. 507–520. doi: 10.2307/2625554
de Haas, H. (2007) 'Morocco's migration experience: a transitional perspective', *International Migration*, 45(4), pp. 39–70. doi: 10.1111/j.1468-2435.2007.00419.x
Engbersen, G., Snel, E. and Van Meeteren, M. (2013) 'Declining migration from Morocco to the Netherlands and the diminutive causation of migration' IMI Oxford Working Paper Series, No. 73, Oxford: International Migration Institute, University of Oxford. Available at: www.migrationinstitute.org/publications/wp-73-13 (accessed 2 October 2019).
Entzinger, H. (2006) 'Changing the rules while the game is on: from multiculturalism to assimilation in the Netherlands', in Bodemann, Y. and Yurdakul, G. (eds) *Migration, Citizenship, Ethnos: Incorporation Regimes in Germany, Western Europe and North America*. New York: Palgrave Macmillan, pp. 121–144.
Entzinger, H. (2014) 'The growing gap between facts and discourse on immigrant integration in the Netherlands', *Identities*, 21(6), pp. 693–707. doi: 10.1080/1070289X.2013.828616
Guiraudon, V. (2004) 'Ethnic migrant minorities and transnational claims. making in Europe: opportunities and constraints', in Flemming, C. and Ulf, H. (eds) *The Politics of Multiple Belonging. Ethnicity and Nationalism in Europe and East Asia*. Farnham: Ashgate, pp. 61–76.
Ireland, P. (1994) *The Policy Challenge of Ethnic Diversity: Immigrant Politics in France and Switzerland*. Cambridge, MA: Harvard University Press.
Karrouche, N. (2013) 'Where national histories and colonial myths meet: "historie croisée" and memory of the Moroccan-Berber cultural movement in The Netherlands', in Hefner, R.W., Hutchinson, J., Mels, S., and Timmerman, C. (eds) *Religions in Movement: The Local and the Global in Contemporary Faith Traditions*. London: Routledge, pp. 114–132.
Kastoryano, R. (1996) *La France, l'Allemagne et leur immigrés: négocier l'identité* [France, Germany and Their Immigrants: Negotiating Identity]. Paris: Armand Colin.
Khosravi, S. (2018) 'A fragmented diaspora: Iranians in Sweden', *Nordic Journal of Migration Research*, 8(2), pp. 73–81.
Levitt, P. and Jaworsky, N. (2007) 'Transnational migration studies: past developments and future trends', *Annual Review of Sociology*, 33, pp. 129–156.
McAdam, D. (1986) 'Recruitment to high-risk activism: the case of Freedom Summer', *American Journal of Sociology*, 92, pp. 64–90.
Moreno, L. (1997) 'Federalization and ethnoterritorial concurrence in Spain', *The Journal of Federalism*, 27(4), pp. 65–84.
Østergaard-Nielsen, E. (2003) 'The politics of migrants' transnational political practices', *International Migration Review*, 37(3), pp. 760–786.
Penninx, R. and Schrover, M. (2001) *Bastion of Bindmiddel? Organisaties van immigranten in historisch perspectief* [Bastion or Binder? Organizations of Immigrants in Historical Perspective]. Amsterdam: IMES.
Quinsaat, S. (2013) 'Migrant mobilization for homeland politics: a social movement approach', *Sociology Compass*, 7(11), pp. 952–964.
Rietveld-van Wingerden, M., Westerman, W., and ter Avest, I. (2009) 'Islam in education in the Netherlands: history and actual developments', in Alvarez Veinguer, A., Dietz, G., Jozsa, D.P., and Knauth, T. (eds) *Islam in Education in European Countries. Pedagogical Concepts and Empirical Findings*. Münster: Waxman, pp. 69–93.
Ruiter, J.J. de, Spotti, M., and Grande, F. (2012) *Mother Tongue and Intercultural Valorization: Europe and Its Migrant Youth*. Milan: Franco Angeli.
Suárez-Collado, Á. (2013) 'El movimiento amazigh en el Rif: Identidad, cultura y política en las provincias de Nador y Alhucemas' [The Amazigh movement in the Rif: Identity, culture and politics in the provinces of Nador and Al Hoceima]. PhD thesis, Universidad Autónoma de Madrid.
Suárez-Collado, Á. (2016) 'La esfera virtual del activismo amazigh en Europa: una arena alternativa de identificación para las segundas generaciones' [The virtual sphere of Amazigh activism in Europe: an alternative arena for second generation's identity], in Lobillo, G., Castro-Higueras, A., Sedeño, A. and Aguilera, M. (eds) *Prácticas culturales juveniles y movimientos sociales en el Mediterráneo ¿Un cambio de época?* [Youth Cultural Practices and Social Movements in the Mediterranean: A Change of Era?]. Málaga: Círculo de Estudios Audiovisuales Ad Hoc, pp. 273–283.
Suárez Collado, Á. (2018) 'L'activisme de la diaspora amazighe en Espagne: opportunités et limites pour une action continué' [The activism of the Amazigh diaspora in Spain: opportunities and limits for sustained action], in Desrues, T. and Tilmatine, M. (eds) *Les revendications amazighes dans la tourmente*

des « printemps arabes » [Amazigh Claims in the Turmoil of the 'Arab Springs']. Rabat: Centre Jacques-Berque, pp. 255–288. doi: 10.4000/books.cjb.1369

Van Amersfoort, J.M.M. and Van Heelsum, A. (2007) 'Moroccan Berber immigrants in the Netherlands, their associations and transnational ties: a quest for identity and recognition', *Immigrants & Minorities*, 25(3), pp. 234–262. doi: 10.1080/02619280802407343

Van Hear, N., Pieke, F., and Vertovec, S. (2004) 'The contribution of UK-based diasporas to development and poverty reduction', Centre on Migration Policy and Society (COMPAS). Available at: www.compas.ox.ac.uk/wp-content/uploads/ER-2004-Diasporas_UK_Poverty_Reduction_DfID.pdf (accessed 12 September 2019).

Van Heelsum, A. (2003) 'Moroccan Berbers in Europe, the US and Africa and the concept of Diaspora'. *UCLA: Center for European and Eurasian Studies*. Available at: https://escholarship.org/uc/item/3f35d97x (accessed 2 October 2019).

Vasta, E. (2007) 'From ethnic minorities to ethnic majority policy: multiculturalism and the shift to assimilationism in the Netherlands', *Ethnic and Racial Studies*, 30(5), pp. 713–740. doi: 10.1080/01419870701491770

Vertovec, S. (2005) 'The political importance of diasporas', Working Paper No. 3, Centre on Migration, Policy and Society. Available at: www.compas.ox.ac.uk/wp-content/uploads/WP-2005-013-Vertovec_Political_Importance_Diasporas.pdf (accessed 12 September 2019).

8
THE DIASPORIC AMAZIGH MOVEMENT IN FRANCE
Articulating indigeneity

Jonathan Harris

One quiet Saturday afternoon in July 2016, on the premises of Azul Espace Franco-Berbère Créteil, a long-standing cultural association in the Parisian *banlieue*, a group of around 50 Amazigh (Berber) activists and association leaders came together to discuss federating their respective groups to create a new platform to challenge the French government to do more for the Imazighen (Amazigh pl.) of France. The meeting had been called by activists from the Congrès Mondial Amazigh (CMA) around a month previously, in reaction to changes in language education policy affecting those of North African origin in France announced by then French Education Minister Najat Vallaud-Belkacem, herself of Moroccan Amazigh parentage. Arabic (along with other 'languages of origin') was no longer to be taught by foreign teachers employed by origin states but by teachers employed by the French state, like any other foreign language. Seeing their chance to advance Amazigh interests in France, this diverse group of Amazigh activists and association leaders called for the incorporation of Amazigh languages into the portfolio of languages taught in French schools, as this, they argued, was their true 'language of origin'.

The crowded meeting took place in the association's main meeting room. The walls were a colourful mural representing Amazigh scenes from across North Africa – a Tuareg tent pitched in the desert, distinctive *ghorfa*, *igherman* and *agadir* (fortified granaries of Tunisia, Algeria and Morocco respectively), *axxam* (the Kabyle house) and prehistoric wall painting in the style of the *Tassili N'Ajjer*. Words in *Tifinagh*, the Amazigh script, named Berber heroes – ancient king Micipsa (ⵎⵉⵛⵉⵒⵙⴰ) and female anti-colonial resistance leader Lalla Fadhma N'Soumer (ⵍⴰⵍⵍⴰ ⴼⴰⴷⵎⴰ ⵏⵙⵓⵎⵔ). The CMA's Secretary-General, Belkacem Lounes, opened the meeting by saying that those in attendance were 'united by Tamazgha'.

Tamazgha in France

This chapter examines how the Amazigh diaspora, networked in France's Amazigh cultural associations, village committees and political movements, constructs an imaginative geography of North Africa, which they call Tamazgha, partly through articulations of Indigenous identity. France is home to a large Amazigh diaspora; hundreds of organisations group together hundreds of thousands of individuals who are united by a common interest in the preservation and promotion of *Amazighité*, that is, the quality of being Amazigh. Indigenous to North Africa and distinct from Arabic, Amazigh language (Tamazight)[1] and culture are under threat in the eyes of the diaspora's leaders, not only as the children of Amazigh migrants grow up as 'French', but as Imazighen across North Africa and the diaspora are being 'arabised'. Arabisation, they argue, is the result of state policies introduced during the colonial period and accelerated following independence, which privilege(d) Arabic as the language of administration, education, literature and media as well as religion, and coded Algerian, Moroccan, Tunisian and Libyan national identities as exclusively 'Arabic'. As a result, the activities of the Amazigh diaspora associations are necessarily political in their motivation and content.

The Amazigh diaspora today is diverse, complex and divided, but nonetheless remains as a category of cultural, linguistic and ethnic affiliation outside the nation-state, comprising various regional sub-groups (such as Kabyles, Tuaregs, Chawis, Chleuhs, Mozabites and Riffians). In France, it is over a century old, with first North African labourers arriving to work in France's factories and mines and later their families coming to join them, and today many of those attending and animating Amazigh associations are second- or third-generation French citizens. The diaspora does not merely exist as an automatic consequence of immigration but is continually reproduced and constituted by the multiple structures, events and practices that articulate Amazigh identity. As such, the Amazigh diaspora cannot be conceptually dissociated from the Amazigh movement; by referring to it as 'the diasporic Amazigh movement', this chapter constantly positions the diaspora and Amazigh identity in ongoing processes of becoming, as well as making a distinction between the Amazigh movement 'in Tamazgha' and 'in diaspora'.

This chapter, based on a mixed-method ethnographic study carried out from 2015–2017, therefore approaches the Amazigh diaspora as its primary object within a relational analysis that eschews methodological nationalism. One of the key demands of the diasporic Amazigh movement is for Amazigh people not to be amalgamated and subsumed within state or religious categories of identity, which they see as secondary. Taking inspiration from Indigenous scholars who have challenged the state's categories of governance by aligning with Indigenous claims to self-determination (Tuhiwai Smith, 2004; Hunt, 2014), this chapter resists categorising the Amazigh diaspora according to their or their forebears' sending-state as in much of the existing literature (Silverstein, 2004; Lacroix, 2012; Aïtel, 2013). It also problematises the other categorisation through which the Amazigh diaspora are amalgamated in much of the literature that informs their governance: as Muslims (Fredette, 2014; Beaman, 2017). Of course, these categories are not entirely absent, but rather are understood as secondary to the self-ascribed identity claim of the members and leaders of the Amazigh diaspora. Amazigh diasporic experience is therefore defined by heterogeneity and hybridity, and the cultural- or religious-boundary maintenance often associated with diasporas (Brubaker, 2005) is diffuse and multi-faceted.

Throughout this chapter, I focus on the ways in which Indigenous articulations are (re) produced in the Amazigh diaspora in France. The counter-intuitive combination of 'rooted' indigeneity and 'routed' diaspora sheds light on the complex relationships to place and mobility in the postcolonial Middle East and North Africa.

Indigenous articulations

At first, the idea that a diaspora can be Indigenous might seem like a contradiction, as diasporas are so frequently imagined to be mobile and Indigenous peoples fixed in place. However, James Clifford (2013) argues that more scholarship on global indigeneity should engage with populations in the urban, diaspora environment. Rather than assume that Indigenous territoriality must necessarily entail continuous residence, Clifford's theorisation of 'Indigenous diaspora' points to the 'complexly routed and rooted experiences' (ibid., p. 83), where 'diasporic displacements, memories, networks, and reidentifications are recognised as integral to tribal, aboriginal, native survival and dynamism' (ibid., p. 71). Clifford draws on Stuart Hall's concept of *articulation*, which he proposed as a way of understanding how seemingly disparate 'ideological elements come, under certain conditions, to cohere together within a discourse' (Hall, 1996, p. 141). It is achieved discursively and politically (and not necessarily consciously), with the consequence that a range of different *positionings* may be linked so that 'people begin to recognise themselves in all of them' (Hall, 1988, p. 61). Such a perspective offers a way of dealing with the essentialist tendency in approaches to indigeneity that reify cultural difference and therefore seek to establish things like 'authenticity' (Gagné, 2016) or to see indigeneity as purely 'invented' or 'constructed' and therefore meaningless or dangerous (Kuper, 2003; Amselle, 2012).

One of the limitations of this articulation approach, however, is that it can become overly focused on discursive and textual representations at the expense of the practised, situated and embodied ways in which Indigenous subjectivity is (re)produced (Radcliffe, 2017). To address this, I also draw on the language of performance as modelled in recent ethnographic work concerning Indigenous people (Oiry-Varacca, 2013; Loyola-Hernández, 2018). Performances are 'explored as practices rather than expressions of essential identities' (Jeffrey, 2013, p. 6) wherein subjectivities and relationships are repeatedly reworked through embodied and situated actions and processes. Performing Indigeneity is an embodied legitimising practice that gives Amazigh diaspora leaders a voice and visibility related to a status and a quality as Indigenous, 'culturally authentic' and therefore within the bounds of acceptable difference in French society. However, when I argue that indigeneity is articulated in the diasporic Amazigh movement, I do not then mean that it is imported as a coherent set of ideas, but rather that it has been 'inflected and reworked as it has travelled' (Li, 2000, p. 155). This inflected and reworked indigeneity joins a set of discourses, political subjectivities and histories that are specific to the diasporic Amazigh movement, and is referred to and articulated without necessarily being identified as such.

The remainder of the chapter uses Tuhiwai Smith's (2004) 25 'Indigenous projects', referred to in italics below, as a non-prescriptive starting point for identifying a series of positionings that articulate indigeneity in the diasporic Amazigh movement. The first section focuses on how Amazigh leaders position themselves within the wider, global movement of Indigenous peoples, *claiming* indigeneity as a putatively fixed and knowable category in an *indigenising* process. The second part raises the common discourse of ongoing 'Arabo-Islamic' colonisation, as diaspora Imazighen bear *testimony* to episodes of violent repression in their home regions and *celebrate survival/survivance*. The third section details how the performed Amazigh difference in the diaspora is manifested in *revitalising and regenerating* the Tamazight language and public displays of 'traditional' costumes, which articulate *gendered subjectivities*. The fourth section examines village territoriality as an Indigenous positioning, expressed through the continued institution of village committees, traditional forms of village sociability and politics, habitation and *restoration*, and a continued practice of *returning* exemplified in repatriating the deceased for burial. I conclude by suggesting that as the concept and politics of indigeneity translate into the Middle East and North Africa, it is worth paying attention to its mutability, relationality and diasporic manifestations.

Articulating indigeneity on the international stage

The diasporic Amazigh movement's most self-evident articulations of indigeneity position the Imazighen within the global movement of Indigenous peoples, *claiming* indigeneity as a putatively fixed and knowable category of ethnic identity. A clear example can be found by returning to Paris-based NGO the CMA, referenced in the opening vignette. Secretary-General Belkacem Lounes described the group's beginnings when activists met 'under the guise of indigeneity at the UN' in the early 1990s when the issue of Indigenous rights was gaining momentum:

> These first Indigenous meetings [were where the CMA began to take form], even though we all already had the idea of the *Amazighité* of North Africa ... But we didn't know how to reach each other until at the UN in Geneva.

The UN Permanent Forum on Indigenous Issues (of which the 2017 chair, Mariam Wallet Aboubakrine, is Tuareg), the UN Human Rights Council's Expert Mechanism on the Rights of Indigenous Peoples, and the African Commission on Human and Peoples' Rights are all examples of platforms where CMA activists network with and are exposed to the political arguments of Indigenous delegates from across the globe. CMA delegates, such as human rights lawyer Hassan Id Balkassm or activist Kamira Naït Sid, use these fora as platforms for raising awareness of the Amazigh movement; they attend a range of international meetings as representatives of the Imazighen, exchange statements of solidarity with other Indigenous leaders and activists, and challenge state governments by bringing human rights cases to the attention of relevant experts. These practices repeatedly draw comparisons between the Amazigh struggle and those of Indigenous peoples around the world, particularly from the New World, comparisons that are then articulated in the wider diasporic Amazigh movement.

Each comparison serves a purpose in the discursive positioning of the Imazighen, as not all Indigenous peoples and geographies are equal (Coombes, Johnson and Howitt, 2012). For example, one diaspora leader referred to the Imazighen as the 'Aborigines of North Africa', while another, Chawi autonomist Yella Houha explained; 'We had an immense territory, but we now have nothing – no language, no recognition of our identity – we are the Apaches of Algeria.' These comparisons with Indigenous peoples, whose historic struggles with and near-extermination by European settlers are well known and dramatic, serve to emphasise the minoritised and dispossessed status of the Imazighen. In contrast, Mohamed Bennana, a Moroccan Amazigh association leader who told me he had visited an Indigenous reserve in Labrador, said he would 'prefer to speak in terms of "First Peoples"'. Bennana's comparison serves rather to assert the potential for more effective political recognition and autonomy through the discourse of Indigenous rights, as First Peoples in Canada have achieved to a comparatively high degree. Though he said he had no illusions as to the difficulties of life on a reserve, Mohammed also recognised the economic and political rights that Indigenous groups in Canada had vis-à-vis the state. Whatever their emphasis, these comparisons position the Imazighen within the constellation of Indigenous peoples worldwide (Silverstein, 2015). For Bennana, this positioning legitimises Amazigh claims to the rights associated with Indigenous peoples. He explained the articulation of indigeneity as part of a political evolution from a cultural, to a political/economic, to a regional/territorial struggle, where the Amazigh movement in North Africa has begun to position itself as Indigenous to claim territorial rights after decades of cultural and later political/economic activism (Oiry-Varacca, 2013). In a similar vein, association leader and open supporter of Kabyle independence, Cyprien Hamadouche argued that '[the issue of] independence goes past Algeria, to the UN and its statutes for Indigenous peoples'.

While many comparisons with other Indigenous groups around the world provided a means for articulating their own Amazigh Indigenous identity, for Rahma Houzig, president of

Tamaynut-France, a meeting of 'Indigenous African Women' held in her native Agadir in 1998 was a formative experience in terms of building transnational links across North Africa:

> I have friends in Libya and in Egypt, luckily. In 1998, we did an event in Agadir on *'Les Femmes Autochtones'* that gathered women from across Tamazgha. It was a shared moment. We shared things like clothes, jewellery, songs.

This 'shared moment' of transnational networking is just one example of many instances where Amazigh leaders have been exposed to and participated in wider Indigenous networks and discourses. In these instances, Amazigh leaders articulate indigeneity as if it were a fixed and knowable quality rather than viewing indigeneity as constantly being (re-)made; they are Indigenous by association.

A similar and parallel articulation is made through performances of inter-community solidarity with other ethnic minorities. In France, Amazigh association members draw lines of comparison with Breton, Occitan, Corsican, Basque and Catalan groups, who, they argue, represent the victims of the same French 'Jacobinism'[2] that has seen the enforcement of repressive language policies in its North African ex-colonies. Nationalist groups like the Kabyle MAK-Anavad engage in a mimicry of state diplomacy (see Harris, 2020c) with representatives of these ethno-linguistic minorities, offering congratulations on successes, holding joint press conferences, and organising actions together. A key locus for this activity is the European Free Alliance (EFA) at the EU, which represents several European 'stateless nations' and has invited numerous 'diplomatic delegations' from the MAK-Anavad, performing solidarity with the Kabyle nationalist cause through signed agreements and declarations. Similarly, representatives of several stateless nations such as Panjab attended the creation in Rotterdam in 2014 of the Riffian separatist *'Mouvement 18 Septembre'*, and, in 2018, a Kabyle national football team mainly comprising players from the diaspora competed with other stateless nations such as Tibet, Western Armenia and Panjab in the CONIFA World Cup in London (see Harris, 2020a).

These links with the global Indigenous groups and Europe's ethno-linguistic minorities are 'not necessary, determined, absolute and essential for all time' (Hall, 1996, p. 141). They are articulated by Amazigh diaspora activists seeking to position themselves outside the state narratives of identity and belonging in France and North Africa. In *claiming* indigeneity in relation to these other groups and structures, they are working out and redefining the meanings and subjectivities of indigeneity in the diaspora. As such, these seemingly straightforward articulations of indigeneity on the international stage are only a small part of the picture of the diasporic Amazigh movement, whose everyday practices and politics performed in associations are unpacked in the following sections.

The colonial present

The experience of colonialism is perhaps the one unifying trait of Indigenous subjectivities. Indigenous peoples 'share experiences as peoples who have been subjected to the colonisation of their lands and cultures, and the denial of their sovereignty' (Tuhiwai Smith, 2004), and this key articulation of indigeneity reappears often in diaspora Amazigh discourse. Through the common discourse of ongoing 'Arabo-Islamic' colonisation, diaspora Imazighen bear *testimony* to episodes of violent repression in their home regions and *celebrate survival/survivance*. Emotional and affective language of suffering, violence, and trauma frames the experience of colonialism in a way that highlights its psychological and embodied nature and effects on the individual and the group. In diaspora members' narratives, the sense of instability and underdevelopment in Amazigh regions over the long term is punctuated by episodes of inter-ethnic and state violence against Imazighen in North Africa. These are widely publicised and protested by diaspora Imazighen, through street demonstrations, press statements, social media and reports to international institutions. Often diaspora Imazighen frame these episodes as 'colonial' using descriptive vocabulary such as 'apartheid', 'genocide', 'racist' or 'ethnic cleansing', such that Amazigh culture itself is understood to be under attack or dominated in a colonial system, as well as highlighting colonialism's racial-ethnic dimension.

A key example of the diaspora Amazigh movement's articulation of a colonial present in recent years lies in how it represented the inter-community violence that erupted periodically in the Mzab, a remote group of oases in central Algeria, between 2013 and 2016. Several instances of looting and killing were reported by Amazigh activists as having been inflicted on the Amazigh population by the local Arabophone population with police support as part of a government-sponsored programme of ethnic cleansing. The official discourse of the Algerian government and the mainstream press framed the violence as sectarian and minimised the role of the security services. Amazigh diaspora activism aimed at drawing international attention to the Mzab and securing the release of scores of Mozabites held under preventive detention continued into 2015–2016. The version of events as established in this activism explicitly framed the Mozabites as victims of violent colonisation, as Arabophone mobs took possession of Mozabite ancestral lands (cemeteries and palm groves particularly), with apparent state endorsement. The historical autonomy of the Mzab, its pre-colonial political institutions, and its cultural specificities were framed as being under threat:

> This war unfolds through a policy of confining the Mozabites within a few isolated islands on their historic territory … The objective is clear: to flood these territories with exogenous populations in order to upset the urban organisation of the region and make the Mozabites a minority in their own territory.
> (Izmulen pour les droits des At-Mzab, 'The Algerian Government continues its war against the Mozabites' 23 December 2015, https://izmulen. wordpress.com/2015/12/)

> Mr. Secretary General Ban Ki Moon … we would like to draw your attention to the institutional violence … perpetrated against the At-Mzab (indigenous Amazigh of the Mzab valley) … an ancient civilization listed since 1982 as UNESCO world heritage. The At-Mzab are under attack by men of the "Chaamba" Arabic community with the known support of the Algerian police force.
> (CMA Open Letter to UN Secretary-General Ban Ki-Moon, 3 March 2016, www.amazighworld.org/ human_rights/index_show.php?id=642022)

> They [Chaamba] say 'we are nomads, and for a long time we used this place as a base for our tents. We are the first.' The Mozabites say no, it was them. We have our walled towns; we structured the environment. That's a deep debate between the two communities. And of course, the Mozabites consider themselves to be Indigenous.
> (Sliman Tounsi, Collectif des Mozabites en Europe, interview with author)

This example may seem to be an extreme case, particularly when presented using the rhetoric of groups like *Izmulen*, but it is not alone in its representation as an instance of present colonialism. MAK-Anavad activists routinely refer to the Algerian state as the 'colonial state' in communiqués, on social media and in public discourse, particularly in reference to the activities of the Algerian *gendarmerie* in Kabylia where they are framed as constituting a 'force of occupation'. This discourse presumes a sovereignty that has been illegitimately usurped. Other Amazigh activists use the same vocabulary to describe the Moroccan state's presence in the Rif and the recent French military interventions in the Tuareg regions of Mali and Niger, positioning them as illegal and illegitimate attacks on the sovereignty of local Amazigh groups. Through this discursive articulation of episodes of conflict in North Africa with colonialism, the Amazigh diaspora's activists position themselves as Indigenous.

Regarding the diaspora itself, the linkages between colonisation and emigration are well documented in Amazigh scholarship (Chaker, 1985; Dirèche-Slimani, 1997). Abdelmalek Sayad, the pre-eminent Franco-Kabyle sociologist of immigration, defined the diasporic condition as a 'double absence' wherein the emigrant feels viscerally detached from the place and people they have left but is equally unable to avoid exclusion in their new home (Sayad, 1999). The psychological and affective conditions of 'double absence' demonstrate how social alienation is central to lived experiences of the diasporic as well as the colonised condition. The two are bound together in the memory of exile, land appropriation and the threat of violence, but even more fundamentally in their logics of assimilation that compel the racial or migrant 'other' to aspire to join the hegemonic social group. Amazigh leaders in the diaspora frequently describe themselves as exiles rather than emigrants, in part to eschew the stereotypes of race and class associated with the term *immigré* , and in part to articulate a colonised subjectivity based on alienation from the homeland. Riffian activist Fikri El Azrak expressed his position in this way: 'I feel exiled, not emigrated. Even if I'm here, I'm in the Rif ... I feel that I'm far from my home. I want to be there, but the regime has chased me out.'

For Malika, who was born and brought up in Paris, starting an Amazigh association was a way of working through a feeling of alienation:

> I have an awareness of what's at stake – the politics of it, Tamazgha, Berber ... it's affective and I need to transmit ... It's important for me but it's not easy, to manage this double culture. I don't belong totally to either. It's a sort of cobbling together of a third identity.

If Amazigh diaspora discourse 'articulates, or bends together, both roots *and* routes' (Clifford, 1997, p. 251), then it does so in a way that highlights the colonial forces that have shaped and continue to shape those roots and routes. The diaspora's members materially and metaphorically locate themselves between French and Arabic cultures and colonialities. Third spaces of cultural hybridity are far more complex in this inter-colonial schema, but Amazigh leaders tend to celebrate Franco-Amazigh hybridity over Arabo-Amazigh. Writer Kateb Yacine famously opposed the Arabisation policy of the post-independent Algerian state, saying that 'the deepest alienation for an Algerian is not to think that he is French but that he is Arab' (Aïtel, 2013, p. 64). French-born Malik Houha explained his admiration for 'the [French political] party "*Indigènes de la République*"' which presents injustices in French society as being a continuation of colonial power relations, but could not agree with them as 'they only talk about being Arabs, and the colonialism and imperialism they talk about is only Western. But my problem is the colonialism of Arabo-Islamism.'

Performing the 'authentic' *authochtone*

While other details may be negotiable, the main identity claim of the Amazigh movement is to be at once North African and non-Arab. Preceding Arabic civilisation by over a thousand years, this is also a claim to cultural 'authenticity' that is performed and embodied as well as discursive. Performed Amazigh difference in the diaspora is manifested in *revitalising and regenerating* the Tamazight language and public displays of 'traditional' costumes, which articulate *gendered subjectivities*.

Since at least the 1940s, the Amazigh diaspora has played a central role in revitalising and regenerating Tamazight through literary production, media and academic work. From the desire to preserve and transmit Tamazight to the next generation, the vast majority of Amazigh cultural associations in the diaspora operate weekly language classes. Amazigh leaders frequently see the language as the essential vehicle of Amazigh identity and describe Arabisation as a form of 'cultural denial', 'erasure' or even 'extermination'. Therefore, most diaspora Amazigh associations try to create 'a secure linguistic environment in [the] mother tongue' (Rubio-Marín, 2003, p. 56), where Tamazight occupies a privileged place within association life. For example, even if French is the universal language, most conversation classes and cultural and literary events are zones of linguistic exclusivity. Early in Tamazight classes at the *Association de Culture Berbère*, beginners are taught a Kabyle proverb '*Agdud mebla idles am wemdan mebla iles*', which translates as 'a people without culture is as a being without a tongue', the teacher explicitly linking a wider imperative of cultural survival to the project of education in the language. As such, many classes are as much about identity formation and performance as everyday literacy. This is evidenced in the way that the distinction of Tamazight from Arabic is a central concern of Tamazight teachers and scholars. Tamazight includes several loan words from Arabic, and their identification and consequent 'correction' are disciplined by the members of Amazigh associations. In the words of one long-term association member, 'We're all learners ourselves. Often, I correct myself and others.' As Houria Labou, an association leader in the Parisian suburbs, said, 'We tolerate French, but never Arabic. For us it was a way of resisting, against forgetting our memory, our identity.'

Amazigh costume in its diverse forms is worn by organisers and attendees of numerous Amazigh diaspora events such as *Yennayer* and *Tafsut*, as a way of performing and embodying Amazighité. Diaspora Imazighen wear these costumes as spectacular rather than functional garments – Tuareg men in music groups wear the attire of the desert including vast enveloping headscarves when performing and Kabyle women pull their dresses on over their 'Western' clothes when they arrive at the venue for a special event. At one such event on the 8 May 2016, around 2,000 people gathered on the 'Esplanade of Human Rights' opposite the Eiffel Tower for Paris's first *Journée de la Robe Kabyle* (Day of the Kabyle Dress). The organisers knew that the event would draw a crowd, emphasising the force for unity that the Kabyle dress represents:

> Everyone feels implicated by the Kabyle dress. I don't think a single Kabyle household in France is lacking one. Very few Kabyle women don't have one, and they're worn at weddings etc. … And we know that we barely ever go out wearing traditional dress, so here we said let's go, a good event for families, it was a dream.

Colourful Kabyle dresses were worn by about a third of the women at the event, and a handful of the men present wore the male costume, the *burnous*. Several women wore henna tattoos of the 'Aza' (ⵣ),[3] and even more wore the symbol in jewellery form. The event had a festival atmosphere that was unmistakably North African, while embodying non-Arabic *Amazighité*.

Although wearing Amazigh costume performs indigeneity by embodying an aesthetic of alterity to both the 'Western' and the 'Arabo-Islamic', it can also, however, be silent, passive and gendered in a way that essentialises, disempowers and fixes it. As Sarah Hunt writes, 'in order to be legible [to Western eyes], Indigenous geographic knowledge must adhere to recognised forms of representation' (2014, p. 29), and Amazigh costume worn as an 'authentic' cultural object fixes this knowledge on the bodies of the (female) diaspora population. Identified in the anthropological literature as the 'trap of visibility' or the 'cunning of recognition' (Povinelli, 2002), this means that being acknowledged as Indigenous through performing cultural 'authenticity' frequently entails behaving in ways that reinforce the stereotypes and expectations of wider society. Indigenous peoples often have limited power to define what is 'authentic' vis-à-vis state hegemony. However, diaspora Imazighen articulate these claims to cultural authenticity with other forms of diaspora activism in relation to home and host societies. Always 'out of place', at a distance to the imagined and essentialised Amazigh subject of rural North Africa, embodiments of Amazigh indigeneity can be made dynamic, political and vocal through the activism of diaspora members: the subaltern speaks through the diaspora.

In other words, wearing Amazigh costume and exclusively using Tamazight, written or spoken, does political work. The tones and cadences of the language are markers of difference, which, like the Amazigh costume, are put on display at specific times and in circumscribed spaces in the diaspora. To quote Hunt's formulation that the embodiment of indigeneity is 'lived, practiced, and relational' (2014), speaking Tamazight achieves this embodiment because it requires making a distinctive sound, hearing, understanding and dialogue with other people; whereas the Amazigh costume is silent and passive, speaking Tamazight is active and vocal. These are only two examples of how the Amazigh diaspora performs Indigenous authenticity and makes visible its difference. As with the 'cunning of recognition', the benefits of this visibility for preserving and promoting *Amazighité* exist in tension with the essentialisation of Amazigh culture that comes with it. Aware of this, diaspora association members invest considerable time, energy and resources in the ongoing use of Tamazight as the vehicle for Amazigh thought and cultural expression. Diaspora associations remain key sites for language revitalisation due to their ability to create 'secure linguistic environments' and articulate a moral politics of authenticity based on the minoritised status of language and the knowledge associated with it.

Village territoriality

Finally, village territoriality is also a key part of the Amazigh diaspora's Indigenous positioning, expressed through the continued institution of village committees, traditional forms of village sociability and politics, habitation and *restoration*, and the continued practice of *returning* exemplified in repatriating the deceased for burial. Nassim Amrouche argues that if the Amazigh village is presented as 'a timeless or eternal place, inscribed in a legendary continuity, the foundation of indigeneity, it also offers a solid anchoring in time and a historical conscience that is reintroduced in the political struggle' (2013, p. 59) of the Amazigh movement. Rooting in the material environment of the village in this way underlines the Indigenous territoriality of the Imazighen, in contrast to the cultural hegemony of urban, Arabic-speaking North Africa.

Amazigh diaspora members trace their origins to a specific village and/or lineage, and encourage each other to recover knowledge of these origins if it has been 'lost'. For example, the MAK-Anavad's *Carte d'Identité Kabyle* (CIK) identifies the bearer's village (*taddart*) and confederation (*aarch*), deliberately evoking pre-colonial political institutions (Roberts, 2014) and prompting applicants to research their family heritage. The enduring importance of village connections articulates Amazigh identity with rurality and 'traditional society'. Tamazight language classes, despite being taken in classrooms in urban Paris or Marseille, constantly position the language within the imagined rural village setting. Beginners learn vocabulary related to village life ('paths' rather than 'roads', 'field' rather than 'office'), study dialogues set in village settings, and are constantly reminded of the rurality of the language in the French and Arabic loan words used to describe urban phenomena and modern technology (e.g. *Takarrost* = Car [French *carrosse*]). Associations frequently hold and display village artefacts such as different clay jars or bridles, brought back by their members from their usually annual return visits. Village committees, informal organisations that regroup, represent and govern the diaspora population of a given village, are both an important part of the organisational structure of the diaspora and a commonly evoked Indigenous political institution.

Amazigh village committees, particularly Kabyle ones, have operated in France for several decades (Lacroix, 2012). Principally, they act as a support network for new migrants, pooling resources to pay for infrastructural improvements in the village of origin and to repatriate the bodies of their members for burial. Their organisation reflects the *tajmaât* (meeting place), which captured the imagination of the mostly French ethnographers, administrators and missionaries of the colonial period, who saw this village-level political institution as 'unchanged' and 'ancient', unique to the purportedly 'secular' and 'democratic' Berber society. Though this assessment has been challenged and nuanced by political historians (Roberts, 2014; Temlali, 2015), these received ideas remain strong in the Amazigh movement today. In its essential and idealised form as explained by Kabyle leaders in the diaspora, the *tajmaât* includes every man[4] in the village and takes place in a designated common space. Decisions are taken unanimously, and so lengthy debates are aimed at building compromise and convincing those in opposition to a given idea, rather than a 'majority rules' version of democracy. Every man's opinion needs to be heard on a given issue and every man's voice should have equal weight, and consequently a man's ability to deliver good speeches, drawing on poetic forms and classical themes, is admired. In practising *tajmaât* as an enduring pre-colonial political institution unique to the Imazighen, diaspora members position themselves as Indigenous by articulating cultural difference, anteriority, a rejection of state institutions and an insistence on the village as the basic unit of political organisation.

Diaspora village committees practise village territoriality by funding infrastructural improvements and repatriating the deceased for burial. With each repatriation costing upwards of €2,000, the collective insurance that the village committee represents is a strong draw for its members. Burial amongst ancestors in the home village forms part of a cosmology of the presence of ancestors in the lives of their families, evidenced in ethnographic work in Amazigh villages (Scheele, 2009; Silverstein, 2015), but also in art and popular culture. For example, Mouloud Feraoun's *La Terre et le Sang* (1953) [Land and Blood], a favourite novel often included in Amazigh diaspora book sales, features an Amazigh man returning to his village with his French wife and includes several scenes in the village cemetery where the living characters go to be with the dead, play and socialise. More recently Nora Chaouche's *L'étrangère française* (2011), exhibited at the ACB in November 2015 as part of their monthly literary event, includes the dead grandmother of a young Amazigh immigrant as one of the novel's key characters. Regardless of the extent of popular belief in the continued presence of ancestors in the world of the living, repatriation for burial remains sufficiently important for village committees to raise significant funds to achieve it and remains focused on the village cemetery.

The rehabilitation of particular sites within the village environment, notably the *tajmaât* and the *tala* (fountain), which are seen as central places of Amazigh sociability, is often funded by the diaspora population. A member of *IDmediterranée*, a France-based development organisation focused on Amazigh regions in North Africa, explained her part in the rehabilitation of the village *tala*:

> I'm very attached to the fountain of my village. The fountain is a symbol … For me, this place is important even though we have piped water these days. I've worked so that these fountains might be rehabilitated, embellished, for the pleasure of the village.

This nostalgia for a fading Amazigh village society, whose social, political and economic institutions should be preserved in the face of transformative forces and processes, is widely shared by diasporic Imazighen. The traditional house (*axxam*) is mapped, reconstructed and actively restored, and its loss in the landscape bemoaned by diaspora Amazigh association members:

> My sisters were raised in a traditional house. And now my uncle has torn it down and put a garage over it. My sisters are really angry. They [the villagers] don't have a clue about architecture and its value. There are architects now working on [restoring traditional architecture] because it's part of the landscape, our culture.

The *axxam* remains a powerful imaginary for the Kabyle diaspora, removed from 'home' and nostalgic for it. If it is relatively well known amongst sociologists, it is because it figures as a central example of Pierre Bourdieu's concept of 'habitus', which he developed following fieldwork carried out amongst Kabyle refugees during the Algerian War (Goodman and Silverstein, 2009). However, the *axxam* he describes, with all its perfectly balanced dualisms, symbolic forms and structures, was always an idealised version of the real houses left behind, remembered through the collective memory of an exiled group. Today, in the Amazigh diaspora in France, this idealised *axxam* remains a powerful identity symbol as well as a locus of territoriality. It is a prized possession, the subject of poems and songs, the setting for Amazigh theatre adaptions, the inspiration for interior decoration in many Amazigh activists' homes, even as it disappears from the landscape in rural North Africa. By enrolling the *axxam* as an identity symbol, diaspora Imazighen articulate indigeneity within a quintessentially non-Western, non-Islamic cosmology.

As Amrouche (2013, p. 61) argues: 'The (re)construction of language, tribe and village is in the image of the projected culture: an attempt to give form to an imagined past and community.' This 'attempt to give form' can be understood as territoriality, which, in the Amazigh diaspora, determines relationships of exteriority and alterity in relation to an Indigenous subjectivity. The village, embodied difference in Amazigh costume and spoken Tamazight discourses of colonisation and exile, as well as solidarities and articulations with the Indigenous Movement globally all point towards the Indigenous diaspora. The diaspora's projection of 'Tamazgha', which in turn is a projection of its own groupness, centres on idealised village spaces under colonial oppression, traditional costume and Tamazight in the face of enforced Arabisation, and a place among the global constellation of Indigenous peoples.

Conclusion

The diaspora does not merely exist as an automatic consequence of immigration but is continually reproduced and constituted by the multiple structures, events and practices that articulate Amazigh identity. As such, the positionings outlined above, articulated together within the discourse and practice of the diasporic Amazigh movement, do political work. Much of this work is intended to legitimise claims to the resources of the state, to sovereignty, and to acceptable difference in the French postcolonial context. It is therefore important that these articulations are secular and culturally defined, non-essentialist, and generally commensurate with French

Republican worldviews (Harris, 2020b). In fact, by specifically claiming and embodying non-Arab, non-Islamic identity within an Indigenous framing, the diasporic Amazigh movement has appealed to the nativism and Islamophobia of the French Right (Harris, 2020c).

This chapter has explored four key positionings in which disparate subjectivities are articulated with indigeneity in the discourse and practices of the diasporic Amazigh movement. First, diaspora Imazighen articulate *Amazighité* and indigeneity through the Global Indigenous Movement. Second, they position themselves and their homeland populations as colonised people. Third, they perform cultural authenticity within an 'Indigenous project' of cultural preservation and revitalisation. Fourth, diaspora Imazighen, particularly Kabyles, practise a village territoriality that articulates with indigeneity through the privileging of rurality and pre-colonial political institutions. These positionings are not always explicit strategies of the diasporic Amazigh movement, nor are they only the product of the agency of its members. They are constantly negotiated and reiterated, performed through the everyday politics of diaspora life. These four positionings are not exhaustive, but highlight the diverse, relational ways in which indigeneity is articulated in diaspora. It is significant that the discourse and politics of indigeneity have been led by the diaspora and are only very recently emerging in the Amazigh movement 'on the ground' in North Africa – reflecting the role of the diaspora as an enduring space of political and cultural innovation for the Amazigh movement. As the concept and politics of indigeneity translate into the Middle East and North Africa, it is worth paying attention to its mutability, relationality and diasporic manifestations.

Notes

1 For continuity within this chapter, I refer to Tamazight as the catch-all term for all Amazigh language(s).
2 Appearing during the founding years of the French Revolution in Robespierre's *Club des Jacobins*, this core element of French political culture radically asserts the equality of individual citizens. This has made French political culture particularly resistant to forms of regionalism and multiculturalism.
3 The Aza (ⵣ) is the first letter of the Tamazight alphabet, Tifinagh. It is found on the Amazigh flag, symbolising freedom and the Amazigh movement generally.
4 Women are not widely admitted to *tajmaât*, though some are changing as Kabyle women struggle for gender equality.

References

Aïtel, F. (2013) 'Between Algeria and France: the origins of the Berber movement', *French Cultural Studies*, 24(1), pp. 63–76.
Amrouche, N. (2013) 'La représentation du village dans la revendication berbériste', *Ethnologie française*, 43(1), pp. 55–63.
Amselle, J. (2012) 'Au nom des peuples: primitivismes et postcolonialismes', *Critique*, 776–777(1), pp. 165–177.
Beaman, J. (2017) *Citizen Outsider: Children of North African Immigrants in France*. Oakland, CA: University of California Press.
Brubaker, R. (2005) 'The "diaspora" diaspora', *Journal of Ethnic and Racial Studies*, 28(1), pp. 1–19.
Chaker, S. (1985) 'Berbérité et émigration kabyle', *Peuples Méditerranéens*, 31–32, pp. 217–225.
Clifford, J. (1997) *Routes: Travel and Translation in the Late Twentieth Century*. London: Harvard University Press.
Clifford, J. (2013) *Returns: Becoming Indigenous in the Twenty-First Century*. Cambridge, MA: Harvard University Press.
Coombes, B., Johnson, J. and Howitt, R. (2012) 'Indigenous geographies II: the aspirational spaces in postcolonial politics – reconciliation, belonging and social provision', *Progress in Human Geography*, 37(5), pp. 691–700.

Dirèche-Slimani, K. (1997) *Histoire de l'émigration kabyle en France au XXe siècle; Réalités culturelles et politiques et réappropriations identitaires*. Paris: L'Harmattan.
Fredette, J. (2014) *Constructing Muslims in France: Discourse, Public Identity, and the Politics of Citizenship*. Philadelphia, PA: Temple University Press.
Gagné, N. (2016) 'The waxing and waning of the politics of authenticity: the situation of urban-based Māori through the lens of municipal politics', *City and Society*, 28(1), pp. 48–73.
Goodman, J. and Silverstein, P. (2009) *Bourdieu in Algeria*. Lincoln, NE: University of Nebraska Press.
Hall, S. (1988) 'The toad in the garden: Thatcherism among the theorists', in Nelson, C. and Grossberg, L. (eds) *Marxism and the Interpretation of Culture*. Urbana, IL: University of Illinois Press, pp. 35–74.
Hall, S. (1996) 'On postmodernism and articulation: an interview with Stuart Hall', in Morley, D. and Chen, K.-H. (eds) *Stuart Hall: Critical Dialogues in Cultural Studies*. London: Routledge, pp. 131–150.
Harris, J. (2020a) 'Assembling the diasporic nation: Kabylia at the CONIFA World Football Cup', in *Sport and Secessionism*. Abingdon: Routledge, pp. 196–210.
Harris, J. (2020b) 'Imazighen of France: articulations of an indigenous diaspora', *Journal of Ethnic and Migration Studies*, pp. 1–16. doi:10.1080/1369183x.2020.1788382
Harris, J. (2020c) 'Nativist-populism, the internet and the geopolitics of indigenous diaspora', *Political Geography*, 102124.
Hunt, S. (2014) 'Ontologies of Indigeneity: the politics of embodying a concept', *Cultural Geographies*, 21(1), pp. 27–32.
Jeffrey, A. (2013) *The Improvised State: Sovereignty, Performance and Agency in Dayton, Bosnia*. Oxford: Wiley-Blackwell.
Kuper, A. (2003) 'The return of the native', *Cultural Anthropology*, 44(3), pp. 389–402.
Lacroix, T. (2012) 'Transnationalisme villageois et développement: Kabyles algériens, Chleuhs marocains en France et Panjabis indiens en Grande-Bretagne', *Revue européenne des migrations internationales*, 28(1), pp. 71–84.
Li, T.M. (2000) 'Articulating Indigenous identity in Indonesia: resource politics and the tribal slot', *Comparative Studies in Society and History*, 42(1), pp. 149–179.
Loyola-Hernández, L. (2018) 'The porous state: female mayors performing the state in Yucatecan Maya municipalities', *Political Geography*, 62, pp. 48–57.
Oiry-Varacca, M. (2013) 'Les revendications autochtones au Maroc. Pour une approche postcoloniale pragmatique', *Espace, populations, sociétés*, 1(1), pp. 41–54.
Povinelli, E.A. (2002) *The Cunning of Recognition: Indigenous Alterities and the Making of Australian Multiculturalism*. Durham, NC: Duke University Press.
Radcliffe, S. (2017) 'Geography and indigeneity II: critical geographies of indigenous bodily politics', *Progress in Human Geography*, 42(3), pp. 1–10.
Roberts, H. (2014) *Berber Government: The Kabyle Polity in Pre-Colonial Algeria*. London: I.B. Tauris.
Rubio-Marín, R. (2003) 'Language rights: exploring competing rationales', in Kymlicka, W. and Patten, A. (eds) *Language Rights and Political Theory*. New York: Oxford University Press, pp. 52–79.
Sayad, A. (1999) *La Double Absence*. Paris: Le Seuil.
Scheele, J. (2009) *Village Matters: Knowledge, Politics an Community in Kabylia, Algeria*. London: James Currey.
Silverstein, P. (2004) *Algeria in France*. Bloomington, IN: Indiana University Press.
Silverstein, P. (2015) 'The diaspora and the cemetery: emigration and social transformation in a Moroccan oasis community', *The Journal of North African Studies*, 20(1), pp. 92–108.
Temlali, Y. (2015) *La Genèse de la Kabylie: Aux origines de l'affirmation berbère en Algérie (1830–1962)*. Algiers: Barzakh.
Tuhiwai Smith, L. (2004) *Decolonizing Methodologies*. London: Zed Books.

9

VALORISING SOME AND MARGINALISING OTHERS

The diasporic field in the making of Lebanon

Paul Tabar and Wahib Maalouf

Scholarly writings on diaspora have broadly focused on developing the definition of the concept by making it more suitable for analysing cross-border engagements of migrant communities with their country of origin (Cohen, 2008; 2009). In this context, scholars have examined the role of diaspora communities and their contribution to the politics of their homelands (e.g. voting, contribution to peacebuilding or war-making) and their economies (e.g. remittances, economic development and investments, skill transfer). Another contribution to the understanding of modern diasporas comes from scholarly discussions on nationalism instigated by Benedict Anderson's seminal book *Imagined Communities* (Anderson, 1991). An innovative work on the origin and characteristics of nationalism, Anderson's book also discussed 'long-distance nationalism' in which he shed light on the role of exiles and migrants in the formative process of creating national identities. Nina Glick-Schiller (2005), among others, later joined the debate and provided a more nuanced understanding of 'long-distance nationalism', arguing that the latter takes four different forms. Taking the 'anti-colonial' form as a starting point in our discussion, we introduce the concept of a diasporic political field (Tabar and Maalouf, 2016), believing that it enables researchers to further understand diasporic contributions to home politics, and more particularly, to capture the complexity and power relations involved in the nation-building process culminating in the creation of Greater Lebanon in 1920.[1]

Our introduction of the concept of a diasporic political field stems from two reasons. First, we choose diasporic and not transnational to describe this political field because, while the two overlap, they are not the same. Broadly speaking, transnational activities refer to cross-border relations between groups and individuals regardless of their ethnic and national identities and the geographical orientation of their activities. Diasporic relations, on the other hand, are formed and enacted by actors sharing a common ethnic-cum-national identity and are oriented towards their country of origin. Diasporic relations are transnational, but not all transnational relations are diasporic (Tabar, 2019).

The concept of 'field' is borrowed from Pierre Bourdieu's writings.[2] Although this concept is used to analyse a nation-state bounded society, we use it here to examine cross-border diasporic relations. More importantly, the concept helps us to frame diasporic political relations beyond the simple relations implied by long-distance nationalism. In other words, it enables us

DOI: 10.4324/9780429266102-11

to reveal the constellation of power relations that develop out of these cross-border relations, the struggles they generate and the state investment in these relations as a regulatory power. Before 1920, of course, the Lebanese nation-state did not exist; rather, it was a highly contested project in the making. This reality gave a greater role for state (Ottoman and later colonial European states) and non-state actors (the diaspora originating from what later became part of Greater Lebanon) in determining the outcomes of the struggles that were taking place in the diasporic political field around the objective of creating a new Lebanese nation-state. The diaspora originating from Mount Lebanon, *wilayat* Beirut (an Ottoman administrative province) and the surrounding regions was engaged in a twofold project: on one hand, they were advocating a variety of conflicting nation-building projects, and, on the other, they were taking part in creating a state necessary for upholding and valorising their particular nationalist identity and its associated activities.

In sum, we examine the role of the diaspora in the creation of Greater Lebanon by focusing on its political and historical-cultural (i.e. symbolic) contribution to this highly contested process. The recent work by Fahrenthold (2019) notwithstanding, writings on the subject have been scattered and highly descriptive. Most importantly, they are rich in primary sources on which we draw to provide a more focused and analytical reading of the diaspora and their activities directed at their place of origin. We also argue that drawing critically on recent writings on long-distance nationalism and Bourdieu's concept of field, as well as accounting for the diaspora's transfers to their country of origin in terms of political and symbolic remittances, allow us to examine an as of yet neglected chapter in the history of modern Lebanon.

Emigration and politics prior to the outbreak of the First World War

Starting in the first decade of the twentieth century when Mount Lebanon was under the rule of the Mount Lebanon Mutasarrifate (*mutasarrifiyyah*),[3] emigrants from Mount Lebanon living abroad sought liberation from the Ottoman rule by appealing to the foreign powers, especially the French, who acted as the protectors of Christians in Lebanon in the face of Ottoman rule. Christian émigrés like Boulous Noujaym and Yousef al-Sawda played a vital role in deepening the national sentiments in the homeland and abroad by advancing a strong economic, political and historical case for the expansion of the borders of the Mutasarrifate to the borders of Greater Lebanon (Zamir, 1985).

Other emigrants, most notably in Egypt, France and the United States, founded diasporic political associations of Lebanese nationalist leanings that were engaged in activism and lobbying efforts in Western capitals, all aimed at achieving liberation from Ottoman rule and establishing an independent Lebanese nation-state.[4] These emigrants and diasporic political associations benefited from the free climate present in the countries of their residence, as opposed to the restrictions they faced in their place of origin, and were influenced by the nationalist ideas prevalent in Egypt at the time, which added more momentum to their political engagement aimed at achieving Lebanon's independence (Kaufman, 2004).

The totality of diaspora activities originating mainly from Mount Lebanon and directed towards establishing an independent Lebanese entity took two forms: first, the formulation of historical and literary narratives (i.e. symbolic capital) aiming to legitimise the establishment of this new nation; and, second, taking up political positions and engaging in political activities that sought to build the political capital required to establish this nation. We discuss these two forms of engagement in the next sections to illustrate the diasporic political field and the emergence of the Lebanese nation-state.

The production of symbolic capital for an emerging Lebanon

The migrants who contributed symbolically to the creation of Greater Lebanon were part of the first wave of emigration from Mount Lebanon, stretching from the mid-nineteenth century until the end of Ottoman rule (Labaki, 2019). During this period, Mount Lebanon underwent important external and internal transformations: migration on a large scale, the growing penetration of European economic, cultural and political influence, and the development of Western-style education,[5] resulting in the emergence of a new educated elite who 'found it difficult to adapt to the existing economic, social and political structures' (ibid., p. 28). This 'educational outburst' contributed to 'feeding the migration waves, especially towards Egypt and the United States of America' (ibid., p. 29).

The diasporic intellectuals who emerged during the first two decades of the twentieth century were part of these migration waves. More importantly, their contribution to the building of the symbolic capital essential for the creation of Greater Lebanon was prolific and significant, but also conflictual, as it reflected the diverse and sometimes contradictory political and ideological outlooks often held by the diaspora. These contributions can be seen as part of an emerging symbolic historical sub-field which was, in turn, part of the emerging diasporic field. It is an emerging field because, as mentioned earlier, the nation-state associated with this field did not exist before September 1920. Hence, before this date, the Ottoman Empire acted as the regulatory power in this emerging diasporic field (and all its sub-fields) in that it had the ultimate power to determine the legitimacy of any narrative or action or value circulating within it. These diasporic historical narratives were circulating in the field but lacked recognition by the Ottoman authorities, who held the ultimate power to provide the legitimate political 'vision of the social world' (Bourdieu, 2000, as quoted in Kim, 2018, p. 265). The proponents of these narratives were competing with the Ottoman Empire's narrative and with each other for exclusive legitimacy until the state of Greater Lebanon was finally founded and valorised the historical narrative favouring its creation.

Between 1905 and 1920, migrant intellectuals, such as Ferdinand Tyan, Boulus Noujaym, Yousef al-Sawda and Jack Tabet, formulated different and sometimes conflicting historical narratives related to the identity of the nation-states they were battling to create in the post-Ottoman period. Hence, these writings became a site of struggle over the identity and political system of the Arab territories previously attached to the disintegrating Ottoman Empire, including the idea of a Christian Mount Lebanon under French guardianship, a Syrian federal state with Phoenician identity (also under French tutelage) and an independent Greater Lebanon (Firro, 2003).

The main proponents of the Lebanist[6] national narrative, namely Boulus Noujaym, Yousef al-Sawda and August Adib, were emigrants who acquired university education and professional experience in France and Egypt, which, we believe, brought them recognition and reputation among the public in the 'homeland' and abroad.[7] This acquired status, in our view, granted their writings and political views more influence and credibility in the eyes of the receiving audience both at home and abroad. In the language of Bourdieu, they were able to exercise a considerable degree of 'symbolic power' by making this audience accept their narratives unquestioningly.[8]

According to Elise Salem's (2003) study on the cultural and literary evolution of Lebanon as a nation, the writings of these immigrant intellectuals acquired greater significance because they were largely consistent with many historical and literary narratives that appeared in the second half of the nineteenth century. The first historical narrative was the Lebanese Phoenician narrative, whose origin can be traced to the year 1864 when French nationalist thinker Ernest Renan published his book, *Mission en Phenicie*, after a team of French archaeologists discovered the remains of ancient Phoenician antiquities on the Lebanese coast (Salem, 2003). These discoveries likely gave substantial support to the narrative of the Phoenician origin of modern Lebanon formulated by various Lebanese migrant Christian intellectuals.

One of the nascent writings about a Lebanist national narrative was emigrant Ferdinand Tyan's booklet *La Nationalité Maronite* (The Maronite Nationality). Published in Paris in 1905, it called for the establishment of an independent Maronite Emirate in Mount Lebanon (Hakim, 2013). However, it was Bulus Noujaym's book *La question du Liban* (The Lebanon Question that was the first and most elaborate study that presented a strong case in favour of the establishment of an independent Lebanese entity, calling for the expansion of the Mutasarrifate that was established in 1861. Noujaym published his book in French in 1908 under the pseudonym of Jouplain, after living for a few years in Paris, during which he completed a doctorate in law and another in political science (ibid.).

The importance of Boulus Noujaym's view of Lebanon is that it is far from being chauvinistic and is closer to the pragmatic view that takes into account the 'geopolitical' factors that had started to gain currency in Europe during his stay in France (Kattar, 1998). This perspective goes a long way to explain the author's call to annex fertile agricultural areas such as the *Bekaa* (where the Assi and Litani rivers pass) and *Marje'youn* to the Mutasarrifate, in addition to Saidon, Beirut, Hula, Akkar and Tripoli. In doing so, Noujaym also invoked the economic justification for the creation of Greater Lebanon. By capitalising on his migrant cultural capital[9] (i.e. university degree) and publishing a book on the history of Lebanon, Noujaym could be construed as sending symbolic (cultural-historical) remittances to the 'homeland', which played a pivotal role in crystallising and justifying the idea of Greater Lebanon. With the publication of his dissertation in 1908, Noujaym's argument for Greater Lebanon was coming to have an effect on certain educated elites who were theorising for, and working towards, establishing a Lebanese state within the Mutasarrifate.

Noujaym's book was followed two years later by the publication of 'The Lebanese Issue', a book by a Lebanese migrant in Egypt, Yousef al-Sawda. In this book, al-Sawda stressed the independence of the Lebanese entity and, in line with Noujaym's ideas, called for the annexation of the Bekaa region to the Mutasarrifate to support its economy. Al-Sawda travelled to Egypt after completing high school and joined the French law office in Cairo, obtaining his degree in 1908. He then practised law in Alexandria and lived there until 1922 before returning to Lebanon. During his stay in Egypt, as Middle East historian Asher Kaufman (2004) notes, al-Sawda was influenced by the nationalist ideas of Mustafa Kamel, the Egyptian activist against British colonialism. However, it was in 1919, during the convening of the Peace Conference in Paris, that al-Sawda published his book *Fi Sabeel Lubnan* [For Lebanon's Sake] in Egypt, which included his more elaborate vision of Lebanese nationalism. In it, he formulated a historical narrative of Lebanese nationalism premised on glorifying the Phoenician origins of the Lebanese people – 'civilisation was born on the slopes of Lebanon's mountain, and ripened on its shores, and from there, the Phoenicians carried it to the four corners of the Earth' (ibid., p. 62).

As Kaufman's (2004) historical account shows, another migrant in Egypt during the same period, August Adib, also contributed to the Lebanese national narrative through his book *Le Liban après la Guerre* (Lebanon After the War), published in Paris in 1918. Adib's book clearly stated that the Lebanese are descendants of the Phoenicians, providing a historical context and serving as a bedrock for the political demands that followed the end of the First World War, calling for the establishment of an independent Lebanese national entity in its present borders. Adib, much like al-Sawda, contributed to the construction and spread of the 'Phoenician ancestry of Lebanon' narrative and, as Kaufman observes, 'his Phoenician-Lebanist ideas were a product of his stay in Egypt where he was influenced by the Egyptian National movement that had also called for a separatist Pharaonic version of the Egyptian national identity' (ibid., pp. 62–63).

It is striking here that the historical narratives of Noujaym, al-Sawda and Adib share a common feature: the use of ancient history to 'invent traditions', a concept coined by British historian Eric Hobsbawm, who argues that many 'traditions' that 'appear or claim to be old are often quite recent in origin and sometimes invented' (Hobsbawm, 1983, p. 1). That is, old materials are used here to build 'invented traditions' of a new type and for entirely new purposes. This phenomenon is particularly evident in the modern development of the concepts of nation and nationalism.

From our perspective, Boulus Noujaym's claim about the size of Lebanon as equivalent to the territories that came under the reign of Emir Fakhreddine (1590–1633) and the Shehabist emirs (1697–1840) lacks historical accuracy, as the territorial concept of the state was relatively new in the region and saw its realisation only after the end of the First World War. As for the writings of al-Sawda and Adib, stressing the 'Phoenician origin' of Lebanon and the historical continuity of the 'Lebanese nation' since the time of the Phoenicians, they completely dismisses the subsequent cultural transformations that 'Lebanon' had since witnessed.

The invention of tradition aims primarily to unify the group, enhance its cohesion and give it a psychological and moral refuge from decline in the face of the narratives and traditions of rival groups that may be stronger, more numerous and more advanced. In this sense, the invention of tradition leads to the unification of the group and contributes to its transformation into 'an imagined political community – and imagined as both inherently limited and sovereign', as defined by Benedict Anderson (1991, pp. 6–7).

The other historical narrative competing for dominance with the Lebanese narrative was the Syrian narrative, mainly represented by three diasporic intellectuals: Khairallah Khairallah, George Samneh and Jacques Tabet. According to historian Kais Firro, Khairallah conflated Syria with Greater Lebanon, Samneh called for an autonomous Greater Lebanon within Syria, while Tabet advocated for a Syrian federal union in which Lebanon would play a leading role. Tabet also emphasised the Phoenician identity of Syria as distinct from Arab identity (Firro, 2003).

Clearly, the intellectuals (journalists, lawyers and political activists) within the diaspora were active in producing historical narratives in line with their vision of the nation-state they wanted to be founded. Of course, any of these narratives is insufficient in itself to lead to the creation of the sought-after nation-state. However, this chapter seeks to acknowledge the symbolic and central role played by these intellectuals in providing a comprehensive 'historical' narrative necessary to valorise the political project of creating the nation they had in mind and in inventing the 'traditions' attached to this narrative.

In the symbolic 'literary sub-field' that was emerging as part of the diasporic field, early seeds of the formation of the Lebanese nation can be found in the writings of Lebanese immigrants, particularly Gibran Khalil Gibran. Born in 1883, poverty led Gibran to immigrate to Boston with his mother and siblings in 1895 (Salem, 2003). He lived in Boston and later New York, where he formed himself as a painter and writer and participated, in 1920, in founding the Pen League.[10]

In his first literary works in Arabic, which were gaining growing popularity in Lebanon and Syria under Ottoman rule, Gibran recurrently used the Phoenician dimension, often 'juxtaposed to other ancient civilisations, or religions, constructing an image of Lebanon that is rich in cultural heritage' (ibid., p. 18). For example, in his novel, *The Broken Wings* (Gibran 2008 [1912]), first published in 1912, Gibran associates the land that later became part of Greater Lebanon with a Phoenician past extensively.

Another example of Gibran's contribution to establishing the Lebanese national narrative was through imbuing this Phoenicianism with a spiritual meaning, 'as his Phoenician references were often linked to gods and temples located within a Lebanese landscape' (Salem, 2003, p. 19). Sometimes, that spirituality was clearly linked to Christian symbols, which made it resonate in a developing nationalist setting, 'as it instils sacred substance into the secular idea of the nation' (ibid., p. 19).

Gibran infused Lebanese nature with Phoenician elements and ancient religious and Christian symbols, thus drawing a picture of a place that is distinct in relation to its surroundings. It is quite significant that Gibran's descriptions occurred during a period when the idea of the Lebanese nation was still forming. This gave his writings a formative value, evidenced in their appropriation by the dominant symbolic field that emerged after the creation of Greater Lebanon in 1920. The nation-building process in Lebanon still presents Gibran as an icon of the Lebanese identity.

Moreover, Gibran used a literary style that was influenced by the vernacular language, an aspect that differentiated it from the Arab writers in the same period. It was a literary style characterised by clarity and simplicity of expression, in contrast with the ornamentation and verbosity typical of classical Arabic prose at the time. After the publication of *The Broken Wings*, Mikhail Naimy, a literary figure from Mount Lebanon and a member of the Pen League, described its writing style as 'the dawn of a new literary era' (1978, pp. 150–151). Soon after the creation of Greater Lebanon, Gibran's writing style became the dominant style of writing in Lebanese literary and journalistic circles. We believe that it is this literary style more so than the content of Gibran's writings that was appropriated by the Lebanists after 1920, to give a literary identity to their conception of Lebanese nationalism. In this sense, it could be argued that Gibran contributed indirectly to the foundation of a Lebanese trend in Arabic literature, which also played a role in defining the newly emerging Lebanese identity. More importantly, the dominance of the Lebanese national narrative after 1920 allowed the Lebanists to appropriate Gibran's writings for their own purposes and sideline his support for a non-Arab Greater Syria. That said, the 'victory' of the Lebanese national narrative was not only an outcome of the struggle in the symbolic literary/historical field but also made possible by the outcomes of various other 'struggles'. In the following section, we examine the political struggle as it manifested itself in the diaspora.

Remitting politically for Greater Lebanon

Diasporic associations were engaged in diverse political activities geared towards achieving liberation from Ottoman rule and establishing an independent imagined homeland. Similar to the status of the historical writings examined above, these activities were often conflictual in character, reflecting the opposing political projects they aimed to serve, and are also best understood as part of the nascent diasporic political field. These activities included writing articles and signing petitions in support of the national liberation movement in the homeland, sending memorandums to the foreign embassies of the Great Powers for the same purpose, and even attending and participating in the Paris Peace Conference. All these activities can be termed as forms of political remittances.[11]

After 1909, both Yousef al-Sawda and Khairallah Khairallah, while in Egypt and Paris respectively, were engaged in sending political remittances to the homeland by issuing memorandums to the 'The Big Seven' countries, including the Allies. In these memorandums, they advocated for the expansion of the Mutasarrifate and the restoration of its 'historical and geographical borders'. Al-Sawda and Khairallah were also members of two active diasporic associations known for their strong Lebanese nationalist leanings, 'The Lebanese Union' in Egypt and 'The Lebanese Association in Paris', respectively (Karam, 2003).

According to Karam, prominent members of the Lebanese Union, which had branches in many Egyptian cities, engaged in various activities, such as conducting meetings, writing and publishing articles, poems and books, all aiming to educate the 'Lebanese people' in the homeland and abroad and strengthen their sense of national identity. In addition, the Union kept the officials of the Great Powers informed about the activities in support of the Lebanese cause. It was easy for the Lebanese Union to make its position public, given its links with the press in Egypt. In fact, Lebanese migrants were running important Egyptian newspapers, including *Al-Ahram*, which was founded by the Takla brothers, one of whom, Gabriel, was an active member of the Union (ibid.). Similarly, Karam argues that *Al Houda*, Noam Moukarzel's New York-based newspaper, played an important role in disseminating the political views of the Lebanese Union in the United States of America, while the Parisian newspaper *Le Temps* covered its activities and published some of its political statements. One of the editors of *Le Temps* was Khairallah, who at the same time supported the Union's political objectives (ibid.).

Karam divides the political activities of the Lebanese Union into three phases: before, during and after the First World War. In the pre-war period, the Union focused on preserving the independent status of Mount Lebanon by countering attempts to annex it to the Ottoman Empire. It promoted the idea of a Lebanese political entity among the Lebanese communities abroad and encouraged them to support the idea of an emerging Lebanese nation. The Lebanese Union's efforts also resulted in the emergence of other associations, adopting similar political principles, the most active of which were the Lebanese Renaissance in New York and the Lebanese Committee in Paris. In the period before the First World War, the Lebanese Committee in Paris focused its activities on informing European political circles about the Lebanese cause (ibid.).

The analysis provided by Karam states that, in 1914, the Lebanese Committee in Paris was divided into two groups: one supporting Greater Lebanon and the other calling for a French Greater Syria. As a result, Shukri Ghanem, an activist and poet in the French language, founded a new association in 1916 called the Syrian Central Assembly. The Lebanese Committee in Paris raised two basic demands: (1) creating Lebanon as a fully independent country; and (2) defining its borders in line with what Noujaym and al-Sawda called its historical boundaries. During the Peace Conference in Paris in 1919, the association sent a letter to the Secretary-General of the conference requesting him to give it the right to present its political outlook, particularly since the conference had listened to Prince Faisal's call to include Lebanon in the proposed Arab kingdom,[12] and the Syrian Central Assembly's proposal for Greater Syria. The association also sent a copy of its letter to the French foreign minister (ibid.).

As noted earlier, the Syrian Central Assembly was established after the secession from the Lebanese Committee in Paris. Shukri Ghanem chaired the Syrian Central Assembly, and George Samneh was its secretary. However, the French government was behind the idea of establishing this association (Labaki, 2019). Reportedly receiving payments for his activities from companies in Lyon and Marseille, Ghanem called for the creation of a Syrian federation under the French mandate, in which Lebanon would enjoy local self-government (Firro, 2003; Labaki, 2019). Here, the Syrian Central Assembly, through its close ties with the centres of French decision-making, was engaging in sending political remittances in support of Greater Syria, in contrast with the remittances sent by diasporic associations with a Lebanese nationalist outlook in favour of the creation of an independent Lebanese nation-state.

Firro (2003) explains that, in relation also to the rising expectations of a Greater Syria, in 1917, the Lebanese Union submitted a memorandum of protest to the commissions of France,

Britain and Italy in Cairo. Indeed, in 1917, the idea of 'French Syria' or Greater Syria was a priority in French official circles and the chambers of commerce linked to them. The French government aimed at merging Lebanon with a wider political entity, Greater Syria, which would either be linked to the French state or be part of a proposed Arab kingdom (ibid.).

Karam (2003) argues that, when the French government eventually sponsored the first option and abandoned the second, the Lebanese Union focused its efforts mainly on confronting the Syrian-French current, which posed the greatest danger to an independent Lebanon. As Karam's narrative explains, a meeting took place in Cairo in January 1918 between representatives of the Lebanese Union and the French diplomat, Georges Picot. Picot wanted to convince the Lebanese independence movement of the benefits of the French new policy towards Lebanon (ibid.). However, the representatives of the Lebanese Union remained attached to their basic demand for an independent Lebanese entity. Following this meeting, the Lebanese Union became suspicious of the new French policy plans (ibid.).

In response, the Lebanese Union sent a memorandum to the Allied powers and published it in newspapers, emphasising 'Lebanon's independence within its natural borders, with the guarantee of the great powers' (ibid., p. 68). The expression 'with the guarantee of the great powers' was in line with the thirteenth item of the principles announced by US President Woodrow Wilson as well as Article XIV, relating to the establishment of the League of Nations, whose objective was to 'guarantee the independence of the smaller states'. This memo, published in *Le Temps*, displeased French officials, according to Karam (ibid.), and it was denounced by the Syrian Central Assembly.

French official circles portrayed the claim of the Lebanese Union for independence as an act of 'ingratitude and hostility to France' (ibid., p. 69). French propaganda went even further and portrayed the call for independence as an attempt to weaken France's position in front of the Allied powers. The Lebanese Union continued to resist this trend, setting up parties and meetings and engaging in journalistic activities, stressing that its claim to Lebanon's independence 'serves an abstract belief' and identifies with the new international climate supporting the liberation of weak peoples and their independence (ibid., p. 69).

The Lebanese Union also had to confront the Syrian Arab trend that emerged during the war, based on the agreement to establish an Arab kingdom that included Lebanon between Al-Hussein, the Sharif of Mecca, and the British (ibid.). After the end of the war, the Lebanese Union had to confront the Hijazi-Syrian project aimed at linking Lebanon to a broader political entity, Greater Syria, which might become part of the Arab kingdom of Sharif Al-Hussein. In March 1920, Karam states, the Syrian conference met in Damascus, declaring Syria's independence within its natural borders and pledging allegiance to Prince Faisal, the son of Sharif Hussein, as its king, and stating that the Lebanese national aspirations would be taken into account within the borders of Mutasarrifate, excluding the city of Beirut from its conception of Lebanon (ibid.). The Lebanese Union protested and sent a telegram to the administrative council of Mount Lebanon denouncing the idea of keeping Beirut outside Lebanon, and urging the council to defend firmly 'Lebanon's right to independence and its natural borders' (ibid. pp. 77–78). The battle over the national identity of Mount Lebanon and surrounding regions was reaching its climax.

On 31 August 1920, General Gouraud, the French High Commissioner, issued a decision extending the borders of Lebanon. The next day, 1 September, the general announced the establishment of the state of Greater Lebanon with French assistance. Despite this crucial step, the idea of Greater Syria, including Lebanon, remained in circulation and the Lebanese Union continued to oppose it. The Lebanese Union issued a memorandum on the subject on 1 February 1921 to officials and newspapers in Paris and Lebanon, as well as to newspapers of the diaspora. The memo indicated, among other things, the legal gain achieved for the Lebanese cause after the establishment of the state of Greater Lebanon, represented by 'France's recognition of Lebanon's independent entity, within its natural borders' (ibid., pp. 78–79).

As mentioned earlier, the Lebanese Renaissance League, which was founded in 1911 in New York by Noam Moukarzel, the owner of *al-Huda* newspaper, was a sister association of the Lebanese Union. According to Karam, the Lebanese Renaissance League, however, advocated for a Lebanon ruled by France (ibid.). In May 1919, Moukarzel represented the Lebanese Renaissance League at the Peace Conference held in Paris and sent a message to the Maronite Patriarch Elias Al-Houwayek (also participating in the conference) urging him to adopt the League's demand that Lebanon be independent in its natural and historical borders under the auspices of France. In March 1920, he also sent a letter to the President of the Republic of France, appealing to him to achieve the main demands of the League: the independence of Greater Lebanon under the French mandate and the rejection of any relationship that might link Lebanon with Prince Faisal bin Al-Hussein (ibid.).

Another active association in the diaspora during the First World War was the League of Liberation of Syria and Lebanon, which presented the Lebanese Union with another threat. The League was founded in 1917 in New York City, and its administrative body consisted of the physician Ayoub Tabet as president, the philosopher Amin Rihani as vice president, Gibran Khalil Gibran, editor-in-chief in English, and Michael Naimy, editor-in-chief in Arabic. Its programme was based on two points: 'making Syria a federal state consisting of autonomous units that include Mount Lebanon with its ancient borders, and under the direction and protection of France', and 'separating the Syrian issue from the Hijazi movement and from other Arab movements' (ibid. p. 122). The association also sought to free Syria from Turkish control with the help of France and its allies.

One of the association's main activities was a petition sent by Ayoub Tabet in 1918 to US President Wilson and to US Secretary of State Robert Lansing, in which he expressed the association's hopes to end the Turks' control of Syria, in line with President Wilson's principles. In early February 1919, after the Peace Conference started its work in Paris, the association sent another petition to the President of the United States and to the heads of governments of France, Great Britain and Italy, protesting against 'the demands of the delegate of the Hijaz to the conference, claiming that the Syrians favoured putting Syria and Palestine under Arab domination' (ibid., p. 123). The petition stated that Syrians are not Arabs, and that they wanted Syria to become a federation consisting of administratively independent units sponsored by France 'because of the cultural, civilizational and historical ties between the two countries' (ibid., p. 123). In August 1919, the League sent a petition to the heads of the Allied countries in which it renewed its basic demands. In November 1919, Ayoub Tabet presented another memorandum to the first assistant to the United States Secretary of State, in which he opposed 'Faisal's attempts to control Syria, and demanded the implementation of his association's program under the auspices of France, because this sponsorship is the only guarantor of developing Syria' (ibid., p. 124).

In these instances, two diasporic associations – the League for the Liberation of Syria and Lebanon and the Syrian Central Assembly – were engaging in the emerging and conflictual diasporic field by remitting politically to Lebanon and Syria in favour of Greater Syria as a distinct political entity separate from any Arab nation or identity. These remittances also stood in opposition to those favouring an independent Lebanese entity sent by diasporic associations with Lebanist nationalist leanings. But as mentioned above, Greater Lebanon was finally created on 1 September 1920, and the process of valorising the claims for Greater Lebanon began on stronger institutional and legal grounds. Based on our reading of the events, counterclaims for

Greater Syria and a United Arab Syrian federation started to recede and lose support from the emerging local and French authorities. In 1926, a constitution for Greater Lebanon was promulgated. French mandatory authorities and emerging state institutions and authorities were by definition against any Syrian or Arab political trends.

According to Middle East historian Stacey Fahrenthold, another type of diasporic political engagement was the Syrian diaspora's pro-Allies military mobilisation, which began in 1916 with the formation of the Légion d'Orient. Since 1916, Syrian and Lebanese emigrants in both North and South America had also been engaging in political practices aimed at achieving 'Syrian' and 'Lebanese' independence from the Ottomans under the sponsorship of Western/American political support. These practices included the enlistment of around 10,000 Syrian emigrants into the armies of the Allies, particularly the United States Army after 1917 (Fahrenthold, 2016). A mixed infantry regiment consisting largely of Armenians under French officers, the Légion d'Orient employed 550 Syrian and Lebanese emigrants recruited from Egypt, Europe and the Americas. The Paris-based Syrian Central Committee (SCC) under Shukri Ghanem and George Samneh led the effort of recruiting emigrants for the Légion between 1916 and 1917, and hence many saw the project as part of SCC's pan-Syrian nationalist politics. Nevertheless, the 'Lebanists', represented by the Lebanon League of Progress, provided most of the Légion's recruitment services. In New York, Naum Moukarzel's Lebanon League of Progress raised US$100,000 to support emigrants in joining the Légion d'Orient, with a large portion of this coming from the French government. And despite the sharp ideological divisions that later erupted between Syrianist and Lebanist leaders, they still collaborated on diasporic recruitment, in the shared belief that 'France will liberate [our] country and break the heavy Turkish yoke that has treated us so severely, subjecting us to famine and starvation' (ibid. p. 93).

The perception, however, that the Légion d'Orient was a Syrianist project serving French colonial interests prompted recruiters of Lebanese and Arab nationalist leanings alike to endorse enlistment in the US Army as an alternative. After June 1917, Noam Moukarzel started to write in *al-Huda* in support of Syrian (and Lebanese) enlistment in the US Army instead of the Légion d'Orient. New York's community of Syrian and Arab nationalists did the same, 'in a bid to build a partnership with Wilson's America for their respective movements' (ibid., p. 97).

Indeed, after the United States entered the war in April 1917 and President Wilson declared his commitment to fighting 'for the liberation of nations and oppressed peoples around the world', Syrian immigrants were eager to support the call to arms (ibid., p. 97). In the United States, the same newspaper editors who welcomed America's war effort also led the first campaigns to enlist Syrians in the army: Naum Mukarzil (*al-Huda*), Shukri Bakhash (*al-Fatat*), Ibrahim al-Khuri and Wadi' Shakir (*Fatat* Boston, *al-Fatat*'s sister publication), among others (ibid., p. 98). In other words, the Syrian emigrant community linked its support for American war goals with the liberation of the Syrian homeland. This was reflected in the Syrian community's recruitment campaigns using the language of Wilsonian self-determination and setting 'establishing the right of peoples to determine their future' in Syria and Mount Lebanon as the main goal (ibid., p. 101). In this sense, as Fahrenthold notes, enlisting in the US Army on behalf of Syrians still 'under the Turkish yoke' became 'an explicitly political act, reframing "Syrian" (or "Lebanese") identity into nationalist categories' (ibid., p. 101).

The diaspora's involvement in military mobilisation also reflected the ideological and political divisions between rival recruiters and among Syrian immigrant associations. Rival groups of Syrianists, Lebanists and Arab nationalists each sought to raise their profile in Wilson's army, to attract American sympathies for their respective political projects regarding post-Ottoman Syria.

Conclusion

In this chapter, we endeavoured first to highlight the presence of an active diaspora originating from a territorial space at a time when the political identity of this space was in question. Second, we showed that this diaspora engaged in a variety of activities (political, historical and literary writings, journalism) targeting the creation of a nation-state that was meant to represent their newly imagined national/political identity. We argued that the significance of these activities is best captured analytically by deploying the concept of a diasporic field, which introduces several important analytical tools essential for this chapter's argument. First, it introduces the conflictual character of diasporic activities. Second, it shows that the overarching objective of diasporic activities is to let the emerging local and international authorities 'valorise' and 'legitimise' their particular claims. Finally, the dominant authority (i.e. the Ottoman state until November 1918 and the French colonial rule until November 1943) in place when these conflicting claims were made had the ultimate regulatory power to confirm the 'legitimacy' of these claims to the exclusion of others.

As indicated above, the publication of *La question du Liban* (The Lebanon Question), followed by *The Broken Wings* represented foundational symbolic contributions to the formulation of a Lebanese national narrative. We have also shown how many diasporic associations lobbied for the creation of an independent Lebanese state. In addition, we highlighted the conflictual character of the emerging diasporic political field, as it included other political players or associations, promoting the establishment of a Syrian homeland, a federal Syrian state including Lebanon, or an Arab nation. The diasporic Lebanist and Syrianist associations in this field sent competing political remittances to their imagined homeland and also engaged in military mobilisation with the Allied forces in an attempt to secure French, but mostly American, support for their post-Ottoman political projects. Recruiters in the diaspora were expecting that their work with the US Army would lead to an American endorsement of their Lebanese and Syrian aspirations for independence. Instead, diasporic demands calling for a separate and distinct Lebanese nation-state were fulfilled through the declaration of Greater Lebanon in September 1920 by the French mandate and the support of the League of Nations. While it can be argued that a multiplicity of factors (local, regional and international, which are outside the scope of this chapter) played varying roles in the establishment of Greater Lebanon, this chapter has clearly shown the contribution of the diaspora in this foundational moment of September 1920. Indeed, the diaspora played a role in the birth of the Lebanese nation-state necessary not only in granting legitimacy to the political field specific to Lebanon, but also to all the other fields associated with this newly emergent state and society.

Notes

1 This field includes, by definition, the parties and associations in the diaspora involved in political activities directed towards the country of origin and the parties and associations in the country of origin that are engaged with the diaspora regarding this kind of activities. See Tabar and Maalouf (2016, pp. 99–120).
2 For a discussion of the concept of 'field', see Swartz (2013, pp. 47–79).
3 Following the sectarian strife of 1860, Mount Lebanon was created as an autonomous Mutasarrifate (province) within the Ottoman Empire in 1861.
4 In the absence of modern political parties in the period (1900–1914), associations served as the medium for political activism by Lebanese emigrants.
5 This period witnessed the establishment of two universities, 'The Syrian Protestant College' (which later became the 'American University of Beirut') in 1866 and 'Saint Joseph University' in 1875.

6 A Lebanist narrative is a narrative that commits and advocates for Lebanese nationalism and Lebanese identity in opposition to narratives that deny this identity to present-day Lebanon (e.g. Arabist and Syrianist narratives).
7 During their migration periods, Noujaym earned a doctorate in political science and al-Sawda a law degree. Both al-Sawda and Adib had successful professional careers during their stay in Egypt, with the latter becoming an eminent civil servant in the Egyptian finance ministry.
8 For more on Bourdieu's concept of symbolic power, see Swartz (2013, pp. 82–106).
9 Pierre Bourdieu identifies four basic types of capital: economic, social, cultural and symbolic. He defines cultural capital as possessing 'information, knowledge, and educational credentials'. See Swartz (2013, p. 50).
10 The Pen League was the first Arabic language literary society in North America, formed initially in 1915, and re-formed in 1920 by Mahjari (migrant) writers in New York, led by Gibran Khalil Gibran. The League dissolved in 1932. Its aim, in the words of its secretary Mikhail Naimy, was 'to lift Arabic Literature from the quagmire of stagnation and imitation, and to infuse a new life into its veins so as to make of it an active force in building up the Arab nations'.
11 In other publications, Tabar (2014) and Tabar and Maalouf (2016), we argue for the use of political remittances as distinct from economic and social remittances, to point to migrants' transfers to the homeland of, for example, political values, positions, practices and claims. Political remittances can be measurable and immeasurable.
12 Prince Faisal, the third son of Hussein bin Ali, the Grand Sharif of Mecca, headed the Northern Army of the Arab rebellion that confronted the Ottomans between 1916 and 1918. With the end of Turkish rule in Damascus in October 1918, Faisal set up a new Arab government in Greater Syria and was proclaimed king in March 1920. After France was given the mandate for Syria, Faisal was expelled from the country and later made King of Iraq in 1921.

References

Anderson, B. (1991) *Imagined Communities: Reflections on the Origin and Spread of Nationalism*. Revised and extended edn. London: Verso.
Bourdieu, P. (2000) *Pascalian Meditations*. Stanford, CA: Stanford University Press.
Cohen, R. (2008) *Global Diasporas: An Introduction*. 2nd edn. London: Routledge.
Cohen, R. (2009) 'Solid, ductile and liquid: changing notions of homeland and home in diaspora studies', in Ben-Rafael, E. and Sternberg, Y. (eds) *Transnationalism: Diasporas and the Advent of a New (Dis)order*. Leiden: Brill, pp. 117–133.
Fahrenthold, S. (2016) 'Former Ottomans in the ranks: pro-Entente military recruitment among Syrians in the Americas, 1916–18', *Journal of Global History*, 11, pp. 88–112.
Fahrenthold, S. (2019) *Between the Ottomans and the Entente: The First World War in the Syrian and Lebanese Diaspora, 1908–1925*. New York: Oxford University Press.
Firro, K. (2003) *Inventing Lebanon: Nationalism and the State Under the Mandate*. London: I.B. Tauris.
Gibran, K. (2008 [1912]) *Al Ajniha al mutakasira* [The Broken Wings]. 8th edn. Beirut: Nawfal.
Glick-Schiller, N. (2005) 'Long-distance nationalism', in Ember, M., Ember, C., and Skoggard, I. (eds) *Encyclopedia of Diasporas*. Boston: Springer, pp. 570–580.
Hakim, C. (2013) *The Origins of the Lebanese National Idea, 1840–1920*. Berkeley, CA: University of California Press.
Hobsbawm, E. (1983) 'Introduction: inventing traditions', in Hobsbawm, E. and Ranger, T. (eds). *The Invention of Traditions*. Cambridge: Cambridge University Press, pp. 1–14.
Karam, G. (2003) *Ahzab al lubniniyin wa jameeytihum fi al rubh al waal min al qarn al eshreen (1908–1920)* [Lebanese Parties and Associations in the First Quarter of the Twentieth Century]. Beirut: Dar Annahar.
Kattar, E. (1998) *Mouarikhoun min lubnan* (Historians from Lebanon). Beirut: Amchit Press.
Kaufman, A. (2004) *Reviving Phoenicia: The Search for Identity in Lebanon*. London: IB. Tauris.
Kim, J. (2018) 'Migration-facilitating capital: a Bourdieusian theory of international migration', *Sociological Theory*, 36(3), pp. 262–288.
Labaki, B. (2019) *Hijrat al lubnaniyin 1850–2018: masarat awlamah mubkirah* [Lebanese Emigration, 1850–2018: Early Globalised Trajectories]. Beirut: Dar Saer al Mashriq.
Naimy, M. (1978) *Gibran Khalil Gibran*. 8th edn. Beirut: Nawfal.
Salem, E (2003) *Constructing Lebanon: A Century of Literary Narratives*. Gainesville, FL: University Press of Florida.

Swartz, D. (2013) *Symbolic Power, Politics, and Intellectuals: The Political Sociology of Pierre Bourdieu*. Chicago: The University of Chicago Press.
Tabar, P. (2014) '"Political remittances": the case of Lebanese expatriates voting in national elections', *Journal of Intercultural Studies*, 35(4), pp. 442–460.
Tabar, P. (2019) 'Transnational is not diasporic: a Bourdieusian approach to the study of modern diaspora', *Journal of Sociology*, 56(3), pp. 455–471.
Tabar, P. and Maalouf, W. (2016) 'The emergence of a diasporic political field: a case for political remittances', in Nowicka, M. and Serbedzija, V. (eds) Migration and *Social Remittances in a Global Europe*. London: Palgrave Macmillan, pp. 99–120.
Zamir, M. (1985) *The Formation of Modern Lebanon*. London: Croom Helm.

10
TRANSNATIONAL NETWORKS IN TUNISIA'S DEMOCRATISATION

Diaspora activism in France and Italy

Alessandra Bonci

Introduction

While previous studies on the Tunisian diaspora have focused on cyber activism (Graziano, 2012), development activities (Ragab, McGregor and Siegel, 2013), external voting (Jaulin and Björn, 2015), business activities (Delahaye and Tejada, 2019) and identity processes (Carment and Sadjed, 2018), few have examined the political influence of diasporic associations on the 2011 Tunisian Revolution and the post-revolutionary democratic transition. In this chapter, I contend that historical events such as revolutions and democratic transitions are always the result of factors and actors that are at once multiple, internal, and external or diasporic, and I build on the scholarship that highlights the role of transnational networks in democratisation processes such as diaspora activism, international non-governmental organisations and great power statecraft to provide an analysis of the role of diaspora associations in the Tunisian case. Existing accounts provide insights into the role of transnational actors and networks in the case of Tunisia. For example, Marzo (2019) outlines the role of German foundations in supporting local Tunisian NGOs and in developing projects linked to the spreading of a democratic culture during and following the Ben Ali presidency. Marzo (2020) also analyses how the United States contributed to the undermining of Ben Ali's regime by favouring individuals and groups that were to become central to the revolution and the transition. In addition to the literature highlighting the role of international actors, my analysis is also informed by the new social movements framework. The new social movements literature advocates analysing activism through a constructivist lens that highlights the framing, building and shifting of contemporary identities (Scott, 1985). New social movements do not necessarily aim to wield political power; rather they are seen as seeking 'autonomy or independence vis-à-vis the system' (Melucci, 1980, p. 220). According to Sökefeld (2006), the formation of diasporas is directly connected with the dynamics of new social movements. In fact, the main dynamics guiding new social movements, such as political opportunities, mobilising structures and practice and framing, also shape the diaspora 'as transnational imagined communities' (ibid., p. 268). Following the same rationale, I explore how Tunisia's diasporas have been crucial in carrying out durable projects which have influenced and shaped the country's transitional politics since the 2011 revolution.

Given the prominence of the notion of identity to new social movements and diasporas, it is important to first acknowledge that identity is not a homogeneous and fixed concept. Stuart Hall (1991) explains that the notion of identity is far from being stable and organised. According to Hall, collective identities of race, class, gender and nation are to be conceived of as incomplete, unstable and *in process*. It follows that diaspora identity is equally incomplete and processual. Rather than being grounded in national narratives or ethnic background, diasporic identities take form and manifest themselves in collective efforts to reach a specific goal. Brubaker (2005) postulates three core diaspora elements: (1) dispersion, (2) homeland orientation, and (3) a boundary-maintaining attitude, all of which must be read with a certain nuance. Even if one assumes that there is consensus over the idea that diaspora entails dispersion, the meaning of dispersion remains contested. Homeland orientation is equally complex and can be polysemic, invoking a mythical ideal of return, a commitment to maintaining economic and/or personal bonds in the homeland or advocacy and political activism for the homeland, though not all the members of the Tunisian diaspora share the goal of returning home. Finally, the boundary-maintaining attitudes of the diaspora should equally be considered because of the diaspora's fluidity and syncretism. Indeed, before 2011, members and groups of the Tunisian diaspora in France and Italy were already well integrated within human rights, immigration and social assistance programmes and forms of activism. Melucci (1995) investigated the mechanism of collective action that are found among diasporic social movements and in so doing defines collective action as the process of building a system of action. First, these systems are organised through rituals and practices that seek to sustain the goals of the movements. Second, since the action is collective, there must be a network of individuals who debate, negotiate, decide and solve problems. Finally, the 'degree of emotional investment which enables individuals to feel like a community' is crucial for the 'action' to be carried out collectively (ibid., p. 45). Indeed, a programme or a network of associations and the emotional involvement of its members seem crucial for contemporary transnational diasporic identities, and the Tunisian diasporas in France and Italy are no exception.

In this chapter, I focus on Tunisian diaspora associations in Italy and France – the countries with the largest Tunisian immigrant communities.[1] The Tunisian diaspora plays an active role in strengthening the ongoing democratic transition in Tunisia. In this chapter, I focus my analysis on the first few years following the Tunisian revolution (2011–2014). The Tunisian diaspora organisations that my analysis draws upon developed and maintained a form of silent dissidence towards the Ben Ali regime despite its concerted efforts to censor Tunisians abroad. When the revolution broke out in 2011, Tunisian associations in the diaspora were ready and able to contribute to the struggle. However, after 2014, their 'resistance capital' seemed to have diminished and was no longer convertible into the 'capital of participation' (Geisser, 2012). Instead, these associations began to compete over forms of representation and belonging to a Tunisian cause that was differently imagined by the different groups. As my analysis shows, starting in 2014, secular Tunisian organisations in France and Italy defined their cause as engaging with their host societies and transcending ethnic and national boundaries. Conversely, Islamist associations maintained an identity based on ethno-national bonds thanks to the relative boundedness of their common political project.

My argument is based on semi-structured interviews with the leaders and members of four diaspora associations in France and four in Italy. In France, I engaged with the Association of Tunisians in France (ATF), the Association of Tunisians of France (ATDF), the Union for Tunisia (Uni'T) and the Young Ennahda France. In Italy, I interviewed leaders and members of PONTES,[2] the Association of Tunisians in Italy (ATI), the Association New Voice Tunisia (AVNT) and Young Ennahda Italy. I also interviewed Imen Ben Mohamed, the Ennahda MP for the Tunisian diaspora constituency in the Tunisian parliament. My argument is articulated in two main sections. The first opens by contextualising the secular and Islamist diaspora in France and Italy, focusing on three points: the pre-2011 'capital of resistance', the achievements of the diaspora in the aftermath of the revolution, and the different trajectories of the secular and Islamist diaspora associations. In the second section, I first turn to the dynamics of diasporic belonging in relation to specific dynamics of the democratic transition, highlighting three main events: (1) diasporic patriotism in 2011; (2) the decline of patriotism and the de-mobilisation of the secular diaspora; and finally, (3) the dynamics of identity beyond ethno-national ties.

The secular and Islamist diaspora: same background, different trajectories

The Tunisian diaspora emerged out of the migration of unskilled migrants who were considered an over-supply of labour in the developing country under President Bourguiba's rule. In 1988, the government created the Office of Tunisians Abroad (OTE) which is still in charge of carrying out various cultural and social assistance programmes as part of Tunisia's diaspora policies (Pouessel, 2017). During the harsh period of political repressions under Ben Ali (1987–2011), the OTE became an important instrument of control on Tunisian citizens abroad. The authoritarian ruler saw the diaspora as a diplomatic tool, useful for negotiating with European governments, and often mentioned the diaspora in state propaganda as a symbol of nation-building and a source of remittances. Control over Tunisians abroad, however, was a continuous struggle instead of a foregone conclusion.

My comparison of the two Tunisian diasporas, in France and Italy, highlights some of the common features observed in the two contexts, but it is also important to stress that the two diasporas have distinct experiences with associational activism. In Italy, there are fewer diaspora stories of political resistance than in France. Indeed, as Adel Chehida, president of the ATI, explained to me, the Tunisian diaspora in Italy is not as educated as the one in France; most Tunisians in Italy are working-class. Therefore, many of their associations are not involved in political debates concerning Italy or Tunisia. Many Tunisians in Italy, who cannot count on the historical network of dissent found in France, engaged in local and non-political associations for fear of reprisals from the Tunisian secret services before the revolution.

A common background in silent resistance

The Tunisian diaspora was politically engaged in homeland politics long before 2011. In fact, since the Bourguiban era, Tunisians in France have belonged to multiple dissident groups with diverse political motivations and ideologies (such as nationalists, leftists and Islamists), all of whom were opposed to the regime. Emigration has always been 'an ambiguous social fact' in Tunisian history (Dini and Giusa, 2020, p. 25). On the one hand, it was a relief for the economy during times of chronic unemployment, and the government has continuously attempted to engage with the diaspora economically. On the other hand, the diaspora has always been a threat, a hub of political dissent, which the government attempted to control.

Up to the fall of the Ben Ali regime, the main obstacle blocking the Tunisian diaspora's political engagement with the homeland lay in the regime's refusal to tolerate any criticism and its desire to focus on economic engagements (Pouessel, 2017, p. 209). Although Ben Ali began a so-called support programme for Tunisian emigrants in 2009, his intention was to use this programme to surveil, control and occasionally harass critics of his regime overseas (ibid.,

p. 209). As such, state-diaspora relations up until the Tunisian revolution in 2011 reflected the desire to fulfil the two goals of political control and, to a lesser degree, provision of economic remittances.

During the 20 years of the Ben Ali regime, political dissidents, including leftists and Islamist activists, chose exile over repression and found political asylum in France and Italy. Contrary to the exiled leftists, members of Ennahda, the Tunisian Islamist political party, have built their credibility on the idea of eventually returning to the homeland. Zederman (2020) highlights that during the years of political repression in Tunisia under Ben Ali, ideological differences did not prevent Islamist and secular dissidents from gathering in the diaspora. In 1991, a collaborative project called *Tunisie: Démocratie* started in France, composed of leftist, nationalist and Islamist dissidents. The project aimed to build a democratic system in Tunisia, defend political prisoners, their families, and refugees, as well as denounce human rights violations in Tunisia (ibid.). While this specific experiment was somewhat short-lived, a second period of détente between Islamists and leftists came in 2002 in response to Ben Ali's attempts to institute a presidency for life. A special congress was held in Paris to gather the dissidents and to denounce the constitutional referendum. Zederman considers this event part of the 'progressive learning' that Islamists and leftists started to acquire together in France during the Ben Ali era (ibid.). In 2003, in Aix-en-Provence, members of the Congress for the Republic, the Democratic Forum for Labour and Liberties, Ennahda and the Progressive Democratic Party, as well as members of associations, journalists and independent activists, met to discuss their perspectives on human rights and homeland politics. The meeting in Aix-en-Provence marked the beginning of the intellectual reconciliation between the Islamists and other political movements. From the 2000s onwards, many Tunisian activists in France started mobilising to advocate for the defence of human rights in their homeland, regardless of their ideological orientations. For example, the second-generation Tunisian association Uni'T advocated for the right of Muslim women in Tunisia to wear the hijab as part of a campaign to counter a proposed ban on the public display of religious symbols. The political polarisation between Islamist and secular groups was reactivated after the revolution when the scramble for power took hold, which I discuss below.

In the 2000s, increased police surveillance in Tunisia and abroad became increasingly justified by and aligned with the US-sponsored War on Terror. Taking advantage of this unique moment and the anti-terrorism powers it conferred upon him, Ben Ali promoted his brand of authoritarianism and surveillance as the best antidote to terrorism. All forms of dissent were thus targeted even more forcefully by the Tunisian security services, both within Tunisia and in the diaspora (Dini and Giusa, 2020). Several Tunisians abroad supported the institution of the Friendship Societies (*amicales*), which are government-sponsored cultural institutions meant to maintain a certain level of control over the diaspora. Brand (2014) describes how the *amicales* provided a space to preserve ties with the homeland for Tunisians abroad. At the same time, members of these societies acted to dissuade anti-regime political activism abroad (Geisser 2012). Apart from the *amicales*, powerful diaspora-oriented media such as *Canal 7* and the private channel *Nessma TV* were used for pro-regime propaganda. Owned by two businessmen, the Tunisian Nabil Karoui and the Italian Silvio Berlusconi, *Nessma TV* sought to nurture a 'Maghreb identity that includes the diaspora' (Pouessel, 2017, p. 217). Yet as Geisser (2012) reports, notwithstanding the threat of repression inflicted upon their families in Tunisia, many diaspora members unsubscribed from the consular lists, refused to vote in rigged elections and boycotted *Canal 7*. Although these actions were not revolutionary and occurred in silence, they helped to articulate dissent in the diaspora.

The return of the secular and Islamist elites

As Pouessel (2017) explains, the Tunisian diaspora remained 'silent' for decades, but when the revolution broke out, diaspora organisations contributed to the rebuilding of the country. With the overthrow of Ben Ali and the beginnings of democratisation, the Tunisian political elite was the first to change its attitude towards the Tunisian elite abroad, considering its members to be political partners. Thus, the diaspora organised and coordinated a 'lobby' (ibid.), with many of its members diaspora associations that advocated for the return of their compatriots to Tunisia. The Tunisian elite abroad asked for political participation and many politicians residing abroad returned, such as the secular Moncef Marzouki and the Islamist Rached Ghannouchi. This led an increasing number of elite Tunisians in the diaspora to return to their homeland (ibid.). The youngest members of the *Association Tunisienne des Grandes Écoles* (ATUGE), for instance, participated in the reconstruction of the Tunisian political environment after their return to Tunisia by appointing three ATUGE ministers in the provisional government in 2011 (Bel Haj Zekri, 2011). Training and studying abroad are not a new phenomenon for Tunisian politicians – even Habib Bourguiba himself studied and worked in France. However, as Bel Haj Zekri argues, the inclusion of diaspora technocrats in the government is new (ibid.). In addition, networks of online activism made it possible to circumvent security controls, in both Tunisia and in the host countries, in the pre- and post-revolutionary years (Lecomte, 2009; Graziano, 2012) and made diaspora politics a more potent node of Tunisian politics. To sum up, after 2011, emigrants were no longer uniquely perceived as a source of remittances, as they became an important point of inclusion in the Tunisian transition to democracy.

The ATF, founded in Paris in 1971, is the oldest extant group of Tunisian leftist dissidents in France. Since its foundation, the ATF has had a powerful influence over the Tunisia diaspora while keeping an eye on the homeland's political scene and has been suspected of harbouring links with the Ettajdid (Communist) Party (Ben Abdesselem, 2018). After the 2011 revolution, the president of the ATF wrote a letter demanding the right of representation in the homeland for the Tunisia diaspora. In October 2011, the right to vote from abroad in elections for the National Constituent Assembly was secured (Boubakri, 2013). The right to vote was a crucial step for the Tunisian diaspora in formalising its role in national politics and inaugurating a remote and transnational form of citizenship. As Pouessel (2017) observes, the 2014 elections showed a 'restorationist' tendency, as 7 out of 18 diaspora MPs joined the Nidaa Tounes Party, which contained members of the old regime. 'But at the same time, there has been an increasing number of children of exiles in the Assembly, who are MPs representing Tunisians abroad for the electoral district of France and Italy, where they grew up' (ibid., p. 214). This was also the case for children of Ennahda dissidents, Imen Ben Mohamed and Oussama al-Saghir, both Ennahda deputies for the Italian constituency, who followed their parents into exile and eventually started their political activism from abroad.

Different trajectories of the secular and Islamist associations

The Tunisian diasporas promptly intervened in the wake of the uprising, in part, because they had been trained and were committed to activism in the diaspora for decades. However, they did not direct their efforts towards the same objective, as Melucci's (1995) mechanism of collective action prescribes. In fact, the secular associations implemented numerous projects in Tunisia oriented towards the urgency of the revolutionary moment. Secular associations in France and Italy were not as coordinated and could not establish networks in Tunisia as quickly as Ennahda did. Furthermore, secular associations relied mainly on ethno-nationalist ties and the leftists could not channel participation into a coherent political goal, while Islamist associations based their activism on both a political *and* religious cause. Arguably, once secular diasporic associations moved away from ethnic-nationalist understandings of identity and towards placing economic and social rights at the core of their efforts, they struggled to focus on Tunisia as the goal of their activism, as has been the experience of Uni'T, ATDF, ATI and AVNT.

Islamist associations followed a different path, which leads one to distinguish between the trajectories of secular and Islamist groups. While secular diaspora associations initiated cooperative projects with the homeland, the efforts became fragmented as they were not oriented towards the same political goal. The Islamists, in contrast, were united in the goal of winning the elections. Indeed, the absence of shared goals between secular associations progressively facilitated their withdrawal from politics in Tunisia while maintaining their activities in their host countries. Secular diaspora organisations seemed to encounter a general disinterest in the homeland concerning their status abroad. As the resident of ATDF Zemni told me, many diaspora members abroad were disappointed with the treatment the Tunisian government showed them in the years after the revolution. Therefore, they instead focused on acquiring social and political positions in their host countries.

Dynamics of belonging during the transition to democracy

The revolution was hailed as a milestone in Tunisia's history and accelerated the political engagement of many diaspora activists (Geisser and Limam, 2018). The advocacy work done by the diaspora since Ben Ali's removal of the right to vote is an example of this new political engagement. The new political commitment of the Tunisian diaspora developed in two distinct periods: (1) the enthusiastic momentum in the aftermath of the revolution (2011–2013); and (2) a period of stagnation (2013–2017).

Diasporic patriotism following the revolution

Immediately after 2011, the diaspora was cohesive, intending to support democracy in Tunisia. At first, thousands of Tunisians took to the streets in many European cities[3] to celebrate the fall of Ben Ali's regime and to call for democracy. Interestingly, the most politically active members of the diaspora were not the only ones to march in the streets; citizens who previously had not been politically engaged and families and young people who had never taken part in demonstrations before also came out to support the calls of political activists (Geisser, 2012). Moreover, many second- and third-generation Tunisians in France, who only conceived of Tunisia as a holiday destination, came to identify themselves with the revolution *au bled* (i.e., in the homeland; ibid.). Many old activists put on hold their more provincial preoccupations to devote time and energy to the Tunisian cause. Among the associations born from the first Tunisian migration in France and Italy were the ATDF, the FTCR (Federation of Tunisian Citizens of the Two Banks) and the UTIT (Union of Tunisian Immigrant Workers). After the revolution, these associations, mostly leftist and secular 'were all able to access the Tunisian public space and join forces with the Community Service Organisations in Tunisia (old and new) in migration actions, advocacy and events' (Boubakri, 2013, p. 21). In addition, a myriad of new associations flourished in this first phase, all united by the cause of the revolution and ready to mobilise for its sake.

The ATDF was founded in 2003 in Argenteuil and is composed only of volunteers. As its president, Mohsen Zemni, explained to me, there are around 500 annual members who manage hundreds of requests for bureaucratic and administrative assistance every day (concerning how to navigate French institutions, demands for copies of the document from Tunisian administrations, follow-up of immigrants' status in France, etc.). The association is devoted mostly to humanitarian, social and cultural activities. It was only after 2011 that the ATDF became involved in Tunisia itself and set up 54 humanitarian projects in the country, such as the delivery of medical equipment. The ATDF had a partnership with the 'Lions Club', the Tunisian Union of Social Solidarity which is linked to the Ministry of Social Affairs, and the SOS Tunisia Collective. The ATDF has always encouraged Tunisians to vote, in France or Tunisia. The volunteers also distributed leaflets reminding people to vote, and their office became a polling station in both 2011 and 2014.

Other diasporic associations followed a similar path of orienting their gaze towards the homeland following the revolution. Uni'T is a leftist association promoting the interests of French Tunisians in France, but in the aftermath of the uprising, many Tunisians, especially young French citizens of Tunisian descent, felt the need to mobilise for democracy in Tunisia. During his tenure, Bader Lejmi, Uni'T treasurer in 2016, explained that his group organised many debates in cafés and conferences to discuss Tunisian politics.

Part of the diasporic patriotism phenomenon can also be found in the youth branch of Ennahda in France. The leader of the Office for the Tunisian Students Abroad argues that while the Young Ennahda France is part of the Ennahda Party, it is considered a wider community. The leader of the Office for the Tunisian Students Abroad shared that young members are between 18 and 35 years old and come from different socioeconomic backgrounds. My interviewee is a Tunisian who moved to France in 2016, while other members are third- or fourth-generation French Tunisians. The official had previous experience in the UGETE, the Islamic student association in Tunisia. In France, Young Ennahda supports Tunisian students and organises debates and sports events. He added that Young Ennahda France is strongly connected to the broader civil society, including MPs and the youth of Ennahda in Tunisia, and that their goal is to sustain the party with their ideas and contributions. During the interview, he stressed that he feels Ennahda can grow thanks to the youth wing's political vision and ideas.

In Italy, too, many associations engaged in diasporic patriotism by supporting the revolution after 2011. For instance, they organised activities and carried out projects to participate in the Tunisian democratisation movement. PONTES has done advocacy work in Italy since 2006 and is the only NGO in Italy that focuses on development in Tunisia, but it does not engage in opposition politics. Ouejdane Mejri, president of the association, explained that PONTES opened a branch in Tunis in 2011 to foster two projects, *Repit* and *Comact Diaspora*. *Repit*, which stands for 'Re-Utilisation, Circular Economy and Participation Italy/Tunisia' is funded by the Tuscany regional government and is focused on building circular economy projects for local administrations in urban areas in Tunisia. *Comact Diaspora* is specifically oriented towards strengthening the Tunisian diaspora in Italy by supporting Tunisian-led businesses in the country and encouraging Tunisian investors to build start-ups in both Italy and Tunisia. After 2014, PONTES focused on public health reform through international cooperation. In addition, PONTES promoted the investment of Tunisian Residents Abroad in Tunisia, by mapping the socioeconomic profile of Tunisians in Italy and inquiring about their aspirations, both Tunisian entrepreneurs in Italy who want to go back to Tunisia and export their business or Tunisian entrepreneurs in Tunisia who have business partners in Italy. Finally, PONTES started a campaign addressed to youth on the theme of illegal migration.

Conversely, ATI is engaged in a special kind of patriotism. Adel Chehida, a Tunisian doctor, set up the organisation in 2017 to help Tunisian students in Italy navigate the local bureaucracy. The association started as a mediator between the Tunisian diaspora and Italian institutions and has maintained this profile without directly intervening in Tunisia. Chehida is against the political engagement of ATI in Tunisia because he claims that partisanship could hinder its goal of helping Tunisians in need of support in Italy. As Chehida stated during the interview, 'We have a serious problem of school dropouts, as many second-generation Tunisians feel affected by the unstable economic condition of their parents. So, our goal is to be useful in Italy first.' Yet, Chehida asserted that ATI cooperated with PONTES to send goods to and create projects in Tunisia.

A history of personal political engagement and patriotism in the diaspora is represented by the president of the apolitical AVNT, Lotfi Ben Hammouda. In fact, Ben Hammouda personally engaged in Tunisian politics in 2011 in a secular electoral list to help draft the constitution. But after Ennahda won the 2011 elections, Ben Hammouda lost hope in Tunisian politics: 'I don't feel represented by them [the Ennahda Party]; and in Italy, secular associations are more useful than Nahdawis.' Ben Hammouda officially created the association after the revolution; however, its members were already active in Parma before the uprisings. AVNT's goals are to help the Tunisian diaspora in Italy navigate the Italian bureaucracy, provide social services and organise cultural events. The association is connected to the larger civil society in Tunisia, especially to the OTE to make information accessible to diaspora members.

One of the most authoritative representatives of Tunisian Islamists in Italy is Imen Ben Mohamed, daughter of a *Nahdawi*[4] exile. She shared with great pride that the members of the Ennahda Party consider themselves activists because of their past resilience and resistance to the Ben Ali regime. Indeed, some of the *Nahdawis* exiled in Italy and France pushed Tunisian politicians to make diaspora members part of the electoral process and provided a crucial contribution to the writing of the new constitution. Moreover, Ennahda also proposed a project called 'The High Consultative Committee of Tunisians in Diaspora', to give Tunisians living abroad the possibility of having a voice on matters they are concerned with. Ennahda in Italy and France maintains affiliations with many Islamist associations. However, Ben Mohamed prefers not to talk about them, stating: 'If you are committed in a party, you cannot be engaged in the civil society too.' Affiliated to Ennahda is the Islamist association Young Ennahda Italy. Its president, Hamdi M'barki, a second-generation Tunisian, told me that his group is still young and that they focus more on civil activism than on politics. They are no more than 50 members and, according to M'barki, while second-generation Tunisian activists are numerous, they are not necessarily coordinated or well organised.

Indeed, highlighting their role in the resistance to the Ben Ali regime, organisations from the independent left and the Islamist movement have imposed themselves de facto in the diaspora as the moral and political references of the democratic transition (Geisser, 2012). It seems that, during the revolution, diaspora Tunisians who had some experience with resistance to the old regime were one of the main centripetal forces of the diaspora, as they mobilised to rescue and support their fellow Tunisians in the homeland. Such a background served for a time as a cohesive dynamic.

The decline of patriotism and de-mobilisation after 2014

Diasporic patriotism and the sense of urgency fostered by the revolution functioned as dynamics of cohesion until political disillusionment replaced the hopes of young Tunisian revolutionaries at home and in the diaspora. After 2012, the diaspora organisations considered in this chapter experienced a progressive de-mobilisation from engagement with the homeland. In fact, after 2011, four out of the eight associations in France and Italy started focusing more on activities in the diaspora: ATDF, Uni'T, ATI and AVNT. The exogenous causes are linked to the post-2011 political events in Tunisia. Indeed, between 2012 and 2016 a stream of political assassinations and violence shocked many in the homeland and abroad. The leftist-oriented diaspora associations in Italy and France felt both betrayed by the failure of Marzouki's project, and threatened by the second victory of the Islamist Ennahda in the 2014 elections. In addition, the murder of the leftist activists Mohamed Brahmi and Chokri Belaid and the rampant phenomenon of Salafism in Tunisia reminded many of old tensions between the leftist and the Islamist associations in the diaspora. Hence, the endogenous causes are linked to the dynamics within diaspora associations, where old ideological, class and generational divisions resurfaced. Additionally, many organisations that emerged in response to the 2011 uprisings disappeared. Today, many diaspora associations exist only on paper and are no longer active. Their telephone numbers and emails are no longer in operation and their Facebook pages are outdated, reporting events from 2012–2013. This political environment pushed the cooperative associations to diversify further. Some of them focused uniquely on implementing projects in Tunisia, like ATF and PONTES, while others specialised in activities (for Tunisians and other ethnicities) in their country of residence, like ATDF and ATI.

In Italy, as in France, the Tunisian diaspora nowadays is also fragmented because of specific partisan agendas and competition between associations. In Italy, for example, according to Ben Hammouda (AVNT), Tunisian associationism is still threatened by Tunisian political forces that want to control the diaspora as they did before the revolution. Ben Hammouda described how there are numerous divisions and a general lack of trust between the different associations. 'People think that Ennahda will be the solution. However, it is not the case, as they are corrupt,' he exclaimed. The president of PONTES, Ouejdane Mejri, did not hide her disappointment vis-à-vis the diaspora in Italy: 'The Tunisian diaspora is more *Nahdawi* in Italy than in Tunisia.' Also, Adel Chehida, president of ATI, explained that the political cleavage is deep among the Tunisian associations in Italy. According to Chehida, if the associations in Italy before 2011 were all pro-Ben Ali's government, many are now under the umbrella of the Ennahda Party. It is therefore difficult to create a common project between Islamist and secular associations like his own, despite (or perhaps because of) ATI's apolitical agenda.

For many secular diaspora activists, it is important to claim their role as historical opponents of Ben Ali and to discredit the Islamists. In France, ATF was born as a politically oriented association, clearly of leftist orientation and with strong ties to the UGTT (Tunisian General Labor Union) and the intellectual elite in Tunisia. Lalla, president of ATF, during the 1990s, bitterly reflected: 'We were deeply contemptuous of the Islamists. However, we turned out to be short-sighted as they managed to take roots in the society way better than we did.' He added that the French government, instead of fostering secular associations, encouraged the spread of Islamic ones. This is because religious associations, in his analysis, worked as watchdogs by discouraging the presence of drug abuse and alcoholism in disenfranchised neighbourhoods.

Still, the secularists' competitive attitude was oriented against Ennahda. For example, Zemni, founder of the ATDF, decided to build a new association because of his disappointment with the partisan strategy of the ATF. Unquestionably, the ATDF was born as a rival to the old ATF, competing on a regional level. Zemni recalled:

> While registering my son at the consulate in 2001, I was insulted and treated like an animal by a civil servant. When I contacted the ATF to report this fact, they were of no help. Thus, I told myself that I had to create an association that could defend Tunisians in France and grant them real help and respect.

Zemni describes the associative phenomenon after 2011 as '*événementiel*'[5] because, during the revolution, 'some people genuinely helped, and other associations or volunteers organised activities only to get noticed.'

A recent World Bank survey provides data in support of the thesis on diaspora de-mobilisation after 2011. The survey shows that many respondents' interest in the home country decreased after the revolution (Malouche, Plaza and Salsac, 2016). One of the many explanations for this transformation could be the expatriates' loss of confidence in diaspora institutions, such as the OTE. If Tunisian institutions before 2011 perceived diaspora members as a mere source of remittances devoid of rights, the diaspora expected a substantial change after the revolution. Thus, members of the Tunisian diaspora hoped that the Tunisian government would consider them as Tunisian citizens, not only migrants. Indeed, in 2012, a new institution to coordinate the diaspora, the State Secretariat for Migration and Tunisians living Abroad (SEMTE) was born. However, it was short-lived as it was disbanded in 2014, and its responsibilities fell to the poorly organised OTE. Due to such institutional failures and the post-revolutionary political fluidity in Tunisia, many diaspora associations and actors felt side-lined and forgotten. Thus, the 'well established perception of the Tunisian diaspora that historically perceived itself as instrumentalised by the homeland' has resurfaced in large measure (Pouessel, 2020, p. 386). After the early enthusiasm associated with the revolution, a phase of disenchantment followed between 2014 and 2017. Zemni, president of the ATDF, explained that:

> More recently, the ATDF has denounced the increase in consular tariffs by over 300%, so we sent a letter to the Prime Minister and the Minister of the Economy and Finance. Taxing Tunisians abroad is deeply disrespectful: we refused to be treated as a 'cash cow.' Unfortunately, the OTE is linked to incompetent politicians with unclear immigration policies. One need only remember that the official invitation we received from the Tunisian embassy called us a *Tunisian colony in France*. We are not under supervision. We are a diaspora! It means that they do not know how to value and respect their diaspora. Because of this, our association in 2018–2019 mounted a campaign to boycott the deputies who represented Tunisians in France.

Dynamics of belonging to the Tunisian cause: nationality and multiple loyalties

If nationality played a role (among other factors) in shaping the early dynamics of the mobilisation of the Tunisian diaspora in France and Italy, it was not sufficient to maintain the engagement in the Tunisian cause over time. As the de-mobilisation started, it was apparent that national ties are not essential for maintaining social networks in the long run, if they are not based on shared goals and, most importantly, on results. When some associations, such as the ATI, the AVNT, and the ATDF in France de-mobilised from the Tunisian cause and reoriented their activities to local volunteering, they also assisted French and Italian citizens in need and were not only confined to helping their Tunisian compatriots. In other words, multiple interests shape 'multiple loyalties' to multiple worlds (Abdelhady, 2006). Hence, there appears to be a shift from the focus on nationality to the notion of identity, which is crucial to make sense of multiple loyalties, as it is linked not only to national ties but also to more general goals. Yet, like the national bond, the feeling of belonging is conditional and can evolve or fade over time. As Abdelhady observes in the case of the Lebanese diaspora (ibid.), when a diasporic community frames its members in a stereotypical and artificial version of nationality, members of the diaspora sometimes feel that they no longer belong. Diaspora associations in France and Italy have in a way reshaped and redefined the grounds of belonging to the Tunisian cause. Established leftist political activists and exiled Islamists, mostly Arabic-speaking, continue to claim to be the standard-bearers of the Tunisians' cause. As a result, younger, apolitical, binational and often

French-speaking members of the diaspora have been cast as less than authentic and unfit to be part of or speak for the Tunisian cause (Geisser, 2012). The result of these membership debates has been a major fragmentation within associations. The disappointment with the revolution made Tunisians abroad aware of a revolution of meanings, where belonging and identity do not exclusively lie on ethno-national ties any longer. The old cohesion, as Stuart Hall taught us, has given way to a new one, products of multiple interests and worldviews.

Conclusion

This study shows that the Tunisian diaspora in France and Italy took advantage of political opportunities and mobilisation structures and practices. I illustrated how the Tunisian diaspora, both secular and Islamist, jumped on the political opportunities available in the host countries by 'taking up "homeland" issues that could not be articulated in the country of origin' (Sökefeld, 2006, p. 270). Indeed, the Islamists managed to implement religious *da'wa* (preaching) outside Tunisia, whereas leftist activists fostered their party activities in France and Italy without fear of being imprisoned. The diaspora took advantage of these political opportunities to implement their own political ends, but these also allowed the dynamics of resistance to the Tunisian regime to flourish. In addition, the effectiveness of the diaspora in the Tunisian democratisation efforts was possible thanks to the mobilisation of structures and practices: neighbourhoods, ethnic groups, kin networks and communities, which all contribute to mobilising collective action, as the history of the associations show. Finally, my analysis also shows how the diaspora's concerns are anchored in notions of identity and belonging. Indeed, the specific events that characterise the history of the community constitute the identity of the different diaspora communities (ibid., p. 271).

Interestingly, my examination of the mobilisation trajectories shows that the Tunisian diaspora did not improvise civic engagement in 2011, as it had some experience with resistance to the regime. The diaspora members in France and Italy came from the leftist and union ranks, as well as from the Islamist groups. They all inherited a tradition of resistance in Tunisia, which they kept alive mainly through the work of the ATF in France and the AVNT in Italy. They were often engaged in civic activism despite the oppressive reach of the Tunisian security services in France and Italy. Thanks to such a rich, albeit neglected, historical background of silent resistance, Tunisians in the diaspora contributed their part to the regime change in Tunisia.

The associations in Italy and France managed to support civil society mobilisation in Tunisia through different means and connections. Some of the associations directly influenced the process of drafting the constitution and strengthened the power of the diaspora, such as the AVNT, the ATF, the ATUGE and Ennahda; others, like ATI, Uni'T and ATDF, made people sensitive to the democratic culture in their host countries, while associations like PONTES and the ATF engaged in cooperation projects with Tunisia. Each association engaged in its own particular way: through sending material aid to Tunisia, supporting the electoral process via debates and demonstrations, or by encouraging Tunisians in the diaspora to return to the homeland to be part of the revolution. Moreover, in the first phase, projects of cooperation and support from the diaspora to the homeland emerged suddenly and unexpectedly. In fact, the quick responses from the diaspora just after the revolution were unexpected as they happened despite the ideological, political, generational, class and regional differences among activists.

Unfortunately, once the enthusiasm for the revolution faded, political and goal-related cleavages emerged. Indeed, in the 2013–2017 period, the major diaspora associations withdrew from seeking to influence homeland politics, as the activists' efforts increasingly focused on their countries of residence. Interestingly, many associations in both France and Italy also expanded the reach of their voluntary work to non-Tunisians, showing that the contemporary nature of the Tunisian diaspora is linked less to nationality and more to collective identities that are not always defined along traditional categories of membership (nationality and ethnicity). Thanks to civil activism in the diaspora, the secular Tunisian associations developed a new understanding of identity that is not solely based on national ties. Indeed, when disillusionment set in, the diaspora partially renounced its national roots and its national identity to assume a collective identity based on sharing the same goals beyond national background. If being one people fighting for freedom is a powerful engine, however, it also risks being illusory. According to Anderson (1983), the nation is nothing more than the result of a collective illusion, an imagined community that citizens share with their fellow co-citizens. The diaspora's notion of a shared community was a fundamental aspect during crucial political changes. Yet, once the disenchantment with the revolution set in, the power of imagination left room for conflicts and unmasked the myth of the diasporic unity. The decline in emotional investment, as explained by Melucci, leads to a decline in the social movement, as observed by the Tunisian diaspora experience.

Notes

1 According to Poussel (2017), France is home to more than half of Tunisians abroad (625,864) followed by Italy (169,099).
2 From the Latin, *pontes* means 'bridge', which means that the association aims at bridging the Italian and Tunisian culture through solidarity.
3 ANSA, Italian National Associated Press Agency, 2011. "Cortei e manifestazioni in Italia". Available at: www.ansa.it/web/notizie/photostory/primopiano/2011/01/15/visualizza_new.html_1640216050.html?idPhoto=1
4 In Tunisian dialect, this term designates the members and affiliates of the Ennahda Party.
5 Related to a specific event.

References

Abdelhady, D. (2006) 'Beyond home/host networks: forms of solidarity among Lebanese immigrants in a global era', *Identities: Global Studies in Culture and Power*, 13(3), pp. 427–453.
Anderson, B. (1983) *Imagined Communities: Reflections on the Origin and Spread of Nationalism*. London: Verso.
Bel Haj Zekri, A. (2011) 'La dimension sociopolitique actuelle de la migration en Tunisie', CARIM Analytic and Synthetic Notes, CADMUS Research Repository, 48. Available at: https://cadmus.eui.eu/handle/1814/18474.
Ben Abdesselem, S. (2018) *Du rêve au cauchemar: genèse de la constitution tunisienne entre deux campagnes électorales. Chroniques de l'Assemblée nationale constituante vécues de l'intérieur*. Tunis: Nirvana.
Boubakri, H. (2013) 'Revolution and international migration in Tunisia', *Migration Policy Center*, 04. Available at: https://cadmus.eui.eu/handle/1814/294544
Brand, L. (2014) 'Arab uprisings and the changing frontiers of transnational citizenship: Voting from abroad in political transitions', *Political Geography*, 41, pp. 54–63.
Brubaker, R. (2005) 'The "diaspora" diaspora', *Ethnic and Racial Studies*, 28(1), pp. 1–19.
Carment, D. and Sadjed, A. (2018) 'Introduction: coming to terms with diaspora cooperation', in Carment, D. and Sadjed, A. (eds) *Diaspora as Cultures of Cooperation: Migration, Diasporas and Citizenship*. London: Palgrave Macmillan, pp. 1–26.
Delahaye, S.G. and Tejada, G. (2019) 'Transnational investments of the Tunisian diaspora: trajectories, skills accumulation and constraints', in Elo, M. and Minto-Coy, I. (eds) *Diaspora Networks in International Business: Perspectives for Understanding and Managing Diaspora Business and Resources*. New York: Springer International Publishing, pp. 105–126.
Dini, S. and Giusa, C. (2020) *Externalizing Migration Governance through Civil Society: Tunisia as a Case Study*. London: Palgrave Macmillan.

Geisser, V. (2012) 'Quelle révolution pour les binationaux? Le rôle des franco-tunisiens dans la chute de la dictature et dans la transition politique', *Migrations Société*, 5(143), pp. 155–178.

Geisser, V. and Limam, W. (2018) 'L'an prochain à Tunis? Les binationaux franco-tunisiens au prisme des héritages militants et des subjectivités diasporiques', in Allal, A. and Geisser, V. (eds) *Tunisie: une démocratisation au-dessus de tout soupçon?* Paris: CNRS Éditions, pp. 413–432.

Graziano, T. (2012) 'The Tunisian diaspora: between "digital riots" and web activism', *Social Science Information*, 51(4), pp. 534–550.

Hall, S. (1991) 'Old and new identities, old and new ethnicities', in King, A.D. (ed.) *Culture, Globalisation and the World System: Contemporary Conditions for the Representation of Identity*. London: Macmillan, pp. 41–68.

Jaulin, T. and Björn, N. (2015) 'Voting at home and abroad: the Tunisian diaspora since 2011', *Revue Européenne des Migrations Internationales*, 31(3), pp. 41–71.

Lecomte, R. (2009) 'Internet et la reconfiguration de l'espace public tunisien: le rôle de la diaspora', *TIC & Société*, 3(1–2), Available at: https://journals.openedition.org/ticetsociete/702#quotation

Malouche, M.M., Plaza, S. and Salsac, F. (2016) 'Mobilizing the Middle East and North Africa diaspora for economic integration and entrepreneurship', Washington, DC: World Bank. Available at: https://openknowledge.worldbank.org/bitstream/handle/10986/26307/111806-REVISED.pdf?sequence=7&isAllowed=y.

Marzo, P. (2019) 'Supporting political debate while building patterns of trust: the role of the German political foundations in Tunisia (1989–2017)', *Middle Eastern Studies*, 55(4), pp. 621–637.

Marzo, P. (2020) 'Solving the security-democracy dilemma: the US foreign policy in Tunisia post 9/11', *Third World Quarterly*, 41(7), pp. 1181–1199.

Melucci, A. (1980) 'The new social movements: a theoretical approach', *Social Science Information*, 19(2), pp. 199–226.

Melucci, A. (1995) 'The process of collective identity', *Social Movements and Culture*, 44, pp. 41–63.

Pouessel, S. (2017) 'Tunisia and its diaspora: between protection and control', in Weinar, A. (ed.) *Emigration and Diaspora Policies in the Age of Mobility*. New York: Springer International Publishing, pp. 205–220.

Pouessel, S. (2020) 'Diaspora policies, consular services and social protection for Tunisian citizens abroad', in Lafleur, J.M. and Vintila, D. (eds) *Migration and Social Protection in Europe and Beyond*, vol. 3, Berlin: Springer, pp. 375–387.

Ragab, N., McGregor, E., and Siegel, M. (2013) 'Diaspora engagement in development: an analysis of the engagement of the Tunisian diaspora in Germany and the potentials for cooperation', UNU-MERIT. Available at: www.merit.unu.edu/publications/uploads/1380291166.pdf

Scott, J. (1985) *Weapons of the Weak: Everyday Forms of Peasant Resistance*. New Haven, CT: Yale University Press.

Sökefeld, M. (2006) 'Mobilizing in transnational space: a social movement approach to the formation of diaspora', *Global Networks*, 6(3), pp. 265–284.

Zederman, M. (2020) 'L'union fait-elle la force face à l'autoritarisme tunisien? Dynamiques d'alliances transidéologiques en France dans les années 2000', *Critique Internationale*, (88), pp. 91–110.

11
SECULARISM, SECTARIANISM AND THE TRANSNATIONAL CONNECTIVITY OF THE LEBANESE DIASPORA IN SENEGAL

Mara A. Leichtman

The Lebanese constitute one of the oldest and most widespread modern diasporas. West Africa has long been a destination of Lebanese migrants and refugees, yet surprisingly little is known about these West African Lebanese communities and the important role they play in Lebanon today. Migrant remittances from Africa have aided in the reconstruction of war-torn Lebanon, and there are even streets in southern Lebanon named 'Senegal' or 'Nigeria'. Lebanon's most powerful Shi'i politician, Speaker of Parliament Nabih Berri, was himself born in Sierra Leone. Musa al-Sadr, the legendary leader of Lebanon's Shi'a who disappeared in Libya in 1978, visited West Africa in the 1960s to gain support for his cause. Furthermore, 'Abdul Mun'am al-Zayn, Senegal's Lebanese Shi'i shaykh who was sent to Dakar by al-Sadr to cater to the spiritual, social and cultural needs of Lebanese migrants, helped negotiate the crisis of French hostages taken by Hizbullah in the 1980s by travelling between Paris, Beirut and Tehran.

Brubaker (2005, pp. 5–6) narrows in on three defining conditions of a diaspora: (1) dispersion in space; (2) orientation to a 'homeland'; and (3) boundary-maintenance 'involving the preservation of a distinctive identity vis-à-vis a host society (or societies)'. Migrants left Lebanon due to economic and political factors, and over time formed a diaspora in Senegal in response to colonial and post-colonial pressures. Lebanese became embedded in Senegalese society, building social, economic and political ties, while they were considered a community apart. It was during times of insecurity in Senegal, resulting from French colonial anti-Lebanese campaigns and Senegalese independence, when the Lebanese community sought to (re)invent its identity in the diaspora, which adapted over time from religious sectarianism to 'secular' ethnicity. There was not a second wave of immigration to Senegal during the Lebanese Civil War (1975–1990), as there was, for example, to the Ivory Coast, which reinforced community tensions (Bierwirth, 1999). This means that Lebanese in Senegal are primarily second-, third- and now fourth-generation migrants. This chapter, a summary of the first half of my book (Leichtman, 2015), provides an overview of the history of Lebanese migration to West Africa and explores shifts in the religio-political identities of Lebanese in Senegal.

Diaspora, as suggested by Brubaker (2005, p. 12), can 'represent a non-territorial *form* of essentialised belonging'. Brubaker also makes a case for thinking of diaspora as a *stance*: 'As a category of practice, "diaspora" is used to make claims, to articulate projects, to formulate expectations, to mobilise energies, to appeal to loyalties' (ibid.). As Lebanese migrants transitioned into becoming a diaspora in Senegal, religion ceased to divide Muslims and Christians and instead became a shared element of Lebanese diasporic culture. Ethno-national identity exhibited by those in the diaspora can sometimes be a response to their exclusion from national belonging in their country of residence.

Yet religious rituals can be another way of reinforcing belonging to the homeland while unintentionally representing the host society as *not* home (Leichtman, 2010). More recently, external constraints have threatened Lebanese coexistence in Senegal as the 2006 Lebanon War revived sectarian divisions. Responses to the war from Dakar were particularly significant because a majority of Lebanese in Senegal had never visited Lebanon. Shi'i Islam began to stand for Lebanese nationalism, as Lebanese in Senegal linked religious observance to ethno-national belonging. The events of 2006 in Lebanon motivated Lebanese Shi'a in Senegal to (re)new transnational attachments to Lebanon, which altered the community's diasporic identification by replacing 'secular' Lebanese culture in Senegal with nationalistic religious performances. This case study suggests that recent traumatic political events can result in a shift in identity, in which an established diasporic community detached from the homeland embraces newfound transnational connections. In this example, transnationalism can be an impediment to diasporic belonging.

History of Lebanese migration to West Africa

Amrika was the generic term for any land – far, far away from the political strife and poverty-stricken Levantine villages of the late nineteenth and early twentieth centuries – to where Lebanese living under Ottoman rule, and later the French Mandate, dreamed of escaping. Lebanese intellectuals and politicians, aware from the very beginning that their country's greatest resource was the massive body of human resources abroad, developed an ideology of emigration. Linking Lebanese migration to ancient Phoenicians (thereby detaching Lebanese history from Arab history) became an ideological tool in constructing a specifically 'Lebanese' (as opposed to Greater Syrian) nationality (Kaufman, 2004; Gualtieri, 2009; Brand, 2010).

Different historical periods in Lebanon (Ottoman rule, French rule, independence, Israeli and Syrian dominance) contributed to various waves of migration. Migrants began to leave Lebanon in the nineteenth century seeking better economic opportunities abroad to improve their local social rank (Taraf, 1994; Khater, 2001), fleeing the 1860 massacres (Hitti, 1957; Makdisi, 2000), and later avoiding conscription in the Ottoman army following the 1908 revolution in Ottoman Turkey. Lebanese migrated to all five continents, but first arrived in West Africa as early as the 1880s, and especially during the 1920s, via Marseilles, the transportation hub of the time. Emigrants planned to continue on to the Americas, where there had been previous Lebanese immigration (Hourani and Shehadi, 1992; Lesser, 1999; Khater, 2001; Alfaro-Velcamp, 2007; Karam, 2007; Abdelhady, 2011). According to the tale told by today's Lebanese of Senegal, their ancestors boarded ships heading for the Americas but never reached their destination. Ships docked at Dakar or elsewhere on the West African coast, and Lebanese found work as intermediaries in the peanut trade between the French in the cities and Senegalese peasants in the rural areas. Other sources state strict health requirements for immigration to the United States, and some Lebanese failed to make the cut because they suffered from trachoma. Additionally, many emigrants spent most of their money in Marseilles while waiting for transport and could no longer afford to complete the journey to the Americas (Boumedouha, 1987). The best solution to these difficulties was to settle in West Africa, where fares were cheap, health requirements lax and French reports favourable (Crowder, 1968; Boumedouha, 1987).

Immigration to West Africa depended on factors affecting both Lebanon and West Africa. Labaki (1993) divides Lebanese migration to Africa into different stages, with the first wave of travel occurring between the two world wars when Lebanon and parts of West Africa were under French rule. The second wave of immigration took place from 1945–1960, before African independence. Migration slowed from 1960 to 1975, due to independence and the accompanying politics of Africanisation. After 1975, migration increased again, due to the Lebanese Civil War, in concurrence with activities in African receiving countries.

Van der Laan (1992) establishes 1920–1955 as the period of Lebanese internal migration from coastal cities to the West African interior with the introduction of lorries for transportation of goods. By the end of the 1950s, Lebanese began to withdraw from villages and return to cities, due to African independence, government intervention in produce trade, falling prices and the desire for better housing and comfort. In Senegal, this was also due to President Senghor's 1961 nationalisation of the groundnut industry with which he established cooperatives in towns and villages of the interior. This meant that most Europeans and Lebanese who had acted as local agents in the groundnut trade were deprived of jobs in buying centres and were forced to move to Dakar (Cruise O'Brien, 1972).

There has been confusion regarding the historical origins of the Lebanese community of Senegal. Before the end of the First World War, the Ottoman Province of Syria contained all of present-day Lebanon and Syria. Emigrants from this province were called 'Syrians' without distinction, yet most were from Lebanon proper. After the Ottoman Empire's collapse in 1918, the former Province of Syria was divided by France in 1920 into two administrative units: Syria and Lebanon. After the French Mandate's establishment, immigrants became technically and legally Lebanese; nonetheless, the names *Syriens* and *Libano-Syriens* continued to be used in French West Africa (*Afrique Occidentale Française*) as late as the 1950s in administrative reports and newspapers (van der Laan, 1975; Boumedouha, 1987). The community today identifies itself and is referred to by Senegalese exclusively as 'Lebanese'.

Lebanese settlement in Senegal was first patterned by temporary migration, with the intention of returning to Lebanon to retire and reinstate children in the country of origin. Economic opportunities kept many Lebanese in Africa, and later conflict in Lebanon eliminated the possibility of return. Lebanese pride themselves on having contributed to the development of Senegal and refer to themselves as pioneers of the land. They see themselves as Senegalese yet distinct from the Senegalese, and as Lebanese but not like those in Lebanon. Lebanese in Senegal are fluent in Wolof or other local languages and enjoy Senegalese cuisine. Their shops range from small grocers to importers of European fabric and clothing, household items, shoes, furniture, and electronics. They own numerous fast-food restaurants and finer French-style bakeries and cafés that include Lebanese specialities. Responding to the changing Senegalese economy and increased competition in retail, second and third generations have moved into industry and the professions, dominating the plastic, paper and cosmetics sectors and even holding a share in the African textile-manufacturing industry. Traditionally, many Lebanese learned their trade through working their way up to leadership positions in family-run businesses. Some of those with economic means send their children to universities in Europe, Lebanon and North America. Among the Lebanese of Senegal are also doctors, lawyers, dentists, pharmacists, tailors and mechanics. Those who can afford to visit Lebanon quickly realise that the social status and standard of living they have secured for themselves in Dakar could never be reproduced in Beirut.

Currently, there are between 20,000 and 25,000 Lebanese in Senegal.[1] While Senegal is a majority Sunni Muslim country, 95 per cent of the Lebanese community today is Shi'i Muslim, with a small Christian population and an even smaller Sunni Muslim presence. Muslim and Christian demographics were more evenly balanced in the first generation of Lebanese in Senegal. Although religious differentiation has remained strong in Lebanon, my informants emphasised that 'there are no problems between Muslims and Christians in Senegal'. Over time, Lebanese religious differences began to be accommodated by the religious institutions as the community transitioned from immigrant group to ethnic group. The boundaries between 'Muslim' and 'Christian' melted away as interreligious marriages became more frequent, children of different religions studied together in Christian or Muslim schools, and all Lebanese community members, Muslim and Christian alike, celebrated weddings, funerals and even religious holidays together in mosques and churches. The Lebanese of Senegal lived through the Lebanese Civil War from a distance. Most Lebanese Muslims did not distinguish between the Sunni and Shi'i denominations; only when they visited Lebanon were they confronted with religious differences. Changes in Lebanese religious identity in the diaspora took place in three stages: (1) the establishment of the Lebanese community in Senegal under French colonialism (1880s–1960); (2) Senegalese independence until the July 2006 Lebanon War (1960–2006); and (3) from the 2006 war until the present.[2] Each historical period involves various configurations of ethnic, national and religious expression shaped in different ways by the changing background of Lebanon and Senegal.

French colonial policy towards Lebanese in *Afrique occidentale française* (AOF)

In Senegal, Lebanese have constructed their diasporic identities in response to imperial politics and colonial rivalries, which caused continuous tensions between religion, ethnicity, race and nationalism. Lebanese in Senegal are a community defined as much by others as by self-definition. Whereas, in Lebanon, religion was the dominant identifier, in Senegal, race and country of origin became the community's distinguishing factors and served as the unifying characteristic of migrants. French administrators recruited Lebanese as economic intermediaries then later opposed their immigration. They soon grew concerned over increasing numbers of Arab immigrants to West Africa and began to see the Lebanese in particular as a threat. Lebanese at this time were very much in touch with the motherland. They not only were involved in the flow of literature between Lebanon and West Africa and supported the reformist Shi'i movement in Lebanon, but they also followed other regional political events with fervour (see Arsan, 2014).

French colonists first lured Lebanese to Senegal to work as intermediaries in the peanut trade at the height of French economic expansion and prosperity in West Africa. The French did not look upon Lebanese immigration with disfavour during this period, nor did they disapprove of the natural inclination of Lebanese to integrate in Senegal. The economic depression of the 1930s, combined with nationalist sentiments spreading through the Arab world, led to a change in French views of Lebanese. Rita Cruise O'Brien (1972, p. 51) attributes this shift in French policy to the fall in the world price of groundnuts, Senegal's monocrop, between 1929 and 1931. Capital no longer circulated freely in Africa, and credit became more difficult for traders to obtain. French colonists in AOF became wary of those Lebanese traders who skilfully competed with their economic control.

In the 1930s and 1940s, French administrators responded with anti-Lebanese campaigns. These included a policy of segregating Lebanese from Africans to prevent the spread of pan-Islamism, pan-Arabism and anticolonial sentiments, restricting the use of Arabic in the colonies, exercising greater control over the importation of publications in Arabic and prohibiting Lebanese Muslims from praying in Senegalese mosques and attending local Qur'anic schools (Harrison, 1988). The French began complete surveillance of *Libano-Syrien* activities. The archives report on individual Lebanese suspected of dispersing banned literature, conspiring against the French, or being too political or pan-Islamic (Archives Nationales de Sénégal). French administrators introduced stricter immigration controls on Lebanese and Syrian populations in 1938. Archival data have illustrated that the French perception and treatment of Lebanese as a threat resulted in Lebanese unity (regardless of sectarian divisions) against the French (Leichtman, 2015).

While French colonists attempted to separate Lebanese from Senegalese, thereby inhibiting Lebanese integration in Senegal, they recognised the Arabic language and Muslim religion formed a bond between the two. Nonetheless, their obsession with Islam was a religious concern paired with the fear of a nationalist Muslim rebellion against the French. French colonial administrators sought to separate Arab migrants who practised Islam (or even Christianity) from Africans to prevent their religious – and political – ideas from spreading to the native population. French officers developed the notion of *Islam noir* by comparing Islam in North and West Africa, albeit in racist and hierarchical terms. *Islam noir* captured the colonial perception of Islam south of the Sahara defined as the product of spiritual and ritualistic transactions between Islam and 'African traditional religions'. African Islam was seen as less 'pure', less literate and more magical than Arab Islam, and flexible enough to be incorporated into French so-called 'Muslim policy' (Robinson, 2000). The French also understood African Islam to be docile, and from the French point of view a harmless religion, where West African Muslims were perceived to be immune from pan-Islamism.

Ethnic particularism (*politique des races*) was a central theme of colonial administration in West Africa until the Second World War. This directive was about ensuring Africans' right to progress on their own terms and reinforcing French commitment to respect African customs. In particular, Africans were given the 'right' to be governed by leaders drawn from their own people (Conklin, 1997). Through this proclamation of the Republican principle of ethnic self-determination, French administrators set about eroding the alliance of *marabouts* (Islamic clerics) and community chiefs by ensuring that Muslims were not placed as chiefs over non-Muslim peoples, so as not to encourage the extension of Muslim clericalism over 'fetishists'.

Not only did *politique des races* aim to divide and conquer indigenous African ethnic and religious communities by ensuring that Muslims did not rule over non-Muslims, but in conceiving of West African autochthony as fundamentally pre-Islamic and incapable of conforming to foreign religious traditions, it sought to segregate *Islam noir* from Arab Islam. French administrators built French-controlled Islamic schools (*médersas*) in the name of colonial modernity, demonstrating their openness to Muslim civilisation but expecting in return to educate a local Muslim leadership supportive of the French civilising mission (Brenner, 2001). The French never strayed from their conviction that progress and improvement could only develop in an Africa open to superior European Christian ways. French colonial policies had a lasting effect, resulting in various local reactions. Lebanese internalised French perceptions and treatment of their community and began to unite as an ethnic group. The *médersa* served as a catalyst for alternative forms of Senegalese – and Lebanese – Islamic education. Ongoing struggles for religious authority and authenticity continued to position themselves against the French model.

In sum, France's 'Lebanese phobia' operated on several levels. On the religious level, the French had a fear of Islam in general, and in particular that Lebanese 'Arab Islam' would co-opt African *Islam noir*, which they were trying to mould to their own needs. Politically, the French feared an outburst of pan-Arabism and pan-Islamism that would unite Arabs and Africans and undermine their authority in West Africa. These fears can be seen by French colonial actions banning publications in Arabic and surveilling Lebanese activities. Finally, on the economic level, the French were fully aware of the Lebanese ability to compete with them and win their market share in West Africa. As a result of these concerns, French administrators aimed to both prevent Lebanese from integrating with Senegalese and impede their contact with Lebanon. They chose not to differentiate between Lebanese in Senegal, nor did they give preferential treatment to Christians, as they did in Lebanon. They classified all Lebanese, even Christians, as the Arab Islamic economically and politically powerful enemy. It was thus the French who first envisioned Lebanese in Senegal as one homogeneous group, regardless of sectarian differences.

By implication, over time, Lebanese grew together in response to the colonial power. Lebanese blame the French for maintaining a Lebanese ghetto in Dakar and not only forbidding Lebanese integration with Senegalese but also keeping Lebanese at a distance from the colonial power. Since Lebanese religious practices were prohibited from externally conforming to those of the Senegalese, Lebanese sectarian divisions were instead internally accommodated as the community united in opposition to French policy. As the French created ethnic, racial and religious divisions in AOF, Lebanese maintained their own boundaries, and a diaspora was formed.

Senegalese independence

Senegal gained independence from France on 20 June 1960, leading to another transition for the Lebanese community. As an ethno-racial minority and a powerful business community, Lebanese encountered hostility from the Senegalese population. Becoming socially and politically invisible was the key to Lebanese economic success as the community remained a vulnerable minority in Senegal. Clandestine patron–client relationships suited the Lebanese, whose economic actions depended on such collaboration, as well as Senegalese politicians, who benefitted from Lebanese financial support but preferred not to publicise it. The Lebanese sensed change was underway well before independence and established good relations with Senegal's nationalist parties, especially the *Bloc Démocratique Sénégalais* of Leopold Senghor. When Senegal became independent, some of these Lebanese were 'rewarded' by receiving Senegalese citizenship, and the community as a whole was assured of continued protection (Boumedouha, 1987).

During the colonial period, a large number of Lebanese had both Lebanese and French nationalities. Some felt threatened at independence and their decision to apply for Senegalese citizenship was out of necessity to keep their jobs in certain sectors or to address Senegalese suspicions that the Lebanese community continued to identify with and send remittances to the homeland. Opting for Senegalese citizenship reaffirmed Lebanese commitment to the new nation, and by the end of the 1960s, the Senegalese government exerted pressure on Lebanese with Senegalese citizenship to revoke their original nationalities. Many Lebanese in Senegal resented what they perceived to be continuous treatment as foreigners and scapegoats even though they had Senegalese citizenship.

Although the transition from colonial to African administration was relatively smooth, it had been easier for the Lebanese to integrate economically in Senegal under French colonialism. After independence, newspaper and magazine articles portrayed the Lebanese community as an obstacle to the nationalisation of the Senegalese economy. For example, an article entitled

'Lebanese in Africa: Parasites or Agents of Development?' reports survey results on Senegalese and Ivoirian views of Lebanese. The overwhelmingly negative responses revolved around recurring topics resembling earlier French grievances against Lebanese:

> They are just parasites, non-producers, whose purely commercial occupations no longer have any economic or social basis; they gain wealth at the expense of nationals by depriving them of a job or rigging the game of commerce and employment; they are too exclusively "seekers of profit" and it is merely in appearance that they are integrated into African society.
>
> *(Thibault, 1976, p. 14)*

Lebanese were required to employ more Africans in their family-run businesses. They were also affected by rural development policies, as the independent government first nationalised the production of the peanut monocrop and then slowly diversified the economy, encouraging other food crops (Gellar, Charlick and Jones, 1980). Many Lebanese were forced to leave the groundnut trade and consequently migrated from the interior of Senegal to Dakar. Meanwhile, Senegalese textile importers circumvented official circuits and undersold Lebanese merchants with untaxed goods. By the late 1970s, Dakar's major Lebanese textile importers began to retreat from the trade (Boone, 1992). Those with financial capabilities moved their activities into new fields of investment.

Independence raised additional questions of Lebanese belonging. The community continued to unite in the face of new insecurities, Africanisation policies and Senegal's neo-colonial challenges. The nationalisation of the peanut industry forced the Lebanese to take over positions once dominated by the French. Lebanese were thus seen as replacing the colonial power and became Senegal's scapegoats due to their white skin and economic success. Lebanese profit derived from flexibility in adapting businesses to Senegal's changing needs and the ability to differentiate themselves from both French and Senegalese. Accused of racism for not intermarrying and thereby integrating, Lebanese continued to be viewed as one united minority, despite Muslim-Christian religious divisions shared with the host society.

Lebanese were excluded from Senegalese society as the economic, racial and religious Other. Community leaders countered accusations against them by proof of their good deeds, envisioning themselves as hard-working and successful, and citing how Lebanese were major employers in Senegal. They highlighted the community's active involvement in charity work and financing mosques, churches, schools and hospitals. Occasionally the government would request large financial contributions from wealthy Lebanese to assist in certain infrastructural projects. Boumedouha (1992) notes contributions increased considerably after 1975, the start of the Lebanese Civil War, when Lebanese had little choice but to invest more in Senegal. Lebanese publicly donated to important causes that won them necessary appreciation and strengthened the protectionist system. They continued to establish good relations with Senegal's political parties. Lebanese politicians were few in number, yet the community remained politically influential. Many voted in presidential elections, split among various political parties. Upon Abdoulaye Wade's election in 2000, a delegation of influential Lebanese men met with the new president to discuss issues important to their community.

Lebanese in Senegal developed two strategies for survival. On the one hand, they clung to cosmopolitan linkages: the Arabic language, international business ties, French education and multiple passports. On the other hand, they renegotiated the integration debate and made a case to be formally recognised as a Senegalese ethnic group, attempting to claim autochthony (Leichtman, 2015). Lebanese in Senegal have an ambivalent racial status; perceived not only as 'Arab' but also as 'white' by the African population, they were not welcome in French 'white-only' social clubs during colonial times. Treated as a scapegoat for many of Senegal's ills, Lebanese are caught in between black and white, Senegalese and French, and, as middlemen, are often considered a race of their own – Lebanese. Senegal offers a unique situation for Lebanese, whose racial status and economic success are what set the community apart and were not a basis for its integration.

These factors also contributed to the coming together of Lebanese Muslims and Christians. It is difficult to separate racial discrimination, based on skin colour, from social class discrimination, based on economic success, from religious discrimination, based on not belonging to Senegal's economically and politically influential Sufi orders. Lebanese are identified in Senegal as a wealthy elite community, yet the Lebanese community itself is divided along lines of social class. Poor Lebanese depend on the community's charity. It was during times of insecurity due to French colonial policies and post-independence politics of Africanisation that Lebanese in Senegal became a diaspora and sought to (re)invent their collective identity, uniting as a secular ethnic group. Meanwhile, in Lebanon, the primary form of identification was religious difference, not ethnicity. Shi'i identity further differentiated Lebanese from Senegalese Sufi Muslims and connected them to their homeland.

Lebanese Shi'i institutions, the 2006 Lebanon War, and increasing sectarian tensions

Shaykh 'Abdul Mun'am al-Zayn arrived in Dakar in 1969, almost a century after the establishment of the Lebanese community. Born and raised in Lebanon, and trained in the Shi'i seminaries (*hawzas*) in Najaf, Iraq, Shaykh al-Zayn's arrival came only shortly before the Lebanese Civil War (1975–1990) and the Iranian Revolution (1979), two important events in the making of a global Shi'i movement. Shaykh al-Zayn's work founding Dakar's Islamic Social Institution in 1978 led to an identity shift in the Lebanese community, with a 'return' to patriotic Lebanese Shi'i sentiments. The shaykh brought religious education and Arabic language instruction to Senegal, and his influence led to an increase in women wearing the veil and participation in religious charity events. He formalised the commemorations of 'Ashura[3] and Ramadan and facilitated ties to Lebanon.

Shaykh al-Zayn understood that inclusive, rather than exclusive, religious politics would be most successful in Senegal. He welcomed Sunni Muslims into his institution and joined Christians in affairs concerning the Lebanese community as a whole. Shaykh al-Zayn succeeded in making the Lebanese diaspora community in Senegal better Lebanese. His powerful sermons, lessons from Lebanese textbooks, visitors from Lebanon, an increase in marriages with women from southern Lebanon, and stories told by those who have gone 'back', inform Lebanese who have never been to Lebanon about their country, implanting in them the ethno-religious pride of being Lebanese. Furthermore, satellite television illustrates the shaykh's efforts more forcefully than he ever intended. The nationalist message of Hizbullah's channel *Al-Manar* informs Lebanese Shi'a in Senegal of their history, rise to power and current struggles, exemplified by the 2006 war. This leads to tensions in Senegal between Lebanese Shi'a and Christians or Sunnis who do not sympathise with Shi'i political endeavours. Frictions go beyond the shaykh's attempt to teach Shi'i pride through religious accommodation in Senegal.

The 2006 Lebanon War was a challenge for Lebanese unity in Senegal. Round-the-clock coverage by *Al-Manar* and the horrific images of death and destruction moved Lebanese Shi'a in Senegal to action for the first time. This was unlike the community's reaction to Lebanon's Civil War, which, I was told, Lebanese in Senegal followed in a detached manner through

French TV reporting in an era before the spread of Arabic satellite television. On 20 July 2006, the Lebanese community organised a large protest against the war, estimated at 3,000 people. Those in attendance waved signs denouncing Israeli attacks and thanking Senegal for its hospitality. I was told the Lebanese shaykh spoke more about politics at this occasion than during the usual religious ceremonies, whereas he had previously been careful not to demonstrate any attachments to Lebanese political parties. A silent vigil also took place at Dakar's Independence Square where Lebanese and some Senegalese lit hundreds of candles commemorating the victims of the Lebanon War. Lebanese Shi'i youth draped the Senegalese and Hizbullah flags over their backs, while others wore t-shirts of the Lebanese flag with the image of a clenched fist next to the cedar tree commanding '*Résistons!*' (Leichtman, 2010). This symbolism is important, as Lebanese in Senegal joined those in Lebanon in following the ideology of Hizbullah and not passively accepting their persecution as Shi'a. Taking a public stance against the war broke with the community's previously cautious public profile as a minority not fully accepted in Senegal and can be analysed as a culmination of their emerging transnational Lebanese identity (ibid.).

Moreover, the 2006 war increased tensions between Lebanese Muslims and Christians in Senegal (for more information on Lebanese Christians in Senegal, see Leichtman, 2013). In Lebanon, the war brought about an increase in sectarian divisions. Certain Christians and Sunni Muslims were outraged at the destruction, yet blamed Hizbullah for provoking Israeli attacks and feared the increasing power of Hasan Nasrallah, its Secretary-General. The war re-emphasised the divergence of the Maronite Catholic vision of Lebanon from Hizbullah's nationalism, which pushed for an Islamic and Arab nation (Shaery-Eisenlohr, 2008). Politics were heightened among Senegal's Lebanese Christians as well, who quietly objected to the increasing pro-Hizbullah sentiments of their Shi'i neighbours. In response, some backed former general Michel Aoun, then Maronite Member of Parliament, who led Lebanon's Free Patriotic Movement and publicly aspired to be a *secular* Lebanese leader.[4] Despite his declared secular leanings, Aoun was a divisive figure, in particular resulting from his surprise alliance with Hizbullah in 2006 (and break with other Maronite politicians in the 14 March coalition). Lebanese in Senegal had become noticeably more politicised as a result of the 2006 war, and, for the first time, some even voted in the 2009 Lebanese general elections.[5]

Through responses to the 2006 Lebanon War, the Arab-Israeli conflict played out in Senegal for the first time through public Lebanese demonstrations (see Leichtman, 2010; 2015, for further details). Yet the war was not the only Lebanese political event commemorated in Senegal. Hizbullah and Amal deputies came regularly to Dakar for the celebration of the liberation of the south of Lebanon (25 May 2000). The Islamic Institute and Maronite Mission held several private religious services over the previous four years commemorating 'martyrs' of Lebanon, including Prime Minister Rafik Hariri, killed on 14 February 2005; Jibran Twayni, a parliamentarian assassinated in December 2005; and Pierre Jumayil, an anti-Syrian cabinet minister and Christian leader killed in November 2006. There were also more general commemorations for all Lebanese who died during the 2006 war and the siege of the Nahr al-Barid Palestinian refugee camp near Tripoli in June 2007.[6] Although Lebanese religious institutions in Senegal denounced violence in Lebanon and officially commemorated martyrs regardless of religion, the 2006 war altered the delicate balance between religion and secular ethnicity among members of the Lebanese diaspora in Senegal. Although the war heightened sectarian tensions between Shi'i Muslims and Christians in Senegal, Christians in Lebanon were split in two, with some joining the Hizbullah-led alliance along with many Shi'i Muslims, and others joining the Hariri-led alliance with numerous Sunni Muslims (see Norton, 2007, pp. 152–153).

On the one hand, Lebanese in Senegal were linked to a distinct *Lebanese* ethnic identity not fully detached from wider politics of sectarianism in Lebanon. On the other hand, this very identity enabled unity in the diaspora as a *secular* Lebanese ethnic group to claim what McGovern (2013, p. 67) has termed 'fictive autochthony', constructed from the community's long history and economic, political and cultural contributions to Senegal. The 2006 Lebanon War impinged on this harmony, indicative of difficulties faced by Lebanese religious institutions in the diaspora in continuing to embrace secularism and distancing themselves from sectarian politics in Lebanon. Yet the 2006 war in Lebanon, while having arguably weakened the Lebanese nation-state, had conceivably strengthened national identity among Lebanese in the diaspora, who became more emotionally tied to the embattled homeland. Thus, newfound transnationalism can at times be an impediment to diasporic belonging.

Conclusion

Members of ethnic groups are often categorised according to which religious communities they belong to and if they speak the same languages and follow certain social practices. Lebanon, in contrast, is characterised by religious difference, which has been exploited throughout history by foreign powers. Yet, in Senegal, distance from the homeland and the altered and multi-layered dynamics of transnational religious politics enabled the ethnic network of Lebanese in the diaspora to develop over time to become expansive and 'secular' enough to include Christians and Muslims. While not immune to divisive events, exemplified by the 2006 Lebanon War, Lebanese in Senegal are too small a minority for the community cohesion that has characterised the diaspora as an ethnic group not to persevere, despite continuous political and economic pressures. Demographics (in addition to internal and external factors) may also determine when religious groups come together as a united ethnicity, or when ethnicities supersede religion as the dominant form of identity. The Senegalese example suggests that ethnic group integration on the secular, not religious, level is greater when there is some degree of ethnic pluralism and where society is marked by uneven numbers in different religious groups.

Lebanese in Senegal are a difficult community to define. They are not a homogeneous group in terms of religion, social class or period of immigration. Lebanese and Senegalese governments do not officially classify them as 'Lebanese' or 'Senegalese'. They are a community defined as much by others as by themselves. Lebanese in Lebanon envision those in Senegal as having originated in Lebanon generations earlier, surviving by hard work in a foreign land. They hope that Lebanese in Senegal will continue to hold strong affections for Lebanon and will invest financially in their homeland. Senegalese do not identify Lebanese in Senegal by national origin but group them as 'Arabs', discernible by their skin colour. This derogatory categorisation is further marked by the perceived high socioeconomic status of Lebanese, of which many are envious. This identity raises questions of nationalism and inclusion, and whether an Arab community, born and socialised on African soil, can ever be considered 'true' Senegalese or Lebanese. In providing an overview of the history of Lebanese migration to Senegal and the social, economic and religious development of a diaspora over several generations, this chapter has illustrated the Lebanese community's agency in strategically advocating for and claiming their place in Senegal. They effectively minimised religion as their dominant identifier and in its place opted for shared ethnicity over race or country of origin.

Yet the Lebanese diaspora in West Africa struggled to leave behind sectarian tensions in Lebanon in embracing religious differences in the formation of a Lebanese ethnic group. Exclusion from Senegalese society simultaneously led to increasing political solidarity with Lebanon while enhancing efforts to establish 'fictive' autochthony in Senegal. Over the distinct historical periods marked by French colonialism, Senegalese independence and the 2006 Lebanon War, Lebanese in Senegal created a secular ethnic network that included all Lebanese religious denominations and was responsive to both local and global change. This was not about completely adapting to Senegal or maintaining an exact tradition from Lebanon, but about creating a modern public civic space in the diaspora. The Lebanese of Senegal gained a national ethnicity they never shared in Lebanon by downplaying their strong religious identities, sharing secular and religious rituals and allowing religious institutions to represent their minority community as a whole, regardless of denomination. Migrant perceptions of serious differences between Muslims and Christians transformed throughout various historical periods into perceptions of limited differences in selected spheres of religious and cultural activity, particularly when juxtaposed with their collective differences from Senegalese society at large.

Lebanese in Africa are an important, while understudied, example of South-South migration and ethnic and religious diasporic identity formation. Looking forward, analysis of post-2020 dynamics in Lebanon should likewise not ignore the role of transnationalism and the Lebanese diaspora. Recent tensions in Lebanon continue to resonate with the Lebanese diaspora in Senegal, including Hizbullah's involvement in the Syrian civil war since 2012, Lebanon's ongoing political and financial crises, the 2019 anti-government protests that united Lebanese across religious sect and social class, and the 2020 coronavirus pandemic and tragic explosion in Beirut's port. With the collapse once again of the Lebanese state, and increased pressures on Lebanon's struggling population to seek a more stable future for their families elsewhere, Lebanese diaspora communities will continue to play a crucial role in Lebanon, with perhaps increasing significance with new waves of migration. As with the case of the 2006 war, current tensions will alter community interactions once again – in Lebanon as well as in the Lebanese diaspora. This historical narrative can therefore shed light on understanding future dynamics, where the West African example adds a transnational dimension to the relationship between religion and nationalism in the Middle East, and beyond.

Notes

1 Formal statistics on the Lebanese population of Senegal do not exist. According to a former Consulate Officer at the Lebanese Embassy of Dakar, there were approximately 25,000–30,000 Lebanese in Senegal in 2000. However, a previous Director General of the Ministry of Emigrants in Beirut believed there were 30,000 Lebanese in Senegal in the past, but only 15,000 in 2000. The higher number from within Senegal demonstrates the Lebanese community's efforts at emphasising their importance and their identity as a Lebanese emigrant community. Likewise, the lower number quoted by the Lebanese Ministry of Emigrants is symbolic of the government deflating the importance of the Lebanese of Senegal, and likewise the flow of resources to the community. Furthermore, this discrepancy is due to the difficulty of estimating the number of Lebanese in Senegal, as not all have Lebanese nationality, many are not registered with the Lebanese embassy and it is difficult to categorise children of mixed marriages. The community has faced additional decline since 2000.
2 This chapter is a summary of my book (Leichtman, 2015) and I have not conducted recent fieldwork among the Lebanese community in Senegal.
3 The first ten days of the Islamic month of Muharram, which commemorate the martyrdom of Imam Husayn (the Prophet Muhammad's grandson) at the battle of Karbala in Iraq in 680 CE, represent a critical aspect of collective identity for Shi'a around the world. Lebanese metonymically refer to this period as "Ashura', which means 'ten'. Technically, the term refers only to the tenth of the month, when the battle at Karbala took place. 'Ashura is both the remembrance of a battle of righteousness against corruption and evil and a tribute to a key moment in Shi'i history. See Leichtman (2015, Chapter 4).
4 His Free Patriotic Movement was comprised of thousands of Lebanese members from different religious sects, including a significant number of Muslims. Aoun became President of Lebanon in 2016.
5 Lebanese political parties flew some with Lebanese citizenship from Senegal to Lebanon in order to vote.
6 Victims included relatives of those in Senegal.

References

Abdelhady, D. (2011) *The Lebanese Diaspora: The Arab Immigrant Experience in New York, Montreal and Paris*. New York: New York University Press.
Alfaro-Velcamp, T. (2007) *So Far from Allah, So Close to Mexico: Middle Eastern Immigrants in Modern Mexico*. Austin, TX: University of Texas Press.
Archives Nationales de Sénégal (ANS) 'Series 21G23(17)'.
Arsan, A. (2014) *Interlopers of Empire: The Lebanese Diaspora in Colonial French West Africa*. Oxford: Oxford University Press.
Bierwirth, C. (1999) 'The Lebanese communities of Côte d'Ivoire', *African Affairs*, 98(390), pp. 79–99.
Boone, C. (1992) *Merchant Capital and the Roots of State Power in Senegal, 1930–1985*. Cambridge: Cambridge University Press.
Boumedouha, S. (1987) 'The Lebanese in Senegal: a history of the relationship between an immigrant community and its French and African rulers', PhD, University of Birmingham.
Boumedouha, S. (1992) 'Change and continuity in the relationship between the Lebanese in Senegal and their hosts', in Hourani, A. and Shehadi, N. (eds) *The Lebanese in the World: A Century of Emigration*. London: I.B. Tauris, pp. 549–563.
Brand, L.A. (2010) 'National narratives and migration: discursive strategies of inclusion and exclusion in Jordan and Lebanon', *International Migration Review*, 44(1), pp. 78–110.
Brenner, L. (2001) *Controlling Knowledge: Religion, Power and Schooling in a West African Muslim Society*. Bloomington, IN: Indiana University Press.
Brubaker, R. (2005) 'The "diaspora" diaspora', *Ethnic and Racial Studies*, 28(1), pp. 1–19.
Conklin, A.L. (1997) *A Mission to Civilize: The Republican Idea of Empire in France and West Africa, 1895–1930*. Palo Alto, CA: Stanford University Press.
Crowder, M. (1968) *West Africa under Colonial Rule*. London: Hutchinson.
Cruise O'Brien, R. (1972) *White Society in Black Africa: The French of Senegal*. Evanston, IL: Northwestern University Press.
Gellar, S., Charlick, R.B., and Jones, Y. (1980) *Animation Rurale and Rural Development: The Experience of Senegal*. Ithaca, NY: Rural Development Committee, Center for International Studies, Cornell University.
Gualtieri, S.M.A. (2009) *Between Arab and White: Race and Ethnicity in the Early Syrian American Diaspora*. Berkeley, CA: University of California Press.
Harrison, C. (1988) *France and Islam in West Africa, 1860–1960*. Cambridge: Cambridge University Press.
Hitti, P.K. (1957) *Lebanon in History from the Earliest Times to the Present*. London: Macmillan.
Hourani, A. and Shehadi, N. (eds) (1992) *The Lebanese in the World: A Century of Emigration*. London: I.B. Tauris.
Karam, J.T. (2007) *Another Arabesque: Syrian-Lebanese Ethnicity in Neoliberal Brazil*. Philadelphia, PA: Temple University Press.
Kaufman, A. (2004) *Reviving Phoenicia: In Search of Identity in Lebanon*. London: I. B. Tauris.
Khater, A.F. (2001) *Inventing Home: Emigration, Gender, and the Middle Class in Lebanon, 1870–1920*. Berkeley, CA: University of California Press.
Labaki, B. (1993) 'L'émigration libanaise en Afrique occidentale sud-saharienne', *Revue Européene des Migrations Internationales*, 9(2), pp. 91–112.
Leichtman, M.A. (2010) 'Migration, war, and the making of a transnational Lebanese Shi'i community in Senegal', *International Journal of Middle East Studies*, 42(2), pp. 269–290.
Leichtman, M.A. (2013) 'From the cross (and crescent) to the cedar and back again: transnational religion and politics among Lebanese Christians in Senegal', *Anthropological Quarterly*, 86(1), pp. 35–74.
Leichtman, M.A. (2015) *Shi'i Cosmopolitanisms in Africa: Lebanese Migration and Religious Conversion in Senegal*. Bloomington, IN: Indiana University Press.
Lesser, J. (1999) *Negotiating National Identity: Immigrants, Minorities, and the Struggle for Ethnicity in Brazil*. Durham, NC: Duke University Press.
Makdisi, U. (2000) *The Culture of Sectarianism: Community, History and Violence in Nineteenth-Century Ottoman Lebanon*. Berkeley, CA: University of California Press.
McGovern, M. (2013) *Unmasking the State: Making Guinea Modern*. Chicago: University of Chicago Press.
Norton, A.R. (2007) *Hezbollah: A Short History*. Princeton, NJ: Princeton University Press.
Robinson, D. (2000) *Paths of Accommodation: Muslim Societies and French Colonial Authorities in Senegal and Mauritania, 1880–1920*. Athens, OH: Ohio University Press.

Shaery-Eisenlohr, R. (2008) *Shi'ite Lebanon: Transnational Religion and the Making of National Identities.* New York: Columbia University Press.

Taraf, S. (1994) 'L'espace en mouvement. Dynamiques migratoires et territorialisation des familles Libanaises au Sénégal', PhD, Université de Tours.

Thibault, J. (1976) 'Les Libanais en Afrique: parasites ou agents de développement?' *Voix d'Afrique*, 24, October 4–17.

van der Laan, H.L. (1975) *The Lebanese Traders in Sierra Leone.* Mouton: The Hague.

van der Laan, H.L. (1992) 'Migration, mobility and settlement of the Lebanese in West Africa', in Hourani, A. and Shehadi, N. (eds) *The Lebanese in the World: A Century of Emigration.* London: I.B. Tauris, pp. 531–547.

PART III

Expressive terrains of contestation

PART III

Explanation and understanding

12
THE SEMANTICS AND SUBSTANCE OF CONTESTING TURKISHNESS IN THE DIASPORA

Pinar Dinc

Being an immigrant from Turkey in Sweden, over the past three years I have often been asked 'Are you a Turk?'. The question was usually asked by other citizens of Turkey, who had just met me or heard me speaking Turkish. My response to this question has always been, 'I am from Turkey' (*Türkiyeliyim*), with which I would firmly but respectfully refuse to reproduce the imposition of Turkishness and excluding 'others' (e.g., Kurds, Alevis and Armenians) in the description of Turkey's national identity. In the summer of 2020, during a visit to the Haga Neighbourhood in the city of Gothenburg with a group of friends from Turkey, we stopped at a local café. Two of my friends went inside to place our orders and returned to our table with a man whom they introduced saying, 'This gentleman is the owner of this coffee shop, and he is from Turkey.' The café owner, who greeted us, was pleasantly surprised by this introduction. He quickly explained that he was originally from Urfa, a south-eastern province of Turkey, and migrated to Sweden several decades ago. He was a Turk from his mother's side and a Kurd from his father's side. In our short conversation, he said he would be criticised by one side if he described his identity as a Kurd, and the other would be offended if he said he was a Turk. 'It is always a problem for me,' he said, 'both in Turkey and in Sweden.' With his mixed ethnic belongings, he liked to be referred to as *Türkiyeli* [from Turkey].

A few weeks after my encounter with the *Türkiyeli* coffee shop owner in Sweden, a video interview with Hakan Taş, an MP from the *Die Linke* Party in Germany, was released. In this interview, Taş talks about himself as an Alevi Kurdish, gay, socialist immigrant who grew up in Istanbul and moved to Germany at the age of 14. Taş mentioned that he is from Germany and also from Turkey. When the interviewer Şafak Salda frames his follow-up question to refer to Taş as a 'Turk', Taş corrects him immediately, saying '*Türkiyeli*. *Türkiyeli*. To me, there is a difference between Turk and *Türkiyeli*. That is why I am a bit sensitive about this' (Salda, 2020).

Historically, the designation 'Turk' has had diverse meanings. For example, the Muslim population under the Ottoman Empire, regardless of their ethnic identity, were viewed as 'Turks'. Migrants who left the Ottoman Empire and went to North America in the late 1800s were also identified as Turks. Since the establishment of the Republic of Turkey as a nation-state in 1923, however, the concept has taken an increasingly homogenising meaning and citizens were expected to fit into 'Turkishness' as an ethno-religious category. Building on Mills's (1997) framework of the racial contract, Ünlü (2016, p. 398) uses the concept of the 'Turkishness contract' to refer to the written and unwritten terms that give the Sunni-Turkish majority a position of privilege. Placed at the apex of the ethnic hierarchy 'the Turks' are both privileged and indifferent or blind to the unequal treatment that the non-Turks have been subjected to since the early 1900s (Ünlü, 2016). Therefore, the 'Turk' no longer simply refers to an ethnically mixed group of people from the Ottoman Empire, or equal citizens of the Republic of Turkey, but a specific group composed of religiously Sunni-Muslim and ethnically Turk individuals. Disagreeing with the use of 'Turkish' or 'Turk' to define the diverse ethno-religious composition of Turkey's citizens and diaspora communities in Europe can therefore also be understood as a way of breaking this contract, and the increasing use of terms like *Türkiyeli*, particularly in the diaspora, can be understood as taking into account the heterogeneity of Turkey's peoples.

Being from Turkey, *Türkiyeli*, is an umbrella term that embraces different identities in Turkey, based on civic citizenship (Grigoriadis, 2007). The concept, which is also referred to as 'Turkeyman, Turkeyish, Turkeyan, Turklander, Turkeyiot' (Öktem, 2017), prioritises the civic identity of being from Turkey instead of an ethnic Turkish identity. In a way, the concept offers an important conceptual framework for breaking the binds of methodological nationalism. Interestingly enough, the notion of *Türkiyeli* has already been used in Turkey's diaspora communities across Europe since the 1960s, such as the European Federation of Socialists from Turkey (*Avrupa Türkiyeli Toplumcular Federasyonu*, ATTF), the Foundation of Teachers from Turkey (*Türkiyeli Öğretmenler Derneği*), the Union of Workers from Turkey (*Türkiyeli İşçiler Birliği*), the Union of Progressives from Turkey (*Türkiyeli İlericiler Birliği*), the Confederation of Workers from Turkey in Europe (*Avrupa Türkiyeli İşçiler Konfederasyonu*, ATİK), and the North-Rhine Westphalia Writers from Turkey Working Group (*Kuzey Ren Vesfalya Türkiyeli Yazarlar Çalışma Grubu*[1]). Some of these organisations were ideologically in line with the Workers' Party of Turkey (*Türkiye İşçi Partisi*, TİP), and the socialist ideology in general.[2] The founding documents of the ATTF, for example, emphasise the federation's desire for democracy and peace in light of socialism and identifies itself as serving Turkey's peoples instead of Turks or Turkish people. However, the ATTF is often translated as the European Federation of Turkish Socialists in English, and *Föderation Türkischer Sozialisten in Europa* in German, despite the federation's use of the concept of *Türkiyeli*, and not Turk or Turkish. Although this suggests that the *Türkiyeli* concept has been doomed to be lost in translation, the concept remains an important analytical framework for explaining Turkey's diverse diaspora communities.

In light of this background, my aim in this chapter is twofold. First, I deliberate the insufficiency of the ethnically loaded hyphenated identity of 'Euro-Turks' in defining the diverse diasporic community of Turkey's citizens and/or their descendants in Europe. Second, I lay out the advantages and disadvantages of using the *Türkiyeli* concept as an alternative to the hyphenated identity Euro-Turks, which allows people and observers of Turkey to acknowledge and emphasise the heterogeneity of Turkey's diasporas in Europe. In doing so, I show how the *Türkiyeli* identity was introduced by Turkey's leftist diaspora groups in Europe in the late 1960s but has also been contested by Turkey's different diaspora groups themselves. Additionally, I discuss how the specific meaning of the term gets lost in translation when converted into other languages (i.e. English, French, German). To better understand the contestations around identity among members of Turkey's diaspora, the chapter begins with an overview of the theoretical literature on collective identity construction and diaspora, followed by a description of the heterogeneity of Turkey's diaspora(s) in Europe. This heterogeneity and contestation are well represented by the Kurdish and Alevi communities in Europe that have been key in challenging the concept of 'Turkishness'. The last section of the chapter focuses on the concept of *Türkiyeli* and the attendant advantages and disadvantages of using the term to represent Turkey's diverse diaspora groups. In concluding, I argue that the concept of *Türkiyeli*, despite the difficulties in translating it, is an important expression of selfhood and critique of the homogenising and exclusionary agendas and ventures of the Republic of Turkey within and outside of the nation-state.

Collective identity (re-)building in the diaspora[3]

Identity is not a fixed entity but 'a project, a non-settled accomplishment' that is constantly in the making (Calhoun, 1994, p. 15), and identity production – 'identisation' as Melucci (1995) explains – is an ongoing and fluid process whereby identities are interactively made. In the literature on new social movements, successful collective actions are linked to clearly defined collective identities. Whittier (2009, p. 105) emphasises that groups 'need to know who "they" are' before they can make demands to authorities, but she also notes that these identities are not always consciously created or with clear agendas. The following passage, put forward by Polletta and Jasper (2001, p. 298), provides a comprehensive definition of collective identity:

> Collective identity describes imagined as well as concrete communities, involves an act of perception and construction as well as the discovery of pre-existing bonds, interests, and boundaries. It is fluid and relational, emerging out of interactions with a number of different audiences (bystanders, allies, opponents, news media, state authorities), rather than fixed. It channels words and actions, enabling some claims and deeds but delegitimating others. It provides categories by which individuals divide up and make sense of the social world.

Being relational, collective identity is not independent of 'historically situated and entangled' power relationships (Weeden, 2009, p. 80). Political opportunity structures (McAdam, McCarthy and Zald, 1996), cultural opportunities or constraints, and targeted audiences play a role in how identity frames are shaped, characterised and determined (Benford and Snow, 2000). Diaspora is an important milieu in which the above-mentioned factors interplay.

Like collective identity, diaspora is also far from being a fixed entity, and diaspora communities, likewise, do not have fixed definitions to their identity. Rather, they are in a process of making and negotiating who they are. In his acclaimed article, 'The "Diaspora" Diaspora', Brubaker discusses the literature's wide-ranging use of the term 'diaspora' and argues that the term refers to a hybrid and fluid 'category of practice, project, claim and stance' (2005, p. 13). Citing Sheffer, Brubaker argues that the conceptualisation of diaspora communities as 'bona fide actual entities' leads to a failure in recognising their heterogeneity (ibid., p. 10, see also Sheffer, 2003).

In her critique of Brubaker, Alexander (2017) draws attention to the ways claims-staking and remaking identities also take place within the existing power structures that sustain practices of exclusion. Accepting this critique, Brubaker (2017, p. 1559) explains the promise of diaspora as a framework in which:

> The language of diaspora contributes to 'making up people' and to 'creating new ways for people to be' [n]ot because it is imposed on them ... but because the language of diaspora, as it is appropriated *by* them, enables telling of new sorts of stories and the shaping of new sorts of self-understandings and subjectivities.

The fluidity and multiplicity of identities and diasporas show that diaspora identities, like collective identities, are not fixed or natural but outcomes of historical contingencies and mobilisations (Sökefeld, 2006). Given this fluidity, the next section questions the ways of tracing the changing identities of Turkey's heterogeneous diaspora communities in Europe. Over time they have been described as 'guest workers', then 'Turkish diaspora' and sometimes 'Euro-Turks', which have in turn been challenged by other formations of collective and diaspora identities by Kurds and Alevis from Turkey, among others.

Rethinking the concept of 'Euro-Turks'

As of August 2020, the population of 'Turkish people' living abroad is reportedly over 6.5 million, 5.5 million of whom live in Western Europe (Turkish Citizens Living Abroad, n.d.). Germany hosts the largest number of immigrants from Turkey among the European Union states with an estimated 1.6 million as reported in 2018 by the Ministry of Foreign Affairs in Turkey. The first wave of migration from Turkey to Europe was characterised by labour migration in the 1960s. From the 1970s onwards, political conflicts in Turkey culminated in new waves of migration to Europe,[4] particularly to Germany and Sweden.[5] Following Turkey's authoritarian turn in the 2010s, and particularly in the aftermath of the failed 15 July 2016 coup d'état, there has been a new wave of migration from Turkey to Europe. Various sources reported that nearly 30,000 people from Turkey migrated to the United Kingdom, Germany and France between 2013 and 2018 (Lowen, 2017) when 'religious politics came to the fore' (Adamson, 2019, p. 224). While the first-generation workers desired and planned a return to Turkey, their children realised they were likely to stay in Europe. These political migrants in Europe have 'thereby changed the composition of the respective diasporas from predominantly apolitical guest worker communities to networked and homeland-oriented political activist organisations' (Eccarius-Kelly, 2002, p. 91). Over the decades, Turkey's diaspora communities became important actors in their host countries, while their ties to Turkey also remained strong.

Today, Turkey's diaspora communities are no longer only perceived as a group as 'remittance machines' but are understood to be a settled group in Europe (Østergaard-Nielsen, 2003, p. 95). The realisation that the 'Euro-Turks' were here to stay in their new host societies changed how they were perceived, adding a political layer for both Turkey and the host countries. Since the 1990s, various groups (such as Kurds, Alevis and political Islamists) have been politically active in Europe, with a significant impact on Turkey's domestic politics. For example, during the Gezi protests in Turkey in 2013, hundreds to thousands of people joined the protests from the streets of Brussels, Amsterdam, Stuttgart, Berlin, Hamburg and other European cities (Giglou, Ogan and d'Haenens, 2018). With the positive role of Turkey's European Union candidacy and democratisation process through political and legal reforms in the early 2000s, Turkey's diaspora community in Europe became a 'potential source of soft power and influence', which has led to the establishment of the Presidency of Expatriate Turks and Related Communities (*Yurtdışı Türkler ve Akraba Topluluklar Başkanlığı*, YTB) in 2010 (Adamson, 2019, pp. 224–225).[6] Despite this initial step forward to reach out to its citizens abroad, the YTB was in 'selective engagement with certain segments of external citizens who form AKP's electoral base abroad' and exclusionary towards other communities, including Kurds and Alevis from Turkey in Europe (Yanasmayan and Kaşlı, 2019, p. 28). In the same period, the AKP government also allowed Turkey's citizens outside Turkey to vote in national elections and referenda from the 2014 presidential elections onwards.[7]

Those who migrated to Europe in the 1960s and 1970s have previously been labelled 'guest workers' (*Gastarbeiter* in German) and foreigners. When Kaya and Kentel (2005) used the

Euro-Turks term, they underlined that their intention was not to essentialise and enforce the 'Turkishness' of these transnational migrants and their descendants but to allow a hyphenated identity based on civic citizenship in their host countries in Europe. However, conceptualisations such as the Turks in Europe, the Turkish Diaspora, those with a 'Turkish descent' in Europe and Euro-Turks have been gradually challenged by various political movements that stress the concept's indifference to the various ethnic, linguistic, religious and cultural identities in Turkey and its diaspora.

Besides the literature on the heterogeneity of diasporas (Gabaccia, 2000; Brinkerhoff, 2008; Lyons and Mandaville, 2010; Afful, 2016; Adamson, 2019), some studies address the multifaceted identity structures among the 'Euro-Turks' and the insufficiency of the term in taking into account the multiplicity and contentious nature of Turkey's diasporas (Østergaard-Nielsen, 2003; Kaya and Kentel, 2005; Lelie et al., 2012). According to Østergaard-Nielsen (2003, p. 81), the Euro-Turks concept has a complex structure with a 'visibly heterogenous collection of ethnic (Kurdish, Laz, Zaza, etc.) and religious (Sunni, Alevi) subgroups'. These subgroups are also heterogeneous, 'fractionalised, and contentious' (Adamson, 2019, p. 212) and 'multipolar' (Massicard, 2013, p. 51). No precise statistical data exist, but among the 5.5 million 'Turks' in Europe, there are an estimated one million Kurds (Baser, 2013) and between 400,000 to 600,000 Alevis (Massicard, 2017). These Kurdish and Alevi communities also overlap, as there are Alevi-Kurds and Sunni-Kurds, or Turkish-Alevis and Kurdish-Alevis. In other words, the different diaspora communities of Turkey are not homogeneous either, and while some oppose the imposition of Turkishness upon them, it is hard to say that they agree on the definition of their identity.

It is also important to highlight Europe's political, legal and social context, which has transformed Turkey's different diaspora communities and also allowed them to 'develop discursive strategies to legitimate their demands for recognition' (Özyürek, 2009, p. 235). Europe was not only a hub for existing political movements but also allowed new identity frames based on ethnic, religious, linguistic, cultural and other belongings to emerge and mobilise. For the Kurds, Europe was a space that differed significantly from the oppressive Turkish state, for the Alevis, it was a transnational space in which they could emphasise their unique religious identity and benefit from the official recognition and state support in their host country, something that they lacked in Turkey. The same goes for other groups, including certain Zaza and Kirmanc (Dersimli) communities that have dissociated themselves from both Turkish and Kurdish belongings to emphasise their unique national/regional/ethnic identities.

Kurdish and Alevi movements from Turkey in Europe have yielded ample study in the literature. Some works discuss the 'emergent identity [of] Euro-Kurdishness' (Soguk, 2008, p. 176), or 'Euro-Kurdistan' as 'a space where painful experiences are channelled into a creative process of nation building driven from below' (Ayata, 2008, p. 23). The concept of Euro-Kurds, like Euro-Turks, refers to a heterogeneous group in which divergent actors and individuals are involved. As Baser (2015) explains, in 1979, before the Kurdistan Workers' Party (*Partiya Karkerên Kurdistanê*, PKK) established its hegemony over the Kurdish political movement, there were already 30 Kurdish associations in Europe, which were united under a federation called the Federation of Kurdish Workers' Association (KOMKAR). KOMKAR was active in several countries, including Germany, the Netherlands and Sweden, and functioned as 'a home for many Kurdish migrants who arrived in Europe and needed a place to gather and find support' (ibid., p. 71).[8] Although the Kurdish movement in Europe today is largely associated with the PKK's ideology and leadership, there were, and to some extent still are, other Kurdish movements in Europe. For decades, the Kurds as non-state actors have drawn on international norms and engaging with the supranational structures of the European Union (EU) by using institutional and discursive opportunity structures (Berkowitz and Mügge, 2014). The transnational role played by the Kurdish movement(s) in Europe has been defined as 'the "EU-ising" of *Kurdi*(sh)ness' (Tekdemir, 2019, p. 877; see also p. 897, emphasis in original), a project that goes hand in hand with the radical democratisation approach of the Kurdish movement. Furthermore, this process of identity-formation led to the acceptance of multiple definitions of Kurdishness, an acknowledgement of 'many Kurdishnesses' including different sub-identities (ibid., p. 877). It is also possible to talk about the struggles of the Kurdish diaspora and its attempts to secure and discard their identities through 'ethnic entrepreneurial labouring', where they actively learn and unlearn to 'de-Turkify' to 'salvage and reconstruct Kurdishness in diaspora' (Demir, 2017, p. 277).

As the case of the ethno-religious Dersim diaspora shows, some diaspora groups interact and intersect with the Euro-Turks, Euro-Kurds and Euro-Alevis while also creating their distinctive diaspora (i.e. Dersimli, Zaza or Kirmanc) identities. Diaspora institutions established by members of the Dersim diaspora, such as the European Federation of Dersim Associations (*Föderation der Dersim Gemeinden in Europa*, FDG), and the Association of Reconstruction of Dersim (*Dersim Yeniden İnşa Cemiyeti*, DYİC), also differ in their definition of collective identity. While the FDG emphasises Dersim's Alevi identity and highlights the Zazaki and Kurdish languages spoken by the Dersim community, the DYİC views Dersim as part of the Kurdish identity and movement (Dinc, 2021). As a result of this difference, both institutions blame each other for seeking to 'assimilate' or reduce Dersim's identity to a single ethnic group (ibid.).

Given the heterogeneity of Turkey's diasporas in Europe, I argue that the Euro-Turk concept fails to fully conceptualise and, therefore, reflect the multiplicity of ethnic, ideological and cultural identities within the groups defined under the terms (ibid.). Despite the acknowledgement of the heterogeneity of diasporas, the narratives of Turkey and host countries, academics, and journalists alike still predominantly use concepts of 'Turk' and 'Turkish' for Turkey's diaspora communities. The last part of this chapter suggests why an alternative concept such as *Türkiyeli* could allow a more inclusive language and approach to understanding Turkey's heterogeneous diaspora in Europe.

Türkiyeli as an alternative?

Article 66 of the Constitution of the Republic of Turkey (1982) reads, 'Everyone bound to the Turkish State through the bond of citizenship is a Turk.'[9] The use of the 'Turk' identity in this citizenship definition has been widely discussed in the academic literature under the civic versus ethnic/cultural nationalism dichotomy (Cagaptay, 2006; Al and Karell, 2016; Goalwin, 2017). Despite the state narrative that the 'Turk' in the Constitution is used to refer to a civic and not an ethnic identity, state policies, starting particularly from the early Republican period, have treated 'Turkishness' as an upper, superior identity into which non-Turk citizens of the republic were expected to assimilate (Yegen, 2009).

Turkey's national identity description has been subject to debate since the second half of the 1990s. With Turkey's candidacy for EU membership in 1999, the EU's anchor role for Turkey's democratisation became stronger. Factors such as the EU's attention to Turkey and the Turkish governments' efforts to gain accession to the EU were combined with the 'pressure of domestic and international human rights organisations and Kurdish diaspora activists who had largely focused on these violations that were taking place in Kurdish majority provinces of the southeast' (Casier, 2009, p. 8). In line with these discussions, the definition of Turkey's national identity also became a focal point. 'The Minority Rights and Cultural Rights Working Group Report' drafted by the Human Rights Advisory Board (2004), established under the supervision of the office of the Turkish Prime Minister at the time,[10] played a key role in setting the framework of this discussion.

The report, published in 2004, begins with a definition of the minority concept, its meaning in the context of Turkey, and continues with a brief discussion of legislation and court judgments in Turkey. Building on the concepts of 'supra identity' and 'sub identities', the report emphasises that the concept 'Turk' in the Constitution refers to ethnically Turk and religiously Muslim groups, excluding others. Instead, the report offers the inclusive supra identity of *Türkiyeli*, saying:

> This supra identity will embrace all sub identities living on these territories without any exception and it will ensure that the concepts of "nationality" (being of a particular ethnic origin) and "citizenship" (the legal bond between the individual and the State) are taken up as separate and independent concepts, which used to be considered as identical terms. There is no doubt that a nation composed of "voluntary citizens" would be much more willing to embrace the State.
>
> *(ibid., p. 6)[11]*

Although the Working Group Report was an important moment in the discussion of Turkey's national identity, leading to a heated debate with its proposition of rewriting it in non-ethnic terms, the chair of the Advisory Council (İbrahim Kaboğlu) and chair of the council's working group (Baskın Oran) were later charged with 'denigrating Turkishness' and 'inciting hatred and hostility among people' for proposing the *Türkiyeli* concept.[12] A few years later, the Turkish Economic and Social Studies Foundation (TESEV, 2012) published a report showing that the majority of Turks (61.4 per cent) and Sunni Muslims (56.8 per cent) believed that the Constitution should only include the ethnically 'Turkish' identity. The Kurds (71.6 per cent) and Alevis (57.3 per cent), on the other hand, thought that all ethnic identities should be included in the Constitution (TESEV, 2012, p. 58). Another attempt at the elimination of the term 'Turk' from Article 66 was proposed by the AKP in 2013, at a time when the peace process between Turkey and the PKK was still ongoing. The AKP had parliamentary support from the Peace and Democracy Party (BDP) for this change in the Constitution, but the attempt eventually failed[13] due to a strong reaction from the Republican People's Party (*Cumhuriyet Halk Partisi*, CHP) and the Nationalist Movement Party (*Milliyetçi Hareket Partisi*, MHP).[14]

Besides the political setbacks, there have been other critiques of the use of *Türkiyeli*. One line of argument suggests that the concept might as well become exclusionary, given that Kurds from Turkey could say they are 'not really from Turkey' (Somer, 2005, p. 85) and that the concept does not comply with the fact that the Kurdish movement is motivated by its Kurdishness (Öktem, 2017). These ideas are evident in the findings of Baser's (2015) fieldwork, conducted between 2008 and 2012. Baser (ibid., p. 185) explains that there are both Kurds and Turks in the diaspora with 'nationalistic sensitivities', whereby Turks deny Kurdish rights and the existence of a place called 'Kurdistan', while Kurds resist the hegemony of Turkey and Turkish national identity by emphasising Kurdishness as their ethnic identity and Kurdistan – not Turkey – as their home country. Demir's (2017) research also shows how Kurdish interlocutors in London struggle for de-Turkification. These examples hint that an emphasis on Turkeyification (*Türkiyelileşme*, becoming from Turkey) and *Türkiyeli* concepts would be perceived as a sacrifice of the Kurdish national identity for some Kurds. Nonetheless, it should also be underlined this has been challenged by the Peoples' Democratic Party (*Halkların Demokratik Partisi*, HDP), which aimed to position itself as a *Türkiyeli* political party, rather than a pro-Kurdish party like its predecessors (Bora, 2017, p. 901). When the HDP was established in 2012, its aim was not only to win the Kurdish votes but also to 'unite and reinvigorate Turkey's fragmented left within a common struggle for democracy and equality' (Gunes, 2020, p. 747). The HDP's 'Turkeyification' attempts from 2013 onwards continue despite the AKP's deviation from its aim of accession to the EU and the remilitarisation and re-securitisation of Turkey after the collapse of the peace process between the PKK and Turkey in the summer of 2015 and the alleged coup attempt in July 2016.

In the meantime, being labelled as 'Turkish' has a whole different meaning from the European perspective. In an op-ed, Türkmen (2019) explains how the 'But you don't look Turkish!' sentence addressing some of the immigrants from Turkey, arguably as a compliment, implies a certain way of portraying 'Turkish' people in Europe. Türkmen rightly argues that this comment is not only about their ethnicity or national identity but also their socio-economic status, their religious belonging, as well as, in this case, the German perceptions of immigrants from Turkey. And there are various ways in which migrants respond to this comment, some of whom say, 'I am different from the Turkish people living here' or explaining how 'Turkey is a diverse country with varying skin colours' or how the ethnic diversity in Turkey makes it 'home to people with different phenotypic features'. As Türkmen argues, the host societies would also benefit from replacing 'Turkishness' with an alternative phrase to acknowledge the plurality of Turkey's, and not Turkish, diaspora communities.

Shifting the narrative from Turkish to *Türkiyeli* becomes particularly important, given that we are talking about a diverse group of people coming from different ethnic, cultural and socio-economic backgrounds when we talk about the immigrants from Turkey in Europe. Some migrated to Europe decades ago as guest workers with no intentions of adapting to the host society at the time, as they planned to return to Turkey; some migrated as part of family reunification mechanisms or through marriage; some were born and raised in Europe or went to Europe to study; some were political exiles or asylum seekers; others were white-collar workers; some started their own business in Europe; some were looking for a better future in the wake of authoritarianism in Turkey; and some escaped from homo/transphobia. The Euro-Turk concept has so far been challenged by Kurdish and Alevi identities of Turkey's diaspora communities in Europe, who have emphasised their unique ethnic/religious identity as opposed to the ethnic Turkish identity imposed on them. There are examples from the past, which I introduced at the beginning of this chapter, where a *Türkiyeli* identity was used from the late 1960s onwards, primarily by Turkey's leftist and worker diaspora groups in Europe.

Although empirical research is limited, the *Türkiyeli* concept has been re-introduced in the diaspora, particularly with the growing number of immigrants from Turkey in the aftermath of the Gezi protests in 2013, the end of the peace process in 2015 and the failed 'coup attempt' in 2016. Bek's (2020) recent study on Turkey's new migrants in Europe in the post-Gezi process and their use of the digital sphere shows two examples in which the concept of *Türkiyeli* has been underlined in newly established diaspora initiatives. The first is a blog called Expatriate Data Bank (*Gurbet Veri Bankası*), which aims to bring together stories from *Türkiyeli* people who live abroad. The second is a civil society organisation called Culture Initiative from Turkey (*Türkiyeli Kültür İnsiyatifi*), established in Berlin, Germany, in 2017, to support artists from Turkey. There is also the Initiative of Migrants from Turkey in Sweden (*Türkiyeli Göçmenler İnsiyatifi/İsveç*), a Facebook group followed by fewer than 500 people as of January 2021. Needless to say, more research needs to be conducted to empirically investigate the meaning and future of the *Türkiyeli* concept for different diaspora communities, as well as the policy-makers in Turkey and the host countries. These examples point to the re-emergence of *Türkiyeli* as an avenue to bring people together without resorting to the traditional affinities of ethnicity and religion.

One of the main setbacks before popularising the *Türkiyeli* concept has to do with language. Öktem (2017) rightly argues that *Türkiyeli* is a term that would 'increase the legal chaos' in the international sphere due to linguistic problems. The fact that *Türkiyeli* is a word in the Turkish language, which simply translates to English as 'people from Turkey' and to French as '*le gens de la Turquie*', shows the difficulty of popularising this concept to an international audience. The second problem has to do with the absence of an extensive *Türkiyeli* subjectivity among Turkey's diverse diaspora communities. The diaspora communities are 'transnational imagined communities' (Adamson, 2012, p. 41) that are constantly challenged, reinterpreted and redefined. What we see in Turkey's diaspora is that there are various definitions proposed and used by different diaspora communities, who identify themselves, for example, as Euro-Turks, Euro-Muslims, Euro-Kurds or Euro-Alevis. The (Euro-)*Türkiyeli* identity is an alternative that has been proposed by some and received some positive reactions from those who want to break the binds of nationalism. Although the concept offers to break away from methodological nationalism by contesting the homogenising and exclusionary modernist projects of the statecraft in Turkey, it is in Turkish and there is a difficulty in translating the concept into global languages. This is an important problem to tackle.

I began this chapter with two vignettes, where two immigrants from Turkey in Europe, a coffee shop owner in Sweden and an MP in Germany, stressed that they were not (Euro-) Turks but *Türkiyeli*. I conclude with another, which was reported in a few non-mainstream media channels through the end of 2020. The news, with video footage, shows what happened when Turkey's ambassador to Austria, Ozan Ceyhun, was told by the interviewer that four MPs with origins from Turkey were elected to the Vienna Federal Assembly. Ceyhun responds to the interviewer, saying: 'One of them does not count herself as *one of us*, so I do not want to comment on that' (Duvar English, 2020, emphasis mine). The politician referred to as 'the other' is Berîvan Aslan, a Kurdish-Austrian from Turkey, who identifies herself as *Türkiyeli*. Aslan described the comment as a diplomatic scandal in her tweet, where she said that the ambassador was uncomfortable by the interviewer's emphasis on the *Türkiyeli* description of the MPs: 'It's shameful for a diplomat to use discriminating language!' (Aslan, 2020). As this incident shows, the *Türkiyeli* concept has several challenges ahead. But despite such shortcomings, it may serve as a more inclusive and flexible concept allowing for ethno-national, cultural or other differences to be understood and examined under an umbrella term that acknowledges the heterogeneity of Turkey's peoples in Turkey and its diasporas.

Notes

1 This working group, established by a well-known novelist from Turkey, Fakir Baykurt, was renamed the Authors from Turkey in Europe Initiative (*Avrupa Türkiyeli Yazarlar Girişimi*, ATYG) in 2013.
2 TİP was the political organisation in which the Kurds, voicing their demands for their ethnic identity, were active. Several Kurdish members of the TİP were also active in the 'Revolutionary Culture Clubs of the East' (*Devrimci Doğu Kültür Ocakları*, DDKO). Hence, the TİP was a political milieu of the left-wing people, who were thinking about ethnic claims and nationalism. The replacement of Turk by *Türkiyeli* cannot be understood properly without acknowledging Kurdish activism within the TİP.
3 The theoretical discussion of this chapter builds heavily on the discussion in my article, 'Euro-who?: Competition over the definition of Dersim's collective identity in Turkey's diasporas' (Dinc, 2021).
4 Sirkeci (2003, p. 204) argues that ethnic conflicts have been a 'direct push factor' for migration from Turkey to Germany, suggesting that it is 'a motivating factor, while not the most influential one'.
5 According to The Integration of the European Second Generation (TIES) research, in 2009, 5.7 per cent and 16.6 per cent of the second-generation Turks' fathers in Germany and Sweden, respectively, came to Europe as asylum seekers (Lelie, Crul and Schneider, 2012).

6 These identities and movements flourishing in Europe have also transformed Europe. Turkey's diaspora community in Europe has gradually been used by right-wing populist actors 'as an "othering" element and culturally polarising issue within European societies, by employing the theme of cultural security' (Özerim and Öner 2020, p. 78).
7 Unsurprisingly, Turkey's diaspora communities did not act as a united whole when it came to supporting the AKP government in Turkey. The Peoples' Democratic Party's (HDP) electoral gains in the June 2015 general elections in Turkey were not only due to the electoral support it received in Turkey, but also its extraterritorial support. The grassroots associations in Europe and the HDP's success in building 'bottom-up alliance associations', mainly with the support of the Kurdish and Alevi organisations in Europe, were important factors for the HDP's electoral success (Yener-Roderburg, 2020, p. 232).
8 In 2009, KOMKAR branches in Europe came together under a confederation called KOMKAR-EU. For a more detailed account of KOMKAR, see Baser (2015).
9 Although the *Türkiyeli* concept was used in the discussions over the drafts of the 1924 Constitution of the Republic of Turkey, it was ultimately replaced with the 'Turk' concept (Oran, 2005; Toprak, 2013).
10 The Human Rights Advisory Board was established 'to provide a platform for consultation and information exchange between academics, NGOs and other civil society actors dealing with human rights'. The Advisory Board and the Working Group were chaired by İbrahim Kaboğlu and Baskın Oran, respectively, and the Working Group report was presented to the Prime Ministry under Recep Tayyip Erdoğan on 22 October 2004.
11 The report included recommendations for the government to harmonise Turkey's existing laws with the EU acquis and to sign, ratify and implement international conventions and universal norms of human rights and the Framework Convention of the Council of Europe, in particular. This meant that the Constitution of the Republic of Turkey needed to be rewritten in a way to guarantee equal citizenship based on liberal, pluralistic and democratic values.
12 Both Kaboğlu and Oran were later acquitted of the charges by the Supreme Court of Appeal's Plenary Penal Committee decision. Kaboğlu and Oran took their case to the European Court of Human Rights in 2008 and 2010, which fined Turkey in 2018 'over the failure of local Turkish courts to strike a fair balance between the rights of two applicants to respect for their private lives and freedom of the press'.
13 The pro-Kurdish political party, the Democratic Society Party (DTP) was banned by the Constitutional Court in 2009. The party was replaced by the Peace and Democracy Party (BDP), which was later succeeded by the Peoples' Democratic Party (HDP) in 2014.
14 Another reason for the failure can be explained through the fact that the AKP and Erdoğan were trying to do opposite things at the same time, by embracing 'an all-inclusive identity of Turkiyelilik pointing to a geographical-historical notion like the American identity' while using the unitary slogan of 'one nation, one flag, one fatherland, one state' (Taşkin, 2013, p. 307).

References

Adamson, F.B. (2012) 'Constructing the diaspora: diaspora identity politics and transnational social movements', in Lyons, T. and Mandaville, P. (eds) *Politics from Afar: Transnational Diasporas and Networks*. London: Hurst and Company, pp. 25–45.
Adamson, F.B. (2019) 'Sending states and the making of intra-diasporic politics: Turkey and its diaspora(s)', *The International Migration Review*, 53(1), pp. 210–236.
Afful, A. (2016) 'Wild seed: Africa and its many diasporas', *Critical Arts*, 30(4), pp. 557–573.
Al, S. and Karell, D. (2016) 'Hyphenated Turkishness: the plurality of lived nationhood in Turkey', *Nationalities Papers*, 44(1), pp. 144–164.
Alexander, C. (2017) 'Beyond the "The 'diaspora' diaspora": a response to Rogers Brubaker', *Ethnic and Racial Studies*, 40(9), pp. 1544–1555.
Aslan, B. (2020) Tweet, Twitter, 29 November. Available at: https://twitter.com/Berivan_Aslan_/status/1333019922138607618?s=20 (accessed 23 December 2020).
Ayata, B. (2008) 'Mapping Euro-Kurdistan', *Middle East Report*, 247, pp. 18–23.
Baser, B. (2013) 'The Kurdish diaspora in Europe: identity formation and political activism', Research Report DPF 2013-RR 01. Boğaziçi University-TÜSİAD Foreign Policy Forum. Available at: https://cadmus.eui.eu/bitstream/handle/1814/28337/Bahar_Baser_RR_01_2013.pdf?sequence=1&isAllowed=y (accessed 28 October 2020).

Baser, B. (2015) *Diasporas and Homeland Conflicts: A Comparative Perspective*. Abingdon: Routledge.

Bek, M.G. (2020) 'Contesting home, nation, and beyond: the digital space of new migrants from post-Gezi Turkey', in Stein, D., de Laforcade, G., Laws, P.R., and Waegner, C.C. (eds) *Migration, Diaspora, Exile: Narratives of Affiliation and Escape*. London: Lexington Books, pp. 227–244.

Benford, R.D. and Snow, D.A. (2000) 'Framing processes and social movements: an overview and assessment', *Annual Review of Sociology* 26(1), pp. 611–639.

Berkowitz, L. and Mügge, L.M. (2014) 'Transnational diaspora lobbying: Europeanization and the Kurdish question', *Journal of Intercultural Studies*, 35(1), pp. 74–90.

Bora, T. (2017) *Cereyanlar: Türkiye'de siyasi ideolojiler*. İstanbul: İletişim Yayınları.

Brinkerhoff, J.M. (2008) 'Diaspora identity and the potential for violence: toward an identity-mobilization framework', *Identity*, 8(1), pp. 67–88.

Brubaker, R. (2005) 'The "diaspora" diaspora', *Ethnic and Racial Studies*, 28(1), pp. 1–19.

Brubaker, R. (2017) 'Revisiting "The 'diaspora' diaspora"', *Ethnic and Racial Studies*, 40(9), pp. 1556–1561.

Cagaptay, S. (2006). *Islam, Secularism and Nationalism in Modern Turkey: Who Is a Turk?* 1st edn. Abingdon: Routledge.

Calhoun, C. (1994) 'Social theory and the politics of identity', in Calhoun, C. (ed.) *Social Theory and the Politics of Identity*. Oxford: Basil Blackwell, pp. 9–36.

Casier, M. (2009) 'Contesting the "truth" of Turkey's human rights situation: state-association interactions in and outside the Southeast', *European Journal of Turkish Studies*, 10. https://doi.org/10.4000/ejts.4190

Demir, I. (2017) 'Shedding an ethnic identity in diaspora: de-Turkification and the transnational discursive struggles of the Kurdish diaspora', *Critical Discourse Studies*, 14(3), pp. 276–291.

Dinc, P. (2021) 'Euro-who? Competition over the definition of Dersim's collective identity in Turkey's diasporas', *Turkish Studies*, 22(1), pp. 49–73.

Duvar English (2020) 'Turkey's envoy denies Turkish origins of Kurdish-Austrian politician', 30 November. Available at: www.duvarenglish.com/turkeys-envoy-denies-turkish-origins-of-kurdish-austrian-politician-berivan-aslan-news-55252 (accessed 23 December 2020).

Eccarius-Kelly, V. (2002) 'Political movements and leverage points: Kurdish activism in the European diaspora', *Journal of Muslim Minority Affairs*, 22(1), pp. 91–118.

Gabaccia, D. (2000) *Italy's Many Diasporas*. London: UCL Press.

Giglou, R.I., Ogan, C., and d'Haenens, L. (2018) 'The ties that bind the diaspora to Turkey and Europe during the Gezi protests', *New Media & Society*, 20(3), pp. 937–955.

Goalwin, G.J. (2017) 'Understanding the exclusionary politics of early Turkish nationalism: an ethnic boundary-making approach', *Nationalities Papers*, 45(6), pp. 1150–1166.

Grigoriadis, I.N. (2007) 'Türk or Türkiyeli? The reform of Turkey's minority legislation and the rediscovery of Ottomanism', *Middle Eastern Studies*, 43(3), pp. 423–438.

Gunes, C. (2020) 'The transformation of Turkey's pro-Kurdish democratic movement', *Journal of Balkan and Near Eastern Studies*, 22(6), pp. 746–761.

Kaya, A. and Kentel, F. (2005) 'Euro-Turks: a bridge or a breach between Turkey and the European Union? A comparative study of German-Turks and French-Turks', in EU-Turkey Working Papers, 14. Available at: www.ceps.eu/ceps-publications/euro-turks-bridge-or-breach-between-turkey-and-european-union-comparative-study-french/

Lelie, F., Crul, M., and Schneider, J. (2012) *The European Second Generation Compared: Does the Integration Context Matter?* Amsterdam: Amsterdam University Press. Available at: www.oapen.org/record/426534.

Lowen, M. (2017) 'Turkey brain drain: Crackdown pushes intellectuals out', BBC News. Available at: www.bbc.com/news/world-europe-42433668 (accessed 28 September 2020).

Lyons, T. and Mandaville, P. (2010) 'Think locally, act globally: toward a transnational comparative politics', *International Political Sociology*, 4(2), pp. 124–141.

Massicard, E. (2013) *The Alevis in Turkey and Europe: Identity and Managing Territorial Diversity*. Abingdon: Routledge.

Massicard, E. (2017) 'Alevi communities in Western Europe: identity and religious strategies'. Available at: https://halshs.archives-ouvertes.fr/halshs-00801075/document (accessed 28 October 2020).

McAdam, D., McCarthy, J.D. and Zald, M.N. (1996) *Comparative Perspectives on Social Movements: Political Opportunities, Mobilizing Structures, and Cultural Framings*. Cambridge: Cambridge University Press.

Melucci, A. (1995) 'The process of collective identity', in Johnston, H. and Klandermans, B. (eds) *Social Movements and Culture*. Minneapolis, MN: University of Minnesota Press, pp. 41–63.

Mills, C.W. (1997) *The Racial Contact*. Ithaca, NY: Cornell University Press.

Oran, B. (2005) *Türkiye'de azınlıklar: kavramlar, teori, Lozan, iç mevzuat, içtihat, uygulama*. Istanbul: İletişim Yayınları.

Öktem, E. (2017) 'The legal notion of nationality in the Turkish Republic: from Ottoman legacy to modern aberrations', *Middle Eastern Studies*, 53(4), pp. 638–655.

Østergaard-Nielsen, E. (2003) 'Turkey and the "Euro Turks": overseas nationals as an ambiguous asset', in Østergaard-Nielsen, E. (ed.) *International Migration and Sending Countries: Perceptions, Policies and Transnational Relations*. London: Palgrave Macmillan UK, pp. 77–98.Özerim, G. and Öner, S. (2020) 'What makes Turkey and Turkish immigrants a cultural polarization issue in Europe? Evidence from European right-wing populist politics', in Norocel, O., Hellström, A., and Jørgensen, M. (eds) *Nostalgia and Hope: Intersections Between Politics of Culture, Welfare, and Migration in Europe*. Cham: Springer, pp. 67–81.

Özyürek, E. (2009) '"The light of the Alevi fire was lit in Germany and then spread to Turkey": a transnational debate on the boundaries of Islam', *Turkish Studies*, 10(2), pp. 233–253.

Polletta, F. and Jasper, J.M. (2001) 'Collective identity and social movements', *Annual Review of Sociology*, 27(1), pp. 283–305.

Salda, Ş. (2020) 'Milletvekili Hakan Taş: "Babam eşcinsel olduğumu öğrendiğinden beri 35 senedir benimle konuşmuyor"'. Available at: www.youtube.com/watch?v=ZfDkZT4oUYI (accessed 22 December 2020).

Sheffer, G. (2003) *Diaspora Politics: At Home Abroad*. New York: Cambridge University Press.

Sirkeci, İ. (2003) 'Migration from Turkey to Germany: an ethnic approach', *New Perspectives on Turkey*, 29, pp. 189–207.

Soguk, N. (2008) 'Transversal communication, diaspora, and the Euro-Kurds', *Review of International Studies*, 34(S1), pp. 173–192.

Sökefeld, M (2006) 'Mobilizing in transnational space: a social movement approach to the formation of diaspora', *Global Networks*, 6, pp. 265–284.

Somer, M. (2005) 'Defensive- vs. liberal-nationalist perspectives on diversity and the Kurdish conflict: Europeanization, the internal debate, and Türkiyelilik', *New Perspectives on Turkey*, 32, pp. 73–91.Taşkin, Y. (2013) 'Hegemonizing conservative democracy and the problems of democratization in Turkey: conservatism without democrats?', *Turkish Studies*, 14(2), pp. 292–310.

Tekdemir, O. (2019) 'The social construction of "many Kurdishnesses": Mapping sub-identities of "EU-ising" Kurdish politics', *Ethnicities*, 19(5), pp. 876–900.

TESEV (2012) 'Anayasaya Dair Tanım ve Beklentiler'. Available at: www.tesev.org.tr/wp-content/uploads/rapor_Anayasaya_Dair_Tanim_Ve_Beklentiler_Saha_Arastirmasi.pdf (accessed 10 December 2020).

The Human Rights Advisory Board (2004) 'Minority and Cultural Rights Report'. Available at: https://baskinoran.com/belge/MinorityAndCulturalRightsReport-October2004.pdf (accessed 8 December 2020).

Toprak, Z. (2013) *Türkiye'de popülizm: 1908–1923*. Istanbul: Doğan Kitap.

Turkish Citizens Living Abroad (n.d.) 'The expatriate Turkish citizens,' Republic of Turkey Ministry of Foreign Affairs. Available at: www.mfa.gov.tr/the-expatriate-turkish-citizens.en.mfa (accessed 28 September 2020).

Türkmen, G. (2019) '"But you don't look Turkish!": the changing face of Turkish immigration to Germany', *Reset Dialogues on Civilizations*. Available at: www.resetdoc.org/story/dont-look-turkish-changing-face-turkish-immigration-germany/ (accessed 20 December 2020).

Ünlü, B. (2016) 'The Kurdish struggle and the crisis of the Turkishness contract', *Philosophy & Social Criticism*, 42(4–5), pp. 397–405.

Weeden, L. (2009) 'Ethnography as interpretive enterprise', in Schatz, E. (ed.) *Political Ethnography: What Immersion Contributes to the Study of Power*. Chicago: Chicago University Press, pp. 75–95.

Whittier, N. (2009) 'Sustaining commitment among radical feminists', in Goodwin, J. and Jasper, J.M. (eds) *The Social Movements Reader: Cases and Concepts*. Oxford: Wiley-Blackwell, pp. 105–116.

Yanasmayan, Z. and Kaşlı, Z. (2019) 'Reading diasporic engagements through the lens of citizenship: Turkey as a test case', *Political Geography*, 70, pp. 24–33.

Yegen, M. (2009) '"Prospective-Turks" or "pseudo-citizens": Kurds in Turkey', *Middle East Journal*, 63(4), pp. 597–615.

Yener-Roderburg, I.O. (2020). 'Party organizations across borders', in Kernalegenn, T. and van Haute, E. (eds), *Political Parties Abroad: A New Arena for Party Politics*. London: Routledge, pp. 218–237.

13
DE-ORIENTALISING QUEER IRANIAN DIASPORIC IDENTITIES

Farhang Rouhani

Queer, Iran, diaspora

Appropriate Behavior is a romantic comedy set mostly in the hipster paradise of Brooklyn, New York. Written and directed by Iranian American film director, producer, screenwriter and actress Desiree Akhavan, the film stars Akhavan herself as Shirin, a bisexual Iranian American woman in Brooklyn seeking to rebuild her life after breaking up with her girlfriend. The film unfolds through a series of vignettes in which she contends with all aspects of her life, and through a series of flashbacks that tell the story of her failed romance with Maxine. Throughout the film, Shirin traverses her complicated worlds of work, love and family to find her way as a young adult. While the film has earned mixed reviews for its artistry and impact, I argue that it profoundly reflects and can be used as an entry to understanding significant themes of queerness, Iranianness, race and diaspora.

In her recent masterful work, *Unruly Visions: The Aesthetic Practices of Queer Diaspora*, Gayatri Gopinath (2018, p. 172) seeks to 'map the subterranean points of crossing and collision, relationality and encounter, between bodies, histories, and temporalities that are typically submerged within standard epistemologies, and that only come into view when deploying a queer optic', with the ultimate goal of showing how 'the aesthetic practices of queer diaspora suggest strategies for bringing other worlds into view that attest to our conjoined pasts, presents, and potential futures' (ibid., p. 175). A queer optic, thus, is necessary both to unearth the histories and geographies hidden from view because they do not fit the dominant narrative of the diaspora, and to provide a lens with which to question, challenge and creatively produce alternatives to the norms.

The development of queer diasporic studies in recent years has served to infuse dynamism in both queer theory and diaspora studies. As Gayatri Gopinath (2006, p. 11) argues, 'The concept of a queer diaspora enables a simultaneous critique of heterosexuality and the nation form while exploding the binary oppositions between nation and diaspora, heterosexuality and homosexuality, original and copy.' In mainstream studies of diaspora, the tensions between immigrants and non-immigrants tend to take primary focus, occluding differences such as sexuality within the immigrant group. Beginning from a queer diasporic perspective enables us to avoid essentialising the meanings of nationality and homeland. While focusing diaspora studies on queerness helps to complicate understandings of family, nation and nostalgia, a centring on diaspora helps to bring the much-needed questions of race, colonisation and globalisation to the centre of queer studies. This combined perspective provides a framework from which to complicate assumptions about immigrant identity groups and to create new opportunities for being and relating with others (Fortier, 2001; Manalansan, 2010; Garvey, 2011; Shakhsari, 2012).

The result is a perspective we could call 'queer un-belonging'. Within this construction, there are no assumptions made about the opportunities for belonging within an already identified diasporic community. Instead, the ideas of belonging and not belonging are held in a suspended, often highly imaginative and yet still grounded state of un-belonging. While from a dominant stance, queerness appears as an impossibility, the spaces that people in the queer diaspora create, under intense conditions of multiple forms of marginalisation and oppression, result in the highly creative spaces of un-belonging that suggest new opportunities, identities and spaces for diasporic futures.

A specific focus on Iranian queer diasporic experiences requires attention to the special role that Iranians in particular and Middle Easterners in general play as US immigrants on the edges of whiteness. Compellingly argued in the recent work of Neda Maghbouleh, Iranian Americans are considered both 'white' by official census measures and as a marginalised 'other' by all other accounts of everyday American life (Maghbouleh, 2017, see Gualtieri, 2009 , for a similar argument made about Arab Americans). Maghbouleh uses two related concepts to address the complications that result: 'racial hinges', which refer to how the geographic, political and pseudoscientific aspects of Iranians as a racially liminal group can be used by powers from above as a symbolic hinge that opens or closes the door to whiteness; and 'racial loopholes', which emphasise the everyday contradictions that develop when the legal categorisation of a group conflicts with its social racialisation. As such, a focus on Iranianness allows for an examination of the outer fringes of whiteness, the top-down and bottom-up processes of racialisation, and the realities of immigrant diasporic assimilation and integration. Recent discourses around creating a Middle Eastern census category and limiting the migration of people from a set of countries including Iran further heighten this racialisation. My research seeks to build on this work by considering how queer Iranians in particular navigate the space between legal invisibility and everyday racial hypervisibility to create dynamic new liveable spaces out of what seems to be an impossible contradiction.

Ultimately, as scholars of Middle East media studies have pointed out, a de-orientalising mode of reading and textual analysis is necessary to help us unlearn these dominant constructions and contradictions (Alsultany, 2012). Inspired by the work of Edward Said and the critical studies of orientalism that followed, a de-orientalising mode of analysis starts from the perspective of rejecting the dominant geopolitical lens that, from imperialism to the Cold War to the post-Cold War period, has started from the perspective that non-Western people and places are essentially inferior. Interestingly, while the critique of orientalism has been effective in deconstructing the idea of 'the East' as a monolithic whole, at least in the academic realm, it has made little progress in deconstructing 'the West' in the same way (Hassan, 2011). By focusing on immigrant narratives, I seek to contribute to a growing body of work that uses this orientalist critique to deconstruct 'the West' and Westerners as well as 'the East' and Easterners.

In this chapter, I analyse the film *Appropriate Behavior* using a queer optic, with specific examinations of how it recasts dominant understandings of Iran and Iranianness, how it seeks to transform perspectives on sexuality and queerness within the diaspora, and how it uses the genre of comedy to contribute to the creation of a de-orientalising gaze, ultimately reproducing Brooklyn as a diasporic 'queertopia' in transit. My aim, ultimately, is to contribute to the development of an anti-orientalist lens that uncovers lost histories and geographies of diasporic living and seeks out alternative diasporic futures to those that are normatively scripted.

Reimagining Iranianness in the diaspora

In the years since the Iranian Revolution of 1979, Iranian scholars abroad have embarked on powerful analyses of Iranianness and the Iranian diaspora through the burgeoning lens of Iranian American Studies. While in the earlier scholarship, the terms 'refugee', 'exile' and 'immigrant' were most commonly used, the concept of the 'Iranian diaspora' has increasingly come to the fore, centring around the complexities and contradictions of nostalgia, civic and political engagement, hybrid identity construction, and the connections with and disconnections from Iran (Elahi and Karim, 2011). Shakhsari (2012) warns against the tendency to assume ease of mobility and movement and the idealisation of the homeland as represented through a homogeneous heteronormative community. Instead, her research compellingly argues that research deploying ideas of diasporic Iranianness needs to be carried out in a grounded, non-essentialising way that does not assume internal cohesion about the meanings, experiences and power relations of Iranianness as an identity category. This is a vital insight not just for examinations of Iranianness but diasporic experiences in general, as prominent scholars of diaspora studies have shown in their move away from the objectifying and essentialising of what 'diaspora' means in normative terms (Brubaker, 2005; Dufoix, 2008).

Added to this complexity, Maghbouleh's (2017) research, addressed above, aids in theorising how Iranianness develops in connection with other identities in the context of countries such as the United States, through the racialisation of the diaspora in connection to whiteness and otherness, and through complex processes of incorporation and marginalisation. Some of the most powerful vignettes that Akhavan paints in the film concern these inter- and intra-diasporic community complications. While these scenes are often brief and fleeting, they serve as vital thought-provoking moments through which to understand Iranianness in a diasporic context.

Many immigrants will relate to a scene, for example, in which Shirin is asked to weigh in on the 'whole situation over there', meaning the political situation in Iran. Underlying Shirin's pained, fatigued facial response lies a world of painful labour in how immigrants, and not just first-generation ones, are cornered and held up as native informants in a way that is deeply racialising and othering. The assumptions in the question are that as an Iranian American, Shirin represents authoritative knowledge and a perspective on Iranian politics, and if she does not, she certainly should. Even though Shirin was raised in the United States, this statement assumes she has intimate, expert knowledge of an Iranian homeland. The impact of the question is to racialise Shirin as an 'other' and mark her un-belonging in an awkward, problematic moment of racism. While the reasons behind the question itself may be entirely benevolent, the effect is to separate, alienate, racialise and put Shirin on the stop as a native informant and expert.

Another scene along similar lines occurs when a prospective boss gets very excited to hear that Shirin has travelled to Tehran. Tehran, to him, is an exotic wonderland. He says that he has watched documentaries about the 'whole underground hip-hop scene', and asks if she is into that at all. Patiently, with a wearied look, Shirin says no and that her visits to Tehran mostly involve visiting her grandmother and watching Disney movies. Shirin's weariness and response are an attempt to deflect the exotification of Iran's underground arts scene, the latest orientalisation of Iranian culture. The prospective boss is clearly disappointed, having hoped for stories of oppression and resistance and cool underground subcultures. This scene relays, on one hand, the cluelessness of some in the dominant culture in exotifying and alienating others. Like the question discussed in the previous paragraph, the boss here is speaking from a benevolent place of curiosity and interest but without enough self-introspection to consider the effect of what he is doing. Furthermore, it suggests the difficulties and complexities of building a meaningful ethnic identity as an Iranian in a context where there are so many external expectations, ranging from critiques of Iranian politics to self-exotification.

These two scenes reveal the two sides of the orientalisation and racialisation of Iranianness through the lenses of Iran as a dangerous place (the situation) and Iran as an exotic place of hijabs and subversion. Through these two scenes, Akhavan conveys the labour that immigrants undertake in explaining their lives. Representing and explaining her Iranianness in the face of exotification and orientalisation are a part of her everyday life. Shirin's tactic of undercutting this reality by talking about grandmothers and Disney provides a hilarious, important moment of de-essentialising perceptions of Iranianness, but it also reveals the constant work it takes to be held as a representative of a group, to be isolated and racialised as a result, and to have to listen to and thoughtfully respond in a way that will help uncomprehending Americans to unlearn their assumptions. Shirin's tired responses draw attention to the need to move beyond essentialised notions of identities and replace them with an understanding of simultaneous commonality and difference.

The complexities of Iranianness are also revealed in vignettes of Shirin's relationship with white Maxine, largely centred around the fact that Shirin has not come out to her parents and has not revealed the romantic nature of their relationship. Responding to a frustrated Maxine, Shirin defends herself by saying, 'I come from Iran, Maxine. You know, where they stone gay people?' And Maxine accuses Shirin of 'playing the Persian card'. Clearly for Shirin, referring to the treatment of gays in this way is a moment of strategic essentialism, trying to explain herself in a desperate moment when she feels so misunderstood, while Maxine is equally harsh, if not more so, in her racialised accusation that Shirin is using her identity to get herself off the hook. While they are both clearly frustrated and angry, what they do not discuss is the underlying assumption of 'coming out' as the norm of what people are supposed to do, something that could perhaps lead to mutual understanding. Instead, they focus on two problematic extremes – Iran as dangerous, and racialisation as an excuse – in a way that leads to alienation and separation. This is another scene in which, while struggling with her own sexual and ethnic identity, Shirin is forced to see how little compassion and understanding white American culture has to offer. Challenging Shirin's belonging to a queer norm that is set by white Maxine, this scene exemplifies diasporic belonging that finds no comfort in either an ethnic community or a (white) queer intimacy.

The most endearing moments of expressing Iranianness in the film are by way of Shirin's relationship with her family, consisting of her parents and brother who all appear to be successful and well-adjusted, leading beautiful lives. By contrast, Shirin, who has a master's degree in journalism, struggles with finances and employment. While Akhavan effectively shows the deep love that exists in the family, the family relationship becomes another way of communicating Shirin's complicated relationship with her Iranianness, through how she struggles while the rest appear to have mastered the immigrant success narrative, and through her sexuality. When Shirin finally comes out to her mother and says that she is bisexual, after a series of humorous lies and deflections, her mother's response is to say, 'No, you're not.' Some reviews of the film have panned this scene, arguing that the mother's blunt response is not in keeping with her character's depiction as a cosmopolitan, loving mother. But from a queer diasporic perspective, it is not difficult to imagine how the construction of the heteronormative diasporic family would be so strong that a bisexual daughter would appear as an impossibility. Moreover, it reveals one more layer of Shirin's complex relationship with her sense of Iranianness, at the closest core at the family level. Shirin is thus forced to grapple with the notion that however she comes to understand herself, sexually and ethnically, will need to start from a position of creating something out of what appears to be impossible.

One final example of how *Appropriate Behavior* deals with issues of Iranianness in the diaspora comes during a scene where there is a raucous Persian Nowruz party and Shirin spends her time critiquing the excesses of diasporic Iranian culture. While on the surface, this scene could be seen solely as another example of Shirin's alienation from Iranianness, I see this as a moment of expressing negative pride, when a cultural insider cultivates a sense of belonging by 'reading' her culture with friends. Elsewhere, I have examined cultivating a sense of home through cultivating a critical queer sense of belonging, and I see this as an extension of that: a certain level of comfort and belonging, though in a qualified, suspended way, that comes with having the insider experience to be able to humorously make fun of one's own culture (Rouhani, 2019).

In various ways, these scenes help to develop a more complex, nuanced, problematised understanding of Iranian diasporic identity. On one level, they serve to critique and complicate the dominant heteronormative representation of home, family and nation in the diaspora through Shirin's complicated relationships with her family and larger immigrant culture. But perhaps more importantly, they reveal the difficulties of identification within a context of constant orientalisation from the dominant culture, something that deserves much more attention in diasporic studies. Shirin's struggles, and her sometimes humorous, sometimes heart-wrenching efforts to respond, reveal the difficulties of diasporic belonging and being, but also suggest new opportunities to cultivate and develop something meaningful, dynamic and new in tension with those pressures from above.

Sex, sexuality and frankness in the diaspora

Autobiographical and semi-autobiographical memoirs written by Iranian immigrant women have been central to the popular consumption of Iranian culture in recent decades. I think it is useful to consider how Akhavan's film fits in relation to this genre through which a large number of Americans and Europeans have come to understand and interpret Iranian American women and to consider how she contributes to the enlargement or transformation of this genre. While the film is not in any traditional sense a memoir, Akhavan has stated that the various scenes were inspired by her own experiences with family, sexuality, and being the child of Iranian immigrants (Freeman, 2015). These works include widely read and discussed titles such as Azar Nafisi's (2008) *Reading Lolita in Tehran*, Marjane Satrapi's *Persepolis* series (2008), Azadeh Moaveni's (2005) *Lipstick Jihad* and Firoozeh Dumas' (2004) *Funny in Farsi*. They have grown in popularity to the point of becoming a lucrative industry in the telling of Iranian women's lives. Some of the major elements of the genre include relating the experiences of expatriation and exile, providing insight into the practices of urban Iranian domestic life abroad, and using the narrative device of returning home as a way of examining Iranian politics, with central themes of nostalgia and loss, immigrant assimilation and integration, and the development of hybrid cosmopolitan identities (Whitlock, 2008). Their power lies within the authority and perspective that comes with first-person narrative experience and fulfilling a market desire among Westerners for an insider's perspective (Malek, 2006). While these memoirs have ranged in topic and perspective, they tend to shy away from explicit and frank discussions of sex and sexuality, and here is where Akhavan's film makes a significant contribution. In the process of presenting Shirin's sexuality, Akhavan provides an inspiringly vibrant, frank, and realistic representation of diasporic sexuality. This is a representation that does not claim universality by any means, and which, through its awkward realness, manages to avoid the orientalism and exoticism that often accompany representations of Middle Eastern and Muslim women's sexualities. Based on a queer optic, this form of representation complicates our understanding of family, nation and sexuality as opposed to the often essentialising and self-orientalising tendencies found in the autobiographical and semi-autobiographical genre.

One of the film's scenes that received the greatest attention and praise in reviews is one in which Shirin engages in a three-way sexual encounter with a heterosexual couple. The encounter goes weirdly wrong when the man suspects that his partner is into Shirin in ways that he does not like. Through realistic, un-romanticised blocking and dialogue, Akhavan conveys sex in a way that is awkward and fumbling, sexy, and painfully lonely all at the same time, in a matter of minutes. While candid and simultaneously erotic and painful to watch, the scene contributes to the larger theme of Shirin's efforts and inability to connect with other people and ventures into brave, realistic territory seldom seen in the cultural media products of the Iranian diaspora. Awkwardness in this context becomes a way to simultaneously communicate sexual desire, miscommunication and realism.

Another evocative scene is a humorous encounter in a lingerie store, where Shirin receives self-esteem coaching from a sales associate. The associate, noticing Shirin's awkwardness and exuding self-assured sexual positivity, tells her that she deserves a great bra. 'Just because your breasts are small', she says, 'it doesn't mean that they're not legitimate.' This scene is important on a personal level in Shirin's growth, to support her gradual transformation into someone who can feel confident and positive about herself and her sexuality. While it serves as a comedic put-down moment regarding the smallness of her breasts, it is also an incredibly earnest, sweet and positive moment in her burgeoning sense of self. She is constantly self-effacing. In another scene, in response to someone who tells her she could be a model, Shirin responds, 'Yeah, a before model for Accutane.' I see scenes such as this as vitally important when one considers the extent to which Middle Eastern and Muslim origin women have largely been sexualised through an orientalist lens from above, which are most incisively critiqued through Lila Abu-Lughod's (2013) *Do Muslim Women Need Saving?*, and also Meyda Yegenoglu's (1998) classic *Colonial Fantasies*, and rarely do we see such frank, positive representations of sex and sexuality. Akhavan is in control of the narrative here, not what a Western audience might desire or expect, and she takes this control courageously to show sex and sexuality in all its awkwardness, eroticism and humour. In other words, it feels real and compelling in a way that we seldom see in other cultural products, such as popular memoirs.

This frankness is equally evident in the vividness of how Akhavan conveys Shirin's doomed relationship with Maxine. Much of the humour surrounding Shirin's discomfort about coming out to her family, for example, revolves around the question of why they share a bed. These silly excuses range from the economics and the expense of beds to vague allusions to European practices and the film *Beaches*. While these moments serve as humorous interludes and as a narrative device that expands the growing wedge between Shirin and Maxine, I see them as also relating cultural discomforts concerning discussions of sex and sexuality. The bed, in this way, stands in for a diasporic cultural awkwardness and difficulty in speaking frankly about sexual matters. It serves as a compelling way to show the complexities of dealing with and negotiating sexuality within diasporic experiences.

While there was clearly a warm centre to the relationship between Shirin and Maxine, much of Shirin's sadness about the break-up concerns the larger context of their relationship within the world of New York relationships. She bemoans the fact they were an 'It Couple', a couple to be admired and emulated, focusing more on the social status she had and lost than the personal companionship. And the loss of the relationship has real-life economic consequences, as the break-up forces Shirin to move from the lovely one-bedroom Park Slope apartment they shared into a curtained share with multiple odd stranger roommates in Bushwick. In the world of New York/Brooklyn sexualities, the loss of the relationship has real-world cultural and economic capital consequences. Here is another important, candid representation of diasporic sexuality and intimacy that manages to avoid the pitfalls of romanticisation: diasporic sexuality and intimacy are not just about the expression of the self, but a form of social engagement and belonging with significant consequences.

As much as she portrays Shirin as desiring to belong to this cosmopolitan Brooklyn queer community, Akhavan is deeply critical in her representation of urban queerness. In one scene in particular, but pervading through the film, cosmopolitan queers are shown to be a bubble community of self-importance, pseudo-intellectualism and general egocentric fakery. It becomes apparent over the course of the film that this seemingly cosmopolitan city is in fact quite superficial. In many ways, this portrayal parallels Akhavan's portrayal of the New York Iranian community as made up of gossiping and hypercritical affluence. In both of these communities to which she is supposed to belong, Shirin feels deeply the limitations they have in allowing her to be who she wants to be: they are both communities that have profoundly limiting constraints for what constitutes 'appropriate behaviour' for belonging. Instead of immersing in bitterness over a lack of belonging, though, Akhavan has Shirin go through all kinds of humorous and profound awkwardness, in a way that is engaging, profound and ultimately liberating in how it rises above the surrounding superficiality. Shirin's awkwardness in the different communities she traverses questions the utility of traditional forms of belonging, whether based on ethnonational identification or sexuality.

Shirin's sexual and ethnic awkwardness in her communities, in essence, serves a productive end as a source of queer un-belonging. In place of either a fantasy of belonging or a tragedy of bitter not belonging, what we have here is this creative, suspended force by which Shirin engages with these communities, seeks out her own way, and hopefully leads to new paths through which they can be enlarged and transformed. This is conveyed most dramatically through her smile sitting in a subway car at the end of the film, after having renewed her commitments to work, family and relationships. Through her engagement, Akhavan significantly expands the boundaries of diasporic Iranian women through her characterisation of Shirin's sexuality in a way that never panders to the demands of an audience that craves the romanticism and exoticness that the popular Iranian women's memoirs often provide. Importantly, by way of Shirin, it manages to avoid representing Iranian diasporic and queer cultures as unified wholes. Shirin's struggles instead signal vital problems and possible spaces from which those communities can be transformed. The way that Akhavan frames and constructs the narrative of the film is essential to her ability to create and contribute to a new way of seeing diasporic Iranian cultures. By leaving the ending scene open-ended, yet hopeful, we are left to imagine the multiple ways Shirin can choose to continue negotiating her belonging and un-belonging in open-ended creative ways that are yet to be written, instead of prescribing a script for performing particular forms of identity and belonging.

The transformative genre of queer diasporic romantic dramedy

In the multiple reviews and press releases that followed the release of the film, *Appropriate Behavior* was most often framed as a hybrid of Woody Allen's New York romantic comedies, most notably *Annie Hall*, and Lena Dunham's acclaimed and panned HBO television show *Girls*. The similarities to Allen exist in the bittersweet nostalgia that pervades the telling of Shirin and Maxine's romance by way of flashbacks, the use of self-deprecating humour to lighten the story, and the significant role of urban New York as background and actor in the story. Where Akhavan departs from Allen, though, is in the use of a more cool deadpan form of humour that depends on a set of colourful outlandish hipster-type characters, and of course a queer optic that constantly questions presented norms.

The similarities to Dunham are evident in their mutual immersion in 'millennial' generational culture, their concern for a range of structural issues such as employment and housing, and their frankness and realness in representing sex and sexuality in a positive, though certainly not glossy, way. At the same time, I am troubled by the extent to which Akhavan has been represented as the Iranian or Middle Eastern Lena Dunham. This is troubling on the level of orientalist critique, the fact that Akhavan becomes reduced to her immigrant ethnic identity in such representations. They assume that you can simply take a formula, then add an ethnic dimension to it, and the result is reduced to the addition of those two things. Instead, the creative product that Akhavan achieves through a queer diasporic lens is much greater and more dynamic than simply adding an ethnic dimension to an existing formula. And the fact that her work would be represented as the Iranian 'something else' leaves truly troubling questions about the limits through which Iranian diasporic subjects continue to be viewed through an orientalist lens.

I have mentioned Akhavan's use of humour before, but it is important to emphasise here how this use of humour is an important creative force in the project. There are other cultural products of the Iranian diaspora that have used humour to tell a diasporic story, most notable Firoozeh Dumas' popular *Funny in Farsi*, but Akhavan's humorous inflections are a specific generational New York deadpan, simultaneously laugh and gasp style of humour that serve the larger queer project of questioning and reimagining social norms. It is used, for example, in contrasting Shirin's questioning of herself and the worlds around her, and Maxine's confident, humourless, judgemental nature. There's even a moment in which Shirin, trying to develop the bond between the two, wryly states, 'I hate so many things too!' The humour always has a sharp edge to it that seeks to question norms, whether focused on the diasporic Iranian community, the New York queer community, or other aspects of New York cosmopolitanism. It becomes an essential force within Akhavan's cultivation of a queer lens of critique.

The film is clearly at least somewhat autobiographical, as it is written, directed and starring Akhavan herself through a character that resembles much of Akhavan's own life. This also adds a compelling dimension, much like the popular memoirs, and it is interesting that Akhavan chooses a different name for her heroine: Shirin. A popular Iranian name that is used widely in diasporic communities because of its ease of pronunciation, Shirin means 'sweet' in Persian. The fact that it is being used for a character that is anything but sweet is another incisive layer of humour and queer critique of appropriateness. The film's low-budget, sometimes haphazard and abrupt style, while criticised by some reviewers, also adds an important layer showing the multiple conflicting, jarring dimensions of Shirin's life.

While praised by many for its humour, the film has also been panned on a few levels, and I think it is instructive to examine these as a way of understanding how Akahvan's work fits within a larger culture of desires and expectations. Much of this critique concerns questions of authenticity in Akhavan's portrayal of diasporic Iranian cultures (for example, Coffin, 2015; Hassenger, 2015; O'Donoghue, 2015; Semerone, 2015). These include criticisms that Akhavan underplays the cosmopolitanism of the parents, devolves to stereotypes in representing gossiping Iranians at the Nowruz party, and does not fully and authentically represent young Iranian American lives. While the critique of narrowness in the representations is somewhat warranted, it is important to note the real issues that Shirin has with them, that she expresses by way of a queer lens. The questions of authenticity and representation, moreover, put Akhavan in the difficult position of having to model Iranianness to a Western audience. One review, for example, states that the film 'does not provoke any serious commentary into the sexual mores of contemporary Persian female behavior' (O'Donoghue, 2015). I would argue that the problem does not lie with Akhavan but with the dominant cultural expectations that the film should teach us something along a traditional anthropological point of view, and in a highly reductive way. What Akhavan seeks to present and teach us is far more nuanced, critical and queer than engaging with such representative, essentialising demands. For someone to approach the film through the criteria of ethnic and national representation, again, reveals the limits in what Western audiences expect and desire, thus simultaneously extending a critique of the normative pressures faced within diasporic communities and the opportunities for creatively subverting and moving past these pressures. These critiques end up highlighting the novelty of Akhavan's film as one that disrupts essentialised understandings of ethnicity, belonging and identity by questioning the possibility of coherence within these realms and forcing the audience to consider incomplete and ambivalent identification with self and other.

Finding 'queertopia', deploying a queer optic

While certainly not perfect, nor intending to be, Desiree Akhavan's *Appropriate Behavior* is a vital example of what we can get by way of a queer optic, as theorised by Gopinath. On one level, it helps to expand the framing of the Iranian diaspora, which through its development has largely hidden the experiences of queer Iranians from view. Through her creation of the character of Shirin, Akhavan provides an opening for considering who is being left out of dominant diasporic narratives. On another level, it questions and challenges the comfortable assumptions held within the diaspora, by the dominant culture about the diaspora, as well as within New York queer cultural circles. As such, the film highlights the importance of un-belonging as an element of diasporic identification and experiences.

While most of the film concerns these moments of discomfort, questioning, and challenging of the norms of appropriateness, its conclusion suggests the creation of an alternative. The film ends, perhaps somewhat abruptly, with Shirin in subway transit, with a transcendental smile on her face. The scene recalls the classic ending of *The Graduate*, where after a set of trials and tribulations, the young couple escape together in the back of a bus with the Hollywood ending of 'happily ever after', but with uncertain and anxious looks on their faces. In Shirin's case, having dealt with the normative pressures of family and New York social life, she is on her way to finding a different kind of future, one in which her desired queer diasporic identity and belonging are possible. This ending moment to me suggests the pleasure and awareness that can come from unearthing something that appears to be impossible. At that moment, Shirin has discovered a queer diasporic utopia, or queertopia, in the crazy impossibilities of transiting cultures, and the imaginative result, the potential it holds, is downright enchanting.

References

Abu-Lughod, L. (2013) *Do Muslim Women Need Saving?* Cambridge, MA: Harvard University Press.
Alsultany, E. (2012) *Arabs and Muslims in the Media*. New York: New York University Press.
Brubaker, R. (2005) 'The "diaspora" diaspora', *Ethnic and Racial Studies*, 28(1), pp. 1–19.
Coffin, L. (2015) 'Review: *Appropriate Behavior* thinks it's better than it actually is', *The Mary Sue*, January 21.
Dufoix, S. (2008) *Diasporas*. Berkeley, CA: University of California Press.
Dumas, F. (2004) *Funny in Farsi: A Memoir of Growing Up Iranian in America*. New York: Random House Incorporated.Elahi, B. and Karim, P. (2011) 'Introduction: Iranian diaspora', *Comparative Studies of South Asia, Africa and the Middle East*, 31(2), pp. 381–387.

Fortier, A. (2001) '"Coming home": queer migrations and multiple evocations of home', *European Journal of Cultural Studies*, 4(4), pp. 405–424.

Freeman, H. (2015) 'Desiree Akhavan on *Appropriate Behaviour* and not being the "Iranian bisexual Lena Dunham"', *The Guardian*, March 5.

Garvey, J. (2011) 'Spaces of violence, desire, and queer (un)belonging: Dionne Brand's urban diasporas', *Textual Practice*, 25(4), pp. 757–777.

Gopinath, G. (2006) *Impossible Desires: Queer Diasporas and South Asian Public Cultures*. Durham, NC: Duke University Press.

Gopinath, G. (2018) *Unruly Visions: The Aesthetic Practices of Queer Diaspora*. Durham, NC: Duke University Press.

Gualtieri, S. (2009) *Between Arab and White: Race and Ethnicity in the Early Syrian American Diaspora*. Berkeley, CA: University of California Press.

Hassan, W. (2011) *Immigrant Narratives*. Oxford: Oxford University Press.

Hassenger, J. (2015) '*Appropriate Behavior* is a flawed but promising debut from a new *Girls* co-star', *AV Club*, January 15.

Maghbouleh, N. (2017) *The Limits of Whiteness*. Stanford, CA: Stanford University Press.

Malek, A. (2006) 'Memoir as Iranian exile cultural production: a case study of Marjane Satrapi's *Persepolis* series', *Iranian Studies*, 39(3), pp. 353–380.

Manalansan, M. (2010) 'Diasporic deviants/divas: how Filipino gay migrants "Play with the world"', in Patton, C. and Sanchez-Eppler, B. (eds) *Queer Diasporas*. Durham, NC: Duke University Press, pp. 183–203.

Moaveni, A. (2005) *Lipstick Jihad: A Memoir of Growing Up Iranian in America and American in Iran*. New York: Public Affairs.

Nafisi, A. (2008) *Reading Lolita in Tehran: A Memoir in Books*. New York: Random House Trade Paperbacks.

O'Donoghue, D. (2015) '*Appropriate Behaviour*', *Film Ireland*, March 9.

Rouhani, F. (2019) 'Belonging, desire, and queer Iranian diasporic politics', *Emotion, Space and Society*, 31, pp. 126–132.

Satrapi, M. (2008) *Persepolis I & II*. New York: Random House.

Semerone, D. (2015) 'Review: *Appropriate Behavior*', *Slant Magazine*, January 15.

Shakhsari, S. (2012) 'From homoerotics of exile to homopolitics of diaspora: cyberspace, the war on terror, and the hypervisible Iranian queer', *Journal of Middle East Women's Studies*, 8(3), pp. 14–40.

Whitlock, G. (2008) 'From Tehran to Tehrangeles: the generic fix of Iranian exilic memoirs', *Ariel*, 39(1–2), pp. 7–27.

Yegenoglu, M. (1998) *Colonial Fantasies: Towards a Feminist Reading of Orientalism*. New York: Cambridge University Press.

14
QUEERING DIASPORA THROUGH VISUAL ART
Contesting the double binds of homonationalism

Andrew Gayed

The art of the queer diaspora offers a rich vantage point from which the relationships of colonial trauma and displacement can be read. Furthermore, they complicate notions of homeland by exposing and alluding to the experiences of living with and through a transnational sexual identity. The cultural production of the queer diaspora and diasporic sexuality can help complicate and disturb the meta-narrative that characterises Middle Eastern cultures as sexually oppressive and intolerant, on the one hand, and Western cultures as sexually liberated and accepting, on the other. I explore these themes through the lens of visual art, and in particular through the works of three diasporic artists: Jamil Hellu, Laurence Rasti and Nilbar Güreş. Through his art, Hellu, a Syrian American visual artist, explores non-Western ways of being queer that are informed by diaspora consciousness. Laurence Rasti is an Iranian-Swiss visual artist who photographs queer Iranian refugees in Turkey, while Nilbar Güreş, a diasporic Turkish visual artist living and working in Vienna, sheds light on the immense violence and trauma that queer and trans subjects face both in the Middle East and the diaspora.[1]

Queering diaspora

Queer diasporic art often cites the links between and critique of the colonial past and the present, creating powerful points of relationality between visual culture and diasporic consciousness. 'Diaspora consciousness' has been understood as a strong and enduring group consciousness of the homeland, in which feelings of solidarity are more or less shared by the members of a diasporic collectivity in a host country or new setting (Cohen, 1997). Here I argue that beyond this definition, which seems well suited to capture some of the more historically prevalent experiences of diaspora, there are nuances and permutations in the present that might also constitute diaspora consciousness. One such site of diaspora consciousness is the art of queer diasporic Middle Eastern subject, where colonial histories, trauma and loss are embedded within expressions of everyday queer diasporic experiences. There are productive links between diasporic consciousness, on the one hand, and identity, on the other. Paul Gilroy (1999, p. 318) argues that 'identity provides a way of understanding the interplay between our subjective experience of the world and the cultural and historical settings in which that fragile subjectivity is formed'. However, as Gilroy cautions, identity is not simply that which is shared, rather 'it is always particular, as much about difference as about shared belonging' (ibid.). For James Clifford (1999, pp. 256–257):

> diaspora consciousness is [thus] constituted both negatively and positively. It is constituted negatively by experiences of discrimination and exclusion … [it] is produced positively through identification with world-historical cultural/political forces, such as 'Africa' or 'China.' The process may not be as much about being African or Chinese, as about being American or British, or wherever one has settled, differently.

In a similar vein, I argue that an interplay of sameness and difference underpins the queer Arab diaspora's search for belonging. Since the late nineteenth and early twentieth century, same-sex desires have been marked by derision in the modern Middle East, eventually leading to the open hostility towards queer identity we find today. Homophobia in the Middle East has often been explained as a legacy of colonialism and symptomatic of postcolonial nation-building projects. The resultant assumption of Middle Eastern homophobia can be felt in diasporic settings like North America and Europe, where there is a heightened sense of difference between 'us' and 'them', that is, the assimilationist process that marks 'good' immigrants from bad. Sherene Razack (2008, p. 117) describes a common trope in Middle Eastern and Muslim immigrant experiences which she explains as 'the story of the unassimilable, fatally pre-modern Muslim community encountering an advanced [Western] civilization'. Within this logic, the gay or queer Muslim and/or Middle Eastern subject must be unproblematically 'homonormative' in the West and live in awe of the liberal values that grant them the 'right' to be gay. This orientalising trope enforces a strict binary between same-sex desire and being Muslim, a dichotomy felt both in the Middle East and the diaspora.

Nadine Naber interrogates the dichotomies that ensnare Arab communities as they clamour for a sense of safety and belonging in the United States. Naber (2012, p. 234) argues that 'conventional nationalisms rely on a patrilinear heteronormative reproductive logic that maintains community boundaries through the ideal of heterosexual marriage and reproduction'. In their edited collection, Rebab Abdulhadi, Evelyn Alsultany and Nadine Naber (2011, p. xxii) argue that when articulating Arabness in the United States, the diaspora has been shaped by an assemblage of different visions of how Arabs survive in North America. They stress that

> historical and contextual factors related to the imperialist relationship between the United States and the Arab world have produced distinct forms of racism against and criminalization of individuals and communities perceived to be Arab or Muslim, especially in the aftermath of September 11, 2001.

This means that the racism and cultural differences Arab families often experience in the West can lead to an intensification of nationalism and a reification of some sort of authentic cultural heritage. For diasporic subjects, this means that difference and dichotomies are heightened, and notions of what it means to be Arab in North America are radically different from being

Arab in the Middle East. Importantly, Naber argues that for the Middle Eastern diaspora in the United States, gender and sexuality are among the most powerful symbols consolidating an imagined difference between Arabs and Americans. This has, more often than not, cast out queer Arabs and Middle Easterners from what it means to be an integrated part of the diaspora. As Naber (2012, p. 4) reflects: 'I learned that many of the Arabs I knew in the [San Francisco] Bay Area had more socially conservative understandings of Arab concepts of religion, family, gender, and sexuality than their counterparts in Jordan.'

Naber's signalling of a contradictory flow between the diaspora and the imagined homeland ca n also be found in Ramy Aly's work on Arabs in London, where the tropes of cultural authenticity can often involve modes of auto or self-orientalism in visual depictions of Arabness.[2] In considering some of the ways that young British-born or raised Arabs represent themselves, Aly notes that:

> fashions and aesthetic orientation in the Arab world and the Arab diaspora seem to flow in opposite directions. While middle-class Arab lifestyle magazines in the Middle East abound with images of Arabs in the latest Western fashions and interiors as testament to their inclusion in (a European) modernity, Arabs in London draw on folkloric Arab past to make the same kind of self-validating visual statements about themselves within the context of multicultural London.
>
> *(2015, p. 181)*

It is through the analysis of visual culture that these complex and often contradictory expressions of Arabness can be seen and read in an alternate visual language. Thus, the visual in the context of diaspora offers an opportunity to add layers to what it means to visualise belonging.[3]

The Islamicate queer subject becomes disruptive not only to ideas of authenticating diasporic cultural projects of survival but equally to a larger set of imperialist dynamics whereby Islamicate queer subjects in the diaspora are used as part of a Western homocolonial project. Following Marshall Hodgson's (1974 pp. 57–59) definition of the Islamicate rather than the less precise terms *Arab*, *Middle Eastern* or *Islamic*, I use the notion of Islamicate sexualities referring not directly to the religion of Islam itself, but to the social and cultural complexities historically associated with Islam, Muslims, and inclusive of non-Muslims living within the same region and other regions of the world that share colonial histories.[4] Momin Rahman (2014) argues against the erroneously assumed mutual exclusivity between queer and Middle Eastern and/ or Asian cultures and aims to illuminate the intersections and complexities of current binaries between and within Muslim communities and families, gay communities and culture, and wider Western political culture and discourses. Most importantly, Rahman argues that we must accept that the Muslim experience of sexual diversity politics is significantly different from the Western experience and that this reality undermines any assumption that the processes of 'Muslim modernisation' will inevitably lead to the same outcomes around sexuality as those experienced in the West. Thus, Middle Eastern homosexuality, including in the diaspora, will never look the same as Western homosexuality. Rahman goes on to define homocolonialism as 'the deployment of LGBTIQ rights and visibility to stigmatise non-Western cultures and conversely reassert the supremacy of the Western nations and civilization' (ibid., p. 7). Specifically, Rahman characterises 'Western exceptionalism as the primary political idea that is triangulated through the process of homocolonialism' (ibid., p. 118). Rahman posits that the queer Muslim subject is intersectional in the spaces they take up in society, and they naturally challenge the monolithic, monocultural versions of queer Western identity politics and the positioning of queer politics both in the Middle East and the diaspora. Here, the sheer existence of queer diasporic Muslims destabilises Western queer discourse and the ways in which queer subjectivity is 'knowable'.

Articulations of Arabness are then grounded in Arab traditions and sensibilities about family, selfhood and ways of being in the world, but they are also hybrid and historically contingent. Benedict Anderson (2006) has argued that nation, nationality and nationalism have all proven notoriously difficult to define, let alone to analyse. He argues that 'nationality', 'nation-ness' and 'nationalism' are cultural artefacts that require interrogation, especially their coming into being and the ways their meanings have changed over time. Therefore, I propose to study the art of diasporic queer Middle Eastern subjects as artefacts of postcolonial nation-ness. This is all the more necessary, given that a queer Middle Eastern diaspora has traditionally been excluded or written out of what it means to be Arab, Middle Eastern and Muslim. Thus, in turning to them, new ways of imagining and reading postcolonial subjectivity in the diaspora can be afforded. Visual culture often provides another language to better articulate these complex identities and subjectivities. I, therefore, explore the potential that visual art of the queer diaspora has to disrupt authentic notions of Arabness and to expose a Western, neo-imperial, homogeneous gay identity that remains a site of violence for the queer diaspora.

Visualising homocolonialism in the art of Jamil Hellu

While the interplays of race and sexual desire are not new, looking at these sites within the context of queer diasporic art is noteworthy. Jamil Hellu is a San Francisco-based visual artist whose work revolves around representations of identity and transnational interpretations of queer sexuality. Born and raised in Brazil with a Syrian father and a Paraguayan mother, Hellu uses photography, video, performance and mixed-media art installations to create contrasting metaphors about the politics of cultural identities and the fluidity of sexuality. His art is about reclaiming and redefining what it means to be Middle Eastern and/or queer. Hellu explains:

> My father's family is from Syria, originally from a town called *Mashta al-Helu*, from which I bear my last name. Looking for ways to voice my despair over homophobia and violence in the Middle East, I started to produce works claiming my own Arab roots. My latest projects explore my identity as a gay man in relation to my Syrian heritage and Arab ethnicity.
>
> *(Soldi and Hellu, 2016)*

In his 2016 installation, *Be My Guest* (Figures 14.1–14.4), Hellu presents two refurbished antique chairs with a footrest positioned between them, creating an intimate seating area. The two chairs face each other at an angle and are flanked by white curtains matching the same pattern on the furniture. The white fabric used in the furniture and curtains is adorned with figurative representations of Middle Eastern men engaging in various scenes of intimacy and undress. Sometimes kissing, hugging, wrestling and dancing, these representations of men are stamped repeatedly in black ink onto the white textile to create a repetitive design. In *Be My Guest*, Hellu cites the taboo of male homosexuality in both the Victorian-era empire and the Arab context that it colonised by using Victorian furniture as a metaphor for the cultural history of sexual repression in the Middle East.[5]

To be identified as Middle Eastern, the men are visibly hairy, play instruments that are popular in the Middle East and wear clothing and headdress that are identifiably Middle Eastern. The tension here between East and West, modern and Victorian, Orientalism and Occidentalism, all work in complex ways with one another (see Manalansan, 2003). These

Queering diaspora through visual art

Figure 14.1 Be My Guest. Installation: mirror, ottoman, 2 chairs, 2 pillows. Upholstered life-size furniture with textile pattern digitally printed on fabric.
Source: J. Hellu (2016).

Figure 14.2 Be My Guest. Detail of chair. Installation: mirror, ottoman, 2 chairs, 2 pillows. Upholstered life-size furniture with textile pattern digitally printed on fabric.
Source: J. Hellu (2016).

scenes of homosexual intimacy and leisure were rendered invisible in the Middle East during the Victorian era (El-Rouayheb, 2005; Najmabadi, 2005; Ze'evi, 2006; Boone, 2014). By upholstering these tender and intimate depictions of Arab men onto the Victorian furniture, they now define the very surface that they cover. In this defiant act of colonising the pristine

Figure 14.3 *Be My Guest*. Detail of pattern. Installation: mirror, ottoman, 2 chairs, 2 pillows. Upholstered life-size furniture with textile pattern digitally printed on fabric.
Source: J. Hellu (2016).

white surface of the furniture with depictions of racialised same-sex intimacy, this installation ensures that these depictions are encrypted with the very Victorian discourses of sexual repression and knowledge production that sought to erase them.

After nations in the Global North started decriminalising homosexuality, the goalposts of modernity moved and homosexual liberation became inextricably tied to being a modern

Queering diaspora through visual art

Figure 14.4 Be My Guest. Detail of Oud Player. Installation: mirror, ottoman, 2 chairs, 2 pillows. Upholstered life-size furniture with textile pattern digitally printed on fabric.
Source: J. Hellu (2016).

nation.[6] Homosexuality and gay liberation are thus insidiously used as a newly changed endpoint of Western modernity, excluding the Middle East from ever reaching progress as defined by the Global North. As Hiram Pérez (2015, p. 3) argues, 'Neither gay liberation politics nor queer activism has ever fully reckoned with the tacit, if complex, participation of gay modernity in U.S. [and Euro-American] imperialist expansion.' The hostility that queer people feel in the Middle East today is in part tied to this colonial history. Thus, Hellu symbolically and visually traces the violence inflicted upon homosexuals in the Middle East to the Victorian period while simultaneously linking this homocolonialism to the violence experienced by contemporary queer subjects today. This uncomfortable reminder seeks to critique and problematise the often heteronormative agendas of the West as the saviour and defender of queer subjects in the Middle East.

Be My Guest fuses the aesthetics of Islamicate same-sex desire, such as facial hair and the conventions of homosociality, alongside markers of gay sex synonymous with the Global North, like BDSM harnesses, jockstraps, and sexual scenes that allude to cruising categories of gay male identification in the West, like being a bear, otter or cub.[7] Furthermore, the male figures in this artwork display the variety of styles and ways in which Middle Eastern headdresses are worn, using multiplicity and repetition as a visual strategy. Illustrating cultural variation in this way means that figures wearing their Palestinian *keffiyeh* over their heads are seen alongside the traditions in other locales, like figures wearing the *ghutra* and *agal*, which are more commonly associated with the Arabian Gulf. Bringing these representations together cites the tensions their specific histories of gender, sexuality and nationalism represent while simultaneously grafting the macro-aggressions and frictions associated with being Arab and being gay.

In creating a link between diaspora consciousness and sexual imperialism in the Middle East, artists like Hellu offer a 'long overdue look at the way concepts of community and belonging are made across the diaspora, and produce insight into the possibilities for decolonising Arabness or rearticulating Arabness beyond Orientalism or reverse Orientalism' (Naber, 2012, p. 9). The double bind of the queer Middle Eastern diaspora brings with it the racialisation of their sexuality in the Global North, creating frictions with an imagined hegemonic gay community. Racial stigmatisation of queerness in the Global North is echoed by Rahman's (2014) assertion of the ostensibly Muslim queer subject lying outside of normative Western queer politics, pointing to issues of genuine difference and incompatibility. Linking racial difference and the queer diaspora in the Americas to Western imperialism and colonialism, Hellu's artwork uses a complex homocolonial history to outline a coloniality that continues to inflict violence, isolation and trauma to this day.

Queer migration in the art of Laurence Rasti

To illustrate the complexities of becoming a queer subject for the diasporic individual and how these experiences intersect with queer discourses in the Middle East, I turn to Laurence Rasti's photographic series, *There Are No Homosexuals in Iran* (2017). Rasti was born to Iranian parents in Geneva, Switzerland. Using both Swiss and Iranian cultural codes, Rasti's photographs explore gender, identity and migration. In *There Are No Homosexuals in Iran*, Rasti focuses on Iranian President Mahmoud Ahmadinejad's 2007 speech at Columbia University where he proclaimed: 'In Iran, we do not have homosexuals like in your country' (ibid., Preface). Coupled with interviews that voice the personal experiences of anonymous migrants, Rasti photographs asylum-seekers in Denizili, Turkey, where hundreds of gay Iranian refugees are stuck in a transit zone. 'Set in this state of limbo, where anonymity is the best protection' (ibid.), Rasti's photographs juxtapose and reimagine the facelessness these migrants experience in the transit zone with Ahmadinejad's attempts to erase their sexual identity from Iranian public consciousness. In one image in the series (Figure 14.5), two women obscure each other by gently cupping their hands to each other's faces. This interplay of visibility and self-preservation is important within refugee and migrant experiences but also to queer experiences both in the Middle East and the diaspora. It is important to dispel the myth of a utopian gay liberation for the queer Middle Eastern diaspora in the Global North, for racial and community violence can be the source of physical and emotional pain as homophobic logics become entwined with articulating Arabness outside of the Middle East. As the historical-colonial heterosexualisation of the Middle East inevitably led to criminalising same-sex desires, so too does a heterosexualisation take place in the diaspora as Middle Eastern cultures are forced into strongly held binaries based on anti-Muslim and anti-brown racism in the Global North. The queer diaspora is, unfortunately, one of the casualties of the racist and homophobic forces that come from both host and home cultures.

For the two women in Figure 14.5, their Iranian identity is in direct (and manufactured) conflict with their Iranian-ness and their queerness. The ways in which their Iranian nationality should somehow make them immune to feeling same-sex desire, and the attitude that gay love can only exist in the West, are both signs of sexual exceptionalism. Sexual exceptionalism occurs through stagings of a US nationalism, for instance, that works in tandem with sexual othering, one that exceptionalises the identities of US citizens often in contrast to Orientalist constructions of perverse 'Muslim sexuality' (Puar, 2007, p. 4). Sexual exceptionalism is understood here as the possession of a feature, like the West's ostensible championing gay rights or Iran condemning homosexuality, that gives a unique mission to a state or a polity and is seen as an anchor to its national identity. This means that sexual exceptionalism, an example of which can be seen in Ahmadinejad's assertion in 2007 that 'In Iran, we do not have homosexuals like

Queering diaspora through visual art

Figure 14.5 There Are No Homosexuals in Iran. Inkjet print.
Source: L. Rasti (2014).

in your country', puts Iranian racial identities in direct opposition to a singular, and reductive, queer identity that corresponds to and comes out of the exceptionalism of the American empire's sexual freedoms. This dualism and 'national homosexuality' is part of what Puar (2007, p. 2) terms 'homonationalism', and is a significant part of queer diasporic migrant experiences.

The antagonistic dualism created when one's sexual identity seemingly contradicts one's cultural identity is a tension that aims to define a normative script for both homosexuality and nationalism, placing aspects of racialised queer subjectivity in assumed conflict with one another. Not all subjects in Rasti's photographs are anonymous, some reveal their faces in these scenes of intimacy. Figure 14.6 shows two men standing outside, one embracing the other with his face nuzzled behind his companion's neck. The man being hugged, however, is fully visible to the viewer, closing his eyes in a peaceful embrace. Figure 14.7 similarly portrays two individuals embracing one another, this time with a man holding his partner's hips from behind as he shields his face. His partner, however, adorns bold make-up, painted nails and long curly hair in a purple silk dress. The gender-fluid figure in the forefront makes eye contact with the viewer, ensuring that the heavy eyeliner, pink lips and unshaven beard do not go unnoticed. In this scene both gender conventions and norms of beauty are questioned, revealing the very dualism that at once makes homosexuality punishable by death in Iran and racially stigmatised outside of the Middle East. This brand of homosexuality that the Middle East deems too American and America deems exceptional, as Puar argues, 'operates as a regulatory script not only for normative gayness, queerness, or homosexuality, but also of the racial and national norms that reinforce these sexual subjects' (ibid., p. 2). What does this tell us about the sociological and political landscape of the queer diaspora? As Gayatri Gopinath (2005, p. 11) suggests, to understand queerness as diasporic and diaspora as queer is to recuperate 'desires, practices, and

Figure 14.6 *There Are No Homosexuals in Iran*. Inkjet print.
Source: L. Rasti (2014).

subjectivities that are rendered impossible or unimaginable within conventional diasporic or nationalist imaginaries'. Such a critical framework of a 'specifically queer diaspora ... may begin to unsettle the ways in which the diaspora shores up the gender and sexual ideologies of dominant nationalism on the one hand, and processes of globalisation on the other' (ibid., p. 10).

Homocolonialism, homonationalism and human rights

It is important to contextualise decolonisation as it pertains to homosexual tolerance and liberation in the Middle East. The arguments thus far presented take issue with the historical upset of Middle Eastern sexualities by an intolerant Western colonialism, and more recently what Joseph Massad (2008) terms 'The Gay International'. These imperialist projects have in turn shaped local sexual discourses in the Middle East, which were more fluid and community-oriented and not identity-based, forcing a Western binary gender identity model of heteronormativity onto the so-called Other in the Middle East. At the height of these colonial projects from the nineteenth and twentieth centuries, homosexuality was also illegal in the legal systems of the colonisers and, consequently, the prohibition of homosexuality in the Middle East was a measure taken as part of a broader formula of mimicking Western modernity.[8] The legacies of Western imperialism on local sexual discourses were a catalyst for homophobic attitudes that more recently have sought to identify 'primitive' sexual discourses in the Middle East and contrast these to the liberal sexual exceptionalism of the United States.

This dilemma is precisely where homocolonialism and homonationalism intersect. As a critique of lesbian and gay liberal rights discourses, homonationalism attends to how such

Queering diaspora through visual art

Figure 14.7 There Are No Homosexuals in Iran. Inkjet print.
Source: L. Rasti (2014).

discourses produce narratives of progress and modernity that continue to advance civilisational discourses in some contexts and limit the progression of the 'backwards' Other (see Dryden and Lenon, 2016). As Euro-American homocolonialism sought an erasure of same-sex desires in the Middle East, Euro-American homonationalism now champions the same-sex desires they once crushed in an effort to align gay liberation with modernity. Jasbir Puar argues that, for the queer subject, national recognition and inclusion are 'contingent upon the segregation and disqualifications of racial and sexual others from the national imaginary' (2007, p. 2). While homosexuality is currently restricted and criminalised in Middle Eastern societies but is relatively protected in certain Western cultures, contemporary discourses of sexual liberation need to be attentive to these histories of imperial violence at the risk of replicating the same coloniality that led to gay criminalisation in the first place.[9] The only way to correct these historical-colonial dynamics that caused irreparable damage[10] for sexual discourses in the Middle East is a human rights advocacy that does not centre protecting people's sexuality today in a monolithic version of queerness that is manufactured in and exported from the Global North.[11] Echoing Massad's (2008) claims, this suggests that human rights discourses that seek to replicate Western queer models of identity will only reproduce imperial control over sexual discourses in the Middle East.

Dangers of heterosexualisation in the art of Nilbar Güreş

These sexual codes of conduct have lasting effects on the Middle Eastern diaspora, both in the queerness of diasporic subjects, illustrated through Hellu's artwork, and on an exilic

 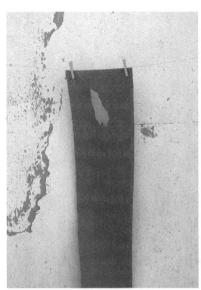

Figure 14.8 Still image from video *Torn*. HD video, colour, sound, 6:00 min.
Source: N. Güreş (2018).

formation of people who flee the region to escape persecution, as seen in the subjects of Rasti's photographic series. The heterosexualisation of a Middle Eastern culture that actively denies the existence of same-sex desires has very real consequences. The violence inflicted upon queer bodies can be seen in the photo-video installation *Torn* (2018) by diasporic artist Nilbar Güreş, a Turkish artist who lives and works in Vienna. Güreş' artwork explores female identity, the relationships between women and domestic/public spaces, as well as intersectional, transnational and transcultural queer identity. Güreş uses video and photography to tell the story of her friend Didem, a transgender woman who was continually discriminated against and aggressively harassed for being queer in Turkey. In the installation, a one-channel video shows Didem standing defiantly in the centre of the frame, arms crossed as she stares into the camera, meeting the viewers gaze (Figure 14.8). Behind her is a rectangular textile with deep orange and red patterns that frames her head like a halo. The video slowly zooms in on Didem while a low guttural sound reverberates through the speakers. She stands still throughout the video, making each scene reminiscent of a photograph capturing a moment in time. It is only in moments when the wind gently blows through her hair or with fluttering blinks of her eyelashes that the audience realises that Didem is actively present and standing witness by looking back at the viewer. The video ends with Didem walking away from the frame and revealing the full textile that was partially hidden behind her. Hanging on the rooftop balcony in Didem's hometown of Izmir, the viewer sees a large tear in the textile, once concealed by Didem's presence in the frame. This slash tells the tragic story of when Didem was brutally dragged into a car in Istanbul, robbed and almost murdered when attackers slit her throat. In the textile, Güreş uses scissors to cut a large, elongated hole in the shape of the scar on Didem's neck. According to Güreş, the cut in the cloth 'references the violent emptiness of society that tries to cover itself up through its victims. LGBTQAI [Lesbian, Gay, Bisexual, Trans, Queer, Asexual, Intersex] people are the victims of hate crimes' (Cornell, Eiblmayr and Schmutz, 2018, p.78).

Considering Güreş' artwork in relation to Hellu's and Rasti's visual art brings interesting connections and frictions to the notion of queer diaspora. In *Torn*, Nilbar Güreş is creating art from the diaspora about the trauma and violence her queer loved ones experience in her homeland of Turkey. Laurence Rasti is creating art from the diaspora about queer migration, and the struggle for queer refugees from Iran patiently waiting for asylum from their transit zones in Turkey. Jamil Hellu produces visual art from the diaspora about the history of colonial violence and sexual imperialism relating to his Syrian heritage. These examples provide a rich site to interrogate: What makes an artwork queer? What makes an artwork diasporic? If 'diasporic art' as a didactic and visual category demands that the art itself be produced in the diaspora, this signals that the artists' diasporic identity is the driving force in determining the diasporic nature and content of the art. When asking what makes an artwork queer, similar slippages happen to the logic that governs our understanding of complex formations of race, sexuality and visuality. Does the queerness of an artwork lie in the queer content of the artwork or in the queerness of the artist? One then has to question the reductive nature to categorise and delimit certain visual practices as belonging to 'gay art' or 'minority art' and instead see the potential of queer diasporic formations. When freed from the disciplinary and academic distinctions between discursive categories such as 'queer' or 'diasporic', queer diasporic visual practices that foreground the personal can 'create deeply affective counter-archives of regional (un)belonging' (Gopinath, 2018, p. 11), regardless of place. Gayatri Gopinath's newest study on the aesthetic practices of the queer diaspora teaches us that asking these questions and creating these disciplinary ruptures within our logics illuminate the unexpected convergences between seemingly disparate sites of analysis. In particular, part of the rubric for the 'aesthetic practices of the queer diaspora' that Gopinath puts forth is the unexpected convergences between

> the interrogation of the visual field and the limits of a politics of visibility and representation, on the one hand, and on the other hand queerness as an optic and reading practice that brings alternative modes of affiliation and relationality into focus.
>
> *(ibid., p. 10)*

Diasporic bodies and queer world-making

To better situate these artistic expressions and literature within ideas of a queer diaspora, it is useful to think of identity formation in relation to queer world-making. This means reassessing the gatekeeping mechanisms that have dictated some bodies as queer, diasporic, both and, depending on the transnational context, neither. As this analysis of contemporary visual art illustrates, queerness finds a way to dwell and remain in seemingly 'inhospitable' places like the Middle East, Africa and Asia. It begs the question: who defines queer hospitality? The answer, of course, is Western queerness and its unquestionable authenticity. The frictions and tensions that queer bodies can have within the Middle East might be lessened in other locales, but these places can be sites in which diasporic bodies are the source of racial tensions and violence. The queer diaspora is often the queer black and brown body, and the process of racialisation, as well as sexualisation, is the site where the queer diaspora is constituted. To demystify the fallacy that it is contradictory to be both brown and queer, it is vital to challenge the concept of stable or fixed identities that foreclose other ways of being. Postcolonial theorist Homi Bhabha (2004) argues that cultural hybridity results from various forms of colonisation and leads to cultural collisions and interchanges. In the attempt to assert colonial power and to create civilised subjects, 'the trace of what is disavowed is not repressed but repeated as something different—a mutation, a hybrid' (ibid., p. 111). This hybrid subject, or the contemporary queer diaspora, contradicts both the attempt to fix and control indigenous cultures and the illusion of cultural authenticity or purity. Here, the notion of the in-between is relevant, for the queer diasporic is then left with opposing views of Western and non-Western sexual practices, a tense historical framing of Arab-sexual discourses, all the while being measured by Western narratives of modernity, progress and enlightened (Euro-American) sexual identity. In these performances and failures, belongings and exclusions, recognitions and disidentifications, the postcolonial queer subject articulates nation-ness in complex ways, a process that is better informed by the visual culture they produce.

Notes

1 I define the Middle East loosely as the geopolitical designation of western Asia and North-east Africa that includes the nations on the Arabian Peninsula, Egypt, Iran, Iraq, Israel, Jordan, Lebanon, Syria, and Turkey. Even though some of these regions, like Iran and Turkey, are not technically a part of the Middle East, a historiographical emphasis makes it integral to include regions that were connected by empire, culture and language. It is worth noting that Arab is an ethno-linguistic category, identifying people who speak the Arabic language as their mother tongue. Arabs trace their national roots to the 22 member states of the League of Arab States: Egypt, Sudan, Jordan, Syria, Lebanon, Iraq, Saudi Arabia, Kuwait, Bahrain, Qatar, United Arab Emirates, Oman, Yemen, Djibouti, Somalia, Eritrea, Libya, Tunisia, Algeria, Comoros, Morocco and Mauritania. Religiously, they include Muslims (Sunnis, Shiites, Alawites and Ismailis), Christians (Protestants, Catholics, Greek Orthodox, Coptic Orthodox, Caldeans, Assyrians and Maronites), and Jews. Unlike Arabs, Middle Eastern people are defined to come from countries of the Arabian peninsula: Iraq, Syria, Lebanon, Jordan, Palestine, Israel, Kuwait, Turkey, Egypt and Iran.
2 Orientalism is defined as the West's patronising representations of 'the East' and the overall exoticisation of the societies and peoples who inhabit countries in Asia, North Africa and the Middle East. According to Said (1979), Orientalism is inextricably tied to the imperialist societies that produced it, which makes much Orientalist work inherently political and central to power.
3 For instance, in her seminal book *Impossible Desires*, queer theorist Gayatri Gopinath (2005) examines film and literary texts, what she calls a public culture, to dissect the ways in which discourses of sexuality are inseparable from histories of colonialism, nationalism, racism and migration. In examining cultural texts that are produced by the South Asian diaspora, Gopinath extends the power of this cultural production as even influencing the homeland. Here, cultural texts going back and forth between homeland and diaspora then contribute to and create a shaping of both sets of cultures, falsifying the notion of diaspora only being oriented towards and dependent on homeland.
4 In 1974, Marshall Hodgson coined the term 'Islamicate' as a way of opening up the borders posed by modern scholarship. Hodgson identifies the issue in using the term Islam and Islamic in unspecific ways, arguing that the more we speak of Islamic art, literature or sexuality, the less we actually speak about Islam as a faith. The Islamicate does not refer directly to the religion of Islam itself, but to the social and cultural complexities historically associated with Islam. It is also inclusive of non-Muslims living within the same regions. Geographically, it also opens up the limits of only studying places such as 'the Middle East', and encompasses other geographic regions where Islam is dominant both religiously and culturally, such as Iran and parts of Asia (Hodgson, 1974, pp. 57–59).
5 The artist states that they use the Victorian-era layout of domestic spaces and furniture as a metaphor for the cultural history of sexual repression. It should be noted that the furniture design within the installation is emblematic of the work of Thomas Chippendale, an eighteenth-century Georgian furniture maker who popularised Rococo and Neoclassical furniture in Britain and the United States.
6 As Jasbir Puar (2007, p. 4) notes, sexual exceptionalism occurs through stagings of US nationalisms that work in tandem with a sexual othering, one that exceptionalises the identities of US citizens often in contrast to Orientalist constructions of perverse 'Muslim sexuality'. As a critique of lesbian and gay liberal rights discourses, homonationalism attends to how such discourses produce narratives of progress and modernity that continue to advance civilisational discourses in some contexts, and limit the progression of the 'backwards' Other (Dryden and Lenon, 2016).
7 For example, 'bears' comprise of a subculture of gay men who valorise the larger, hairy body. For critical writing on gay subcultures, see Hennen (2005).

8 El-Rouayheb (2005, pp. 119–121) outlines detailed descriptions of how *liwāt* (sodomy) was criminalised and handled in Islamic law, specifically in the four acknowledged schools of law in the Ottoman Empire: Hanaf'i, Shafi'i, Hanbali and Maliki. Historian Dror Ze'evi (2006, pp. 168–169) also argues that historically, major conflicts about the permissibility of same-sex relations simply did not exist. Though legally frowned upon, same-sex desires were taken to be part of life and their illegality were usually ignored until modernisation (and Westernisation) led a previously invisible part of life to suddenly become an object for observation and comparison with Victorian cultural norms.

9 Language is one of the sites that conditions sexual experiences in the Global South. Tarik Bereket and Barry Adam's (2006) research on gay identities in Turkey contends that the contemporary concept of 'gay' is a particularly generational and classed identity category dependent on a certain social status and education level. However, in MSM (men who have sex with men) relations, for instance, terms such as 'active' and 'passive' dictate how the individual performs their masculinity and are more socially relevant categories at the local level. These ideas of masculinity scripts are relatively in line with Judith Butler's (2015) notion of performativity, reiterating a type of masculinity that serves to define an individual's identity as being either active or passive; the passive subject refuses to take on the active image of the hyper-masculinised, as it conflicts with his identity script as passive.

10 Homosexuality is illegal in 10 of the 18 Arab countries in Western Asia (Bahrain, Egypt, Iraq, Jordan, Kuwait, Lebanon, Libya, Mauritania, Morocco, Oman, Palestine, Qatar, Saudi Arabia, Sudan, the Syrian Arab Republic, Tunisia, the United Arab Emirates and Yemen). Homosexuality is punishable by death in six of these 18 countries. All sexual orientations are legal in Bahrain, Cyprus, Lebanon, Jordan, Turkey, Palestine, and Israel. Female homosexual activity is legal in Palestine and Kuwait; however, female homosexuality in Egypt is sporadically policed. Even though female homosexuality is less consistently punished when compared to men having sex with men, few of these countries recognise legal rights and provisions for gay individuals. Male homosexual activity is illegal and punishable by imprisonment in Kuwait, Egypt, Oman, Qatar and Syria. It is punishable by death in Iran, Iraq, Saudi Arabia, Qatar and the United Arab Emirates. In Yemen and Palestine, the punishment might differ between death and imprisonment depending on the act committed. For more detailed information, see Human Rights Watch (2018).

11 Walcott (2015, p. viii) states that 'Canada is deeply involved in exporting its homosexual rights agenda elsewhere, and even within its borders, its homosexual rights agenda differentiates across race, sexual practices, and place of "origin".' An example of this is the inauguration of Pride House as part of the 2010 Winter Olympic Games, which were held in Vancouver and Whistler, to position Canada as a gay haven. Imagining itself as a safe space where sexual minorities (both athletes and their allies) from around the world were welcome, 'Pride House showcased Canadian (sexual) exceptionalism on a world stage' (Dryden and Lenon, 2015, p. 3).

References

Abdulhadi, R., Alsultany, E. and Naber, N.C. (2011) *Arab & Arab American Feminisms: Gender, Violence*. Syracuse, NY: Syracuse University Press.

Aly, R.M.K. (2015) *Becoming Arab in London: Performativity and the Undoing of Identity*. London: Pluto Press.

Anderson, B. (2006) *Imagined Communities: Reflections on the Origin and Spread of Nationalism*. New York: Verso.

Bereket, T. and Adam, B. (2006) 'The emergence of gay identities in contemporary Turkey', *Sexualities*, 9(2), pp. 131–151.

Bhabha, H.K. (2004) *The Location of Culture*. London: Routledge.

Boone, J.A. (2014) *The Homoerotics of Orientalism*. New York: Columbia University Press.

Butler, J. (2015). *Gender Trouble: Feminism and the Subversion of Identity*. London: Routledge.

Clifford, J. (1999) *Routes: Travel and Translation in the Late Twentieth Century*. Cambridge, MA: Harvard University Press.

Cohen, R.L. (1997) *Global Diasporas: An Introduction*. Seattle, WA: University of Washington Press.

Cornell, L., Eiblmayr, S. and Schmutz, H. (2018) *Nilbar Güreş: Overhead*. Linz, Austria: Lentos Kunstmuseum Linz.

Dryden, O.H. and Lenon, S. (2015) *Disrupting Queer Inclusion*. Vancouver, BC: University of British Columbia Press.

El-Rouayheb, K. (2005) *Before Homosexuality in the Arab-Islamic World, 1500–1800*. Chicago: University of Chicago Press.

Gilroy, P. (1999) 'Diaspora and the detours of identity', in Woodward, K. (ed.) *Identity and Difference*. London: Sage and Open University, pp. 299–346.

Gopinath, G. (2005) *Impossible Desires: Queer Diasporas and South Asian Public Cultures*. Durham, NC: Duke University Press.

Gopinath, G. (2018) *Unruly Visions: The Aesthetic Practices of Queer Diaspora*. Durham, NC: Duke University Press.

Hennen, P. (2005) 'Bear bodies, bear masculinity: recuperation, resistance, or retreat?' *Gender & Society*, 19, pp. 25–43.

Hodgson, M.G.S. (1974) *The Venture of Islam*, vol. 1: *The Classical Age of Islam*. Chicago: University of Chicago Press.

Human Rights Watch (2018) 'Audacity in adversity: LGBT activism in the Middle East and North Africa'. Available at: www.hrw.org/report/2018/04/16/audacity-adversity/lgbt-activism-middle-east-and-north-africa (accessed 11 March 2021).

Manalansan, M.F. (2003) *Global Divas: Filipino Gay Men in the Diaspora*. Durham, NC: Duke University Press.

Massad, J. (2008) *Desiring Arabs*. Chicago: University of Chicago Press.

Naber, N.C. (2012) *Arab America: Gender, Cultural Politics, and Activism*. New York: New York University Press.

Najmabadi, A. (2005) *Women with Mustaches and Men without Beards: Gender and Sexual Anxieties of Iranian Modernity*. Berkeley, CA: University of California Press.

Perez, H. (2015) *A Taste for Brown Bodies: Gay Modernity and Cosmopolitan Desire*. New York: New York University Press.

Puar, J.K. (2007) *Terrorist Assemblages: Homonationalism in Queer Times*. Durham, NC: Duke University Press.

Rahman, M. (2014) *Homosexualities, Muslim Cultures and Modernity*. Basingstoke: Palgrave Macmillan.

Rasti, L. (2017) *There Are No Homosexuals in Iran*. Zürich: Edition Patrick Frey.

Razack, S. (2008) *Casting Out: The Eviction of Muslims from Western Law and Politics*. Toronto: University of Toronto Press.

Said, E. (1979) *Orientalism*. New York: Pantheon Books.

Soldi, R. and Helu, J. (2016) 'Q&A: Jamil Hellu.' *Strange Fire*. Available at: www.strangefirecollective.com/qa-jamil-hellu (accessed 11 October 2019).

Walcott, R. (2015) 'Foreword: the homosexuals have arrived', in Dryden, O.H. and Lenon, S. (eds) *Disrupting Queer Inclusion*. Vancouver, BC: University of British Columbia Press, pp. vii–ix.

Ze'evi, D. (2006) *Producing Desire: Changing Sexual Discourse in the Ottoman Middle East, 1500–1900*. Berkeley, CA: University of California Press.

15
POST-*TARAB* IDENTITIES IN DIASPORA
A sonic imaginary of Arab Canada

Jillian Fulton-Melanson

A queer counter-public

Throughout this chapter, I illuminate the sonorous world that takes place within electronic dance music (EDM) culture in Canada in regard to both the way that Arabic music lives in various EDM genres today and how that life, in turn, creates life for my interlocutors who are active participants in EDM spaces. My work sounds the Arab diaspora by drawing attention to the individual, lived experiences of my interlocutors, which inform their senses of Arabness and the Arabness they bring to EDM culture. I use the concept of post-*tarab* to theorise the shifting performativity of Arabness in diaspora that my Arab interlocutors undergo.[1] As further defined in the next section, post-*tarab* frames the modulation from the Arabic classical music genre, *tarab*, to EDM in parallel with the pivot from ethnonormative and heteronormative pan-Arabism to queer Arabness. It is argued that the Arabness of Arab people is being redefined, and as such, the Arabness of Arabic music is also being redefined.

The concept of post-*tarab* is employed to describe and analyse EDM as what Arjun Appadurai termed a scape (Appadurai, 1990; 1996; Rantanen, 2006) in combination with R. Murray Schafer's soundscape (1977). These post-*tarab* soundscapes index the musical and affective interpellation of Arabic folk music and culture into the urban contexts that my interlocutors occupy, embody and contest.[2] The post-*tarab* soundscapes *sampled* from Arabic music and heard in EDM tracks are collected from old folk songs from the Arab world. Producers thus *collect* these folk songs from the Arab world and *bring* them to Canada. I suspend these terms because producers do not have to physically collect these songs from one geographic location and transport them to another; rather, through online networks, producers are able to collect and collaborate with other producers and musicians internationally. The collected Arabic music samples thus appear in new performance contexts, such as EDM, and they are heard in geographic locales outside of their original music society, the Arab world. Because of the movement of both sound and people, I argue that my interlocutors are not only part of an Arab immigrant community, but also a sonic Arab diaspora that features genres lying outside of the World Music market.[3] In this way, post-*tarab* soundscapes traverse the distance between home and diaspora and can be used to analyse the tensions that emerge through my interlocuters' claims about identity-making and belonging.

Through the lens of EDM subgenres, house and techno, this chapter covers the diasporic experience of Arab music producers, DJs, dancers and participants who have sought out EDM scenes as a place they can call home. EDM, a countercultural genre for both Canadian and Arab societies, is a sonic environment that hosts a counter-public of individuals. There are many different groups – or what Michael Warner (2002) terms publics – that my interlocutors identify with outside of the EDM counter-public. EDM is a counter-public and counter-culture because its members are acutely aware that underground EDM spaces oppose the rules and guidelines of heteronormative society (Hirschkind, 2006). Outside of EDM, they could be part of religious or spirituality-based publics, publics based on political views, or publics who meet, based on their ethnicity or nationalist sentiments. Because of this, I prefer to think of EDM enthusiasts as being part of a sonic imaginary that serves to connect them to each other through sound and experience.

My interlocutors are connected to each other by music, and they have created not only an alternative imaginary through which they find their senses of self, but also a responsive imaginary. This response is, first and foremost, to the mainstream, ethnonormative account of what it means to be Arab and heteronormative (Aly, 2015). Unfolding through their individual narratives and alongside Arabness, my interlocutors each ascribe to different intersectional identities that lie outside of the realm of heteronormativity. Not only do they express Arabness counter-culturally by being associated with EDM, but they also identify with queerness, an ambiguous, non-binary identifier for gender and sexuality, inherent to the foundation of EDM.[4] Queerness is neither exclusive to same-sex relationships, nor is it limited to 'mismatched' expressions of gender and sexuality (Fleeger, 2014). It also includes alternative ways of living. As such, some of my interlocutors identify as genderqueer, some have fluid sexualities, and some choose to live outside of the 'nine-to-five grind'. Queerness, in this manner, creates tension among those who crave binary categories. In the words of José Esteban Muñoz (2009, p. 1), 'Queerness is essentially about the rejection of a here and now and an insistence on potentiality or concrete possibility for another world.' My interlocutors display their queerness in a social world where heteronormative living is preached as the model for how to achieve success in adulthood. In this way, they are not only individually queer, but the collective itself is also queer because it consists of individuals who are brought together by the soundscape of EDM rather than by gender, ethnicity, social class or ideologies that they do not necessarily share. Writing about a queer collective creates space for new ways of life to be constructed and lived in the contracting and expanding grip of society (Bogard, 2007; Farsakh, Kanaaneh and Sheikaly, 2018; Kapadia, 2019).

The sonorous world of EDM constructs a social platform for the production of queer, Arab identities that are reproduced through performance and participation. The term Arab is used throughout this chapter to describe a relationship between each of my interlocutors, where they or their ancestors have lived before, and where they live now.[5] I use the term diaspora to refer to the Arab sounds and communities that have moved from the Arab world to Toronto and Montreal, acknowledging that there are different ethnic and national groups within these. One of the main threads throughout this chapter is the bond or category of Arabness and my interlocutors' varying degrees of acceptance, rejection or complacency with the term. Arabness performed by a queer, Arab collective co-produces a radical response to heteronormativity, ethnonormativity and media and public narratives about Arab people.

The ethnographic substance I present demonstrates that affective moments hold political potential for creating a 'politics of belonging' filled with acts of sharing, dialogue and exchange. Although EDM is a subaltern countercultural scene, EDM enthusiasts do not necessarily aim to redraw existent relationships of power (within heteronormative Canadian society, or within the ethnonormativity of the greater Arab-Canadian public). Rather, they are carving new spaces where they can belong, desire, hope and imagine their pasts, presents and futures.

I began 'walking alongside' my interlocutors in 2016; this methodology for both fieldwork and writing comes from Trinh T. Minh-Ha (2016) and allows me to witness the everyday lives of my interlocutors while I engage in continuous dialogue with them. Walking through musical encounters at both performances and everyday experiences, I describe the way that the nodes of home, identity and belonging, as well as hoping and desiring, are conceptual points of departure for the conversations and moments we experienced together. Home, identity and belonging and hoping and desiring act as two separate nodes that are attached to the central experience of Arab people living in diaspora. Between these two nodes, I locate the tensions my interlocutors feel as a result of their expressions of self. I conceptualise post-*tarab* as the central node encompassing each of these experiences. On that account, post-*tarab* is a temporal encounter that entangles Arab ethnicities, identities and musical expressions as interwoven elements that cannot be separated, and that differ from person to person.

From *tarab* to post-*tarab*

In November 2017, I asked one of my interlocutors, Ibrahim – a queer percussionist from Tunisia living in Montreal – what they thought about *tarab*. They responded by saying that *tarab*, the genre, was 'certainly not' being composed any more. This response made me think about *tarab* as not only a genre with accompanying affects and performance spaces, but as an era that held particular importance for the Arab community. As Ibrahim stated, this era of *tarab* has come to a close, but its cultural effects continue to linger. While sitting in one of Ibrahim's band rehearsals one Friday night in Montreal, I thought about the post-rock music they were playing and how rock music had evolved beyond its genre label. While I still assert that *tarab*'s elements are felt and heard in EDM, the music is not *tarab* any more. The Arab+EDM equation is post-*tarab*, a concept that encompasses experiences, genres, temporalities and philosophies of transcendence.[6]

Post-*tarab*, in the manner I elaborate it, works as a provisional, theoretical lens to discuss the temporal continuum of what it means to be Arab in the contemporary, postcolonial era. I use post-*tarab* to reference EDM that incorporates the classical *tarab* elements described below. Post-*tarab* generally includes direct samples from old Arabic songs, samples of electronically produced Middle Eastern instruments, and the musical structure of *tarab*, which features hour-long sets, repetition, improvisation and detemporalisation. These classical *tarab* elements also incorporate a similar affective capability. The use of the word *tarab* in Arabic can either refer to the musical genre, its affectual experience, or a mixture of the two.

Though I use *tarab* as a term encompassing more than merely a musical genre, *tarab* in its original form is an Arabic music genre hailing from Cairo, Beirut and Damascus. *Tarab* music incorporates vocal and instrumental pieces that range in length from 30 to 60 minutes. These pieces use methods of improvisation, repetition and detemporalisation to create an affected ecstasy or enchantment (*tarab*'s English equivalents) in the music's various participants (Danielson, 1999; Frishkopf, 2001; Racy, 2003). It is considered to be an Egyptian genre, where it peaked between the 1940s and 1970s. It was particularly culturally relevant to Nasser's Egypt during the 1950s and played an important role in spreading pan-Arab sentiments (Danielson, 1999). *Tarab* was contextualised by everything from the gender politics of turn-of-the-century Cairo, which caused the famous *tarab mutrib* (solo vocalist), Umm Kulthum (1898–1975), to perform dressed as a boy to hide her femininity, to the nightclubs of Egypt filled with booming sound systems, alcohol, hashish and sex workers. *Tarab* also observed the addition of the electric guitar to the traditional Arabic orchestra (the *takht* ensemble). In this fashion, *tarab* reflected ideas of modernisation and was able to open up to new contexts and technical innovations in music.

Tarab literally means ecstasy. A.J. Racy writes extensively about *tarab* as a concept, genre, and setting (1991; 2000; 2003). Racy explains that in order to create the ambience of *tarab*, musicians must be in the right state of mind to produce *saltanah*, the ecstatic state that only the performer can achieve. The performer's ecstatic state of *saltanah* is required to invoke *tarab* in their audience. *Saltanah* is usually generated pre-performance through vocal warm-ups in particular *maqamat* (Arab modal system), but it can also be invoked once on stage by prolonging a particular *maqam* at the beginning of a performance. There are dozens of *maqamat* to choose from, and each is said to carry its own unique, distinct mood or personality. Although these Arabic compositions move between specific *maqamat*, each piece traditionally has a home or 'reigning' *maqam* (Marcus, 2007, p. 18) that establishes its particular mood sonically, resonating throughout the body of the singer or the instrument and instrumentalist, creating the *saltanah* that is then passed on to the audience as the ecstatic state of transcendence called *tarab*.

The structure of EDM runs parallel to *tarab* structure, as the DJ's musical set is comprised of the same techniques as *tarab*: the set is at least an hour in length, features repetitive or 'looping' melodic and percussive elements, and incorporates detemporalisation by suspending the bass and adding euphoric improvisatory sounds. As the bass re-emerges, bringing the dance floor back into time, participants can often find themselves experiencing ecstasy in a continuous, cyclical process that ebbs and flows throughout the night. The DJ must carefully select their setlist in advance while also leaving room for the emergence of improvisatory avenues, depending on the reaction the audience has to each track. The DJ often also 'warms up' or prepares their headspace before performing, a process that can be considered similar to *saltanah*. Like the transmutation of *saltanah* into *tarab* transferred over the feedback loop between audience and performer, an EDM event is often conceived of as a spiritual experience (Hutson, 2000). In Arabic terms, we could say that the DJ acts as the *tarab mutrib*. As a result, EDM participants are entranced by the DJ and placed into a state of *tarab*.

EDM and *tarab* are an uncanny pair. Although different in context and instrumentation, bassline-driven house and techno (genres of EDM that emerged from Chicago and Detroit in the 1980s) mirror *tarab* in structure, hold events with similar contextual qualities, and also map the city beyond their events by reaching into different spaces with musical recordings. Like Chicago house, Detroit techno, Berlin techno and various other musical hubs, *tarab* as a genre uses the concept of a home base – Al-Andalus, Aleppo, Beirut and Cairo – where various national elements within the genre are emphasised based on locale (Racy, 2000). An Arab DJ in Montreal producing Berlin techno with samples from Beirut *tarab* creates a sonic diaspora. An EDM track with each of these national elements reflects multiple locales. The placement of elements from one musical locale alongside another evokes a 'techoustemological' understanding of the world – a sonic knowing through technological reproductions and travels of music (Bijsterveld and van Dijck, 2009).[7] *Tarab* and EDM produce parallel states of affect, and are thus powerful entities to combine.

Home, identity and belonging

Postcolonial conditions produce displaced and decentred identities, and as such, my interlocutors define home in multiple ways depending on the reason for their displacement (Gupta and Ferguson, 1992; Alajaji, 2015). Some feel nostalgic for their homeland, while others want to forget it because of how they associate it with traumatic experiences. Some have migrated to Canada of their own accord and can visit their home regularly. Others were born in Canada or other diasporic settings and have a limited experience of 'home' that is often bound to nostalgic relations and imaginations. Because underground EDM events featuring post-*tarab* soundscapes are often cultivated by an Arab-imagined sensorium, immersing participants into a form of home, I would argue that underground EDM *creates* a sonic place for participants and performers to briefly feel at home in new ways. Feeling at home, even for a brief moment, allows one to identify with their home in diaspora while simultaneously feeling nostalgic for their place of origin. In this manner, post-*tarab* soundscapes engage the nostalgic process, which relates not only to the memory of the past but also to present experiences and imagined social futures (Boym, 2001), dynamically connecting homeland and diaspora.

Home is a place filled with memories or references to the past as it has been lived (Dosse, 1999; Ricoeur, 2000; Berliner, 2005). These references to the past can be utopic or heterotopic (Foucault, 2008 [1967]), and the lines between these possibilities are often blurry to the individual accessing the memories. People choose to remember and forget certain components of home because of their personal experiences with home and the way that home has changed. Nostalgia, in this case, the longing for a home that no longer exists or has never existed, isolates home in time and space, imposing feelings of loss and displacement, but it also has the power to create a romantic or utopic fantasy (Boym, 2001).

Memories of home, as well as memories of efforts to recreate a sense of home, came across in my interlocutors' narratives and practices at various events in Toronto and Montreal. Mohammed is a deep house DJ and producer in Toronto. He was born in Iraq, where he spent the first ten years of his life. His family relocated first to India and then Egypt before moving between Germany and Canada, where they eventually settled in 2008. Born in 1988, the year the Iran-Iraq War came to an end, Mohammed says he has no recollection of living in an Iraq without war; the war with Kuwait began not more than two years later, followed by the Gulf War, the 1991 uprisings, and the subsequent sanctions regime, which brought economic hardship for Iraqis and in turn created an environment 'perfect for Saddam to do his dictatorship', as Mohammed put it. He described his childhood as having been akin to living in 'a North Korea ... But at the same time, it was beautiful in its own [way]'.

Mohammed often expresses his longing for home using the music he produces. Standing in the middle of a dance floor one night in 2017, I asked Mohammed about a pre-mastered track he had sent me called *Nostalgia*. I told him that I wanted to understand it; I could hear sadness and mourning in it, but I wanted to know how he conceptualised its relationship to club culture. I asked if it was produced for at-home listening as opposed to nightclub play. He looked at me, then turned his gaze to the floor, and nodded: 'Yeah, you got it. It's more for listening to at home and being introspective.' I could tell by his body language that he felt uncomfortable discussing his track at the time, so I chose not to push the conversation further. *Nostalgia* was not released until 2020 and Mohammed mentioned in interviews that the music he produces about Iraq is a lament for his homeland and an outlet for his grief.

Mohammed told me about the green spaces, rivers, and cuisine that demarcated his memory of Baghdad during a conversation about his last visit to Iraq. He cut the trip short because he had been unable to relive the fond memories he holds of home:

> I was supposed to stay for a month, but I only stayed for twenty days because it was so bad. It was curfew at 10:00 p.m., the American soldiers were there, and the Iraqi army [was] on the streets, everything [was] fucked. The police are corrupt ... Ever since then, it's more like sadness – so much sadness. I gave up on it in a way. Something you kind of give up on [is] the dream of going back home one day, and [how] amazing [it will be] – I'm over that. A lot of Iraqis are over that already. It's not gonna happen.

A lot of countries are in a similar situation. At the same time, does that reflect a different type of love? Of course.

Mohammed's choice to no longer return to Iraq is reflected in his nostalgic tracks about a home that is lost and in his past, yet he does not limit himself to producing tracks reflecting his Arab and Iraqi identity. While he maintains a deep and complex relationship of love, loss and yearning for his nostalgic Iraqi home, he believes he must move past Iraq, both musically and personally. Thus, through his music, Mohammed's relationships with Iraq can be heard, and his tracks equally cite his post-Iraq or post-*tarab* life in Canada, a point which I shall return to later in this chapter.

Dalia, a Lebanese sound artist, micro house and micro tech producer in Montreal, infuses elements of *tarab* into the EDM she produces. She described her relationship with Arabic music to me in the following terms:

> I'm Lebanese and I grew up to really traditional, old, Arabic music, [which has a] very emotional, very interesting sound. It's something [that is] a part of me [although] I'm not trying to combine it into my music [in order] to make it 'Oriental' or 'minimal' or anything. It just really speaks to me, and there's certain strings that – when I play in my live set – hit people differently. I see [people's] emotions going because [the music] is very emotional, and it's beautiful. So, I sample a lot of [Arabic music] and I fuse it into my music.

In Montreal, she has witnessed people, Arabs and non-Arabs alike, being moved to tears during her live sets because of the emotional qualities that Arabic music possesses.[8] There is no one absolute pitch within Arabic music that makes it so emotionally moving. Rather, a combination of intervals, microtones, personifications and moods attached to each individual *maqam* is what gives Arabic music this emergent quality. Scholars, dating back to the early writings of Guillaume André Villoteau (1826) and Ahmad Faris al-Shidyaq (2013 [1855]), have shown how traditional *tarab* contexts created intense emotional experiences for listeners and participants and the ways in which those experiences inhered in the spaces of *tarab* (Racy, 2003; Shannon, 2003). As Dalia explains:

> When you create a 'live set', you're creating everything from scratch. When you play live, you're composing everything on the fly, so [with] every string that you play, you're pulling [on] people's emotional strings. Oriental [music] pulls people's emotions on another level, and [since] I grew up to that, I know that on 'this' string, [that's] how 'that' is going to feel. Seeing how people are going to react from different perspectives – it's really interesting. So, that's why I put [Arabic music]; since I grew up to that and it's *in me*, I fuse it into the music. Also, to connect with people – just to see how they react – it's very interesting to me as a Lebanese person and as a musician. [The connection] is what I look for when I [play Oriental].

Mohammed's and Dalia's narratives point to how *tarab* is transformed into post-*tarab*. Both have a personal connection with Arabic music and use samples of it in different genres that have different moods and contexts in EDM. Depending on the genre, EDM provides a variety of spaces that allow for nostalgic dreaming, remembering, mourning, ecstasy, authenticity, pride and reinvention on the dance floor. The emotional connections that audience members share with each other bring them back to the scene repeatedly, creating a sense of comfort and belonging, to both the music and each other. However, the way the Arabic samples are used also have the potential to invoke contrasting opinions in taste and energy and can result in tensions between DJs, producers and audience members.

Post-*tarab* tensions

The post-*tarab* equation, Arab+EDM, is located at the intersection of various influences from the Middle East, North Africa, Europe and North America. The Arabness heard in a track depends on the producer's situatedness within the culture-scapes of their current locale, who they are surrounded by, and where their home in the Arab world is. They might produce typically Arab sounding music, drawing on the Orientalist tropes of the World Music market, and they might not. Questions surrounding what it means to be Arab and produce music that aligns with so-called Arabness are complicated by the fact that each Arab identity is multifarious and heterogeneous. The complicated contexts surrounding the idea of home create a problematic assumption of what music from home should sound like and what music Arab producers should be producing (Nickell, 2020). Many of my interlocutors whose tracks are uninfluenced by Arabic music are critiqued by their audiences for not producing or playing music from home, in other words, that their repertoire is not authentically Arabic music.

When I began my fieldwork, one of the emerging record labels in Toronto that produced Arab-influenced deep house marketed their label and products using reclaimed Orientalist tropes such as images of belly dancers and fonts that attempt to stylistically mimic the Arabic script. Under the subgenre, Oriental deep house, this label incorporated sonic and visual elements to remind listeners of the Arab world.[9] As time went on, the genre became more popular. Oriental deep house flooded the market by 2017, becoming 'a bit cliché' in the words of Anas, a DJ and producer from Montreal who witnessed and participated in the development of the genre. Around this time, some of my collaborators expressed the concern that they did not want to be boxed into the category of producing only 'Oriental-sounding' electronic music. When my interlocutors performed at Arab-themed or Arab-influenced events, they said that they were given less room to be creative, and as such, felt trapped in the pre-determined categories imposed on them because of their ethnicity and the assumptions and expectations that flow from it. The Arabness of Arabic music is now being redefined and reshaped through the dynamic relationships between home and diaspora that each of my interlocutors lives through. Despite the processes I witnessed where new modes of musical expression were being forged, often my collaborators were left with a flattening and binary question, 'do I make Arabic music, or do I not?'

Selma, a DJ and producer from Belgium, who participated in an artistic retreat in Toronto from 2016 to 2017, conceptualised and curated events using the concept of the *souk* or market. Selma evokes the *souk* because, in her opinion, it is a site of cultural mixing and bricolage. A souk-themed event then is a heady mix of deep house, a little bit of Arabic funk, some electro- *dabkę* industrial techno, Sahara blues, electro-*chaabi* and/or minimal techno. Selma is a queer woman of Belgian and Tunisian descent, and as such, a person of complex intersectional identities. She perceives her performances as a representation of herself, a fusion of East and West. She does not feel that she should have to define or constrain herself to one aspect of her identity, and similarly, she does not feel that she needs to limit her sonic repertoire to Arabic music for the entirety of her *soirée*. She often ends her parties with dark, driving techno, and I have heard audience members express surprise about her non-Arab library. One night, after Selma transitioned from Arab+EDM into acid techno, some people on the dance floor leaned over the DJ booth making requests for 'Arab' tracks. At EDM events, song requests are not part of the culture, as a DJ's set is considered to be an artistic compilation reflecting their unique taste. Selma smiled and placed her hand at the side of her forehead, offering a satirical military salutation. To get them 'off her back', she was giving them the impression that she would incorporate their requests, but instead, she continued on the techno journey she had transitioned into. Music played by Arab DJs carries with it the expectation of a specific Arab sound, and often these expectations have little interest in what music Arab DJs and musicians are actually making in contexts like Toronto and Montreal. Not only were there ethnonormative expectations that DJs with Arab-sounding names or connections should play Arab tracks but equally, there were moments where a DJ's choice of music made them too Arab.

When Selma lays down an Arab+EDM track, she often plays samples from music that might be heard at mainstream wedding celebrations. In contrast, Oriental deep house is a genre with subtle, dark, minimal melodies sampled from the '*ud*, for example. Selma's performance of Arabness has made some Oriental deep house enthusiasts feel uncomfortable:

> Standing in the central rear of the dancefloor, swaying from side to side, I glanced at my friend, Mehdi – a deep house enthusiast from Iraq, living in Toronto. He had been translating the lyrics to the vocal line for me, smiling. Suddenly, his smile morphed, and he smirked, 'She can't do this!'
> 'She can't do what?' I asked.
> 'This… you know? It's like I'm at a wedding or something!'
> Instead of responding vocally, I raised my eyebrows and nodded my head in acknowledgement. Then I scanned the dancefloor. The venue was filled to capacity, shaking with movement, laughter and ululations. She was doing it.

The music that Selma was playing made Mehdi feel uncomfortable because it was 'too Arab' for him. As Chris Nickell's work suggests, an individual has to be 'just brown enough' to be accepted (2020, p. 240). The example of Selma shows that one can be critiqued for playing too far on the EDM spectrum, as well as for playing too far on the Arab spectrum: one should be Arab, but not too Arab. They should be 'just Arab enough'. Here the expectations of audiences, much like the expectations of wider society, seem to demand a very delicate cultural balancing act from those who are cast as ethnic.

Mohammed and his group of friends, including Mehdi, do not enjoy music or events that are what they call 'too Arab':

> Lately, I've started – I don't like to post things about politics. Even if I have my opinion, I don't have to share it publicly. My opinion – in a passive way [but] also personal – is this performance. It has depth, and it's important to have depth and meaning. If you're going to listen to my set, I'm going to play some music that is Oriental, to give it that kind of sound. I like to balance. Some artists are trying to represent *only* the Arab thing, and that's nice, but it's another extreme.

Instead, Mohammed and his circle enjoy *subtle* nuances of Arabness in EDM. In his own words 'This music is my *jihad* against orthodox Islam. For me, it's subtle, but it's there.'

Mohammed believes that the mainstream media portrayal of Arab people has forced Arabs to become better representatives for their own people:

> Now you want to rebel against that, fix the image, fix the way that people see it in general. Not an 'in your face' kind of way, but I just don't want to push it in people's

faces: 'I'm an Arab, I'm an Arab, I'm an Arab' – No! Be a good person, always be up front, that's the most important. *Then* you can say, 'I'm an Arab', like winning an award or something. Not just saying it. I think that's our problem. We have no good representation, you know?

Mohammed believes one should avoid performing Arabness unless the performer is also willing to become a positive referent. In this sense, we can see how the music scene in Toronto and Montreal can become sites where images of Arabs as a threatening and problematic group in Canadian society are challenged, resisted and contested. For Mohammed, the performer must become a 'good immigrant neighbour' to challenge the 'Arab villain' so commonly portrayed in media. Thus, for Mohammed, visual and sonic performances are ways of doing and representing a situated Arabness within Canadian EDM culture, within the Arab-Canadian diaspora, and within Canada more generally. Mohammed's insistence on 'good representation', along with Mehdi's dissatisfaction with Selma's choice of music, point to the ways the diasporic EDM of my interlocutors struggles with its own norms of sounds and representations, and that such sounds and representations should not be understood as cohesive agreed-upon practices.

Mohammed was not alone in expressing the desire to produce music that made sense to the setting in which he lives rather than any abstract or assumed ideas about the Arabness of his tastes. Anas offered the following:

With the music that I play, I don't really think about where it was made or its roots. Being from Montreal, I try to create something from Montreal – there's a certain sound that's poppin' out of there. As for me trying to show that I'm Egyptian, that's not really me. I'm trying to create a sound that comes out of Montreal, but that's kind of like a 'label' version with the sounds I'm trying to create … whatever sounds good, I just make it happen, but I don't think that deep into it as for its roots.

Some of Anas' DJ sets and track productions have included Arab samples, and others have not. His interest in making music that 'just sounds good' appears to eliminate the tensions that arise in the debate about whether or not music is too Arab. It situates diasporic music and post-*tarab* in the cultural landscape of Montreal rather than in the expectations and constraints of ethnonormativity. The examples I draw upon here do not resolve but rather allude to post-*tarab* tensions between performers and audiences and between musicians concerning what Arabness *is* and how it *should be* performed. These tensions arise because post-*tarab* is a reflection of the queering of Arabic music as much as it is about the queering of Arabness in the diaspora.

Ethnomusicologists have taken a particular interest in the Arab folk revival, where, since the Arab uprisings in 2011, Arab youth have been revamping old folk tunes in new political contexts as they fight for a brighter future (Lornell and Rasmussen, 2016). I argue that, today, Arab EDM is a prominent part of this folk revival. Through the use of sampled folk songs, edited and altered with new music production technologies, Arabic music is being spread far beyond the contexts of acoustic performances by musicians and audiences who are already largely familiar with the repertoire. My extensive time in the scene's various spaces has shown me that Arab+EDM spreads onto dance floors and into the homes of EDM enthusiasts, not limited to the Arab population of that community, nor its Arabic music lovers. A song that came to life in Cairo is now being sampled by a producer in Berlin, released on a label in Amman, sent to Mohammed for remixing in Toronto, and played by Anas in a nightclub in Montreal. Through these cultural routes, varying expressions of Arabness and home are elucidated; *tarab* morphs into post-*tarab* through situated diasporic negotiations of the self through the sonic.

Post-*tarab* can be seen as a temporal term that encompasses EDM and the performativity of Arabness in some diasporic settings, and that reflects the affective complexity of expressing diasporic selves. Within the sonic imaginary of EDM, post-*tarab* identities improvise within the realm of queerness and respond to ethnonormative impressions of what it means to be Arab. While redefining Arabness, it also offers a new lens through which we can analyse the polyrhythmic, non-linear movement of sound and sentiment between individual, collective, home and diaspora. Post-*tarab* can help in reading and hearing ways of being Arab in the aftermath of pan-Arab sentiments imposed on people living in the Arab world during the time of *tarab* music. The post-*tarab* equation of Arab+EDM simultaneously echoes nostalgia for home in the Arab world and feels in place in diaspora. However, as I hope to have demonstrated, the expectations of being normatively Arab in the diaspora are challenged by post-*tarab* musicians who attempt to reflect self and collectivity in complex and challenging ways.

Notes

1 The ethnomusicologist Michael A. Figueroa has traced the term post-*tarab* back to both the Egyptian writer Ammar Mnla Hassan's review of post-rock demo releases in 2016 and 2019 and Syrian-born composer/producer Abdo Ineni's use of the term, both in metadata for a track in 2016 and as the title of an EP in 2017. According to Figueroa, in both instances, Hassan and Ineni talk about post-*tarab* as a concept and process for fusing genres during which music is deconstructed and reconstructed (Figueroa, 2022, p. 6).
2 My use of post-*tarab* draws upon Ryan Thomas Skinner's (2015) concept of *Afropolitanism*, which he uses to discuss the tensions present in African cosmopolitan music from Mali. My interlocutors ascribe their identities to major cities internationally, and continue to relocate in different metropolitan environments. Their Arabness is, therefore, influenced by the array of urban environments they have encountered.
3 Thomas Burkhalter describes the World Music market, 'World music was created by British record producers in the 1980s with the goal of diversifying the Euro-American market in order to sell more music. Consequently, world music is based on "musical difference" and "Otherness" in its core idea' (2013, p. 90).
4 The techno and house 'underground' was created by black, queer individuals in response to the white, gay clubs in Detroit and Chicago where black and queer individuals were denied entry. The term queer exists on a spectrum that includes both gender and sexual fluidity. A same-sex couple may or may not identify as queer, depending on the means by which they define the boundaries of their relationship, their lifestyle and familial relations. Although same-sex desire can be considered part of queer identification, queer individuals generally locate themselves on a continuum of sexuality and gender identities that is broader than that encompassed by such acute and binary terms as gay and straight. To the white, gay scene, black and queer individuals were too different to be welcome. The techno and house underground provided black, queer individuals with an escape route from such discrimination.
5 I recognise that many individuals from South-West Asia and North Africa (SWANA) do not identify as Arab, but for the sake of consistency and clarity, I use Arab and Arabness to refer to the undoing of a pan-Arabist identity throughout this geographic area.
6 I use Arab+EDM in alignment with Dylan Robinson, who uses the term 'Indigenous+art music' to show that the two sound practices are conjoined and not merged. It is a political statement that 'disrupt[s] "intercultural music's" implication of union, hybridity, syncretism, and reconciliation' (2020, p. 9).
7 According to Bijsterveld and van Dijck:

> Thomas Porcello has coined the term "techoustemology," as a notion that foregrounds "the implication of forms of technological mediation on individuals' knowledge and interpretations of, sensations in, and consequent actions upon their acoustic environments as grounded in the specific times and places of the production and reception of sound." Porcello has derived this notion from "acoustemology," the contraction of "epistemology" and "acoustics" used by Steven Feld to describe how the members of a non-Western nation understood their world in terms of sound.
>
> (Porcello, 2005, p. 270; in Bijsterveld and van Dijck, 2009, p. 16)

8 A live set occurs when the DJ uses digital audio workstation (DAW) software to compose music and build on tracks during a performance. This is in contrast to a DJ set, where DJ software is used to mix and layer tracks.
9 Oriental deep house is an informal term used to identify deep house music with an Arab influence. Although it is not used by everyone, it is the most commonly used term for the subgenre. I use the term Oriental to refer to this genre because that is how my interlocutors describe such music.

References

Alajaji, S.A. (2015) *Music and the Armenian Diaspora: Searching for Home in Exile*. Bloomington, IN: Indiana University Press.

al-Shidyaq, A.F. (2013 [1855]) *Leg Over Leg*. Vol. 1, trans. Humphrey Davies. New York: New York University Press.

Aly, R.M.K. (2015) *Becoming Arab in London: Performativity and the Undoing of Identity*. London: Pluto Press.

Appadurai, A. (1990) 'Disjuncture and difference in the global cultural economy', *Public Culture*, 2(2), pp. 1–24.

Appadurai, A. (1996) *Modernity at Large: Cultural Dimensions of Globalization*. Minneapolis, MN: University of Minnesota Press.

Berliner, D. (2005) 'The abuses of memory: reflections on the memory boom in Anthropology', *Anthropology Quarterly*, 87(1), pp. 197–211.

Bijsterveld, K. and van Dijck, J. (2009) *Sound Souvenirs: Audio Technologies, Memory and Cultural Practices*. Amsterdam: Amsterdam University Press.

Bogard, W. (2007) 'The coils of a serpent: haptic space and control societies', *CTheory* td057. Available at: http://ctheory.net/ctheory_wp/the-coils-of-a-serpent-haptic-space- and-control-societies/#bio (accessed 4 June 2020).

Boym, S. (2001) *The Future of Nostalgia*. New York: Basic Books.

Burkhalter, T. (2013) 'Multisited avant-gardes or World Music 2.0?: Musicians from Beirut and beyond between local production and Euro-American reception', in Burkhalter, T., Dickinson, K. and Harbert, B.J. (eds) *The Arab Avant-Garde: Music, Politics, Modernity*. Middletown, CT: Wesleyan University Press, pp. 89–118.

Danielson, V. (1999) 'Moving toward public space: women and musical performance in twentieth century Egypt', in Asfaruddin, A. (ed.) *Hermeneutics and Honor: Negotiating Female "Public" Space in Islamic/ate Societies*. Cambridge, MA: Harvard Center for Middle East Studies, pp. 116–139.

Dosse, F. (1999) 'La méthode historique et les traces mémorielles', in Morin, E. (ed.) *Le défi du XXIe siècle: relier les connaissances*. Paris: Editions du Seuil, pp. 317–326.

Farsakh, L., Kanaaneh, T., and Sheikaly, S. (2018) 'Queering Palestine', *Journal of Palestine Studies*, 47(3), pp. 7–12.

Figueroa, M. (2022) 'Post-*tarab*: music and affective politics in the US SWANA diaspora', *Ethnomusicology*, 66(2).

Fleeger, J. (2014) *Mismatched Women: The Siren's Song Through the Machine*. New York: Oxford University Press.

Foucault, M. (2008 [1967]) 'Of other spaces', in Dehaene, M. and De Cauter, L. (eds) *Heterotopia and the City: Public Space in a Postcivil Society*. New York: Routledge, pp. 13–29.

Frishkopf, M. (2001) '*Tarab* ("enchantment") in the mystic sufi chant of Egypt', in Zuhur, S. (ed.) *Colors of Enchantment: Theatre, Dance, Music, and the Visual Arts of the Middle East*. Cairo: American University in Cairo Press, pp. 239–276.

Gupta, A. and Ferguson, J. (1992) 'Beyond "culture": space, identity, and the politics of difference', *Cultural Anthropology*, 7(1), pp. 6–23.

Hirschkind, C. (2006) *The Ethical Soundscape: Cassette Sermons and Islamic Counterpublics*. New York: Columbia University Press.

Hutson, S.R. (2000) 'The rave: spiritual healing in modern western subcultures', *Anthropological Quarterly*, 73(1), pp. 35–49.

Kapadia, R.K. (2019) *Insurgent Aesthetics: Security and the Queer Life of the Forever War*. Durham, NC: Duke University Press.

Lornell, K. and Rasmussen, A. (2016) *The Music of Multicultural America: Performance, Identity, and Community in the United States*. Jackson, MS: University Press of Mississippi.

Marcus, S. (2007) *Music in Egypt: Experiencing Music, Expressing Culture*. New York: Oxford University Press.

Minh-Ha, T.T. (2016) *Lovecidal: Walking with the Disappeared*. New York: Fordham University Press.

Muñoz, J.E. (2009) *Cruising Utopia: The Then and There of Queer Futurity*. New York: New York University Press.

Nickell, C. (2020) 'Masculinities under pressure in Beirut's independent music scenes', PhD thesis, New York University.

Racy, A.J. (1991) 'Creativity and ambience: an ecstatic feedback model from Arabic music', *The World of Music*, 33 (3), pp. 7–28.

Racy, A.J. (2000) 'The Arab taqasim as a musical symbol', *Ethnomusicology*, 44 (2), pp. 302–320.

Racy, A.J. (2003) *Making Music in the Arab World: The Culture and Artistry of Tarab*. New York: Cambridge University Press.

Rantanen, T. (2006) 'A man behind scapes: an interview with Arjun Appadurai', *Global Media and Communication*, 2(1), pp. 7–19.

Ricoeur, P. (2000) *La mémoire, l'histoire, l'oubli*. Paris: Editions du Seuil.

Robinson, D. (2020) *Hungry Listening: Resonant Theory for Indigenous Sound Studies*. Minneapolis, MN: University of Minnesota Press.

Schafer, R.M. (1977) *The Tuning of the World*. New York: Knopf.

Shannon, J.H. (2003) 'Emotion, performance, and temporality in Arab music: reflections of tarab', *Cultural Anthropology*, 18(1), pp. 72–98.

Skinner, R.T. (2015) *Bamako Sounds: The Afropolitan Ethics of Malian Music*. Minneapolis, MN: University of Minnesota Press.

Villoteau, G.A. (1826) *Description de l'Égypt: de l'état actuel de l'art musicale en Égypt*, vol. 14, 2nd edn. Paris: Imprimerie de C.L.F. Panckoucke.

Warner, M. (2002) 'Publics and counterpublics', *Public Culture*, 14(1), pp. 49–90.

16
RESISTING MARGINALISATION, RENEGOTIATING GENDER

Intersectional narratives of diaspora experiences

Dalia Abdelhady

A large body of literature attests to the centrality of the Lebanese diaspora within the context of Middle East migrations. Lebanon's recent history and present circumstances mean that migration is an increasingly desirable reaction to a collapsing economy and political corruption. Despite the significance of the Lebanese case, little research explores the gender dynamics of its diaspora communities, reflecting a larger gap in the analysis of Middle East diasporas and immigrant communities in general. In this chapter, I explore the interplay between gender, sexuality, class and migration contexts in shaping diasporic lives by drawing on the narratives of Lebanese immigrants in New York, Montreal and Paris. The chapter draws on my earlier publications on the Lebanese diaspora (in particular, Abdelhady, 2006; 2008; 2011; 2015) which are based on multiple waves of fieldwork in the three cities between 2001 and 2011. My aim here is to reflect the complex system of power relations in which women and men of the Lebanese diaspora are socially embedded and the ways gender informs diasporic experiences in intersectional ways. As described by Farahani (2017, p. 1), diaspora narratives allow us to explore how immigrants 'resist, accept, (re)negotiate, adjust, conform, seize, and challenge the conflictual cultural norms that organize their (sexual) lives'. In what follows, I illustrate the ways Lebanese men and women renegotiate, resist and challenge the cultural norms and traditional understandings of social positions imposed on them.

Lebanon is considered one of the world's most emigration-prone countries, resulting in a large diaspora whose numbers exceed that of the population in the home country (Abdul-Karim, 1992). Historically, the Lebanese immigrants' first destinations were New York in the United States and Montreal in Canada (Abu-Laban, 1980). Since the outbreak of the Lebanese Civil War in 1975, Paris has become a destination equal in popularity to the two North American cities (Hourani and Shehadi, 1992). The three cities continue to serve as magnets for present-day Lebanese immigrants for several reasons. First, the three cities are major port cities and international, commercial, educational and cultural centres, and thus form 'diasporan capitals' (Butler, 2001) where communities from many diasporas congregate. Second, New York and Montreal provide strong networks that have traditionally linked the Lebanese immigrant communities with the home country. Finally, the French milieu (as a result of colonial history), which is congenial to many Lebanese immigrants in Montreal and Paris, has facilitated their acceptance of (and in) the host societies. As such, the three cities are important not only due to the presence of a large Lebanese community, but because they provide strategic arenas for the development and articulation of diasporic identities and communities. These three settings vary in terms of the contexts of immigrant reception, where assimilation and multiculturalism take on different meanings, and consequently result in different immigrant experiences that produce diverse dynamics of life in a diaspora. Despite the specific differences among and within the three Lebanese communities in terms of their placement within the general racial/ethnic structures of their hostlands, reasons for migration and class background, my analysis focuses on commonalities in experiences, which are aided by global narratives of migration and belonging.

My analysis of intersectional narratives of diaspora experiences highlights three central (interconnected) strategies or themes along which my interlocutors narrate their understandings of migration and belonging. Being diasporic entails reconfiguring gendered selves as a process that helps some to cope with gendered expectations and ambitions, which may lead them to pursue contradictory trajectories. At the same time, my interlocutors also articulate diasporic positions in the ways they resist their simultaneous marginalisation in the homeland and their new settings. Finally, by expressing their positions within global narratives and forms of social engagement, my respondents challenge traditional forms of identification and articulate their interests in affecting their surroundings. I discuss these strategies individually and then move to consider their interconnectedness in the conclusion.

Reconfiguring gendered selves

Farah and I met at a coffee shop in Montreal, after I was given her name and phone number by her sister in New York. Since I was a friend of the sister, Farah wanted to invite me to her home. She preferred meeting me at the coffee shop, however, since our meeting allowed her a break away from her family. At the beginning of our conversation, Farah described her feelings when she first arrived in Canada:

> People were so hospitable to us when we first came here, it felt like everyone was saying 'welcome'. In two hours, we felt that we have everything we need. We felt so much at home, it was like we never left.

Farah, who is a married mother of three children, moved to Montreal in 1993 and stressed that French-speaking immigrants are always welcomed there. She moved shortly after getting married to her husband, who works as a taxi driver, since they both realised that their chances for economic mobility were limited, given their limited resources in Lebanon following the civil war. Thus, they migrated to create a family and allow their children a better life. Towards the end of our meeting, Farah insisted that I accompany her home to meet her husband and children. At home, I met Elias, the husband, and the three children who were busy playing video games. It was a good opportunity to talk about family issues and witness some of the disagreements that Farah and Elias had.

Farah, like other married women in Montreal, emphasises that her family is the reason for migration to Canada. At the same time, these women recognise that they left their families behind to come to Canada and thus broke with an important Lebanese tradition, making their experience with migration difficult. Instead of expressing the loss of strong family ties to describe their lives in Canada, however, this group of women emphasises that the main reason for their migration is the pursuit of their families' well-being. For example, they often stress access to good-paying jobs, education for their children, as well as healthcare and retirement benefits as things that they would not find in Lebanon. Farah explained her reasons for moving to Montreal:

> The kind respect for humanity that you get here, the acknowledgement of your basic right, to equal treatment, to healthcare, and good education for your children, these are things that we know we won't get in Lebanon since we don't have the right family background or the right connections.

Farah still has family members living in Lebanon who struggle to obtain basic healthcare, proper education for their children or well-paying jobs. She is reminded daily of her privilege compared to those relatives in Lebanon and, as a result, her difference from other Canadians who, according to her, only know of social welfare and equal opportunity.

Elias does not share Farah's positive attitude towards family well-being in Montreal. On the contrary, he emphasises the added threats posed by living in Canadian society such as the possibility of divorce, premarital sex and the social independence of children. Unlike many of the women I spoke with, Lebanese immigrant men lament the loss of family values as a result of migration. Children's independence at a young age and the possibility of divorce (which is strongly prohibited in the Lebanese Catholic community to which Farah and Elias belong) mark a loss in status for many men who reap more benefits from a patriarchal family structure. Accordingly, these men lament the weaker family ties in Canada when compared to Lebanon. The respect for the patriarchal family in Lebanese culture is the main axis along which this group of men draw their distinction from Canadian society and emphasise their transnational ties with their families in Lebanon. All these views notwithstanding, Elias and other men I spoke to emphasise that being away from Lebanon facilitates their roles as fathers who are capable of providing for their families, given the limited opportunities for economic survival in Lebanon. As such, both Farah and Elias express the importance of being able to fulfil their traditional parental gendered roles, offered by being in Canada.

Farah's migratory experience challenges parts of the traditional gendered script in the sense that she believes that she is not a good daughter who stayed close to her parents to take care of them during their old age. At the same time, the stressful life in Lebanon resulting from their economic position would increase the likelihood of divorce, the very same fear her husband associates with being in Montreal. In Farah's calculation, being in Montreal allows her to fulfil more dictates of her gendered role as a mother and wife, while going back to Lebanon would only allow her to fulfil her role as a daughter, and only to a limited degree (as a result of being unable to support her parents financially). As such, being in Montreal allows Farah as well as Elias to negotiate gender expectations and roles but not to challenge them entirely.

State policies play an important role in shaping women's experiences with migration, as illustrated by Farah's emphasis on policies of social welfare alleviating the daily guilt associated with her new position of privilege compared to her family members who are left in Lebanon. Similarly, Canada's multicultural policies are considered to be equally important in facilitating transnational identities. For example, one of Farah's children was about to join a high school that offered Arabic language classes, and she believes that only in Canada can her children have such an opportunity as children of immigrants.

Farah's and Elias' narratives allow us to understand the ways that gendered understandings of the self are shaped within a complex web that takes into account definitions of gendered roles in the homeland and state policies in the new setting. Much of the literature on gender and diaspora underscores the emancipatory space offered for women in contexts of immigration, as women escape the limits of traditional patriarchy often associated with the homeland (Pasura, 2008; Tinarwo and Pasura, 2014; Rao Mehta, 2015; Batisai, 2016). Looking at the ways gendered narratives are constructed within complex negotiations between homeland obligations, state policies and family goals, as illustrated by Farah and Elias, allows us to go beyond the emancipation/restriction binary to understand the ways traditional gender roles can be reconfigured in new contexts. As Pessar and Mahler (2003) explain, the multiple locations immigrants occupy bring about different sets of disciplinary dynamics. At the same time, the diasporic subject can formulate their own narrative of location and position. Consequently, the understanding of diaspora as a process of narrating the self and forging belonging allows us to understand the ways multiple social axes shape the reconfigurations of diasporic identities and relations in different social locations.

Women migrants in my study prefer to stay in their new societies instead of returning to Lebanon. A number of authors have illustrated similar patterns among various groups of migrants, where women are more likely to develop strategies consistent with long-term or permanent settlement in the host societies (see, for example, Hondagneu-Sotelo, 1994; Goldring, 1998). Among Lebanese immigrant women, strategies such as buying property, investing in their children's marriage in the diaspora, or bringing elderly parents to accompany them abroad all featured in marking their desire to stay outside Lebanon for the foreseeable future. Men, on the other hand, are more likely to pursue strategies that get them closer to their eventual return, such as buying a house in Lebanon, emphasising the importance of family vacations in the homeland or, for a few, engaging with transnational businesses that require their travel back and forth between Lebanon and the host society. These differences in desires and strategies for family cohesion often bring tension into the marital relationship, as I witnessed between Farah and Elias. Class seems to play an important role in mediating that tension. For those like Elias, visiting Lebanon or buying property there is a costly endeavour that their meagre financial resources cannot afford. As a result, the difference between Farah and Elias remains one of opinion. Wealthy businessmen, and especially those living in Paris and making use of the geographic proximity, are more able to travel between the two countries and maintain stronger social and financial ties. Their wives, who still did not wish to return to Lebanon, were confronted with the need to resolve the conflict once and for all. In most cases, the women stayed with the family in the diaspora and possibly sacrificed their own careers to keep the family together while the husband commuted to and from Lebanon.

In these narratives, my respondents were motivated by their desire to 'do what is good for the family' and therefore were not interested in negotiating gender norms. Instead, the outcome of their diasporic position and desire to bring about a better life for their family members resulted in a reconfiguration of the traditional gender roles. Other respondents found themselves in a position to resist traditional understandings of their identities, as I describe in the next section.

Resisting multiple forms of marginalisation

Abeer moved from Lebanon to pursue a degree in medicine. She lived in Boston for two years and then moved to New York City where we met. Abeer explains how she was faced with exclusion in generally passive ways, such as people hanging up on her during a phone conversation, which made her uneasy establishing social relationships with white Americans.

> What I saw from whites dealing with me as a foreigner, I felt very ostracised. Just because I speak with an accent, people would shout at me, hang the phone on me or not answer me. They would make believe that they don't understand what I'm saying.

Since people did not necessarily identify her as Lebanese or Arab, she was not confronted with Arab slurs or ethnicity-based harassment. She was viewed as an immigrant, however. As a self-identified lesbian, Abeer's sense of alienation in the United States was further strengthened as she sought relationships with American women when she first moved from Lebanon. In her experiences, the American-born women she encountered could only accept her if she had denounced her Arab culture, which they perceived as totally negative. Abeer could not relate to the simplistic understandings of her cultural background and moved on to form relationships with other immigrant women who face similar predicaments in American society. As Abeer expressed, experiences of prejudice and exclusion were taken to mark immigrants' distance from the host society and strengthen their sense of belonging to a negatively stereotyped minority group. The inability to conform to the expectations of American-born and particularly white women led Abeer to seek relationships with Arab and South-east Asian women, who are stereotyped in similar ways in American culture.

Experiences with discrimination, like those shared by Abeer, play an important role in strengthening my interlocutors' ethnic identification. These experiences, however, are gendered, especially as they emphasise the construction of Lebanese/Arab men as terrorists and women as docile. Roy illustrates the ways discrimination strengthened his ethnic identification. Roy, a 34-year-old graduate student, lived in New York City when we met. His initial reaction to being in a foreign environment was to affirm his Arab and Lebanese identification. During the first few years after leaving Lebanon, affirming his ethnic Lebanese identification was his response to the rejection he encountered in the new setting:

> It's a normal reaction, I think, when you are in a strange country, and you feel alienated from the society at large, the normal reaction is to get back to your identity as the past beckons. In Lebanon, I never cared that I was Lebanese. The idea didn't mean anything to me. I didn't care I was Arab. It didn't mean anything as well. It's only in the time I came to the US, when people started describing me as such, in a pejorative manner. As a reaction, there was a period when I was very involved in affirming my identity. I am not like that anymore. I think the whole idea [of identity], the whole notion is silly.

In Roy's experience, affirming his ethnic identification was an outcome of his experiences of prejudice and discrimination and his way of distancing himself from his new, hostile environment. Ethnic identification can also provide a source of pride to compensate for experiences of exclusion and refuse the imposition of positions of inferiority. When I asked if he could relate specific encounters, he commented:

> There are two instances that stick in my mind. During the [first] Iraq war, I was working out at a gym. I left one of the weights lying about. And the attendant came and asked me to remove the weights. Then, he turned his back and said, 'Those fucking Arabs.' So, I went to the reception, wrote a complaint, voided my membership, and got my money back. [Another instance was] after September 11, I was walking in the mall, about two hours after the planes struck. And some guy who was walking by looked at me, and started screaming at me: 'Bastards, these bastards are

gonna win.' I didn't beat the crap out of him, which I could've easily done. I let it go. But it struck me. You feel accused in certain instances, accused without doing anything, accused in a transcendental manner; your state of being is one of being accused.

Both instances are specifically gendered. In Roy's view, the gym is a masculine space. The attendant's comment was meant to assault not only his ethnic origins but his masculine identification as well. Roy further explains that, while the mall is a gender-neutral space, the person who harassed him was able to identify him as Arab because of his gender. Roy believes that unless an Arab woman is veiled, and is thus marked as Muslim, she is less likely to be identified as Arab. For men, however, given the constant media portrayal of Arab/Muslim male terrorists, men like Roy with dark hair and an olive complexion were more frequently targeted as well as feared. Roy's remark that he could have physically attacked his accuser at the mall asserted his superiority in a specifically masculine way.

For many of my interlocutors, discrimination in the new setting was exacerbated by alienation from the homeland, as they experienced being labelled 'foreign' by people in Lebanon. For example, Abeer refers to the way people in Lebanon remark on her foreign accent when speaking Arabic, which is compounded in her case, since people in the United States made similar comments about her foreign accent when speaking English. Referring to the consequences of her first visit to Lebanon, Abeer illustrates an ambiguous state of not belonging to either society:

> People thought that I'm very Americanised in my gestures, my values, the way I dress, the way I behaved myself and the way I started speaking. For them, I speak Arabic with an accent, which I cannot see but they see it, so I don't know why. And for them, I'm like their American friend. When I'm here, they know I'm a foreigner, and when I go there, they know I'm a foreigner. So that's a very silly state.

Abeer's experience shows that her lack of compliance with gender norms in Lebanon, in the ways she spoke or carried herself, led to her exclusion from her Lebanese circles as people considered her foreign and Americanised. Lack of belonging to either a homeland or a host society leads to an ambivalent position, or as Abeer stressed, a silly state. Abeer asserted that her lack of belonging to Lebanese society did not and would not translate into her belonging to American society. At first, Abeer explained that she sought membership in a Lebanese professional group that was oriented towards addressing the Lebanese diaspora in general. The group, however, quickly alienated her:

> I didn't like their politics and I felt that I'm dealing with a male-dominated society where women really have no voice, and there was a lot of totalitarian politicians that have the mentality that Lebanon is their possession, and I don't want to deal with this, I left Lebanon for this whole patriarchal mentality, and I'm not ready to embrace it back here again.

In Abeer's example, belonging to a Lebanese diasporic community is not necessarily empowering as it maintains gender discrimination. The replication of Lebanese social and political problems in the diaspora leads Abeer and many others to stay away from any sort of formal organisation that aims at unifying Lebanese immigrants.

For Abeer, the initial sense of alienation from both Lebanese and American societies is based on her ethnicity and her sexual orientation. She holds that Lebanese society is not accepting of homosexuality in general. Still, in her experience, a gay community in New York is not accepting of her Arab heritage either:

> Among Arabs, I am not accepted since I am a lesbian. And among lesbians, I am not accepted since I am Arab, and proud of it. Arabs want me to give up my lesbian identity. I tried. I used to dress and act like the girl they want me to be, especially among family members. I did not do a good job at it, so I stopped. Among lesbians, they don't like the fact that I am proud to be Arab. They emphasise that Arab culture is oppressive to women and queers. They are right, but they do not understand that I am proud of this part of my identity. I am both lesbian and Arab; yet I am not accepted in either group.

As a result, Abeer found that the community she could best relate to was that of gay Arabs:

> To me, it is very important to be able to relate to other gay Arabs, because I share more common grounds with them than other gays and other Arabs. It joins two identities for me that were practically incompatible before.

Abeer's case may be considered unique if one chooses to emphasise that she is an outspoken queer activist. At the same time, her narrative portrays common experiences shared by many of my interlocutors. As experienced by Abeer and others, migration is disruptive to one's sense of self and the way one relates to their social surroundings. At the same time, diaspora offers a space for the rearticulation of the self and experimentation with different modes of belonging.

Being diasporic to my interlocutors involves a heightened awareness of one's precarious social position, and experience with the fragmentation of traditional identities and communities. These feelings, however, do not translate into efforts to restore a sense of coherence (which can be envisioned in identifying with a homeland, a diaspora or even assimilating to a host society). Instead, there is a rejection of the form of social coherence offered by traditional identities. As Roy explains, all identities are rather problematic:

> I have an issue with identity right now. I tend to consider it more and more as a very bad idea; as something that's always causing trouble and without any validity. So, what constitutes my identity? [Pause] I tend to abandon the idea of identity as such. I don't like it anymore; I don't enjoy it. It doesn't give me the same glow it used to.

In Roy's account, the rejection of all efforts towards identification is an active choice that some immigrants make in response to the conditions of their migration and displacement. As expressed by Roy, a sense of not belonging adds to his feeling of ambivalence but also this 'liminality' can be a comfortable location when there were common issues that might temporarily unite people. For Roy, participating in anti-war campaigns and labour-related activities allows him to forge a feeling of commonality with others that he does not feel through traditional forms of identification.

Challenging hegemonic narratives

In *Black Feminist Thought*, Patricia Hill Collins (2000, p. 285) explains that the hegemonic domain of power is primarily engaged with the shaping of consciousness 'via the manipulation of ideas, images, symbols, and ideologies'. As a result, narratives of the self should be understood in relation to their ability to resist dominant ideologies and hegemonic workings of power. For Collins, 'the hegemonic domain becomes a critical site for not just fending off hegemonic ideas from dominant culture but in *crafting counter-hegemonic knowledge that fosters changed consciousness*' (ibid., emphasis added). For members of diasporas who find themselves subjected to multiple hegemonic domains of power, investigating the ways they craft counter-hegemonic narratives also needs to account for the multiple sites in which such narratives are produced. In my account of *The Lebanese Diaspora* (Abdelhady, 2011), I describe the ways Lebanese immigrants contest hegemonic narratives of belonging to a homeland, host society and the diaspora. Instead of revisiting this argument here, I limit the discussion to one strategy of contesting hegemonic narratives of identification and belonging. My interlocutors produced counter-hegemonic understandings of themselves and were interested in cultivating changed consciousness in various ways. Making claims to global citizenship, however, is an over-arching narrative that allows them to contest multiple forms of marginalisation both in the homeland and their new settings, which I demonstrate in this section through Sophie's narrative.

When we met in Paris, Sophie was working as a sculptor. She had a long career for the United Nations and expressed her passion for working in the social development field. She started doing sculpture while working but eventually decided to pursue her art full-time. Walking me through the different pieces decorating her lavishly styled apartment located in one of Paris' wealthiest neighbourhoods, she described the different figurines of couples as belonging to her earlier pieces:

> The first part of my work emphasises harmony, an image of comfort, of love, and understanding. It's quiet, and it's passionate. It's because when I started, I wanted to express what I would like to see in Lebanon. For me, a couple is the two parts of Lebanon: one part Christian, one part Muslim. The couple is one and the other. It's the beginning of every social or political group. [Through my work] I expressed how I can live in Lebanon, how I would like Lebanon to be: harmonious, and equal.

Having experienced the civil war in Lebanon and the sectarian political configuration that followed, Sophie wanted to disrupt the conflict narrative that is associated with war and political divisions. She crafts her sculptures as representations of an idealised vision of Lebanese society, one that may not reflect reality but a desire for a harmonious future.

A desire for a harmonious society reflects Sophie's experience growing up but, in her description, it applies to other places and connects to her desire to see peace all over the world. That peaceful message that she wanted to communicate in her earlier work, however, changed over time, as her work began to have a clearer political interest. Sophie went on to explain the most recent sculpture she was working on at the time of our meeting – silent figures. These silent figures have an important political message that she wishes to express. Specifically, she referred to her latest figurine of a tied-up seated man with a bandage on his mouth, which was much appreciated in Lebanon as people there felt that Sophie's sculpture expressed feelings they were unable to express themselves. When I asked her about the specific message that the figurine represents, her response was firm: 'Rebellion.'

Sophie's response was somewhat surprising, as I did not see the rebellious aspect of the sculpture, and instead, I thought it reflected restrictions on individual freedoms and especially freedom of expression. Sophie agreed with me and went on to explain that the bandage on the mouth prevents a person from expressing their opinions and from having their voices heard as they are unable to speak. The sculpture, however, communicates that the bandage cannot be enforced forever and that at some point, the tied-up man has to protest the bondage, speak up and present a different perspective that so far has not been allowed. For Sophie, this was the vision she had when working on the sculpture. That vision did not only relate to the lack of freedom of expression that ties people in Lebanon and most of the Arab world. As Sophie described, it related to any context where people were denied the opportunity or the ability to present their own narrative and have their voices heard.

The tied-up man also reflects Sophie's professional experience. Sophie has access to valuable social and cultural capital in Paris and through her professional success. At her previous job, and throughout certain interactions in French society, however, Sophie experienced several frustrations. Her long career eventually led her to the conclusion that working for international organisations will not necessarily have a direct impact on people's lives, especially those who are among the most disadvantaged. Similarly, despite occupying a position of privilege in French society, Sophie was critical of the ways Arabs, and immigrants in general, were represented and othered. The two forms of frustration came together and led her to quit her job to focus on crafting narratives about social change, agency and migration through her sculpture. Occupying a position of relative privilege, for Sophie, does not preclude the experience of othering or the desire to draw attention to inequality and marginalisation as social processes. Being an immigrant, according to Sophie, makes one more sensitive to these issues, and in her case privilege means a responsibility to be an agent of social change.

The desire to contest power over narratives of truth circulating in society, for Sophie and others, is a global one. It applies to societies that restrict access to forms of participation and representation, like Lebanon or other Arab countries. It equally applies to societies where there is relatively more open access to forms of representation, such as Europe and North America, but where immigrants and especially those from the Middle East are denied the ability to participate in debates over or express their own narratives and experiences. In Sophie's example, immigrants were othered in French society and denied an opportunity to voice their visions and experiences of French society. Othering is a process that denies the other the opportunity to represent oneself.

Like Sophie, many of my interlocutors resorted to global narratives and imaginaries of their social position in ways that were directly connected to their experiences of being Lebanese, migrating and experiencing life in a new setting. Many of my interlocutors shared a heightened awareness of occupying positions of privilege. A privileged class position does not have to be based on absolute economic capital, as reflected in Sophie's narrative; Farah also expressed an awareness of her privileged class position compared to her family members in Lebanon. In addition to class, my interlocutors were also aware of their privilege living in more stable societies (socially, economically and politically), and that awareness resulted in their desire to impact the lives of those who were less fortunate. At the same time, many were also aware of their precarious situation, as Arab/Middle Eastern immigrants in countries that associated their place of origin with conflict and violence. Lebanese immigrants' awareness of their precarious situation motivates most of my interlocutors to challenge traditional forms of belonging and identification.

Key to contesting flat, unitary identities is an ability to engage in practices of social change that occur at the global level. Facing exclusion in their new contexts and Lebanon, they were motivated to be effective in changing the different societies of which they are members. The kinds of social changes they were interested in are global in nature, as they realise the broad forms of inequality and exclusion that they faced. Since global problems call for global efforts, Lebanese immigrants understand their positions as cosmopolitan citizens who are interested in global social change. These changes, however, can only be realised in specific societies and at the local level. Lebanese immigrants' attachment to their homeland and host societies was expressed in their interest in challenging social norms and engaging in activities that aimed at social change in both contexts. Issues of sectarian divisions, class inequalities, gay visibility, corruption and illiberal ideas (economic and political) were among the topics that Lebanese immigrants engaged with in their homeland. In their host societies, they took on similar concerns for more equality, desegregation and multiculturalism. Such interests were global in nature and many Lebanese immigrants emphasised their experience with migration as informing their understanding of the world as an interconnected place.

Conclusion

Similar to all social experiences, diasporic experiences are racially and socially gendered. As Anthias and Yuval-Davis (1993) argue, these experiences usually rely on specific notions of 'manhood' and 'womanhood'. However, as with the experience of other groups of migrants, being in the diaspora can provide space for challenging and negotiating discourses of identity and nationality (Batisai, 2016). The narratives of Lebanese immigrants that I illustrate here demonstrate ways that migration provides opportunities for both men and women to question hegemonic social structures (such as those imposed by class, gender and nation) and to entertain alternative understandings of gendered lives and social relationships in general. Their positions are shaped by different power dynamics that operate at various levels – locally, nationally and transnationally. These power dynamics also influence the migrants' sense of belonging and experiences with inclusion or exclusion. Nonetheless, the migrants' ability to exert agency and participate in processes of change are central to their ability to make sense of their social positions and experiences.

Beyond simplistic gender differences, however, using the lens of diaspora and emphasising the geographies of power allow for a more complex understanding of the ways men and women negotiate their roles and relationships to different social spaces. For Lebanese immigrant women, their entanglement in webs of kin and friends that stretch across vast distances and international borders shapes their ability to negotiate gendered positions and forms of belonging. Farah, Abeer and Sophie renegotiated the meaning of womanhood, based on their experiences with transnational connections that involved different forms of inclusion and exclusion. Relative disadvantage dictated by the position of an immigrant was accentuated by disadvantageous class position (in Farah's case) and marginalised sexual identity (in Abeer's case). However, these positions also interacted with sources for empowerment that these women built on in achieving a positive sense of self (being a good mother and wife for Farah and a successful physician and queer activist for Abeer). Together, the various social positions these two women occupy allow them to renegotiate gendered identities and personhood. Being able to draw on such positive notions of self illustrates immigrant women's ability to exercise agency in navigating the social hierarchies that are dictated to them and consequently traverse social structures in important ways.

In their analysis of the relationship between globalisation processes and community networks, Gupta and Ferguson (1997) stress that communal ties are constructed within a wide set of social and spatial relations and suggest that 'it is fundamentally mistaken to conceptualize different kinds of non- or supra-local identities (diasporic, refugee, migrant, and so forth) as spatial and temporal extensions of a prior, natural identity rooted in locality and community' (p. 7). For many Lebanese immigrants, and especially the women among them, their relationship to the homeland and membership in an ethnic diasporic community are fraught with disagreement and a sense of exclusion. Objecting to sectarian divisions, class inequalities, bigotry, corruption and a lack of democracy, many of my respondents underline the different perspectives that they have gained from having left Lebanon. These respondents also stress their critical views of Lebanese society and their ability to participate more effectively in processes of change while in the diaspora. As these respondents 'pick quarrels' with their homeland, they also become more active in their host societies and diasporic communities (Said, 1990). Similar to their criticism of Lebanese society, many members of the Lebanese diaspora also find that the diaspora itself is a site where many of the homeland's problems are reproduced. The sense of exclusion from the diaspora weakens my respondents' identification with their co-ethnics, which leads them to question the logic of privileging national and ethnic identities. Focusing on social change also allows them to understand Lebanese social problems within a global context and seek more global solutions. Similarly, demanding full participation in the host society allows them to gauge bases for inclusion and participation. These concerns, while motivating participation in the host society, also trigger a cosmopolitan sense of belonging and more global forms of involvement. For example, Abeer's quarrels with Lebanese society, the gay community in New York and, to some extent, the gay Arab community ought to be considered foci of social involvement in the three societies that she considers herself part of, as opposed to markers of exclusion and marginalisation. Importantly, these positions of 'picking quarrels' lead my interlocutors to forge affinities with other immigrants from various backgrounds which foster further detachment from ethnicity and nationality as sources for communal belonging and identification.

Enacting agency does not end with empowering the migrants themselves but extends to include the wish to empower the communities they see themselves as members of as well. Immigrant women in my study did not simply wish to participate in actions that would help others in an interest in philanthropic goodwill. Instead, they were interested in transforming their communities towards being more just, harmonious and inclusive. As illustrated by Sophie, such interests are indeed based on a strong cognitive imagery that allows them to imagine a different type of society. Their ability to take the initiative to act as agents of change is an important aspect in their engagement with given power geometries and willingness to transform them. Godin (2019, p. 159), refers to 'diasporic critical spaces' that allow the diasporic subject to interrogate the position of the other. These critical spaces, as illustrated by the experiences of my interlocutors, connect personal histories of roots and routes to global trajectories and dramas.

Arif Dirlik (1997) argues that the social construction of in-betweenness and cosmopolitan history are strategic mechanisms to cope with conditions of displacement and diaspora. As a product of historical experiences, diasporic communities construct forms of solidarity that are shaped by past experiences of displacement, present problems of inequality and exclusion, and future interests in solidarity and freedom. In the process, they challenge traditional forms of attachments that are based on nationality, ethnicity or religion. The context of globalisation facilitates the construction of social relations that transcend national boundaries. More than providing the structure for global solidarity, globalisation makes global solidarity necessary, at least in the experience of immigrants who wish to challenge the traditions of both their homeland and host societies.

References

Abdelhady, D. (2006) 'Beyond home/host networks: forms of solidarity among Lebanese immigrants in a global era', *Identities: Global Studies in Culture and Power*, 13(3), pp. 427–453.

Abdelhady, D. (2008) 'Representing the homeland: Lebanese diasporic notions of home and return in a global context', *Cultural Dynamics*, 20(1), pp. 53–72.

Abdelhady, D. (2011) *The Lebanese Diaspora: The Arab Immigrant Experience in Montreal, New York and Paris*. New York: New York University Press.

Abdelhady, D. (2015) 'Lebanese women transnational immigrant experiences: a gendered geographies of power approach', in Stephan, R., Hourani, G. and Horn, C. (eds) *In Line with the Divine: The Struggle for Gender Equality in Lebanon*. Beirut: Abelian Academics, pp. 128–148.

Abdul-Karim, A. (1992) 'Lebanese business in France', in Hourani, A. and Shehadi, N (eds) *The Lebanese in the World: A Century of Emigration*. London: The Centre for Lebanese Studies, pp. 698–714.

Abu-Laban, B. (1980) *An Olive Branch on the Family Tree: A Study of Arabs in Canada*. Ottawa: The Multicultural Programme.

Anthias, F. and Yuval-Davis, N. (1993) *Racialized Boundaries: Race, Nation, Gender, Colour and Class and the Antiracist Struggle*. London: Routledge.

Batisai, K. (2016) 'Transnational labour migration, intimacy and relationships: how Zimbabwean women navigate the diaspora', *Diaspora Studies*, 9(2), pp. 165–78, doi:10.1080/09739572.2016.1185236

Butler, K. (2001) 'Defining diaspora, refining a discourse', *Diaspora*, 10(2), pp. 189–218.

Collins, P.H. (2000). *Black Feminist Thought: Knowledge, Consciousness, and the Politics of Empowerment*. New York: Routledge.

Dirlik, A. (1997). *The Postcolonial Aura: Third World Criticism in the Age of Global Capitalism*. London: Routledge.

Farahani, F. (2017) *Gender, Sexuality, and Diaspora*. London: Routledge.

Godin, M. (2019) 'Intersectionalizing diaspora studies', in Cohen, R. and Fischer, C. (eds) *The Routledge Handbook of Diaspora Studies*. London: Routledge, pp. 154–162.

Goldring, L. (1998) 'The power of status in transnational social spaces', in Guarinzo, E. and Smith, M. (eds) *Transnationalism from Below*. New Brunswick, NJ: Transaction Press, pp. 165–195.

Gupta, A. and Ferguson, J. (1997) 'Culture, power, place: ethnography at the end of an era', in Gupta, A. and Ferguson, J. (eds) *Culture, Power, Place: Explorations in Critical Anthropology*. Durham, NC: Duke University Press, pp. 1–29.

Hondagneu-Sotelo, P. (1994) *Gendered Transitions: Mexican Experiences of Immigration*. Berkeley, CA: University of California Press.

Hourani, A. and Shehadi, N. (1992) 'Introduction', in Hourani, A. and Shehadi, N. (eds) *The Lebanese in the World: A Century of Emigration*. London: The Centre for Lebanese Studies, pp. 3–11.

Pasura, D. (2008) 'Gendering the diaspora: Zimbabwean migrants in Britain', *African Diaspora*, 1(1), pp. 86–109. doi: 10.1163/187254608X346060

Pessar, P. and Mahler, S. (2003). 'Transnational migration: bringing gender in', *International Migration Review*, 37.(3), pp. 812–846.

Rao Mehta, S. (2015) 'Revisiting gendered spaces in the diaspora', in Rao Mehta, S. (ed.) *Exploring Gender in the Literature of the Indian Diaspora*. Cambridge: Cambridge University Press, pp. 1–15.

Said, E. (1990) 'Reflections on exile', in Ferguson, R., Gever, M., Minh-ha, T.T., West, C., and Gonzales-Torres, F. (eds) *Out There: Marginalization and Contemporary Culture*. Cambridge, MA: The MIT Press, pp. 357–366.

Tinarwo, M.T. and Pasura, D. (2014) 'Negotiating and contesting gendered and sexual identities in the Zimbabwean diaspora', *Journal of Southern African Studies*, 40(3), pp. 521–538, doi: 10.1080/03057070.2014.909258

17
CREATIVITY AS A CONTESTED SITE OF IDENTITY-MAKING
Careers, gender and diaspora for Sydney's Lebanese Australians

Sherene Idriss

This chapter explores the lived experiences of creative and cultural workers who come from Lebanese Australian backgrounds. I use an 'ethnographically grounded' (Peteet, 2007) application of the increasingly elastic concept of diaspora (Tabar, 2020) and ask, how do Lebanese Australian creative workers construct their ethno-cultural identities and what is at stake in their careful management of cultural expression? Drawing on narratives of craft and creativity, I aim to understand how place and gender are lived out through their creative-based careers. The overarching aim of tracing this trajectory is to examine how personal forms of cultural expression and community attachments are manifestations of diaspora experiences (Abdelhady, 2011) and how gendered norms, particularly around heterosexuality and patriarchy, within the Lebanese Australian diaspora are disrupted and complicated by creative identities and aspirations.

Following a cultural studies approach, the discussion of diaspora presented here moves away from the centrality of the state to instead trace the 'efforts, strategies and affects' (Obeid, 2013, p. 367) involved in performing ethnicity, articulating 'home' and living out 'culture' within specific institutions and spaces (Aly, 2015). Diaspora is employed conceptually to do two things. The first is to explore the psychic processes that underscore the gendered identity-making among second- and third-generation Lebanese Australian young people from working-class backgrounds. Second, building on this, the chapter analyses how diaspora consciousness is mobilised as a resource by those young people in their career-making strategies within the multiculturalist funding structures of segments of the creative industries.

In the context of minoritised young people and career-making, a focus on the performativity of ethnicity offers a departure from the corpus of the literature. Ethnicity is generally viewed as either a constraining or useful social category but the expressions of which are ultimately peripheral to the individual's chosen career and educational pathways (see, for example, Reay et al., 2001). In contrast, creative and cultural labour requires the cultivation of personal aesthetics, style and cultural capitals that can emphasise ethnicity (Abdelhady, 2007). For minoritised artists, the burden of representation requires them to personally and continually confront their situatedness within power relations (Spivak, 1990; Bhabha, 1994). The strategic essentialism (Spivak, 1990) involved in reproducing Lebaneseness and/or Arabness through creative and cultural projects, as I show in this chapter, becomes a core component of an individual's career identity, narrated by participants themselves as a kind of capital for carving out a niche market but which ultimately involves a number of challenges.

The young women and men who took part in the research that informs this chapter are predominantly 'second generation'; born and raised in the cities of Sydney and Melbourne, but frequently travelling to their parents' homelands across their life course. In the first project on which this chapter is based, I conducted an ethnographic study of Arab Australian young men from working-class backgrounds with aspirations to work in the creative and cultural industries in metropolitan Sydney between 2010 and 2014 (Idriss, 2017). In it, I employed an intersectional approach to understanding the entanglement between masculinity, class, ethnicity and creativity when looking at the discursive strategies of Arab Australian young men as they navigate the challenges of developing creative vocational aspirations. Over 12 months, I conducted participant observation at several key community arts organisations across South Western Sydney, where filmmaking, writing workshops and photography classes were taught alongside regular showcases by emerging and established local, migrant and Indigenous artists. The participant observation was complemented by in-depth biographical interviews with 20 Arab Australian young men from socio-economically disadvantaged backgrounds who had broader aspirations to work in the creative and cultural industries.

The second project, taking place in 2018–2019, built on this, working exclusively with young women from a range of non-white migrant backgrounds involved in community arts-based creative and cultural work. The young women in this study align with what might be culturally regarded as 'high achievers' whose attitude to work was defined by 'hustling' strategies of survival (Idriss, 2021). They had performed well in their final school years, had completed or were completing tertiary education, and held paid positions in the creative and cultural industries. The primary focus was to capture narratives of young women from non-white ethnic minority backgrounds working in creative and cultural sectors, in a range of fields such as publishing, music, film, media and fine arts, to better understand how their ideas about and experience of creativity, craft and political participation are shaped by markers of gender, class and race.

All of the participants in this second project were between 18 and 30 years of age and were recruited via a number of channels, including initial contact with local arts organisations in Western Sydney that offered residencies to artists of colour and consultation with a local community arts organisation in West Melbourne that similarly developed initiatives for artists from migrant backgrounds. The relationships I had with these organisations allowed me to conduct participant observation of their programmes and build rapport with artists and artists in training, who then agreed to face-to-face, one-on-one interviews. A total of 12 interviews were conducted, five with Arab Australian women. The interviews were biographical in nature, structured chronologically where possible, and generally lasted between 90 minutes and 2 hours.

In this chapter, I combine insights collected from the two projects to construct an argument about diasporic forms of expression as narrated by my interlocutors. I suggest that the recitations of Arabness, and specifically Lebaneseness, are contingent in one sense on the state requirements to fit within multiculturalist regimes of difference and diversity. What I show is that this invocation of an imagined Lebanese homeland, contrasted with their sense of Otherness in Australia, does not map neatly onto their personal desires and aspirations as they negotiate a plurality of social locations across different aspects of their everyday lives. In what follows, I provide a brief background to the Lebanese Australian diaspora, particularly concerning Australian multiculturalist constructions of ethnic hierarchies and the bearing this has on the sectors of employment that these communities are commonly associated with. I then briefly trace how representations of Lebanese Australian communities have accounted for place, gender and enterprise thus far, before moving on to an in-depth look at two case studies – Layal and Ziad – to explore how they navigated creative labour in the broader context of their lived experiences. Building on the scholarship that suggests that diaspora refers to material and symbolic border making and crossing/s (Brah, 1996; Abdulhadi, Alsultany and Naber, 2011; Tabar, 2020), in each of the case studies presented here I consider what kind of bordering of the self these diasporic subjects engage with. This question is interrogated particularly as it relates to the transformation and reconfiguration of gendered identity-making across generations within the Lebanese Australian diaspora.

The Lebanese Australian diaspora: a brief historical overview

Migration from Lebanon to Australia dates back to 1876, but the largest wave of migration took place at the outbreak of the Lebanese Civil War towards the end of 1975 (Batrouney and Batrouney, 1985). In this period, Australia saw an end to the official assimilationist 'White Australia' policy under Whitlam's Labour government in favour of multiculturalism that focused on cultural and religious tolerance. With the end of assimilationist programmes, the Lebanese community that settled in this post-1975 era enjoyed robust multicultural policies in which settlement services were available in the migrants' own languages along with free English classes, for the first time in Australia's history (Monsour and Convy, 2008). As Tabar (2014, p. 447) notes:

> after 1990, the number of Lebanese immigrants began to decline considerably. This was mainly due to the restructuring of the Australian economy, which started in the 1980s, leading to the downsizing of the industrial sector and the expansion of the service sector and the so-called knowledge economy.

State funding for ethnic community organisations and a cultural shift whereby ethnic minorities were actively encouraged to express their ethnic identities allowed Lebanese migrants to form stable but complex diasporic community networks and political organisations (Humphrey, 2001; Tabar, Noble and Poynting, 2010). Formal and state-sanctioned expressions of Lebanese culture continue to take place through cultural festivals like Harmony Day and through Special Broadcasting Service media where news and programming are delivered in Arabic, among other languages. Institutions like the Immigration Museum also played a part in this new cultural landscape, in which Lebanese migrants' contributions to Australian society are quite literally on display. Other networks such as the Council for Australian-Arab Relations, the Lebanese Muslim Association, the Australia Arab Chamber of Commerce and Industry, as well as a broad array of local village-based, sectarian and politically affiliated organisations work to maintain bonds between Australia and Lebanon (Tabar, 2014). They also offer advice on faith-based and culturally appropriate ways to live 'a good life' particularly for the second generation of Lebanese Australians who are often seen as being subject to contradictory pressures, as Hyndman-Rizk (2016) explores in her ethnography of arranged Lebanese marriages in Australia.

Unlike other Lebanese communities living in the diaspora, first-generation migrants to Australia mostly arrived through non-skilled visa programmes; subsequent generations arrived through family reunification and/or humanitarian schemes. They are not the 'highly educated professionals' that make up Lebanese migrant communities in other global cities (see, for example, Abdelhady, 2011). The socio-economic make-up of these communities contributed to their racialisation as Other in the Australian context. Jumana Bayeh (2017) has explored how the sprawling suburban landscape has served as an important resource and signifier for Arab Australian writers making sense of diaspora and belonging. Bayeh compares how second- and third-generation diaspora literature reflects values wholly at odds with an imagined Lebanon with its dense cities, and is simultaneously distinct from the experiences of Lebanese migrant communities in New York, Paris and London who also found themselves in the heart of busy cosmopolitan cities with longer-established non-white communities nearby (Aly, 2015).

As Brah (1996) argues, diaspora needs to be interrogated in relation to the specific material conditions and power relations under which the diasporic group is made. This has intergenerational effects on the psychic and affective dimensions of how diasporic subjects imagine their positionality within society and how they sustain a sense of home and culture. The specificities of location, place and migration dynamics are reflected in the ways that the diasporic Lebanese subject in France, for example, can articulate their ethnicity as wholly compatible with a French social system and distinguish themselves as cosmopolitans, away from other, tribal, non-assimilatable Arab subjects, as seen in Abdelhady's (2011) research. In Australia, Lebanese Australian migrants and their children have been imagined as socially deviant and Othered subjects. In particular, Lebanese Australian Muslims have long been associated with motorbike gang crime, assault weapons smuggled from the Middle East, and the infamous Bilal Skaf rape case (see, for example, Rawsthorne, 2019), all of which received highly racialised media coverage that was reflected in police profiling policies and the establishment of a dedicated 'Middle Eastern Crime Squad' in the early 2000s (Dagistanli, 2007). Young Lebanese Australian men were at the centre of these moral panics about ethnicised protest masculinity, gang-related crime and sexual assault (ibid.). Many of the symbols associated with Lebanese Australian communities are place-based and also code for socio-economic disadvantage, like 'Telopea Street' in Punchbowl, an infamous street for drug busts in the late 1990s and 2000s, or Punchbowl Boys High School, which was cast as a notoriously violent school mostly attended by 'Lebs' and Muslims. Rob White (2007) explains how being Lebanese has been transformed through socio-cultural and political processes into code for social deviance specifically for young men, most of whom were born or raised in Australia but are nevertheless treated as outsiders.

In establishing the context in which the Lebanese Australian diaspora is situated, it is important to note that the corpus of scholarship has tended to be assumedly gender-less or, where gender is emphasised, takes for granted the primacy of male migrant experience. Thus the literature on second- and third-generation Lebanese Australian women is almost always about Muslim women. Research has shown how they experience exclusion most commonly due to Islamaphobia, where Arabness and Islam are conflated and signified in similar ways (Harris and Hussein, 2018). In the aftermath of the Afghanistan War in 2001, the Iraq War in 2003 and the growing carnage in places like Syria, the number of refugees arriving in Australia from these countries has only increased (Bayeh, 2017). Conservative politicians and media commentators have depicted these refugees as a cultural, economic and security threat to Australia, who among other things are perceived as a welfare burden, while the conflation between Muslims and terrorists frames them as a threat to the safety of Australians. Thus, 'already subject to economic disadvantage and social marginalisation, a generation of young people has grown up in a social atmosphere that is very hostile to their culture, to their community, to their religion and to their very presence' (ibid., p. 71). What I show in the case studies that follow is that this local context significantly shapes the multiple modalities of belonging, the performativity of gender, and expressions of creativity for the Lebanese Australians involved in the research in as much as their affective attachments to Lebaneseness.

Reclaim the space: Layal

Layal was 26 years old when I interviewed her and comes from a Lebanese Maronite family. She grew up and lived in South West Sydney with her mother and younger sister. Her mother had arrived in Australia as a teenager, completing secondary school and technical college; her father migrated a decade later in the late 1980s when in his late twenties. He worked for himself as a garden landscaper. Layal described her mother as a 'housewife'. She describes her upbringing as 'tough' coming from a low socio-economic background where 'my dad was always, always working and my mum was doing a million things to help him with his business because he couldn't speak English well'. The racial prejudice her father experienced shaped Layal's view of home and sense of belonging, saying;

> He could never settle in here, he just always wanted to go back but we couldn't afford to and it just wasn't an option after a while. So he always has that mentality and would always say to us, 'this isn't your home'. That always impacted me and I would see Australia in the same way sometimes.

The family had moved to Lebanon on a number of occasions for periods of up to six months, but each time the money her father had saved in Australia ran out. They were never able to commit to staying in Lebanon because of the remoteness of her family's village and the lack of opportunities for Layal and her sister. Her parents separated when she was 16 but her father did not move out of the family home until a year or so later; this was very disruptive to her senior school years. Before their separation, Layal's parents' relationship was 'intense' and 'unstable'. She says,

> Sometimes he'd be amazing to be around, other times he was awful ... just drinking so much and depressed and that's when he'd come up with these plans to go back to Lebanon because we could have a fresh start and of course it would never work out and then it was the same cycle over and over. Just very clichéd. My mum couldn't do anything, she'd go along with these plans thinking it would stop his drinking but obviously that didn't work either.

When her parents divorced, her father lived in Lebanon for six months each year, and Layal and her sister set up a social media account for their mother to establish a Lebanese catering business so that she could be self-sufficient. The enterprise became quite successful in the local South West Sydney suburbs. Layal does not describe her mother's transition to self-employment as a deviation from Lebanese gendered scripts of femininity and domesticity; nor does she elaborate on the ramifications of her parents' divorce in her extended Maronite family and community. Instead, she draws on her travels to Lebanon throughout her life and invokes diasporic memories to situate her mother's journey as emblematic of a certain strength and entrepreneurship that are inherent to Lebanese womanhood. She told me, 'my grandmother, like a lot of Lebanese grandmothers, really runs the show in her village and has such a strong presence that I've always admired'.

When it came time for Layal to make post-schooling choices, she drew both on her parents' respective unconventional work arrangements, saying 'the idea of a 9-to-5 never inspired me' as well as the nostalgia and fond memories of her extended family's rural home and lifestyle in Lebanon, where she spent many of her school holidays. She enrolled in a fine arts degree at a prestigious university in Sydney, majoring in sculpture and painting, a choice she deeply regrets. She reasons that

> [The department was] extremely purist. Just a bunch of dinosaurs that have hive mind; the head of department hired his student who hired his student and on and on so they just come from one stream of thinking. And that is that there is a right way to do art. They were just heavily misogynistic and really racist. Like, I was working with clay and rolling it out and they'd make horrible comments like 'you're in your element, Lebanese woman cooking' stuff like that. It was so gross. And the curriculum was so Western and Eurocentric.

The double bind of racialisation and gender stereotypes are an enormous burden for Arab Australian women, especially so for Muslim women who are subjected further to Islamophobia (Harris and Hussein, 2018). For Layal, it is the invocation of a diasporic transnational identity that helps her get through the course and challenge the outdated myths associated with Lebanese womanhood. She said:

> I could not fight the curriculum but I had so many questions, like, about the Indigenous peoples of this land and my family's history, and why are we being taught that art began in this Western space? Why is that the root of it? And why should my practice speak to that? Um, I ended up just, through the internet, connecting with Lebanese artists in Sydney and other artists' spaces in the Middle East.

Connection with artists in Lebanon, as well as other racialised artists in Australia, is a strategy commonly employed by diasporic artists looking to carve out a space to build community and develop their craft outside the white gaze. As Abdelhady (2007) found in her research with Lebanese artists in the diaspora, belonging in between two or more cultures, as Layal does, can be interpreted not as a problem but instead 'as an important source for artistic imagination' (p. 49). Indeed, this is the path that Layal finds herself on, where her cultural attachments and the performativity of Arab womanhood become increasingly part of her craft artist identity. When we met, Layal was a freelancer involved in a number of publicly funded art programmes across Western Sydney. At the time of our interview, her exhibition was heavily infused with themes of cultural identity. She makes rose water in one show, while she is scrubbing carpets with a friend in a public square at her university in another. She explained,

> It's not about the actual rose water but the symbolism of the rose and it's not about the clean rug but the actual practice and the process behind it, of the women who are cleaning the rug. And it's this loaded symbolism of the Orientalist rug in this specific space (the elite art school) and it's subversive that way. My friend whom I did that exhibition with was Iraqi and we were speaking Arabic during that work and it was a way for us to reclaim language and reclaim the space. And we filmed it and made it into a digital installation.

Her narratives about developing subversive projects that speak to her ethnicity and gender echo Liu's study of Chinese Australian professionals who insist on 'the fluidity of their ethno-cultural identity' even though they 'perform a stable, even stereotypical, Chinese identity to their colleagues …'. Liu calls this a form of 'mythbusting' where 'Chinese Australian professionals deliberately engaged in self-Orientalism to secure recognition from white Australians, yet contested and subverted Orientalist images in other ways' (Liu, 2016, p. 796). We can see similar processes taking shape in Layal's narratives of craft and creativity in which she explicitly invokes strategic essentialism through the motif of an 'Orientalist' rug in her show to subvert it. She is limited in her ability to do so, however, because she has to operate within established and contained ethnic identity categories. Her reflexivity in recognising this as a strategy for 'reclaiming the language and reclaiming the space' can best be understood, in one instance, as the way Arabness, and Lebanese womanhood more specifically, act as 'repertoires of "doing", achieved through the imperfect repetition of culture over time and space' (Aly, 2015, p. 1). Doing ethnicity includes speaking Arabic in public settings, as Layal does here to highlight her non-white visibility and to perform pride in her heritage (as seen in ibid. as well as Poynting et al., 2004).

Beyond this recitation of ethnicity through visual expression, what is interesting about Layal is that while she was frustrated with the way that her teachers at the art school essentialised her identity and wrapped it in Orientalist images of Arab female domesticity, that imagery, of Arab womanhood and domesticity, became central to her practice. Ethnicity is at once a burden and a resource to be leveraged, or, in Aly's terms, a 'narrative of redemption and crisis' (Aly, 2015). In Aly's study, British Arab artists engage in a process of 're-appropriation' of Orientalist imagery, intending to subvert and challenge white hegemony. Yet he argues that these attempts at re-appropriation are:

> grounded on rather apologetic and muted grounds, encrypted with an anxiety which proclaims: 'We are not all extremists', 'We have a worthy civilisation too', 'We are like you', 'We are not ugly, we are beautiful'. These utterances are addressed first and foremost to the (ethnic subject) British Arabs as a form of self-affirmation. Yet that self has within it an encrypted other, namely the Euro-American culture which has vilified and subordinated Arab and Islamic 'cultures' in the process of its own self-realisation.
>
> *(ibid., p. 167)*

Here, 'reclaiming the space' is additionally laden with attempts by Layal to carve out a career in the multicultural arts sector that positions ethnicised artists in highly specific niche boxes from which there is little room to escape or transcend. Further, the themes of Layal's installations and the creative decisions she makes to incorporate essentialising motifs invite a broader discussion about the enduring effects of racism and the model of Australian multiculturalism. This model welcomes those in the Lebanese Australian diaspora to perform cultural identity in specific ways that position them as offering unique insights into 'authentic' representations of a community. Layal's narratives of work reveal the specific way she participates in the commodification of ethnicity and femininity as a strategy of survival. Diasporic expression is thus a set of situated and embodied aesthetics within circuits of knowledge and artistic production. In Layal's case, these forms of diasporic expression can be mobilised as useful for navigating limited career possibilities in highly competitive creative industries.

Layal told me the community response to her work has been mostly positive, with other Lebanese Australian young women telling her, 'oh, my God, this is great, my mum does this [the rose water and carpet cleaning] and it's great to have those stories represented.' I relayed to her my surprise at this feedback. As a member of the Lebanese Australian community myself, my cultural education was that domestic duties were to be performed in the home but a good *sit bayt* never wants to reveal just how much hard work takes place behind the scenes to maintain a pristinely clean home. Layal noted that perhaps this was a class or geographic issue. Where my extended family was urban poor, she came from a 'really remote village':

> LAYAL: My grandparents and my older aunts and uncles in Lebanon look after their land and their animals, it's not like they had cleaners or like it was a secret that they were hard workers.
> SHERENE: OK, but you're talking about cleaning a rug and cooking for people in Australia.
> LAYAL: Actually, in one of my residencies at the gallery, I got my mum to host *wara enab* cooking classes. So each week Australian women, and some men, would come and learn how to make it and they absolutely loved it. She [her mother] loved it too, like just giving people a sense of what our culture is about.
> SHERENE: That's so interesting because in my experience my mother and my grandmother would say to me, 'all we did is clean and cook we hope you don't have to do that and you can get a good job' but you're right, maybe it's an urban thing?
> LAYAL: [pause] Well, you know, now that you say that, even though I do this stuff and they're really proud of the exhibitions themselves, I still always feel like I can't just say I'm an artist because, what is that?

Although expressing pride at having 'their stories' told to a mainstream audience, Layal still has to find other ways to justify her vocational pathway to friends and family. To get their full approval, she highlights her role as a board member at an exclusive art gallery or the teaching she does in the community art sector. These narratives about the value and purpose of creativity – as a skillset which can then be taught or recognised as valued by prestigious and established institutions – is a common one across the Lebanese Australians involved in research; as one young woman put it in a different interview, second-generation Lebanese Australians are treated in the community as 'corsages on their parents' jackets' (Morgan and Idriss, 2012).

Layal's narratives are also highly gendered. Aly (2015) explains that gender performativity within Arab diasporic communities is differentiated in particular ways; women's attachments and reference points tend to be around family life. Furthermore, Arab women in the diaspora often recite differing and usually competing versions of themselves to satisfy different audiences (ibid., p. 96). Management of these competing demands is difficult to sustain over a long period; when the mask slips, there are often consequences. Layal was in a long-term relationship with an Arab woman at the time of our interview. This was something few people knew about her, certainly, her family was not privy to that part of her life even though they knew her partner well – 'as a friend'. Unlike the young women in Aly's research, Layal says she never experienced any limitations on her personal freedoms. Her family were not exceptionally religious or conservative and their volatile relationship meant she could 'get away with a lot of stuff. It's not like I ever lied to them; they were just busy with their own shit and didn't realise I came home late or whatever.' This relationship with a woman is her first time having to manage multiple versions of herself, as she enters her late twenties and questions about marriage and motherhood will invariably become intensified.

To escape the demands of heterosexual femininity within the local community, Layal tells me about the queer spaces and communities she learned about in her most recent travels to Lebanon, saying:

> It was just so beautiful to see that there are these culturally safe spaces that are open to everyone who needs it really and it's run by these two artists – actually, I had been

connecting with them online for a while beforehand and we've come up with a way to do a project together so next time I go there hopefully we'll be doing that, but we're trying to work out the angle first and where to apply for funding.

In this connection with a 'global diasporic public sphere' (Abdelhady, 2011), Layal demonstrates a continual oscillation between hybrid, plural and sometimes competing forms of belonging and identification concerning her ethnicity and gender. At the same time, because of her position competing for public arts funding under multicultural programmes, this fluidity and hybridity have to be represented in neatly bounded ways to make sense to a general audience who lack, by and large, nuanced understandings of her cultural background.

In what follows, I trace the working experiences of Ziad who, like Layal, was involved with community arts projects. Through those experiences, questions of gender and Otherness are also brought to the fore in his life history narrative but, by embodying and performing masculinity norms and expectations, he has some different perspectives of the role of creativity for living out an Arab Australian diasporic identity.

Opting out: Ziad

Ziad was 23 years old at the time of our interview and comes from a mixed Lebanese Iraqi Muslim background. He worked as a freelance multimedia designer and was contemplating returning to university to complete a Master of Fine Arts because of the limited contracts he had been able to secure in recent months. In July 2016, I was invited by Ziad to attend a workshop on diversity in the arts in Western Sydney. The panel he was part of spoke to the constraints on artists of colour, particularly refugees, to constantly have to navigate what they described as the 'war porn' industry. The panellists, Ziad in particular, were frustrated by the underlying racism in the sector and, in tandem, a sense that diversity and inclusion were often dealt with in tokenistic ways. This was echoed across almost all the interviews I conducted (Idriss, 2017), and something Ziad felt acutely and actively tried to manage. In direct contrast to Layal embracing an exoticised, feminine version of Lebanese identity, he told me,

> I don't want to make stuff that's right in your face about 'oh, poor oppressed Muslims and Arabs'. Yeah, there's a huge problem of getting work [in the creative industries] when you're a refugee or ethnic but, I don't know, my work is more abstract than that and I have heaps of things I'm really into. Like Parkour is a huge thing for me and that whole [subcultural] world really feeds into what I sketch but then you get galleries and places [at local arts organisation] who are, like, 'hey, can you help some Year 8 students talk about what it means to be Muslim in Australia through sketching or some other visual method?'. I do it, because that's one part of me that's still important to my identity, being part of this community and giving back, helping kids get involved in art and it's nice when we hold the exhibition and everyone comes with their parents and they feel proud. But, me being Muslim or Arab, it's not my be-all and end-all. And it can't be part of all my design ethos, that's just way too limiting to me. And boring, you know!

Like Layal, Ziad was directly involved in community arts programmes that were directed to the Sydney Lebanese community where direct links between ethnicity, culture and creative expression are encouraged. This approach mostly focuses on social cohesion and inclusion but requires clear binaries between the home country and the host state. Ziad expresses here that his creative and subcultural interests are 'more abstract', diverse and diffused and this presents a challenge for the available creative vocational templates afforded to minoritised artists. One of the fundamental reasons for the tokenism experienced by minoritised artists is because creative workers more generally, to be successful, are encouraged to be 'culturally omnivorous' (Prieur and Savage, 2013). That is, to be able to capture the *zeitgeist*, be adaptable to trends and be at the forefront of popular culture. The white gaze circumvents funding bodies and audiences (in the context of publicly funded creative projects) from seeing minoritised subjects as capable of producing genre-bending, innovative and global art; instead, emerging non-white creative workers have their productions and outputs consumed, critiqued and reviewed, almost always in relation to their representations of culture (Spivak, 1990). Under multiculturalist structures, the Lebanese Australian artists in my research were simultaneously pulled in on account of their unique contribution and pushed out to the fringes of a multicultural arts scene. In my work I explored how several Arab Australian emerging artists from socio-economically disadvantaged suburbs of Western Sydney followed a similar trajectory by becoming community brokers, facilitating particular modes of creative expression that centred their voices in response to racism, Islamophobia and moral panics (Idriss, 2017). Though he recognised these structures as effectively forcing minoritised artists to compete against one another, he found it hard to escape its constraints, saying, in an ideal scenario:

> I would be able to do more to advocate for artists to get a foot in the door who are like me, you know, brown and Muslim or refugees, but sometimes I just worry, can there only be, like, one Lebanese artist? Like, you know what I mean, am I in competition with them because there's not enough room for, like, that much diversity?

Ultimately, Ziad was not interested in becoming a community broker or re-appropriating culture, as Layal is, to navigate the sector. He told me he was planning to 'get out of the whole workshop scene and just build a different kind of brand'. This desire to escape was partly because of his ambivalence within the local ethnic community, where heteronormative masculine templates pushed him to the fringes of the community and his subcultural interests, like Parkour. Furthermore, his pursuit of a creative-based career was seen as 'weird' and openly mocked by his cousins. Indeed, in my interviews with Arab Australian young men, most explained that creative expression was something that remained hidden from view within their immediate family and extended ethnic community. Creative expression and any exhibitions they were involved in were downplayed to family members out of fear of homophobic slurs and judgement about not fulfilling communal aspirations of social mobility. I asked Ziad about the communal pressure and how his creative interests fit within his family's expectations:

> SHERENE: It sounds like your parents are OK with your choice to pursue graphic design?
> ZIAD: For now, I think. Maybe because I want to go back and do a Masters, it's like that makes it OK ... [trails off]
> SHERENE: Yeah, but I guess, they haven't openly said they aren't happy with it or anything?
> ZIAD: No, they don't. Honestly, I think they think I do IT. Like, it's just something I'm thinking about now. They don't really know what graphic design is. Just something you do on the computer and that's probably enough for them.
> SHERENE: I can understand that. My parents don't fully get what a sociologist is but they know I had to do a PhD for it.
> ZIAD: Yeah! (laughs) They probably tell people I'm an engineer ...

In this excerpt, like Layal's management of her queer identity, Ziad is reluctant to too harshly critique his parents' lack of engagement with the substance of his work and this reluctance is heightened when we compare his reaction to white audiences at the community arts workshop, who also have limited and rudimentary engagement with his craft. Abdulhadi, Alsultany and Naber have captured this tension in their reflections of Arab American communities saying 'certain issues [are] "cultural" and "private" and therefore distinct from "political" and "public issues"' ((2011, p. xxxviii), like racism and sexism, for example. In Ziad's case, the 'doing' of ethnicity in the public domain demands of him to perform reified versions of inclusion and exclusion on account of his Muslim and Arab background, a demand he hates and attempts to reject. But in private spaces, where his creative vocational identity is misunderstood or reduced by his parents and peers, the doing of ethnicity requires him to silently adhere to patriarchal templates of Arab masculinity and play along with the high value placed on credentials (Idriss and Morgan, 2018); this kind of performativity of Lebaneseness is more palatable for Ziad at this moment in his life.

Like Layal, he draws on a transnational diasporic community to achieve a sense of confidence in his interests in vocational choices. He says:

> Actually my cousins and my family in Lebanon and Iraq are pretty creative and it's not seen as 'gay', immoral or anything. I could show them that side of me, they'd understand that what I do for work, like being a designer, is actually a great job. It's more the guys here in Sydney.

Like the other young Arab Australian men in my research, Ziad's creative and leisure interests are discursively understood as at odds with Arab forms of hegemonic masculinity where the other 'guys in Sydney' subscribe to, as Aly similarly finds in the British context, 'notions of "Arab" loyalty and solidarity during struggle or hardship, a central component and expectation of Arab fraternity' (2015, p. 76). Ziad's Otherness in the creative industries, compounded with his isolation in the Sydney Lebanese Australian community, is never fully resolved in the context of our interview. Instead, the excerpt here shows that, like Layal, he turns to diasporic repertoires of gender, which he identifies as more fluid and where his creative interests are validated as within the scope of what it means to be an Arab man rather than threatening that part of his identity.

Configurations of place and gender in the Lebanese Australian diaspora

Taken in conversation with each other, Layal and Ziad's narratives shed light on contemporary affective and performative dimensions of diaspora. I have highlighted how, for some second-generation Lebanese Australian artists, ethno-cultural markers become constitutive of their craft, partially as a way to carve out a niche market but partially out of necessity due to overlapping process of racialisation, class-based inequalities and community expectations about respectable gendered career pathways. Ethnicity operates as a resource that is embodied and performed in particular ways to achieve personal and collective projects of mobility in the case of Layal but, as we see with Ziad, this approach to creative work is limited in that it requires the diasporic subject to rely on somewhat fixed and unproblematic notions of an ethnic community.

I have focused on the 'doing' of ethnicity by artists who produce 'collective memories' of what it means to be Lebanese Australian beyond mere translations of 'Lebanon' but rather by participating in a 'diasporic global public sphere' (Abdelhady, 2007) where gender norms and expectations across generations and in specific places are questioned and articulated. At first glance, both Ziad and Layal were invested in diasporic affiliations as central to their craft and this forms part of their broader work identities. They are called into the framework of multicultural arts on account of their transnational points of belonging but, as we see, both run into problems when their personal aspirations, interests and gender performativity challenge the simple templates available to them in these sectors. The differentiated ways in which young Lebanese Australian men and women carefully manage expressions of 'culture' as they pursue careers in highly competitive and exclusionary employment sectors were thus explored here to contribute to grounded accounts of how diasporic attachments are lived out in and across different settings.

References

Abdelhady, D. (2007) 'Cultural production in the Lebanese diaspora: memory, nostalgia and displacement', *Journal of Political and Military Sociology*, 35(1), pp. 39–62.

Abdelhady, D. (2011) *The Lebanese Diaspora: The Arab Immigrant Experience in Montreal, New York, and Paris*. New York: New York University Press.

Abdulhadi, R., Alsultany, E. and Naber, N. (2011). *Arab and Arab American Feminisms: Gender, Violence, and Belonging*. Syracuse, NY: Syracuse University Press.

Aly, R.M.K. (2015). *Becoming Arab in London: Performativity and the Undoing of Identity*. London: Pluto Press.

Batrouney, A. and Batrouney, T. (1985) *The Lebanese in Australia*. Melbourne: AE Press.

Bayeh, J. (2017) 'Arab-Australian fiction: national stories, transnational connections', *Mashriq & Mahjar: Journal of Middle East and North African Migration Studies*, 4(2), pp. 66–96.

Bhabha, H.K. (1994) *The Location of Culture*. London: Routledge.

Brah, A. (1996) *Cartographies of Diaspora: Contesting Identities*. London: Taylor & Francis.

Dagistanli, S. (2007) '"Like a pack of wild animals": moral panics around "ethnic" gang rape in Sydney', in Poynting, S. and Morgan, G. (eds) *Outrageous! Moral Panics in Australia*. Hobart: ACYS Publishing, pp. 181–197.

Harris, A. and Hussein, S. (2018) 'Conscripts or volunteers? Young Muslims as everyday explainers', *Journal of Ethnic and Migration Studies*, 46(19), pp. 3974–3991.

Humphrey, M. (2001) 'Lebanese since 1970', in Jupp, J. (ed.) *The Australian People*, 2nd ed. Cambridge: Cambridge University Press, p. 561.

Hyndman-Rizk, N. (2016) 'No arranged marriages here: migration and the shift from relations of descent to consent in the Lebanese diaspora', *Journal of Intercultural Studies*, 37(3), pp. 303–319.Idriss, S. (2017). *Young Migrant Identities: Creativity and Masculinity*. London: Routledge.

Idriss, S. (2021) 'The ethnicised hustle: narratives of enterprise and postfeminism among young migrant women', *European Journal of Cultural Studies*, doi: 10.1177/1367549421988948

Idriss, S. and Morgan G. (2018) 'The inertia of masculinity: narratives of creative aspiration among Arab-Australian youth', in Walker, C. and Roberts, S. (eds) *Masculinity, Labour and Neoliberalism*. Basingstoke: Palgrave, pp. 219–241.

Liu, H. (2016) 'Beneath the white gaze: strategic self-Orientalism among Chinese Australians', *Human Relations*, 70(7), pp. 781–804.

Monsour, A. and Convy, P. (2008) 'Sydney's people: the Lebanese', *Sydney Journal*, pp. 70–78.

Morgan, G. and Idriss, S. (2012) '"Corsages on their parents' jackets": employment and aspiration among Arabic-speaking youth in Western Sydney', *Journal of Youth Studies*, 15(7), pp. 929–943.

Obeid, M. (2013) 'Home-making in the diaspora: bringing Palestine to London', in Quayson, A. and Daswani, G. (eds) *A Companion to Diaspora and Transnationalism*, 1st edn. Malden, MA: Wiley-Blackwell, pp. 366–380.

Peteet, J. (2007) 'Problematizing a Palestinian diaspora', *International Journal of Middle East Studies*, 39, pp. 627–646.

Poynting, S., Noble, G., Tabar, P., and Collins, J. (2004) *Bin Laden in the Suburbs: Criminalising the Arab Other*. Sydney: Institute of Criminology.

Prieur, A. and Savage, M. (2013) 'Emerging forms of cultural capital', *European Societies*, 15(2), pp. 246–267.

Rawsthorne, S. (2019) 'Gang rapist Mohammed Skaf: his life behind bars', The Sydney Morning Herald, 30 June. Available at: www.smh.com.au/national/gang-rapist-mohammed-skaf-his-life-behind-bars-20190627-p5220c.html. (accessed 26 February 2021).

Reay, D., Davies, J., David, M., and Ball, S. (2001) 'Choices of degree or degrees of choice? Class, "race" and the higher education choice process', *Sociology*, 35(4), pp. 855–874.
Spivak, G.C. (1990). *The Post-Colonial Critic: Interviews, Strategies, Dialogues*. London: Routledge.
Tabar, P. (2014) '"Political remittances": the case of Lebanese expatriates voting in national elections', *Journal of Intercultural Studies*, 35(4), pp. 442–460.
Tabar, P. (2020) 'Transnational is not diasporic: a Bourdieusian approach to the study of modern diaspora', *Journal of Sociology*, 56(3), pp. 455–471.
Tabar, P., Noble, G., and Poynting, S. (2010) *On Being Lebanese in Australia: Identity, Racism and the Ethnic Field*. Beirut: Lebanese American University Press.
White, R. (2007) 'Lebanese young people in a climate of conflict', in Jupp, J., Nieuwenhuysen, P. and Dawson, E. (eds) *Social Cohesion in Australia*. Melbourne: Cambridge University Press, pp. 70–79.

PART IV
Class, livelihood and mobility

18
EXPLORING THE CREATIVE ISRAELI DIASPORA

Reading class and profession in the diaspora

Nir Cohen and Steven J. Gold

Introduction

The past two decades have seen much criticism of the use of ethno-nationally bounded conceptualisations of diaspora (Werbner, 2002). Inspired by postmodernist theories, critics have called for the abandonment of the exclusively ethnic prism and for greater attention to be paid to variegated sub-categories within the general group, as suggested by the critique of methodological nationalism (Wimmer and Glick Schiller, 2003; Brubaker, 2005). The problem of 'groupism', as it was commonly referred to, not only render diasporas a reified and unitary actor, and privileges the place of origin ('homeland') in the formation of its members' identities (Anthias, 1998), but helps conceal salient differences that exist among them. Paying attention to these differences, including *inter alia* gender, ethnicity and race, is important to understand diasporas as heterogeneous social groups whose members affiliate in radically different ways with each other, as well as 'outsiders' (Mavroudi, 2007).

Yet, despite a growing literature about this process of de-clustering, primarily concerning gender and ethno-religiousness, relatively little attention has thus far been paid to other cleavages that exist within diasporas. Missing, in particular, are accounts detailing the importance of class and/or professional identities in the formation of sub-diasporic groups (but see Nessi Garcia and Guedes Bailey, 2019). Such accounts are needed for three main reasons. First, increasing international mobility, primarily to a handful of Northern destination countries, not only has enlarged existing diasporic communities in these countries but also further diversified them. The result is an unprecedentedly (super)diverse diaspora (Jones, 2020), whose members differ considerably on a range of parameters, class included (Lan, 2012). Second, diasporas, like other social collectives, experience rising levels of internal economic disparities. Fuelled by existing global inequalities, but also the faster economic advancement of *some* of their members, these disparities bring class identities to the fore in diasporic sub-group formation processes. Third, many diaspora strategies, namely policy initiatives 'aimed at developing and managing [sending state] relationships with a diaspora' (Ancien, Boyle and Kitchin, 2009, p. 3) segment their target populations by class/profession. Programmes designated to court diasporic subjects possessing high levels of economic (e.g. business owners, investors) or cultural (e.g. academics) capital have

DOI: 10.4324/9780429266102-22

proliferated in recent decades, producing ever more class/professional segmented diasporas (see Dickinson and Bailey, 2007).

In this chapter, we explore the emergence of a specific professional/class sub-group within the Israeli diaspora. Taking after Florida's (2002) notion of the Creative Class, namely individuals whose primary economic function is 'to create new ideas, new technology and/or new creative content',[1] we posit that this group constitutes a new class-based formation within the general Israeli diaspora. In addition to being highly educated/skilled and employed in white-collar professions in fields like science and engineering, architecture and design, arts, music and entertainment, group members share several important characteristics. First, their migration is motivated by an assortment of pecuniary and non-pecuniary reasons, most notably professional advancement and a more broadly engaged lifestyle in destination countries. Second, they are disproportionately concentrated in global city-regions (e.g. New York, San Francisco, London and Berlin) and, often, in specific areas within them. Third, they show high rates of entrepreneurship or self-employment in their chosen fields of specialisation. Fourth, they possess high levels of cultural capital (e.g. good command of English, dual citizenship), and as a result, tend to be more mobile and hold more liberal and cosmopolitan sociopolitical views. Finally, their privileged socio-professional profile allows them a smoother integration into labour markets in destination countries, and appreciation for culturally specific products and symbols, including urban amenities and job-specific benefits.

Conceptualising creative Israelis as a discrete (sub-)group requires some early clarifications. First, we are *not* claiming that they are entirely disconnected from the broader (Israeli and Jewish) diasporas. Indeed, many admit they retain a strong sense of affinity with both groups, particularly at times of rising anti-Semitism – or anti-Israel sentiments – in some destination countries. Still, because of their advanced levels of economic and cultural capital, creatives may well be seen as a distinct group that maintains 'soft' boundaries vis-à-vis the broader ethno-religious/national diaspora. Second, the creative diaspora is by no means a fixed social category; rather, its porous boundaries are socially constructed and constantly change. These changes result partly from the specific spatio-temporal contexts within which group members live, work and socialise, as well as the relationships they forge vis-à-vis social and political agencies in both Israel and destination countries. Finally, while a small but growing proportion of Israeli creatives who reside abroad are (Muslim or Christian) Arabs, for purposes of brevity, this chapter draws on the experience of Jewish Israelis only.

The chapter consists of four sections. We first survey the literature on creative professionals, including their migration patterns. We then provide the necessary background on the history of skilled migration from Israel, focusing primarily on recent decades. Later we describe the socio-demographic and geographic characteristics – and draw the porous contours – of what we term 'the creative Israeli diaspora'. We conclude by discussing the benefits of using a class/professional perspective in diaspora studies.

Creative migration: a theoretical prelude

The Creative Class is a geographical-economic thesis developed in a series of publications by Richard Florida (2002; 2005; 2006). Its central tenet is that for cities to remain economically competitive, they must strengthen their capacity to attract a specific professional class, termed 'creatives'. These are individuals who produce economic value through their creativity, that is, their ability 'to create new ideas, new technology and/or new creative content' (Florida, 2002, p. 8). Alongside a 'core' group, which consists of '[P]eople in science and engineering, architecture and design, education, arts, music and entertainment' (ibid.), this class also includes

'[A] broader group of *creative professionals* in business and finance, law, health care and related fields … [which] engage in complex problem solving that involves a great deal of independent judgement and requires high levels of education or human capitals' (ibid). Creatives of both groups differ from other (working and service) classes in their enhanced autonomy and flexibility in their professional engagements as well as environments, known as the 'No-Collar Workplaces' (ibid., pp. 116–117).

These qualities, along with the 'footloose' nature of their professions, which could be put to use in multiple locations, make creatives a fairly mobile class (Comunian, Faggian and Li, 2010; Hansen and Niedomysl, 2009). Despite continental variations (Martin-Brelot et al., 2010), the geography of creatives seems to follow consistent patterns and they are drawn primarily to so-called 'Creative Centres', large cities that offer them '[A]bundant high quality amenities and experiences, an openness to diversity of all kinds, and above all else the opportunity to validate their identities as creative people' (Florida, 2002, p. 218). The availability of 'Technology, Talent and Tolerance', acronymically known as the three T's, makes these centres an '[I]ntegrated eco-system or habitat where all forms of creativity can take root and flourish' (Florida, 2005, p. 35). These centres are not necessarily traditional corporate communities or even climatically-friendly (e.g. Sun Belt) cities; rather, in North America, they include such city-regions as the San Francisco Bay Area (Silicon Valley), Boston, Austin and Seattle (ibid.), and in Europe – Amsterdam, Barcelona, Berlin, Copenhagen and Dublin (Martin-Brelot et al., 2010).

Little empirical research exists on the international migration patterns of creatives (King, 2011). However, studies using close proxies, like high levels of human capital (e.g. researchers and scientists), entrepreneurship or advanced technological expertise, show they generally correlate with higher-than-average cross-border mobilities (Solimano and Pollack, 2004; Regets, 2007; Bach, 2008). These findings are consistent with the self-selection model in migration studies, which posits that migration is driven by a basic mismatch between individuals (e.g. workers) and places (e.g. countries of origin). The greater the mismatch, the likelier the worker is to leave his country. Consequently, workers with the highest levels of human capital are the likeliest to emigrate from countries in which their skills are (monetarily) under-valued (Borjas, Bronars and Trejo, 1992).

The over-representation of the highly skilled – and creatives specifically – among migrant populations calls for a more nuanced inquiry of their profile, primarily in relation to other diasporic sub-groups. For example, do creative migrants differ geographically, socio-economically or culturally from non-creative migrants originating from the same country, and if so, how? Although a definite answer to this question requires an advanced (quantitative) analysis of the creative group, our objective in this chapter is to present in broad brushstrokes the salient characteristics of its members and argue that these qualify them as a new class/profession-based (diasporic) formation. Before honing in on these characteristics, let us briefly discuss contemporary patterns of emigration from Israel.

Skilled migration from Israel: an overview

Emigration from Israel is as old as the state (Cohen, 2013), estimated at 575,000 total outward migrants (Nathan, 2017), approximately 6.5 per cent of its current population. The volume of Israeli emigration has always been a contentious issue, but recent years have seen greater concerns over the socio-professional make-up of those departing. The rapid drain of Israeli brains was attributed to socio-economic conditions, but also rounds of regional violence, notably the second Palestinian Intifada (2000–2004) and the second Lebanon War (2006), as well as massive cuts in higher-education budgets. Studies show that Israelis with advanced professional skills who are in high demand in destination countries are more likely to emigrate (Gould and Moav, 2007) and remain abroad, but also maintain transnational ties, compared with their low-skilled co-nationals for whom the migratory process is more expensive, tumultuous and, often, temporary (Gold and Hart, 2013). Data reveal that while the plight of the highly educated cuts disciplinary boundaries, it is particularly acute for those in academic STEM fields and medical doctors. Figures were even higher among PhD graduates in the biological sciences, engineering, architecture and information technology-related fields (Israel National Brain Gain Program, 2016).

High rates of out-migration were also recorded among graduates of non-STEM academic disciplines. It is estimated that the annual net migration balance for education, humanities and social science graduates at all levels combined exceeds 1,200 (ibid.). A large proportion of individuals are in core artistic industries, including architecture and design, culinary, media, music and visual arts. The current wave of creatives is made up of mostly young, aspiring individuals who seek international recognition as a means to be acknowledged in the home country.

Creatives, like Israeli migrants more generally, gravitate towards a handful of highly developed, mostly English-speaking countries. In 2000, two-thirds (66 per cent) of the 164,000 first-generation adult migrants (over 15 years of age) Israelis in 25 OECD countries were living in the United States (Cohen, 2011). An additional fifth (20 per cent) lived in Canada, the United Kingdom and Australia. Sizeable, though smaller, émigré communities also exist in France, Germany (15,000–20,000 each) and the Netherlands (10,000). In addition to their liberal political systems and dominance of English in conducting business affairs, the high proportion of skilled Israelis in Western democracies is attributed to these destinations' prospering economies, which allow them to maximise returns on their professional capital.

Israeli creatives: a profile

Owing to their skills and lucrative occupations, the earnings of Israeli migrants, and those in creative sectors, in particular, are considerable. In the United States and Australia, for example, the median household income of Israeli-born individuals is significantly higher than native-born (Rebhun and Lev-Ari, 2010; Porat, 2015; Gold, 2016). But it is not only economic comfort, reflected in higher earnings, that pulls Israeli creatives to destination countries. Since many of them were doing well *prior* to emigration, most attributed their relocation to a mixed set both pecuniary and non-pecuniary – mostly professional and cultural – reasons.

The experiential life (Florida, 2002, pp. 165–189) sought by creatives is reflected in part through their passion for exploring new cultural terrains. Yet, their quest for such multidimensional experiences does not preclude the need to make ends meet, especially among older creatives. The oscillation between the rationally economic and culturally open outlook of many creatives is captured in the words of Aviel, a software engineer who spent four years in China before moving to the United States with his family:

> You see, we've always wanted to move somewhere. Ever since we were students, we wanted that. Both of us like to travel, like adventures. We've always looked for that experience and it didn't work out. We always thought about the US, but when I had the opportunity it wasn't what I had in mind because it practically meant eating up our savings. So, when the opportunity in China presented itself, it was more challenging professionally and [more rewarding] economically.

In line with Florida's prediction (2002), softer socio-cultural considerations also play a critical role in creative migration. Thus, for example, qualitative studies show that Israeli creatives seek more serene lives (Cohen and Kranz, 2015). Peacefulness overseas is defined in one of two ways; first, at the macro-level, as a (temporary) getaway from the consequences of geopolitical regional instability. Though small, a surge in the number of departing Israelis was observed, for example, during the wave of Palestinian suicide bombing attacks in 1995–1996 and, later, the second Intifada (2000–2004) as well as following the second Lebanon War (2006). Some of the departed during these times, though certainly not all, were creative professionals, for whom the option of international mobility was always imminent, and who decided to capitalise on it when tensions mounted. The following depiction by Meirav, a Data Security Manager who immigrated to Israel from Russia as a young girl, is illustrative of this motivation:

> When my son was born, it was during the last operation in Gaza [Operation Protective Edge] … The rockets [fired from Gaza] were scary, and we were living in Central Tel Aviv at the time. It was scary to go down to the bomb shelter with a baby, in the middle of breastfeeding. I guess I took it too hard … some of my [native] Israeli friends took it less seriously, but somehow it had a big effect on me. And right there in the bomb shelter I told my husband, 'go on, look for [employment] options [overseas]'. [Laughing] I guess he took my words literally.

Second, other creatives, especially those with a history of activism in Israel, expressed disillusionment with the social and political impasse, both internally (between liberals and hardliners) and externally vis-à-vis the Palestinians. Thus, for example, some young professionals who were leading figures in the 2011 social protest have reportedly left the country since. One of them, stating his disappointment with its outcomes was quoted as saying, 'I don't want a monologue about leaving for ideological reasons, but I have big and bubbly anger about the way in which this whole business is run and we, citizens, pay the price' (cited in Arad, 2013). More recently, a small but growing out-migration of critical Israeli academics has also been documented. Interviewed for a newspaper article, one of them explained his decision to leave by the loss of hope for political change:

> People with a similar political profile to mine have the feeling that we have been defeated and that we will no longer be able to exert a meaningful influence in Israel. In a profound sense, we do not see a horizon of repair, of true peace or a life of quality. A great many people understood this and looked for another place to live. There is something quite insane in Israel, so to look at it from a distance is at least a little saner.
> *(quoted in Littman, 2020)*

A more common search for peacefulness is found in the desire expressed by many to live in less stressful everyday social environments. Although most are doing well economically, creatives in Israel, especially those who are in their thirties and forties and parent young children, are challenged by their time-consuming social obligations. Expected to work long hours, raise families and fulfil customary social roles (attend/host family dinners and care for ageing parents), many creatives described the carefree environment in their new places of residence in very positive terms. As Uri, a web-designer in San Francisco, recalls:

> After we landed here [the US], and the first weekend approaches, and then Friday, when everybody starts relaxing, and then Saturday kicks in, and then Sunday, and

you sit relaxed in your back yard and say to yourself, 'Wow, wait a minute, what an improvement'. I mean, the weekend has turned from being about last-minute shopping of Friday in Israel, where you run around like crazy trying to get everything you need before stores close, to Saturday *and* Sunday – everything is open, you can take road trips as much as you want ... and, I hate to admit it, but it's nice that the family gets off your back.

Others were similarly fond of the social and cultural amenities their chosen urban environments had to offer them. Miri, for example, who relocated to Berlin with a humanities degree claims that in addition to its affordability, '[T]he atmosphere [in the city] is serene ... [and] I believe that the overall energy of the place you live in affects you' (cited in Shtauber and Fortuna, 2016, p. 14). Irit, an architect pursuing a PhD in Cambridge, similarly explains, 'I cannot get enough of the urban space, the beauty and serenity of it, a lifestyle that is embedded in the city ... [it] allows for intellectual creativity and freedom' (Drukker, 2013, p. 18). Ron, an Amsterdam-based data security analyst also emphasises the stress-free environment in his new city of residence:

Work-life balance is much better here. In Israel, when I was returning home at 8 p.m., my wife would say 'Oh, you came home early today'. Here, I finish working at 7 p.m. and there's no one around ... because everyone is gone by 4:30 or 5 p.m. People give their eight hours, drop everything and go home. What's more, no one calls you [after working hours], and if they do, they are apologetic. [So] ... you have time ... to have hobbies, travel, [things which] in Israel you simply have no time for.

Another determinant, which many creatives cited, was Israel's limited opportunities for professional development. Particularly in constantly evolving technological niches or those requiring engagement with specialised markets, being in proximity to 'where things happen' was often quoted as a main reason for leaving the country. The following description by Noa, a Director of Growth in a business consulting firm in New York, is typical of the migratory trajectory of many creatives we have interviewed since the early 2000s:

I realised that our market was in the US. That's where our clients are today, that's where our organic growth takes place, and if you want to catalyse it, it's there. So, my proposal ... was, 'we must open offices there, we must have [direct] contact with the market'. So, we realised that it needs to be done and that I need to be the one to open our New York office in order to move things along.

Creatives in the IT sector typically justified relocation by referring to the need to ensure that their firms acquire and assimilate cutting-edge technologies not readily available in Israel. While all were unanimous that Israel is a major hub of innovation, they admitted that the United States, and Silicon Valley in particular, remains the most important IT cluster globally. Avishay, an entrepreneur, who sold two start-up firms to giant US-based corporations, claimed that despite Israel's thriving IT ecosystem, moving to the Valley was inevitable. In his words, 'It's like [John] Lennon said, "If I'd lived in Roman times, I'd have lived in Rome." So today Silicon Valley is the Rome of technology, so I had to move here.'

Although their advanced skills could potentially open the doors for them in multiple locations, creatives settle primarily in global cities (Florida, 2005). Israeli migrants are no different in this respect. It is estimated that the largest concentrations of Israeli creatives include New York,

Boston, San Francisco, London, Berlin and Amsterdam. In addition to ample job opportunities, these global city-regions provide them with liberal, culturally dynamic urban environments, and put them near other skilled migrants – co-nationals and others. Consequently, many creatives prefer living in ethnically diverse urban sections (e.g. Berlin's Neukolln) and not in traditionally Jewish neighbourhoods (e.g. London's Golders Green, West Los Angeles and New York's Forest Hills), where earlier waves of less-skilled Israeli migrants gravitated towards (Gold, 2018).

Retreating from these locations allows them to maintain spatial – but not necessarily social – distance from established diasporic Jews, but also from other (non-)creative Israelis. For some, this results in dispersed residential geographies, which elevates their sense of 'social' freedom while enabling them – and their children – to choose their (creative) Israeli friends selectively. Shira, for example, a biomedical engineer in Silicon Valley, noted having Israelis in their township was 'not a consideration, [because] if he wants to see his [Israeli] friends after school its only 15–20-minute drive, so it's really no big deal'.

Miki, a development engineer in the Hague, admits that 'keeping distance' from other co-nationals and co-ethnics was a deliberate decision:

> We chose to send our kids to an English-speaking private school, which is already a statement about disengagement from the [Israeli] community but also 'Native' Dutch. Being near Israelis wasn't a consideration ... [But] I don't even know if it is a good idea [to live in neighbourhoods that have a high percentage of Jewish/Israeli residents] because you then enter an Israeli Ghetto, you lose the experience of the place, and you totally disconnect [from the Dutch environment]. Because you *do* want the excitement, to feel the 'other'.

Havah, whose family resides in Silicon Valley, describes Israelis' difficulty in relating to diaspora Jews:

> There is a big inability to relate to American Jews . . . If I meet an East Coast kind of typical Jew, I don't know what I should do. I feel that there is a minority mentality there that I can't decipher. It is very embarrassing for me. He is trying to communicate in a way that is fathomable to another American Jew and I can't figure it out.
>
> *(cited in Gold, 2018, p. 139)*

In the United States, Israeli creatives like Havah tend to concentrate in culturally diverse, economically innovative and intellectually vibrant communities on the East and West Coasts (e.g. Boston, New York, the San Francisco Bay Area) while avoiding more prosaic locations. Outside the United States, Israeli migrants are well integrated in the United Kingdom, where their number is estimated at 23,000 (Graham, 2015). London, where 60 per cent of them reside, is especially bustling with Israeli creativity. Some of its chief representatives include *inter alia* renowned chefs (Yotam Otolengi and Sami Tamimi), architects (Ron Arad), critical academics (Eyal Weizmann, Ilan Pappe), musicians (Sagi Hartov, Doron Erez) and photographers (Uri Gersht). Migrants play an active role in the city's IT industry as well as those of adjacent Cambridge (aka 'Silicon Fen') and Oxford. The so-called 'Golden Triangle' is home to an excess of 70 Israeli start-up firms specialising in a range of fields, including fintech, digital media and online marketing (Orpaz, 2016). Recent initiatives to institutionalise relations with these firms and draw additional creative entrepreneurs from Israel include the UK-Israel Tech

Hub at the British Embassy in Tel Aviv and 'Mind the Tech', a London-based conference which aimed at matching British investors and Israeli start-up firms (Videl, 2019).

In recent years, Berlin has also become a hub for Israeli creatives. Its multicultural environment and modest cost of living have drawn many visual artists, musicians, designers and graduate students. With one quarter of arrivees reportedly equipped with EU citizenship,[2] many within the 10,000-strong community in the city engage in creative sectors (Kranz, Rebhun and Sünker, 2015). The popular image of 'Israeli artists who conquered Berlin' (Friedman, 2012) is corroborated by qualitative studies showing the high concentration of creatives in the city. Thus, the majority of subjects interviewed for a Technion-sponsored study on Israelis in Berlin were employed in creative industries, including high technology, academia, music and the arts (Shtauber and Fortuna, 2016). In contrast to the cultural commercialisation of some artistic fields in Israel, they found the city's thriving arts scene particularly appealing. As Michal, a cellist, explained: 'I came to Berlin because I wanted to live off the music I love playing – Brahms and Beethoven, not Lior Narkis[3] and Bar Mitzvahs' (ibid., p. 13).

Israeli migrants are found among the highest rates of entrepreneurship of all national-origin groups in the United States and other points of settlement, including Europe, South Africa, Australia and Asia (Gold, 2004; Davone, 2007). Their success is achieved partly by cultivating extensive economic cooperation among themselves. In the past, these collaborations were formed in more traditionally ethnic (i.e. Jewish) economic concentrations, such as diamonds, garments, retail trade, cultural activities and kosher foods (Freedman and Korazim, 1986; Cohen and Gold, 1996; Gold and Phillips, 1996). Since the 1990s, with the advent of new technologies and the de-stigmatisation of Israeli emigration (Cohen, 2007), new forms of web-based, ethnic professional networks have emerged. Though some remain place-based, anchored primarily in destination city-regions like Israeli Career Networking in New York City, Israeli Musicians and Artists in Berlin and Israeli Business Club (IBC) London, others extend well beyond, tying creative Israelis from Israel and destination countries in (trans)national networks. The Israeli Executives and Founders Forum (IEFF) is a case in point. Conceived as a platform for networking, exchanging ideas and providing mutual assistance among Israelis in the IT sector who reside in Silicon Valley, it has gradually been joined by Israel-based professionals who visit the area frequently for business purposes. With over 1,000 subscribers communicating daily through a vibrant listserv, the forum sponsors meet-ups, business skill-enhancement workshops and TED-style talks for the benefit of its increasingly transnational membership base.

In contrast to regular ethnic networks, ethno-professional networks catering to creatives are focused exclusively on embedding them within their specific (trans)national sector – from finance to healthcare. While over time some networks may evolve and become platforms for other purposes than those for which they were originally established, they still retain a strong sense of professional sentiments, ushering in the production of 'soft' class-based boundaries with other less-skilled Israelis.[4]

At the same time, the class position of creative Israelis – both economically and intellectually – is often based on their high levels of education and earnings that allow them to pursue meaningful work, erudite social circles and stimulating environments. In contrast, less educated and affluent Israel immigrants associated with traditional Jewish occupations and communities are far less focused on such concerns (Bellah et al., 1985; Gold, 2018). Eyal, for example, a financial analyst who holds an MBA from Cambridge, characterises Israelis he socialised with in the area as 'the crème de la crème ... [who] represent quality ... socio-demographic'. Similarly, Ravit, a product manager at a health-tech firm in San Francisco, admits that those in her social milieu constitute a distinct group in professional/class terms that stands apart from Israelis in other destinations cities:

> You feel that they are all educated, BA at least, if not higher than that, and much higher than that. People for whom education is very important. Most are either IT professionals or postdocs in fields, like you won't find here a postdoc in gender studies, but more in the area of computational linguistics, at least these are the people I have encountered.

However, they also admit there was a whole other group of Israeli migrants in these (and other) cities, who are markedly different. Drawing the professional/class and cultural, but also moral and geographic contours of that group, Meirav reminisced that in Vancouver, where she once resided, '[I] didn't have any [social] network, because Israelis [there] work in sales and all they want is to get high every evening', and Eyal proclaimed:

> There's also the other side here, you know. Folks of the 'mall kiosks' [Hebrew *Agalot*]. But they don't come to Silicon Valley. Cost of living here is too high, so it filters these things, but if you go down to Los Angeles, for example … you know, [Israeli] people move there for completely different reasons. These are people that flee the country [Israel] … you know, non-professionals, who only want to, you know, 'fuck the system', the Mall Kiosk people, we call them.

In some cases, these class/professional boundaries were also carried over to the political realm. Creatives interviewed shortly after one of Israel's recent rounds of national elections were particularly sensitive to the left-leaning, liberal orientation of their reference group. Arik, characterising Israelis in Silicon Valley said, 'They are very enlightened and Tel Avivians … I mean, very progressive in their worldview' and Ravit cynically summarised, 'When people ask where have the Knesset [Israeli parliament] seats of the Zionist Camp and Meretz[5] disappeared in the last elections? Well, three or four of them are here in Northern California.'

Since the 1990s, migration scholars have noted the growing prevalence of skilled migrants who acquire multiple citizenships for reasons related to practical and economic concerns and prestige rather than political loyalty or residential preference alone (Ong, 1999). Creative Israelis are well represented among this group (Harpaz and Mateos, 2019). Many of our interviewees had relatives (and spouses) or family origins in affluent Western societies as well as in nations with EU membership. Secure legal status and effective ties, personal and familial, to destination countries allow them unrestricted access to national job markets and enhance their chances to benefit from federal and city-sanctioned social and economic services, especially in the welfare states of Central and Western Europe. Ori, an Amsterdam-based web systems analyst, describes the advantages of his EU passport as follows:

> Once I got it [the job], it was easy. All I had to do was move here. I accepted [the job] in May and landed here in July. I needed no visa because I have a German passport. I zoomed through border control. [They gave me] no problems whatsoever. It was pretty fast and easy.

In many cases, the family lore and cultural baggage of Israeli migrants are rich with stories of – and techniques for coping with – life in foreign settings. Creatives who frequently hail from more privileged geographical and ethno-class backgrounds (urban communities in central Israel, upper-middle class, veterans of elite military units and academic institutions, Ashkenazim) are in a particularly advantageous position. In addition to their skills and citizenship status, many possess a cultural orientation and personal trajectories that are compatible with life outside Israel. Whether having spent time overseas as children of academic parents on sabbatical or travelled extensively in the course of their previous careers in Israel, creatives are often better prepared for the challenges associated with life away from home. Noy, an e-commerce specialist in Amsterdam, describes how her personal background affected her decision to relocate:

> As a child, I lived six years ... in European capital. Through my mom's work who was in high technology. I see my parents' decision, this act, as a formative experience. I was 3–9 years old. Those years had an enormous influence on me and gave us skills and tools that I could directly link to them. And now I give it to my children. It challenged me, and them now, to confront things we would have otherwise not. Adaptation to a new place, flexibility, problem solving, emotional strength to deal with changes, new language, new culture.

For Noy, and others, migration is a strategy to attain (or maintain) class-based advantages. Whether they remain abroad or opt to repatriate, the migratory experience allows them – and their children – to acquire considerable cultural capital that could easily be converted to professional and economic capital in either location. This process of class reproduction fortifies their position within the Israeli (diasporic) class structure and hardens boundaries vis-à-vis other co-nationals in Israel or abroad.

Conclusion

The chapter offers a new reading of Israeli migrants. Drawing on Florida's (2002) model, we suggest that highly skilled and educated Israeli migrants constitute a new ethno-professional segment within the broader diasporic community. Conceptualised as 'creative diaspora', this emerging group displays specific socio-demographic, cultural and geographic characteristics. In addition to being employed in such fields as science and engineering, architecture and design, arts, music and entertainment, 'creatives' are disproportionately concentrated in global city-regions, exhibit high rates of entrepreneurship, socialise and form ethno-professional networks with other creatives, and possess high levels of cultural capital, which facilitate their integration in destination countries.

While creatives are *not* entirely disconnected from the broader (Israeli) diaspora, due to their advanced levels of social, economic and cultural capital, they may well be seen as a distinct profession/class-based group with 'soft' boundaries vis-à-vis the broader ethno-national community. Such boundaries tend to 'soften' at times of rising anti-Semitism or Middle East conflicts, as creative and non-creative Israeli migrants come together in defence of what they perceive as an existential threat to themselves and/or the homeland. Accounting for these boundary-(un)making processes is not possible within the space of this chapter, but future studies should further explore them as well as their variations across destination countries.

Applying the creative lens may contribute to diaspora studies both conceptually and empirically. Conceptually, the creative angle facilitates an analysis that is simultaneously broader and more focused. On the one hand, it allows a more nuanced exploration of sub-diasporic groups, analysing them along socio-economic, geographic and professional lines. Simultaneously, drawing on creativity, and professional skills more generally, is potentially helpful in transcending tendencies towards the ethno-racial 'groupism' that is still prevalent across the field of diaspora studies.

Empirically, placing creativity at the heart of our analysis requires a closer engagement with the professional lives of migrants. By this, we not only mean their skill level or formal educational attainments but a broader outlook on their professional trajectories (e.g. career history), pre- and post-migration. From using (trans)national professional networks to adapting to culturally diverse working environments, creativity differs considerably across – and within – diasporic groups. In this respect, for example, the observable experience of Israeli creatives who are women is markedly different from their male co-nationals. Future research should account for these differences in different national contexts.

Finally, creative migrants are part and parcel of many diasporas. From Korean and Indian IT professionals in Silicon Valley to Syrian, Iraqi and Turkish physicians in German hospitals, these first-generation migrants constitute a growing segment within their respective groups. Yet, while their levels of education and professional qualifications may be on par with – or exceed – those of our Israeli interlocutors, their integration into destination labour markets may prove more difficult on account of their migratory trajectories, national background, or ethno-racial and religious identities. Thus, the experience of creative Israelis, who are predominantly White and hail from privileged socio-economic and national backgrounds, may be markedly different from creatives from those other groups. Against the backdrop of rising Islamophobia and a more general xenophobic discourse and policy towards (even the most skilled) asylum seekers in many destination countries, the creative experience is becoming ever more differentiated. An intersectional perspective, which juxtaposes class/profession with other salient identity markers, must inform future studies of diasporas.

Notes

1 'The Creative Class' (and 'Creative Economy' or 'Creative Industries') form a fuzzy concept with multivalent meanings, which has been subjected to various critiques (Peck, 2005). It includes '[L]arge lumpy occupational categories … [created] largely on the basis of educational attainment and credentials', and therefore '[E]xcludes all creative workers without degrees' (Markusen et al., 2008, pp. 26–27). Yet, interchangeable terms, like 'Cultural Economy' or 'Knowledge Economy', are also problematic because of their ostensibly economic orientation, focus on organisational outputs, or '[T]he production of novel ideas that subsequently lead to new or improved goods and services and organizational practices' (Powell and Snellman, 2004, p. 201; for critical reviews of both concepts, see, for example, Gibson and Kong, 2005; Smith, 2000). We therefore find creativity, namely the inventive and imaginative capacities that are embedded in individual – and groups of – workers, to be a more useful term in a chapter dealing with class formations.
2 This figure was reported for Germany as a whole, but since the overwhelming majority of Israelis in the country reside in Berlin, we believe it can be extrapolated.
3 A famous Israeli pop singer.
4 We realise, of course, that 'skill' is a socially constructed concept whose meanings vary considerably across time and space (see Liu-Farrer, Yeoh and Baas, 2021).
5 Left-leaning Israeli political parties.

References

Ancien, D., Boyle, M. and Kitchin, B. (2009) 'Exploring diaspora strategies: An international comparison: Lessons for Ireland'. NIRSA Working Paper.
Anthias, F. (1998) 'Evaluating 'diaspora': beyond ethnicity?' *Sociology*, 32(3), pp. 557–580.
Arad, R. (2013) 'Two years after the height of the protest, many activists are not in Israel anymore', *Haaretz Online*, August 14. Available at: www.haaretz.co.il/news/education/.premium-1.2095840 (accessed 4 March 2021).

Bach, S. (2008) 'International mobility of health professionals: brain drain or brain exchange', WIDER Research Paper, No. 2006/82, Helsinki, Finland: The UN University World Institute for Development Economics Research.

Bellah, R., Madsen, R., Sullivan, W.M., Swidler, A. and Tipton, S.M. (1985) *Habits of the Heart: Individualism and Commitment in American Life*. Berkeley, CA: University of California Press.

Borjas, G.J., Bronars, S.G. and Trejo, S.J. (1992) 'Self-selection and internal migration in the United States', *Journal of Urban Economics*, 32(2), pp. 159–185.

Brubaker, R. (2005) 'The "diaspora" diaspora', *Ethnic and Racial Studies*, 28(1), pp. 1–19.

Cohen, N. (2007) 'From overt rejection to enthusiastic embracement: changing state discourses on Israeli emigration', *GeoJournal*, 68(2–3), pp. 267–278.

Cohen, N. (2013) 'From nation to profession: Israeli state strategy toward highly-skilled return migration, 1949–2012', *Journal of Historical Geography*, 42, pp. 1–11.

Cohen, N. and Kranz, D. (2015) 'State-assisted highly skilled return programs, national identity and the risk(s) of homecoming: Israel and Germany compared', *Journal of Ethnic and Migration Studies*, 41(5), pp. 795–812.

Cohen, R. and Gold, G. (1996) 'Israelis in Toronto: the myth of return and the development of a distinct ethnic community', *The Jewish Journal of Sociology*, 38(1), pp. 17–26.

Cohen, Y. (2011) 'Size and selectivity patterns of Israeli born immigrants in OECD countries', *International Journal of Comparative Sociology*, 52(1–2), pp. 45–62.

Comunian, R., Faggian, A. and Li, A.Q. (2010) 'Unrewarded careers in the creative class: the strange case of bohemian graduates', *Papers in Regional Science*, 89(2), pp. 389–410.

Davone, R. (2007) 'Diasporas and development', Washington, DC: World Bank. Available at: http://documents.worldbank.org/curated/en/2007/01/7527868/diasporas-development. (accessed 15 July 2020).

Dickinson, J. and Bailey, A.J. (2007) '(Re)membering diaspora: uneven geographies of Indian dual citizenship', *Political Geography*, 26(7), pp. 757–774.

Drukker, T. (2013) 'Finding the words', *Jewish Renaissance*, Special Issue: 'Britain's Israelis', October. Available at: www.jewishrenaissance.org.uk/october-2013 (accessed 4 March 2021).

Florida, R. (2002) *The Rise of the Creative Class: And How It's Transforming Work, Leisure, Community and Everyday Life*. New York: Basic Books.

Florida, R. (2005) *Cities and the Creative Class*. New York: Routledge.

Florida, R. (2006) 'The flight of the creative class: The new global competition for talent', *Liberal Education*, 92(3), pp. 22–29.

Freedman, M. and Korazim, J. (1986) 'Israelis in the New York Area labor market', *Contemporary Jewry*, 7, pp. 141–153.

Friedman, L. (2012) 'That's how Israeli artists conquered Berlin', Mako News Online, September 9. Available at: www.mako.co.il/news-world/international/Article-1897da4a3540a31017.htm (accessed 7 March 2021).

Gibson, C. and Kong, L. (2005) 'Cultural economy: a critical review', *Progress in Human Geography*, 29(5), pp. 541–561.

Gold, S. (2004) 'Immigrant entrepreneurs and customers throughout the 20th century', in Foner, N. and Fredrickson, G.M. (eds.) *Not Just Black and White: Historical and Contemporary Perspectives on Immigration, Race and Ethnicity in the United States*. New York: Russell Sage Foundation, pp. 315–340.

Gold, S.J. (2016) 'Russian-speaking Jews and Israeli emigrants in the US: a comparison of migrant populations', in Gitelman, Z. (ed.) *The New Jewish Diaspora: Russian-Speaking Immigrants in the United States, Israel and Germany*. New Brunswick, NJ: Rutgers University Press, pp. 103–122.

Gold, S.J. (2018) 'Israeli infotech migrants in Silicon Valley', *RSF: The Russell Sage Foundation Journal of the Social Sciences*, 4(1), pp. 130–48. doi: 10.7758/RSF.2018.4.1.08

Gold, S.J. and Hart, R. (2013) 'Transnational ties during a time of crisis: Israeli emigration, 2000 to 2004', *International Migration*, 51(3), pp. 194–215.

Gold, S.J. and Phillips, B.A. (1996) 'Mobility and continuity among Eastern European Jews', in Pedraza, S. and Rumbaut, R.G. (eds) *Origins and Destinies: Immigration, Race and Ethnicity in America*. Belmont, CA: Wadsworth, pp. 182–194.

Gould, E.D. and Moav, O. (2007) 'Israel's brain drain', *Israel Economic Review*, (5)1, pp. 1–22.

Graham, D. (2015) *Britain's Israeli Diaspora: A Demographic Portrait*. London: The Institute for Jewish Policy Research.

Hansen, H.K. and Niedomysl, T. (2009) 'Migration of the creative class: evidence from Sweden', *Journal of Economic Geography*, 9(2), pp. 191–206.

Harpaz, Y. and Mateos, P. (2019) 'Strategic citizenship: negotiating membership in the age of dual nationality', *Journal of Ethnic and Migration Studies*, 45(6), pp. 843–857.

Israel National Brain Gain Program (2016) 'PhDs: numbers and employment data. Final Presentation'. Jerusalem: Ministry of Economy.

Jones, D. (2020) *Superdiverse Diaspora: Everyday Identifications of Tamil Migrants in Britain*. Cham: Springer.

King, K.M. (2011) 'Technology, talent and tolerance and inter-regional migration in Canada', in Andersson, D.E., Andersson, A.E. and Mellander, C. (eds) *Handbook of Creative Cities*. London: Edward Elgar Publishing, pp. 169–186.

Kranz, D., Rebhun, U. and Sünker, H. (2015) 'The most comprehensive survey among Israelis in Germany confirms the image: secular, educated, and left', *Spitz Magazine*, 4.

Lan, S. (2012) *Diaspora and Class Consciousness: Chinese Immigrant Workers in Multiracial Chicago*. London: Routledge.

Littman, S. (2020) 'After losing hope for change, top left-wing activists and scholars leave Israel behind', *Haaretz Online*, May 23. Available at: www.haaretz.com/israel-news/.premium.MAGAZINE-losing-hope-for-change-top-left-wing-activists-and-scholars-leave-israel-behind-1.8864499 (accessed 2 March 2021).

Liu-Farrer, G., Yeoh, B.S. and Baas, M. (2021) 'Social construction of skill: an analytical approach toward the question of skill in cross-border labour mobilities', *Journal of Ethnic and Migration Studies*, 47(10), pp. 2237–2251.

Markusen, A., Wassall, G.H., DeNatale, D. and Cohen, R. (2008) 'Defining the creative economy: industry and occupational approaches', *Economic Development Quarterly*, 22(1), pp. 24–45.

Martin-Brelot, H., Grossetti, M., Eckert, D., Gritsai, O. and Kovács, Z. (2010) 'The spatial mobility of the "creative class": A European perspective', *International Journal of Urban and Regional Research*, 34(4), pp. 854–870.

Mavroudi, E. (2007) 'Diaspora as process: (de)constructing boundaries', *Geography Compass*, 1(3), pp. 467–479.

Nathan, G. (2017) 'International migration Israel: 2016–2017: Annual Report', The OECD Expert Group on Migration. Available at: www.israel-sociology.org.il/uploadimages/26102017_4.pdf (accessed 2 March 2021).

Nessi García, L. and Guedes Bailey, O. (2019) 'The Mexican European diaspora: class, race and distinctions on social networking sites', *Journal of Ethnic and Migration Studies*, 45(15), pp. 3007–3022.

Ong, A. (1999) *Flexible Citizenship: The Cultural Logics of Transnationality*. Durham, NC: Duke University Press.

Orpaz, O. (2016) 'Relocation to the kingdom: Israeli startups take over London', *The Marker Online*, 1 May.

Peck, J. (2005) 'Struggling with the creative class', *IJURR*, 29(4), pp. 740–770.

Porat, R. (2015) *Ausraeli Jews in Australia: Profile of Israeli-born Australian Jewish Residents*. Melbourne: Monash University, The Australian Centre for Jewish Civilization.

Powell, W.W. and Snellman, K. (2004) 'The knowledge economy', *Annual Review of Sociology*, 30, pp. 199–220.

Rebhun, U. and Lev Ari, L. (2010) *American Israelis: Migration, Transnationalism, and Diasporic Identity*. Boston: Brill.

Regets, M.C. (2007) 'Research issues in the international migration of highly skilled workers: a perspective with data from the United States', Working Paper SRS 07-203. Arlington, VA: Division of Science Resources Statistics, National Science Foundation.

Shtauber, S. and Fortuna, G. (2016) *Israelis in Berlin: A Community in the Making*. Haifa: Technion, Samuel Neeman Institute for National Policy Research.

Smith, K. (2000) *What Is the 'Knowledge Economy'? Knowledge-Intensive Industries and Distributed Knowledge Bases*. Sydney: University of Western Sydney.

Solimano, A. and Pollack, M. (2004) 'International mobility of the highly skilled: the case between Europe and Latin America', Washington, DC: Inter-American Development Bank, Special Office in Europe.

Videl, E. (2019) 'Investors in London Conference: Israeli ecosystem is great', *Calcalist Online*, September 14.

Werbner, P. (2002) 'The place which is diaspora: citizenship, religion and gender in the making of chaordic transnationalism', *Journal of Ethnic and Migration Studies*, 28(1), pp. 119–133.

Wimmer, A. and Glick Schiller, N. (2003) 'Methodological nationalism, the social sciences, and the study of migration: an essay in historical epistemology' *International Migration Review*, 37(3), pp. 576–610.

19
MAKING MIDDLE-CLASS LIVES
Diaspora and belonging among Pakistanis in Dubai

Gennaro Errichiello

Introduction

Today, migrants to the Gulf Cooperation Council (GCC)[1] countries include a wide range of nationalities, though Indians, Pakistanis and Bangladeshis remain among the most prominent in terms of the scale of migration (Errichiello, 2012; De Bel-Air, 2018). Migrants in the GCC are considered temporary workers, and their status is regulated by the sponsorship system (*kafāla*)[2] which defines their ability to travel and work. The *kafāla* system ties migrants to a local employer (either a citizen or a firm). Until recently, contracts were limited to three years and, despite being renewable, the short duration of these arrangements has influenced the understanding of migration in the GCC as being both temporary and precarious.[3] While temporariness might entail detachment and limit what is often understood as modes of 'belonging', it has not impeded the feeling of 'home' making among diasporic subjects (Shah, 2017). Instead of assumptions about temporariness, lack of belonging and longing for home, diaspora formations draw our attention to the ways that home and belonging are actively constructed and negotiated in people's everyday life (Abdelhady, 2008).

At the heart of diaspora as an analytical concept, there is the idea of a population dispersed from an original homeland to two or more territories. Thus, 'home' and 'homeland' have become formative concepts that 'help us to map the contemporary field of diaspora studies' (Tölölyan, 2019, p. 22). The 'homeland forms the basis for collective memory, and for ethno-communal solidarity and consciousness' (Abdelhady, 2011, p. 11), representing a symbolic element around which diasporic subjects construct the myth of return. However, transnational migrants are considered as members of diaspora when they 'develop some familial, cultural and social distance from their nation yet continue to care deeply about it not just on the grounds of kinship and filiation but by commitment to certain chosen affiliations' (Tölölyan, 2019, p. 27). In his discussion of integration to the hostland among diasporic subjects, Sheffer (2013, p. 14) argues that even though some diasporans adjust to and accept 'norms, laws, patterns of behaviour, etc. that are prevailing in the countries of residence', they still retain their strong emotional and affective features and links with their homeland. In other words, the extent to which diasporans integrate with their new country of residence depends on a balance between their acceptance of the norms and laws of the host country and their feelings of connection to their original homeland (Sheffer, 2013). Diasporic subjects, especially the second and third generations, renegotiate their identity in light of the context in which they live, developing a hybrid culture and multiple loyalties, and exploring a sense of belonging that is constructed in everyday practices (Howell, 2000). The concept of class is of primary importance in how diasporic subjects understand and locate themselves as it affects and informs their modes of consumption and political orientation (ibid.; Leonard, 2000).

Transnationalism 'refers to some combination of plural civic-political memberships, economic involvements, social networks, and cultural identities reaching *across* and linking people and institutions in two or more nation-states in diverse, multi-layered patterns' (Morawska, 2011, p. 155, original italics). Beyond transnationalism, diaspora is a process, a project (Brubaker, 2005) through which diasporic subjects construct their sense of belonging. Diaspora is conceived of 'as an idiom, stance, a claim' (ibid., p. 12) endowed with symbolic capital, represented, among other things, by collective memory, communal consciousness, and notions of 'homeland' that allow diasporic subjects to 'overcome the – often considerable – obstacle of distance separating its communities' (Bruneau, 2010, pp. 35–36). Therefore, diaspora tends to emphasise emotional and affective ties existing within a dispersed community, and the sense of belonging that is, in turn, constructed in people's everyday lives (Suzuki, 2019).

Informed by fieldwork I conducted among Pakistani middle-class migrants in Dubai, this chapter provides an understanding of the modalities of belonging of diasporic subjects in the Gulf States. I use the notion of diaspora as a framework to identify how my interlocutors construct their sense of belonging in light of the hierarchies and exclusionary practices in place in the GCC countries in which they live and work. In these lives and contexts, diaspora emerges as a 'strategic resource', whereby the Pakistani middle-class migrants I interviewed in Dubai tend to preserve their Pakistani identity and background in such a way as to construct their sense of belonging within and beyond ethnic boundaries alone, for example, through class and culture consumption. Therefore, broadly understood as also involving practices and feelings about class, consumption and belonging, diaspora represents a resource that is strategically relevant insofar as it allows diasporic subjects to feel part of their homeland and host society in multiple ways.

Although the migration systems in the GCC countries rely on temporariness, middle-class migrants often stay for many years, repeatedly renewing their residence permits and in many cases having children, which has led to second generations become an emerging feature of the migration dynamics of the Gulf region (Ali, 2010; Shah, 2017; Akinci, 2019). My focus is therefore on the construction of belonging and the creation of a 'home away from home' in a context in which migration is expected to be temporary but ends up being a permanent or semi-permanent aspect of immigrants' lives and narratives. Following Vora (2013, p. 30), I include 'temporary' migrants from South Asia in the Gulf region as diasporic subjects and part of the broader South Asian diasporas who construct their sense of belonging and their claims about rights and citizenship in ways that are important and worth exploring. Whether they are legally construed as being permanent or temporary, migrant workers share with diasporic communities around the world a collective memory, racial and ethnic consciousness and a sense of belonging to the homeland. In turn, exploring these diasporic life worlds allows us to understand how subjects cope with the complexities and challenges of life in the Gulf region.

In the next section, I provide an overview of the literature on South Asian diaspora in the Gulf countries, which points to the use of diaspora as a framework to understand middle-class migrants in particular. I then draw on insights from my fieldwork among Pakistani middle-class migrants in Dubai where the relationships between belonging and class emerge. In doing so, I hope to demonstrate that while diasporic subjects feel a strong sense of belonging to their homeland and traditions, they also tend to construct an elaborate sense of belonging to the context in which they live, even when those contexts are characterised by uncertainty.

Class and the South Asian diaspora in the GCC countries

Diaspora is a multidimensional concept that 'challenges the discourse on assimilation by introducing concepts like nostalgia, hybridity, and diaspora space' (Vora, 2013, p. 28). In particular, diaspora scholarship has focused on the links between migrant communities dispersed across different countries and their homeland. Ethnographic accounts of South Asian migrants have mostly focused on their ability to cope with the complexities of the migration experience in the GCC countries (Gardner, 2010; Buckley, 2012; Vora, 2013; Kathiravelu, 2016). In her research on Indian middle-class elites in Dubai, Vora (2013) starts from the observation that the presence of South Asian migrants in the Arab Gulf countries became prominent after the discovery of oil, but that their presence in the diaspora literature has mostly been overlooked. She argues that the Indian diaspora in Dubai resembles that in the Global North, particularly when considering dynamics related to gender, class and religion. However, some differences are evident, and for Vora, these differences stem from the specific migration context in Dubai, and she argues that we need to think of diaspora not as a bounded socio-cultural unit, but rather as internally stratified and formed of different subjectivities. Indian middle-class elites in Dubai identify themselves as 'Indian' to position themselves 'against whites and Arabs. However, their racial consciousness also relies on separating themselves from both working-class labourers and elites' (Vora, 2008, p. 402). Such differences are evident in their practices of consumption, which are designed to distinguish them from 'Indians who took abuse and worked in demeaning position … and Indians who flaunted their wealth and were corrupted by the materialism of Dubai' (ibid., p. 402).

Gardner's (2010) research on the Indian community in Bahrain considers the Indian diasporic elite formed of professionals, skilled workers, and merchants, who bring their families with them to Bahrain. They are diasporic in the sense that they maintain ties with Indian diaspora communities around the globe. Gardner describes 'strategic transnationalism' as the ability of the Indian diasporic elite to construct transnational networks to reduce the vulnerability that non-citizens face in Bahrain while seeking to profit from local labour market opportunities. This has led Gardner to conclude that even members of the Indian diasporic elite are subjected to a certain extent to the vulnerabilities and constraints of the transnational proletariat. However, unlike the Indian working class, the Indian elite is able to cope with the vulnerabilities of the sponsorship system because they have the means and opportunities to opt for convenient strategies to relocate their family, work and invest in several places and locations through their links with Indian diasporic communities around the globe.

These studies demonstrate the relevance of social ties within diasporic communities, and how notions of home and belonging have to be renegotiated in light of their migration experience. It is also evident that class affects migration at least in the sense that resources available to low- and highly-skilled subjects determine how they cope with the difficulties and complexities of the migration experience in the GCC countries.

Making a home in Dubai and beyond

The The United Arab Emirates (UAE) is characterised by the presence of many foreign communities, cultures and religions; its population is socially, ethnically and religiously diverse. The first large-scale oil explorations in the 1950s and its exportation in the 1960s, the creation of the UAE federation in 1971 and the oil boom in the 1970s required a foreign workforce to implement development projects because of the small size of the local population and the lack of the necessary skills and vocations among the locals (Davidson, 2005). In the UAE, foreigners now comprise 88 per cent of the workforce (Rutledge, 2018); most of whom are employed in the construction sector and are overwhelmingly men from South Asian countries (Abdul-Aziz, Olanrewaju and Ahmed, 2018). The presence of foreigners represents both opportunities and anxieties for the UAE authorities because it has led to a so-called 'demographic imbalance' meaning that non-Emiratis outnumber Emiratis.

At the beginning of the twenty-first century, Dubai 'erupted onto the world stage as a media and tourism spectacle' (Vora, 2013, p. 6). Dubai's fascinating history, characterised in the nineteenth and twentieth centuries by extreme poverty and small population, dramatically changed between the 1950s and the 1970s when the oil economy transformed the poor and mercantile emirate into a modern and global city (Abdulla, 2006).

The links between South Asia and the Gulf States, especially the port cities, is historically documented; over several centuries these links have led large numbers of foreign merchants to settle in the coastal areas and port cities, such as Dubai and Abu Dhabi (Potter, 2009; Kanna, 2011). At the beginning of the twentieth century, the Indian and Iranian communities were the most important foreign communities in Dubai, whose merchants not only traded but also supported the rulers of the city financially. They constituted communities that were closely linked to political power, allowing them to push local authorities to naturalise some Iranians and (maybe) Indians.[4] Some Indian merchants did become (in)formal citizens of these newly independent states based on their historic links and privileges but in practice are considered 'half-citizens' (Vora, 2013). Between the 1950s and 1970s, the discovery of oil, the oil boom and the subsequent drive for development triggered new waves of migration, which led to Pakistanis becoming numerically relevant. In 1971, Pakistan was one of the first countries to recognise the UAE federation by establishing its embassy in the country (Ahmed, 1984). This official recognition led to a strengthening of the links between the two countries and fostered migration from Pakistan to the UAE. Pakistanis in the UAE numbered 1.2 million (De Bel-Air, 2018). According to data obtained from the Pakistani Consulate in Dubai, a third of Pakistanis in the UAE are employed in the construction sector and another third are employed in service jobs,[5] which suggests that the majority works in low-skilled jobs and are mostly men living in the labour camps. There are a few Pakistanis employed as professionals, however, and this group is the focus of my study.

The division of labour in the Gulf States has often led to nationals or locals being employed in the public sector and foreigners in the private sector (Baldwin-Edwards, 2011), which has intensified existing cultural, social and economic differences between nationals and foreigners. As Kathiravelu (2016) argues, such divisions create ethno-racial and gender hierarchies. For Vora (2013), these hierarchies are evident in local and transnational companies, which establish employees' payment scales based on nationality rather than skills. Consequently, South Asian employees are paid less than those originating from the Global North, who are sometimes less qualified and less experienced. Ethno-racial hierarchies go hand in hand with gender hierarchies: 'Occupations in the UAE are often divided along the lines of gender and nationality as well, with companies actively recruiting employees from certain parts of the world for gendered occupations' (ibid., p. 78). In the Gulf region, the majority of migrant women are employed as domestic workers (Fernandez, 2014). This specific niche of the local labour market, as Gamburd suggests, is not only gendered but also ethnically and religiously stratified: 'In the UAE, for example, within the housemaid category, housemaids from the Philippines are paid more than those from Indonesia, Sri Lanka, Ethiopia, and Bangladesh in that order. Racial, ethnic, religious, and national stereotypes predetermine wages' (2009, p. 70).

Vora shows how racial and class hierarchies among Indians in Dubai work and underlines how the Indian middle class tend to blame other migrants 'for the racism they experienced in their own lives, arguing that because uneducated and unskilled workers constitute the majority of South Asians in the Gulf, people assume all Indians are uneducated and unskilled' (2013, p. 131). Discrimination is thus embedded within a system of class differentiation in which the perception of the 'Other' (e.g. Indians) is stereotyped. Class and socio-economic status shape the self-understandings and social positionings of middle-class, working-class and elite Indians and determine benefits and advantages. Coming from the same country of origin does not necessarily entail being equally included in diasporic life (Amelina and Barglowski, 2019) but, as Vora (2013) emphasises, discrimination and exclusionary practices within the same migrant community are common.

In this context, characterised by economic development, historical links between South Asian and the Gulf countries and hierarchies, I conducted my field research. In this chapter, I draw on unstructured interviews and informal conversations with 20 Pakistani middle-class migrants in Dubai between 2014 and 2015. The 15 men and 5 women I focus on had varying occupations, such as managers and executives, doctors and teachers, and were also diverse in being Baluchi, Punjabi and Sindhi. All my respondents saw themselves as Muslim, with most of them being Sunni Muslims, while one participant was an *Ismāʿīlī* Muslim and one was an atheist with an Islamic background. The majority of them were first-generation migrants, meaning they were the first of their household to migrate to the GCC countries, but some of my participants were members of the second generation of Pakistanis who were born and brought up in the UAE or in other Gulf countries. Only one participant belonged to the third generation, whose grandparents migrated to Kuwait in the 1950s. The interview data have been anonymised and pseudonyms are used.

Temporariness, ethno-racial hierarchies and discriminatory practices in the Gulf States seem to conspire against the idea of belonging among diasporic subjects (Errichiello and Nyhagen, 2021). In this section, I analyse how belonging is constructed to demonstrate that, despite their temporary status, Pakistani middle-class migrants can be considered to be members of a Pakistani diaspora insofar as their family ties, transnational connections and networks are considered as a resource to be deployed to cope with the challenges posed by the GCC migration system.

Belonging is constructed in everyday experiences and practices (Yuval-Davis, 2011), it is more than shared values as it relates to locations, emotional and affective ties. Through a translocational lens, it is possible to treat 'lives as being located across multiple but also fragmented and interrelated social spaces of different types' (Anthias, 2015, p. 15). As migrants interact in the workplace and in their everyday lives with other nationalities including GCC nationals, they construct flexible modes of belonging to different communities. Belonging is thus fluid, dynamic, situational and flexible (May, 2011).

For my interlocutors, attachment to the homeland is a powerful tool for identification and belonging. For example, Abdallah (aged 49), a doctor who has spent more than ten years in Dubai, emphasised how his Pakistani passport is important for him and an expression of his Pakistani identity. Although he has spent many years working abroad, he has never thought of renouncing his Pakistani passport:

> I preserve my [Pakistani] passport, despite staying in Africa for so long. I still keep my own passport and I am very proud of it. I have travelled all over the world with it and never had any problems with it. It remains my identity and I am proud of it.

Abdallah's Pakistani passport is a material object with a strong symbolic and semiotic meaning for his sense of self as well as standing for the consistency of his emotional attachment to his homeland despite his long-term absence from it. Similar attachments to the homeland are expressed and reflected in the ritualised celebration of Pakistan Independence Day, which entails particular kinds of consumption practices. Independence Day (14 August) is considered by the Pakistani community in Dubai as one of the most significant events in the calendar, where listening to Pakistani music, watching Pakistani movies, speaking Urdu and displaying pictures of Pakistani leaders serve to manifest links within the Pakistani diaspora to the homeland. Importantly, they recreate a 'home away from home' rather than simply citing the Pakistani nation-state. The materiality of the passport and the consumption of media, food and clothing allow Pakistanis in Dubai to claim a 'Pakistaniness' that is situated in the UAE.

Attachment to the homeland and its cultural products and symbols does not preclude attachment to the Emirati context, especially as this context is multicultural and global. Some of the middle-class Pakistanis I interviewed had managed to forge relationships with Emirati nationals despite the hierarchies of separation created by the labour market. Leila (aged 36) moved to Dubai in 2000 when she got married and now works in business development for a private company. Although she emphasised the importance of preserving her Pakistani identity, especially for her daughter, she has also made clear that she feels at home in Dubai:

> I travel back [to Pakistan] often in order to maintain connections with her [daughter's] roots, so she has to know, where she comes from. She speaks Urdu ... fluently ... she has to know the language and where she comes from ... I do have Emirati friends ... my husband has got good and close Emirati friends who come over and they treat us as part of a big family ... I am saying the Emiratis who are known to us, once you know them, you are part of them.

Leila's emotional attachment to her homeland and her Emirati friends demonstrates that flexible belonging is constructed through shared values and customs as well as experiences and practices of everyday life in Dubai. Her close contact with Emiratis is a luxury that is afforded to very few non-nationals. Nonetheless, the absence of establishing friendships with Emiratis did not always mean a lack of attachment to the Emirates as a home. A more common form of interaction between Emiratis and migrants is characterised by cordial albeit superficial nature. Ibrahim (aged 74), who was a Chief Financial Officer at a public sector institution, said:

> They [Emiratis] have been very good whatever relations I have had, working with them or non-working with them. There are certain people [Emiratis] who sit downstairs in the cafeteria [ground floor of the building where he works], and they come for prayers. I do not know their names and they do not know mine. Every time I go for prayers, they come with me and we just share a laugh or a little joke. Wherever I worked, for example, I worked for two Emirati companies earlier, I worked with Emiratis and other Arab nationals they have been very friendly.

The friendliness Ibrahim describes underlines the good relations with Emiratis but only on a superficial level. As Ali (2010, p. 146) argues, migrants often have good relations with nationals, but it seems 'not to go beyond that'. Nonetheless, inhabiting and dwelling in the same places and institutions create some level of conviviality and sense of commonality.

While Dubai's global and multicultural make-up encourages contacts and exchanges among different diasporic communities and allows migrants to share affinities that move beyond similarities based on nationality or ethnicity, opportunities for sociality are often marked by class. Contacts with other diasporic communities are part of migrants' everyday life and motivate diasporic forms of flexible belonging. Farida (aged 28), who lives on her own in a gated community in Dubai and works for an international company, put it this way: 'I made a lot of friends from different nationalities at work. In school, I had mostly Indians, Bangladeshis and Pakistanis, and Arabs. Then in my neighbourhood, I used to have a Filipino family, some Chinese neighbours.' Farida emphasises the presence and coexistence of many different nationalities with whom she can live together and share the same spaces. Sometimes, these spaces reflect regional affinities, for example, Zia (aged 53), who owns his own company in Dubai, said: 'I have many friends, but they are mostly from Pakistan, and some Indians as well, not so much of Western people.' Zia emphasised a sense of belonging and cohesiveness with other diasporic communities, especially Indians. Hamza (aged 65) who arrived in Qatar in 1973 and then moved to Dubai where he spent the last few years working in a media company, shared an experience similar to Zia's:

> Even where I live, in my neighbourhood we meet every month, we have a potluck, which means that everybody brings one dish. It is about 10, 12 families, we are the only Pakistanis in there, the rest are all Indians. We are very good friends.

These social activities and contacts with other diasporic communities may represent modes of cosmopolitanism where diasporic subjects construct their belonging by crossing boundaries of ethnicity (Anthias, 1988). While they may engender a sense of belonging to the context, they remain marked by the ethno-class hierarchies and possibilities that are afforded by the context itself.

The Pakistani middle-class migrants feel that they belong to Dubai where they have spent many years, where some of them were brought up, where their children were born and where some of them have also established their own businesses. In the Emirati context, belonging for migrants is thus characterised by fluidity and flexibility but equally by structured constraints. Pakistani middle-class migrants in my study articulate the ways the multicultural milieu in Dubai allows them to simultaneously belong to people of the same ethno-national community in Dubai, in Pakistan and in other countries, and with individuals of different nationalities with whom they share everyday life, experiences and practices (Anthias, 2015). Naseer (aged 59) moved to the UAE following a short stay in Saudi Arabia at the end of the 1970s. He is now retired and has established his own company in Dubai:

> I belong to Pakistan, and I was born in Lahore, a beautiful city of Pakistan, the second-largest city, most populated, I feel very proud of my country ... I have lived a good 35 years in Dubai and three and a half in Saudi, you are totally assimilated, you cannot live anywhere else.

Naseer has expressed a strong attachment to his homeland, his customs and traditions, but, at the same time, he described his life in Dubai as being completely assimilated because he has spent 35 years in the city – more than half his life. It is noteworthy that the migration systems and structures in the Gulf States are explicitly designed to avoid assimilation as it is understood in a Western context. Yet, belonging is not only *determined* by formal structures of inclusion and/or exclusion, but it is also informed by experience, and it is often construed by migrants as part of a process of narrating their journey and sense of self in place (Errichiello, 2021). It is important for diaspora scholarship to recognise the complexity, opportunities and constraints that formal citizenship and/or a specific political project such as integration or assimilation have on diasporic subjectivities while always avoiding the conclusion that these *determine* belonging. In her account on Indian middle-class migrants, Vora contends that while they perceive Dubai as 'a place they did not belong' to, Dubai is also perceived and experienced 'as an "Indian" cultural space above all else, and therefore [they] described their reasons for being in the Gulf and their experiences there as impacted by more than just their jobs' (2008, p. 382).

For Vora (2013), diasporic communities are internally stratified and formed of different subjectivities evident in the way middle-class Indians position themselves against the Indian labourers and elite. This social stratification was also manifest among the Pakistani middle-class migrants I interviewed in Dubai; however, they expressed recognition of this stratification while also choosing to underplay its divisive nature. Hamza (introduced earlier) said:

> they [Pakistani low-wage migrants] are from a different mindset; they do not have education at all. So, they are accepted, we coexist, that's not the problem. The gardener in my house is Pakistani, and we treat him well, no discrimination against him … we treat him well.

Hamza is conscious of his status, which is marked in part by living in a gated community with other middle-class migrants from different nationalities. His positionality is reflected in consumption practices that are typically associated with the middle class. He can afford to hire a (Pakistani) gardener but class asymmetries in this relationship did not detract from his attachment to Pakistanis with different circumstances. Indeed, these class-based relationships between more and less privileged Pakistanis in the diaspora may reinforce ethno-national consciousness and ways of expressing and maintaining 'Pakistaniness' and status. Farida (introduced earlier) provides another example:

> I help whoever. For instance, a Pakistani colleague in our office passed away recently, he was 33 years old, we do something for his family, we have ex-colleagues who contact us and their family and they are suffering and we do something for them as well.

Farida's support moves within and beyond ethno-national consciousness. Relying on the help of her South Asian and European colleagues, she managed to provide assistance to the family of her Pakistani colleague, who worked as a cleaner in the office and passed away.

Religious support is equally important and builds on ethno-national affinities. Mahmud (aged 45), who arrived in Dubai in 2000 to become an entrepreneur, is a member of the *Ismāʿīlī* community in Dubai whose members are mostly of Pakistani origin. He explained how the community supports its members:

> One of our commitments is working with workers who are labourers, for example, we would try to get them driving licences or improve their job skills. If they are labourers, we would try to help them become technicians and if they are technicians, we try to help them to become supervisors. So, we support them, we educate them and help them move forward.

There is an ethnic, national and religious consciousness that leads Pakistani professionals to support their fellow nationals (and sometimes those belonging to other nationalities). Mahmud and members of the *Ismāʿīlī* community are in a privileged position that allows them to be charitable and redistribute their knowledge, experience and contacts to improve lower-class migrants' status.

Temporary middle-class migrants in the GCC countries are more likely to establish transnational connections and networks with diasporic communities to move to other countries than temporary working-class and/or unskilled migrants who are more likely to return to their country of origin (Gardner, 2010; Vora, 2013; Errichiello and Nyhagen, 2021). In his research, Gardner (2008, p. 74) used the term 'strategic transnationalism' to argue that the Indian elite in Bahrain rely on 'historic networks forged in the colonial and postcolonial era, and transnational networks that connect them to multiple continents'. When faced with the need to leave Bahrain, the Indian elite migrants that Gardner studied used their transnational connections to find a way to settle in a different country. The narratives of Pakistani professionals I interviewed in Dubai, to a certain extent, reflect the same strategy (Errichiello and Nyhagen, 2021). While their middle-class status has not prevented them from being exposed to precariousness, the Pakistani professionals I interviewed use transnational connections and family ties with members of diasporic communities already settled in other countries to migrate upon leaving Dubai, for example, in the United States or the United Kingdom. Sometimes, these transnational networks are also developed to facilitate the return to Pakistan. Some of my participants expressed a strong attachment to their country of origin and had already decided to return to Pakistan, where they may have bought a house. For example, Zia (introduced earlier) said:

> I have my own house [in Pakistan] … I have no intention to go to any other country. I will feel more relaxed and happier if I go to Pakistan rather than if I go and settle in Canada because, for example, my son is a Canadian resident now. So, he intends to call us to settle there, but I have no intention of going and spending the rest of my life there. I would rather be in Pakistan than in any other place.

Zia emphasised his emotional and affective ties with his home country and family. This emotional attachment has not hampered him from buying a house in Dubai, which demonstrates the attachment to Dubai, but equally reflects how mobile global middle classes use their economic and social capital to navigate and plan opportunities and curate attachments. Like Zia, other participants also stressed the wish to return to Pakistan and elaborated the meanings of feeling relaxed that Zia refers to. In Naseer's (introduced earlier) explanation, being free from the bureaucratic negotiation of his status and being able to put an end to his temporary status was important:

> I have my own house, I have a plot … since I was born there [in Pakistan] and I have too much love for my country and I am positive actually that I will be happy there … it is my own country, I do not have to renew my residence, I do not have to ask for a visa, I do not have to ask for a local sponsor there. And I feel proud of that actually.

Nasser's account points to the consequences of the formalised precarity of life in Dubai. As such, Pakistan is presented as a space of permanence, of inalienable rights and stability which, in his narrative, is reflected in an unbridled sense of belonging, even though he has not lived there for most of his adult life. In this instance, diasporic imaginings create spaces of belonging that are affective and practical. In contrast to Pakistani migrants who have settled in places like

Britain, return is not as mythological but rather a real and ever-present prospect that must be planned for both emotionally and practically (Anwar, 1979).

Equally, I encountered people who do not want to return to Pakistan but want to go to other diasporic locations. This was the case for Hamza who said he would 'move maybe not to Pakistan but maybe Canada or maybe America, we have our family there'.[6] It is common practice to join family members already settled in another country because, among other reasons, it is easier to get citizenship and sometimes to maintain their lifestyle. One of my participants, who has children in both the United States and in the United Kingdom, is likely to move to either of these two countries instead of returning to Pakistan. The different strategies and places where the Pakistani professionals I interviewed plan to move to upon leaving Dubai exemplifies diaspora as a 'strategic resource' that allows them to cope with challenges posed by the context and local rules.

Diasporic subjects share their everyday lives with different people who live side by side, such as in middle-class enclaves; go mostly to the same workplaces, schools and spaces; and share the same interests, ways of acting, tastes, dispositions, experiences and practices. Despite the temporariness and uncertainties of the migration experience, members of the Pakistani diaspora consider Dubai as a 'home' because some of them were brought up in the city and, even if they go to study in the United States or the United Kingdom, they prefer to return to Dubai as they feel that they belong to the Emirati context. For example, Aminah (aged 38), who works in an IT company, said:

> For university I went to America to study my bachelor then I came back, and I worked in Dubai for five years. Then I went to London to study for one year, then came back again and I continued my work over here. I grew up in Dubai and I was working in Dubai as well. I was used to this fast life, quick things, lots of things happening. Because, I have grown up here, I am very multicultural. I have friends with whom I grew up from school.

Aminah exemplifies the sense of belonging to the place where she grew up, the relevance of diasporic ties in the city where she had lots of friends, and where her ex-husband lives, who is able to support her being a single mother. Pakistani migrants use diasporic connections as a resource to cope with the challenges and difficulties of the migration experience in Dubai and to relocate themselves when they have to leave the country. Thus, assimilation may not just refer to a national context but to a diasporic condition itself where multiple places, particular lifestyles and transnational connections constitute a mode of life beyond the ethno-national framework (Errichiello, 2021).

Conclusion

In this chapter, I have discussed diaspora, belonging and class in the context of Dubai, one of the major cities in the GCC and a migrant hub. While analyses of diasporic communities and forms of attachment largely focus on contexts of permanent settlement in the Global North, this chapter analyses diasporic formation in the case of temporary middle-class migrants. As my research among Pakistani middle-class migrants demonstrates, temporary workers in the GCC countries express their sense of belonging and construct a 'home away from home' even if they cannot assimilate to their immigration contexts (Errichiello, 2021). Their temporary status does not prevent them from forging attachments within diasporic communities (Errichiello and Nyhagen, 2021), particularly when they use their transnational connections and networks in other countries to move and relocate themselves and their businesses elsewhere.

As Brubaker (2005, p. 12) argues, '"diaspora" is used to make claims, to articulate projects, to formulate expectations, to mobilize energies, to appeal to loyalties'. For the Pakistani middle-class migrants in Dubai, diaspora is a 'strategic resource' enabling them to deal with the uncertainties of the migration experience in the Gulf States. Like lower-class migrants, middle-class subjects are exposed to the vulnerabilities and constraints of the particular migration system. However, the latter are in a more privileged position than the former because they can use their diasporic ties to move and invest in a third country. As such, their settlement process in a Western country, for example, can be easy because they have the capital to move, and some of their family members have already settled there. Middle-class migrants tend to move to the West both to maintain their lifestyle, to get citizenship and become permanent residents.

Notes

1 The GCC members are Bahrain, Kuwait, Oman, Qatar, Saudi Arabia and the United Arab Emirates.
2 The transliteration of Arabic terms relies on the system used by the *International Journal of Middle East Studies*. The only exceptions are those terms that are commonly used in English (e.g. participants' names and geographical names).
3 However, the sponsorship system has recently undergone some changes (Zahra, 2019). In 2019, the UAE authorities implemented new rules allowing some categories of migrants to obtain a long-term visa. See www.government.ae/en/information-and-services/visa-and-emirates-id/residence-visa/long-term-residence-visas-in-the-uae (accessed 3 February 2020).
4 Naturalised Indians, or 'Indian Emiratis', have been mentioned in Vora's work (2013, p. 103), however, the real existence of this figure has not been proved; she 'never [found] this mythical Indian Emirati'.
5 Numerical data on the proportions of professionals and construction workers were provided by the Pakistani Consulate in Dubai to the author in November 2014.
6 In 2018, he moved to Canada where his son lives. Email received on 2 July 2018.

References

Abdelhady, D. (2008) 'Representing the homeland: Lebanese diasporic notions of home and return in a global context', *Cultural Dynamics*, 20, pp. 53–72.
Abdelhady, D. (2011) *The Lebanese Diaspora: The Arab Immigrant Experience in Montreal, New York, and Paris*. New York: New York University Press.
Abdul-Aziz, A.R., Olanrewaju, A.L. and Ahmed, A.U. (2018) 'South Asian migrants and the construction sector in the Gulf', in Chowdhury, M. and Irudaya Rajan, S. (eds) *South Asian Migration in the Gulf: Causes and Consequences*. London: Palgrave Macmillan, pp.165–189.
Abdulla, A. (2006) 'Dubai: the journey of an Arab city from localism to cosmopolitanism', *Al-Mustaqbal al-Arabi*, 323, pp. 57–84 (in Arabic).
Ahmed, S.A. (1984). '"Dubai Chalo," Problems in the Ethnic Encounter between Middle Eastern and South Asian Muslim Societies', *Asian Affairs*, XV(III), pp. 262–276.
Akinci, I. (2019) 'Culture in the "politics of identity": conceptions of national identity and citizenship among second-generation non-Gulf Arab migrants in Dubai', *Journal of Ethnic and Migration Studies*, 46(11), pp. 2309–2325.
Ali, S. (2010) *Dubai: Gilded Cage*. New Haven, CT: Yale University Press.
Amelina, A. and Barglowski, K. (2019) 'Key methodological tools for diaspora studies: combining the transnational and intersectional approaches', in Cohen, R. and Fisher, C. (eds) *Routledge Handbook of Diaspora Studies*. Abingdon: Routledge, pp. 31–39.
Anthias, F. (1988) 'Evaluating "diaspora": beyond ethnicity?', *Sociology*, 32(3), pp. 557–580.
Anthias, F. (2015) 'Interconnecting boundaries of identity and belonging and hierarchy-making within transnational mobility studies: framing inequalities', *Current Sociology*, 64(2), pp. 172–190.Anwar, M. (1979) *The Myth of Return*. London: Heinemann.

Baldwin-Edwards, M. (2011) 'Labour immigration and labour markets in the GCC countries: national patterns and trends', Kuwait Programme on Development, Governance and Globalisation in the Gulf States, LSE, Number 15.

Brubaker, R. (2005) 'The "diaspora" diaspora', *Ethnic and Racial Studies*, 28(1), pp. 1–19.

Bruneau, M. (2010) 'Diasporas, transnational spaces and communities', in Baubӧck, R. and Faist, T. (eds) *Diaspora and Transnationalism: Concepts, Theories and Methods*. Amsterdam: Amsterdam University Press, pp. 35–49.

Buckley, M. (2012) 'From Kerala to Dubai and back again: construction migrants and the global economic crisis', *Geoforum*, 43, pp. 250–259.

Davidson, C.M. (2005) *The United Arab Emirates: A Study in Survival*. Boulder, CO: Lynne Rienner.

De Bel-Air, F. (2018) 'Asian migration to the Gulf States in the twenty-first century', in Chowdhury, M. and Irudaya Rajan, S. (eds) *South Asian Migration in the Gulf: Causes and Consequences*. London: Palgrave Macmillan, pp. 7–34.

Errichiello, G. (2012) 'Foreign workforce in the Arab Gulf states (1930–1950): migration patterns and nationality clause', *International Migration Review*, 46(2), pp. 389–413.

Errichiello, G. (2021) Migration, integration and belonging: Pakistani migrants in Britain and the United Arab Emirates, in Profanter, A. and Maestri, E. (eds) *Migration and Integration Challenges of Muslim Immigrants in Europe. Debating Policies and Cultural Approaches*. London: Palgrave Macmillan, pp. 55–89.

Errichiello, G. and Nyhagen, L. (2021) '"Dubai is a transit lounge": migration, temporariness and belonging among Pakistani middle-class migrants', *Asian and Pacific Migration Journal*, 30(2), pp. 119–142.

Fernandez, B. (2014) 'Essential yet invisible: migrant domestic workers in the GCC', Gulf Labour Markets and Migration. Available at: http://gulfmigration.eu/ (accessed 1 September 2020).

Gamburd, M.R. (2009) 'Advocating for Sri Lankan migrant workers: obstacles and challenges', *Critical Asian Studies*, 41(1), pp. 61–88.

Gardner, A.M. (2008) 'Strategic transnationalism: the Indian diasporic elite in contemporary Bahrain', *City & Society*, 20(1), pp. 54–78.

Gardner, A.M. (2010) *City of Strangers: Gulf Migration and the Indian Community in Bahrain*. Ithaca, NY: Cornell University Press.

Howell, S. (2000) 'Cultural interventions: Arab American aesthetics between the transnational and the ethnic', *Diaspora*, 9(1), pp. 59–82.

Kanna, A. (2011) *Dubai: The City as Corporation*. Minneapolis, MN: University of Minnesota Press,

Kathiravelu, L. (2016) *Migrant Dubai: Low Wage Workers and the Construction of a Global City*. Basingstoke: Palgrave Macmillan.

Leonard, K. (2000) 'State, culture, and religion: political action and representation among South Asians in North America', *Diaspora*, 9(1), pp. 21–38.

May, V. (2011) 'Self, belonging and social change', *Sociology*, 45(3), pp. 363–378.

Morawska, E. (2011) *A Sociology of Immigration: (Re)Making Multifaceted America*. Basingstoke: Palgrave Macmillan.

Potter, L.G. (ed.) (2009) *The Persian Gulf in History*. New York: Palgrave Macmillan.

Rutledge, E.J. (2018) 'Labour markets in the Gulf and the South Asian migration', in Chowdhury, M. and Irudaya Rajan, S. (eds) *South Asian Migration in the Gulf: Causes and Consequences*. London: Palgrave Macmillan, pp. 101–122.

Shah, N.M. (2017) 'Kuwait is home: perceptions of happiness and belonging among second plus generation non-citizens in Kuwait', *Asian Population Studies*, 13(2), pp. 140–160.

Sheffer, G. (2013) 'Integration impacts on diaspora–homeland relations', *Diaspora Studies*, 6(1), pp. 13–30.

Suzuki, T. (2019) 'Embodying belonging: diaspora's racialization and cultural citizenship', in Cohen, R. and Fisher, C. (eds) *Routledge Handbook of Diaspora Studies*. Abingdon: Routledge, pp. 63–70.

Tӧlӧlyan, K. (2019) 'Diaspora studies: past, present and promise', in Cohen, R. and Fisher, C. (eds) *Routledge Handbook of Diaspora Studies*. Abingdon: Routledge, pp. 22–30.

Vora, N. (2008) 'Producing diasporas and globalization: Indian middle-class migrants in Dubai', *Anthropological Quarterly*, 81(2), pp. 377–406.

Vora, N. (2013) *Impossible Citizens: Dubai's Indian Diaspora*. Durham, NC: Duke University Press,

Yuval-Davis, N. (2011) *The Politics of Belonging: Intersectional Contestations*. London: Sage.

Zahra, M. (2019) 'The legal framework of the sponsorship system of the Gulf Cooperation Council Countries: a comparative examination'. Explanatory Note N. 4/2019. Gulf Labour Market and Migration. Available at: http://gulfmigration.org/media/pubs/exno/GLMM_EN_2019_04.pdf (accessed 18 January 2020).

20
DIASPORIC BEFORE THE MOVE
China's Hui Muslims' trade and ties with Iran and Muslimness

Man Xu

Introduction

In the winter of 2020, I met Mr Su at his office in a Muslim neighbourhood in Yiwu, a city near the eastern coast of China. Yiwu is a major trading hub that exports Chinese goods all around the world and hosts the world's largest market for small commodities – the Yiwu International Trade Market. Mr Su is the co-owner of a trade and logistics company in Yiwu who studied Persian in Iran in 2000 and came to Yiwu in 2003. He used to run a company that facilitates trade between China and Iran and his customers were primarily Iranians. Since the Trump administration tightened sanctions on Iran in 2018, his company has seen a decline in business with Iranian clients and he began to collaborate with another Hui Muslim entrepreneur to expand his enterprise. Today, his customers include wholesalers from a range of Middle Eastern countries, such as Iraq, Palestine, Morocco and Iran, and he also provides shipping services for numerous Chinese trade companies, some of which are run by returned Hui migrants in Yiwu. After a few rounds of polite greetings, Mr Su asked me how long I had been in Yiwu and how many and which Hui Muslim merchants I had interviewed. I was surprised to hear that he knew most of the Hui informants I had contact with, many of whom are returned migrants from Iran. He said jokingly, 'Well, you don't need to talk to me any more, our stories are all the same.'

Indeed, Mr Su's migration and entrepreneurial trajectories share many similarities with other Hui Muslims in Yiwu. Many of them studied Arabic or Persian at Islamic schools in China, had similar experiences of working and studying in the Middle East and all returned to Yiwu to participate in international trade. In this chapter, I argue that this shared experience has become a basis for a group of Hui Muslims to develop diasporic social ties and to construct an imagined community to which they belong – one that extends beyond their geographic location in China. Mr Su's story is a tale that illustrates how, in the last three decades, many Hui Muslims have strategically deployed the resources in their ethnic and religious community to become mobile entrepreneurs. It is also a story of the formation of new transnational networks and symbolic connections between Hui Muslim migrants who have become active participants of social-economic exchanges between China and the Middle East. These transnational social spaces (Faist, 2015), I argue, are building blocks that aid in the development of their diasporic identification and forms of belonging (Levitt, 2001).

In his critical assessment of the concept of diaspora, Brubaker (2005, p. 12) contends that diaspora should be understood as 'a category of practice, project, claim and stance, rather than as a bounded group'. The constructive approach to diaspora directs attention to the ways in which the diasporic condition is embodied through an individual's everyday practice and claims-making and through the process of diaspora identity and community formation (Butler, 2001; Brubaker, 2005). While diaspora and transnationalism overlap significantly in their focus on cross-border connection and social identification that transcends nation-based identity (Faist, 2010, pp. 9–24), a distinctive dimension of diaspora is its emphasis on the connection between geographically dispersed populations and the sense of global identity that extends beyond homeland and hostland attachments (Abdelhady, 2006).

I build on these theoretical arguments to investigate the experiences of Hui migrants in China and Iran. With a few exceptions (for example, Ho, 2013; Wang, 2018), Chinese Muslim diasporas remain underexamined by scholars of Chinese migration. Moreover, existing studies of Chinese Muslim diasporas tend to focus on migrants' participation in exchanges between their various host societies and the homeland, and their negotiation of the 'dual' ethnic identity as Chinese and Muslim, paying less attention to the interconnection between geographically dispersed Chinese Muslim migrants and identification with a diasporic community. Furthermore, few scholars of Chinese diaspora have considered how diasporic connections and consciousness can exist among prospective and returned migrants, whose everyday life is just as much an embodiment of transnationalism and de-territorialised belonging as that of migrants.

In this chapter, I expand current studies of Chinese Muslim migrants through a diasporic perspective. My study shows that the concept of diaspora has analytical purchase for us to understand Hui Muslim migrants' experiences beyond the focus on transnationalism and their 'dual' identity. Moreover, I move beyond a view of migration as unidirectional processes and shed light on the circular movement and multidimensional global engagement of Hui Muslims. Chan's (2015) theorisation of diaspora as a series of historical moments that produce diasporic identity provides a fruitful analytical framework for the discussions in this chapter. The conception of 'diasporic moment' allows us to think of diaspora as processes and specific junctures that reveal diasporic members' complex senses of belonging and strategies to engage with national development and global change (ibid.).

In the following sections, I situate Hui Muslims' transnational movement in the broad context of the new Chinese migration to Iran since the 1980s and discuss the historical and current socio-economic conditions that give rise to this migration flow. Then, I shed light on three moments that shape the Hui diasporic community and consciousness: education at Islamic schools in China, migration to Iran and return migration and settlement in Yiwu, China. By incorporating diasporic experiences prior to and following their migration to Iran, my analysis emphasises the processual formation of diaspora communities and identification that are concretised in daily experiences traversing nation-state boundaries beyond the actual experience of migration.

This chapter draws on data collected from participant observation and interviews undertaken between June 2019 and December 2020 in China and Iran. My informants include Chinese exchange students in Iran and employees at state-owned enterprises (SOEs) dispatched to Iran for work. The exchange students are Chinese undergraduates and graduate students majoring in Persian at prestigious universities in China and went to Iran to study for 6–12 months. Another group of participants are self-employed entrepreneurs, self-funded students who went to Iran voluntarily, of whom Hui Muslims are a major component. I also interviewed many Hui Arabic and Persian interpreters in Yiwu who facilitate trade business between China and the Middle East. Many of these Hui interpreters are returned migrants from Iran and other Middle Eastern countries.

The new Chinese migration to Iran and the role of Hui Muslim migrants

The new Chinese migration to Iran began in the 1980s and peaked in the 2000s. Since the 2000s, US and international sanctions on Iran have resulted in a significant amount of trade diversion on Iran's side (Habibi, Alizadeh and Hakimian, 2014) and China replaced many of its former trade partners, such as Japan, South Korea, India and the European countries, to become the top exporter to Iran and the main importer of Iranian oil and gas (Bhat, 2012; Habibi, Alizadeh and Hakimian, 2014). The increase in bilateral trade between Iran and China is not only a result of China's rising energy demand but also Iran's increasing imports of consumer goods from China (Bazoobandi, 2015).

The emerging trend of new Chinese migration to Iran is a manifestation of the growing economic relationship between the two countries. Large Chinese SOEs and private Chinese companies began to invest in Iran in the late 1990s, sending Chinese managers and contract labourers to build a range of infrastructure projects, such as highways, metro systems and dams throughout the country (Lu, 2017). There is also a sizeable stream of migration to Iran by Chinese entrepreneurs, students and independent labourers (Ji, 2015; Lu and Huang, 2016). The influx of Chinese private businesses to Iran reached its peak in 2016 after the signing of the Iran nuclear agreement which temporarily lifted international sanctions. Following the agreement, Chinese hotels and restaurants sprang up in Tehran and the number of Chinese travellers to Iran reached about 70,000 in 2017, of whom 60–70 per cent travelled for business purposes (Hu and Qu, 2019).

As China deepened its economic relationship with Iran over the past three decades, there has been an increase in demand for people with Persian language skills to work for Chinese SOEs, government agencies and private firms trading with Iran. However, Persian language training has been underdeveloped in Chinese higher education – only five universities in China offered a Persian language major up until 2010. These market dynamics explain the increased number of Chinese students who go to Iran to study and the continuation of trade migration over the past three decades.

Hui migrants have been the main participants in trade and cultural exchanges between China and Iran during the last three decades. Since the 1980s, an increasing number of Hui Muslims have travelled to the Middle East to study or conduct business (Armijo, 2008; Ji, 2015). Historical connections and the present political dynamics shape the distinctive position of Hui people in the contemporary relations between China and Iran. The Hui people are commonly understood as descendants of Persian and Arab immigrants who settled in China in the seventh century (Lipman, 1997). The exchanges between China and the Middle East emerged when traders from Central Asia and the Middle East travelled to China and established the ancient Silk Road. Since then, a conspicuous number of Arab and Persian merchants have visited and settled in China (Zhu, 1978; Ma, J.C., 2019). Their presence led to the formation of the Chinese-speaking Muslim or Hui ethnic group and shaped the unique linguistic, religious and social practices of the Hui people.

Whereas the Hui people predominantly speak Chinese, they maintain some Arabic and Persian phrases in their language, especially in denoting religious activities (Abidi, 1981; Ding, K., 1999). I heard many fascinating stories when I asked my informants about the first time they heard or learned Arabic and Persian. The most memorable tale comes from Mr Ma, a Hui Muslim trader in Yiwu. Mr Ma is from Ningxia province, a Hui autonomous region in northwestern China. He said that his grandparents used a Perso-Arabic script called 'Xiao Er Jing' (小儿经) to write Mandarin because they are illiterate in Chinese but learned Arabic and Persian at mosques. These linguistic practices reveal the mixed cultural heritage of the Hui and the deep historical connections between Chinese Muslim communities and the Middle East. They are also moments that my informants constantly revisit and grapple with and are important for their process of identification and awareness of their links to the Middle East.

In the next section, I discuss how historical ties and a mixed cultural identification facilitate the ability of Hui people to capitalise on the opportunities offered by China-Iran trade. In the process, their diasporic identifications and communal belongings extend beyond imaginations based on shared ancestry and linguistic heritage to include concrete experiences of global encounters with the Middle East.

Connecting to the diasporic community: Islamic education in China

Many theorists emphasise a historical approach to the study of diaspora. For example, Alexander (2017) argues that historical and current conditions intertwine to produce a range of 'mobility capital' that shapes the construction of diasporic networks and membership. In the last two decades, a range of historically shaped conditions in Hui communities generated new forms of mobility capital that enabled the Hui to venture abroad and to become brokers and entrepreneurs in China-Iran trade. In particular, Islamic education, which is a legacy of the Silk Road exchanges, plays a crucial role in Hui people's migration to the Middle East.

Since at least the thirteenth century, Chinese Muslim scholars have taught Arabic and Persian and translated Arabic and Persian works into Chinese (Ding, K., 1999; Ding, J., 2004). Today, Arabic and Persian languages are taught at Chinese Islamic schools and are used by Hui Muslims in their religious practices (Yang, 1996; Ma, Y., 2012). As part of China's counter-terrorism policies, however, the Chinese government has imposed restrictions on the practice and study of Islam in China and connections between Chinese and foreign Muslim groups (Dillon, 2003). Nevertheless, these restrictions are not evenly applied to all groups of Chinese Muslims (Gladney, 1996). Hui people – who share the same language and closer cultural affinity with Han Chinese, the ethnic majority in China – have enjoyed more freedom in expressing their ethno-religious identity, compared to other Muslim groups such as Uyghurs (Bird, 2017, p. 124; Wang, 2018).

Islamic schools in China are important sites for the formation of Hui cultural and religious identity. My research highlights the role of two particular types of Islamic schools in Hui Muslim's migration: madrasas (经堂学校) and private language schools (阿语学校). Classes at madrasas often involve the teaching of Arabic and sometimes Persian and the foundations of Islamic beliefs (Ding, K., 1999). Language schools are also established and funded by local mosques. Yet they tend to integrate Islamic education with vocational training to benefit students' opportunities for future employment (Alles, 2003; Ma, X.F., , 2014). Madrasas and language schools in China place equal weight on the dissemination of Chinese and Islamic culture (中阿并重) and often offer courses such as classical and modern Chinese alongside Arabic and Persian training and combine classes about the world history of Islam with courses on the history of Islam in China and of the Hui ethnic group (Ma, H.P., 2013, pp. 104–128). As previous research shows, this curriculum design fosters Hui students' mixed cultural membership in the Chinese and Islamic communities (ibid.).

Education at Islamic schools provides the first chance for some of my informants to gain a deeper understanding of their religion, setting the foundations for them to develop global ties through shared Islamic beliefs. A few informants stressed that not all Hui are Muslim, and many Hui people are secularised – they neither understand Islamic religion nor practise it. Mr Sha, a Hui trader in Yiwu, who learned Arabic at a language school said, 'before studying at Islamic schools, most Hui youths attend national schools and do not learn about Islam. We may know that we are Hui, we believe in Islam, but in fact, we are not so different from Han people.' The construction of Muslim identity through Islamic education has an impact on Hui people's future development of cross-cultural relationships with Muslims from other countries. According to the Hui students and merchants whom I met in Iran and Yiwu, being Muslim allows them to establish trust and rapport with Muslims from the Middle East because Islam entails a shared worldview and business ethics that facilitate their communication and mutual understanding. This suggests Hui people's view of Islam as a world religion and shows the influence of Islamic identity on the development of their diasporic connections beyond the Chinese and Chinese Muslim communities.

Islamic schools are also crucial sites in which Hui people establish social ties with other diasporic members that make their migration possible. During my fieldwork in China, I met Mr Li, a Chinese Muslim from Gansu province in northwestern China. After graduating from middle school, he went to study at a mosque in the province through a friend's recommendation. This mosque offers both Arabic and Persian classes as part of its religious training and many teachers are returned migrants who studied Persian in Iran. Mr Li said that his teachers know the admission officers at Al-Mustafa University in Iran well and they helped to send Chinese students to the university every year. He told me that the teachers from Iran's Al-Mustafa University visited China regularly to recruit students. Through his teacher's connection, he attended the admission exam in 2015 and was accepted. Mr Li's experience represents many Hui people's pathway of migration to Iran. Besides Iranian universities, educational institutions in other Middle Eastern countries, such as Egypt and Saudi Arabia, also visit cities with Chinese Islamic schools to recruit students. Many teachers at Islamic schools are themselves returned migrants who studied in the Middle East, some of whom have ongoing contacts with the overseas universities they attended. Islamic school can thus be seen as a critical constituent of the Chinese Muslim diasporic network. This network connects prospective Hui migrants in China, returned Hui diaspora, and educational institutions overseas and plays a crucial role in channelling Hui people's migration to the Middle East.

In his reflection on the Chinese diaspora, Ma Mung (1998; 2004) emphasises that the geographical dispersal of diasporas in multiple countries and the interconnection between diasporic members constitute a form of spatial resource. Hui students' migration manifests their deployment of diasporic networks as a resource to enable their migration. Mr Li, for instance, used his social ties with the returned diaspora to pursue an educational opportunity in Iran.

Moreover, as Ma Mung (1998) suggests, the use of diasporic networks as a resource signifies and induces a diasporic perspective because it transforms the meaning of locality and the ways in which one sees the world. Ma Mung argues that diasporic consciousness arises when one becomes aware of and knowledgeable about the places where one's peers live and realise the opportunity of migrating to these places due to one's peers' presence. Many Hui informants told me that they have aspired to study overseas from a young age because they have acquaintances in the Middle East who can help them go there, and they were motivated by the migration stories of these pioneers in their communities to follow suit. For example, Mr Li said that he decided to go to Iran when he began to study at the mosque school because 'it was a common thing among students there' and his teachers encouraged him to go abroad. A diasporic consciousness is embodied in these accounts because they illustrate how one learns about different places through diaspora stories and comes to see the world through diasporic networks that transcend national boundaries. This view of the world manifests a sense of extraterritoriality – a key feature of diasporic consciousness (Ma Mung, 2004). Both Mr Li and Mr Su, the Hui entrepreneur whose story I share at the beginning of the chapter, told me that they knew very little about Iran before going there. It was not so much their knowledge about Iran but rather the presence of their peers in the country that determined their choice to travel. When Mr Su described his migration decision to me, I was surprised by how easy it seemed to be. He said: 'I had relatives in Malaysia and Iran, so I considered going to either of the two countries.' This seemingly 'unthoughtful' decision-making process nonetheless reveals how diasporic networks allow distinctive localities, such as Iran and Malaysia, to appear similar and transform a foreign land into a potential 'home'. This way of imagining the world through diasporic connections, rather than a nation-based framework, is an integral part of diasporic consciousness.

Migration to Iran: negotiating marginality

Despite the diasporic imaginings that are initiated in the context of the language schools, most Hui informants see their decision to go to Iran as a strategic choice that allowed them to capitalise on their own social resources and opportunities that emerged as part of the growing China-Iran trade economy. Many Hui youths at Islamic schools who subsequently went abroad are from poor families in rural China and had dropped out of public education at primary or secondary school (Ma, H.P., 2013; Mu, 2013). Some of them chose to study in Iran due to the relatively low cost of living and the free education at Iranian public universities.

Among the Hui students, some are self-funded. They mostly study at the Persian language centres in Tehran and Qazvin. However, a significant number of Hui students attended the religious programme at Al-Mustafa International University in Qom and the other five branches of the university in Tehran, Mashhad, Isfahan, Gorgan and Qeshm. These universities charge no tuition fees and provide free accommodation, meals on campus and a monthly stipend for foreign students. According to Al-Mustafa University's official website, the main objective of these programmes is 'disseminating Islamic teachings' (Al-Mustafa International University, 2017). However, many Hui informants told me that they went there mainly to learn the Persian language so that they would have better opportunities to find employment.

The disadvantaged class background of Hui students prompts them to look for jobs throughout their study in Iran. Participation in part-time work during student years shapes Hui migrants' complex position in the Chinese migrant community, their knowledge of the Iranian host society and their role as the economic and cultural middlemen between China and Iran. Hui students' involvement in part-time work often came up in my interviews during my fieldwork. A few Hui informants joked apologetically that they were 'bad students' because they took on many part-time interpreter jobs and barely attended school. This view is also shared by the more affluent Chinese migrants. A remark that I heard several times from Chinese exchange students (who are from prestigious universities in China) and elite migrants describes Hui students as low *suzhi*, because they often skipped classes or failed to complete their studies in Iran. *Suzhi* is a Chinese word that refers to 'physical, psychological, intellectual, moral, and ideological qualities of human bodies and their conduct' (Jacka, 2009, p. 524) and serves as a form of distinction and social differentiation (Lam, 2017). Hui students' background and practices in Iranian educational institutions do not conform to the conventional expectation that knowledge mobility is an elite exercise to accumulate high cultural capital. As a result, they are seen as inadequate students tarnishing the reputation of Chinese students in Iran.

Part-time jobs, however, provide opportunities for Hui students to acquire deeper knowledge about Iran and become cultural translators and brokers in China-Iran trade – a position that ultimately helps them to obtain upward mobility. Hui informants told me that their jobs as interpreters sometimes took them on week-long trips to marketplaces and trade expos in different Iranian cities. This allowed them to gain insights into Iranian society and international trade business. They also expanded their social networks through interactions with various Chinese and Iranian merchants and professionals during part-time work. Moreover, working as an interpreter requires Hui students to assume the role of cultural middlemen and brokers in the China-Iran trade market. In this process, they learn to live 'in translation', to switch between Chinese and Iranian cultures and develop cross-cultural competencies that are crucial for their future ventures in transnational trade.

Many scholars of Chinese overseas studies have criticised the use of 'diaspora' as a totalising concept implying a uniform 'Chinese' identity and nationalist loyalties (Shih, 2013; Hsu, 2019). These critiques lead to attempts to move beyond a nation-based understanding of Chinese diasporas and to pay more attention to the heterogeneity of Chinese overseas. Recent studies have investigated how various factors, such as class, religion, regional identities and dialect, shape Chinese diasporic networks and belonging (McKeown, 1999; Lam, 2017; Le, 2019). Hui Muslims' experiences with cultural brokerage and marginalisation in Iran demonstrate social distinctions among the Chinese migrant community in Iran and reveal a diasporic condition that cannot be accounted for by either their nationality or ethno-religious status alone. On the one hand, many Hui informants had close ties with the larger Chinese migrant community in Iran and they capitalised on resources in this community for employment. For instance, some informants said that the Chinese Student Association in Iran and the Chinese Embassy were important sources of information about part-time jobs. Mr Bai is a Hui entrepreneur who runs a trade company in Yiwu facilitating export from China to Iran. He went to Iran in 2003 and spent 12 years studying and working in the country before returning to China in 2015. Mr Bai told me that he frequently attended events at the Chinese Embassy in Tehran, and sometimes worked or volunteered as an interpreter at these events. On the other hand, Hui Muslims' participation in part-time jobs marks their disadvantaged status within China, a position that followed them in Iran and informs their fragmented belonging to the Chinese migrant community in Iran.

Migration not only reveals Hui Muslims' complex position and sense of belonging to the Chinese community but also generates new ties with the host country. Hui migrants develop Persian language skills, complex knowledge about Iranian society and a sense of affinity with Iran. When I conducted my fieldwork in Tehran, I met Mr Gao, a Hui student who was completing a degree in Iranian studies at the University of Tehran. He told me that he wanted to become a scholar of Iranian studies in the future. He believes that there are deep cultural linkages between China and Iran and that the Persian culture has a profound influence on the Hui community in China:

> We are the descendants of Persian Muslims; our religion is *Persian* Islam. For instance, we say our daily prayer and the prayer before *Iftar* partly in Persian language, we still use the Persian classic book *Golestan* in many Chinese mosques. Sufism also has an important influence on Chinese Islam. These cultural similarities make it easier for us to understand Iranian culture.

In this account, Mr Gao emphasises the Persian influence on the Hui community, a belief that helps him to relate to the new host society and eases his adaptation to life in Iran. At the same time, the process of 'making home' in a new place produces sentimental ties with the host land. Mr Bai, the Hui entrepreneur I mention above, said to me: 'we lived in Iran for a long time.

I may not understand a Chinese person as well as my Iranian friends and clients. It's almost like we've spent the best time of our life on the land of Iran.'

Cultural ties notwithstanding, few Hui Muslims see Iran as a permanent home, and many eventually return to China to participate in trade. Some informants explained that migration allowed them to realize the gap in the level of economic development between China and Iran and to see more clearly the economic opportunities in China. Mr Su, for example, visited Yiwu for the first time during his third year of study in Iran and was 'amazed' by the scope of global trade businesses and the level of economic development he witnessed. He said he decided immediately that he would stay in Yiwu and he never went back to complete his studies in Iran. Because of the transient nature of their residency in Iran, many Hui migrants do not show a strong sense of belonging to Iran or the Chinese migrant community there. Their experiences in Iran, however, contribute to their diasporic identification as it informs their connection to a global entrepreneurial trade network spanning across China and the Middle East, as I describe in the next section.

Returning home: becoming diasporic entrepreneurs

When I conducted fieldwork in Yiwu in the fall of 2020, I met many Hui people who have lived in Iran and returned to China to run businesses facilitating trade between the two countries. Since the end of the 1990s, a rising number of merchants from Iran and other Middle Eastern countries have come to settle in Yiwu, turning the city into one of the main nodes in the transnational commodity chain between China and Iran (Ma, Y., 2012; Wang, 2015). According to statistics from the Yiwu Government, Iran was among the top three importer of goods from Yiwu from 2012 to 2018 (Yiwu Government, 2020). The growing presence of Middle Eastern merchants in Yiwu creates a demand for Persian and Arabic interpreters and intermediate agencies that facilitate trade activities between China and the Middle East (Ma, Y., 2012; Wang, 2015). Hui Muslim returnees' Persian skills and first-hand knowledge of Iran become important assets for them to assume the brokerage role in China-Iran trade activities.

Mr Su is one of the Hui Muslim returnees who became successful entrepreneurs in Yiwu. As the story at the beginning of this chapter shows, Mr Su's clientele is not limited to Iranians but includes traders from many Middle Eastern countries as well as returned Hui migrants. Moreover, the diverse clientele also provides an opportunity for Mr Su to use his proficiency in Persian and Arabic that he acquired at the Chinese Islamic school. He told me that he has provided services of both Arabic and Persian interpretation for Middle Eastern traders.

As Mr Su's experience illustrates, returning to China does not mark the end of Hui migrants' transnational engagement. Instead, it opens up new opportunities for more extensive global connections beyond those between China and Iran. In his study, Guo (2016, p. 168) conceptualises his Chinese Canadian informants in China as the 'double diaspora' whose transnational movement signifies a form of diasporic journey that is 'neither unidirectional nor final, but rather multiple and circular'. The mobile Hui Muslims in this study share this characteristic of the double diaspora. They left China after becoming engaged in a diasporic space created through Chinese Islamic schools and went to Iran and forged ties with other Chinese in Iran and with Iranian society. Upon their return, their diasporic connections are expanded and performed on a daily basis.

The transnational lifestyle and what Guo describes as a circular movement of these returned diasporans are illustrated in their frequent cross-border travels and continued relationship with Iran. Mr Su, for example, has regularly gone to Iran to visit his clients throughout the past 20 years. He also maintains contact with some Chinese friends in Iran and occasionally collaborates with them for business. Apart from actual movement across borders, transnationalism and global engagement also characterise the everyday life of returned Hui diasporas like Mr Su. Because of their involvement in global trade business, they are keen observers of social and political events and market changes in Iran and other potential markets. Some of them regularly read Persian news on Iranian websites and BBC Persian. The main components of their daily job include communication with foreign clients online and hosting foreign customers who visit Yiwu to purchase products. These activities are not only part of the demands of their entrepreneurial lifestyle but are also informed by their conceptions of themselves as a particular diasporic minority in China that has linkages with the Middle East.

Furthermore, the diasporic connections of returned Hui migrants are also multiplied, and, in the case of my informants, extend beyond Iran. Yiwu is a place where returned Hui migrants develop new social relationships with other Hui Muslim traders, many of whom have studied Arabic and sojourned in other Middle Eastern countries such as Egypt, Syria and Saudi Arabia. During my fieldwork, I was often invited to have tea at social gatherings of these Hui Muslim entrepreneurs. Some Hui traders talked about the many common links they share with their friends: they may be from the same hometown, have been at the same Islamic school in China or studied in the same country before coming to Yiwu. It is worth noting that the relationships between Hui Muslim traders in Yiwu are highly complex and are often characterised by competition and even mistrust. Nevertheless, the similarities they share do help them to establish a certain level of trust, thus laying the groundwork for business partnerships and the creation of diasporic bonds.

The extensive connections among returned Hui diasporans with shared ethnic identity and migration experiences also lead to new forms of diasporic imaginations. Many Hui informants spoke proudly about the success of Hui entrepreneurs who are actively involved in trade business between China and the Middle East. For example, Mr Gao, the Hui student I met in Tehran, talked about the successful Hui entrepreneurs in his family and social circle. He commented on these stories emotionally:

> These Hui entrepreneurs did not take up educational resources from our country, but they made huge contributions to China-Middle Eastern trade relations ... Most people participating in Sino-Middle Eastern trade today are Hui. This is because as Muslims it's easier for us to communicate with foreign Muslims.

As I discussed in the previous section, Islam as a global religion provides a common ground for mutual understanding and trust between Chinese and Middle Eastern Muslim traders in the transnational market. At a time when Muslims are often depicted by Chinese public discourses and international media as risky subjects, Mr Gao's narrative portrays Islamic identity as an asset for Hui Muslims to become successful entrepreneurs and grassroots ambassadors between China and the Middle East. Moreover, Mr Gao's account constructs an imagined diasporic community constituted of accomplished Chinese Muslim students and entrepreneurs who have made significant economic and cultural contributions to their homeland. Against the prejudice of Hui Muslim migrants as low *suzhi* subjects, members of the Hui migrant community construct an alternative understanding of themselves as accomplished Chinese citizens with a heightened awareness of their Muslim identification and diasporic modes of belonging.

Conclusion

In this chapter, I examine Hui Muslims' transnational migration between China and Iran. I discuss how different moments of Hui people's migration contribute to the formation of diasporic ties and imaginations. I argue that Hui Muslims become 'diasporic' even before they migrate to Iran. Experiences with migration allow Hui people to acquire cross-cultural competency and knowledge about global trade and complicate their sense of belonging to China and Iran. While in Iran, their inability to totally belong to a Chinese migrant community, as a result of their limited access to economic and cultural capital, marks their difference and estrangement from a coherent Chinese diaspora. At the same time, they rely on the Chinese migrant community as a source of social capital that grants them access to job opportunities while in Iran. These experiences contribute to their ability to succeed upon their return to China. Their transnational ties and diasporic connections do not end but expand after their repatriation, leading to a new imagination of diasporic communities. Throughout my analysis, I conceptualise migration as a circular, open-ended process rather than a unidirectional relocation. Furthermore, I argue that while diasporic disposition is closely connected to cross-border travelling, it is, more importantly, a way of being and of understanding the world that can be embodied by those who are not on the move and by migrants who have returned and resettled in the homeland.

My analysis also contributes to studies of Chinese diaspora. I discuss how the historical legacy of China-Middle East exchanges produce new opportunities for Hui Muslims today to venture abroad and become brokers and grassroots ambassadors between China and the Middle East. I use the concept of diaspora to illustrate Hui migrants' diverse social ties and complex senses of belonging to China, Iran and the diasporic community. This analysis reveals the need to move beyond an ethnic or nation-based framework for understanding the Chinese diaspora.

References

Abdelhady, D. (2006) 'Beyond home/host networks: forms of solidarity among Lebanese immigrants in a global era', *Identities: Global Studies in Culture and Power*, 13, pp. 427–453.
Abidi, A. (1981) 'Iran-China relations: a historical profile', *China Report*, 17, pp. 33–49.
Alexander, C. (2017) 'Beyond the "The 'diaspora' diaspora": a response to Rogers Brubaker', *Ethnic and Racial Studies*, 40, pp. 1544–1555.
Alles, E. (2003) 'Muslim religious education in China', *China Perspectives*.
Al-Mustafa International University (2017) 'About us'. [Online]. Available at: http://en.miu.ac.ir (accessed 1 March 2021).
Armijo, J. (2008) 'Muslim education in China: Chinese madrasas and linkages to Islamic schools abroad', in Noor, F.A., Sikand, Y., and van Bruinessen, M. (eds) *The Madrasa in Asia: Political Activism and Transnational Linkages*. Amsterdam: Amsterdam University Press, pp. 169–190.
Bazoobandi, S. (2015) 'Sanctions and isolation, the driving force of Sino-Iranian relations', *East Asia*, 32, pp. 257–271.
Bhat, M.A. (2012) 'Iran-China relations: a challenge for US hegemony', *Quarterly Journal of Chinese Studies*, 3, p. 113.
Bird, J. (2017) *Economic Development in China's Northwest: Entrepreneurship and Identity along China's Multi-Ethnic Borderlands*. London: Taylor & Francis.
Brubaker, R. (2005) 'The "diaspora" diaspora', *Ethnic and Racial Studies*, 28, pp. 1–19.
Butler, K.D. (2001) 'Defining diaspora, refining a discourse', *Diaspora: A Journal of Transnational Studies*, 10, pp. 189–219.
Chan, S. (2015) 'The case for diaspora: a temporal approach to the Chinese experience', *The Journal of Asian Studies*, [Online], pp. 107–128.
Dillon, M. (2003) *Xinjiang: China's Muslim Far Northwest*. London: Routledge.

Ding, J. (2004) 'The contribution of Hui Muslims to Arabic language education in China', *Journal of Northwest Minorities University*, 6 [回族穆斯林对中国阿拉伯语教学事业的贡献. 西北民族大学学报], 6.

Ding, K. (1999) 'The position and impact of Persian education and classics in the history of Chinese Islamic culture', *Journal of Hui Muslim Minority Studies*, 2. [波斯语教学及经典在中国伊斯兰文化史上的地位及影响. 回族研究,], 2.

Faist, T. (2010) 'Diaspora and transnationalism: what kind of dance partners?', in Faist, T. and Bauböck, R. (eds) *Diaspora and Transnationalism: Concepts, Theories and Methods*. Amsterdam: Amsterdam University Press, pp. 9–34.

Faist, T. (2015) 'Transnational social spaces', *Ethnic and Racial Studies*, 38, pp. 2271–2274.

Gladney, D.C. (1996) *Muslim Chinese: Ethnic Nationalism in the People's Republic*. Cambridge, MA: Harvard University Asia Center.

Guo, S. (2016) 'From international migration to transnational diaspora: theorizing "double diaspora" from the experience of Chinese Canadians in Beijing', *Journal of International Migration and Integration*, 17, pp. 153–171.

Habibi, N., Alizadeh, P. and Hakimian, N. (2014) 'The Iranian economy in the shadow of sanctions', in Alizadeh, P. and Hakimian, N. (eds) *Iran and the Global Economy: Petro Populism, Islam and Economic Sanctions*. London: Routledge, pp. 172–198.

Ho, W.Y. (2013) 'Mobilizing the Muslim minority for China's development: Hui Muslims, ethnic relations and Sino-Arab connections', *Journal of Comparative Asian Development*, 12, pp. 84–112.

Hsu, M. 2019. 'Decoupling peripheries from the center: the dangers of diaspora in Chinese Migration Studies', *Diaspora*, 20, pp. 204–215.

Hu, Y.W. and Qu, X.Y. (2019) 'Chinese enterprises trying to survive in Iran despite policy shifts, US bluffs'. [Online]. Available at: www.globaltimes.cn/content/1135325.shtml (accessed 20 December 2020).

Jacka, T. (2009) 'Cultivating citizens: Suzhi (quality) discourse in the PRC', *Positions: Asia Critique*, 17, pp. 523–535.

Ji, KY. (2015) 'Studies on the overseas Chinese in the Middle East', *Middle East Studies*, 1. [中东华侨华人若干问题研究. 中东问题研究], 1.

Lam, K.N.T. (2017) *Chinese State-Owned Enterprises in West Africa: Triple-Embedded Globalization*. London: Taylor & Francis.

Le, A.S.H. (2019) 'The studies of Chinese diasporas in colonial Southeast Asia: theories, concepts, and histories', *China and Asia*, 1, pp. 225–263.

Levitt, P. (2001) *The Transnational Villagers*. Berkeley, CA: University of California Press.

Lipman, J.N. (1997) *Familiar Strangers: A History of Muslims in Northwest China*. Seattle, WA: University of Washington Press.

Lu, J. (2017) 'Strategies of development for Iran in the context of "The Belt and Road" Initiative', *World Affairs*, 3 [伊朗发展战略怎样对接 "一带一路". 世界知识], 3.

Lu, Z. and Huang, R. (2016) 'Chinese diasporas in Iran – a country at the crossroad of "The Belt and Road" Initiative', in Lu, Z. and Huang, R. (eds) *Building Bridges: Chinese Overseas and "The Belt and Road" Initiative*, pp. 120–124 ["一带一路"交会重镇—伊朗的华侨华人. 搭桥引路：华侨华人与"一带一路"], pp. 120–124.

Ma, H.P. (2013) *Contemporary Hui Education*. Ningxia: Ningxia People's Publishing House [当代回族教育. 宁夏人民出版社.].

Ma, J.C. (2019) 'The Middle Eastern trade caravan in the "Maritime Silk Road" from the seventh to fifteenth centuries', *Journal of Chinese Historical Studies*, 1 [公元7—15世纪 '海上丝绸之路' 的中东商旅. 中国史研究,], 1.

Ma, X.F. (2014) 'From Jingtang education to Arabic school', in Buang, S. and Ghim-Lian Chew, P. (eds) *Muslim Education in the 21st Century: Asian Perspectives*. London: Routledge, pp. 70–89.

Ma, Y. (2012) *The Migration Practice of Faith Community: An Ethnography of the Social Life of Muslims in Yiwu*. China Minzu University Press [一个信仰群体的移民实践：义乌穆斯林社会生活的民族志. 中央民族大学出版社].

Ma Mung, E. (1998) 'Groundlessness and utopia: the Chinese diaspora and territory', in Sinn, E. (ed.) *The Last Half Century of Chinese Overseas*. Hong Kong: Hong Kong University Press, pp. 35–47.

Ma Mung, E. (2004) 'Dispersal as a resource', *Diaspora: A Journal of Transnational Studies*, 13, pp. 211–225.

McKeown, A. (1999) 'Conceptualizing Chinese diasporas, 1842 to 1949', *Journal of Asian Studies*, 58(2), pp. 306–337.

Mu, Q. (2013) 'Arabic language opens doors for Chinese'. [Online]. *China Daily*, August 5, 2013. Available at: http://usa.chinadaily.com.cn/epaper/2013-05/08/content_16484949.html (accessed 10 April 2020).

Shih, S.M. (2013) *Sinophone Studies: A Critical Reader*. New York: Columbia University Press.

Wang, Y. (2015) 'Between the sacred and the secular: living Islam in China', in Possamai, A., Richardson, J.T. and Turner, B.S. (eds) *The Sociology of Shari'a: Case Studies from Around the World*. Cham: Springer, pp. 155–174.

Wang, Y. (2018) 'The making of China's "Good Muslims" from middleman minority to cultural ambassadors', *China Review*, 18, pp. 131–154.

Yang, Z, (1996) *The Language and Culture of Hui Ethnic Group*. Ningxia: Ningxia People's Publishing House [回族语言文化. 宁夏人民出版社].

Yiwu Government (2020) *Yiwu Statistical Yearbook*. Available at: www.yw.gov.cn/col/col1229442729/index.html (accessed 14 March 2021).

Zhu, J.Q. (1978) 'The historical relationship between China and Iran', *Historical Research*, 7. [中国和伊朗历史上的友好关系. 历史研究], 7.

21
A DIASPORIC BALANCING ACT
Syrian entrepreneurs in Turkey, Egypt and Jordan

Ching-An Chang

In this chapter, I investigate the business activities of expatriate Syrian entrepreneurs and suggest that, although they have physically moved away from Syria and adapted to the local rules and business customs, their specific values and practices regarding business have accompanied them to their new settings. Maintaining specific values and practices is due not only to not being integrated in host countries but also due to a higher level of communal trust among members of the Syrian business diaspora communities. By examining the business practices of expatriate Syrian entrepreneurs, I argue that their business practices are closely related to and dependent on the balancing of diasporic ties. On the one hand, diasporic ties with co-national entrepreneurs help my respondents counter the difficulties they encounter when re-establishing their enterprises within the host country. On the other hand, ties to the homeland in the form of governmental repression, family connections and property further constrain the entrepreneurs' behaviours in their host countries.

Like other types of diaspora, the study of business diasporas stresses connections to the homeland. In the general study of migrant entrepreneurs, and specifically, that of diaspora entrepreneurs, ties with home have been described quite positively. For example, diasporic networks are found to facilitate entrepreneurial activities in host countries (Portes and Bach, 1985; Massey et al., 1994; Kitching, Smallbone and Athayde, 2009). Ties based on the same ethnicity and knowledge about their home countries can provide a competitive edge that local competitors in host societies lack (Leblang, 2010; Ojo, Nwankwo and Gbadamosi, 2013). Additionally, members of diaspora communities transfer money to, or invest in, their home countries based on a range of practical and emotional attachments to their homeland (Curtin, 1984; Gillespie et al., 1999; Cohen, 2008; Nielsen and Riddle, 2009). As my analysis shows, the experiences of Syrian diasporic entrepreneurs in Turkey, Egypt and Jordan highlight that attachment to the homeland can also constrain business practices in the host societies. The difficulties migrants have in finding jobs in the host societies and the experiences of being discriminated against by local institutions have led some to change their business practices or gravitate towards self-employment (Kloosterman and van der Leun, 1999; Shneikat and Alrawadieh, 2019). I suggest that in the case of Syrian entrepreneurs, diaspora networks act as a shield in the face of institutional barriers in the host society, especially for solving challenges from the local regulatory systems and finance sectors.

The scale of the emigration of Syrian entrepreneurs after the 2011 uprising was substantial. Countries neighbouring Syria received the largest numbers of those forcibly displaced, including entrepreneurs. It is believed that thousands of Syrian entrepreneurs fled Syria for Turkey after 2011 and that by the end of 2015, more than 10,000 Syrian companies had been established (Turk Press, 2015). Egypt was considered a popular destination, especially for wealthier Syrians, due to its welcoming policies, particularly under the Morsi presidency. In Jordan, 25 per cent of the 9,024 foreign-registered companies were owned by Syrians in 2014 (Al-Sa'di, 2014). The scale of migration of Syrian entrepreneurs to these three countries should not overshadow the various tensions between Syrian refugees and members of the host communities. As has been reported, locals have sometimes been hostile towards the arriving Syrians due to competition in local labour markets, increases in national budgets and worsening security conditions (Dahi, 2014; Doganay and Demiraslan, 2016; Rayes, 2019).

In this chapter, I draw on fieldwork among Syrian entrepreneurs in Turkey, Egypt and Jordan who were forced to flee Syria as a result of the 2011 uprisings and ensuing civil war. I collected ethnographic material for this chapter during a nine-month field research stay in Turkey, Egypt and Jordan between the middle of 2014 and the end of 2015. Specifically, I conducted 191 interviews with Syrian entrepreneurs. I chose to conduct interviews with any Syrian who had had investment activities in Syria and who was registered in the Syrian Chambers of Commerce and Chambers of Industry before the 2011 uprising, or any Syrian who relocated to a host country after 2011 and then embarked on economic investment and registered with the local chambers. The chambers in Syria are ostensibly private institutions, yet they have been used by the Syrian regime as a system of patronage to privilege its preferred business allies (Haddad, 2012; Donati, 2013). The interviews focus on five themes: (1) the respondents' former professional activities in Syria; (2) their reactions to the 2011 uprising; (3) the rationales for their departure and choices for resettlement; (4) the ways in which they interacted with fellow Syrian entrepreneurs and local residents; and, finally, (5) their reasons for and their means of business activities within the host countries. Among the 191 interviewees, only three were women. As a male researcher, it was not easy to arrange interviews with female entrepreneurs. Moreover, it has been argued that female entrepreneurs in Arab countries encounter more difficulties than male entrepreneurs and that there are far fewer of them as a result (Hattab, 2012; Ameen and Willis, 2016). Due to the ongoing conflict in Syria and the strong hold of the Syrian regime on its citizens within and outside Syria, I have anonymised my data and omitted information that might lead to my respondents being identified.

Business cultures and the culture of business

As argued by Abdelhady (2006, p. 433), the distinction between diaspora and transitional communities is that 'the extension of attachments and affinities beyond the home/host dichotomy of specific nation-states to include a larger diaspora that is spread around the world'. For diasporic Syrian entrepreneurs, the homeland is not merely an intangible idea to which they are emotionally attached. Instead, diasporic ties with fellow Syrians in exile, the Assad regime and families and fixed assets back home sometimes facilitate and at other times constrain their business practices in host countries; thus, I argue that their business practices are conducted by balancing their diasporic ties. In the following two sections, I discuss how the host and home countries affect business owners in the Syrian diaspora.

Adaptation to local contexts

Conducting business in a foreign country is not easy; varying degrees of discrimination from the host society may arise (Wauters and Lambrecht, 2008, p. 910) as well as the attendant legal, political and social challenges. To facilitate business activities in Syria in the pre-2011 era, many of the entrepreneurs I interviewed resorted to bribes in exchange for help from those in positions of power. In many cases, bribes would work to decrease the amount of tax that they needed to pay or even lead to obtaining tax exemption altogether (Haddad, 2004, pp. 46–54). After establishing their investments in their new countries, they could not rely on privileged networks to facilitate their work in the diaspora. Instead, they have to obey local rules and regulations. An Aleppine machine-trading businessman in Gaziantep explained his observations of his fellow Syrian entrepreneurs:

> Now we need to pay taxes and meet all the requirements that the Turkish government asks us to meet. Honestly, it is not easy because before [in Syria] we just paid money to officials we knew and they would facilitate things for us.

Sometimes, following local practices meant resorting to old strategies of paying bribes. Some interviewees in Egypt who did not officially register their business investments instead applied 'the old tactics' which involved finding a *wasta* (connection) for their work. They indicated that this is a fairly common practice for conducting business in Egypt. Nevertheless, they were required to follow the business regulations of the host countries.

Among the three host countries, the main differences in business regulations were the required amount of capital needed to establish a company and the regulations to establish a commercial company. Egypt provided the lowest threshold for opening a new investment project, followed by Turkey and Jordan (PKF Progroup, 2011; LexMundi, 2012; ADMD, 2017). Jordan had the lowest requirements of tax payment for Syrian companies, such that the tax to be paid in Jordan was only half that of Turkey or Egypt (PWC, 2020a; 2020b; 2020c). The regulations for foreign investors to establish a commercial company in Turkey are different from those in Egypt and Jordan. The regulations in Egypt allow foreign investors to have 100 per cent ownership of the companies. Nevertheless, both limited liability companies and joint-stock companies do not allow foreign investors to import from outside Egypt (PWC, 2019). For Jordan, foreign investors can hold 100 per cent of the shares of their companies, but 'Foreign entities may not, however, have ownership in excess of 50% of construction and certain other commercial ventures', according to Jordanian investment law (PKF Progroup, 2011). Turkey did not have any of the above-mentioned limitations for foreign investors to establish companies (Investment Support and Promotion Agency of Turkey, 2020). In most cases, Syrian entrepreneurs work in similar economic sectors to those they operated in before relocating to host countries, since they are not only more familiar with the fields of activity but can also continue business with their old customers.

Politically, the Turkish, Egyptian and Jordanian governments have held different stances on the Syrian uprising. The Turkish government changed its position from being a mediator of the conflict in Syria to publicly condemning the Assad regime in mid-2011 (Taşpınar, 2012). Egypt was dealing with its own political transition from the ousting of Hosni Mubarak after three decades of rule. Between the beginning of 2011 and 30 June 2012, the Egyptian government was temporarily ruled by the Supreme Council of the Armed Forces. During this period of just over a year, the Egyptian policy towards the Syrian uprising remained vague due to Egypt's internal situation. When the newly elected president Muhammad Morsi took office in mid-2012, Egyptian policy towards the Syrian regime shifted, but still followed the Arab League's position which was broadly opposed to the Assad regime for geopolitical reasons. However, support of the Syrian uprising ended after the military coup on 3 July 2013 when General Abdel Fatah al-Sisi became the de facto leader of Egypt. After Sisi officially assumed the presidency in 2014, the government started to treat the Syrians based in Egypt more harshly than before (Abdul-Aziz, 2015). Jordan's policy on the Syrian uprising was ambiguous and cautious, neither supporting the Syrian regime nor standing in opposition to it (Muasher, 2014).

Since the local governments' attitudes towards the Syrian entrepreneurs were not stable and could take sharp turns at any time, Syrian entrepreneurs often needed to adjust their behaviour and calibrate what they said in public to accommodate the political climate in the host countries. Syrian entrepreneurs were also required to demonstrate an adjustment of their political leanings depending on the local government's position towards the Syrian conflict. In Egypt, Syrian entrepreneurs either had to leave the country or remain silent on their differing political views, especially after the 2013 coup.

In many cases, adopting local business practices entailed a change in the ways Syrian entrepreneurs carry out some essential business activities. I observed two ways that local business customs were different from Syrian business customs. The first adaptation to business transactions is the use of cheques. My respondents had been used to cash transactions while in Syria and were not accustomed to receiving bank cheques. Nevertheless, after they relocated and started engaging local businesses in Turkey, Egypt and Jordan, they were required to use cheques; otherwise, their business could not be sustained in the host countries. 'If we are doing businesses with other Syrian or Iraqi businessmen, we can use cash. But the locals will not do business with you unless you accept their cheques', stated a Damascene household cleaning products industrialist in Mersin.

Return policies in Egypt constitute a second form of adaptation that Syrian entrepreneurs had to accept. In Egypt, local business owners have their own ways of buying and selling goods. A Damascene clothes businessman stated that 'If Egyptian entrepreneurs order goods from you at the beginning of the year, and if they do not finish selling them by the end of the year, they will return the goods to you and you need to give them back their money.' This particular way of conducting business was common in the Egyptian business community but new and unfamiliar to my Syrian respondents in Egypt, who found that they had no choice but to accept it. An important feature of diaspora communities is the maintenance of certain boundaries from members of their host societies (see, for example, Brubaker, 2005). In the following section, I show that despite adapting to local regulations and business customs, there are certain practices that businesspeople continue to rely on which serve to mark their boundaries from local business owners.

Staying in business: communal capital and risk

In their daily business practices, my respondents continued to depend on and apply traditional customary practices in their business operations through their diasporic ties with other Syrian entrepreneurs. When my respondents experienced financial issues or business disputes, they sought help using the customary practices which they had used in pre-uprising Syria. Two traditional practices were found to be popular even after leaving Syria: non-interest loans and informal arbitration.

My respondents complained about the difficulties they face when accessing loans from banks in the host countries. They said that the difficulties in getting loans were due to either the sanctions from Western countries or discrimination against Syrians. Making the situation even worse, many could not manage to bring their money with them when fleeing the conflict in Syria. Since they could not take loans from banks in the host countries and did not hold enough capital to start or run a business, they had to seek out a solution to gain access to the capital necessary to establish and sustain a business. Using non-interest loans is an informal economic activity that is neither contract-based nor legally binding. My respondents explained two types of non-interest loans: one in the form of goods and the other in the form of cash. Many of my interviewees provided examples whereby they would give goods to other Syrian entrepreneurs whom they considered trustworthy before receiving payments for said goods. This practice entailed significant risk: if the recipient did not pay in full, my respondents would lose their money. To minimise the risk, most non-interest loans were given to those who had a reputable name in the market or to those whom my respondents had already known for a long time and trusted.

When a Syrian entrepreneur arrived in a host country with a need for capital to establish new investments, seeking help from their former business friends by way of a non-interest-bearing loan was considered the most viable option. Although Syrian entrepreneurs have relocated to different cities in different countries, the use of such non-interest-bearing loans was the same regardless, and its application solidified diaspora ties beyond national boundaries. For example, an Aleppine plastic industrialist in Amman contacted his former Aleppine friend who was a raw material provider in Istanbul for financial help to set up a factory in Jordan at the end of 2012. 'He lent me all the machines I needed in the beginning without any charge. The machines he lent me were worth more than $1 million. Later, I returned the money to him after I started to make a profit.' These non-interest loans are commonly used among expatriate Syrian entrepreneurs and attest to the strength of communal ties based on friendship, shared interests and circumstances. This kind of loan is prevalent in business practices in exile, going beyond national borders, as suggested by my informants and my observations through field research.

Communal ties between members of the business communities in my study were also concretised through the use of traditional arbitration practices. When a business dispute would arise between Syrians in a particular country, the Syrian entrepreneurs I interviewed would usually not seek a solution from the local judicial system. As new arrivals, they sought to avoid resorting to the local courts which they did not trust at any rate. An Aleppine tanker industrialist explained his worries about the local courts in Turkey:

> How long will it take for arbitration here in Turkey? Three months? Five months? Or even longer? It's not only because it may take a long time to get the result of the arbitration, but it's also because we want to be 'clean' – we do not want to have any negative judicial labels from the country we live in now after we left our home. God knows what will happen then.

As mentioned previously, Syrian entrepreneurs were required to conduct their entrepreneurial activities according to the local regulations and adapt to the business customs to operate their businesses in the host countries. Although they conform to the local rules, they believe they are treated unfairly compared to the locals. An Aleppine restaurant owner put it this way:

> My restaurant was intentionally damaged by a Turkish taxi driver due to some misunderstanding. Although I have Turkish citizenship, and I sued him in the [Turkish] court providing all the evidence, the judgement was in his favour. How will you expect me to go to the court here? In the end, I'm still a foreigner in their eyes.

Statements similar to this were repeated by many of my respondents. They reflect an awareness of a boundary between locals and immigrants, which can disturb the latter's life and ability to conduct business activities in the host country, even if they attempt to adapt to local rules and ways. According to my respondents, informal arbitration is the preferred practice for solving business disputes among Syrian businesspeople. One of my respondents, an Aleppine automobile industrialist, was often asked to be the arbiter in business disputes and explained the process:

> It is based on Islamic law (*Sharia*). The two disputers would both agree on an arbitrator who is pious and experienced, and each of them would find another person from their side to participate in this arbitration. The disputer who raised the arbitration is called 'oppressed' (*maẓlūm*), and he would need to prepare the evidence of receipts, contracts or other witnesses regarding the business dispute. The other disputer who is being charged is the 'denier' (*munkar*) of the charges. If he denied all the charges, he would put his right hand on the Quran and claim that he rejects the charges (*ḥilf al-yamīn*). The arbiter needs to let these two disputers sign a blank paper to show that they would accept the arbitration. The results of arbitrations were accepted by our courts in Syria if the informal arbitrations were conducted with the help of two witnesses. Before, in Aleppo, this kind of informal arbitration was prevalent not only for businesses but also for marriage or other disputes. Usually, the arbiters would be 'knowledgeable ones' (with knowledge of Islamic laws) or from religious families.

Difficulty in navigating the judicial system and modes of discrimination in host countries are not the only reasons Syrian entrepreneurs preferred traditional means of arbitration and dispute resolution. Relying on these established informal practices was seen to involve a better chance of receiving money and resolving their business problems. Since these customary practices have no legal effect, their application indicates that the users have, to a certain extent, enough trust in each other, or that they can at least be assured that the result of these arbitrations represented a form of justice they had faith in.

Trust in the context of the extension of credit and arbitration did not always require a direct personal relationship. As explained by a Damascene clothing businessman:

> We might not know them [as individuals], but we know their fathers, their uncles, and their brothers. So we know this person is from a good and honest family and we will not overthink the case, rather, we'll give them the loan directly.

This shows that when they apply these informal and customary practices, they reproduce notions of 'Syrianness' in the host countries as well as create new networks. Indeed, these practices can be seen as points of convergence with the practices of businesspeople in host countries like Egypt and Jordan where informal credit networks and arbitration are common (Gemmell, 2006; Al-Ramahi, 2008).

Staying in line: the Syrian state and threat as a disciplinary mechanism

While some ties to the homeland have been seen to have a positive impact on easing business practices in the host societies, ties to the Syrian regime and the potential of harm coming to families and fixed assets in Syria showed a different side of the story. The idea of *home* in the study of diaspora is mostly understood to be one of positive longing and nostalgia. The hope of returning exists among diasporans (Safran, 1991; Clifford, 1994; Van Hear, 1998). However, for expatriate Syrian entrepreneurs, the image of home, or, more specifically a regime that makes itself synonymous with the homeland, creates layers of complication. The idea of home bears two opposite meanings: on the one hand, it is the place where they learned and started their businesses and spent time with their families and friends for decades. While living in diaspora, ties to their friends could, to a certain extent, support their business activities, as shown above. On the other hand, it is also the place where they had to monitor their every action and avoid crossing red lines set by the regime that could have grave consequences. Detention and imprisonment were not uncommon experiences after the eruption of the 2011 uprising – 19 out of the 191 interviewees were arrested on account of their participation, remaining in prison for anything between a few days to two years. A dozen more interviewees also explained that their relatives or friends had been imprisoned or had disappeared. Businesspeople whose families and kinship networks had historically been against the regime or were associated with the uprising received threats from the state intelligence agency (*mukhabarat*). Fear of the regime was still prevalent in the lives of the expatriate entrepreneurs, even though they were no longer living in Syria, and led them to censor their behaviour in certain ways.

After interviewing an Aleppine dessert industrialist in his factory in the 6th of October City in Egypt, he promised that he would try to arrange some interviews with other Syrian friends. However, he called three days later to apologise. He told me, 'Trust me, my friend, all my friends think the Syrian *mukhabarat* sent you here.' Those who accepted to be interviewed provided narratives that reflected similar fears of the Syrian regime. The fear of the regime was not imagined, the regime did occasionally threaten entrepreneurs outside of Syria. As described by Pearlman (2016, p. 25), the stronghold of the Syrian regime has been 'carried beyond the homeland'. The Syrian government was notorious for monitoring its people through its intelligence service. The monitoring of Syrians abroad is not new, with embassies in places like London in the 1960s and 1970s orchestrating numerous assassinations of dissidents (Aly, 2015). My research suggests that threats are not limited to those involved in dissident political movements but increasingly to entrepreneurs in both Syria and abroad. The *mukhabarat* have been reported to 'ask' businesspeople to become business partners, sometimes without providing any capital to the businesspeople. This meant that businesspeople had two choices: either accept the offer or stop their business activity altogether. One Aleppine plastic industrialist recounted a story of a fellow Aleppine businessman working in the food industry. Once the investment of my respondent's friend had become popular, the *mukhabarat* came to him and asked to become business partners with him. The man refused at first, but then the *mukhabarat* told him that 'If you refuse, we will buy the lands next to you, and build up the same products as yours but with a bigger factory than yours [then you will close your factory by yourself].' In the end, he had no choice but to accept this demand to partner with the *mukhabarat*.

Also, businesspeople were not allowed to go against the regime's norms of speech and behaviour as they would be killed or put in prison for such acts. One of my respondents lost his father in the 1980s in Syrian prisons. The father was a wood industrialist who participated in the uprising against the Syrian regime at the time. He was later arrested by the regime and died at their hands. The son, who was in the food business, did not want to face the same fate as his father and leaving Syria appeared to be the only step towards avoiding the same fate. As indicated by the statement from my respondents above, the fear of the *mukhabarat* meant that life in the diaspora was disciplined: speech, actions and trust have to be carefully managed to minimise potential repercussions.

Having families and fixed assets in Syria strengthened the grip of the regime over members of the diaspora. Expatriate Syrian entrepreneurs do not simply work for themselves in exile, they often struggle to assure the livelihood and security of their family members and their real estate in Syria. An Aleppine textile businessman explained:

> Even though we are in Turkey, we still need to be careful about what we say and who we meet. Because our houses and relatives are all in Syria. If we criticise the regime or meet with opposition groups here, then all our stuff and our relatives may be put in danger.

Transnational oppression, such as physical threats and verbal warnings from the Syrian intelligence service to many of my respondents and their relatives within Syria, also reminded them to 'behave' while in exile. An Aleppine food industrialist noted:

> A businessman in Turkey told me that a few weeks previously the *mukhabarat* had gone to his house in Aleppo and asked for him. His parents told them that he was in Turkey. They told his parents to warn their son not to criticise the regime on his Facebook page.

Despite the continuing dangers and threats in Syria, some expatriates who have settled in the host countries have not given up the hope of returning or visiting their families in Syria. 'Some of my relatives are still in Syria, and I want to visit them. My house is still there. If I do anything that could anger the regime here, then my relatives and house may be in trouble', stated a Turkey-based Aleppine money-transfer businessman. The majority of my respondents had real estate in Syria, with some owning factories and companies that were operational at the time of the interview. It was not easy for many of my interviewees to give up on their assets as some had worked tirelessly for decades to accumulate them. Their homes, company premises or factories that they established constitute additional ties with home which concern them while they are away from Syria. These sentiments best capture the diasporic bind that many Syrians face on a daily basis, namely that resettlement has not relieved them of the dynamics of state brutality; they are constrained not only by the difficult process of resettlement but by their ongoing ties to Syria in the grip of a vengeful regime.

Even when Syrian entrepreneurs had been in exile for a few years, the mental burden of the separation from their relatives and material assets marked their daily activities. The separation from and the uncertain circumstances of their relatives caused my respondents to suffer significantly. One 60-year-old Aleppine art dealer left his interview to answer a phone call. When he returned to our conversation, it was clear from his eyes that he had been crying. He explained:

> My wife just called me from Aleppo. When I answered the phone, I said 'hello' to her, but she did not answer. I said 'hello' again and she just started to cry without saying anything. I did not know what to do so I just cried with her. She was with me in Turkey last month, but because she wanted to take care of our daughter who is still in Aleppo, she went back to Syria. But now she cannot return because the border between Turkey and Syria was shut down since ISIS is getting closer to the border.

In addition to the emotional connections, ties with the homeland affect the daily life of the entrepreneurs since there is social pressure to take responsibility for supporting their family members back home. Sending money home could lead to repercussions for people living abroad since migrants not only need to adjust themselves to new environments but also work hard to make a living out of it. This social responsibility of helping the people back home sometimes increases stress and anxiety in exile (Al-Ali, Black and Koser, 2001; Lindley, 2009). Diasporans in particular have a collective responsibility, which originated either from their bonds with their home based on sentiment or from imposition by their social networks back home (Tyler, 2011; Lo, 2016; Horst, 2018). Having ties to their homeland requires them to support their relatives back home. More importantly, familial ties sometimes turn into a mental burden for those living in the diaspora. Many repeatedly received calls from their family members who were still in Syria, sometimes asking for money and sometimes giving news of the loss of another relative. This limited many of my respondents' ability to devote themselves to and concentrate on their new investments in the host countries.

It is not the focus of this study to go into the unbalanced composition of the Syrian entrepreneurs. However, at the same time, it is important not to neglect how gendered entrepreneurial activities influence the shaping of businesses (Marlow and Martinez Dy, 2017). Entrepreneurship has been portrayed as masculine in general (Hamilton, 2013). An examination of the business practices of expatriate Syrian entrepreneurs focusing on gender shows that almost all their practices are operated by male entrepreneurs. One position is that a male entrepreneur is 'a somewhat solipsistic, aggressive individual, focused only on his own wealth, status and happiness' (Giazitzoglu and Down, 2015, p. 14). However, as Giazitzoglu and Down argue, not all male entrepreneurs possess the same entrepreneurial masculinity as suggested in the extant literature. Instead, ethnographic work shows 'the complex, multiple sorts of masculinities enacted, and rejected'. For instance, many of my respondents stated that they did not live and work for themselves but that, in contrast with the individualistic orientation described above, they also struggled to protect their family members and their property in Syria. By supporting their families, they were demonstrating an *altruistic* form of masculinity (see, for example, Reed, 1996, pp. 108–109 on Australian entrepreneurs). As expatriate Syrian entrepreneurs support their families at home in Syria, they also demonstrate that altruistic behaviours provide support for success in business and maintaining diasporic ties.

Conclusion

From the investigation of the business practices of expatriate Syrian entrepreneurs, in this chapter, I have shown that their business activities are conducted in a transnational context between homeland and host societies and through reliance on diasporic networks that span multiple nation-states. The expatriate Syrian entrepreneurs are required to change some of their ways of conducting business to the local forms, and they carry out their activities according to the rules and political contexts of the host countries. Nevertheless, adaptation to local customs and rules does not detach them from their reliance on diaspora networks. Instead, their experiences concretise the importance of these networks for their ability to persevere and succeed in their new environments. The maintenance of specific values and practices is due not only to their unintegrated situations in the host countries but also to their diasporic ties with their fellow Syrian entrepreneurs in various contexts. Additionally, I argue that the idea of *home* is a mixture of bitter and sweet for the expatriate Syrian entrepreneurs. On the one hand, diasporic ties can facilitate migrant entrepreneurs' ability to counter the difficulties associated with starting a business in a new society. On the other hand, the ties between the diasporic entrepreneurs and their homeland might further constrain their behaviours in the host countries. The business practices of expatriate Syrian entrepreneurs are thus closely related to and dependent on how they balance their diasporic ties.

Experiences of accessing local banks or courts show that they are not fully integrated into the local society despite adapting to local customs and rules, as the boundaries between locals and foreigners persist. On the one hand, while encountering difficulties in doing business in the host societies, their diasporic ties become one of the main strategies for solving problems, particularly those related to capital and business disputes. High levels of communal trust among members of the Syrian business diaspora communities encourage them to apply these traditional mechanisms in the host societies. It also motivates them to maintain their positive reputation and embeddedness in the diasporic community. On the other hand, *home* might become a certain constraint for them while living in the diaspora. Although living away from the Syrian regime, they are not immune to its exercise of transnational authoritarianism (see Moss, 2016; Pearlman, 2016). While conducting business in the diaspora, they are mentally attached to their family members and fixed assets in Syria. What happens (or what might happen) to their beloved families or to their assets further distracts them in the host countries. Nevertheless, their diasporic ties are an indispensable part of their lives away from home. Although these ties might become mental burdens in certain circumstances, Syrian entrepreneurs could not and would not be disconnected from their attachment to home. Not only could they rely on their ties to other diaspora entrepreneurs to improve their business practices, but they were also constantly reminded of their 'Syrianness' from these diasporic ties.

The ties between the expatriate Syrian entrepreneurs and their home regime continue to remind them of their identity as 'Syrians'. Regardless of which country they have relocated to, the shadow of the regime accompanies them. Their ties to the regime become a more serious issue, especially when they are linked to the safety of their families or assets back in Syria. Their ties to the homeland have also affected their ways of doing business since they are required to monitor their speech and actions to avoid angering the regime while living in the diaspora. They are not working as individuals without attachment to their home in the host countries. Rather, they have a sense of living at home in diaspora since they are not mentally or materially detached from their families or fixed assets back in Syria. This shows that the ties have not only constrained business practices but also remind them of their Syrian identity, despite being away from home.

Acknowledgements

This work was supported by the Ministry of Science and Technology, Taiwan (R.O.C) [108-2636-H-004-002-].

References

Abdelhady, D. (2006) 'Beyond home/host networks: forms of solidarity among Lebanese immigrants in a global era', *Identities: Global Studies in Culture and Power*, 13(3), pp. 427–453.

Abdul-Aziz, H. (2015) 'The Egyptian policy on the Syrian crisis', *MEMO: Middle East Monitor*. Available at: www.middleeastmonitor.com/20150528-the-egyptian-policy-on-the-syrian-crisis/ (accessed 11 August 2020).

ADMD (2017) 'How to incorporate in Turkey'. Available at: www.admdlaw.com/how-to-incorporate-in-turkey/#.WSzEGmiGM2w (accessed 11 August 2020).

Al-Ali, N., Black, R. and Koser, K. (2001) 'The limits to "transnationalism": Bosnian and Eritrean refugees in Europe as emerging transnational communities', *Ethnic and Racial Studies*, 24(4), pp. 578–600.

Al-Ramahi, A. (2008) 'Sulh: a crucial part of Islamic arbitration'. Research paper 08-05. London: London School of Economics.

Al-Sa'di, S. (2014) 'sharikāt Sūriyya tuwāṣil al-hijra … ilā al-Urdunn' [Syrian companies continue to migrate … to Jordan]. Available at: www.almodon.com/economy/2014/8/21/%D8%B4%D8%B1%D9%83%D8%A7%D8%AA-%D8%B3%D9%88%D8%B1%D9%8A%D8%A9-%D8%AA%D9%88%D8%A7%D8%B5%D9%84-%D8%A7%D9%84%D9%87%D8%AC%D8%B1%D8%A9-%D8%A5%D9%84%D9%89-%D8%A7%D9%84%D8%A7%D8%B1%D8%AF%D9%86. (accessed 11 August 2020).

Aly, R. (2015) *Becoming Arab in London: Performativity and the Undoing of Identity*. London: Pluto Press.

Ameen, N.A. and Willis, R. (2016) 'The use of mobile phones to support women's entrepreneurship in the Arab countries', *International Journal of Gender and Entrepreneurship*, 8(4), pp. 424–445.

Brubaker, R. (2005) 'The "diaspora" diaspora', *Ethnic and Racial Studies*, 28(1), pp. 1–19.

Clifford, J. (1994) 'Diasporas', *Cultural Anthropology*, 9(3), pp. 302–338.

Cohen, R. (2008) *Global Diasporas: An Introduction*. London: Routledge.

Curtin, P. (1984) *Cross-Cultural Trade in World History*. Cambridge: Cambridge University Press.

Dahi, O. (2014) 'The refugee crisis in Lebanon and Jordan: the need for economic development spending', *Forced Migration Review*, 47, pp. 11–13.

Doganay, M. and Demiraslan, H. (2016) 'Refugees of the Syrian civil war: impact on reemerging infections, health services, and biosecurity in Turkey', *Health Security*, 14(4), pp. 220–225.

Donati, C. (2013) 'The economics of authoritarian upgrading in Syria: liberalization and the reconfiguration of economic networks', in Heydemann, S. and Leenders, R. (eds) *Middle East Authoritarianisms Governance, Contestation, and Regime Resilience in Syria and Iran*. Stanford, CA: Stanford University Press, pp. 35–60.

Gemmell, A. (2006) 'Commercial arbitration in the Islamic Middle East', *Santa Clara Journal of International Law*, 5(1), pp. 169–193.

Giazitzoglu, A. and Down, S. (2015) 'Performing entrepreneurial masculinity: an ethnographic account', *International Small Business Journal*, 35, pp. 40–60.

Gillespie, K., Riddle, L., Sayre, E., and Sturges, D. (1999) 'Diaspora interest in homeland investment', *Journal of International Business Studies*, 30(3), pp. 623–634.

Haddad, B. (2004) 'The formation and development of economic networks in Syria: implications for economic and fiscal reforms, 1986–2000', in Heydemann, S. (ed.) *Networks of Privilege in the Middle East: The Politics of Economic Reform Revisited*. New York: Palgrave Macmillan, pp. 37–76.

Haddad, B. (2012) *Business Networks in Syria: The Political Economy of Authoritarian Resilience*. Stanford, CA: Stanford University Press.

Hamilton, E. (2013) 'The discourse of entrepreneurial masculinities (and femininities)', *Entrepreneurship & Regional Development: An International Journal*, 25(1–2), pp. 90–99.

Hattab, H. (2012) 'Towards understanding female entrepreneurship in Middle Eastern and North African countries', *Education, Business and Society: Contemporary Middle Eastern Issues*, 5(3), pp. 171–186.

Horst, C. (2018) 'Making a difference in Mogadishu? Experiences of multi-sited embeddedness among diaspora youth', *Journal of Ethnic and Migration Studies*, 44(8), pp. 1341–1356.

Investment Support and Promotion Agency of Turkey (2020) 'Establishing a business in Turkey'. Available at: www.invest.gov.tr/en/investmentguide/pages/establishing-a-business.aspx (accessed 11 August 2020).

Kitching, J., Smallbone, D. and Athayde, R. (2009) 'Ethnic diasporas and business competitiveness: minority-owned enterprises in London', *Journal of Ethnic and Migration Studies*, 35(4), pp. 689–705.

Kloosterman, R. and van der Leun, J. (1999) 'Just for starters: commercial gentrification by immigrant entrepreneurs in Amsterdam and Rotterdam neighbourhoods', *Housing Studies*, 14(5), pp. 659–677.

Leblang, D. (2010) 'Familiarity breeds investment: diaspora networks and international investment', *The American Political Science Review*, 104(3), pp. 584–600.

LexMundi (2012) 'Guide to doing business: Egypt'. Available at: www.lexmundi.com/Document.asp?DocID=4291 (accessed 11 August 2020).

Lindley, A. (2009) 'The early-morning phone call: remittances from a refugee diaspora perspective', *Journal of Ethnic and Migration Studies*, 35(8), pp. 1315–1334.

Lo, J. (2016) 'Diaspora, art, and empathy', in Assmann, A. and Detmers, I. (eds) *Empathy and its Limits*. London: Palgrave Macmillan, pp. 202–216.

Marlow, S. and Martinez Dy, A. (2017) 'Annual review article: is it time to rethink the gender agenda in entrepreneurship research?', *International Small Business Journal: Researching Entrepreneurship*, 36, pp. 3–22.

Massey, D., Arango, J., Hugo, G., Kovaovci, A., Pellegrino, A. and Taylor, J.E. (1994) 'An evaluation of international migration theory: the North American case', *Population and Development Review*, 20, pp. 699–752.

Moss, D. (2016) 'Transnational repression, diaspora mobilization, and the case of the Arab Spring', *Social Problems*, 63(4), pp. 480–498.

Muasher, M. (2014) 'Jordan's ambiguous Syria policy'. Available at: http://carnegieendowment.org/2014/06/09/jordan-s-ambiguous-syria-policy-pub-55832 (accessed 11 August 2020).

Nielsen, T. and Riddle, L. (2009) 'Investing in peace: the motivational dynamics of diaspora investment in post-conflict economies', *Journal of Business Ethics*, 89(4), pp. 435–448.

Ojo, S., Nwankwo, S. and Gbadamosi, A. (2013) 'African diaspora entrepreneurs: navigating entrepreneurial spaces in "home" and "host" countries', *International Journal of Entrepreneurship and Innovation*, 14(4), pp. 289–299.

Pearlman, W. (2016) 'Narratives of fear in Syria', *Perspectives on Politics*, 14(1), pp. 21–37.

PKF Progroup (2011) 'Doing business in Jordan, October 2011'. Available at: www.pkf.com/media/608484/doing%20business%20in%20jordan.pdf (accessed 11 August 2020).

Portes, A. and Bach, R. (1985). *Latin Journey: Cuban and Mexican Immigrants in the United States*. Berkeley, CA: University of California Press.

PWC (2019) 'Doing business in Egypt: a tax and legal guide'. Available at: www.pwc.com/m1/en/tax/documents/doing-business-guides/egypt-tax-and-legal-doing-business-guide.pdf (accessed 11 August 2020).

PWC (2020a). 'Egypt'. Available at: https://taxsummaries.pwc.com/Egypt/corporate/taxes-on-corporate-income (accessed 11 August 2020).

PWC (2020b) 'Jordan'. Available at: https://taxsummaries.pwc.com/Jordan/corporate/taxes-on-corporate-income (accessed 11 August 2020).

PWC (2020c). Turkey'. Available at: https://taxsummaries.pwc.com/Turkey/corporate/taxes-on-corporate-income (accessed 11 August 2020).

Rayes, D. (2019) '"Stuck" in transit: systematic limitations on integration of Syrian refugees in Egypt and its impact on mental health and well-being'. Available at: https://timep.org/commentary/analysis/stuck-in-transit-systematic-limitations-on-the-integration-of-syrian-refugees-in-egypt-and-its-impact-on-the-mental-health-and-well-being-of-a-population-in-flux/ (accessed 30 September 2020).

Reed, R. (1996) 'Entrepreneurialism and paternalism in Australian management: a gender critique of the "self-made" man', in Collinson, D.L. and Hearn, J. (eds) *Men as Managers, Managers as Men: Critical Perspectives on Men, Masculinities and Managements*. London: Sage, pp. 99–122.

Safran, W. (1991) 'Diasporas in modern societies: myths of homeland and return', *Diaspora*, 1(1), pp. 83–99.

Shneikat, B. and Alrawadieh, Z. (2019) 'Unraveling refugee entrepreneurship and its role in integration: empirical evidence from the hospitality industry', *The Service Industries Journal*, 39(9–10), pp.741–761.

Taşpınar, O. (2012) 'Turkey's strategic vision and Syria', *The Washington Quarterly*, 35(3), pp. 127–140.

Turk Press (2015) ''adad al-sharikāt al-sūriyya fī turkiyā yatajāwwaz 10 ālāf sharika', [Number of Syrian companies in Turkey exceeds 10,000 companies]. Available at: www.turkpress.co/node/12286 (accessed 11 August 2020).

Tyler, K. (2011) 'New ethnicities and old classities: respectability and diaspora', *Social Identities: Journal for the Study of Race, Nation and Culture*, 17(4), pp. 523–542.

Van Hear, N. (1998) *New Diasporas: The Mass Exodus, Dispersion and Regrouping of Migrant Communities*. London: University College London Press.

Wauters, B. and Lambrecht, J. (2008) 'Barriers to refugee entrepreneurship in Belgium: towards an explanatory model', *Journal of Ethnic and Migration Studies*, 34(6), pp. 895–915.

22
DIASPORA SYRIANS AND HUMANITARIAN AID IN THE SYRIAN CIVIL WAR

Shawn Teresa Flanigan

Introduction

Members of diaspora groups often have deep emotional connections to their ancestral homelands, and this holds true for many members of the Syrian diaspora. Modern emigration from Syria has a long history, beginning in the nineteenth century under the Ottoman Empire when many Syrian migrants were classified as 'Turks' by receiving countries (Suleiman, 1999). More recently in the 2000s, discussions of Syrian emigration have focused largely on the mass displacement of Syrians during the nearly decade-long civil war, still ongoing at the time of writing. During this conflict, at least six million Syrians have fled their homeland to more than 100 countries (Carlson and Williams, 2020). This chapter discusses Syrian diaspora philanthropy that seeks to aid Syrians displaced by the civil war.

In this chapter, I summarise my prior published work (Flanigan and Abdel-Samad, 2016; Flanigan, 2018; Abdel-Samad and Flanigan, 2019) on a study of Syrian diaspora-founded NGOs providing various forms of humanitarian aid to conflict-displaced Syrians in Europe, North America, the Middle East-North Africa (MENA) region and within Syria itself. The study drew its data from interviews with board members, staff and volunteers of Syrian diaspora-founded NGOs, all Syrian nationals or persons of Syrian descent. These interview data are complemented with numerous hours attending meetings of Syrian diaspora members and visiting sites of service provision to Syrian migrants in Canada, Germany, Lebanon, Turkey and the United States. In this chapter, I endeavour to highlight the commitment of Syrian diaspora members to assisting their fellow Syrians during what some have called the worst humanitarian crisis since the Second World War.

The Syrian conflict and humanitarian need

The Syrian crisis has proven to be an enduring conflict among an ever-shifting constellation of actors, initially sparked with the Arab protests of 2011. At the time of this writing, Syria has spent nearly a decade embroiled in a civil war that has been all but won by the al-Assad regime (Hubbard, 2020). A product of this conflict has been the displacement of nearly half of the Syrian population, with one quarter internally displaced within Syria and another quarter fleeing Syria in search of safer ground. Conflict-displaced Syrians now live in more than 100 nations worldwide, though a majority are in neighbouring Jordan, Lebanon and Turkey, with an ample minority managing to settle in Europe (Carlson and Williams, 2020).

The Syrian civil war and the resulting mass migration have created serious humanitarian needs and vulnerabilities in communities of Syrians within the country and beyond. Over six million Syrians have been internally displaced by the war, pushed out of their home communities by violent conflict (UNHCR, n.d.). The civil war has decimated the Syrian economy, creating dire economic and social needs for many residing in Syria, even those persons who are not conflict-displaced. The United Nations estimates that over 13 million people within Syria require humanitarian aid, three million of whom live in hard-to-reach or besieged locales (ibid.). The violent conflict, particularly the targeting of civilian infrastructure, such as schools, hospitals and water systems, simultaneously increases the need for aid while complicating the risk calculations of traditional aid organisations, which may decide they are unable to operate in conditions of active conflict (UNICEF, 2015). Meanwhile, local service delivery systems find themselves under the dual pressures of heightened need and influxes of new migrants. As of mid-2020, Syria faced a 40 per cent unemployment rate and an approximately 80 per cent poverty rate. These staggering figures are likely to worsen during the COVID-19 pandemic as governments around the world, including in Syria, institute restrictions in an effort to combat the spread of the virus (Hubbard, 2020).

The large majority of Syrians who have fled the country as refugees live in neighbouring Jordan, Lebanon and Turkey. Turkey hosts the largest number of Syrian refugees, with 3.6 million Syrian migrants residing in Turkey (Adah and Türkyılmaz, 2020). However, Lebanon has the highest density of Syrian refugees, with 164 Syrian migrants per 1,000 people (Sieverding and Calderón-Mejía, 2020). Indeed, as early as 2014, many Lebanese towns had more Syrian refugee residents than Lebanese residents (UNHCR, 2014). Neighbouring Jordan hosts close to 700,000 Syrian refugees, compared to 1.5 million in Lebanon (Sieverding and Calderón-Mejía, 2020).

Living conditions are often poor even for those Syrians who have left the country, particularly in neighbouring host states. In Turkey, early refugees were housed in what were largely considered higher-quality refugee camps, but as these quickly filled, most Syrians have become urban dwellers (İçduygu 2015; Adah and Türkyılmaz, 2020). Syrian refugees in Turkey face language barriers and challenges in accessing education for their children and participating in the formal labour market (İçduygu 2015; Adah and Türkyılmaz, 2020). There are reports of Syrian refugee women and children being victimised through informal polygamous marriages to Turkish men (Duman, 2020). In Jordan, a country with a long history of hosting Palestinian refugees, Syrians lack full freedom of movement when attempting to leave refugee camps, which hinders economic opportunity. Syrian refugees also are subject to strict work permit requirements, and more than 90 per cent of Syrian migrants in Jordan face vulnerabilities in meeting their basic human needs (Sieverding and Calderón-Mejía, 2020).

Migrants in Lebanon face similar challenges that are exacerbated by Lebanon's own long history of sectarianism and civil war, with the large and vulnerable refugee population creating pressures on already weak government services and infrastructure (UNHCR, 2014). More recent political upheaval in Lebanon, beginning in autumn 2019, created scarcity for all residents and heightened the vulnerability of Syrians in the country. Economic instability has increased with the rampant devaluation of the Lebanese currency (Mounzer, 2020) and prohibitions on withdrawing US dollars in an effort to prevent a run on Lebanese banks (Hubbard, 2020; Mounzer, 2020). COVID-19 has had a powerful effect on the Lebanese economy, as in many countries, with a poverty rate of about 33 per cent for all Lebanese residents in late 2019 increasing to a rate close to 50 per cent by mid-2020 (ibid.). Poverty among Syrian migrants is typically much higher. A massive explosion in Beirut on 4 August 2020 displaced thousands of people from their homes and exacerbated the already precarious economic and political conditions in the country. The impacts of this disaster on vulnerable Syrian migrants are likely to be extraordinary.

There is some evidence that Syrian migrants to Europe are somewhat less vulnerable and somewhat more affluent than migrants who remain behind in Syria or neighbouring Jordan, Lebanon and Turkey. The long and difficult trip itself requires resources and more often is viewed as a viable option by healthy young men than by mothers of young children, the elderly or individuals with disabilities or health concerns. Upon arrival, Syrian migrants to Europe are generally greeted with more robust legal protection frameworks and better-developed welfare states (Flanigan, 2018). Nonetheless, migrants to Europe face an arduous journey over land and sea and are often viewed with suspicion or open hostility (Carlson and Williams, 2020). Similar sentiments are common in nearby MENA countries as well, with Syrians viewed as stealing jobs, increasing housing scarcity and creating political instability in neighbouring Lebanon and Turkey (İçduygu, 2015; Flanigan and Abdel-Samad, 2016).

The Syrian diaspora and humanitarian aid

Members of the Syrian diaspora have emerged among the constellation of actors attempting to address the humanitarian needs created by the Syrian crisis. While informal, ad hoc aid efforts by diasporas are common (Newland and Patrick, 2004; Sidel, 2008), in this chapter, I discuss findings from a research project examining formally registered NGOs created by Syrian diaspora members. This chapter and previously published work (Flanigan and Abdel-Samad, 2016; Flanigan, 2018; Abdel-Samad and Flanigan, 2019) draw upon interviews with individuals working or volunteering for several NGOs founded by Syrian diaspora members, as well as many hours spent in the field in five countries. About half of the interview participants were themselves recent migrants from Syria who had left due to the conflict, and the remaining interview participants had left Syria in early childhood or were born outside of Syria to Syrian parents. All organisations were led by a combination of more recent migrants (typically economic migrants within the last 20 years) and those with ancestral ties to Syria. The NGOs mostly were involved in providing basic services related to humanitarian aid, health and social welfare, though some organisations engaged in capacity development, for example, operating schools for migrant children or offering job training and résumé services to recent migrants (Garkisch, Heidingsfelder and Beckman, 2017).

The diaspora Syrians who founded and operated these NGOs were not individuals who had been displaced by the current conflict. They had left Syria many years ago or, in many cases, were the children of Syrian emigrants who had never lived in Syria themselves. These interview participants' involvement in diaspora aid usually began before the Syrian crisis, often with less formal, ad hoc relief and education efforts by the diaspora networks to which they belonged. After the onset of the Syrian conflict, these pre-existing efforts were followed by the creation of formal NGOs providing more robust assistance both inside and outside of Syria. The formal organisations were typically registered in Europe or North America as not-for-profit organisations/NGOs by diaspora members living outside the MENA region. The usual justification for registering NGOs outside the region was to facilitate fundraising (for example, so larger donors in the United States could make tax-deductible donations), to make use of more stable banking structures, and to benefit from more progressive legal frameworks that offer protections to not-for-profit and nongovernmental organisations.

A goal of the research project was to explore individuals' personal motivations for becoming involved in philanthropic activity. I also sought to better understand the mechanisms that Syrians in the diaspora use to engage in the region, send money and resources into conflict zones and refugee settings, ensure accountability for those funds and resources, and assess the success of their efforts. Finally, I was interested in individuals' perceptions of the broad political goals of the Syrian diaspora. Interview participants lived in many countries at the time of the interviews, including Canada, France, Germany, Lebanon, the Netherlands, Saudi Arabia, Syria, the United Arab Emirates, the United Kingdom and the United States. I had the good fortune of being able to conduct face-to-face interviews in Canada, Germany, Lebanon and the United States, and to spend many dozens of hours observing meetings of diaspora members and visiting sites of migrant services in Canada, Germany, Lebanon, Turkey and the United States.[1]

The NGOs with which the interview participants were associated provided aid to migrants in Canada, Egypt, Germany, Lebanon, Syria, Turkey, the United Arab Emirates and the United States. While organisations provided aid in a wide variety of locations, the majority of the NGOs' collective work took place in Syria and neighbouring Lebanon and Turkey. Many of the interview participants did not live in the country where aid was provided but travelled frequently as part of their efforts. Most interview participants were involved in more than one Syrian diaspora network that was providing aid and did aid work in more than one country. For most interview participants, this work was not a paid, full-time job but a labour of love, requiring the investment of a great deal of volunteer time, personal financial resources and emotional energy.

The role of diasporas in humanitarian assistance

Many readers will be familiar with diaspora members' deep emotional connections to a shared homeland, and to the attending commonalities in aspects such as culture, language and religious practice. Concern about the difficulties faced by other members of the diaspora around the world often springs from these emotional ties (Brinkerhoff, 2008; 2011), and indeed, assisting fellow diaspora members becomes a means of performing one's own diaspora membership (Werbner, 2002; Nielsen and Riddle, 2009; Brinkerhoff, 2011). Helping fellow diaspora members may also be driven by a cultural expectation, passed across generations, that social needs should be met by the family, clan or ethnic group (Tchouassi and Sikod, 2010; Brinkerhoff, 2011). Assistance also can be motivated by a sense of responsibility or even guilt, when reflecting on one's higher quality of life and greater financial resources in a country of residence outside the homeland (Brinkerhoff, 2008; 2011). This aid, provided across diaspora ties to fellow diaspora members, is sometimes referred to as diaspora philanthropy.

Ancestral ties and a deep connection to the homeland are strong drivers of diaspora philanthropy, and interview participants in this study were powerfully motivated by their emotional connections to Syria and their fellow Syrians. For this research, I define diaspora philanthropy as money, goods, volunteer labour, knowledge and skills, and other assets donated for the social benefit of a community broader than one's family members. This aid is targeted towards a country or region where there is a population with whom the donors share ancestral ties (Flanigan and Abdel-Samad, 2016; Flanigan, 2018; Abdel-Samad and Flanigan 2019). Considering shared ancestry, rather than exclusively categorising by countries of origin and residence, provides room to include, as an example, Syrians in Dubai aiding conflict-displaced Syrians in Beirut. This broader geographic focus more carefully attends to the ambiguous, sometimes contested borders that are an inextricable part of the transnational dimension of diaspora communities.

While Syrians have a long history of emigration, and diaspora philanthropy takes myriad forms, this chapter specifically focuses on humanitarian efforts in response to the effects of the Syrian civil war. The potential contribution of diasporas to economic development, humanitarian aid and peacebuilding is an important topic in the international development profession (Espinosa, 2015). However, diaspora philanthropy is less researched than the adjacent fields of diaspora remittances, business investment and business networks (Gillespie et al., 1999; Newland and Patrick, 2004; Mutume, 2005; Page and Plaza, 2006; Sikod and Tchouassi, 2007; Riddle, Brinkerhoff and Nielsen, 2008; Nielsen and Riddle, 2009; Leblang, 2010; Mehrez and Hamdy, 2010; Newland and Tanaka, 2010; Mullings, 2011; Brinkerhoff, 2012). Diaspora philanthropy is certainly a component of remittances, but philanthropic remittances are difficult to disaggregate from other types of activities supported by money sent back to one's homeland. Because of this methodological challenge, a small but growing body of research focuses on more formal and organised diaspora philanthropy (see, for example, Newland and Patrick, 2004; Merz, 2005; Johnson, 2007; Brinkerhoff, 2008; 2011; 2012; 2014; Sidel, 2008; Dhesi, 2010; Tchouassi and Sikod, 2010; Moon and Choi, 2012; Espinosa, 2015; Flanigan and Abdel-Samad, 2016; Flanigan, 2018; Abdel-Samad and Flanigan, 2019; Carpi and Fiddian-Qasmiyeh, 2020).

This project focuses on a smaller subset of Syrian diaspora philanthropy, conducted by formal, registered NGOs and not-for-profit organisations created by Syrian diaspora members. These types of organisations represent an important mechanism of diaspora philanthropy, allowing a philanthropic intermediary to aggregate and coordinate many, often smaller, donations from a multitude of diaspora donors (Flanigan, 2017). However, the vast majority of diaspora philanthropy is still thought to be largely an informal, ad hoc practice that takes place through individuals or loose networks of diaspora members (Newland and Patrick, 2004; Sidel, 2008).

Motivations for Syrian diaspora aid to migrants in the Syrian conflict

Syrian identity was a powerful motivator of diaspora philanthropy for the individuals in this research. The literature on diaspora philanthropy predicts diaspora identity will be a motivating factor, emphasising the role of diaspora membership, familial ties, and clan and other social obligations in diaspora giving (Werbner, 2002; Brinkerhoff, 2008; Nielsen and Riddle, 2009; Tchouassi and Sikod, 2010; Brinkerhoff, 2011). Many interview participants discussed deep emotional ties to Syria, telling stories of childhood trips to their grandparents' homes or ancestral villages, or stories that had been shared with them by their parents. Perhaps most illustrative of these ancestral ties were how individuals who had never lived in Syria would describe their imagined origins[2] as residents of Syrian communities, prefacing their motivations with phrases such as, 'Because I'm from Aleppo …', or 'Because I'm from Homs …' (Flanigan and Abdel-Samad, 2016; Flanigan, 2018). These statements from individuals who had spent their entire lives in Europe or North America showed the deep sense of membership in this diaspora community.

More recent migrants from Syria noticed this motivation among their diaspora colleagues who grew up outside the MENA region and had ancestral rather than recent ties to Syria. As Amira, a more recent migrant, observes:

> Because [the Syrian diaspora members from outside the MENA region] were brought up abroad they have this mentality of sharing what they have, and improving conditions for the Syrians. The founders never cut that cord between themselves and Syria; it is still there.
>
> (Flanigan, 2018, p. 46)

The important role of identity would likely be common among many diaspora philanthropists worldwide. However, something more unique to the Syrian context and other contexts of conflict-driven migration is the role that conflict itself has had in motivating Syrian diaspora philanthropy. The Syrian civil war created a strong emotional response even in ancestral Syrians observing the conflict from afar. Interview participants explained that they felt called to respond to the Syrian conflict by a sense of solidarity, compassion and sorrow. They described feeling responsibility, and even guilt, due to their family's migration history that arbitrarily blessed them with the good fortune of living outside of harm's way during the civil war. Many interview participants with ancestral ties to Syria described a heightened awareness and salience of their Syrian identity in the early phases of the civil war, a phenomenon also mentioned in other research on Syrian diaspora organisations (Baeza and Pinto, 2016). As Faisal described:

> To be honest, before the uprisings-slash-revolution, I always thought of myself as Arab-Canadian most of the time. I didn't feel a belonging to Syria as the country because for me, what Syria represented as an official entity was not what I ascribed to [referring to her negative opinion of the al-Assad regime]. It was more the people I identified with. I think with the uprising, all of the emotional turmoil that we went through and the Arab Spring and everything, then I think my Syrian identity sort of magically surfaced. So now I speak a lot more about being Syrian than before.
> *(Flanigan and Abdel-Samad, 2016, p. 58)*

The increased identity awareness Faisal described may be missing from much literature on diaspora philanthropy, but it is well discussed in the academic literature on violent conflict. The presence of violent conflict, or the threat of such conflict, increases the salience of individuals' conflict-associated identities (Gurr, 2000; Kaufman, 2001; Tilly, 2003; Flanigan, 2010). This increased identity salience can then lead to a spectrum of actions, including charitable work and service (Flanigan, 2006; 2010). The Syrian diaspora members interviewed for this project often became involved in diaspora philanthropy for the first time because of the Syrian conflict, or shifted and broadened their organisations' mission in light of the conflict. In many cases prior to the conflict, organisations had focused on education, scholarships or school fees, or workforce development. Rima explained:

> The sad part or the exciting part is if it weren't for the crisis I'm sure what we would be doing would be on a much smaller scale. Right we would probably just be hoping to be giving twenty or thirty university scholarships a year, and that would be kind of what we are doing. Just because of everything that has been going on [the Syrian conflict], there's so much need for our and other organisations' services that we've just grown, and it has become this huge thing. And in a lot of ways if it weren't for what is going on [the Syrian conflict], I'm sure that wouldn't have happened.
> *(Flanigan and Abdel-Samad, 2016, p. 58)*

Advantages of Syrian diaspora aid to Syrian migrants

There are many advantages of Syrian diaspora aid in the Syrian crisis, and the identity-based motivations discussed previously are one of those. Diaspora members' strong emotional connections may lead them to be less deterred by risk than other aid providers, and more willing to persevere through challenges and obstacles (Brinkerhoff, 2008; 2014; Flanigan and

Abdel-Samad, 2016; Flanigan, 2017; Abdel-Samad and Flanigan, 2019). This commitment was evident in my research, as Hakim described:

> A lot of NGOs, Syrian or Lebanese or Turkish local NGOs, they are funded by a big funder like the UN and if they stop the funding, the NGO stops the project. But we have so many Syrian donors abroad, if one donor leaves or suspends funds, we can look for other donors and continue the project. Our donors are willing to stick with us even when things get hard, or there is donor fatigue with this migrant crisis.
>
> *(Flanigan, 2018, p. 46)*

Syrian diaspora identity is often accompanied by greater cultural competence, local knowledge and membership in Syrian social networks, which are also crucial advantages of diaspora philanthropy.

Cultural competence and local knowledge

Syrian diaspora donors offer other advantages as well. Many Syrian diaspora members have strong cultural competence and local knowledge, which in the literature is proposed to be an advantage of diaspora organisations vis-à-vis other humanitarian actors (Newland and Patrick, 2004; Johnson, 2007; Flanigan and Abdel-Samad, 2016; Abdel-Samad and Flanigan, 2019). Aspects of cultural competence that were mentioned during the research interviews include language skills, knowledge and understanding of local religious practices, and a set of social skills that allow diaspora members to better understand various ways of interacting with individuals in the field, based on age, gender, social status and urban versus rural cultural norms. Leila, a local Syrian staff member, stated when describing diaspora Syrians:

> Having a board of Syrian expatriates does make a difference, I think mostly for the positive. All of the members on the board now used to visit Syria at least every other year for the summer, so they still have relatives in Syria, they know Syria, they are familiar with the culture. It's not like they left and never went back. And this is very important because they can relate the work to their lives, they can relate to the Syrians there, and they want to work to help their fellow Syrians move ahead. They are passionate about it.
>
> *(Flanigan, 2018, p. 47)*

As suggested in the literature on diaspora philanthropy, Syrian diaspora donors and volunteers also possess important local knowledge that is beneficial to the work of the organisations. This knowledge is particularly useful when organisations provide aid inside Syria. Some examples of local knowledge mentioned in the interviews include an understanding of the presence or absence of certain amenities at the local level, or knowing what businesses existed in a village and whether those businesses were still operational in the context of the civil war. Information about these important questions was obtained through diaspora members' broad and overlapping networks of family members, friends and professional contacts, who could provide information on local conditions inside Syria. For example, an interview participant described efforts to fund the rebuilding of a school that had been bombed, but first needed to know if the local concrete business could provide materials. He learned that the local concrete business was not functioning, but another business several villages away could do the job. Another interview participant described learning through his network that Internet access, which was tightly regulated by the Syrian regime before the civil war, was now widely (if illegally) available in certain villages, making that a new and useful tool for logistical coordination and communication.

Syrian diaspora members are also better able to assess local needs due to having contacts on the ground, including in more remote settings, which is another advantage sometimes espoused in the literature (Brinkerhoff, 2008; 2011). Hasaan describes:

> These programs came because we go and ask people what they need … We basically provided a big tanker, a big oil tanker that was giving out heating fuel, and people lined up in Aleppo, in the outskirts of Aleppo, for heating fuel. But since we have people we trust there, we can find out the greatest need in that moment. And because we are flexible we don't have to stick to a budget that says, 'Well, this money is for clothing.' We can say, 'Forget clothing, use that money to buy heating fuel, that's what people say they need.'
>
> *(Abdel-Samad and Flanigan, 2019, p. 337)*

In addition to benefiting from greater cultural competence and local knowledge, membership in Syrian social networks provides useful forms of social accountability that facilitated the efforts of the NGOs.

Syrian diaspora networks and social accountability

For Syrians involved in diaspora philanthropy, social networks provide benefits beyond the localised knowledge and information about community needs described earlier. Social networks also provide a framework for accountability in the organisations' humanitarian efforts. Particularly when providing services in conflict zones, diaspora organisations face serious logistical and security challenges. Informal tools of social accountability that draw upon social network ties allowed Syrian diaspora members to identify trusted partners, deliver services effectively, and ensure the safe transfer of funds into places where the banking system poses challenges, such as in Syria and neighbouring Lebanon. These tools of accountability worked well due to the trust embedded in the social network, and the tandem roles of reputation and shame in controlling for negative outcomes (Abdel-Samad and Flanigan, 2019). Scholars suggest that these types of diaspora networks have advantages in identifying trustworthy partners, enforcing contracts in the face of weak legal systems when compared to other non-diaspora humanitarian organisations (Newland and Patrick, 2004; Brinkerhoff, 2011).

An advantage of having fellow diaspora members' 'eyes on the ground' was that Syrian diaspora organisations were able to identify trusted individuals and organisations who could serve as partners. For organisations based primarily outside of Syria that needed to get funds into Syria – often in the form of cash during the early years of the conflict – selecting a trustworthy partner was a decision that left no room for error. Diaspora members faced the dual pressures of effectively moving funds and providing services, and being accountable for the appropriate use of their donors' contributions. Syrians in the diaspora addressed this challenge by investigating the backgrounds of partners through their social network ties. As Kareem, a Syrian donor and logistical coordinator, explained:

> We have our networks, we have our contacts, we have our friends and our families [who are still in Syria] who are part of what is going on. So this is how we started; then the good names are easy to figure out.
>
> *(Abdel-Samad and Flanigan, 2019, p. 337)*

Repeatedly, Syrian diaspora members mentioned the importance of finding 'good names' to facilitate logistics inside Syria, and in neighbouring Lebanon, where strict banking regulations towards Lebanon by the United States and some European governments made transferring and withdrawing funds a challenge. The ability to fully trust someone with a 'good name' was solidified by the importance of reputation, and fear of shame, in Syrian culture. In many cultures, reputation is an instrument for rewarding or sanctioning individuals professionally or socially. Syrian diaspora members were deeply concerned about their own and their organisations' reputations and therefore made partnership selections carefully. Interview participants also acknowledged the role of reputation and shame for individuals in their diaspora networks who might make recommendations for partners. Recommending a poor partner could have serious implications for the recommender's own reputation, so diaspora members understood that any recommendation they received had been made thoughtfully. As Fatima explained:

> We feel like we can trust the recommendations of our friends and family because you know, in the Arab world, we're all very shame-based (laughs). And I'm not saying we in [our NGO] would ever intentionally shame someone. But people know that if they give a bad recommendation, if that person performs poorly or does something corrupt, as the recommender, they look bad too. It's their reputation too. And it's not just, like, their reputation at work. This is their reputation with their friends, their cousins, in their home village. And that's everything, that's really big.
>
> *(ibid., p. 339)*

Cultural competence, local knowledge and social accountability derived from Syrian diaspora networks proved to be assets for these organisations. Nevertheless, Syrian diaspora organisations faced challenges including perceived limits to their role as peacebuilders and certain barriers presented by diaspora membership.

Syrian diaspora philanthropy and peacebuilding in Syria

International development professionals often are optimistic about the potential of diaspora organisations to contribute to peacebuilding, despite ample evidence that diasporas also can contribute to violence in their countries of origin (Shain, 2002; Newland and Patrick, 2004; Orjuela, 2008; Van Hear, Pieke and Vertovec, 2010), and sometimes are less open to compromise than individuals currently living inside the country of origin (Newland and Patrick, 2004). In this research, Syrian diaspora members generally had little optimism that Syrians in the diaspora could impact peacebuilding at the highest levels, due to a conviction that there was little hope for policy responsiveness from the al-Assad regime and little ability to intervene in the disorder of non-regime-held areas. Interview participants also acknowledged that, as within many diaspora groups, there were members of the Syrian diaspora who stood both with and against the current regime, and perhaps the only common ground between these groups was a desire for peace and stability (Flanigan and Abdel-Samad, 2016). This perception of a lack of political efficacy held even among individuals who had been political activists in Syria and had since fled the country. As Iman noted:

> Knowing how decisions and things are made in Syria, I don't think it's easy to affect that. Because everything is political, and everything relates back to the leader who says what happens and what doesn't happen. Therefore, the social movements, even though I really appreciate them, and I was a part of many when I was in Syria, and

I would support them all the way to the end, I don't really think they can make a change.

(ibid., p. 59)

Diaspora members had a more optimistic view about the possibility of building peace at the grassroots level by investing in education and training opportunities for individuals inside Syria. Several organisations operated schools for Syrian children and provided scholarships for Syrians to study at universities abroad. One NGO trained Syrian lawyers in international human rights law, inviting lawyers to training sessions on the Turkish side of the Syrian-Turkish border. One NGO trained Syrian refugees to become teachers in refugee schools in Lebanon, with a focus on peacebuilding and conflict resolution in children's education. The short-term goal of this effort was to have Syrian teachers, who were more culturally sensitive to the needs of Syrian children, work with refugee children. Over the longer term, however, the staff talked about how these teachers would later take their new skillset and peacebuilding curriculum with them back to Syria and use them to improve conditions there. Nadia, a staff member of an NGO that provided career training to Syrian refugees in the Gulf States, described the value of simply having Syrians from different backgrounds sitting in the same room, facing the same problems:

Some of them never thought they would be sitting next to someone with completely different political view or from another sect or background, and that they become friends at the end of the workshop. When they discover that they are all having the same troubles, they all left their countries, they all have limited resources, they all have the same troubles, their families, money and future, when they realize that, things back home and their different views don't matter any more … So hopefully whether it's through [this organization] or personally I can somehow educate Syrians on living better lives and building more peaceful communities.

(ibid., p. 60)

Syrian diaspora member's responses echo some themes in the literature on diaspora philanthropy and 'social remittances' (Levitt, 1998), the idea that diasporas send not only money but new behaviours, ideas and values to their country of origin.

The promises and pitfalls of Syrian diaspora philanthropy

This chapter focuses on the advantages of Syrian diaspora organisations in humanitarian aid in the Syrian crisis. However, it is important not to assume Syrian diaspora NGOs are a panacea for the challenges of aid in the Syrian conflict. Rather, Syrian diaspora organisations are but one unique type of actor among an assemblage of humanitarian organisations required to address the Syrian crisis. Importantly, diaspora aid is not welcome in all countries of origin, since governments may view diasporas as politically threatening, especially when violent conflict prevails, as it does in Syria (Shain, 2002; Shain and Barth, 2003; Brinkerhoff, 2011; Moss, 2016). While this chapter discusses the advantages of friend and family networks in the Syrian diaspora, the literature notes that these networks may exclude the most vulnerable communities, since the poorest of the poor are less likely to have connections in other countries (Brinkerhoff, 2008; Bains, 2014). A reliance on friend and family networks also means diaspora humanitarian aid may face the challenge of philanthropic particularism, meaning a tendency to help the donors' own ethnic, religious or geographic group while neglecting (intentionally or not) other, perhaps needier, groups (Salamon, 1995; Van Hear, Pieke and Vertovec, 2010).

Diaspora aid also can be characterised by philanthropic amateurism (Salamon, 1995; Brinkerhoff, 2011), as the efforts of well-meaning donors often are volunteer and amateur rather than professionalised. This amateurism can decrease the effectiveness of humanitarian aid solutions (Salamon, 1995). I witnessed this challenge in the course of this research project, finding myself in the awkward position of explaining to a meeting of Syrian diaspora members that their plan to use iPads and web-based applications in refugee tent schools might be ineffective. The Syrian diaspora members had a deep emotional affinity for Syria, and almost all had flown long distances to be part of a conference of Syrian diaspora members seeking to become more involved in humanitarian aid. However, most had very little lived experience in Syria or the MENA region more broadly, having emigrated as young children, or having been born outside Syria to Syrian emigrants. In fact, few spoke Arabic, and the entire conference was conducted in English. Though I was the only non-Syrian in my break-out group, I was also the only person who had ever visited a Syrian refugee camp. Having visited the specific camp they were targeting, I knew there was no Internet access and only intermittent electricity, making Internet-based solutions likely unviable.

This is perhaps an extreme example since most of the interview participants in the study had spent ample time in Syria, and in the humanitarian contexts where aid was being offered. Nonetheless, more recent Syrian emigrants frequently mentioned the issue of well-intended but misaligned strategies from ancestral Syrians who grew up in Europe or North America. These more recent Syrian migrants spoke of educating ancestral Syrians about living conditions in the MENA region, and about the extended amount of time it takes to accomplish tasks. The more recent migrants explained that ancestral Syrians from the diaspora became more adept at understanding the local context once they had travelled more frequently to sites of service provision (Flanigan, 2018). As Jameela put it, 'Once they come [to the MENA region], the foreign Syrians are pretty quick learners.'

As the Syrian conflict sadly endures and new challenges such as the COVID-19 pandemic unfold, Syrian migrants within Syria and throughout the MENA region will continue to have a high need for humanitarian aid. Syrian diaspora organisations will continue to be important actors in this humanitarian sphere, motivated by their deep emotional connection to their diaspora community and by a salient diaspora identity heightened by the violent conflict. As has been noted here, these diaspora organisations bring important advantages to the humanitarian field that derive from their diaspora membership. These include greater cultural competence and local knowledge than some other actors, and strong forms of social accountability based on reputational concerns in diaspora social networks. However, diaspora aid has its own limitations, some of which are the product of diaspora membership. Some regimes find diaspora efforts politically threatening, and diaspora assistance can be prone to philanthropic amateurism. The same diaspora social networks that facilitate aid can intentionally or unintentionally exclude vulnerable communities external to those networks. Finally, there is a risk of over-reliance on diasporas for humanitarian aid and economic development, making it important to remember that the dire humanitarian needs described here cannot be met without clear political will from the international community and concerted, well-funded efforts by other humanitarian organisations. While diaspora organisations benefit from a committed group of donors who may not be as easily deterred by challenges in the field, the resources of these relatively small organisations cannot compare to those of many larger international NGOs in the broader field of humanitarian aid. Thus, diaspora aid organisations can be only one of myriad actors providing humanitarian aid to those affected by conflict. Nonetheless, as experts such as Kelley (2017) call for greater reliance on national NGOs in humanitarian aid, Syrian diaspora NGOs can be valuable partners in addressing the Syrian crisis.

Notes

1 While I conducted the vast majority of interviews myself in English, I am grateful to Mounah Abdel-Samad for facilitating a focus group interview in Arabic with eight focus group participants in Lebanon.
2 Here I used the word 'imagined' not to mean 'pretend', but in the spirit of Benedict Anderson's (1983) *Imagined Communities*.

Acknowledgements

The author is indebted to anonymous Syrian diaspora members for their participation in this research project, their warm hospitality, and their frank description of their efforts to help their fellow Syrians. I thank Mounah Abdel-Samad for assistance with the translation of Arabic materials and facilitation of an Arabic-language focus group. I am grateful to the United Nations World Institute for Development Economics Research (WIDER), particularly Rachel Gisselquist and Finn Tarp, for helpful feedback on aspects of this research.

References

Abdel-Samad, M. and Flanigan, S. (2019) 'Social accountability in diaspora organizations aiding Syrian migrants', *International Migration*, 57(4), pp. 329–344.
Adah, T. and Türkyılmaz, A. (2020) 'Demographic profile of Syrians in Turkey', in Carlson, E. and Williams, N. (eds) *Comparative Demography of the Syrian Diaspora: European and Middle Eastern Destinations*. Cham: Springer, pp. 57–91.
Anderson, B. (1983) *Imagined Communities: Reflections on the Origin and Spread of Nationalism*. London: Verso.
Baeza, C. and Pinto, P. (2016) 'Building support for the Asad regime: the Syrian diaspora in Argentina and Brazil and the Syrian uprising', *Journal of Immigrant and Refugee Studies*, 14(3), pp. 334–352.
Bains, S. (2014) 'Punjabi diaspora as agents of change', paper presented at Diaspora, Sustainability, and Development Conference. Simon Fraser University, Vancouver, Canada, 20 September.
Brinkerhoff, J. (2008) 'Diaspora philanthropy in an at-risk society: the case of Coptic orphans in Egypt', *Nonprofit and Voluntary Sector Quarterly*, 37(3), pp. 411–433.
Brinkerhoff, J. (2011) 'David and Goliath: diaspora organizations as partners in the development industry', *Public Administration and Development*, 31, pp. 37–49.
Brinkerhoff, J. (2012) 'Creating an enabling environment for diasporas' participation in homeland development', *International Migration*, 50(1), pp. 75–95.
Brinkerhoff, J. (2014) 'Diaspora philanthropy: lessons from a demographic analysis of the Coptic diaspora', *Nonprofit and Voluntary Sector Quarterly*, 43(6), pp. 969–992.
Carlson, E. and Williams, N. (2020) *Comparative Demography of the Syrian Diaspora: European and Middle Eastern Destinations*. Cham: Springer.
Carpi, E. and Fiddian-Qasmiyeh, E. (2020) 'Keeping the faith? Examining the roles of faith and secularism in Syrian diaspora organisations in Lebanon', in Dijkzeul, D. and Fauser, M. (eds) *Diaspora Organisations in International Affairs*. London: Routledge, pp. 129–149.
Dhesi, A. (2010) 'Diaspora, social entrepreneurs and community development', *International Journal of Social Economics*, 37(9), pp. 703–716.
Duman, T. (2020) 'The situation of Syrian women in Turkey', in Carlson, E. and Williams, N. (eds) *Comparative Demography of the Syrian Diaspora: European and Middle Eastern Destinations*. Cham: Springer, pp. 93–107.
Espinosa, S. (2015) 'Diaspora philanthropy: the making of a new development aid?', *Migration and Development*, 5(3), pp. 361–377.
Flanigan, S. (2006) 'Charity as resistance: connections between charity, contentious politics, and terror', *Studies in Conflict and Terrorism*, 29(7), pp. 641–655.
Flanigan, S. (2010) *For the Love of God: NGOs and Religious Identity in a Violent World*. Sterling, VA: Kumarian Press.
Flanigan, S. (2017) 'Crowdfunding and diaspora philanthropy: an integration of the literature and major concepts', *Voluntas: International Journal of Voluntary and Nonprofit Organizations*, 28(2), pp. 492–509.

Flanigan, S. (2018) 'Advantages of Syrian diaspora aid to refugees in Middle Eastern states of the global south', *Journal of Muslim Philanthropy and Civil Society*, 2(2), pp. 35–66.

Flanigan, S. and Abdel-Samad, M. (2016) 'Syrian diaspora members as transnational civil society actors: perspectives from a network for refugee assistance', *Contention: The Multidisciplinary Journal of Social Protest*, 4(1–2), pp. 51–65.

Garkisch, M., Heidingsfelder, J. and Beckman, M. (2017) 'Third sector organizations and migration: a systematic literature review on the contribution of third sector organizations in view of flight, migration and refugee crises', *Voluntas: International Journal of Voluntary and Nonprofit Organizations*, 28, pp. 1839–1880.

Gillespie, K., Riddle, L., Sayre, E. and Sturges, D. (1999) 'Diaspora homeland investment', *Journal of International Business Studies*, 30(3), pp. 623–634.

Gurr, T. (2000) *People Versus States: Minorities at Risk in the New Century*. Washington, DC: United States Institute of Peace Press.

Hubbard, B. (2020) 'Syria's economy collapses even as civil war winds to a close', *New York Times*, 5 June 2020. Available at: www.nytimes.com/2020/06/15/world/middleeast/syria-economy-assad-makhl ouf.html (accessed 17 June 2020).

İçduygu, A. (2015) *Syrian Refugees in Turkey: The Long Road Ahead*. Washington, DC: Migration Policy Institute.

Johnson, P. (2007) *Diaspora Philanthropy: Influences, Initiatives, and Issues*. Boston: The Philanthropic Initiative, Inc., and the Global Equity Initiative, Harvard University.

Kaufman, S. (2001) *Modern Hatreds: The Symbolic Politics of Ethnic War*. Ithaca, NY: Cornell University Press.

Kelley, N. (2017) 'Responding to a refugee influx: lessons from Lebanon', *Journal on Migration and Human Security*, 5(1), pp. 82–104.

Leblang, D. (2010) 'Familiarity breeds investment: diaspora networks and international investment', *American Political Science Review*, 104(3), pp. 584–600.

Levitt, P. (1998) 'Social remittances: migration-driven, local-level forms of cultural diffusion', *International Migration Review*, 32(4), pp. 926–948.

Mehrez, D. and Hamdy, H. (2010) 'Skilled Egyptian diaspora contributions to Egypt', *Education, Business and Society: Contemporary Middle Eastern Issues*, 3(4), pp. 250–261.

Merz, B. (2005) *New Patterns for Mexico: Observations on Remittances, Philanthropic Giving, and Equitable Development*. Cambridge: Global Equity Initiative.

Moon, S. and Choi, S. (2012) 'Ethnic giving versus mainstream giving by foreign-born Korean immigrants in California', *Nonprofit and Voluntary Sector Quarterly*, 42(4), pp. 803–827.

Moss, D. (2016) 'Transnational repression, diaspora mobilization, and the case of the Arab Spring', *Social Problems*, 63, pp. 480–498.

Mounzer, L. (2020) 'In Lebanon, a pandemic of hunger', *New York Times*, 6 May 2020. Available at: www.nytimes.com/2020/05/06/opinion/lebanon-protests-coronavirus.html (accessed 17 June 2020).

Mullings, B. (2011) 'Diaspora strategies, skilled migrants and human capital enhancement in Jamaica', *Global Networks*, 11(1), pp. 24–42.

Mutume, G. (2005) 'Workers' remittances: a boon to development. Money sent home by African migrants rivals development aid', *Africa Renewal*, 19(3), pp. 10–14.

Newland, K. and Patrick, E. (2004) *Beyond Remittances: The Role of Diaspora in Poverty Reduction in Their Countries of Origin*. Washington, DC: Migration Policy Institute.

Newland, K. and Tanaka, H. (2010) *Mobilizing Diaspora Entrepreneurship for Development*. Washington, DC: Migration Policy Institute.

Newland, K., Terrazas, A. and Munster, R. (2010) *Diaspora Philanthropy: Private Giving and Public Policy*. Washington, DC: Migration Policy Institute.

Nielsen, T., and Riddle, L. (2009) 'Investing in peace: the motivational dynamics of diaspora investment in post-conflict economies', *Journal of Business Ethics*, 89, pp. 435–448.

Orjuela, C. (2008) 'Distant warriors, distant peace workers? Multiple diaspora roles in Sri Lanka's violent conflict', *Global Networks*, 8(4), pp. 436–452.

Page, J. and Plaza, S. (2006) 'Migration remittances and development: a review of global evidence', *Journal of African Economies*, 15, pp. 245–336.

Riddle, L., Brinkerhoff, J. and Nielsen T. (2008) 'Partnering to beckon them home: public sector innovation for diaspora homeland investment', *Public Administration and Development*, 28(1), pp. 54–66.

Salamon, L. (1995) *Partners in Public Service: Government-Nonprofit Relations in the Modern Welfare State*. Baltimore, MD: Johns Hopkins University Press.

Shain, Y. (2002) 'The role of diasporas in conflict perpetuation or resolution', *SAIS Review*, 22(2), pp. 115–143.

Shain, Y. and Barth, A. (2003) 'Diasporas and international relations theory', *International Organization*, 57(3), pp. 449–479.

Sidel, M. (2008) 'A decade of research and practice of diaspora philanthropy in the Asia Pacific region: the state of the field'. Available at: https://papers.ssrn.com/sol3/papers.cfm?abstract_id=1127237 (accessed 25 June 2020).

Sieverding, M. and Calderón-Mejía, V. (2020) 'Demographic profile of Syrians in Jordan and Lebanon', in Carlson, E. and Williams, N. (eds) *Comparative Demography of the Syrian Diaspora: European and Middle Eastern Destinations*. Cham: Springer, pp. 109–135.

Sikod, F. and Tchouassi, G. (2007) 'Diaspora remittances and the financing of basic social services and infrastructure in Francophone Africa south of the Sahara', in Paterson, R. (ed.), *Africa Brain Drain Circulation: Beyond the Drain-Gain Debate*. Boston: Brill, pp. 41–58.

Suleiman, M. (1999) *Arabs in America: Building a New Future*. Philadelphia, PA: Temple University Press.

Tchouassi, G. and Sikod, F. (2010) 'Altruistic preferences as motivation for migrants in the diaspora to remit to home communities', *Research in Applied Economics*, 2(1), pp. 1–18.

Tilly, C. (2003) *The Politics of Collective Violence*. Cambridge: Cambridge University Press.

UNHCR. (2014) *Lebanese Communities in Focus: Supporting Communities Protecting Refugees*. Geneva, Switzerland: UNHCR.

UNHCR. (n.d.) 'Syria emergency'. Available at: www.unhcr.org/en-us/syria-emergency.html (accessed 25 June 2020).UNICEF. (2015) 'Humanitarian response plan: Syrian Arab Republic'. Available at: http://reliefweb.int/sites/reliefweb.int/files/resources/2016_hrp_syrian_arab_republic.pdf (accessed 25 June 2020).

Van Hear, N., Pieke, F. and Vertovec, S. (2010) *The Contribution of UK-based Diasporas to Development and Poverty Reduction*. Oxford,: ESRC Centre on Migration, Policy and Society (COMPAS), University of Oxford.

Werbner, P. (2002) 'The place which is diaspora: citizenship, religion and gender in the making of chaordic transnationalism', *Journal of Ethnic and Migration Studies* 28, pp. 119–133.

PART V
Diasporic sensibilities

23
RETURN MIGRATION AND REPATRIATION
Myths and realities in the interwar Syrian *mahjar*

Stacy D. Fahrenthold

Introduction

'I intended to go back [to Lebanon] and practice medicine at home after graduation', began Simon Abdelnour in a 1962 interview with historian Alixa Naff, 'but I was prevented from doing so by the war' (Abdelnour, 1962). It was 1914, and the Triple Entente placed a naval blockade on the eastern Mediterranean, effectively marooning Syrian, Lebanese and Palestinian migrants abroad. Abdelnour had come to the United States as a student, with a group of young men for whom the trip to the *mahjar* (diaspora) was supposed to be a temporary sojourn. Arabic-speaking immigrants in the Americas came from a variety of class backgrounds and worked in a variety of trades: as professionals and students, as labourers, industrial workers and peddlers. Alixa Naff's oral history series reveals how even in this diversity of early Arab American experiences, one common narrative feature presides: the initial expectation that immigration was temporary, eventual return to the Middle East was the goal, and that the force of historical circumstances forced a change in plans post-arrival (Naff, 1985, p. 127). In Abdelnour's case, fluctuating laws governing repatriation frustrated his attempts to return to Lebanon: 'I applied for a passport to go back but they weren't issuing passports; this was in 1919–20 … I came to Los Angeles and gave up the idea of going back to Lebanon' (Abdelnour, 1962). Another of Naff's interlocutors named Alice Abraham (who in 1909 came to America from Ayn Arab, unaccompanied at 15 years old) put it succinctly: 'I came to the U.S. to stay, but I was more sure of that after I got here' (Abraham, 1962, 1:11:40–1:11:50).

Scholars often comment on the ubiquity of return as a feature of Arab American historical narratives, part of an autobiographical storytelling that shapes the *mahjar*'s historical consciousness and upsets the linear 'to America' archetype. Historians insist that return migration to the *Mashriq* (defined here as Syria, Lebanon and Palestine) not only occurred in the interwar period but that it was more common than is popularly assumed. However, even as scholars routinely acknowledge return migration as relevant, the topic remains a vexing and understudied issue in the subfield. A notable exception, Akram Khater's (2001) *Inventing Home*, demonstrates how returning Lebanese emigrants shaped the architectural tastes, aesthetics and feminist debates of Lebanon's middle class, themes also pursued in Palestine studies by Jacob Norris (2017, pp. 60–75) and Nadim Bawalsa (2015). But significant questions remain about the broader issues of

DOI: 10.4324/9780429266102-28

migrant repatriation to the Middle East, with implications for societal impact, cultural hybridity and the politics of citizenship and nationality.

Migration historians approach the concept of diaspora alongside other forms of meso-level analysis. Situated between global, structural, and local determinants, meso-level analysis critiques neoclassical theories of migration rooted in push/pull functionalism, linear models or labour flows between economic cores and peripheries (Lucassen and Lucassen, 1997; Wimmer and Schiller, 2002). Instead, diasporas are held together by migrant social networks and are continually refreshed by ongoing circulations of people, goods and ideas (Clifford, 1994, pp. 302–305). A diaspora is both a social geography and a cultural space that 'is not congruent with physical geography' but is produced by migrant institutions, such as mutual aid societies, employment networks or circuits of information. These institutions maintain and continue to shape diasporic space, simultaneously creating and constraining opportunities for the individuals privy to them (McKeown, 2004, pp. 178–179). This focus on circulation, social geography and the dynamic of agency to structure marks a departure from older notions of diaspora centred on cataclysmic displacement, 'scattering', loss of homeland or permanent exile (Safran, 1991). Most notably, in a diaspora that is multi-centred and shaped by enduring connectivities, both circular and return migration are not only possible, often they are likely (Hoerder, 1999). Still, even with this dynamic theory of diaspora, the impact of return migration remains a road less travelled for historians. A closer look at return migration deepens the conceptual terrain of diaspora, for instance, by challenging the assumptions of the place-based area studies tradition (Arsan, Karam and Khater, 2013). Put another way, diasporas do more than *add to* the social histories of the Middle East; they also *transform* the region.

Rates of return migration from the interwar *mahjar* also reform long-standing notions about the relationship of economic cores to peripheries. Most of the historiography on American labour migration is informed by the settlement studies tradition and consequently focuses on immigrant integration, class mobility and other measures of (usually economic) success after arrival. The 'settlement studies' frame allows scholars to answer important questions about immigrant lives and advocacy abroad, especially concerning ethnicisation, racialisation, and more recently, surveillance and migration restriction in the Global North (Lucassen and Lucassen, 1997, pp. 21–25). However, its hegemony produced a blind spot with regard to circular and return migration. For many Middle Eastern migrant workers in the Americas, the diaspora represented structural economic and legal precarity, not a space of integration, multi-culturalism or success. Towards building a research agenda for analysing return migration to the Middle East, this chapter considers return along three planes: (1) as a scholarly problem; (2) as a set of diasporic myths; and (3) as a reality undertaken by thousands of migrants during the interwar period. It sets out core issues confronting scholars of return migration; introduces relevant historiography and comparisons between the Syrian, Lebanese and Palestine cases; and argues in favour of deeper reflection on return migration as a core facet of Arab Atlantic history.

Return as a scholarly problem

Though enumerating the *mahjar* is a fraught business, historians have arrived at a rough consensus concerning rates of emigration from Ottoman *Mashriq* (Syria, Mount Lebanon and Palestine) between 1880 and 1926, arriving at figures between 300,000 and 500,000 people in the Americas. Mass emigration from the Ottoman Empire began in the 1880s, and Charles Issawi (1982, p. 86) estimates that perhaps 120,000 people left Syria, Mount Lebanon and Palestine before 1900. Emigration sped up in the decade before the First World War, with 15,000 departing greater Syria annually. Most were bound for the United States, Brazil or

Argentina, each country hosting over 100,000 migrants by 1910. Smaller settlements emerged across the Americas, particularly in Chile, Mexico, Honduras, Cuba and Canada. Emigration halted during the war but picked up again in the 1920s. Using French Mandate statistics, Kohei Hashimoto (1992, p. 105) concludes that the Syrian and Lebanese in the Americas numbered 550,000 by 1926, a figure that excludes Palestinians under British Mandate. Emigrants in the Americas represented between 18 and 25 per cent of greater Syria's total population (Issawi 1992, p. 31). The demographic impact of emigration was lumpy and particularly high in places like Mount Lebanon, where some villages sent a third of their population abroad.

Several factors trouble this data, complicating more rigorous quantification of return migration patterns. First, these data derive from port records or census data, imperfect proxies for assessing migration rates. Relying on exit port registries creates blind spots around clandestine migration, for instance, and limits the impact that trajectory had on destinations. Many migrants departed Beirut, for '*Amrika*' and ended up, not in the United States as planned, but in Latin America (Khater, 2001, p. 62). Entry records across the Americas are spotty, non-standard, and notoriously unreliable. Between 1880 and 1920, Atlantic settler states focused on categorising arriving immigrants along racial, ethnic and later national origin categories associated with eugenicist ideas about assimilability. Determining the origins of Middle Eastern migrants is complicated by the shifting classificatory regimes they encountered. Arabic-speaking migrants from the *Mashriq* were variously classified as 'Turks', as 'Syrians' and occasionally as 'Assyrians', categories themselves conflated with religious confession. US immigration registers disaggregated 'Syrian' from 'Turk' in 1899, but the categories were still used unpredictably (Gualtieri, 2009, p. 77). Other Atlantic states employed these national origins markers similarly, conflating geographic terminologies with ethnic, racial or sectarian descriptors (Civantos, 2006, pp. 1–13; Karam, 2007, pp. 71–94). Finally, entry records lacked information on migrant departures; the constant circulation of migrants between *mahjar* and *Mashriq* confounded immigration registration regimes that focused solely on arrivals. Census data can be similarly problematic because imprecise immigration categories were iterated there as well.

With those caveats aside, in this chapter I propose points of entry into the study of interwar return migration, considering the ways that return operated as an idea within the *mahjar*'s transnational milieu before, during and after the First World War. As an ideal associated with notions of exile, sojourning and liberation, return assumed a cultural currency and gave meaning to the lives of individuals, held families together, or comprised a part of a larger diasporic worldview. I then examine actual experiences of return migration and repatriation, observing trends during the 1920s and 1930s. Along the way, I argue that Syrians, Lebanese and Palestinians living abroad grappled with the question of repatriation. Return figured in the *mahjar*'s mythologies, in its politics and as lived experience in the interwar period.

Return as mythology: literary and ideological tropes

The anticipation of return represents a core mythology of diaspora, a preoccupation remarked by scholars of Jewish, Armenian, Chinese and African histories. The terms by which a return to a homeland is imagined vary widely, connected to the circumstances of departure, the material and affective conditions of émigré communities, the prevalence of information or travel technologies (print culture, the telegraph, steamship, rail or air travel), or the emergence of diasporic nationalisms. The return narrative operated at several valances at once. It was a mundane feature of economic migration, an autobiographical story told by migrant workers who arrived abroad. Return also played a role in the *mahjar*'s intellectual imaginary, part of a cultural politics expressed by the Pen League writers of Syrian New York and their interlocutors in Latin

America (for instance, São Paulo's Andalusian League). Finally, the topos of return took on political content after the First World War and was a favourite topic for diasporic nationalist activism in Syrian, Lebanese and Palestinian contexts.

That Arabic-speaking Ottomans came to the Americas as sojourners (not as settlers) represents a point of consensus in the available scholarship. Whether coming as workers, peddlers, students or professionals, migrants described their motivations as economic, their goal to improve on their families' material conditions and return home with enhanced social mobility. Sarah Gualtieri (2009, p. 39) captures this autobiographical narrative, quoting a 1910 newspaper interview:

> If you ask a Syrian in North or South America whether he has emigrated from Syria, he will reply, "Absolutely not. I am away from her for a while. I left in search of wealth, and when I succeed I will return to my homeland."

The theme recurs in oral history testimonies given to Alixa Naff, revealing it as both more and less than nostalgia: it was also a mundane detail, a commonplace expectation (Naff, 1985).

Return also represented a potent literary theme in Arab American literature, connected with transcendental expressions about the relationship between cultures 'East' and 'West'. *The Book of Khalid*, published in English by Ameen Rihani in 1911, tells the story of Khalid and Shakib, two men who left Lebanon to work as peddlers in New York, where they end up in a tangle amid atheists, bohemians and corrupt political functionaries before returning home (Rihani, 2011). Rather than pantomiming the idealised return, which was then common within *mahjar* poetry (Nijland, 1989; Jubran, 2007; Hassan, 2008), Rihani depicts Khalid as the fool who charges back into the Ottoman Levant with reformist pretensions only to be excommunicated from the Maronite Church, cause a riot in Damascus and have his marriage plans spurned (Schumann, 2008, pp. 244–247). He becomes a hermit in the Lebanese Mountains for a time, momentarily reappears amid the 1908 Revolution's tumult, and then vanishes again in the novel's conclusion.

The narration of diaspora as exile also fed specific political patterns. After 1908, Syrian, Lebanese and Palestinian émigré intellectuals employed return as an arm of a larger nationalist politics, politicising the trope by putting it in service to explicit, programmatic claims to a post-Ottoman territory. Their long-distance nationalism differed from earlier articulations of the return trope in two ways. First, by generating 'an emotional attachment that is strong enough to compel people to political action that ranges from displaying a home country flag to deciding to return to fight and die in a land they may never have seen', diaspora nationalists claimed both the migrant generation and their children born abroad as part of a national community stretching beyond territorial borders (Schiller and Fouron, 2001, p. 4). Second, opposing the sentimentality evinced by the exile trope, long-distance nationalist politics prompted dynamic action in service to the homeland, a shared obligation resting on emigrants' shoulders. During the First World War, nationalist parties in the Americas invoked the obligations of Syrian emigrants abroad to save their homeland from the 'Turkish yoke' (*nir al-atrak*), retroactively recoding Ottoman rule as four centuries of hostile occupation by a foreign power. Randa Tawil, for instance, illustrates how Ameen Rihani's wartime writings renarrated Syrian migration as a flight from the empire's 'criminal tyranny' and concomitant indebtedness to the homeland (Tawil 2018, pp. 96–97).

The culmination of this politics came after the Ottoman Empire's 1918 evacuation from the Arab provinces. As the Great Powers negotiated the terms of the region's postwar administration, émigré political associations lobbied their allies on behalf of Syrian, Lebanese and

Palestinian compatriots. Many activists already had ties to the Entente, for instance through war work in intelligence, immigration advocacy and humanitarianism. During the 1919 Paris Peace Conference, these migrant associations petitioned in support of multiple nationalist projects, plotting a spectrum of opinion along the terms of national independence (complete and immediate versus some form of 'aegis', 'technical support' or 'protectorate' status guaranteed by France, Great Britain or the United States) among Arab nationalists, Syrianists and Lebanists (Hakim, 2013, pp. 214–221). The French Foreign Ministry, in particular, cultivated allies in the *mahjar* who submitted petitions of support for a French Mandate (Narbona, 2007). These petition campaigns were so prolific that they have inspired a robust scholarship of their own (Arsan, 2012; Jackson, 2012; Bailony, 2018). As diverse as they were, the idea that returning emigrants would rebuild the Middle East was a constant refrain, evident in this selection of petitions submitted to the peace conference from the Syrian *mahjar*:

> Syrians in the U.S.A. have already become in a way Americanized, and as a large majority of them is expected to return to Syria, once the odious Turkish yoke is lifted off, they will not wish anything better than to continue to breathe the same strong atmosphere of American liberty in their own country.
>
> *(New Syrian National League, 1919, p. 8)*

> This emigration on a large scale of Syrians, has given new economic resources and fresh social and intellectual powers to the country. As a result of being associated, for long years, with highly civilized people abroad the Syrian emigrants have, on their return, brought home many social improvements, sterling democratic principles and up-to-date fashions.
>
> *('Reborn Syria': an appeal to the League of Nations union, 1919, p. 9)*

> Another resultant blessing of American guidance will be the return of the bulk of Syrian emigrants without whom it will take Syria and especially the Lebanon more than a generation to return even to normality ... inducements are needed to reinforce in them the enfeebled attraction of the homeland. It is remembered that the flower of Syrian manhood has perished during the war, and that the moral and material generation of Syria depends ... on the return of her virile manhood from abroad.
>
> *(Tabet, 1919, pp. 10–11)*

These 1919 petitions link three projects into a potent triad: migrant repatriation, postwar reconstruction and nationalist reform. The gendered construction of repatriation as restorative to masculinity was also common within diasporic nationalist writings (Fahrenthold, 2014, pp. 263–264).

That said, return functioned as more than a nationalist rallying cry. In 1920s Arab feminist publications, writers employed the dislocations and estrangements (*ghurba*) experienced by women returning from the *mahjar* as a vehicle for critique of nationalist politics. Though marginalised by the mainstream *mahjari* press (which espoused the views and voices of émigré men's clubs), women writers engaged one another in the pages of women's newspapers produced in Beirut, New York, Boston, São Paulo, and beyond. 'Afifa Karam, Julia Dimashqi, Victoria Tannous and Salwa Salama Atlas (among others) articulated a feminism of the 'new woman' defined by links to the international women's movement; demands for access to rights of employment, education and public spaces; and explicit challenges to the patriarchal leanings of nationalist parties. They folded these demands within established discourses about women as civilisational agents and national mothers (Khater, 2001, pp. 146–159; Baron, 2007, pp. 7–9).

The act of returning took on a particular role in feminist discourse in the *mahjar*. 'Afifa Karam wrote at length about Syrian women abroad, arguing they were privy to the 'civilising benefits' of the American shop floor. In New York City's *al-Akhlaq* in 1920, she wrote:

> [M]ost of us will recall that common saying uttered by our civilised men that 'the [Syrian] women in America behave better than the men', [because] the women work for the benefit of our brothers and sisters ... and at the same time, she does not return as herself; the times and their virtues have impressed themselves upon her.
>
> *(Karam, 1920, p. 7)*

Karam and her contemporaries shaped a discourse around the notion that emigrant women could also offer political education to their homeland sisters. Akram Khater (2001, p. 169) discusses how class-based tensions sat amid *mahjari* feminist discourses, 'as much as emigrants brought back with them the seeds of middle-class society, they also carried along the arguments, debates, and tensions which were part and parcel of that phenomenon'.

For some, migrant repatriation represented neither a culmination of independence nor feminist liberation, but an escape from American racism and xenophobia. Writing to *The Syrian World* in 1927, Dr Michael Shadid opined that Syrian immigrants would never be accepted in the United States and would always face racial discrimination. The solution, he argued, was in return to the Middle East, and *Syrian World* editor Salloum Mukarzil printed his proposal for an organised return to Syria. A debate ensued, with readers writing in to reject Dr Shadid's assertions and tally the cultural costs and benefits of 'Americanism', defined as assimilation, economic integration or hybridisation of Syrian and American cultures. The debate in *The Syrian World* was lengthy and fraught, revealing that even as some migrants endorsed repatriation, others were anxious about whether repatriation projects like Shadid's would undermine the community's right to remain in America (Halaby, 1987, pp. 55–65). In the end, politics alone did not seem to provide much impetus for actual return migration. According to Sarah Gualtieri (2009, p. 107), 'Shadid had justified his "back to Syria" crusade in other than economic terms'. Like the nationalist repatriation campaigns, Shadid's idea came to nought. When Arab emigrants did return home, their motivations were almost invariably economic. Having found either fortune or failure in the *mahjar*, they boarded steamships headed east when the diaspora's economic circumstances shifted into the 1930s.

The politics of migrant repatriation to Syria, Lebanon and Palestine

Although the notion of a planned mass return to the homeland represented a potent societal myth in the *mahjar*, some Syrian, Lebanese and Palestinian migrants did return to the Middle East as tourists, visitors and repatriates. During the Ottoman period, Arab subjects encountered few problems in returning to their home villages, and circular labour migration was a typical configuration. According to Kemal Karpat (1985, p. 186), the Ottoman government's 'basic policy was to allow unlimited freedom of return to all Ottoman subjects, present and former, with no discrimination on the basis of race'. Despite moments of reversal, the empire tended to view repatriation with favour. Both the Hamidian state and the constitutionalist government which followed it funded repatriation campaigns, designed to entice emigrants to invest their earnings in Ottoman industries. Following the 1908 Young Turk Revolution, the Committee of Union and Progress (CUP) government opened new consulates in the United States, Brazil and Argentina to reach Ottomans abroad (Klich, 1993; Hyland, 2011). From those consulates, the government announced a general amnesty for all migrants accused of political crimes, hoping to appeal to Armenians and Arabs in exile.

For the Ottomans, Arab return migration was desirable, but continuing emigration abroad was also the cause of official anxiety. Ottoman law prohibited permanent emigration and expressly forbade expatriation (naturalisation in another country of domicile). Nevertheless, Arab migrants used the internal Ottoman passport (the *mürur tezkeresi*) to travel beyond the empire, and it was widely accepted by immigration authorities at Mediterranean and Atlantic ports (Karpat, 1985, p. 187; Gutman, 2012, pp. 62–66). Ottoman officials worried about the departure of men of conscription age, prompting them to intensify passenger traffic controls through the port of Beirut 1909 and 1913 (Akarli, 1992, p. 110). The CUP also attempted to limit access to travel certificates, and prosecuted agents discovered to have assisted unauthorised migrant departures.

Until the First World War, Ottoman policy towards the *mahjar* remained focused on its economic capacity, encouraging remittances and investment in the homeland. After 1914, Istanbul disengaged with the Americas, closing the empire's consulates, censoring the press and prosecuting émigrés for political crimes. The allies responded by placing Ottoman immigrant communities under close surveillance and restricting their movement across borders. The United States, for instance, imposed a travel ban on Ottoman nationals living in American territories in 1918. Purportedly to protect US war interests, the 1918 Travel Control Act prohibited both arrivals and departures of Ottoman passport holders through US borders, prompting a number of Syrian and Lebanese merchants to seek diplomatic protection and travel passes from the French Foreign Ministry (Fahrenthold, 2019, pp. 115–122).

The Travel Control Act also standardised passport controls in a new way, transforming the passport into the primary means of migration regulation. At the same time, passports assumed new provenance as systems of verifying individual identity, categorising migrant flows and regulating rights of nationality. For Middle Eastern migrants, these processes operated in concert with events that shaped the post-Ottoman eastern Mediterranean: the Paris Peace Conference, the emergence of the League of Nations and its mandates in the region. The resumption of passenger transit in the eastern Mediterranean encouraged a burst of new migration in all directions: across the *mahjar* and between the homeland and its diasporas. Emigration from Syria, Mount Lebanon and Palestine swiftly resumed at levels that surpassed the peaks of the prewar moment (Hourani, 1992, pp. 4–5), raising concerns for the European officials then managing these territories.

On the other hand, emigrants who spent the war abroad also began to return home, hastened by the need to tend to properties or claim nationality status after the Ottoman Empire's disintegration. Historians have recorded return migration patterns of former Ottoman Kurds, Armenians, and Syrian, Lebanese and Palestinian Arabs at varying rates. The highest rates of return seem to be to the new state of Greater Lebanon, created in 1920; there, estimates range from 25 to 45 per cent of all emigrants who departed prior to 1914 ultimately returning during the interwar period (Hashimoto, 1992, p. 87; Khater, 2001, pp. 110–114). This rate of return is slightly higher than European averages but was by no means exceptional; scholars mapping the return of Turkish migrants, for instance, cite rates as high as 90 per cent (Acehan, 2009, p. 21).

Even in periods of heightened return migration, however, new waves of emigration tempered the absolute numbers of returnees. From 1926 to 1933, for instance, new emigrant departures outpaced return migration at a ratio of 2 to 1 (Himadeh, 1936, p. 20). This circulation impacted local cultures in the *Mashriq*. A Brazilian priest visiting Lebanon in 1925 discovered Portuguese speakers in Zahle (Lesser, 1996, p. 54). In the late 1930s, Syria became the top importer of Argentinian yerba mate outside Latin America, driven by returning émigré businesses (Folch, 2010, pp. 26–27). Repatriates to Mount Lebanon brought their red-tile roofs and bourgeois social expectations with them, reshaping the middle class by the mid-century (Khater, 2001, pp. 108–145). In sum, the interwar *mahjar* was conditioned by the continuous circulation of people, goods and ideas, not by the singular experience of migration to America. Likewise, when repatriates returned to their towns and villages of origin, they brought the *mahjar* with them: social capital, consumer items, ideas and prejudices, new idioms or hybrid cultural norms.

The mandates also redefined sovereignty in important ways, influencing who had access to repatriation and under what terms. Syria, Lebanon and Palestine each emerged after 1920 within territorially defined borders drawn by their mandatories, France and Great Britain. In all three places, European administrators fixated on territorial borders as assumed sovereign containers for exclusive, distinct nationalities; such assumptions were instantly challenged by the realities of international migration, the presence of refugees, cross-border transhumance and diasporic claims-making. Similarly, both the French and British were engaged in refugee resettlement programmes, and these programmes encoded the mandates' population policies and stance towards repatriates from abroad (Robson, 2017, pp. 35–64; White, 2017). French policies governing migrant repatriation from the Americas, for instance, emerged alongside a concurrent programme to resettle 150,000 Armenian refugees in Syria and Lebanon (Issawi, 1982, p. 78). In a 1924 report to the League of Nations, the French connected the Armenian relocation to uncontrolled Lebanese emigration:

> they [the Armenians] will contribute a necessary artisan class to Syria and Lebanon, skilled in the trades, and by default they will compensate for the rarefaction of labour, itself a consequence of the traditional emigration of Lebanese to the Americas.
> *(Ministère des Affaires Étrangères 1925, p. 52)*

However, even as mandate authorities shared concerns about the impact of migration on the region and contemplated possibilities for migrant repatriation from the *mahjar*, interwar policies governing migrant rights produced distinct, contradictory results. In Lebanon, the French encouraged selective repatriation of Lebanese Christians from the Americas, creating a system of travel passes to incentivise return migration. In Syria, by contrast, the French were consumed with ongoing anticolonial insurgencies and sought to cut ties with Syrian emigrants instead. In Palestine, the British emphasised policing the mandate's territorial borders, leaving the encounter, screening and detention of migrants up to border guards, with unpredictable results.

In Lebanon, the French Mandate extended some rights of travel, repatriation and nationality to Lebanese emigrants seeking to return home. In a marked departure from state impulses towards other emigrants, French authorities in Beirut imagined the diaspora as a source of needed political legitimacy, leading to the inclusion of 130,000 Lebanese domiciled abroad in Lebanon's first national census in 1921 (they were counted again in 1932). The inclusion of emigrants from the majority-Christian diaspora bolstered the High Commissioner's claims to Greater Lebanon as a Christian-majority state. The diaspora's demography, moreover, influenced the apportionment of seats in Lebanon's representative council and underpinned its confessional system of governance. The French allowed Lebanese emigrants the right to vote in Lebanese elections, but only if they returned to their villages of origin to do so (Hashimoto, 1992, p. 79; Maktabi, 1999, p. 241). The sectarian system of government the French constructed in Lebanon depended on the active maintenance of confessional demography, prompting them to encourage selective repatriation. Returning emigrants were granted a means of securing Lebanese nationality in the 1925 Nationality Code, for instance, and the French instituted consular offices to reach Syrian and Lebanese communities abroad (Ministère des Affaires Étrangères, 1925, pp. 52–53). At those consulates, officials exercised considerable latitude in vetting emigrant passport applications. Lebanese émigrés protested that consular staff rejected their applications on political bases (Fahrenthold, 2019, pp. 157–158).

In Syria, the French were disinterested in emigrant repatriation, and Syrians abroad experienced more trouble travelling to Syria than did their Lebanese counterparts. Continuing anticolonial activism in the Americas led the French to view the Syrian *mahjar* as a political threat. French authorities were alarmed by the possibilities for diasporic material support for armed insurrection, an anxiety that deepened during the 1925–1927 Great Syrian Revolt (Bailony, 2018). When the former Ottoman consul of Buenos Aires, Amin Arslan, condemned French imperialism following the mandate's 1925 bombardment of Damascus, the city's consulate threatened to retract the right of migrants in Argentina to claim Syrian nationality entirely. A crisis ensued and mandate officials backed down, but by 1928, fewer than 10 per cent of Argentina's Syrian immigrants had achieved recognition of any kind (Narbona, 2007, p. 137). In sum, the French treated Lebanese and Syrian emigrants in divergent ways, a politics tied to the mandate's dependence on Lebanese emigrants as a source of legitimacy.

In Palestine, the British Mandate was disinterested in facilitating Arab return migration from the Americas and in most cases expressly prohibited it. Instead, the colonial authorities invested in the affixing of territorial borders and the creation of complex, shifting and bureaucratically opaque border controls designed to make permanent repatriation difficult. Palestinian Arabs both at home and abroad remained formal Ottoman subjects until 1923. In the absence of a nationality law, ambiguity presided over the theoretical right of Palestinian emigrants to return home. Lauren Banko (2016) argues that British officials in Jerusalem exercised an incredible amount of latitude in determining repatriation cases, often refusing to issue passports and visas to Palestinians, some of whom subsequently applied for French passports to Syria. As in the French Mandate, the Treaty of Lausanne offered international recognition of Palestinian emigrants to a post-Ottoman nationality, theoretically opening a window for emigrants from Palestine to return and opt for Palestinian nationality. In 1925, Palestine's Citizenship Order-in-Council was passed, restricting repatriation rights to those born in Palestine (excluding children born abroad), and requiring migrants to hasten their return, meet a six-month residency requirement and claim nationality before July 1926 (Banko, 2012, p. 653). Palestinians in the Americas continued to petition for the right to return after 1926, but the British Mandate was committed to refusing migrant repatriation applications (Bawalsa, 2015, pp. 126–127). This left Palestinians abroad in an awkward legal space as neither British protected persons, nor non-Jewish citizens of Palestine, nor citizens of their countries of domicile.

Despite these bureaucratic obstacles, many migrants did return. Estimates about the scope of return migration vary in the scholarship, maintaining that 20–45 per cent of emigrants from the *mahjar* returned between 1920 and 1946. Higher rates of return to Lebanon are reported than to Syria or Palestine, although Lebanon continued to experience higher rates of new emigration. Though return migration and circulation were constant features of the Mandate Period, two spikes also occurred: a wave of repatriations in the months following the 1918 armistice, and a second increase accompanying the global recession in the early 1930s.

Conclusion

The 1920s were defined by a mood of mounting hostility towards Middle Eastern immigrants. In addition to quota restrictions, popular xenophobia, and the fixation on deportation and 'public charge' legislation in the Americas, the European mandatory states installed in the Middle East after the Ottoman Empire's collapse also favoured the restriction of return migration. This climate of migration restriction pushed against the desires of Syrian, Lebanese and Palestinian Arab migrants seeking permanent repatriation in the region. Whereas the Turkish Republic oversaw the repatriation of Turkish emigrants from the Americas through the 1920s (Acehan, 2009), rates of Arab return migration increased later in the decade as America's heavy industries faltered. Between 1926 and 1929, for instance, the US textile industry went bust: factories in Lowell, Lawrence, Fall River and New York City closed their doors on immigrant workers, and larger firms moved operations to Latin America in pursuit of cheaper labour (Chomsky, 2008). Some Arab workers followed the industry south, relocating from the United States to the Syrian colonies of São Paulo or Ypiranga, Brazil; to Buenos Aires and Rosario, Argentina; to Santiago, Chile; or elsewhere. Unemployed men also sought repatriation to the Middle East, looking for better economic conditions at home. Contrary to pervasive assumptions that the *mahjar* was a place of economic opportunity and the chance to find one's fortune, many workers discovered that the diaspora offered them only bare existence, a structurally precarious position they alleviated by travelling back home. Returnees in the *Mashriq* ran the socio-economic gamut, from the upwardly mobile bourgeoisie whose red-roofed houses dotted Mount Lebanon to the compassionate repatriation of unemployed or disabled Arab workers rejoining their natal families.

These patterns intensified during the Great Depression in the early 1930s, as unemployed workers applied for private welfare to pay for steamship tickets to the Middle East. In 1933–1934, joblessness, homelessness, and privation dogged urban Syrian neighbourhoods in New York, New England, and elsewhere, prompting a reversal of the same economic patterns that had motivated outmigration four decades earlier. Unemployed and impoverished workers depended on mutual aid societies and philanthropic organisations to assist in repatriation. In Mexico, Camila Pastor reveals a complex system of public-private partnerships between immigrant aid organisations and French consular authorities; to compel the French Mandate to accept Lebanese repatriates, their return had to be understood as a benevolent resolution to genuine economic misfortune beyond the migrants' control (Pastor, 2017, pp. 96–98). In Boston, a similar set of connections between American social workers, the Red Cross, and immigrant charities like the Syrian Lebanese Ladies Aid Society negotiated return passage for destitute, disabled or aged workers to Lebanon and Palestine (Shakir, 1987, pp. 133–135). In all cases, repatriation represented a safety valve, an escape from the structural precarity of the Depression-era *mahjar*. At the same time, however, critics of repatriation worried that planning the departure of economically marginalised immigrants might undermine the right of the larger Arab American community to remain. In the context of US debates over public charge deportations involving Mexican, Chinese and other workers in the 1930s, such anxieties were understandable (Hester, 2017, pp.141–169).

Though precise statistics concerning the rates of repatriation from the Arabic-speaking *mahjar* have been elusive, there is abundant room for new research into return migration to the Middle East from this diaspora. Framing diaspora alongside other meso-level networks maintained by migrant communities across oceans and continents, this chapter suggests that examining return as a diasporic fixation, as a political ideology, and as a practical reality for many Syrian, Lebanese and Palestinian emigrants creates opportunities for thinking about the diaspora's impact on the modern Middle East. New methodologies in social history will also lend significant support for scholars pursuing these questions, especially methods drawing on migrant correspondence, the ethnic press and the travel regimes (passports, port records, immigration control and border authorities) that Syrians, Lebanese and Palestinians confronted as they moved around the world.

Finally, the creative and rich borderlands literature in American and Latin American contexts offers a model for thinking through return without dependence on formal archives. Among other boons for the field, a deeper engagement with return will unpack the pioneer bias within immigrant histories, stressing instead the circular migration, transnationalisation of families and civil society, and the continuities that emigrants maintain with their places of origin. Perhaps most compellingly, a focus on return migration might reframe what historians often assume about emigration in the first place: the notion that diasporas represent spaces of comparative wealth, economic liberty and enhanced social mobility. Such rosy pictures of life abroad are themselves part of an immigration mythology that contrasts against the precarity, privation and legal proscription that emigrants often experience.

References

Abdelnour, S. (1962) 'Oral history interview with Alixa Naff'. [Recording and notes, online] Available at Faris and Yamna Naff Arab American Collection, Smithsonian Institution, online at Arab American National Museum. Available at: http://cdm16806.contentdm.oclc.org/cdm/search/collection/p16806coll10/searchterm/Simon%20A./field/partic/mode/exact/conn/and/order/nosort

Abraham, A. (1962) 'Oral history interview with Alixa Naff'. [Recording and notes, online] Available at Faris and Yamna Naff Arab American Collection, Smithsonian Institution, online at Arab American National Museum. Available at: https://cdm16806.contentdm.oclc.org/digital/collection/p16806coll10/id/81

Acehan, I. (2009) '"Ottoman Street in America": Turkish leatherworkers in Peabody, Massachusetts', *International Review of Social History*, 54, pp. 19–44.

Akarli, E. (1992) 'Ottoman attitudes towards Lebanese emigration, 1885–1910', in Hourani, A. and Shehadi, N. (eds) *Lebanese in the World: A Century of Emigration*. London: I.B. Tauris, pp. 109–138.

Arsan, A. (2012) '"This age is the age of associations": committees, petitions, and the roots of interwar Middle Eastern internationalism', *Journal of Global History*, 7(2), pp. 166–188.

Arsan, A., Karam, J. and Khater, A. (2013) 'On forgotten shores: migration in Middle East studies and the Middle East in migration studies', *Mashriq and Mahjar: Journal of Middle East and North African Migration Studies*, 1(1), pp. 1–7.

Bailony, R. (2018) 'From mandate borders to the diaspora: Rashaya's transnational suffering and the making of Lebanon in 1925', *Arab Studies Journal*, 26(2), pp. 44–73.

Banko, L. (2012) 'The creation of Palestinian citizenship under an international mandate: legislation, discourses and practices, 1918–1925', *Citizenship Studies*, 16, pp. 641–655.

Banko, L. (2016) *The Invention of Palestinian Citizenship, 1918–1948*. Edinburgh: Edinburgh University Press.

Baron, B. (2007) *Egypt as a Woman: Nationalism, Gender, and Politics*. Berkeley, CA: University of California Press.

Bawalsa, N. (2015) 'Citizens from afar: Palestinian migrants and the new world order, 1920–1930', in Arsan, A. and Schayegh, C. (eds) *The Routledge Handbook of the History of the Middle East Mandates*. London: Routledge, pp. 123–135.

Chomsky, A. (2008) *Linked Labor Histories: New England, Colombia, and the Making of a Global Working Class*. Durham, NC: Duke University Press.

Civantos, C. (2006) *Between Argentines and Arabs: Argentine Orientalism, Arab Immigrants, and the Writing of Identity*. Albany, NY: State University of New York Press.

Clifford, J. (1994) 'Diasporas', *Cultural Anthropology*, 9(3), pp. 302–338.

Fahrenthold, S.D. (2014) 'Sound minds in sound bodies: transnational philanthropy and patriotic masculinity in al-Nadi al-Homsi and Syrian Brazil, 1920–1932', *International Journal of Middle East Studies*, 46(2), pp. 259–283.

Fahrenthold, S.D. (2019) *Between the Ottomans and the Entente: The First World War in the Syrian and Lebanese Diaspora, 1908–1925*. New York: Oxford University Press.

Folch, C. (2010) 'Yerba mate myths, markets, and meanings from conquest to present', *Comparative Studies in Society and History*, 52(1), 3–36.

Gualtieri, S. M. A. (2009) *Between Arab and White: Race and Ethnicity in the Early Syrian American Diaspora*. Berkeley, CA: University of California Press.

Gutman, D. (2012) 'Agents of mobility: migrant smuggling networks, transhemispheric migration, and time-space compression in Ottoman Anatolia, 1888–1908', *InterDisciplines*, 1, pp. 48–84.

Hakim, C. (2013) *The Origins of the Lebanese National Idea, 1840–1920*. Berkeley, CA: University of California Press.

Halaby, R. (1987) 'Dr. Michael Shadid and the debate over identity in *The Syrian World*," in Hooglund, E. (ed.) *Crossing the Waters: Arabic-Speaking Immigrants to the United States before 1940*. Washington, DC: Smithsonian Institute Press, pp. 55–65.

Hashimoto, K. (1992) 'Lebanese population movement 1920–1939', in Hourani, A. and Shehadi, N. (eds) *Lebanese in the World: A Century of Emigration*. London: I.B. Tauris, pp. 77–107.

Hassan. W.S. (2008) 'The rise of Arab-American literature: Orientalism and cultural translation in the work of Ameen Rihani', *American Literary History*, 20(1/2), pp. 245–275.

Hester, T. (2017) *Deportation: The Origins of U.S. Policy*. Philadelphia, PA: University of Pennsylvania Press.

Himadeh, S. B. (1936) *Economic Organization of Syria*. Beirut: American Press.

Hoerder, D. (1999) 'From immigration to migration systems: new concepts in migration history', *OAH Magazine of History*, 14(1), pp. 5–11.

Hourani, A. and Shehadi, N. (eds) (1992) *Lebanese in the World: A Century of Emigration*. London: I.B. Tauris.

Hyland, S. (2011) '"Arisen from deep slumber": transnational politics and competing nationalisms among Syrian immigrants in Argentina, 1900–1922', *Journal of Latin American Studies*, 43(3), pp. 547–574.

Issawi, C. (1982) *An Economic History of the Middle East and North Africa*. New York: Columbia University Press.

Issawi, C. (1992) 'The historical background of Lebanese emigration, 1800–1914', in Hourani, A. and Shehadi, N. (eds) *Lebanese in the World: A Century of Emigration*. London: I.B. Tauris, pp. 13–31.

Jackson, S. (2012) 'Diaspora politics and developmental empire: the Syro-Lebanese at the League of Nations', *Arab Studies Journal*, 21(1), pp. 166–190.

Jubran, S. (2007) 'Classical elements in Mahjar poetry', *Journal of Arabic Literature*, 38(1), pp. 67–77.

Karam, A. (1920) 'al-Muhajira ka-l-tajira', *al-Akhlaq*, p. 7.

Karam, J.T. (2007) *Another Arabesque: Syrian-Lebanese Ethnicity in Neoliberal Brazil*. Philadelphia, PA: Temple University Press.

Karpat, K. (1985) 'The Ottoman emigration to America, 1860–1914', *International Journal of Middle East Studies*, 17(2), pp. 175–205.

Khater, A.F. (2001) *Inventing Home: Emigration, Gender, and the Middle Class in Lebanon, 1870–1920*. Berkeley, CA: University of California Press.

Klich, I. (1993) 'Argentine-Ottoman relations and their impact on immigrants from the Middle East: a history of unfulfilled expectations, 1910–1915', *The Americas*, 50(2), pp. 177–205.

Lucassen, J. and Lucassen, L. (eds) (1997) *Migration, Migration History, History: Old Paradigms and New Perspectives*. New York: Peter Lang.

Lesser, J. (1996) '(Re)creating ethnicity: Middle Eastern immigration to Brazil', *The Americas*, 53(1), pp. 45–65.

Maktabi, R. (1999) 'The Lebanese census of 1932 revisited: who are the Lebanese?' *British Journal of Middle Eastern Studies*, 26(2), pp. 219–241

McKeown, A. (2004) 'Global migration, 1846–1940', *Journal of World History*, 15(2), pp. 155–189.

Ministère des Affaires Étrangères (1925) *Rapport sur la Situation de la Syrie et du Liban, Année 1924*. Paris: Imprimerie Nationale.

Naff, A. (1985) *Becoming American: The Early Arab Immigrant Experience*. Carbondale, IL: University of Illinois Press.

Narbona, M. (2007) 'The development of nationalist identities in French Syria and Lebanon: a transnational dialogue with Arab immigrants to Argentina and Brazil', PhD dissertation, University of California, Santa Barbara.

New Syrian National League (1919) 'The future of Syria', memorandum submitted to the American Commission to the Peace Conference (12 July 1919) [memorandum]. Held at: National Archives and Records Administration, general records of the Department of State, record group 59 (National Archives microfilm publication M367, roll 382, document 763.72119/1819).

Nijland, C. (1989) 'The fatherland in Arab emigrant poetry', *Journal of Arabic Literature*, 20(1), pp. 57–68.

Norris, J. (2017) 'Return migration and the rise of the Palestinian nouveaux riches, 1870–1925', *Journal of Palestine Studies*, 46(2), pp. 60–75.

Pastor, C. (2017) *The Mexican Mahjar: Transnational Maronites, Jews, and Arabs under the French Mandate*. Austin, TX: University of Texas.

'Reborn Syria: an appeal to the League of Nations union', memorandum submitted to the United States Department of State (January 1919) [memorandum]. Held at: National Archives and Records Administration, general records of the Department of State, record group 59 (National Archives microfilm publication M367, roll 399, document 763.72119/4302).

Rihani, A.F. (1911) *The Book of Khalid*. New York: Dodd, Mead and Company.

Robson, L. (2017) *States of Separation: Transfer, Partition, and the Making of the Modern Middle East*. Oakland, CA: University of California Press.

Safran, W. (1991) 'Diasporas in modern societies: myths of homeland and return', *Diaspora: A Journal of Transnational Studies*, 1(1), pp. 83–99.

Schiller, N.G. and Fouron, G.E. (2001) *Georges Woke Up Laughing: Long-Distance Nationalism and the Search for Home*. Durham, NC: Duke University Press.

Schumann, C. (2008) 'Within or without? Ameen Rihani and the transcultural space between the "West" and the "East"', in Schumann, C. (ed.) *Liberal Thought in the Eastern Mediterranean: Late 19th Century until the 1960s*. Leiden: Brill, pp. 239–266.

Shakir, E. (1987) 'Good works, good times: the Syrian Ladies Aid Society of Boston, 1917–1932', in Hooglund, E. (ed.) *Crossing the Waters: Arabic-Speaking Immigrants to the United States before 1940*. Washington, DC: Smithsonian Institute Press, pp. 133–143.

Tabet, C.N. (1919) 'America and Syria', letter to U.S. Secretary of State Robert Lansing (27 February 1919) [correspondence]. Held at: National Archives and Records Administration, general records of the Department of State, record group 59 (National Archives microfilm publication M367, roll 304, roll 403, document 763.72119/4555).

Tawil, R. (2018) 'Racial borderlines: Ameen Rihani, Mexico, and World War I", *Amerasia Journal*, 44(1), pp. 85–104.

White, B.T. (2017) 'Refugees and the definition of Syria, 1920–1939', *Past & Present*, 235, pp. 141–178.

Wimmer, A. and Schiller, N.G. (2002) 'Methodological nationalism and beyond: nation-state building, migration, and the social sciences", *Global Networks*, 2(4), pp. 301–344.

24

THE EMERGENCE OF DIASPORIC SENSIBILITIES AMONG IRAQIS IN LONDON

Zainab Saleh

Historically, Iraq did not export economic migrants. Rather, beginning in the first half of the twentieth century, Iraqis began to leave Iraq mainly for political reasons. Since its establishment in 1921, the Iraqi state under different regimes – whether monarchical, republican or military – has been responsible for the displacement and expulsion of different segments of the Iraqi population. The forced migration from Iraq has been closely tied to the project of nation-building and different regimes' efforts to assert their sovereignty, govern a diverse country, control and discipline groups that are seen as a threat, and silence political opposition and other national claims (Chatelard, 2012, p. 363). This long history of persecution and migration led to the emergence of Iraqi communities in the Middle East (particularly, Jordan, Iran, Syria, Yemen and the Gulf countries), Europe (especially the United Kingdom, Finland, Sweden and the former Eastern bloc), the United States, New Zealand, Australia and Canada. The forced migration of Iraqis through direct or indirect compulsion was accompanied by measures to limit the mobility of the population within Iraq through restrictions on issuing travel documents under the monarchy and through banning travelling under Saddam Hussein's reign (ibid., p. 367). Different Iraqi communities constituted nascent diasporic groups that created connections with Iraq and the host countries, engaged in political activism that involved different centres of exilic opposition with the aim of changing the status quo in Iraq and building new forms of communities and subjectivities.

The first Iraqi group to arrive in London were Iraqi Jews who were forced out of Iraq in the early 1950s and settled in London, rather than Israel. Following the fall of the monarchy in 1958, elite urban Arab families associated with the monarchy also arrived in the United Kingdom. In the early 1960s, these small communities were joined by Iraqi Assyrians, who began to leave for London due to their military association with the British occupation in Iraq between 1914 and the fall of the monarchy in 1958 (Al-Rasheed, 1994). These communities formed Iraqi enclaves in London whose numbers did not exceed a few thousand.[1] It was not until Saddam Hussein came to power in 1979 that Iraqi communities[2] of considerable size began to emerge in the United Kingdom. In 1979, an already powerful Saddam Hussein seized control and became president of Iraq. His regime was in some respects a continuation of those established by the first Ba'th regime of 1963, and the second Ba'th regime of 1968, which heralded the rise of the one-party system and the consolidation of authoritarian rule. The nature of the Ba'th Party itself began to change when it simply became a means to wield power rather than a brand of pan-Arabism, and when political opponents, as well as critical voices within the party, began to be eliminated. Saddam Hussein's reign began with a cold-blooded purge of the Ba'th Party, the liquidation of the Iraqi Communist Party, the persecution of the Shi'i opposition and Kurdish movements, the expulsion of the so-called Iraqis of Iranian origin, and the elimination and silencing of anyone else who was perceived to represent a threat to his rule (Farouk-Sluglett and Sluglett, 2001; Allawi, 2007; Tripp, 2007; Sassoon, 2011; Khoury, 2013). The emergence of the Iraqi communities in the United Kingdom and other countries in the late 1970s is intimately connected to this political moment in Iraqi history.

In the wake of the 1991 Gulf War, thousands of Iraqis fled the country, swelling the Iraqi communities in Detroit, London, Damascus and Amman. The failure of the uprisings against Saddam Hussein's regime in the north and the south, and the harsh UN-imposed economic sanction from 1990 to 2003 led to further and larger waves of Iraqi refugees in the United Kingdom, when the government began to routinely grant asylum to Iraqis. During the initial phase of my fieldwork (2006–2008), the Iraqi ambassador to London put the number of Iraqis in the United Kingdom at 400,000. The majority of the Iraqi communities in the United Kingdom are thought to reside in London.

My work focuses on Iraqis who arrived in London from the late 1970s onwards, when the British capital emerged as a centre for the Iraqi communities. Iraqis in London, like other Iraqis in other host countries (such as Iran, Syria, European countries, the United States and New Zealand) occupied a peculiar position as migrant communities in that their presence in London was informed by forced absence (Clifford, 2013) since they could not maintain direct connections with Iraq while Saddam Hussein was in power. While the national space of Iraq was closed to Iraqis in London before 2003, these Iraqis were tied to Iraq through their values, family connections, friendship circles and cultural productions about Iraq, characterised by a nostalgia for the 'good old days', and news from Iraq. Though living in London, Iraqis developed long-distance nationalism that reflected their deep commitment to Iraq. More importantly, Iraqi diasporic communities in London played an important role in shaping post-Saddam Iraq as London emerged as the centre of exilic Iraqi opposition to Saddam Hussein's regime in the 1990s. The migrant reality of the Iraqi communities in London over the past four decades raises questions about the nature of the communities. Do Iraqis in London constitute exilic, transnational or diasporic communities? In what ways do different generational experiences with migration and settlement inform conceptions of diaspora and exile? How do Iraqis in London construct new forms of communities and subjectivities to relate to the realities of belonging to multiple spaces? And how did the fall of Saddam Hussein's regime in 2003 shift the narrative of exile and transnationalism into a discourse of diaspora?

The scholarly debate on the concepts of diaspora and transnationalism has informed studies of migration, identity, globalisation and nation. While scholars acknowledge that the two terms overlap and are often used interchangeably, they aim to distinguish between them to show the different modalities of mobility and community formation. Ato Quayson and Girish Daswani approach diaspora as the dispersal of a population that must meet certain conditions, which include

> the time-depth of dispersal and settlement in other locations; the development of a myth of the homeland; the attendant diversification of responses to homeland and host nation; the evolution of class segmentation and conflict within a given diaspora alongside the concomitant evolution of an elite group of cultural and political

brokers: and the ways in which contradictions among the various class segments end up reinforcing different forms of material and emotional investment in an imaginary ideal of the homeland.

(2013, p. 3)

To Quayson and Daswani, the emphasis on the myth of the homeland and the sense of a co-ethnic and cultural community in a diaspora differentiates it from a transnational community, which transcends diaspora precisely because its members are tied together through 'elective modes of identification involving class, sexuality, and even professional interest' (ibid., p. 4). A Buddhist community outside China, Japan or India, and an environmental movement that professes a common cause are examples of transnational communities in this case. In this framework, transnationalism is not limited to the movement of people but includes notions of citizenship, multinational governance, technology and global markets. Despite their efforts to differentiate between diaspora and transnationalism, Quayson and Daswani come close to conflating the two when they describe the research on transnationalism as delineating the experiences of migrants and those who remain behind and share a sense of belonging to two or more nation-states, and who develop nostalgia 'lodged in both homelands and the nations of sojourn at once' (ibid., p. 6). This definition centres the emphasis on co-ethnic and cultural identification and on connections between the homeland and host countries again.

Dalia Abdelhady offers a different reading of the terms diaspora and transnationalism. To her, transnationalism provides an alternative to theories of assimilation and integration and encompasses connections and linkages that reach across the homelands and host countries, particularly political ties that an immigrant community maintains with the homeland (2006, p. 426). Moreover, immigrants can foster transnational ties to their homeland as a mechanism to manage existing racial and ethnic structures in the host country. Abdelhady critiques the concept of transnationalism for implying a hierarchy between a homeland and a host country and foreclosing the possibility of understanding new forms of communities and subjectivity that emerge out of the experience of migration (ibid., p. 430; Abdelhady, 2011, p. 5). To her, the concept of diaspora opens the space to study how immigrants construct notions of subjectivity and community within a global frame of reference (Abdelhady, 2006, p. 431). Taking inspiration from Stuart Hall's assertion that members of diasporic communities realise that they could never be unified in the old sense and that they could belong to multiple homes, she argues that diaspora implies multiple loyalties and attachments that an immigrant community fosters with the host country, the homeland and the larger diasporic community. These multilayered loyalties enable diasporic communities to forge social, cultural, economic and political networks that are at once grounded within and beyond national boundaries (Abdelhady, 2011, pp. 12–13).

Anthropologists have also joined the debate on diaspora and transnationalism. Girish Daswani concurs with other scholars that studies of transnationalism and diaspora have opened the space to challenge the reproduction of the nation-state as the sole frame of reference and to examine how 'transnational movements and affiliations are situated across borders simultaneously' (2013, p. 35). On the one hand, he endorsed James Clifford's argument that a diaspora indicates that a population did not come from another country and that the articulation of diasporic affiliations transcends the normative reality of the nation-state. On the other hand, he proposes that transnational studies are concerned with identities that include multiple national affiliations. As such, transnational studies still take the nation-state as a point of reference in understanding migration while diaspora studies critique the linear narratives implied in the former. Taking diaspora to indicate a multiplicity of meaning and the concept of hybridity, Daswani (ibid., p. 37) argues that diaspora is not only a transnational phenomenon; rather it is 'also about imagining and planting roots, in a place or multiple places, while sharing or contesting memories of having arrived from elsewhere'. Likewise, Neha Vora defines diaspora as the process of 'identity and community formation that occurs through the process of migration, and the ongoing linkages (both material and affective) between a real or imagined "homeland" and the various locations of resettlement' (2018, p. 1). To her, diaspora theories have enabled scholars to move beyond traditional accounts of migration that focus on the push-pull factors and assimilation models. Vora emphasises the fact that the notions of diaspora, hybridity and third space would allow scholars to think about ways of identity and community formation that are not solely rooted in the notions of a homeland and a host country.

Exile has received less scholarly attention in studies of migration because scholars approach it as the antithesis of building networks and connections between a homeland and a host country. James Clifford (2013, p. 73) defines exile as 'a condition of enforced absence with the sustained expectation of returning home as soon as the conditions of expulsion can be corrected'. In exile, the hope of an actual return remains alive and 'it takes concrete political form in land claims and repatriations', while diaspora denotes deferred return and distance from the homeland. Likewise, Nina Glick Schiller and Georges Eugene Fouron (2001, p. 7) argue that an immigrant is someone who uproots herself, forges new forms of loyalties between the homeland and the host country and embraces a new life and language, while an exile is someone who refuses to do these things and waits to return home. Edward Said offers some explanation for the resistance of the exile to let go of her native land, asking:

> Is it not true that the views of exile in literature and, moreover, in religion obscure what is truly horrendous: that exile is irremediably secular and unbearably historical; that it is produced by human beings for other human beings; and that, like death but without death's ultimate mercy, it has torn millions of people from the nourishment of tradition, family, and geography?
>
> *(2000, p. 174)*

In this framework, the exile remains rooted in the homeland while experiencing migration as a form of banishment from the place of origin/nation-state. The host country does not emerge as a home but as a temporary place of sojourn on the way to return. While the notion of diaspora aims to critique the focus on the nation-state, the concept of exile remains firmly rooted within the confines of national borders.[3]

How can these theories of diaspora, transnationalism and exile complicate our thinking about the Iraqi communities in London? In what ways did the Gulf War of 1991 and the US invasion of Iraq in 2003 transform this experience? What opportunities did these political events open and foreclose? In this chapter, I examine how the migratory experience of Iraqis in London has transformed over the past four decades due to political developments in Iraq and the United Kingdom, and to generational differences in forging new forms of subjectivity and community. Iraqis who arrived in London in the late 1970s and early 1980s perceived themselves as exiles who firmly believed that they would go back home once Saddam Hussein's regime was toppled. Given that they fled Iraq for political reasons, that visits to and from Iraq were not possible because of a ban on leaving Iraq, and that Saddam Hussein's regime enjoyed good relations with Western governments, Iraqis in London could not maintain transnational connections with Iraq in the 1980s. They perceived their time in London as defined by enforced absence. However, in the 1990s, following Iraq's invasion of Kuwait and the expulsion of Hussein's agents from London, some Iraqis in London began to develop transnational connections that focused on Iraq as the main frame of reference. They joined the opposition to Saddam Hussein's regime and agitated for regime change in Iraq with the British and US governments. The activity of the opposition denoted the emergence of transnational connections between Iraq and the United Kingdom, which revolved on the status quo in Iraq. Nevertheless, while the US occupation of Iraq enabled visits and connections between Iraq and the United Kingdom, it also foreclosed the possibility of return due to instability and violence. This status quo indicated a shift from a narrative of exile to a discourse of diaspora, especially among the younger generation who began to build new notions of selfhood that transcend the binary notion of homeland and host countries and emphasise the concepts of hybridity and global connections.

From exile to transnationalism

The majority of Iraqis who arrived in the United Kingdom in the late 1970s and early 1980s fled Saddam Hussein's persecution. They perceived their stay in the United Kingdom as a temporary sojourn in a journey back to Iraq once the regime was toppled. They also experienced their forced migration and inability to keep contact with friends and relatives in Iraq as a form of exile (*manfa*). Unlike established diasporas with intricate connections to homelands – such as the relationship of the Ghanaian diaspora in London and New York to Ghana (Shipley, 2013), or the relationship between the South Asian diaspora in London and the Gulf to South Asia (Brah, 1996; Vora, 2013), Iraqis in London during the reign of Saddam Hussein could not maintain diasporic connections with Iraq. The national sphere of Iraq was closed off to them. In the 1980s, visits to and from Iraq were not possible due to a ban on leaving the country and a fear of persecution. Letters in and out of the country were read by state employees to detect criticism of the regime and the exchange of vital information. Phone calls had to be carried out through state operators, which took hours to get through, if at all, and were recorded. Radio and television stations and newspapers were strictly controlled by the state and served as propaganda tools for the regime, and did not reach the community abroad as they circulated within Iraq only. In the 1990s, while the Internet and cell phones provided technological breakthroughs and changed communication patterns between diasporic communities and homelands, Iraqis in London could not make use of them to connect with friends and relatives back home since cell phones and the Internet were not allowed in Iraq.

It is in this sense that I argue the Iraqi communities in London were exilic prior to the fall of Saddam Hussein's regime. Their experiences were informed by enforced absence and an inability to maintain direct connections – characterised by visits, easy contact with relatives and friends, and cultural and political exchange – with Iraq (Saleh, 2021). However, this experience of exile was not a mutually exclusive condition that precluded the rise of long-distance nationalism or the formation of connections with other Iraqi communities abroad that served as a conduit to contact Iraqis in Iraq. While the national space of Iraq was closed off to Iraqis in London prior to 2003, they were tied to Iraq through their thoughts, kinship and friendships, and cultural productions about Iraq. Moreover, this exilic scene was transformed after Iraq's invasion of Kuwait in 1990. The British government severed its relations with Hussein's regime and expelled his agents, who had monitored the political activities of the Iraqi community in London. The consolidation of Hussein's power after the Gulf War of 1991 and the expulsion of his agents from London galvanised the London-based opposition to his reign. In the 1990s, London emerged as a major centre for the Iraqi opposition. The opposition, with its connections to other Iraqi groups in Tehran and Damascus, remained transnational and exilic in its outlook in that the eventual regime change in Iraq would entail return, and that the focus of their politics and cooperation with the US and British governments remained the homeland.

Scholars have looked at migrant communities as productive sites that reshape and reconfigure national politics and transnational activism. On the one hand, migrants may mobilise to bring about changes in their homeland (such as through sponsoring certain candidates in the homeland or voting in the elections) or to make an impact on the host country's policies towards the homeland (through agitating for regime change or the imposition or lifting of sanctions). On the other hand, politicians in the place of origin sometimes seek the support of people abroad for their political projects and rely on remittances that are crucial to the national economy. These transpolitical connections open a space of political engagement that straddle both the place of settlement and the homeland (Silverstein, 2004, p. 216) and reconfigure political trajectories and events in the homeland.

The Iraqi opposition scene in London in the 1990s comprised different religious, ethnic and secular groups, including the Iraqi Communist Party, the Coalition for the Support of Democracy in Iraq, the Supreme Council for the Islamic Revolution in Iraq (SCIRI), the Islamic Call Party (Da'wa Party), the Kurdish Democratic Party (KDP) and Union of Kurdistan (PUK). Some of these parties joined two major umbrella groups, namely Iyad Allawi's Iraqi National Accord (INA) and Ahmed Chalabi's Iraq National Congress (INC). These exilic groups advocated different political ideologies and projects, including militant Islamism, moderate liberal Islam, Arab and Kurdish nationalism, liberalism, and Marxism. Despite major differences in imagining the future of Iraq, they were unified in their desire to see regime change. Unlike in the past, when men and women marched together in demonstrations and advocated for gender equality, women barely had a voice in this political sphere (Al-Ali, 2007; Ali, 2018); men constituted the majority of the membership in parties, groups and conferences. The issue of gender equality was sidelined by the focus on regime change and the desire to acquire power in Iraq.

These opposition groups organised a conference in Salahuddin in Iraq (which was under Kurdish control) in 1992. The Salahuddin Conference – which was boycotted by Iyad Allawi's INA – saw the emergence of the INC as an umbrella for different opposition groups, including Islamist and Kurdish groups. As such, it marked a shift in the Iraqi political scene in that a sectarian discourse displaced the secular discourses of the past, when communism and Arab nationalism dominated the political scene. The INC

> developed an explicit formula whereby seats on various executive bodies were allocated according to sectarian, ethnic and ideological affinities. This formula proved controversial, as it seemed to enshrine the divisions of society according to communal and ethnic considerations. The INC had a leadership council, comprising a Shi'a, a Kurd, and a Sunni. The executive council was also divided proportionately, according to sectarian and ethnic composition/
>
> *(Allawi, 2007, p. 53)*

In the late 1990s, the INC, represented by Ahmed Chalabi, secured a victory in its efforts to commit the Clinton administration to a policy of regime change in Iraq. Chalabi worked with US congressional staffers to write the Iraq Liberation Act (ILA). Signed by Bill Clinton in 1998, the Act stated that 'it should be the policy of the United States to support efforts to remove the regime headed by Saddam Hussein from power in Iraq and to promote the emergence of a democratic government to replace that regime' (ibid., p. 62). The ILA also provided funding for the opposition and recognised seven opposition groups. Despite the announcement of the ILA, the Clinton administration remained equivocal about bringing about regime change in Baghdad.

The election of George W. Bush in 2001, the rise of the neo-conservatives in the new administration, and the failure of the United Nations to uphold the sanctions regime and send weapons inspectors back to Iraq reorganised US policy towards the country. The new administration perceived Iraq as a threat and worked towards regime change – by unilateral means, if necessary (Tripp, 2007, p. 270). The September 11 attack and the War on Terror that ensued sealed the fate of Saddam Hussein. Members of the Bush administration saw the War on Terror as having long-term implications, beyond the immediate overthrow of al-Qaeda, in that it could be employed to reshape the international order according to US interests. The United States turned its attention to regimes that were seen as hostile to its interests and were suspected of developing chemical, biological or nuclear weapons. The case against Iraq was built on the claim that it was developing weapons of mass destruction (ibid.), and the INC became instrumental in promoting this vision by planting defectors who claimed that Iraq had weapons of mass destruction (ibid., p. 271). The truth of these allegations could not be verified since Iraq did not allow UN weapons inspectors inside the country. On March 17, George Bush gave a 48-hour ultimatum to Saddam Hussein to leave Iraq. Two days later, the invasion of Iraq began.

Following the invasion of Iraq, the US administration in Iraq, represented by the Coalition Provisional Authority (CPA) that was headed by Paul Bremer, established the Iraqi Governing Council (IGC). According to Ali Allawi, who was part of the London-based opposition and assumed ministerial positions after 2003:

> [the] selection of the twenty-five members of what was to become the Iraqi Governing Council was done according to certain established formula. These continued to govern the distribution of power subsequently. The first 'cut' was to accept the principle of ethnic and sectarian balance in the governing authority.
>
> *(Allawi 2007, p. 164)*

The second criterion of inclusion in the council was the political affiliations of the members, which encompassed 'Islamists, Kurdish parties, secularists, and liberal democrats' (ibid., p. 164). The third criterion stipulated that tribes would be represented as well. Women got three seats on the council. The CPA – with its Orientalist understanding of Iraq as a place inhabited by Sunnis, Shi'is and Kurds – endorsed the opposition's sectarian discourse of Iraq and reconfigured the political landscape when it institutionalised a sectarian quota system in the country. One-third of the 25 members of the IGC were London-based exiles (Haddad, 2011, p. 251). Other Iraqis in London assumed positions in Iraq, including in ministries and diplomatic missions.

The London-based opposition to Saddam Hussein's regime consisted of elderly men who transformed the political landscape in Iraq through agitating for regime change in Iraq and the endorsement of a sectarian quota system. The activity of the opposition remained transnational in its scope in that it focused on the status quo in the homeland mainly as Iraqi politicians in London aimed to shape the policies of the host country – namely Britain – towards Iraq. However, this transnational landscape that dominated the political scene among the Iraqi community in London began to be replaced by the emergence of a diasporic scene among young Iraqis after the fall of Hussein's regime in 2003.

A diasporic landscape

The US invasion of Iraq both opened and foreclosed possibilities for the Iraqi communities in London, such as by opening new channels of communication. After the fall of Saddam Hussein, dozens of newspapers were published in the country, both in print and online, and new satellite television stations were established that could reach Iraqi communities all over the world. Iraqis abroad and inside Iraq wrote articles for websites that became hubs for political and intellectual exchange. Cell phones were also introduced into Iraq, and calling families and friends became a daily occurrence. More importantly, Iraqis could visit Iraq. Indeed, many of the Iraqis I met in London during my fieldwork (2006–2019) had visited Baghdad at least once after 2003. However, the US invasion also foreclosed possibilities, most prominently by undermining the imagination of Iraq as a progressive, prosperous country. For many Iraqi in the diaspora, the spiralling sectarian violence created a sense of disappointment and bewilderment, whereby the utopian past they yearned for no longer existed. Visits to Iraq only furthered this sense of disenchantment and alienation, as Iraqis found themselves in a country they could not recognise and among people they could not relate to. It is in this sense that Iraqi exiles in London had to live with the realisation that they were no longer exiles waiting to return home. Instead, they had become Iraqis in the United Kingdom, and London transformed from a stopping place on the journey back home into a permanent home. For young Iraqis, who were born in the United Kingdom or arrived there at an early age, the foreclosure of the possibility of return and the opening up of Iraq's national space enabled them to forge diasporic subjectivity. This diasporic subjectivity was the product of several intertwined histories and the experience of hybridity. It also revolved around the cultivation of multiple attachments to different homes, and the maintenance of material and symbolic connections between the homeland, the host country and the larger diaspora communities in other parts of the world.

The life story of Hadjar, a young woman in her mid-thirties when I first met her in 2006, exemplifies the journey to forging diasporic sensibilities over a decade and a half. At the age of 7, she was snatched from the comfort of her middle-class home and taken to the Iran-Iraq border by security agents because her father was *taba'iyya*: an Iraqi of 'Iranian origin'. Her family's deportation was part of the regime's massive expulsion campaign in the early 1980s that targeted Shi'i Arabs and Shi'i Kurds – like Hadjar's family – who had held Persian nationality under the Ottomans and who came to be seen as a threat to the Iraqi nation under Hussein's regime. In Iran, Hadjar's family was confronted with Persian nationalism, which perceived them as others – specifically Arabs, though they are Kurds – who did not belong to Iran even though they are Shi'i Muslims and even though the father had relatives in Iran. After nine years of economic hardship and marginalisation, Hadjar's family relocated to London, where one of her brothers lived and supported the family. The family decided that Britain offered the prospects of a secure and comfortable life, though it was different from the Middle East.

During our conversations, Hadjar dwelled at length on how the questions of selfhood and home became a pressing issue for her from a young age. While in Iran, Hadjar wanted to blend with Iranians to avoid being called an Arab. However, her family attempted to press the idea that she was an Iraqi. After the family moved to London in the late 1980s, faith began to play a central part in her life. Hadjar's religious beliefs became an anchor that prevented her from losing sight of who she was. Faith became a means to construct a Shi'i subjectivity that connected her to her Iranian, Iraqi and Shi'i Kurdish roots. Shi'i Islam was the one thing that she shared with these three groups. In her mid-twenties, Hadjar's feelings of loss and confusion were aggravated. She felt alienated from the Iraqi and Muslim communities in London and no longer felt connected to her faith. She continued to wear the veil out of habit, rather than religious conviction. This period of turmoil came to an end when Hadjar undertook the pilgrimage to Mecca. Going to Mecca for the first time became part of a journey to 'know' herself. On her way, she visited the shrine of Sayyida Zainab in Damascus to connect with her Shi'i faith. These journeys also made Hadjar yearn to visit Iraq – in particular, Najaf and Karbala. However, she could not get an Iraqi visa because her family was deported.

After the fall of Hussein's regime in 2003, Hadjar was finally able to visit Iraq. The trip to Iraq consolidated Hadjar's sense of Iraqiness. She relished the little details that constituted Iraq to her, such as sitting on an Iraqi sofa (*karawita*), sleeping on the roof, walking in Adhamiyya, going to Abboussi Ice Cream, sitting in the garden, seeing the Tigris and eating famous Iraqi dishes, such as *pacha*. To her, these little things represented home and constituted her as an Iraqi. Hadjar had yearned for these experiences all her life as she grew up listening to stories her sisters told about Iraq. The trip presented her with the opportunity to have her own experiences of Iraq. It also enabled her to visit the holy shrines in Najaf and Karbala. Hadjar stayed in Iraq for two weeks and visited different parts of the country and Baghdad. The trip had significant meaning to her in that she began to have her own memories of Iraq. Having first-hand experience of Iraq, Hadjar was able to identify as an Iraqi:

> I'm glad I went to Iraq in 2003. That was it. When I came back, I knew where I came from. I was so proud of myself, so proud of being an Iraqi. I got in touch with Iraqi culture, Iraqi music, Iraqi this, Iraq that … Now I knew what my family talked about. I heard a lot about Iraq from my sisters. Now, I can say I was there. All of a sudden, it is a reality. It was no longer a vision from my sisters … At first, I wanted to go to Iraq in order to visit Najaf and Karbala. I think by going there, everything came to one place, and I was Kurdish, Shi'i, and Iraqi. They all represented one country for me. My identities started to intermix. As a Kurd, I'm an Iraqi. As a Shi'i, I'm an Iraqi. That was it. I'm Iraqi, which means I'm Kurdish-Iraqi, Shi'i Iraqi. That was my identity now … I'm also British-Iraqi. I know I'm not English, but I'm British. This is important because you can still be an Iraqi as well as British. Being British means I can be an Iraqi, and I can be a Muslim. You can be anything because it is a nationality. I studied here. I grew up here. It was my Britishness that allowed me to go to Iraq.

Since I met Hadjar in 2006, she has been to Mecca, Baghdad, Karbala and Najaf many times. She constantly felt the need to make these journeys to affirm her Shi'i faith and her sense of belonging to her Iraqi and Kurdish roots. It was through the performance of religious rituals and mundane Iraqi acts – such as eating certain dishes or taking walks in certain neighbourhoods in Baghdad – that Hadjar cultivated a religious and national subjectivity rooted in these places. These constant journeys, however, were defined by unexpected encounters that shifted Hadjar's notion of home and subjectivity. When I interviewed Hadjar again in 2017, she emphasised the importance of a British identity to her, though she still identified as an Iraqi British. She thought her previous identity as a Shi'i-Iraqi and Kurdish-Iraqi were extenuated due to her frequent visits to Iraq. During her trip to Iraq in 2014, Hadjar decided to get her family's national documents so that they could claim the properties that were confiscated under Hussein's regime. Hadjar's experience with Iraqi bureaucracy shook her Iraqiness. She was faced with a corrupt system defined by long delays and expectations of bribes. She was also vocal when people cut in line. Her attitude – refusing to give bribes and insisting that people wait their turn – made her an object of ridicule. Moreover, during that trip, Hadjar saw more cruelty in Baghdad, such as a woman hiring a child to carry her heavy groceries or a man kicking a child for making a mistake. She thought these cruel acts would not be tolerated in the United Kingdom, where child protection procedures penalised such acts. These experiences made Hadjar feel that she did not 'fit in'. She had seen and felt things during her visit that she did not want to be part of. In addition, daily life in Iraq seemed to get more difficult with each trip. Hadjar remarked:

during that trip, I could see everything. I could see the traffic, the meaninglessness. It was so ridiculous, why do people have to live like that? The fear of bombing. The fear whether you'll come back or not come back.

Though Hadjar felt that she wanted to belong to Iraq, she was happy that she could leave the country. In turn, these trips and experiences made Hadjar feel more British:

When we last spoke [2006], it was much more about being Iraqi, and that meant a lot to me. It is now that but it is no longer a strong part. I'm Iraqi. I'm Kurdish. I'm Muslim. I'm Shi'i. These are all my identities, but I think my Britishness comes up a lot more ... I think being British allowed me to be different. While if you're Iraqi, it is either this or that. Being British means you can be Asian, Chinese, Black African, Middle Eastern. In that way, I always say being British is a combination, and I'm British-Iraqi. Previously, I was Iraqi, Shi'i, Muslim. I'm not sure if that is a major identity for me at this stage. It was at that point in my life. Maybe my Britishness is very much about my ideology in life and the way I see other people.

Over the years, Hadjar grew wary of her Shi'ism, Kurdishness and Iraqiness as the main markers of her selfhood. She thought these identities marginalised and excluded people who are different from her:

If I say I were a Shi'i, it means I reject the Sunnis or I'm prioritising my faith over somebody's else. If I were to say I'm Muslim, it means somebody else is a Christian, not necessarily equal to me. I'm Iraqi, but what about the Iranian side of me? And then I'm Kurdish, but what about the Shi'i in me because the Kurds are Sunnis and they are rejecting Arabs? When I say I'm British, I'm allowed to be everything.

Britishness came to indicate a marker of inclusion not only of Hadjar's multiple identities but also of groups who are religiously and ethnically different. Being British enabled Hadjar to write each of her multiple identities into the social fabric of British society. Moreover, social media and Iraqi websites established by Iraqis inside Iraq and abroad provided an opportunity for Hadjar to maintain contact with Iraqi friends over all the world and debate questions of identity, home and the future of Iraq with Iraqis in different countries. These complex and shifting connections transcended the simple binary of homeland/host country (Abdelhady, 2006; Bernal, 2017).

Home was not a stable, fixed or taken-for-granted thing for Hadjar. Instead, home has been a shifting and contested notion that was the product of intertwining histories and multiple attachments, and that was constantly reaffirmed through journeys to other places. It is rooted in, and routed through, multiple locations, but with the ongoing expectation of homecoming. After 2003, Hadjar constantly embarked on journeys to Baghdad, Najaf, Karbala and Mecca, only to come back home to London, and then start a new journey whenever she had the opportunity. While in London, she yearned for these cities abroad, but as soon as she was away, she yearned for London. It is through these processes of homecoming that Hadjar carved an Iraqi British and Muslim British subjectivity. Each journey made her feel anchored and affirmed some aspect of her identity because these journeys enabled her to establish roots in specific places and enjoy everyday experiences that she missed while she lived in London. Hadjar felt at home whenever she arrived in Iraq, heard Iraqis shout at each other in the Iraqi dialect, sat on an Iraqi sofa, visited and touched the shrines of Imam Ali and Imam Hussein, went on pilgrimage and felt proximity to God and the Prophet, and returned to the gloomy skies and queues of London. She inhabited a subjectivity that was reproduced in processes of homecoming. The search for roots, a home and a sense of selfhood was constantly enacted through routes.

Conclusion

The Iraqi communities in London that were consolidated after the rise of Saddam Hussein to power in 1979 have been transformed from exilic and transnational communities in the 1980s and 1990s, respectively, into diasporic communities after 2003. While the migratory experience of Iraqis in London was defined by enforced absence due to the existence of an authoritarian regime in Iraq that had its agents in Western countries, Iraqis in the United Kingdom began to forge transnational connections that aimed to change the status quo in Iraq. The binary of the homeland and host country denoted an emphasis on the homeland as a site of yearning and eventual return, and a perception of the host country as a temporary place. However, political changes in Iraq and different generational experiences led to the emergence of diasporic sensibilities among young Iraqis who cultivated attachments to multiple places, pushed the boundaries of what it meant to be British and Iraqi, and formed new notions of subjectivity and homes as their lives were informed by intertwined histories and locations. These diasporic realities, moreover, transcended the binary of homeland/host country and challenged the nation-state as the sole frame of reference through the cultivation of a notion of hybridity and a sense of belonging to multiple locations that included the homeland, the host country and the larger diasporic community.

Notes

1 There are no accurate statistics on the number of Iraqis who arrived in London in the early 1950s to the 1960s. Al-Rasheed puts the number of Iraqi Assyrians in London in 1994 at 3,000 to 4,000 (Al-Rasheed, 1994). During my fieldwork (2006–2008), Iraqi Jews estimated that their community consisted of 5,000 members.
2 I use the term 'communities' instead of 'community' intentionally, to emphasise the deep divisions among Iraqis in London along class, sectarian, political and religious lines. Indeed, it is hard to speak of Iraqis in London as one unified community. Rather, different groups constitute different Iraqi communities with different political, social and religious projects and aspirations.
3 Sima Shakhsari provides an alternative reading of the notion of exile as far as the Iranian diasporic communities are concerned, in that the term exile tends to homogenise the diversity of experiences of displacement. Shakhsari argues that:

> [the] exilic economy is established not through challenging the dichotomy of here and there, local/global, but through a masculinist hegemonic situating of the "uprooted" self "here/in exile" in relation to the authentic and fixed "there/home." In this contest for authenticity, a link between people and place is naturalised, while its loss is mourned and grieved by the estranged exile.
>
> (2020, p. 49)

To Shakhsari, a feminist approach to diaspora challenges the essentialist notions of home, identity and nation. However, the term diaspora remains problematic as well in that it can homogenise all forms of border crossing, and in that it could be celebrated as 'a transgressive shift' from the nation. Rather than perceiving diaspora as a valorisation of hybridity and multilocality, Shakhsari draws attention to 'collusion of diaspora with scattered hegemonies that include nationalism, colonisation, imperialism, and militarism' (ibid., p. 50).

Acknowledgements

Parts of this chapter first appeared in Zainab Saleh's *Return to Ruin: Iraqi Narratives of Exile and Nostalgia* (Stanford, CA: Stanford University Press, 2021).

References

Abdelhady, D. (2006) 'Beyond home/host networks: forms of solidarity among Lebanese immigrants in a global era', *Identities: Global Studies in Culture and Power*, 13, pp. 427–453.
Abdelhady, D. (2011) *The Lebanese Diaspora: The Arab Immigrant Experience in Montreal, New York, and Paris*. New York: New York University Press.
Al-Ali, N. (2007) *Iraqi Women: Untold Stories from 1948 to the Present*. London: Zed Books.
Ali, Z. (2018) *Women and Gender in Iraq: Between Nation-Building and Fragmentation*. Cambridge: Cambridge University Press.
Allawi, A. (2007) *The Occupation of Iraq: Winning the War, Losing the Peace*. New Haven, CT: Yale University Press.
Al-Rasheed, M. (1994) 'The myth of return: Iraqi Arabs and Assyrian refugees in London', *Journal of Refugee Studies*, 7(2/3), pp. 199–219.
Bernal, V. (2017) 'Diaspora and the afterlife of violence: Eritrean national narratives and what goes without saying', *American Anthropologist*, 119(1), pp. 23–34.
Brah, A. (1996) *Cartographies of Diaspora: Contesting Identities*. London: Routledge.
Chatelard, G (2012) 'The politics of population movements in contemporary Iraq: a research agenda', in Tejel, J., Bocco, R., Bozarslan, H. and Sluglett, P. (eds) *Writing the Modern History of Iraq: Historiographical and Political Challenges*. New Jersey: World Scientific, pp. 359–378.
Clifford, J. (2013) *Returns: Becoming Indigenous in the Twenty-First Century*. Cambridge, MA: Harvard University Press.
Daswani, G. (2013) 'The anthropology of transnationalism and diaspora', in Quayson, A. and Daswani, G. (eds) *A Companion to Diaspora and Transnationalism*. Malden, MA: Blackwell Publishing Ltd, pp. 29–53.
Farouk-Sluglett, M. and Sluglett, P. (2001) *Iraq Since 1958: From Revolution to Dictatorship*. London: I.B. Tauris.
Glick Schiller, N. and Fouron, G.E. (2001) *Georges Woke Up Laughing: Long-Distance Nationalism and the Search for Home*. Durham, NC: Duke University Press.
Haddad, F. (2011) *Sectarianism in Iraq: Antagonistic Visions of Unity*. New York: Columbia University Press.
Khoury, D.R. (2013) *Iraq in Wartime: Soldiering, Martyrdom, and Remembrance*. New York: Cambridge University Press.
Quayson, A. and Daswani, G. (eds) (2013) *A Companion to Diaspora and Transnationalism*. Malden, MA: Blackwell Publishing Ltd.
Said, E. (2000) *Reflections on Exile and Other Library and Cultural Essays*. London: Granta Books.
Saleh, Z. (2021) *Return to Ruin: Iraqi Narratives of Exile and Nostalgia*. Stanford, CA: Stanford University Press.
Sassoon, J. (2011) *The Iraqi Refugees: The New Crisis in the Middle East*. London: I.B. Tauris.
Shakhsari, S. (2020) *Politics of Rightful Killing: Civil Society, Gender, and Sexuality in Weblogistan*. Durham, NC: Duke University Press.
Shipley, J. (2013) *Living the Hiplife: Celebrity and Entrepreneurship in Ghanaian Popular Music*. Durham, NC: Duke University Press.
Silverstein, P. (2004) *Algeria in France: Transpolitics, Race, and Nation*. Bloomington, IN: Indiana University Press.
Tripp, C. (2007) *A History of Iraq*. 3rd edn. Cambridge: Cambridge University Press.
Vora, N. (2013) *Impossible Citizens: Dubai's Indian Diaspora*. Durham, NC: Duke University Press.
Vora, N. (2018) 'Diaspora', in *The International Encyclopedia of Anthropology*. Hoboken, NJ: John Wiley & Sons, pp. 1–4.

25
HEALED PASTS, MULTIPLE BELONGINGS AND MULTIFOCAL ENGAGEMENTS
A Danish-Palestinian diaspora tour

Nina Gren

'Here it is! The village land begins here!' explains our guide in Arabic. Ibrahim looks around a bit bewildered, before silently kneeling and touching the ground with his forehead. He doesn't seem to care that his white Adidas shorts are getting dirty by the soil. Some of his friends seem a bit embarrassed by his big gesture. Ibrahim and the others then spend about an hour among the remains of his family's Palestinian village, in northern Galilee in today's Israel. The only building that has not been completely demolished is the ruin of a school.

Together with his friend Daoud, who also originates from this place, Ibrahim collects stones, berries, twigs and soil to bring with him to his family in Denmark. The two of them have brought along cookies and juice that they offer us, their 'guests' in their village. Ibrahim later tells me that it would have been even better if they had offered us Arabic coffee as a display of 'genuine Palestinian hospitality'.

Our guide then shows us the way to a Palestinian village nearby that was not emptied during the war and to an old woman who grew up in Ibrahim and Daoud's village. The woman talks about what happened in 1948 in the village we just visited. We are all deeply affected when she recounts the killing of villagers and both Ibrahim and Daoud begin to cry. They have already heard these stories in their families and part of the woman's story is about the killing of their own relatives.

As we drive off that afternoon, I sit in the same rented car as Ibrahim and his friend Fatemeh. Fatemeh asks Ibrahim how he is feeling but she does not really get an answer. Ibrahim keeps his eyes on the road and seems busy driving. Instead, Fatemeh turns to me and explains that she is asking because none of her fellow travellers understood how much the visit to her family village affected her the other day.

The experience described above was part of a tour I joined during eight months of ethnographic fieldwork among Danish-Palestinians in 2011–2012.[1] Ibrahim's and Daoud's visit to their original village is far from a single event; rather, it is part of a well-established practice among Palestinians in the diaspora. When the political situation and their citizenship status (i.e. having Western passports) make it possible, countless people of Palestinian origin living in different parts of the world visit their ancestral family homes in cities such as Jerusalem and Jaffa or in abandoned villages scattered around present-day Israel. Such visits have also been portrayed in documentary films by two Danish-Palestinians: Omar Shargawi's *My Father from Haifa* [*Fra Haifa til Nørrebro* in Danish] (2009) and Mahmoud Issa's *Ancestors' Land* [*Den Fædrene Jord* in Danish] (1995) in collaboration with Gitte Rabøl. Another Danish-Palestinian, Numan Kanafani (1995), has written about his own 'return trip' to Palestine.[2] This chapter focuses on a group of young Danish-Palestinians and their diaspora tour to the Palestinian homeland. Diaspora tours create a sense of political community between people with a common background spread across diverse localities (Kelner, 2010). Palestinian diaspora tourism is a kind of memory work that resembles pilgrimage and involves ritualistic and transformative potential (e.g. Ebron, 1999; Sturken, 2011). As the vignette above shows, they can be emotionally charged and deeply personal as well as collective experiences. In this chapter, I point to the transformative potentiality of diaspora tours on an emotional level, where feelings of grief, self-blame, relief and different kinds of nostalgia flow from the experience (Boym, 2001).

These trips can be understood as ritualised homecomings and as responses to the losses Palestinians have experienced ever since the first Israeli-Arab war in 1948. While Israelis call this the Independence War, Palestinians refer to it as *al-Nakba* or 'the catastrophe' which points to the grave impact it had on Palestinian society, collective memory and nationalism (Abu-Lughod and Sa'di, 2007). The violence and force used to expel Palestinians also turn them into an example of a 'victim diaspora', as Cohen (2008) described it when attempting to typologise diasporas. A victim diaspora is distinguished from other forms of dispersion by the atrocities and military force that compel people to move. Its members often dream of returning to or re-establishing a mythologised homeland (Safran, 1991). In the Palestinian case, return is seen as a right and an obligation. While my interlocutors come from families who migrated as a result of *al-Nakba* and have family members who endured the physical and emotional destruction it brought, my analysis highlights the transformational aspects that come about after they visit their ancestral homeland. In doing so, I approach membership in the Palestinian diaspora as more processual and practice-oriented (Brubaker, 2005) than Cohen's typology implies.

Most of my interlocutors were between the ages of 18 and 30, born and raised in Denmark and had neither experienced *al-Nakba* first-hand nor visited Palestine before. Nonetheless, they had decided to travel to Palestine, sometimes against their parents' wishes. The majority of my interlocutors come from Palestinian families who first fled to Lebanon in 1948. Only later, during the Lebanese Civil War in the 1980s, did my interlocutors' parents end up in Denmark in a second exile. These families had experienced extensive violence during the Lebanese Civil War as well as frequent imprisonment and torture by the invading Israeli forces and other Lebanese militia groups (Kublitz, 2011). Marked by these experiences, many in the parent generation were subsequently hesitant to travel themselves or let their children travel to Palestine – a trip that unavoidably goes through Israel and Israeli border controls. The young Danish-Palestinian travellers had, however, been inspired by peers with the same origins and heard of the tours organised by a Danish-Palestinian association. Their positionality is distinct from that of their parents in the sense that their decision to travel to Palestine represents what Brubaker describes as a 'diasporic stance'. Rogers Brubaker (2005) proposes that research should focus on diaspora as a category of practice that is used to make claims, start projects and mobilise energies. 'It is often a category of strong normative change. It does not so much *describe* the world as it seeks to *remake* it' (ibid., p. 12). Since Palestinian refugees and their descendants are not welcomed to return to Palestine for long-term repatriation (implementing the Right of Return)³ and barely tolerated for shorter visits, a trip to Palestine is a deeply politicised event for them and for the Israeli state.

My argument in this chapter is twofold: First, I claim that the diaspora tour creates and recreates community and relationships with the Palestinian homeland and its people. However, I focus on the ways in which that process of creation and recreation of community involves a sort of catharsis, a transformation not only of identification but also of emotional states. The young Danish-Palestinians negotiated unsettling and dramatic family stories in addition to multiple and complex belongings through their trips. One particularly important part of this transformation occurred during visits to ancestral villages in today's Israel; another vital part was collecting and purchasing 'Palestinian objects'. After the tour, they reported having reached a sense of inner peace. Second, while the experience of the diaspora tour strengthens and recreates a sense of belonging to the Palestinian homeland, such sense of belonging triggers active involvement with diverse and multifocal social issues also in Danish society and in diasporic networks (see also Abdelhady, 2011; Darieva, 2011; Morris, 2012). Before proceeding with unpacking these experiences and arguments, I first turn to a brief overview of the Danish-Palestinian context.

Danish-Palestinians: from dispossession to marginalisation

People with a Palestinian background are estimated to be one of the largest refugee groups in Denmark, numbering approximately 24,000 (Kublitz, 2010, p. 37). The family histories of my young informants are intertwined with multiple losses and experiences of political violence. *Al-Nakba* brought statelessness, but also deep poverty, especially among farmers whose main assets were their fields. In addition to losing their land, Palestinian farmers lost houses, furniture, stocks of food, cattle, tools and clothing (Fischbach, 2003). Many refugees from rural areas ended up in refugee camps in the neighbouring countries. Social networks were shattered since villagers and kin often settled in different locations and were left to grieve the death of relatives and friends who were killed in the process of dislocation and dispossession.

Since most people of Palestinian background in Denmark arrived from Lebanon, their families had not only experienced *al-Nakba* but also lived through the Lebanese Civil War and the War of the Camps (Sayigh, 1979). They had lived through the massive destruction of the refugee camps they inhabited and experienced extensive violence and human loss. The massacres of the refugee camps of Sabra and Shatila in Lebanon have become key events that are commemorated in similar ways to *al-Nakba* (Khalili, 2007). Palestinian refugees in Lebanon are also disadvantaged in comparison to other Palestinians since they have fewer opportunities for work and education than in most other host countries in the Middle East (BADIL, 2018). These historical experiences inform and continue to influence the position of Danish-Palestinians who struggle with unemployment and modes of segregation.

Over the years, Danish-Palestinians have received a great deal of negative media attention linking them to many social problems, ranging from early marriage and poor educational performance to 'ghettos' and gang criminality. In Danish public debates, the word 'Palestinian' not only connotes terrorism, violence and conflict in the Middle East but also crime, social problems and failed integration. However, many of the young adults I met during my fieldwork were enrolled in higher education, even if their parents were often unemployed or had manual jobs despite their education (see also Kublitz, 2011). My interlocutors considered the Danish media and the general public to be pro-Israeli and emphasised the lack of attention given to people with a Danish-Palestinian background and their understanding of the conflict. Demonstrations in Copenhagen that opposed Israeli policies and actions often turned into clashes with the police, which strengthened the negative image of Palestinians in Danish public perceptions. The Muhammed Cartoon Affair in 2005 and the protests it triggered among Muslims in Denmark (Kublitz, 2010) strengthened the sense that Muslims (and Palestinians among them) were not welcome. Moreover, contrary to some neighbouring states, Denmark does not recognise Palestine as an independent state, which has sown distrust among Danish-Palestinians (Forslag, n.d.). Neither is it possible to have Palestine registered as a place of birth in Danish passports and driving licences; instead, the choice is between Israel or 'the Middle East' (Borgerforslag, n.d.). Such events and issues exacerbate feelings of powerlessness and hopelessness among Danish-Palestinians. The influence of the right-wing Danish People's Party (*Dansk Folkeparti*) has contributed further to the negative perceptions of Palestinians who are often seen as unintegrated in Danish society (see Rytter, 2019, for general arguments about integration in Denmark).

The trip to Palestine and village visits

About 15 people signed up for the diaspora tour I joined. They were to be accompanied by more experienced peers who had already visited Palestine.[4] I had established contact with most of the travellers before the tour and they had collectively agreed to let me join them. They did not seem to mind having a researcher around and were happy that someone took interest in their trip and their experiences. The ten-day trip had a full schedule, which included visits to Palestinian-majority towns in Israel, such as Jaffa and Haifa, visits to different areas in the West Bank and Jerusalem (including religious sites), helping farmers pick olives, visits to families who had had their houses demolished by the Israeli authorities, a tour of the infamous Israeli wall, meetings with human rights NGOs and visits to the graves of Yasser Arafat and the Palestinian poet Mahmoud Darwish in Ramallah. Apart from the village visits, the trip seemed similar to tours arranged to the Palestinian occupied areas by pro-Palestinian activist groups based in Europe and North America.

Shaul Kelner (2010, p. xvi), writing on Jewish diaspora tours to Israel, asserts that both nation-states and diaspora organisations have realised tourism's effectiveness when building diasporas and uniting potential members. Tourism is a way to experience a place and to actively position oneself in relation to that place. In contrast to Birthright Tours for Jewish diasporic youth, funded by the Israeli state, the Danish-Palestinians paid for the travel expenses themselves and the organisers were keen on ensuring the low cost of the trip. Palestinian diaspora tourism is much smaller in scale than those organised for the Jewish diaspora. Another striking difference is that Jewish diaspora tourists are welcomed by the Israeli authorities, the very same authorities that often prevent Palestinian youth in the diaspora from participating in diaspora tourism.

During Palestinian diaspora tours, it is common to visit the travellers' original villages, where a series of mini rituals are normally performed, which include praying by abandoned tombs and touching the earth (Ben-Ze'ev, 2004). Descendants of Palestinian refugee families, visiting their lost villages, have been characterised by their desire to feel the village land and the stones of ruined houses. Ben-Ze'ev argues that Palestinian village visits are 'condensed experiences, momentarily erasing the time that has passed and mediating between people's current lives and their pre-dispersion lives' (ibid., p. 141). Daoud told me that he had been able to orient himself in the ruined village thanks to his father's drawings: 'My father had drawn everything for me. The pond, for example. It was weird. In my head, time was winding back: is this where my father played, and my grandparents lived? Today, only the school remains.' In addition to drawings, the fusion of different time periods and the feeling of briefly visiting the past had been initiated by storytelling. Stories continue to transfer knowledge of the family history while simultaneously strengthening a sense of belonging to Palestine (Sayigh, 1979; Slyomovics, 1998). Lara, a 20-year-old university student, had heard her uncles' stories about the village and the past wealth of their family many times. Visiting the village made the stories come alive and gave her relief:

> I had flashbacks of their stories when we were in my village. My stomach was full of butterflies. But I also felt at peace. I've often been angry with my parents because they fled but when I came here, I understood.

Reconciling with the past

Among Danish-Palestinians, what was talked about and what was silenced about past losses seemed to vary from family to family. Some of my young interlocutors were well aware of this. Ibtissam, a 23-year-old university student, told me that her parents never talked about the war in Lebanon but focused on rebuilding their everyday life in Denmark. Whether this was due to an inability to talk about difficult experiences, an attempt to protect their children, or an unwillingness of the youth to listen, it had triggered emotions during the trip to Palestine. Much of my interview with Ibtissam consisted of her story about travelling through Israel on her own and finally breaking down and panicking in an Israeli taxi. She explained to me that being alone among Israelis, among people Ibtissam had learnt to fear, curse and hate for so many years, aroused strong reactions (see also Kanafani, 1995). 'We're a family marked by war and flight', as Ibtissam put it. Past events often linger in refugee families so that '[t]he family becomes not only the site of memorial transmission and continuity across generations but also a trope of loss, longing, and the desire for home' (Hirsch and Miller, 2011, p. 8). When it comes to the past and generational differences among families of refugee backgrounds, Hirsch (2012) uses the term 'post-memory' to understand experiences of having a life overshadowed by memories of a very momentous historical happening lived by older relatives. In the Danish-Palestinian case, Kublitz (2011) has used this concept to understand younger generations of Palestinians, who never lived through *al-Nakba* or other traumatic events in Palestinian history, but who, through their parents' behaviours, stories and silences, are deeply influenced by it (see also Abu-Lughod, 2007). In addition to *al-Nakba*, Palestinians continue to experience ongoing losses due to the Israeli occupation, wars and political turmoil in the countries where they have taken refuge. My young interlocutors were aware of their parents and grandparents' experiences of violence but most of them knew little about the details and the exact sequences of events.

Over my years of research among Palestinian refugees in the occupied territories and in Scandinavia, I have noticed a recurrent theme of guilt and self-blame in stories about *al-Nakba*. *Al-Nakba* is not only blamed on Israelis, the former British colonial authorities and the defeated Arab armies, but also on the refugees themselves (Gren, 2014). Countless Palestinians maintain that the refugees should have stayed and fought and that they should not have been intimidated by the Jewish military forces (Hasso, 2000). Research shows that such feelings of guilt among diasporic groups are common (e.g. Graham and Khosravi, 1997). Lara told me that she had hesitated before travelling because she expected to be treated as a traitor by local Palestinians. However, these fears were unfounded, and all my informants had very positive experiences of encounters with local Palestinians. Others were afraid they would not feel at home and then be left with a sense of eternal homelessness. These fears also did not materialise, and everyone reported that they felt at home.

Other events during the trip evoked rage and fear, such as when my interlocutors were subjected to harassment by Israeli border inspectors. At Ben Gurion Airport, the

Danish-Palestinian group I met with were kept and interrogated for hours. To Israel, the Danish-Palestinians were not tourists or expats, they were judged, suspected and handled as 'security threats' (see also Gren, 2015). The Israeli authorities fear and actively oppose the Right of Return even in this simulated and limited fashion. The mistreatment of Palestinian diaspora tourists seems to be part of a tactic to limit the number of tours. Two of my interlocutors were denied entrance to Israel on a later occasion for no given reason but guessed that it was because of the interviews they had given about their earlier trips to Palestine in local Danish news media. Similar to Khalidi's (1997) description of a Palestinian identity that is established at border crossings, my informants became 'more Palestinian' by such annoyances, since these Israeli practices underlined and confirmed their 'Palestinian-ness'.

Members of the Danish-Palestinian diaspora tour I attended often refrained from showing strong feelings in front of me. They had gathered informally every evening when they processed what they had experienced during the day, but I did not join these as a way of respecting their privacy. During informal conversations and interviews, however, many expressed that they often felt angry and sad during the tour. For most, feelings of peace followed. The trip seemed to be a kind of catharsis, a process where emotions were released, relieved and also renewed. This catharsis was part of a temporary homecoming that resembles a pilgrimage (Slyomovics, 1998; see also Ebron, 1999). The traditional meaning of pilgrimage, as a ritualised trip to a sacred place or holy person, usually includes some form of personal transformation. Similar transformative processes are part of memory tourism within which practices of grieving are mixed with more typical touristic activities, often making it difficult to distinguish one from the other (Sturken, 2011, p. 284). The Danish-Palestinian trip can even more fruitfully be compared to the liminal phase of an initiation ritual (Turner, 1969). In liminality, there is a potentiality for transformation, moving a person or a group from one life stage to another. Much like neophytes in an initiation, the young Danish-Palestinians were taken out of their everyday context and met obstacles and ordeals, for instance, at the Israeli border control, when witnessing the violence of the Israeli army, or when handling their own family past. Moreover, there were also possibilities for forming *communitas* (ibid.) which included new friendships; many of the Danish-Palestinian travellers have kept in contact after the trip. The ritualised practices during Palestinian village visits, such as kneeling, praying, collecting soil and eating together, also include expectations of experiencing intense emotions of sadness, anger and frustration but also peace. Another way to find peace was to comfort oneself with Palestinian souvenirs and other material things.

The comfort of things from Palestine

My interlocutors spent part of the trip buying, collecting and even producing objects that would remind them of Palestine later. The work of Daniel Miller and Fiona Parrott (2009) on materiality and loss help us to understand the sometimes frenetic collection of things during the trip to Palestine. Miller and Parrott argue that there are two main ways to handle grief through material objects: first, there is the possibility of accumulating things, and, second, of getting rid of other things connected to the memory or experience of loss. After the death of a close family member, for instance, we often go through the deceased's belongings, deciding on what to keep as a memory, what to throw away and what to give to charity. This complex process creates a long-term relationship to loss which helps when coming to terms with bereavement. In Miller's (2008) book, *The Comfort of Things*, he argues that the accumulation of objects can also be part of a process of self-constitution, giving the example of a former drug addict who rebuilds the record collection he sold off to finance his addiction. The individual material practices Miller and Parrott write about can also illuminate more collective processes of coming to terms with self, collectivity and loss. During the diaspora tour, items ranging from mass-produced souvenirs to homemade jam reflected my interlocutors' experiences of and attempts to deal with grief and loss.

Ibrahim and Daoud collected herbs and soil from their village that they wanted to bring back to Denmark. They also picked olives, leaves, stones and soil. This was a common practice and part of a cultural script of what to do when visiting lost Palestinian villages. The eating of herbs and fruits from the village is a particularly important practice, and Ben-Ze'ev (2004) argues that the plants act as mnemonic devices and memory containers that allow for a temporary recreation of the past. Many Palestinian refugees also claim that their village had a speciality, for example, that the apricots or almonds grown there were the best in all of Palestine (ibid.). Consuming herbs or fruits that have grown on one's own land seems to be a symbolic way to reunite with the soil and 'once again' become part of it. On a similar note, in Gardner's (1993) work on Bangladeshi migrants, substances of village soil, water and agricultural produce are consumed by villagers living abroad who in this way remain connected to the village and both its social and natural qualities. Substance has also been used to discuss the fluid nature of relatedness; for instance, eating together (i.e. consuming the same substances) often means becoming related (Carsten, 2004). Most Palestinian refugees from Lebanese camps are former farmers who, before their displacement, lived by the land and had most of their savings in the land. It is thus possible that the soil is particularly important for my informants as descendants from such families.

My interlocutors also bought what they referred to as 'traditional food' in shops or at the market. It could be ground coffee with cardamom, nuts, seeds, dates and *kneife* (a kind of cheesecake) as well as spices and herbs used for cooking or tea infusions. To them, these products embodied Palestine and to some extent the Middle East more generally, but were less personally charged than the soil and stones collected in former villages. Homemade foods like honey, jam, olive oil and pickled vegetables occupied a particular status as they were related to and given by family members. Many of my interlocutors did not have close contact with relatives in Palestine but those who did visit family were often given these homemade foods.

Participants in the diaspora tour also collected religious souvenirs from and around holy Muslim and Christian sites. In the alleys of the Old City of Jerusalem, they purchased incense, prayer beads and rosaries. Religious souvenirs were common even among interlocutors who did not claim to be particularly religious. Mounsir, for instance, a father of two and student of medicine, had kissed the ground in his family's hometown as well as in al-Aqsa mosque. In our interview, he claimed that he was not particularly religious but, to him, the mosque symbolised Palestinian existence.

Some objects had a primarily political and nationalistic value, which were popular among my informants, such as Palestinian flags, t-shirts with political messages and *keffiyeh* (the Palestinian chequered scarf). The cartoon drawings of Handala, drawn by the Palestinian cartoonist Naji Al-Ali (1938–1987), are often used as a patriotic symbol, particularly among Leftist Palestinians. Handala is frequently reproduced on t-shirts and necklaces and those were popular purchases. My informants also bought maps of Palestine (i.e. in the shape of the former British Mandate) in different versions. Wissam, whom I interviewed in Denmark about a month after his first trip to Palestine, wore a necklace in the shape of Palestine that he bought in Jerusalem.

> I walk around with this necklace [he grabbed his necklace in the shape of the Palestinian map]. I have been there. I am proud in another way. Earlier when I spoke

with someone who had been there, I couldn't argue or have an opinion or share his experiences.

For Wissam, the necklace seemed to symbolise emotional stability and pride in having experienced Palestine 'on his own body', but it was also an identity marker that showed that he belonged to the Palestinian nation and a proof of his new knowledge of the homeland. Like Wissam, the Danish-Palestinians I accompanied picked objects according to a certain logic – namely, things that would make them more 'Palestinian' in a cultural, political, social and embodied sense. Material culture is important to a process of repair – taking people from the *actual*, back to the relatively *ideal* state of who they should be, or who they should have been if they or their parents and grandparents had not migrated.

In addition, taking photos and filming were also common practices. Nisreen made a film about her first visit to Palestine and her process of 'becoming Palestinian' and politically engaged (see below). Another informant, who was a little older than the group I took the trip with, curated an art exhibition about his first visit to his family's ancestral village. Both the film and the art exhibition were clearly directed to the Danish-majority public and sought to explain the plight of Palestinians from a Palestinian perspective but also served to document the experience for the family left behind in Scandinavia.

Miller and Parrott's (2009) work suggests that people often use material culture when trying to deal with various experiences of loss and separation. Objects are used to both continue and end relationships. In this case, it is the accumulation of objects and how they are used to create what Miller and Parrott call 'an economy of memory and relationships' that is of relevance. An accumulation of objects is used to establish relationships and is about nostalgia rather than separation. Most diaspora tourists accumulate objects on their trips to Palestine. They do not intend to separate from the homeland to get over their loss, but rather to keep or re-establish a dynamic and continuous relationship to loss. The Palestinian expulsion and dispossession have not been resolved. My interlocutors want to belong to Palestine and to continue to make political claims relating to their right to Palestinian citizenship. Nostalgia is not always simply about the past. Rather, diasporic nostalgia can be future-oriented. 'Fantasies of the past determined by needs of the present have a direct impact on realities of the future', writes Boym (2001, p. xvi).

Becoming Palestinian *and* Danish

The diaspora tour established a sense of belonging to Palestine and gave an existential assurance of who one was. For instance, when I asked Lara if she felt Palestinian, she replied that she had not previously been so interested in her origins. While on the tour, she felt 'Palestinian with a capital P'. She assured me that she had become more nationalistic.[5]

One of my interlocutors who most clearly expressed that she felt changed by her trip to Palestine was 19-year-old Nisreen. Nisreen only had 'ethnic Danes' as classmates in elementary school, as she put it. When she strongly asserted that she was not Palestinian but Danish at home, her mother forced her to join a local Palestinian association. There, her interest in the Palestinian homeland developed and she had travelled to Palestine with some friends the year before we met. As mentioned earlier, Nisreen also made a short film about her experiences in Palestine. When asked by an interviewer in the film what home is for her, she answered that it is a place where she feels safe, where she is accepted for who she is and where she is not discriminated against or judged because of her looks, her personality, her headscarf, her religion, her gender or her family. Through the film, the audience can follow Nisreen through her first visit to Jerusalem, where she met family members, and when she visited the village her father left in 1948. She was surprised by all the relatives who wanted to meet her and was delighted to pray in al-Aqsa mosque in the Old City of Jerusalem. On her way to wash before the prayer in the mosque, she addressed her mother in Arabic through the camera, describing what she was doing, the site and the heat. Suddenly the account was broken by Nisreen's tearful voice: 'Oh, mum, let me live here, let me live here!'

Coming to Palestine for the first time was clearly a deeply emotional experience and a sort of homecoming but, according to the film, it was the violence of the Israeli forces that Nisreen witnessed that truly unsettled her. She and her friends were visiting a part of the Palestinian occupied areas where clashes were taking place and they met a 10-year-old boy who had repeatedly been arrested and beaten by Israeli soldiers. The group of Palestinian youth from Denmark also experienced shootings nearby. Nisreen came back to Denmark a changed person, emotionally shaken by the severity of the situation in the place her family originates from and with a new sense of belonging. By the end of the film, she declared that 'No matter what the Israeli soldiers did, I felt at home.' In one of the last clips of the film, she declared that she refused to decide if she was Danish or Palestinian but rather that she is both. She became more outspoken when she turned to the camera saying that she would like people to come to Palestine, not only to visit the beautiful country but to see how people live there and to see what is going on for themselves. Svetlana Boym's (2001) distinction between two different types of nostalgia is relevant in understanding the experience of Nisreen and other Danish-Palestinians. For Boym, restorative nostalgia emphasises truth, tradition and attempts to recreate the lost home. In contrast, reflective nostalgia is about recognising the ambivalence in longing and belonging. Nisreen's film is primarily an example of the latter and gives a sense of nuance, the duality of home and a refusal to label oneself in any simplistic manner.

A few months after we returned to Denmark, I met Ibrahim and Daoud again. They said that they thought about the world and their own lives differently since the tour. They claimed that Palestine and what happened there were constantly on their minds; it had become a kind of a parallel present to their everyday lives in Denmark. Palestine now was 'for real' or had been transformed from being 'a vision to becoming concrete', as Kanafani puts it (1995).

It was not only my interlocutors' relation to Palestine and their sense of being Palestinian that had changed, it was also their views on life in Denmark. When I asked Wissam a few months after the trip if it had changed something in him, he replied that he himself had not changed, but his view on his family's life and circumstances in Denmark had. He had realised that compared to the situation of Palestinians in Palestine, 'the Danish system was nothing to complain about', as he put it. The diaspora tour offered new perspectives and a distance from Danish everyday life. Despite experiences of unemployment, exclusion and Islamophobia, Wissam now thought that Palestinians in Denmark needed to keep going despite all the hardships. Nisreen expressed herself in similar terms:

> The hope [Palestinians in Palestine] maintain is fantastic! They live with the worst circumstances, but there is still hope. And how much they struggle! Since 1948! Here in Denmark, we keep complaining. We should be more grateful for what we have.[6]

Wissam and others stated that the knowledge they had gained about Palestinian society and politics through travelling was part of the process of becoming Danish too. 'Knowing their roots', as some of them said, offered them the opportunity for several belongings and a new sense of purpose when fighting for inclusion in Denmark.

Multifocal engagements after the diaspora tour

> I feel like I'm carrying a heavy concrete lump on my shoulders – since I've seen the situation in Palestine, I have to talk about it. Why do I need to feel this responsibility? But that's just how it is.

This statement was made by Mounsir when I interviewed him in the poor neighbourhood where he lived in the city of Aarhus. Similar to Mounsir, many of the young people who took part in the diaspora tour became more involved in associations working for the Palestinian cause in Denmark, organising film screenings and discussions on the situation in Palestine or inviting NGO activists from the West Bank to speak in Denmark. They also organised demonstrations, held speeches in public and wrote opinion pieces to raise awareness about Palestine. Others travelled to Palestine again to volunteer in activities like picking olives during the harvest season. These were ways in which they could continue to engage with Palestine. There was no consensus as to how one could really help; a few wanted to raise money but most emphasised awareness campaigns. When I asked Wissam if he wanted to help people in Palestine, he replied: 'I don't know. At the Red Cross office [in the West Bank] there was a poster: "If you have come to help us, you can go home, but if you came here to get to know us..." They want us to tell the world [what is happening in Palestine]. Old men took our hands and said, "Please, tell them about this!"' The message on the Red Cross poster can be read as a refusal to accept charity and a motivation for solidarity and outreach work. At the time of the interview a few months after the diaspora tour, Wissam had arranged a weekend event on the Palestinian predicament for young Danish-Palestinians. It was the first time he had been involved in any such activity.

The insights my interlocutors had gained of life in Palestine gave the awareness that a significant part of their struggle was to improve the experiences and opportunities for themselves and other Danish-Palestinians. Some reasoned that only people who were not too busy with their own socioeconomic problems could engage with their Palestinian homeland fruitfully, and only people who were accepted in the majority society would be listened to. This resonates with the avenues for social engagement that my interlocutors started pursuing shortly after their return from the diaspora tour. Many volunteered in various local social projects where they lived, such as homework and leisure activities for children and youth. The diaspora tour highlighted inequality, poverty, discrimination and social injustice in Palestine but these were issues that many of my interlocutors also experienced first-hand to some degree while living in the welfare state of Denmark. Their renewed sense of self and belonging to both Palestine and Denmark following the tour inspired them to proactively work towards the alleviation of these problems. Thus, the involvement in diasporic activities also led to more intense involvement in Danish public life in general. Karen Morris' (2012) reference to multifocality in diaspora politics is of special relevance here. My interlocutors' social and political engagements after the diaspora tour were multifocal in the sense that they were active in different places at different societal levels; these engagements were meaningful as a result of their multiple loyalties. Just like multifocal eye lenses bring a clear and balanced sight both at close and long distances, so do multifocal engagements for my interlocutors.

Conclusion: diasporic grief and nostalgia as transformative practice

A diaspora tour aims to form future diasporic relations and political engagements, but it can also be a way to commemorate and deal with the past and lost places. In this chapter, I have shown the transformation of my young interlocutors as they went from being uncertain about where they belonged (neither to Denmark nor to Palestine) to being sure about their multiple belongings; from being or experiencing themselves as ignorant to being knowledgeable, from being passive to being an active part of both diasporic networks and Danish society. They continued to take a stance and engage in activities, grounded in a new diasporic consciousness and awareness of social issues. Emotionally, they also started to handle the grief and losses they grew up with in their families. Diaspora tours and visits to highly symbolic and charged places of origin thus can have a transformative potential.

Such diasporic trips can be further understood with inspiration from anthropological ritual theory and in particular the concept of initiation. Seen as an initiation, the tour constituted a liminal phase where a *communitas* of young people accumulated knowledge by visiting former home villages as well as human rights organisations, experienced both emotional and violent ordeals, prayed in holy sites and sorted out their emotional baggage with the help of an accumulation of things. They came back to Denmark as partly new people, as responsible and politically aware Danish-Palestinians who were prepared to engage in political and social issues in multiple places. The tour became a rebirth of sorts.

As idiom, standpoint and entitlement, Palestinian diasporic practices and stances are means to formulate belongings and loyalties for Palestinians outside the original homeland. Those who do the formulating might well be an elite or a minority of a larger group, understood as constituting the diaspora (Brubaker, 2005). What is interesting here is not who belongs to the diaspora or the boundaries of the group but what people actually do. I have argued that the decision to visit Palestine was a diasporic stance in itself. Through diaspora, we can understand communities through their actions, how they mobilise, strategise and affect change locally, nationally and transnationally. By taking seriously the transformative potential of practices of diasporic people, we can start to grasp the complexities and ambivalences of belongings, move beyond essentialised understandings of ethnicity and nationality and start to explore the existential, emotional, political and social meanings that enrich people's lives when involved in diasporic practices.

Notes

1 The fieldwork also included in-depth interviews with about 35 individuals and participant observation at events such as public lectures, demonstrations and youth camps and, to some extent, in people's everyday life.
2 Palestine is not an independent state and academic literature often use terms such as the occupied Palestinian territories and Israel or Palestine/Israel when referring to the territory of the former British Mandate of Palestine. In this text, I choose to use the same word, Palestine, as my interlocutors did when referring to their ancestral homeland.
3 The Right of Return refers to UN General Assembly Resolution 194, passed by the end of the first Israel-Arab war in 1948, which defined principles for returning Palestinian refugees to their homes and compensating them for their losses (see UN General Assembly Resolution 194 (III), 1948).
4 The Danish-Palestinian organisation that arranged the tour was also a platform for future political involvement. Although the member base for this organisation was first and foremost Danish-Palestinians, there were also members who did not have Palestinian origins.
5 My findings partly contradict the research in Scandinavia (Kublitz, 2011; Jakobsen and Andersson, 2012) that points out that young people of Palestinian origin and other Muslim backgrounds involved in activism for the Palestinian cause identify themselves mainly as Muslims. According to these studies, young people tend to see the Israeli-Palestinian conflict as a conflict between the West and Islam. However, my study shows that the diaspora travellers renegotiated complex processes of identification in which different national identities, rather than religious, were in focus.
6 These quotes, along with other ethnographic examples, point to the extent of the internalisation of the mainstream discourse on ungrateful immigrants in Danish majority society.

References

Abdelhady, D. (2011) *The Lebanese Diaspora: The Arab Immigrant Experience in Montreal, New York, and Paris*. New York: New York University Press.

Abu-Lughod, L. (2007) 'Return to half-ruins – memory, post-memory, living history in Palestine', in Abu-Lughod, L. and Sa'di, A.H. (eds) *Nakba: Palestine, 1948, and the Claims of Memory*. New York: Columbia University Press, pp. 77–104.

Abu-Lughod, L. and Sa'di, A.H. (eds) (2007) *Nakba: Palestine, 1948, and the Claims of Memory*. New York: Columbia University Press.

BADIL (2018) *Survey of Palestinian Refugees and Internally Displaced People, 2016–2018* vol. IX, Bethlehem: BADIL Resource Centre for Palestinian Residency and Refugee Rights.

Ben-Ze'ev, E. (2004) 'The politics of taste and smell: Palestinian rites of return', in Lien, M. E. and Nerlich, B. (eds) *The Politics of Food*. Oxford: Berg, pp. 141–160.

Borgerforslag (n.d.) 'Stop diskrimination af palæstinensiskfødte danskere, så de kan anføre Palæstina som fødselregistreringssted i deres pas eller kørekort' [Citizen proposal (n.d.) Stop the discrimination against Palestinian-born Danes so they can register Palestine as place of birth in their passport or driving licence]. Available at: www.borgerforslag.dk/se-og-stoet-forslag/?Id=FT-05186 (accessed 25 February 2021).

Boym, S. (2001) *The Future of Nostalgia*. New York: Basic Books.

Brubaker, R. (2005) 'The "diaspora" diaspora', *Ethnic and Racial Studies*, 28(1), pp. 1–9.

Carsten, J. (2004) *After Kinship*. Cambridge: Cambridge University Press.

Cohen, R. (2008) *Global Diasporas: An Introduction*. New York: Routledge.

Darieva, T. (2011) 'Rethinking homecoming: diasporic cosmopolitanism in post Soviet Armenia', *Ethnic and Racial Studies*, 34(3), pp. 490–508.

Ebron, P.A. (1999) 'Tourists as pilgrims: commercial fashioning of transatlantic politics', *American Ethnologist*, 26(4), pp. 910–931.

Fischbach, M.R. (2003) *Records of Dispossession – Palestinian Refugee Property and the Arab-Israeli Conflict*. New York: Columbia University Press.

Forslag (n.d.) 'Forslag til folketingsbeslutning om anerkendelse af en selvstændig palæstiniensisk stat 2011/1 BSF 30' [Proposal for a parliamentarian decision to recognise an independent Palestinian state]. Available at: file:///Users/cme-nag/Downloads/20111BB00030.pdf (accessed 27 November 2020).

Gardner, K. (1993) 'Desh and bidesh: sylheti images of home and away', *Man*, 28(1) pp. 1–15.

Graham, M. and Khosravi, S. (1997) 'Home is where you make it: repatriation and diaspora culture among Iranians in Sweden', *Journal of Refugee Studies*, 10(2), pp. 115–133.

Gren, N. (2014) 'Gendering *al Nakba*: elderly Palestinian refugees' stories and silences about dying children', *St Anthony International Review*, 10(1), pp. 110–126.

Gren, N. (2015) 'Being at home through learning Palestinian sociality: Swedish Palestinians' houses in the West Bank', in Kläger, F. and Stierstorfer K. (eds) *Diasporic Constructions of Home and Belonging*. Berlin: De Gruyter, pp. 229–247.

Hasso, F. (2000) 'Modernity and gender in Arab accounts of the 1948 and 1967 defeats', *International Journal of Middle Eastern Studies*, 32, pp. 491–510.

Hirsch, M. (2012) *The Generation of Postmemory: Writing and Visual Culture After the Holocaust*. New York: Columbia University Press.

Hirsch, M. and Miller, N.K. (eds) (2011) *Rites of Return: Diaspora Poetics and the Politics of Memory*. New York: Columbia University Press.

Issa, M. (1995) *Den Fædrene Jord* [Ancestors' Land] (in collaboration with Gitte Rabøl). Danish Television.

Jacobsen, C.M. and Andersson, M. (2012) '"Gaza in Oslo": social imaginaries in the political engagement of Norwegian minority youth', *Ethnicities*, 12(6), pp. 821–843.

Kanafani, N. (1995) 'Homecoming', *Middle East Report*, 194(25), pp. 40–42.

Kelner, S. (2010) *Tours that Bind: Diaspora, Pilgrimage and Israeli Birthright Tourism*. New York: New York University Press.

Khalidi, R. (1997) *Palestinian Identity: The Making of a Modern National Consciousness*. New York: Columbia University Press.

Khalili, L. (2007) *Heroes and Martyrs of Palestine: The Politics of National Commemoration*. Cambridge: Cambridge University Press.

Kublitz, A. (2010) 'The cartoon controversy – creating Muslims in a Danish setting', *Social Analysis*, 54(3), pp. 107–125.

Kublitz, A. (2011) 'The mutable conflict – a study of how the Palestinian-Israeli conflict is actualized among Palestinians in Denmark', PhD thesis, University of Copenhagen.
Miller, D. (2008) *The Comfort of Things*. Cambridge: Polity.
Miller, D. and Parrott F.R. (2009) 'Loss and material culture in south London', *The Journal of the Royal Anthropological Institute*, 15(3), pp. 502–519.
Morris, K. (2012) 'Diasporic politics, transnational media circulation and the multifocality of Côte d'Ivoire', *City and Society*, 24(2), pp. 240–259.
Rytter, M. (2019) 'Writing against integration: Danish imaginaries of culture, race and belonging', *Ethnos*, 84(4), pp. 678–697.
Safran, W. (1991) 'Diasporas in modern societies: myths of homeland and return', *Diaspora*, 1(1), pp. 83–99.
Sayigh, R. (1979) *Palestinians: From Peasants to Revolutionaries*. London: Zed Books.
Shargawi, O. (2009) *Fra Haifa til Nørrebro* [My Father from Haifa]. Zentropa Productions.
Slyomovics, S. (1998) *The Object of Memory – Arab and Jew Narrate the Palestinian Village*. Philadelphia, PA: University of Pennsylvania Press.
Sturken, M. (2011) 'Pilgrimages, reenactment, and souvenirs: modes of memory tourism', in Hirsch, M. and Miller, N.K. (eds) *Rites of Return: Diaspora Poetics and the Politics of Memory*. New York: Columbia University Press, pp. 280–293.
Turner, V. (1969) *The Ritual Process: Structure and Anti-Structure*. London: Routledge.
UN General Assembly Resolution 194 (III) (1948) 11 December 1948, New York: United Nations. Available at: https://unispal.un.org/UNISPAL.NSF/0/C758572B78D1CD0085256BCF0077E51A (accessed 25 February 2021).

26
IDIOMS OF CARE
Ageing and connectivity among older Turkish migrants in Sweden

Öncel Naldemirci

Introduction

The first-generation of Turkish migrants came to Sweden in the late 1960s and early 1970s and worked in the manufacturing sector (Alpay, 1980; Lundberg and Svanberg, 1991; Erder, 2006). It is well known that Kulu, a small town in Turkey, was the hometown of many immigrants who settled in Sweden (Lundberg, 1991). Yet, during the early years of Turkish migration, the group of migrants who settled in Sweden was more heterogeneous in terms of their pre-migratory backgrounds and cities of departure than is often assumed (Naldemirci, 2017). After the end of the relatively easy pathway to immigration to Sweden in the 1970s (Westin, 2003), immigration patterns started to rely more heavily on asylum applications and the family reunification of former immigrants. In the 1980s, many Kurdish and Assyrian people from Turkey came to Sweden as refugees (see also Başer and Levin, 2017). Today, there is a heterogeneous community of Turkey-born migrant groups, including highly skilled workers, refugees, large families originating from the same towns in Turkey, and descendants of individual families.

By revisiting some arguments that I developed elsewhere (Naldemirci, 2013), my aim in this chapter is to highlight caring relations, ideals and practices in the diaspora by focusing on the *gurbet* or 'being away from home' experiences of first-generation Turkish migrants, as well as their sense of longing (*gurbetlik*) and ideals of care. The experience of having once lost caring relations and ageing within a new web of relations in the diaspora may nourish and reinforce a quest for a diasporic community in older age. This quest emerges as a response to the unknown future and complex fears of solitude, abandonment and isolation in old age, which are reshaped and reinforced in the diaspora. Many of my respondents reconsidered their 'myth of return' to Turkey and their decision to stay in Sweden in terms of their family relations, rights in both Turkey and Sweden, their need for care and medical treatment, as well as a wide range of possibilities for transnational mobility. There is growing research that investigates how transnational families are performed across borders around changing ideals and practices of care (Baldassar, 2001; 2007; Bryceson and Vuorela, 2002; Zechner, 2008). Here, I highlight how the experiences in the diaspora also shape narratives of care and normative expectations about an imagined diasporic community.

The insights into ageing in the diaspora that I present here are based on two years of fieldwork (2011–2013) in a large Swedish city where I had the opportunity to interact with and interview 20 elderly people who self-defined as Turkish. These were evenly split with ten men and ten women making up the group of interlocutors and all were over 60; the women were generally younger than the men, most of whom were over 70. Quite common among the group was that men immigrated first, mainly as labour migrants, while the women joined their husbands later. All of the informants immigrated to Sweden during the late 1960s and early 1970s and were retired and naturalised Swedish citizens. They had chronic illnesses and were familiar with medical institutions in Sweden.

Gurbet and loss of caring relations in the diaspora

Diaspora is considered as a process (Gilroy, 1993; Clifford, 1994) rather than an essential and unchanging state of being or community. Following Parreñas and Siu, I see diaspora as 'an ongoing and contested process of subject formation embedded in a set of cultural and social relations that are sustained simultaneously with the "homeland" (real or imagined), place of residence, and compatriots or co-ethnics dispersed elsewhere' (2007, p. 1).

This contingency helps us to explore how migrants make sense of their affiliations with different subject positions, belongings and identities. Processes of subject formation may coincide with diverse ways of 'doing' belonging. People originating from the same homeland can develop a sense of belonging around a shared story of migration, an ever-changing and often contested cultural repertoire (folklore, religion, language, food), political engagements both in the diaspora and in the countries of settlement, as well as transnational ties that continue to reshape the idea of a homeland. They can deploy new ties in the country of settlement through different channels for socialisation (Naldemirci, 2017), economic collaboration and collective struggle against social ills. They can nourish their sense of community by telling and remembering stories about here and there, past and present (Myerhoff, 1979). However, people can also imagine a diasporic community in response to their vulnerabilities, needs of care and caring relations while they live with vulnerability, destitution, marginalisation and social ills (Dossa, 2020). Older Turkish people participating in the study were willing to tell me, whom they saw as a young and recent immigrant in Sweden, about their difficult beginnings in *gurbet*. *Gurbet* means, in Turkish, anywhere that is far from home, a foreign place or land. It does not necessarily connote being abroad; even in the same country, for instance, in the case of rural to urban migration, people can define their cities of settlement as *gurbet*. Suzan Ilcan defines *gurbet* as 'a *perceived* state of exile and a *longing for belonging*' (2002, p. 7, italics added). This multi-layered definition allows for the interweaving of a myriad of experiences of being uprooted, having no caring relations in a new setting where people attempt to carve out new relations and lives.

Gurbetlik is a colloquial expression deriving from *gurbet*, denoting the emotional burden of the separation from familiar surroundings, nostalgia and homesickness. Similar to 'homing desires', which are 'desires to feel at home achieved by physically and symbolically (re)constituting spaces which provide some kind of ontological security in the context of migration' (Fortier, 2003, p. 163), *gurbetlik* may lead to reconstituting spaces by constructing affective ties in the diaspora. These newly constructed affective ties are emphatically gendered. For instance, while women in my study often referred to other female family and kin members who also resettled in Sweden and Turkish neighbours who were supportive during their first years in Sweden, men mentioned their new friends that they mainly met at the workplace as people to turn to for help (Naldemirci, 2017). The very feeling of being in *gurbet* may have brought together people who would not even be acquaintances if they had stayed in their mutual home country. As migrants, they were far away from their families and friends and in need of new relationships with people with similar backgrounds. Speaking the same language while endeavouring to navigate a new language, sharing similar stories of emigration and immigration, facing similar challenges of resettlement, having similar pre-migratory cultural references, working in similar jobs, having immigrated to a bigger city and living in the same districts triggered new affinities between them. As *gurbetlik* derives from distancing oneself from caring relations in the context of migration, it arguably leads to imagining and building a community of people who have experienced similar difficulties and care about each other, especially those in need of care.

As Myerhoff (1979) poetically reminds us, old age can reinvigorate recollections, reflections and reckonings among older migrants. Similarly, many of my interlocutors harked back to their *gurbetlik* and beginnings in Sweden when asked about ageing and care and they hoped that Turkish family and community would respond to the potential vulnerabilities they may experience in the future.

In the following sections, I first shed light on how the Turkish family is imagined as the haven of caring relations and responsibilities in the diaspora through particular emotional idioms. I then move on to revisiting stories about an older Turkish man who had no family support in his frail old age, and underline how this particular set of emotions circulated among people and helped them imagine a diasporic community.

Turkish family as 'emotional'

The emotionalisation of the family is one underlying discourse in diaspora communities; the family becomes an important site in which diasporic communities articulate their identities and belongings (Skrbiš, 2008). Many interlocutors considered Turkish families as caring and compared this to an often-stereotypical understanding of the Swedish family as less emotional and caring. Memnune had become a blue-collar worker upon her immigration. She never forgot her first difficult years in Sweden, as she needed to combine her exhausting menial work with the care of her five children. She was quite assertive in her way of defining the Turkish family as radically different from the Swedish family. After reflecting on the difficulties she faced in Sweden and how she always showed love and affection for her children, Memnune referred to her Swedish neighbour to describe the Turkish family as she understood it:

> I had a neighbour, my Swedish neighbour ... She had no one [to care for her]. I sometimes cooked and brought food. There was no one at home. When she died, all her sons and daughters came. [Addressing neighbour's children] 'Where have you been until now?' I felt so sorry. *These people are very lonely (*garip*) here. They are lonely in their home country.* I don't know why – because they haven't shown love and affection to their children? They are disconnected; they live separate from each other. They don't give anything to their children, and their children don't give anything back either. We are always giving, we love and protect. They are not like that. This is the big difference.

Gurbetlik can connote *gariplik* or loneliness, having no one to turn to, homelessness and a lack of caring relations. *Garip* is widely used to refer to people who lead a precarious life, or those who have no caring family members. Being in a foreign land was an important period during which many of my interlocutors felt '*garip*'. Memnune reversed this and used it in reference to the Swedish people, who were imagined to be at home but lonely because their caring relations, adult children and friends were indifferent to their loneliness. As *garip* suggests, feeling at home is about having caring people around. In this sense, Memnune saw home-help services as indispensable for the elderly Swedes, because she assumed them to lack caring relations within their family and have no one to 'knock on the door', whereas she felt that as she had invested emotionally in her children, she was assured that she would be always cared about.

Memnune's account is an example of drawing clear and exaggerated boundaries between the Swedish and Turkish families. Many older Turkish people participating in the study oscillated between different subject positions and expectations about familial responsibilities and obligations, articulated in more nuanced ways by evoking emotions. On the one hand, they did not want to see and present themselves like some other migrants or their acquaintances in Turkey who, in my respondents' view, expected 'too much' from their adult children. On the other hand, they considered their families as different from the imagined Swedish families who were thought to have recourse to formal care providers. As Memmune's narrative indicates, many older Turkish interlocutors were ambivalent towards formal care facilities such as home-help services and elderly care homes. This ambivalence was anchored in their ways of perceiving 'the Swedish' as modern and independent but too individualistic and uncaring.

My interlocutors straddled their ambivalence towards caring relationships and formal care. On the one hand, they did not wish to strain their relationship with their children. They were aware that their adult children had their own children, paid work and other responsibilities. On the other hand, they were afraid of 'abandonment', as I illustrate with Mehmet's story later in this chapter. The fear of abandonment and loneliness becomes even more intense in *gurbet* in the narratives I encountered. The desire to avoid overburdening their adult children in old age influences some people's openness to relying on 'some' formal elderly care facilities. Songur (2019) highlights that older migrants refrain from the use of special housing due to the greater accessibility of home-help services and the help they receive from family and relatives in a Swedish context. At the same time, they hope that their children will remain emotionally attached to them and thus responsive to their care needs. Many participants in the study referred to particular emotions such as compassion (*merhamet*), loyalty (*vefa*) (see also Naldemirci, 2015) and affection (*şefkat*), which they considered to mark their difference from native Swedish people.

Here, I revisit *merhamet* (compassion, mercy, altruism, forgiveness) as it gains new meanings in the diaspora, particularly in relation to the imagined Swedish adult children. A number of my interlocutors thought and hoped that their children were more compassionate than the imagined Swedish offspring, and therefore more responsive should their parents need care. I quote below an extract from a long discussion between Esma, Adnan, Selma and myself. Esma was in her late seventies and lived with her adult son, very close to her beloved friends and neighbours, Selma and Adnan, a married couple whom she had known since their immigration. We were discussing different elderly care arrangements when Esma interjected to say that Turkish people were 'self-damaging' and thus more inclined to age early.

> ESMA: Let me tell you this, Adnan, if we were like the Swedish, if we lived like them in Sweden, we would live until we are centenarians.
> ADNAN: You would live, for sure.
> ESMA: Because we have these thoughts, these feelings…
> ADNAN: [*Interrupting*] Worries … Worries damage Turks.
> ESMA: Of course, we have this joy of life, this willingness to live, but we can't be like them. Everything bothers us. Even with strangers [*yedi kat el*], we would sit and talk about troubles, have heart-to-heart talks. We become sorry for them, we keep thinking

about why such a bad thing happened, we are even sorry for the Swedes. God save this feeling inside us, only compassionate [*merhametli*] people have it probably. Does the Swede have it? I doubt it. He only cares about his own life. He does not care about his children, nor his grandchildren. I would not like to live like that, though. Without any feelings.

ÖNCEL: You had told me that your daughter would be very upset if you talked to her about an elderly home …

ESMA: She would kill me, I swear.

ÖNCEL: So, you mean, they [your children] also have this feeling? They look at things differently from the Swedish?

ESMA: Yes, they would not be like them.

ADNAN: Not yet, they are more compassionate [*merhametleri fazla*].

Selma engaged in many transnational care visits. She travelled back to Turkey to take care of her family members, first, her older brother, then her mother. For her, care in old age should be a family responsibility. However, she did not want her son or daughter-in-law to take care of her and offered this view during our conversation:

> We are compassionate [*biz merhametliyiz*], it is my duty to take care of my elders. All in all, I did not become Swedish after more than 40 years. Of course, there are many compassionate Swedes, but not all of them place importance on these kinds of family relations. My mother had cancer and I immediately went there [Turkey] and took care of everything with my sister. But I would not ask the same thing from my son. He has his own life. I know that he loves me but … I completely agree with the idea of an elderly home where he can come to visit me. If I return to Turkey, it would be even more difficult for them to arrange such visits.

In Selma's view, *merhamet* is not only a feeling to demonstrate, it comes with particular caring practices that show how one really cares about someone else. By reminding us of the exception of 'compassionate Swedes', she insisted that being compassionate was anchored not only in her migrant biography (transnational visits to care for her family members) but also in her cultural identity, which is different from the mainstream cultural script in Sweden. By telling this story to me, as a young migrant, and also by underlining the improbability of demanding the same thing from her own son, she knew the limits of demanding the same thing from the younger generations. Her son loved her, but she did not take future family care for granted, the caregiving that she juxtaposed with being *merhametli* could take new forms. If she moved to a care home, her son being *merhametli* and loving would be shown in new forms (by visiting her regularly, for instance). *Merhamet* as an emotion continues to align the individual (Turkish adult second-generation son) with the collective (the Turkish family and community).

Another emotion that was often referred to is *şefkat* (affection, concern), which adds nuance to the complexity of care and distinguishes family care from professional care. *Şefkat* was imagined to be provided mainly by close relations and family members who genuinely care about someone. For instance, Ayşe, as a first-generation Turkish migrant, was proud of how her adult children had carved out successful and independent lives for themselves in Sweden. Both her son and daughter were university graduates and employed in well-known Swedish companies. When we started to talk more about older age, she was angry at the indifference of the Turkish community living in the city to any agenda concerning older members. As she had spent years organising associational activities, she was quite pessimistic about the Turkish community, which she considered to be not modern. She argued that many older Turkish people living in the city were and would be happy to depend on their adult children, and therefore they were reluctant to engage in associations working to establish a Turkish elderly home. Ayşe disagreed with the idea of being dependent on her adult children in old age and was willing to move to an elderly home if she needed care. Yet, she was afraid of not finding şefkat in a care home. She told me:

> When you get old, when you cannot take care of yourself, God save you, it is difficult. Thank God, I manage very well at the moment. But sooner or later, we will all need something. You cannot expect your children to give you everything; they have their own lives. They cannot move to my place nor can I move to theirs. I can, I want to, move to an elderly home. Yet still, you don't know if you will find yourself in affectionate [şefkatli] hands there. There are good people, there are bad people [professional caregivers]. For sure, it won't be like family giving care. It will be like work for them, you cannot expect more from them, can you? I don't expect şefkat from them, it is enough if they do not do any harm.

These idioms of emotion, merhamet and şefkat (see also vefa, Naldemirci, 2015) are well known in a Turkish context but have gained new meanings in the diaspora. For instance, merhamet, a common trope in contemporary Turkey, was actively recited and articulated to reinforce the ideal of the Turkish family vis-à-vis the assumed modern but uncaring Swedish family. However, it was also deployed to nuance their expectations from their adult children so that they did not expect 'too much' as did many other migrants. Şefkat, on the other hand, was used as a critical response to the professional caregiving in Sweden that many idealised as 'the best in the world'. The assumed loneliness and isolation of the Swedish elderly were frightening to those who had once felt garip in gurbet. The emotionalisation of the Turkish family in these new contexts has paved the way for a particular way of assessing enigmatic futures in old age and rethinking their caring relations in gurbet.

Quest for a diasporic community: Mehmet's story

During my fieldwork, I noticed that while these emotions prescribed moral duties to the family in the first instance. and especially to adult children, they could also be deployed to imagine moral subject positions for the Turkish community living in Sweden. The stories about 'some' Turkish people's institutionalisation and solitude in elderly care homes point to the fear of abandonment by family members. A common trope in these stories is the experience of being in gurbet, the need for reciprocity and mutual help. Solitude in an elderly care home, for my interlocutors, was reminiscent of these emotionally difficult times of early beginnings and not feeling at home.

In the early days of my fieldwork, I was looking for older Turkish people who resided in special housing or nursing care homes. All my contacts and informants cautioned that they did not know many Turkish people living in this type of institution and mentioned only two names. The first was an older woman, Hatice, who had severe dementia and resided in a specialised care home. During conversations with my interlocutors, they emphasised that her adult children did not want to move their mother to a care home. However, her aggravating medical condition and increasing care needs made this decision necessary. A common trope in these accounts was the devotion that was reflected in this woman's adult children's visits to their mother every day, where they would spend many hours with her and actively engage in caregiving. As Selma underlined, the severity of the illness and the need for professional care did not absolve filial obligations; rather, it changed the form and place of caring practices.

The other name that came up in these conversations was Mehmet. He was an early-in-life emigrant from a small province in Turkey who arrived in Sweden after short stays in several northern European countries. He settled in Sweden just before restrictions on immigration in 1973. He had a turbulent life with troubles in his family and loose connections to the rest of the Turkish community. He was in his eighties at the time of the fieldwork and had moved to a care home nearly a decade ago when he needed intensive hands-on care.

Mehmet's institutionalisation in his old age and his lack of close friends and family members haunted almost all my interviews, as many informants knew or had heard about him. Mehmet was seen as having fallen victim to frayed family and community ties and the misfortune of being abroad with no one to care about him in his old age. His story must have been much more nuanced than the accounts I was hearing, yet its widespread circulation made me think about the enigmatic futures that many older people were working out or anticipating. Talking about or referring to Mehmet's loneliness and presumed abandonment was a way to project and reject a similar future for themselves. I met Mehmet only once at the care home where he lived but did not interview him as he was in poor health. However, his name and story were often recalled by my conversations with other older Turkish people.

Some of the women in my study cared about and for Mehmet's plight as they wished for a community where members would and should care about each other, especially when one needed care in a foreign land. They did this by invoking emotions like compassion, affection and loyalty to highlight the norms of a genuine Turkish family from which Mehmet had been alienated in *gurbet*. For Selma, who travelled back to Turkey to care for her mother, Mehmet should not have been abandoned and isolated since he was a member of a larger Muslim community; he should rather be surrounded by people who genuinely and compassionately care about him. Selma wished to mobilise the benevolence of practising Muslim Turkish people towards the vulnerable in the community. Another interlocutor, Seda, went through difficult times after her divorce in Sweden; she was first stigmatised and ostracised but never severed her ties with the Turkish community. According to her, both Turkishness and Islamic values were at the core of a future diasporic community but needed to coincide with daily activities of care and support. Yet, a common trope in this multitude of stories about Mehmet was the experience of being in *gurbet*. Mehmet's solitude in an elderly care home in Sweden was reminiscent of having no caring relations after their settlement in Sweden. It also mirrored fears of ageing and being alone in *gurbet*.

I came across two explanations for Mehmet's lonely institutionalisation. The first was a medical and therefore brief one. Selma had never met Mehmet nor visited him. Her husband, Adnan, frequently went to the mosque for his daily prayers, and there he came to hear and know about Mehmet's circumstances. Mehmet had a severe illness and he was frail, his son also had a chronic disease, which led Selma to a fatalist understanding of their plight. This was a tragedy, an epitome of human vulnerability, an ordeal to accept with faith. The prospect of ever being in a similar situation, in frail old age, in isolation and with severely ill family members, was frightening for Selma and it was important not to be judgemental. This fear was anchored in a particular understanding of fate and the relationship between God and his subjects. A popular belief among practising Muslims is that if a person disgraces, despises or reproaches another because of an affliction, then they themselves will fall victim to the same fate. Selma told this story with extreme caution. She too had an only son and, since she did not know what would happen to her and her family in the future, she dealt with Mehmet's story with great sensitivity. Mehmet was a tragic example of ageing and a frightening template on which she had come to think about her own ageing and dependence on family relations. Selma avoided judging his family for admitting him to an institution and thought that the community should be more compassionate (*merhametli*) than judgemental and reproachful.

The second story was more critical of Mehmet's family but also the Turkish community. Mehmet was institutionalised because his family and the rest of the Turkish people who knew him did not care about him. Mehmet's admission to an elderly care home was a drastic rupture from the rest of the community, which also enabled his friends and family to relinquish their responsibilities. When I told Seda that I visited someone called Mehmet at a care home, she was happy to hear that I met him. Seda recounted that during one of these visits to a friend at the care home, a care worker, 'a Bosnian Muslim woman', insisted that Seda came to see if she spoke Turkish. The Bosnian care worker informed Seda that Mehmet had not had any visitors since his admission. When Seda entered his room for the first time, Mehmet was so happy that he burst into tears to have a visitor after three years alone in that room. Seda was touched by this first encounter and by Mehmet's loneliness. She started to visit him twice a week unless it was very cold, or she was unwell. Seda spent one to two hours, sometimes more, with him. She read religious texts, sometimes the Quran to him which she felt he enjoyed. Mehmet did not like the food he was served at the care home and so Seda cooked and brought special Turkish food to him. As he had diabetes, she carefully rearranged her cooking on the days she visited him. When she heard from the care workers that Mehmet did not want them to bathe him since he thought that it was religiously unsuitable for a man to be bathed by women, Seda called a male acquaintance, who came every week with a friend to bathe him. Seda also informed and encouraged her acquaintances and friends to visit Mehmet, which happened occasionally.

Seda told me this story several times, adding new details about new people and incidents each time. She was happy to alleviate Mehmet's pain and solitude to some extent. For her, it was the religious duty of a good Muslim to be compassionate and affectionate to those who are suffering or lonely. As Mehmet was originally from Turkey, it was primarily a moral duty for someone from the Turkish community to provide for a member in need of care. This resonated with the way many older immigrants understand their experience of being in *gurbet*. An elderly care home can offer a good quality of care, but the absence of caring relations should be complemented by others who have similar life stories. This is not only because they share a cultural repertoire, including religious beliefs and the same language, but as migrants, they too would also always need reciprocal help and caring eyes and hands. It was also a gendered way of knowing what can complement formal care practices. Seda is the mother of three children and was very concerned about her close kin members. She took care of her family and cared for her mother when she was ill. Caring about others was linked to her moral subjectivity, which has been shaped by her migrant experience, religious beliefs, and family and community concerns. Seda's epic story came to an end with Mehmet's funeral. Even though his family was not at the funeral, Seda's emphasis was more on the number of people who were at the mosque on a Friday. His funeral prayer was performed by the Muslims who were there for their Friday prayer. The closure of the story was about people of good faith coming together for the last prayer, but the absence of a large and emotionally supportive Turkish community at the funeral was the underlying message.

Ageing in diaspora

Ageing in the diaspora coincides with working out different possibilities of connectivity, care needs and caring relations. As Skrbiš and Svašek (2007) argue, 'mobile individuals are tied to their families and friends "back home," but they also *grow attachments to their new surroundings, learn to express feelings in new ways,* and have particular *hopes and expectations* about what the future may bring' (p. 373, italics added). The particular repertoire and idioms of emotions that I revisit here continue to gain new meanings for older migrants, who continuously renegotiate and make sense of familial care responsibilities and obligations in the diaspora. Besides the particular hopes and expectations that Skrbiš and Svašek highlight, I suggest that older migrants also grow into particular considerations and trepidations in the diaspora.

The experiences of having once lost caring relations and building and giving meaning to new affective ties in the diaspora make many first-generation Turkish immigrants recollect their early beginnings in the diaspora, and work out their needs of care and caring relations for the future. This very experience reshapes their belongings and expectations but also their fear of abandonment and wish for connectivity. As Suad Joseph explains, connectivity consists of 'relationships in which a person's boundaries are relatively fluid so that persons feel a part of significant others' (1993, p. 467). One significant challenge to connectivity in old age is that many lose those relations; some friends whom they came to know after their settlement in Sweden pass away, some suffer from severe illnesses, while others move to other cities and a few return to Turkey after retirement. In such a rapidly changing landscape of social relations and friendships, family, especially children and grandchildren, have become even more significant for their sense of connectivity.

While Mehmet's communal narrative represents perceptions about abandonment and solitude in *gurbet*, I suggest that the widespread circulation of this narrative among older migrants concerns a fearful projection and stimulates a desire for connectivity. Harking back to the definition of the diaspora as an ongoing and contested process of subject formation (Parreñas and Siu, 2007), I argue that reaching older age and facing enigmatic futures and vulnerabilities in the diaspora may reinvigorate cultural and religious ideals of care and coincide with particular and local responses to vulnerabilities and suffering, which can also reshape the understandings of diasporic communities. The homing desires, and aspirations to sustain a revived and reshaped connectivity in older ages, may critically inform the attempts to understand diaspora as a caring community that is responsive to older migrants' idiosyncratic vulnerabilities and wishes.

References

Alpay, Ş. (1980) *Turkar i Stockholm: en studie av invandrare, politik och samhälle* [Turks in Stockholm: A Study of Migrants, Politics and Society]. Stockholm: Liber Förlag.
Baldassar, L. (2001) *Visits Home: Migration Experiences Between Italy and Australia*. Melbourne: Melbourne University Press.
Baldassar, L. (2007) 'Transnational families and aged care: the mobility of care and the migrancy of ageing', *Journal of Ethnic and Migration Studies*, 33(2), pp. 275–297.
Başer, B. and Levin, P.T. (eds) (2017) *Migration from Turkey to Sweden: Integration, Belonging and Transnational Community*. London: I.B. Tauris.
Bryceson, D. and Vuorela, U. (2002) *The Transnational Family: Global European Networks and New Frontiers*. Oxford: Berg.
Clifford, J. (1994) 'Diasporas', *Cultural Anthropology*, 19(3), pp. 302–338.
Dossa, P. (2020) *Social Palliation: Canadian Muslims' Storied Lives on Living and Dying*. Toronto: University of Toronto Press.
Erder, S. (2006) *Refah toplumunda getto* [Ghetto in the Welfare Society]. Istanbul: Istanbul Bilgi Üniversitesi Yayınları.
Fortier, A.M. (2003) 'Making home: queer migrations and motions of attachment', in Ahmed, S., Castaneda, C., Fortier, A-M. and Sheller, M. (eds) *Uprootings/Regroundings: Questions of Home and Migration*. Oxford: Berg, pp. 115–135.
Gilroy, P. (1993) *The Black Atlantic: Modernity and Double Consciousness*. London: Routledge.

Ilcan, S. (2002) *Longing for Belonging: The Cultural Politics of Settlement*. Westport, CT: Praeger.

Joseph, S. (1993) 'Gender and relationality among Arab families in Lebanon', *Feminist Studies*, 19(3), pp. 465–486.

Lundberg, I. (1991) 'Kulubor i Stockholm: en svensk historia' [Kulu Migrants in Stockholm: A Swedish History]. Invandraminnesarkivet Serie A. 4. Stockholm: Tumba.

Lundberg, I. and Svanberg, I. (1991) 'Turkish associations in metropolitan Stockholm', Uppsala Multiethnic Papers, 23, Uppsala.Myerhoff, B. (1979) *Number Our Days*. New York: E.P. Dutton.

Naldemirci, Ö. (2013) 'Caring (in) diaspora: aging and caring experiences of older Turkish migrants in a Swedish context', unpublished PhD thesis. Gothenburg. Available at:. https://gupea.ub.gu.se/bitstream/2077/34304/1/gupea_2077_34304_1.pdf

Naldemirci, Ö. (2015) 'Rethinking loyalty (*vefa*) through transnational care practices of older Turkish women in Sweden', in Milewski, N., Sirkeci, I., Yücesahin, M.M. and Rolls A.S. (eds) *Family and Human Capital in Turkish Migration*. London: Transnational Press, pp. 35–45.

Naldemirci, Ö. (2017) 'Nicknames in diaspora: tracing migrant tales of first-generation Turkish migrants in Sweden', in Başer, B. and Levin, P.T. (eds) *Migration from Turkey to Sweden: Integration, Belonging and Transnational Community*. London: I. B. Tauris, pp. 64–85.

Parreñas, R.S. and Siu, L.C.D. (2007) *Asian Diasporas: New Formations, New Conceptions*. Stanford, CA: Stanford University Press.

Skrbiš, Z. (2008) Transnational families: theorizing migration, emotions and belonging', *Journal of Intercultural Studies*, 29(3), pp. 231–246.

Skrbiš, Z. and Svašek, M. (2007) 'Passions and powers: emotions and globalization', *Identities: Global Studies in Culture and Power*, 14, pp. 367–383.

Songur, W. (2019) 'Older migrants' use of elderly care in Sweden: family affects choice between home help services and special housing', *European Journal of Social Work*, 24(3), pp. 481–491. doi: 10.1080/13691457.2019.1639628

Westin, C. (2003) 'Young people of migrant origin in Sweden', *International Migration Revie*, 37(4), pp. 987–1010.

Zechner, M. (2008) 'Care of older people in transnational settings', *Journal of Aging Studies*, 22(1), pp. 32–44.

27

THE EGYPTIAN MUSLIM BROTHERHOOD IN TURKEY AFTER THE 2013 COUP

Organisational renewal and renegotiation in the diaspora

Lucia Ardovini

Introduction

Walking through the streets of Istanbul one cannot help but notice how, through subtle changes over the years, the city has become a hub for several displaced communities from neighbouring Arab countries. Since the 2011 Arab uprisings, Turkey has been subjected to a steady influx of people fleeing their homelands because of unstable regimes, authoritarian rule or worsening economic conditions. Bringing together hundreds of thousands from across the Middle East and North Africa (MENA) region, Istanbul has now become the stage for a new pan-Arab experience, hosting new experiments of Arab interactions and various projects of political activism (Ali, 2020). Within this larger context, Istanbul has become a 'Brotherhood hub' in the aftermath of the July 2013 coup d'état in Egypt, which violently removed the Muslim Brotherhood (henceforth the Brotherhood) from power and led to the scattering abroad of its members and leaders alike (Ayyash, 2020). As well as hosting several of the Brotherhood's offices, the city also houses its media stations, while the Turkish government directly invests in the movement's branches, offering them a platform to rebuild and reorganise. While key organisational decisions are now being taken in Turkey, the experience of forced exile also poses significant challenges to the core values, principles and structures on which the Brotherhood is organised.

As such, Istanbul is at once the hub from which the Brotherhood leads its various branches and the stage for ongoing conflicts over leadership, ideology and competing responses to repression. During my field research on the Brotherhood, current and former members referred to the experience of forced exile and diasporic formation as opportunities allowing them to re-evaluate the organisation's overarching control over daily activities, careers and individual thought processes. As described by Osama, a current member who thinks of himself as a dissenter:

> After the coup, when we came here [Istanbul], I realised that I had time to think ... how did I get here? Why am I in this? Why am I a member of this organisation? Why should I keep listening to them [the Brotherhood's leaders] if I do not agree with what they are saying?

Once a hardliner when we first met in 2014, Osama vehemently denied suggestions that the movement's often contradictory policies while in power might have contributed to its downfall and spoke harshly of those criticising its leadership. As the years passed, each conversation showcased a more critical side and now he speaks openly of the often painful process of having to rebuild his worldview. His testimony shows the extent to which some members have begun to question the hierarchical organisational structures and strict dogmas they have been socialised into for decades, rediscovering their individual voices and challenging the collective identity the Brotherhood historically relies on. These words are also representative of the experiences of many of my research respondents, which point to diasporic identification among members of the Brotherhood in exile.

In this chapter, I offer an examination of the Brotherhood's diaspora in Turkey, highlighting how the process of settling and rebuilding abroad is creating the space for its members to reconsider the terms of their belonging to the movement. Focusing on the personal narratives of Brotherhood members in Istanbul, I look at diasporic identification to better understand how core principles such as 'listen and obey', isolationism and hierarchical structures are being challenged by a growing number of members in the diaspora. Overall, I find that the unprecedented space for individual agency within the context of forced exile is leading several Brotherhood members to directly question the movement's structures, collective identity and message, therefore generating the potential for organisational renewal.

The findings are informed by a long-term qualitative study of the Brotherhood's organisation and ideology, and on several rounds of ethnographic fieldwork, semi-structured interviews and participant observations that began in 2013. The core of the primary data that informs this chapter is based on conversations held in Turkey between 2017 and 2019 with 30 respondents (only two of whom were women). The sample of participants cuts across the Brotherhood's organisational and generational spectrum and therefore allows going beyond the usual sample of members that informs several studies on the movement. Interviews were primarily conducted in English and, when a translator was employed, they were suggested by the interviewees themselves to make sure that they felt safe and comfortable. All interviews have been anonymised and pseudonyms are used to avoid regime retaliation. I employed grounded theory methodology to assess how members are responding to repression and forced exile, as it allowed me to analyse the data without pre-imposing a specific theoretical question or framework. During the fieldwork, I interviewed some of the participants multiple times.

These ongoing conversations inform the primary data at the core of this chapter. My analysis focuses on the individual perspectives and experiences vis-à-vis that of the movement as a monolithic unit, offering a point of departure to investigate the impact of the diasporic experience on the Brotherhood's tight organisational structure. My fieldwork shows that Brotherhood members in exile face two distinct sets of challenges: those connected to the process of settling into a host country, and those brought about by the organisation's disarray. In turn, these factors also affect other activities generally associated with diaspora communities, such as mobilisation patterns and their stance towards the Egyptian regime (Magued, 2018). Overall, I argue that a diaspora framework helps one better understand the challenges that the organisation faces in the aftermath of 2013, offering new insights into social and political dynamics, ongoing processes of emerging subjectivities, internal fragmentation and questions surrounding belonging.

The exact number of Egyptians in Turkey is difficult to estimate, but it is assumed that there are approximately 15,000–30,000 who fled to Turkey after 2013. Most Egyptians in Turkey live in Istanbul, and most of them are believed to have some connection to the Brotherhood (Ayyash, 2020). Some clear factors have facilitated the Brotherhood's settling in Turkey. First and foremost is the historical relationship between the movement and Turkish Islamic figures who created an ideologically welcoming context (Magued, 2018), as well as then-Prime Minister Erdoğan's overt condemnation of the 2013 coup (Kotan, 2017). Erdoğan has also provided the Brotherhood with the legal and financial backing they need to start building their transnational activism and advocacy networks, making Istanbul a hub of exilic political activities, housing the Brotherhood's headquarters and media channels, as well as being the fighting ground for internal splintering and struggles over leadership. The city also hosts a growing number of research centres and media outlets headed by dissatisfied members who have begun to challenge the organisational and structural constraints (Ardovini, 2020). As my analysis in this chapter shows, the diasporic experience offers the movement's members an unprecedented space to reclaim their agency against the Brotherhood's strict hierarchical structures, with processes of diasporic identification manifesting in different ways. Some members are progressively disengaging from the movement while others choose to maintain their affiliation and attempt to reform the movement from within. These trends are both significant, as the Brotherhood has historically repressed any form of dissent or independent thinking. Therefore, the dimension of forced exile and the disintegration of established chains of command are allowing for the reconfiguration of the relationship between the organisation and its members.

The chapter proceeds as follows. I first offer an overview of the movement's formation, ideology and politicisation, before moving on to the analysis of the diaspora experience. Then, I offer a brief description of my theoretical framework, that of diasporic identification. The next section illustrates the argument that the novelty of forced exile as a movement-wide phenomenon means that the Brotherhood has found itself in deeply unfamiliar circumstances, which invalidates historical hierarchies and strategies to maintain unity. I then explore the analysis of how different members experience diasporic identification, ranging from renouncing their membership to attempts to revive the movement from within. Overall, the disintegration of the Brotherhood's internal structures is allowing members to disengage from a fixed collective identity and to reclaim their agency vis-à-vis the movement, leading to the renegotiation of their belonging and membership. Therefore, looking at the Brotherhood in exile through the framework of diaspora allows us to examine its ongoing transformations in an original way, also shedding light on ongoing processes of organisational change.

Background: the Muslim Brotherhood

Founded in 1928 by schoolteacher Hassan al-Banna, the Brotherhood began as a pan-Arab grassroots religious movement with a strong anti-colonial message. During its early stages, the organisation developed a comprehensive ideology that understood Islamic values as core pillars of society and a way out of social problems, hence its slogan 'Islam is the solution' (Mitchell, 1969, p. 172). It was not long before its religious message began incorporating themes of resistance and identity politics, with activities expanding beyond preaching (*da'wa*) and penetrating into Egypt's political arena (Ayoob, 2008, p. 65). Declared illegal in 1948, the Brotherhood spent the majority of its existence as an outlawed organisation, but such status did not prevent it from evolving into one of Egypt's most organised opposition actors. Deriving legitimacy from its comprehensive message and an unrivalled network of social services – ranging from healthcare provision to education and vocational training – the Brotherhood quickly filled the gap left by the state and became a core component of Egyptian civil society (Brooke, 2017). This made it both a resource and a threat for various Egyptian regimes, subjecting the movement to alternating periods of heavy state repression and short bursts of tolerance and cooperation.

In fact, one of the distinguishing features of the organisation is its ability to survive, even thrive, under heavy repression. Historically, the Brotherhood managed successfully to turn repression into a fundamental marker of its collective identity and a source of unity and loyalty. The ordeal or tribulations that the Brotherhood was subjected to historically (*Mihna*) therefore became 'the glue' that bound its members together (Zollner, 2019), providing a shared experience that boosted their resolve against authoritarianism and reinforced the movement's status as a legitimate opposition actor. This shared sense of victimhood also contributed considerably to the creation of a pervasive collective identity that, coupled with the Brotherhood's strictly hierarchical organisational structures and principles such as 'listen and obey', kept the movement united in the face of repression (Kandil, 2015).

Despite its limited role in the popular uprisings in 2011, the events ushered an unprecedented political opportunity for the movement. When Hosni Mubarak was removed from power, the Brotherhood quickly capitalised on the transitional period, establishing a political party and officially entering the political arena. Relying on its established popular base, the movement moved from the periphery to the centre of Egyptian politics in the space of a few weeks and, despite widespread criticism from both external actors and its own members, fielded a presidential candidate for the 2012 elections. The proclamation of Mohammed Morsi as Egypt's first democratically elected president marked the movement's official foray into electoral politics and signalled that the Islamic project was finally within reach (Pargeter, 2016).

While it is beyond the scope of this chapter to examine the Brotherhood's political behaviour while in power and the reasons that led to its downfall, existing accounts point to the impact of decades of isolationism, the lack of political expertise and the permanence of the deep state to explain the premature end to the movement's experience in government (El Sherif, 2014). On 3 July 2013, Morsi was overthrown by a military coup d'état after one year in power. The toppling of the first Brotherhood-led government was a deeply symbolic moment as it embodied both the fragility at the core of the hopes and dreams behind the outbreak of the uprisings as well as the perceived failure of the Islamist project (Ardovini, 2020). As the military-backed deep state took control of Egyptian politics once again, the Brotherhood entered one of the harshest periods of repression in its history. The regime of Abdel Fattah el-Sisi soon showed its willingness to go to any lengths necessary to suppress the Islamists, proscribing the Brotherhood as a terrorist organisation and commencing the systematic targeting and persecution of its members (Darwich, 2017). In the aftermath of the coup, nationwide protests broke out against the military takeover and the largest sit-in was held in Rabaa al-Adaweya Square, in the northern Cairo district of Nasr City (Middle East Eye, 2018). Some 85,000 protesters from various religious and political backgrounds camped there for six weeks, in a manner that greatly resembled the barricades in Tahrir Square during the 2011 uprisings. On 14 August, army tanks blocked all five exits to the square and security forces used snipers, bulldozers and ground forces to disperse the protesters. The bloodshed that followed killed over 1,000 people and embodies yet another significant milestone for the movement as it marks the beginning of a new, dark era in its history (Pargeter, 2016). Following the massacre at Rabaa al-Adaweya, surviving members of the Brotherhood faced heavy-handed persecution, forcing many into exile and instigating a process of disintegration.

The events catalysed by the July 2013 coup depart quite significantly from the Brotherhood's historical trajectory, forcing the movement into deeply unfamiliar territory. As mentioned before, the movement has operated under illegality and routine crackdowns since the 1940s, but it could not have anticipated just how brutal and unprecedented the repression that followed Morsi's removal would be. The indiscriminate persecution of the movement and its members, which led to its scattering abroad and the formation of the communities at the centre of this analysis, completely invalidated the tools of resistance described above and required the Brotherhood to develop new strategies in the face of repression. Additionally, the loss of leadership, as a result of Morsi's death in prison in June 2019, that of Essam el-Arian in 2020 and the recent arrest of Mahmoud Ezzat, left only two senior members of the Guidance Bureau, Ibrahim Mounir and Mahmoud Hussein (Al Jazeera, 2020), challenging the organisation further. Despite the presence of a Guidance Office in Istanbul, the movement is perceived as lacking clear direction and leadership, which opens space for rank-and-file members not only to question their belonging to the Brotherhood but also to implement organisational changes that they have long asked for. Disengagement from the movement's core ideology, challenging its hierarchical structures and general calls for reform point to diasporic identification among the Brotherhood members in exile, which I highlight in my analysis.

Diaspora as a framework

Because most of the existing studies approach the analysis of the Brotherhood as a movement (e.g. Munson, 2001; Wickham, 2013; Ranko, 2015; al-Anani, 2019), the focus falls on collective action and on the organisation as a unitary entity, overlooking the dynamics pointing to contestation and disintegration since at least 2011, and arguably even earlier. With the exception of Mustafa Menshawy's (2019) book, which examines processes of disengagement from the Brotherhood from 2011 onwards, what is missing from these perspectives is the focus on individual members as the main unit of analysis, as the means for understanding the forces that have shaped the members' trajectories in the aftermath of 2013. Focusing on individual experiences and perspectives is therefore key to better understanding how the diasporic experience affects the relationship between the movement and its members, and how the reclamation of agency against the Brotherhood's fixed hierarchies takes place in the diaspora. Applying diaspora as an analytical framework, particularly focusing on diasporic identification, brings new insights into the study of the Brotherhood and highlights internal struggles over identity and belonging and emerging patterns of transnational advocacy.

The experience of the Brotherhood in Turkey resonates with the ancient, but durable, concept of diaspora, understood as communities created through forces ranging from war and displacement to repressive politics and global capitalism (Gorman and Kasbarian, 2015). The diaspora literature develops around some core themes: perceptions of belonging and identity issues, the politics of belonging in the host state and the relationship with the homeland. While the concept of what constitutes a diaspora is in continuous evolution (Alexander, 2017), a defining characteristic is that while its members have moved, the community still maintains a strong connection with the homeland and holds onto the 'motherland culture' (Pandurang and Munos, 2014). Yet, despite the importance of the homeland as a reference point for collective memory and solidarity, the diasporic experience is a transnational one that sees diasporic populations engaged across multiple spaces, ranging from the homeland to the country of settlement and a larger international community (Lavie and Swedenburg, 1996).

Another characteristic of the Brotherhood's diasporic experience is that, while the 'homeland' is often used as a point of departure to the formation of group cohesion and a shared sense of identity among diaspora communities, in the case of the Brotherhood, religious ideology strengthens these formations even more. The post-2013 waves of Egyptian exiles as a whole are indeed brought together by the shared experience of escalating repression at home, but for the Brotherhood, religious ideology takes the centre-stage as the determining factor of their community. Despite the double forces of the attachment to the homeland and repression based on religious beliefs, the experience of living in exile also provides opportunities to question these forms of belonging instead of following them uncritically.

Therefore, for the purpose of this chapter, I align with the understanding of diaspora as a process of forging identity and belonging beyond traditional forms of membership dictated by nationality, religion or ethnicity (Brubaker, 2005; Abdelhady, 2011) rather than as an entity that members belong to. When analysing the experience of the Brotherhood post-2013, I follow the approach to diaspora as a process of claim-making (Butler, 2001; Brubaker, 2005), which allows for an understanding of diaspora communities as heterogeneous entities, bringing together groups with different needs and encompassing competing internal voices and trends (Baser and Halperin, 2019, p. 216). This is particularly relevant when it comes to the discussion of individuals experiencing contradictory processes of belonging and displacement within the same context, as in the case of the Brotherhood in Istanbul. This is true for both those members who stay and those who leave the movement, as both processes reveal different dynamics of diasporic identification at play.

While the starting point is that, for diasporas to exist, there needs to be a group of people who are somewhat aware of their existence as a collective, this does not exclude the existence of individual voices who do not conform with the collective experience. Diasporas can therefore also be sites of contestation, with competing questions about culture, community and agency outnumbering those centred on national belonging. Recent literature points to the counter-narratives of diaspora, arguing that, alongside the 'essential sadness' of exile (Gorman and Kasbarian, 2015, p. 9), living in a diaspora can also be a liberating experience. This is certainly the case for many of my respondents, who experience forced exile as an opportunity to rethink their commitment to the Brotherhood. Independently of whether or not they choose to stay, it is the uncertainty and novelty that come with the diasporic experience that allow for these processes to take place and should therefore be investigated within this framework. Therefore, agreeing with works that highlight the importance of taking identity politics within diasporas into account (see Hall, 1990; Brah, 1996; Radhakrishnan, 1996), I argue that the Brotherhood's experience in exile is marked by competing processes of diasporic identification and by the ensuing rejection of collective identity and conformity. Vertovec and Cohen (1999) explain that as a form of identification, diaspora embodies a variety of experiences that are grounded within national boundaries but also transcend them. At the root of the process of creating diaspora identification are fragmentation, homelessness and displacement (Abdelhady, 2011). In the case of the Brotherhood, forced displacement and the search for belonging are definite characteristics of the diasporic experience, and the ways in which individual members react to the movement's fragmentation directly influence their positioning towards the organisation and their new reality. This also influences how they perceive their social role both within and outside the movement, often leading to the reclamation of individual agency vis-à-vis the Brotherhood's collective identity.

Diasporic identification can help to unpack several of the issues that the Brotherhood is facing, first and foremost internal fragmentation, competing strategies against repression and the lack of a cohesive narrative. Bauman (2005) refers to the diasporic experience as a perpetual state of unfixed identity that leads to a 'war of liberation', a pursuit of freedom, which is a red thread underpinning most of my conversations with both current and former Brotherhood members in Turkey. Menshawy (2019) writes of several Brotherhood members who left the organisation and its tight-knit community after experiencing Istanbul's social freedoms, which is a widespread phenomenon I also came across during my fieldwork. Additionally, I have come across several others who, while remaining affiliated to the Brotherhood, have begun to pursue greater individual agency and have become openly critical of its hierarchical structure and the levels of social and ideological control the movement seeks to impose on its members. Furthermore, there is also another portion of the Brotherhood membership that has gone dormant during the process of diasporic formation, pausing all activities and almost occupying a 'grey zone' characterised by their indecision towards the movement. While these processes are still very much in flux, it is undeniable that diasporic identification is leading many to rethink their belonging to the organisation, or to at least question some of the core principles on which it has historically rested.

The Muslim Brotherhood in Istanbul

Immediately after Morsi's removal, a few Brotherhood leaders and ministers fled to Qatar, Malaysia and the United Kingdom to avoid arrest and persecution. However, as the intensity of the crackdown escalated, and especially after the Rabaa massacre, lower-ranking Brotherhood members and supporters also found themselves having to flee. With most of its leadership either in jail or scattered abroad, the Brotherhood was faced with the monumental task of having to reform while in exile. This unprecedented dimension led to the emergence of previously suppressed internal tensions and debates. What makes the diaspora experience new to the movement is the fact that exile is no longer restricted to the leadership, but is also experienced by the rank-and-file members. As ordinary members are forced to flee and regroup abroad, they are beginning to question the movement and their belonging to it in novel ways. This is further facilitated by the fact that exile has also brought together members from a variety of social and economic backgrounds and age groups, disrupting the strict organisational structures that the Brotherhood is built upon and creating the space for internal debates, grievances and diasporic identification. Away from the familiar Egyptian context, members are able to question the very bases and tenets upon which the organisation historically rests.

The Brotherhood's fragmentation in exile and the lack of a cohesive strategy against repression are conducive to these questions about identity and belonging, as the movement's once strong collective identity has now been significantly disrupted. Indeed, the process of regrouping abroad has not been smooth and struggles over legitimacy and leadership have taken the centre-stage. This is evident in the creation of competing Guidance Offices, such as the 'High Administrative Committee' in Egypt – which advocates for open confrontation against the regime – and the 'External Muslim Brotherhood Office', which relocates the movement's centre of power abroad (Ayyash and Willi, 2016, p. 5). The latter brings together Brotherhood senior and high-rank leaders, representing the so-called 'Historical Leadership', who remain in charge of the movement's finances and key strategic decisions. Yet, even if the Brotherhood's historical leaders essentially remain in charge of the movement, the emergence of competing offices and factions has considerably impacted their legitimacy.

In the words of Ammar Fayed, former special secretary to Mohamed Morsi, 'Of course the organization hasn't adapted to being in exile … in fact, we have failed to deploy effective opposition ever since the coup' (*World Politics Review*, 2018). This lack of internal coherence is symptomatic of competing approaches towards repression. While the movement's Historical Leadership strongly denies internal fragmentation, throughout several rounds of fieldwork I began to observe the ways in which competing strategies against repression began to create a rift within the organisation. It became increasingly clear to me that a growing number of members were going through the process of exile alone, as single individuals rather than as part of a collective, meaning that their personal trauma, emotions and perspectives directly shape their view on how the movement should react to its current circumstances. Abdullah, a former member in his forties, always aligned with the conservative wing of the organisation and was in Rabaa when the regime's crackdown was unleashed on the Brotherhood and his followers. He managed to escape arrest and has since relocated to the United Kingdom with his family. After the coup, he grew increasingly disillusioned with how the leadership was handling the crisis, and eventually left the organisation in 2017. While walking through a park, he recalls the chaos of the weeks that followed the Rabaa massacre:

> Everyone was running around, we were just trying to survive. Leaders were being arrested, others were running away, but they did not say anything! We needed directions, but everyone was talking over each other and everyone was saying different things! This is not our way. We should have been better prepared.

In turn, this results in a detectable gap between collective and individual responses to repression. Overall, what I have found is that the organisation as a whole has been implementing changes and strategies to accommodate repression but avoiding sweeping changes to its structure and hierarchies, while individual members are taking advantage of their newfound space to put forward independent thinking and initiatives.

Perhaps unsurprisingly, the Historical Leadership's main strategy is largely an inactive one that calls for patience and obedience during what they see as yet another period of repression. The only official strategy adopted by the organisation as a whole has been the development of transnational advocacy media networks, which largely rely on Turkish support and expand on the Brotherhood's pre-existing media platforms (Magued, 2018, p. 481). On the other hand, a growing number of discontented members have taken it upon themselves to establish research centres, opening a dialogue with secular opposition actors and pursue professional development to find a dynamic way to exit the current crisis, openly disregarding orders not to do so (Ardovini, 2020). While maintaining their membership, they are largely frustrated with what they described as a 'wait and see' strategy. Shuruq, once a youth leader in the Muslim Sisterhood, participated in the 2011 uprisings from the very beginning and has now enrolled on a university course in media studies, explained these tensions to me:

> I think this has been the main strategy [wait and see] of the Ikhwan since the 1950s [laughs]. I have internal peace that there is no hope in the Leadership. When I came to Istanbul four years ago I was very proactive and tried to start and get involved in a lot of initiatives, but the Leadership is not going to change. So it is up to us to make it happen.

Therefore, one can say that while members are adapting to their new circumstances, the Brotherhood as an encompassing, unitary movement remains largely immobile. Over seven years since the coup, what this means is that the Brotherhood still lacks a coherent strategy to face the regime and a cohesive sense of identity.

Renegotiating belonging in the diaspora

While fragmentation prevents the Brotherhood as a whole organisation to put forward a coherent strategy against repression, it is opening up the space for greater individual agency and for individual identities to develop. Several respondents described the diasporic experience as the first time they had the opportunity to stop and consider their belonging to the Brotherhood, particularly regarding long-standing issues relating to freedom of thought, expression and debates within the movement. Many made direct reference to this unprecedented space to engage in individual thought, describing the process with powerful statements such as one made by Abdullah, a member now residing in Istanbul. Born into a Brotherhood family, Abdullah was socialised into the movement from childhood and rose relatively quickly through its ranks. He started questioning the limited space for individual freedoms when he became more involved in politics in the early 2000s, but never openly challenged the organisation's hierarchy until being forced to flee Egypt:

> Up until the revolution, there was no space outside the *Ikhwan*, so we had no choice but to operate within it … you were, like, trapped. But after the revolution, there was space, so we said that this is the time to renegotiate what it means to be an Ikhwani.

Abdullah remains a member and vocally argues for internal reforms, but a similar sentiment was also expressed by Mohammad, a young journalist who joined the Brotherhood when he was a student at Cairo University. Deeply committed to the goals of the 2011 uprisings, Mohammad reported daily from Rabaa Square. The organisational fragmentation and struggles over leadership that followed the Brotherhood's ousting have made him lose faith in the authenticity of the movement's message. This disillusionment led him to cut all ties with the Brotherhood, and he refers to his move to Istanbul as the time when 'I saw that the *Ikhwan* was not my door for the world. So I am gaining a wider view. I can say now that the philosophy of the *Ikhwan* does not match with my thoughts.' While diasporic identification led to opposite results in the case of these two members, what is striking here is the common reference to a deeply traumatic event – forced exile – as an avenue that provided unprecedented space for members to breathe and question their belonging to the movement. The opportunity to 'stop and think' was identified by many as an empowering moment that allowed them to disengage from the overarching, top-down narrative of the Brotherhood and consider the options ahead of them. From this, these processes of self-reflection lead to widely different results, ranging from some members completely disengaging from the movement to others choosing to retain their membership and work towards implementing internal change.

These trends reveal that current and former members are experiencing diasporic identification with different results. Fragmentation and the renegotiation of belonging to the movement lead to some falling back on the same socialisation patterns typical of the homeland, seeking comfort in the replication of daily activities and social roles abroad. This means weekly *usra* meetings,[1] regular social activities and a clear pyramidal membership structure. The Brotherhood also offers economic support to those who need it, and legal and bureaucratic advice when it comes to the settling process. While this is somewhat comforting and brings familiarity to the new context that the members find themselves in, many complain that this is preventing them from integrating into Turkish society. Abdullah was a primary school teacher from Alexandria, now a dock worker, and fled to Turkey in 2015 after his brother was arrested for participating in a pro-Morsi demonstration. While he initially found solace in finding the Brotherhood community abroad, he realised that this prevented him from actually settling into his new circumstances. He complained:

> So many people came here and the *Ikhwan* immediately found them a place to stay, and gave them a job [e.g. in the organisation's media channels], but they never learnt

Turkish, they never speak to anyone else … they have been here [in Istanbul] for five years, and if they leave the organisation, they are lost.

Throughout several conversations, Abdullah explained to me how this caused him to feel like he did not belong anywhere, not to the Brotherhood nor to Turkish society, which eventually led him to leave the movement altogether.

Abdullah is not alone in this, as both current and former members now residing in Istanbul told me that they feel increasingly alienated from the movement. They attribute this to what they call a 'copy and paste' process, referring to the Brotherhood's replication of its social and hierarchical structures abroad. Rather than renouncing their membership, some see the diasporic experience as an opportunity to renegotiate their belonging to the Brotherhood and to claim greater agency to reform the movement from within. Indeed, one indication of diasporic identification is that dissenting members believe that they can now change the movement from within, rather than seeing leaving as their only choice. This is the case for Tamer, a Brotherhood member in his early thirties whom I have known since 2013. He joined the Brotherhood while in medical school and, while he often felt constrained by its strict hierarchy, he still believes that the movement is a good embodiment of his religious and political beliefs. Our conversations through the years tell a story of his personal battle for belonging, between not wanting to renounce his membership and his frustration at not being listened to. After fleeing to Istanbul in 2013, he chose to re-train and went back to university to study political sciences, developing friendships with secular activists in exile and dreams of the Brotherhood becoming a more inclusive and less isolationist movement. He considered leaving the movement when he saw that no real strategy against repression was being implemented, but then realised that:

> There is not just one way to be a Brother (*Ikhwani*) any more. I can do what I believe is right, for myself and for the organisation, and we are many who feel this way … The general feeling is that there should be more freedom to take an active part in the decision-making process, and maybe this super-hierarchical structure does not work any more That is why some people left, others are very unhappy. Others, including myself, started pushing to have these kinds of changes taking place within the organisation, because it is not good or advisable to think that *khalas*, this organisation is over, so let's just wipe it out and start something new. This is not wise, especially when we have the kind of resources, structures, history, influence in many countries … this should not be wasted! We should learn from our mistakes and implement changes.

Another much older member recounts experiencing a similar thought process, especially when reflecting on how the diasporic experience changed his stance towards following orders rather than questioning them. Having grown up in a Brotherhood family, up until the coup Mohammad never doubted core values such as 'listen and obey' and followed the movement's educational curricula literally. He hosted weekly *usra* meetings in his home and often reprimanded fellow members who displayed dissent or acted in disaccord with the movement's message. After settling in Istanbul with his family, he remained actively involved in the Brotherhood's daily activities but quickly grew frustrated with the Leadership's dismissal of members' suggestions and individual experiences. He is now part of a vocal group of dissenters arguing for more internal transparency and consultation, but sometimes still struggles to speak up. He says that unlearning such an ingrained pattern of behaviour will require time, but that he could simply not pretend to be his old self after forcibly relocating in 2015:

People are also becoming more vocal. A lot of people don't feel intimidated any more about expressing their own opinion. One of the issues is that, because I am talking to you like this, a lot of those in the leadership would consider me a traitor. They think these are internal issues and they should only be discussed internally. Which is fine, but then they [the Historical Leadership] don't allow us to do that. So we do it anyway.

The belief that members themselves have the power to go against hierarchical structures and implement internal changes is a significant development for a movement like the Brotherhood, which has historically relied on high levels of social and emotional control over its members as a source of unity. While such an approach has worked for decades, there are clear indications that it is not yielding the same results in the diaspora. Greater degrees of individualism and a growing disregard towards the Leadership's orders are leading many to vocally ask for the reformation of the core principles on which the Brotherhood rests, asking for greater pluralism, representation and individual freedoms. These are the three demands that stand out in conversations with both former and current members, with some like Mohammad openly asserting that 'this pyramid structure [the *tanzim*] does not work for us any more'. Others also further articulate what they mean by wanting greater freedom and space for individualism within the movement. Mustafa, an engineer in his forties who represented the Brotherhood in parliament throughout Morsi's rule, believes that the appointment of political position based on loyalty rather than expertise was one of the Brotherhood's main mistakes. He now argues against the same hierarchies that benefited him in the past, and thinks that members should be given more space to voice their opinions within the movement and play a greater role in the decision-making process:

> This is what I always say: we should not be afraid of freedom. It will allow us and everybody else to express ourselves ... But the leadership is not getting the message: we are not talking about the freedoms in the society, we are talking about freedom in the group first, which is the main problem here.

While the popularity of such approaches is hard to measure, there is an undeniable feeling of renewal and proactivity that permeates most of the interviews conducted in Turkey over the past few years, with current and former members from across the generational and organisational spectrum. Indeed, it is also possible to see how individual members are taking advantage of the decreasing legitimacy of the Historical Leadership, pursuing individual initiatives aimed at both personal development and at benefitting the organisation as a whole.

While these are too many to unpack here, these range from creating research centres and think-tanks to enrolling back in university to study topics such as political and social sciences or media studies, which in the long term will affect the membership composition of the Brotherhood and its activities. As I show elsewhere (Ardovini, 2020), these are also members who pursue their own initiatives to kick-start a more tangible form of political mobilisation, establishing dialogue and cooperation with secular activists and other opposition groups in exile.

However, this is not true for everyone and diasporic identification is leading to widely different results. For some, the trauma of unprecedented repression and frustration over the organisation's lack of a cohesive political strategy has led them to reject their own Islamist identity and to leave the Brotherhood, with Mahmoud saying, 'When we left [the Brotherhood], we opened our eyes.' Once a Brotherhood Youth leader and now in his thirties, Mahmoud was born into a Brotherhood family and was therefore socialised into the movement since he was young. He fled Egypt after Rabaa and settled in Turkey in 2015, after first travelling to Sudan,

Qatar and Malaysia. He now refers to the various states of his diasporic experience as a 'soul-searching' process that eventually led him to feel trapped by his belonging to the movement, which prompted him to leave in 2017. In his own words:

> I was unhappy with the leadership, that was the starting point. But then came the ideological problems and through my new thoughts, my new readings, I saw that the *Ikhwan* was not my calling any more. I can also say that all the political Islam movements, they also don't resonate with me any more … I have overcome all of this. Now I am free actually, I feel it. There are many who feel this way, I am not alone.

Diasporic identification is therefore evident in the way in which several members have begun questioning their belonging to the movement, as well as in the reclamation of greater individual agency. Adopting such a lens also allows us to unpack these dynamics in greater detail and to associate specific trends with shifting processes of identity formation, shedding light on the sources of internal fragmentation that the movement has been experiencing since 2013. These processes are still in flux and it is therefore too early to speculate what their results will be, but one can see that they have already begun to affect how members relate to the organisation as a whole. In other words, the novelty of the diasporic experience is allowing individual members to begin to subvert decades-old structures and constraints, which, in the long term, might drastically change the movement as a whole.

Conclusion

Throughout this chapter, I have focused on the Brotherhood diaspora in Turkey to show how the experience of forced exile has severely disrupted the movement's core principles and structures, destabilising old hierarchies and generating the potential for internal renewal. The process of reuniting abroad is indeed giving many members an unprecedented opportunity to reflect upon what their belonging to the organisation means for them, leading to the questioning of its core principles through diasporic identification. Indeed, looking at the Brotherhood's members experience of diasporic identification allows the emergence of key issues that are at the centre of the renegotiation of the relationship between the movement and its members, such as fragmentation and displacement. This is leading to struggles over leadership and competing strategies against repression, and to the emergence of members' subjectivities vis-à-vis the organisation's top-down collective identity. While these phenomena are still developing, in the case of the Brotherhood, the potential for internal renewal and the reassessment of the Islamist projects lies in the diasporic dimension, and therefore needs to be examined as a framework of diasporic identification to be fully understood.

Note

1 Literally 'family' meetings, where members meet in small groups to go through the Brotherhood's curriculum and follow designated activities.

References

Abdelhady, D. (2011) *The Lebanese Diaspora: The Arab Immigrant Experience in Montreal, New York and Paris*. New York: New York University Press.

al-Anani, K. (2019) 'Rethinking the repression-dissent nexus: assessing Egypt's Muslim Brotherhood's response to repression since the coup of 2013', *Democratization*, 26(8), pp. 1329–1341.

Alexander, C. (2017) 'Beyond "the 'diaspora' diaspora": a response to Rogers Brubaker', *Ethnic and Racial Studies*, 40(9), pp. 1544–1555.

Ali, H.M. (2020) 'Exiles on the Bosporus', *Diwan-Carnegie*, 10 March. Available at: https://carnegie-mec.org/diwan/81249 (accessed 26 February 2021).

Al Jazeera (2020) 'Top Muslim Brotherhood leader dies in Cairo prison', 13 August. Available at: www.aljazeera.com/news/2020/8/13/top-muslim-brotherhood-leader-dies-in-cairo-prison (accessed 26 February 2021).

Ardovini, L. (2020) 'Stagnation vs. adaptation: tracking the Muslim Brotherhood's trajectories after the 2013 coup', *British Journal of Middle Eastern Studies*, doi: 10.1080/13530194.2020.1778443

Ayoob, M. (2008) *The Many Faces of Political Islam: Religion and Politics in the Muslim World*. Ann Arbor, MI: The University of Michigan Press.

Ayyash, A. (2020) 'The Turkish future of Egypt's Muslim Brotherhood', *The Century Foundation*. Available at: https://tcf.org/content/report/turkish-future-egypts-muslim-brotherhood/?agreed=1 (accessed 26 February 2021).

Ayyash, A. and Willi, V. (2016) 'The Egyptian Muslim Brotherhood in 2016: scenarios and recommendations', *DGAP Kompakt* pp. 1–6. Available at: https://dgap.org/en/research/publications/egyptian-muslim-brotherhood-2016 (accessed 26 February 2021).

Baser, B. and Halperin, A. (2019) 'Diasporas from the Middle East: displacement, transnational identities and homeland politics', *British Journal of Middle Eastern Studies*, 46(2), pp. 215–221.

Bauman, Z. (2005) 'Identity for identity's sake is a bit dodgy', *Soundings: A Journal of Politics and Culture*, 29, pp. 12–20.

Brah, A. (1996) *Cartographies of Diaspora: Contesting Identities*. London: Routledge.

Brooke, S. (2017) 'Egypt', in Hamid, S. and McCants, W. (eds) *Rethinking Political Islam*. New York: Oxford University Press, pp. 218–230.

Brubaker, R. (2005) 'The 'diaspora' diaspora', *Ethnic and Racial Studies*, 28(1), pp. 1–19.

Butler, K.D. (2001) 'Defining diaspora, refining a discourse', *Diaspora: A Journal of Transnational Studies*, 10(2), pp. 189–219.

Darwich, M. (2017) 'Creating the enemy, constructing the threat: the diffusion of repression against the Muslim Brotherhood in the Middle East', *Democratization*, 24(7), pp. 1290–1291.

El Sherif, A. (2014) 'The Egyptian Muslim Brotherhood failures', Carnegie Endowment for International Peace. Available at: https://carnegieendowment.org/2014/07/01/egyptian-muslim-brotherhood-s-failures-pub-56046 (accessed 26 February 2021).

Gorman, A. and Kasbarian, S. (eds) (2015) *Diasporas of the Modern Middle East: Contextualising Community*. Edinburgh: Edinburgh University Press.

Hall, S. (1990) 'Cultural identity and diaspora', in Rutherford, J. (ed.) *Identity: Community, Culture, Difference*. London: Lawrence and Wishart, pp. 222–237.

Kandil, H. (2015) *Inside the Brotherhood*. Cambridge: Polity Press.

Kotan, B. (2017) 'An overview of Turkish-Egyptian relations since the Arab uprising', *TRT World*, 27 November. Available at: www.trtworld.com/mea/an-overview-of-turkish-egyptian-relations-since-the-arab-uprising-12658 (accessed 26 February 2021).

Lavie, S. and Swedenburg, T. (eds) (1996) *Displacement, Diaspora and Geographies of Identity*. Durham, NC: Duke University Press.

Magued, S. (2018) 'The Egyptian Muslim Brotherhood's transnational advocacy in Turkey: a new means of political participation', *British Journal of Middle Eastern Studies*, 45(3), pp. 480–497.

Menshawy, M. (2019) *Leaving the Muslim Brotherhood: Self, Society and the State*. London: Palgrave Macmillan.

Middle East Eye (2018) 'Rabaa: The massacre that ended the Arab Spring', *Middle East Eye*, August 2018. Available at: www.middleeasteye.net/news/rabaa-massacre-ended-arab-spring (accessed 26 February 2021).

Mitchell, R. (1969) *The Society of the Muslim Brothers*. New York: Oxford University Press.

Munson, Z. (2001) 'Islamic mobilization: social movement theory and the Muslim Brotherhood', *The Sociological Quarterly*, 42(4), pp. 487–510.

Pandurang, M. and Munos, D. (2014) 'Mapping diasporic subjectivities', *South Asian Diaspora*, 6(1), pp. 1–5, doi: 10.1080/19438192.2013.847252

Pargeter, A., (2016) *Return to the Shadows: The Muslim Brotherhood and an-Nahda since the Arab Spring*. London: Saqi Books.

Radhakrishnan, R. (1996) *Diasporic Mediations: Between Home and Location*. Minneapolis, MN: University of Minnesota Press.

Ranko, A. (2015) *The Muslim Brotherhood and Its Quest for Hegemony in Egypt: State-Discourse and Islamist Counter-Discourse.* Hamburg: Springer VS.

Vertovec, S. and Cohen, R. (eds) *Migration, Diasporas and Transnationalism.* Northampton, MA: Edward Elgar Publishing.

Wickham, C.R. (2013) *The Muslim Brotherhood: Evolution of an Islamist Movement.* Princeton, NJ: Princeton University Press.

World Politics Review (2018) 'Why Egypt's Muslim Brotherhood needs to transform to survive', *World Politics Review*, 20 February. Available at: www.worldpoliticsreview.com/articles/24221/why-egypt-s-muslim-brotherhood-needs-to-transform-to-survive (accessed 26 February 2021).

Zollner, B. (2019) 'Surviving repression: how Egypt's Muslim Brotherhood has carried on', *Carnegie*, 11 March. Available at: https://carnegie-mec.org/2019/03/11/surviving-repression-how-egypt-s-muslim-brotherhood-has-carried-on-pub-78552 (accessed 26 February 2021).

PART VI

Plurilocal diasporas, rethinking *mahjar*

28
THE HADRAMI DIASPORA
A plurilocal *mahjar*

Iain Walker

Wadi Hadramawt, the river valley that gives its name to the governorate in Yemen, runs through the arid desert landscapes of the east of the country, parallel to and about 150 kilometres distant from the coast. This fertile and productive region of rain-fed agriculture has historically supported a large population: the now-ruined towns of Raybun and Shabwa were among the oldest urban centres in the world while contemporary cities such as Tarim and Shibam, with their unique mud-brick houses, are scarcely more recent. However, when the rains fail, so do the crops, and over the centuries famine and civil unrest have repeatedly driven emigration, leading to the constitution of a Hadrami diaspora that spans the Indian Ocean. Hadramis are traders too, however, and many of the region's communities were established by merchants who took advantage of the ocean's maritime networks to seek out commercial opportunities. Following these traders, religious leaders, many trained by the scholars of Tarim, also left the homeland, to proselytise and teach. Finally, Hadramis have served as mercenaries and sought service in the armies of rulers on the shores of the Indian Ocean. As a result of all these movements Hadramis, or people of Hadrami descent, were historically found as far afield as Papua in the east and Mauritania in the west, Madagascar to the south and the Gulf States to the north. Today, of course, they are also found further afield.

Diasporic origins

In what follows I present an overview of the history of the Hadrami diaspora in the different regions of the Indian Ocean world, largely constituted before the advent of air travel in the latter part of the twentieth century, before analysing the different strategies, based particularly on kin links and religious practice but also on education and trade, that bind together these different localisations of the diaspora, and the diaspora to the homeland. The Hadrami diaspora has been the subject of much scholarship since the late twentieth century (e.g. Freitag and Clarence-Smith, 1997; Abushouk and Ibrahim, 2009; Brehony, 2017) and as we shall see, what is remarkable about it is its enduring character – the very name Hadramawt is said to derive from Hazarmaveth, a descendant of Noah who is mentioned in the Book of Genesis (Bent, 1894). Unlike many contemporary diasporic populations, Hadramis appear to have long subscribed to a collective sense of identity based on their belonging, whether real or

DOI: 10.4324/9780429266102-34

imagined, to a homeland that itself has an identity that is centuries-old. The use of the *nisba*[1] is ancient – the Prophet Muhammad himself sent his envoy Abu Al-Ala'a Al-Hadrami to convert the people of Bahrain – and Hadramis (among whom the ancestors of the scholars Ibn Khaldun and Al Imam Al-Hadrami) arrived in Spain with the Umayyads in the eighth century (Ṭāhā, 1989).

Although Hadramis travelled west and north, most Hadrami diasporic communities lie on the shores of the Indian Ocean, where migrations were facilitated by trading networks based on the regular annual pattern of monsoon winds that allowed navigators to sail between the Arabian peninsula and India, on the one hand, and the African coast, on the other. The *Periplus of the Erythraean Sea* states that Arabs from Yemen (probably including Hadramis) had settled on the East African coast two millennia ago and describes the networks that linked the Hadrami port of Cana with the Indian subcontinent (Casson, 1989); other authors have demonstrated the long-standing links between these regions (e.g. Hourani, 1951).

These networks probably extended further than India. The Srivijaya kingdom of Sumatra, which reached its peak towards the ninth century, certainly attracted traders from the west (Feener, 2004) and the contemporaneous Tang dynasty saw significant growth in the number of Arabs in China (Tibbetts, 1957; Schottenhammer, 2012) and it would have been surprising if Hadramis had not been among them. Much of this pre- and early Islamic history must remain speculative, however, and it is not until well after the birth of Islam that we have more detailed written evidence of Hadrami movements in the ocean. One reason for the appearance of documentation is the rise of an influential Hadrami religious class, the Ba Alawi.

The Ba Alawi are descendants of Ahmad bin 'Isa al-Muhajir, himself a descendant of the Prophet Muhammad, who left Basra for Hadramawt in the early tenth century. Al-Muhajir ('the migrant') was probably Shia (possibly Zaidi) and he would have found himself in a minority in Hadramawt, largely Ibadhi at the time. Despite traditions attributing to him the conversion of the Hadramis, it was not until the twelfth century that Sunni Islam – and the Shafi'i *madhhab*[2] – finally became dominant in the region (Serjeant, 1957). As Ibadhi antipathy towards the descendants of the Prophet, known as *sada* (sing. *sayyid*), was gradually displaced by Sunni reverence, the status of the Ba Alawi grew. By the fourteenth century, the Ba Alawi *sada* had largely triumphed in their struggles for supremacy against the local high-status learned classes, the *mashaykh*, and assumed the mantle of Shafi'i leaders. At about the same time a descendant of al-Muhajir known as al-Faqih al-Muqaddam, the 'First Jurist', founded a new Sufi order, or *tariqa*, the Alawiyya. Almost from the start, membership of the Alawiyya was restricted to the Ba Alawi, further entrenching their religious authority (Bang, 2003; Ho, 2006).

The conjunction of these events, and the growth in Sufism generally during this period, led to the Hadrami diaspora being dominated, socially and theologically if not numerically, by the Ba Alawi as proselytising scholars began to settle in India, eastern Africa and Southeast Asia. As they spread both the Alawiyya *tariqa* (amongst themselves) and the Shafi'i school more widely, so they established themselves as leaders not only of the Hadramis but of the now-Shafi'i Islamic *ummah* of the Indian Ocean. Literate and often exercising secular as well as religious power, the *sada* have left their mark on the diaspora: the poor who both preceded them and accompanied them – the ship's crews, traders, mercenaries and migrants fleeing famine – were less likely to leave traces of their passage, and suggestions that most migrants were *sada* ignores both the fact that in times of stress it is the lower classes who are most likely to suffer and migrate and the fact that the *sada* are more likely to maintain their histories, their genealogies and hence their authority (see Knysh, 1999; Van der Kroef, 1953).

Africa: from Cairo to the Cape

References to Hadramis in northeast Africa are sparse and there are few *sada* families presumably because, as the region has long been part of Dar al Islam, proselytisation was not required and possibly even unwelcome from Shafi'i jurists in these Maliki communities. The German traveller Heinrich von Maltzan (1865) found a small but influential community of Hadrami merchants, mostly from Wadi Doan, a tributary of the main wadi, in Cairo in the early 1870s, where they had been settled for some time (see Pétriat, 2016). There were several wealthy Hadrami businessmen in the Sudanese port of Suakin (Ewald and Clarence-Smith, 1997), forming a small community, of whom half were permanently settled 'since the old days' (Ingrams, 1937, p. 163) and likewise in Massawa, where the Ba Junayd *sada* family were particularly successful. In Massawa too, some must also have been there 'since the old days': according to Jonathan Miran (2012, p. 133), there are traces of a Hadrami presence in Eritrea in the early Islamic period. It is noteworthy that the earliest Hadrami religious figures that he mentions were not *sada*, their arrival in Eritrea pre-dating the rise to power of the *sada* in Hadramawt itself.

To the south, there was significant Hadrami migration into Ethiopia in the early sixteenth century (Martin, 1974) as well as in the late nineteenth and early twentieth centuries. By the 1920s, more than 700 Yemenis, many of them Hadramis, were registered at the British legation in Addis Ababa, including the members of the Ba Zar'a, al Habshi, Ba Naji and Ba Hajri tribes, also all from Wadi Doan. Some, such as Shaykh Said Ahmad Ba Zar'a and Muhammad Yusuf Ba Naji, amassed considerable fortunes and were among the wealthiest men in Ethiopia (Bezabeh, 2011). The community today has a reasonably cohesive identity and runs a community association, founded in 1942 and open to all Yemenis, that provides support of various kinds, if perhaps not with the same scope as in the past. Although there were *sada* in Ethiopia, most notably the al Bar, again from Wadi Doan, in a Christian environment, their religious leadership was only exercised within their own community. On the coast, the context was slightly different and several locals, religious leaders of Hadrami origin, were politically active. In 1919, al-Hajj Abdul Kadir Ba Wazir demanded that the United States support his claim for an independent Muslim state to be carved out of eastern Ethiopia, a request that appears to have been considered quite seriously (Bezabeh, 2017).

Further south, Hadramis settled on the East African coast. Some followed the trading caravans inland from the ports of Mogadishu, Merca and Brava, opening shops, operating transport companies or acting as wholesalers and middlemen, trading ivory, hides and ostrich feathers from the interior for cloth and manufactured goods from the coast. Some towns seem to have had substantial numbers of Hadrami residents – Leif Manger says that in 1882 there were 200 Arabs, presumably mostly Hadramis, in the small trading post of Goobweyn, north of Kisimayo (Manger, 2010, p. 92). Further south, the Swahili coast seems to have attracted Hadrami from the eastern wadi, and particularly from the villages around Tarim, rather than Wadi Doan. This may be a reflection of the *sada* influence since, unlike the Horn, Hadrami *sada* seem to have been responsible for much proselytisation on the Swahili coast. Among the *sada* lineages in East Africa today, the most prestigious and the best known are the Jamal al Layl, from Tarim, and the Abubakar bin Salim, from Inat, about 20 kilometres east of Tarim. One prominent member of the Jamal al Layl was Habib Salih b. Alawi. Habib Salih was born on the Comorian island of Ngazidja in the mid-nineteenth century but moved to Lamu on the Kenya coast at a young age, where he founded the Riyadha Mosque. It rapidly became a centre for learning, drawing students and scholars from across the region (El-Zein, 1974), and in 1909 he established the Lamu Maulid, which has since become a major annual event in the town, attracting people from around the world, many (although not all) of them of Hadrami descent.

Despite the role of the *sada* in establishing a Hadrami identity, most East African Hadramis are not *sada* – as B.G. Martin observes, 'the migrants were a good cross section of the population' (1974, p. 371). As in the ports of the Red Sea, many Hadramis came as traders or labourers. Poor young men fleeing the regular famines of the homeland often took the first southbound dhow available and disembarked at an East African port: if they had contacts, preferably family, so much the better; otherwise, they would seek out a fellow Hadrami, who would generally look after one of his own, even if this sometimes tended towards exploitation; but Hadramis worked hard, and were expected to put in long hours to succeed. In ports such as Zanzibar, Hadramis historically filled a range of low-status roles such as porters, dockers, coffee sellers, water carriers and small shopkeepers. In the nineteenth century, Hadramis engaged in the Sultan of Zanzibar's army and had a reputation as reliable and trustworthy soldiers. Hadramis moved inland to the Lakes, while further south there are Hadramis in Mozambique and Madagascar (Bang, 2014) as well as the Comoros (Walker, 2011; 2012); somewhat intriguingly the anthropologist Tudor Parfitt (2000) suggests that the Lemba of southern Africa may have Hadrami origins.

By the 1930s, there were perhaps 15,000 Hadramis in British East Africa, with important communities in Zanzibar, Mombasa and Lamu, the rest scattered through the rural areas where they were generally shopkeepers, selling imported goods to the local populations and sending exports to the coast, and they often served as imam of the local mosque, too (Ingrams, 1966). Almost every town in rural eastern Africa had an Arab shopkeeper – to the point that to be a trustworthy shopkeeper one had to adopt an Arab identity (Beckerleg, 2009). As in Ethiopia, and with the implicit encouragement of the colonial administration, the Hadramis of East Africa established community associations that served as a focal point for expressions of community identity. For example, there was a Hadrami association in Zanzibar which, despite being banned by the post-1964 revolutionary government, was reactivated in the 1990s and includes among its members most Zanzibaris who consider themselves Hadrami.

Throughout eastern Africa these migrants married local women, establishing a community of people known today in Hadramawt as *muwalladin*, the foreign-born. Locally the continuity of Hadrami identities was maintained by specific strategies whereby men sent their male children back to Hadramawt for education while the girls were generally left to their mothers.[3] Socialised as Swahili, but with a Hadrami paternal identity, they were ideal marriage partners either for the next generation of Hadrami immigrants or for brothers who returned to the coast from Hadramawt as young adults. Some of these men would have married in Hadramawt before arriving in East Africa, thus maintaining the links between the homeland and the diasporic community from generation to generation (Le Guennec-Coppens, 1991).

Hadramis in India, Hadramis of India

There are scattered references in the literature to an early Hadrami presence in various parts of India as well as in the Maldives and Sri Lanka. In Gujarat, there are tombs of *sada* such as the Saggaf, the Ba Faqih and the Al Aydarus families, including the scholar Abdallah ibn Shaykh al-Aydarus of Ahmadabad (d. 1582), and despite being Shafi'i, these *sada* appear to have remained in favour during the Mughal period (Khalidi, 2004). Non-*sada* were also present. The Sodagar of Patan, also in Gujarat, claim descent from Hadramis who arrived during the Mughal period, while the Arab Ki Sarai in Delhi was allegedly built in the late sixteenth century to house 300 Hadramis who accompanied the widow of the Mughal Emperor Humayun on her return from the Hajj. It was still home to a few residents of Hadrami origin in the early twentieth century but most of the remaining Hadrami Indians of northern India migrated to Pakistan at Partition (ibid.).

Further south, the Mappilas of Kerala are somewhat analogous to the Swahili: a trade-based community who claim (mythologised) descent from Persian and Arab settlers but who are nevertheless quite Indian. Many of these Arabs may have been Hadramis. Ibn Battuta, who visited in the mid-thirteenth century, says Kerala followed the Shafi'i *madhhab* and although the nearby Maldives seem to have been Maliki when Ibn Battuta sojourned there, the vizir was one Abdallah ibn Muhammad al-Hadrami (Forbes, 1981).

Links with Hadramawt were enduring: the Shafi'i *madhhab* was introduced to the Maldives in the late sixteenth century by Muhammad Jamâl al-Dîn Huvadu, who is said to have spent 15 years studying in the wadi (Forbes, 1981), probably in Tarim. Duarte Barbosa, a Portuguese scrivener who lived in Cannanore in the early sixteenth century, was able to identify a community of local resident foreigners, the Pardesis, including Arabs, many of whom were of considerable wealth; and although he does not specifically mention Hadramis, he mentions the trade between Malabar and the Hadrami port of Shihr (Barbosa, 1866).

If most of those of immigrant descent have lost any claim to Hadrami identity over time, the religious leaders – mostly *sada* – were, of course, Hadramis, and explicitly so since their authority derived, if perhaps only partially, from their prestigious and carefully maintained genealogies. Although it is likely that there were already *sada* resident in Malabar – Sheikh Zainuddin Makhdoom I (d.1521) is said to be a scholar of 'Yemeni Arab descent' (Kuzhiyan, 2016, p. 435) – the first documented arrival of Ba Alawi *sada* dates to the mid-eighteenth century when Sayyid Hasan Al Jifri arrived from Tarim and settled in the village of Tirurangadi, south of Calicut. He was later joined by his brother, and then by his nephew Sayyid Alawi b. Muhammad b. Sahl; the honorific title for *sada* in Malayalam is *thangal* and the latter is known locally as Alavi Thangal. His tomb is the site of a *ziyara*. The respect that the *sada* were accorded was accompanied by increased social importance and they assumed leading roles in confronting both the British and the local Hindu elite. Sayyid Alawi and his son Sayyid Fadl were particularly prominent political leaders and were at the forefront of anti-colonial sentiment in Kerala, to the point that in 1852 the British administration forced Sayyid Fadl into exile (Dale, 1990; 1997; Miller, 1992; Jacob, 2019).

The al Jifri are probably the best known of the *sada* families in Kerala, and while they and others fill a niche as religious leaders, others, such as Syed Abdurrahiman Bafaki Tangal and his nephew Ummer Bafaki Tangal, entered politics (Miller, 1992). Others have been successful in business; the Barami family were timber merchants and shipbuilders who built dhows for sale to clients in the Gulf (Dale, 1997; Abdurahiman, 2004). Lower-status Mappilas of Hadrami origin are harder to find, to the point that the terms Hadrami and Sayyid are often used as if they were synonymous. Various authors have referred to non-*sada* Hadramis, but almost in passing; Stephen Dale (1997), for example, who nevertheless highlights the gap in the literature, and Caroline and Filippo Osella, who refer to the prestige attached to (almost mythical) 'Arab food' (2007) and state that, as Arab identity is reappraised in the context of migration to the Gulf, 'Koyas are now re-evaluating their historical connections with Hadrami settlers' but provide no details (ibid.). Indeed, many references are just to Arabs, but whether this reflects a lack of (awareness of) Hadrami ancestry or merely a lack of scholarship is unclear. Abdul Jaleel (2015, pp. 132–134) refers to local scholars who have recorded the tribal names of people of non-*sada* origin, but notes that they are rarely used these days, presumably for political reasons, although he also reports that one informant explained that since there was no prestige attached to the names for non-*sada*, there was little point using them. The Hadrami community in

Kerala today, therefore, seems to be limited to a small handful of *sada* families who maintain their genealogies in support of their (declining) status as religious authorities.

The community in Hyderabad is of more recent origin and was largely constituted by Hadramis who began arriving in the early nineteenth century to serve in the Nizam's army. Among them were Umar b. Awad al Qu'aiti, Ghalib b. Muhsin al Kathiri and Abdullah b. Ali Al Awlaqi, all of whom were appointed *jamadar* in the Nizam's irregular forces, commanding detachments of Hadrami troops. The position of *jamadar* provided these men with land and a labour force that allowed them a substantial income: Umar al Qu'aiti's annual personal income was well over 20,000 rupees (Manger, 2010). These revenues, in turn, financed their activities in Hadramawt, which was politically somewhat chaotic at the time, and it is thanks to his income in Hyderabad that Umar was able to establish the Qu'aiti state, reducing the territories of his Kathiri rivals to the towns of Seiyun and Tarim (Hartwig, 1997; Freitag, 2003) and ousting, with some help from the British, competitors including the Awlaqis.

The Arab troops that these men commanded were also largely of Hadrami origin, numbering perhaps 6,000 by the early twentieth century, and they remained until Indian independence and the annexation of the state of Hyderabad; the commander-in-chief of the Hyderabad State Forces at the time of the annexation of Hyderabad by India in 1948, Syed Ahmed el Edross, was of Hadrami origin. Following the annexation, many Hadrami Indians either fled or were deported 'back' to Hadramawt while others left for Pakistan (Sherman, 2011). Nevertheless, there remains a large community of Chaush, as they are known locally – some sources cite figures of 50,000 or more. They live mostly in and around the Barkas neighbourhood in the southern suburbs of Hyderbad and count several prominent Indians among their number: the poet Sulaiman Areeb, the writer Awaz Sayeed and the latter's son Ausaf Sayeed, who served as Indian ambassador to Yemen (Khalidi, 1997).

Southeast Asia: Irshadis and Sayyids

Hadramis in Hadramawt talk proudly of the Hadrami community in Southeast Asia, asserting that there are fifty million Indonesians of Hadrami origin and that it is thanks to the Hadramis that Indonesia is both Muslim and civilised. Although the Hadramis (however they may be defined) in Southeast Asia are perhaps not quite so numerous, they certainly appear to be ubiquitous and were, in the past at least, influential beyond their numbers. From Aceh to Papua, Vietnam to Timor, they have been economically successful as well as providing both religious and political leadership. Many married into local ruling families and assumed power – the sultans of Pontianak (Kalimantan), Siak (Sumatra) and several of the rulers of the Malay states were of Hadrami origin, as (according to some) is the sultan of Brunei; the second prime minister of Timor Leste, Mari Alkatiri, was, as his name suggests, a Hadrami, likewise former Malaysian prime minister, Abdullah Ahmad Badawi, and the former Indonesian foreign minister Ali Alatas. Several prominent businessmen, particularly in Singapore (we might cite the erstwhile owner of Raffles Hotel, Mohamed Ahmed Alsagoff), are of Hadrami descent, as are many contemporary religious leaders including, perhaps unfortunately, the Islamist cleric Abu Bakar Bashir.

The Hadrami diaspora in Southeast Asia, and in Indonesia in particular, has been the object of considerable scholarship since the 1990s (e.g. Mobini-Kesheh, 1999; de Jonge and Kaptein, 2002; Ho, 2006; Abushouk and Ibrahim, 2009), much of which has focused on the *sada*. This is undoubtedly due to their literacy and their religious leadership, as well as their propensity to maintaining genealogies, and hence a Hadrami identity, but also due to the success of many of the larger families; the Al Kaf, Al Junayd and Al Sagoff families of Singapore, in particular, amassed considerable fortunes and were highly influential both locally and in the political and social development of the homeland. Indeed, such was the success of Hadramis in the colonial period that the Dutch administration commissioned a study of the community that remains a key text today (van den Berg, 1886).

Although there may well have been Hadramis among the Arab traders who visited the region in the early Islamic period, it is not until the seventeenth century that we are able to identify individuals. Among the earliest migrants was Nuruddin ibn Ali al-Raniri, a scholar from Gujarat who arrived in Aceh in 1637 and served for several years at the court of the sultan, Iskandar Thani. Nuruddin's father was of Hadrami origin and his mother may have been Malay (Gibson, 2007; Andaya, 2011). It is likely that scholars such as Nuruddin, and his uncle, Shaikh Muhammed Jailani, who also came to Aceh, were both responsible for and closely associated with the exponential growth in conversions and the widespread adoption of Islam in the Malay world that seems to have occurred between the fourteenth and sixteenth centuries.

Men such as Nuruddin were among the earliest members of a wave of Hadrami migration that followed the European colonial powers in the eighteenth and, particularly, nineteenth centuries, swelling their numbers across Southeast Asia. In Indonesia, the community grew from fewer than 10,000 in 1860 to more than 85,000 by the 1950s (van der Kroef, 1953). Initially present in Palembang and Aceh on Sumatra and Pontianak on Borneo, Batavia (Jakarta) became the more attractive destination once the Dutch had established their capital there. Nevertheless, much as in eastern Africa, Hadramis can be found serving as religious leaders and running small businesses – small retail and manufacturing operations, import and export as well as moneylending (ibid.) – in Sulawesi (Slama, 2011), Ambon (Istiqomah, 2020) the Philippines (Clarence-Smith, 2004) and Papua (Slama, 2015). And, as elsewhere, Hadrami men, unaccompanied by spouses in their travels, took local wives and produced children of mixed descent: the *muwalladin* or, in Indonesian, the *peranakan*, 'tak[ing] the shape of the people who live there' (Walker, 2015, p. 47).

Towards the end of the nineteenth century there began what is termed the *nahdah*, the Hadrami awakening, a growing awareness among the community of their origins in a particular place, Hadramawt. In parallel with, and undoubtedly influenced by, a similar increasing awareness of a collective identity within the Chinese community in Indonesia, and the development of an Indonesian sense of identity that would bring forth independence, Hadramis' sense of their collective identity shifted from being Muslim (shared with other Indonesians) through 'generic' Arab, to Hadrami – with a homeland (Mobini-Kesheh, 1999) – a perception increasingly shared by other Indonesians, particularly in light of the non-native status of the Hadramis in the Dutch system. This was swiftly followed by a split in the community that emerged following a marriage between a *sada* woman and a non-*sada* man, judged *haram* by a leading Hadrami scholar, Sayyid Omar al Attas, since it did not conform to the rule of *kafa'a*, eligibility in marriage. However, a *fatwa* judged the marriage legal (Bujra, 1967), and the episode led to a more substantial contestation of the privileges accorded the *sada* – not simply marriage rules but more pervasive practices such as the right to the Sayyid title and the obligation on the part of non-*sada* to kiss the hands of *sada*.

Out of this split was born Al Irshad, a Hadrami reformist association established in 1914 that undertook a number of initiatives, most notably establishing a network of schools, of which perhaps 50 had opened by 1939. These schools were instrumental in promoting Hadrami identity, and although *sada* were not permitted to serve on the executive committee, the organisation nevertheless attracted some less conservative *sada* who recognised the need for change. The schools were popular, partly because the Dutch educational system had very few schools specifically for Arabs, and partly because, as elsewhere, many Hadramis were reluctant to send their children to the schools of the Christian colonial power for fear of proselytisation (Mobini-Kesheh, 1999).

Hadramis were present elsewhere in Southeast Asia – a small community were even involved in the agarwood trade in Cambodia – and were particularly successful in the Malay peninsula, whether through marriage into the ruling houses or through business activities in British Singapore. There were significant Hadrami communities in several of the Malay states, for example, in Penang (Karim, 2009) and Kedah (Sharifah, 2004). Ulrike Freitag's (2002) overview gives a good idea of both the geographical extent of Singaporean Hadramis' business ventures (across Indonesia and into Malaysia and Vietnam as well as back to the Arabian peninsula) and of their success. The Alsagoff family arrived in Singapore in 1824 from Mecca (tellingly, not from Hadramawt but from elsewhere in the diaspora), established a shipping business and invested in the homeland, while Umar Al Junayd and Salim Bin Talib, the latter allegedly the richest man in Singapore by the 1930s, provided both financial and political support to the Kathiri sultan, Ghalib b. Muhsin, in his struggles for power in Hadramawt. The Al Kaf, who likewise established themselves in Singapore in the mid-nineteenth century, rapidly amassed a fortune in trade and through investment in real estate in Singapore and also repatriated much of their profit. Indeed, Hadrami investment in real estate in Singapore helped to maintain links as local businessmen acted as agents for absentee landlords across the Hadrami diaspora (Freitag, 2002).

Saudi and the Gulf: humble origins

Phillipe Pétriat's (2016) masterful study of Hadrami traders in Jeddah has provided insight into the activities of the community from the late Ottoman to the early Saudi period, when several prominent Hadrami families, foremost among them the Ba Naja, dominated commerce in the town and beyond. Ulrike Freitag suggests that in the mid-nineteenth century, Hadramis accounted for half the population of Jeddah (2020). Following the establishment of Saudi Arabia, however, fortunes shifted as those families close to the sharifs – many of whom viewed the al Saud as Bedouin usurpers – were marginalised and replaced by a new generation of migrants, often poor and of low status. The family narratives are very similar: Mohammed bin Laden, for example, who arrived in Jeddah penniless, found work on a construction site building a royal palace, became close to the royal family and eventually built his construction company into the largest in Saudi Arabia. Likewise, Salem bin Mahfouz, a poor but canny moneylender who eventually founded the National Commercial Bank; or Ahmed Bugshan, the founder of a conglomerate of engineering and construction enterprises (Walker, 2015).

Hadramis in Saudi Arabia have a very different profile from Hadramis elsewhere in the Indian Ocean and engage different strategies of integration. Fundamental to Hadrami practice is the character of Saudi society: unlike Java, Ethiopia or Zanzibar, Saudi Arabia is much like home, indeed, Saudi Arabia *is* home. A land on the fringes of Hadramawt, home to an Arabic-speaking tribal society, with a native Arab population almost all of whom are Muslim and who share a similar culture and similar social structures; on the face of it, there is little difference between Saudi Arabia and Hadramawt. This had two important implications for Hadrami migrants. First, and particularly given the Salafi character of Saudi Arabian Islam, there was (and remains) little scope for the *sada* to exercise religious leadership since Saudi Arabia has its own religious leaders, many of whom claim even greater authority than the *sada* of Hadramawt. Open displays of respect towards the *sada* are frowned upon in Saudi Arabia and they exercise some discretion in how they present themselves publicly. This may be one reason why most Hadramis in Saudi Arabia seem to be from the poorer areas of Hadramawt such as Wadi Doan rather than from the religious centres of the eastern wadi. Second, given that the Arabian peninsula is, from a social perspective, 'home' to Hadramis, there are few restrictions on Hadrami women moving to live with their husbands – indeed, quite the opposite – a woman moving to live with her husband in Mecca is moving up in the world, so to speak. This opportunity for virilocal residence accords Hadramis a slightly different identity from their compatriots elsewhere in the diaspora since there is less intermarriage between Hadramis and the local population, and thus little 'creolisation' (see Mandal, 2018); Hadramis in Saudi Arabia often have two Hadrami parents (Walker, 2015).

Prior to Yemeni unification, Hadramis enjoyed something of a special relationship with Saudi Arabia. In the 1950s, Saudi Arabia established the *kafala* system, under which immigrants required a sponsor to be eligible for a residence permit,[4] but unlike migrants of other nationalities, Hadramis were eligible for collective sponsorship and were not required to work for their sponsor, largely in recognition of the social and cultural proximity of Hadramis and Saudis. This led to some prominent Saudis of Hadrami origin, most notably Ali Abdullah Bugshan, sponsoring large numbers of Hadramis, and although these Hadramis were not permitted to own land or businesses, they were generally able to find Hadrami kin with Saudi citizenship with whom they could work. Many of the Hadramis who were in Saudi Arabia before the 1980s are citizens but more recent arrivals, as well as those who for one reason or another did not bother obtaining citizenship, are not, thus creating a somewhat arbitrary formal separation between the two groups which has become increasingly restrictive, particularly since the imposition of stricter controls on Yemenis – as Hadramis have been since Yemeni unification – in the kingdom.

Elsewhere in the Gulf States, there are Hadramis in the United Arab Emirates, particularly in Abu Dhabi, whose former ruler, Sheikh Zayed bin Sultan Al Nahyan, was particularly well disposed towards them, seeing them as fellow Bedouin, and invited them to come and settle in the city at a time when the population was small and the oil boom yet to come. A number of Hadramis from Hadramawt, as well as from Saudi Arabia and Kuwait, took advantage of his offer and were granted land and citizenship. They remain a small but influential community today. In Kuwait, however, Hadramis seem to have had a status more akin to that of the labour migrants in the Gulf, explicitly stating that they are not like the Hadramis of Saudi Arabia or the United Arab Emirates (Alajmi, 2017).

Relationships with the homeland

Although Hadramawt itself, as a place, has long existed, there has never been a unified Hadrami state, and the notion of a homeland – a greater Hadramawt that encompasses, both geographically and symbolically, more than the wadi itself – owes much to external influences.[5] Natalie Mobini-Kesheh's (1999) suggestion that the development of a Hadrami identity was prompted by analogous political processes in Indonesia, and among the Chinese community as much as among Indonesians, is compelling. The contemporary concept of the nation-state owes much to the colonial effort to establish a coherent set of identities to govern, which in turn prompted nationalist movements that required an equally coherent concept of the state and its people who were claiming independence. In the Dutch East Indies, leaders of the independence movement were faced with the task of promoting a sense of national identity, based on the concept of Indonesia, across hundreds of ethnic groups speaking as many languages and living on thousands of islands. The threat of exclusion of Hadramis from this group contributed to the *nahdah*, a parallel process that likewise required a concept of Hadramawt to claim as a homeland. It is fortuitous, perhaps, that at the same time, the British resident in Mukalla,

Harold Ingrams,[6] was doing much the same thing 'at home': following the consolidation of the two principal sultanates through treaties with the British, and the establishment of the Eastern Aden Protectorate (the Qu'aiti, Kathiri, Mahra and Wahidi sultanates) – itself an attempt at creating states in the European image – Ingrams proceeded to endow them with the requisite symbols: 'modern' flags, postage stamps, passports and the like. Although the name Hadramawt was not used in any official appellation, largely because the British were not quite sure where it was, everyone else knew where Hadramawt lay (Ingrams, 1966, pp. 47–49).

There is a saying amongst Hadramis, 'an old man's wallet won't see the sun until he reaches Hadramawt', a neat encapsulation of the ideally temporary character of emigration and the attractions, both real and symbolic, of a homeland that was very much alive in the imaginations and memories of many in diaspora. However, and despite references to Hadramawt and Hadramis, it is also clear that affiliations and expectations were often shaped by more specific allegiances: to family (or tribe) and to village. It is perhaps these characteristics that define Hadramis as much as any collective sense of belonging to Hadramawt. Thus Hadramis in diaspora return (or arrive, since many were born in diaspora) to visit ancestral tombs, an important symbolic event in an individual's life (Ho, 2006). Visits to ancestral tombs also prompt visits to more collectively symbolic tombs: the tomb of the *sayyid* Abubakar bin Salim in Inat, for example, for members of his lineage; the tomb of Al-Muhajir near Tarim, for all *sada*; or the tomb of the Prophet Hud in eastern Hadramawt, the site of an annual pilgrimage that draws people, mostly of Hadrami descent, from around the world.[7]

As elsewhere, the relationship between diaspora and homeland was (and is) somewhat ambiguous. On the one hand, those who departed left behind family, land, possessions, relationships, entitlements, obligations and memories, and therefore had very real claims to belonging. This allowed them to send their sons back for education, to send money to pay for anything from food for the family to a pump for the well, and to return themselves, to visit, study, marry, claim inheritance or retire. However, the relationships between diasporans and those who remained are permeated with ambivalence. A dependence – and, in Hadramawt, the purely economic dependence on remittances was very real – on absent family members engages a debt that can itself place stress upon relationships, and the maintenance of identity in diaspora, and the return of subsequent generations, those who have perhaps never known Hadramawt, can cause resentment; the successful emigrant returns and, despite his relative wealth, wants his share of the homeland, too. There is a saying in Hadramawt that well represents this ambivalence: 'if you see a snake and you see a *muwallad*, kill the *muwallad*. It is more dangerous than the snake' (Walker, 2012; see also Walker, 2011).

The impact of the diaspora on the homeland has been significant, both economically and culturally. In the pre-colonial period, the sums of money remitted or invested were probably small, but by the nineteenth and twentieth centuries, they were large enough to have a profound effect on the homeland. The incomes of the Qu'aiti and Kathiri sultans in Hyderabad were fundamental to shaping local political configurations, while the immense fortunes amassed by the Hadramis of South and Southeast Asia, and Singapore in particular, were to radically transform the wadi in the early twentieth century. Many Singapore Hadramis left endowments for a variety of purposes in Hadramawt (Freitag, 2002), and families such as the Al Kaf also invested personally, building themselves imposing neo-baroque palaces that still stand in Tarim today. The Al Kafs also not only brought the first cars to the wadi (in pieces, on camels' backs), but a range of consumer goods from refrigerators to teapots, before they finally financed the construction of a road from Tarim to the coast on which to transport all their imports (Mobini-Kesheh, 1999).

More widespread changes also arrived from the east: tea, now ubiquitous in Hadramawt, as well as the consumption of rice and dishes of Asian influence more generally; the *futa*, a wraparound cloth based on the sarong worn by men; and the smoking of tobacco and well as the consumption of alcohol. The latter is of course *haram*, and while some external influences are tolerated or even welcomed, there is also a perception that members of the diaspora, away from the moderating, pious and often austere environment of the homeland, have loose morals, engaging in vices that are quite unwelcome in Hadramawt (e.g. Freitag 2002, pp. 117–118). Young *muwalladin* wearing jeans on the streets of Mukalla are but the thin end of the wedge. Some influences are religious, whether they be Salafi influences from the north or the repatriation of the Irshadi/*sada* conflicts of Indonesia. The latter often find an echo in Hadramawt, where support for the *sada* is perhaps not as strong as it is in diaspora: descendants of the Prophet, perhaps, but they will always be foreigners in the wadi.

The economic contribution of the diaspora has naturally been shaped by political and economic changes outside Hadramawt, most obviously the development of colonial economies. During the Second World War, remittances from Southeast Asia ceased, leading to famine in the homeland, and with the ensuing independence of the Asian and African colonies, the decline in remittances was more prolonged. The establishment of a communist government in South Yemen in 1967 largely put an end to emigration, and even visits were difficult since many returnees had their passports confiscated on arrival and were not permitted to leave again. In the post-communist period, however, and with the discovery of oil in Hadramawt, diasporans, often comparatively well educated, returned to the homeland and took jobs that local members of their families were unable to perform, thus creating further tensions (Walker, 2008).

Being diasporic

Contemporary mobilities provide for the renewal of diasporic identities and certain places are more propitious than others for diasporic encounters. It is sometimes assumed that Hadrami immigrants, much like immigrants elsewhere, lose their Hadrami identities and assimilate into the local population with time. Links with the homeland attenuate, emigration ceases, as do visits and remittances. And yet while this is certainly true of some individuals, this does not seem to be true of the diaspora as a whole. The growing body of scholarship, for example, fosters an awareness of and an interest in the Hadrami diaspora as books and articles become increasingly accessible: barely is a text published than it is circulating on the internet or translated into Arabic and posted on a Hadrami website. Similarly, social media bring together people who in a previous age would never meet; a Google search for Al Attas, for example, returns more than a million results, and Facebook is equally fertile a source for a member of the family to begin networking. If anything, diasporic identities are being reinvented and reaffirmed using the tools of cyberspace. Even if a particular tribal name is unknown, anyone familiar with Hadramis knows that a name that begins with Ba, Bu or Bin is likely to be Hadrami.

In many ways, the Hadrami diaspora is a family diaspora. Philippe Pétriat (2016) has observed that family is often more important than diasporic identities or affiliations and this observation reveals something important about the Hadrami diaspora. A friend once told me the story of how his father-in-law, an Emirati Hadrami, hired an Indian immigrant driver only to find that his name was Al Kathiri. The Indian had no idea that he was of Hadrami origin but his employer immediately took him under his wing, paying his parking fines and generally granting him rather more latitude than he might an employee of non-Hadrami origin. Whether this encounter led the Indian to explore his Hadrami roots is unknown, but it seems likely that such encounters do prompt reconsiderations of personal identity, and they are based on kin links.

Often being a member of a family provides enduring links, but if that family is a Hadrami one, and linked to other Hadrami families by marriage, commercial interests, Sufi practices, and so on, so a diaspora coalesces.

As my friend's father-in-law's story indicates, family names and the potential for a (re)discovery of Hadrami ancestry find a particular conjuncture in the Gulf. The reliance on immigrant labour in several of the Gulf States has led to a mass migration of Asians, among whom are some of Hadrami origin, over recent decades, reversing the migratory patterns that had led to Arabs (including Hadramis) settling in south India. Remittances from migrants in the Gulf had a significant effect on local household incomes at home, but contacts also drove social changes, particularly among those of Hadrami origin, who would start speaking Arabic, wearing Arabic dress, and demonstrating greater religious adherence. In a reversal of established practice, emigrant women of Hadrami origin have married Arab men in the Gulf, thus 'renewing' a sense of and claim to Arab identity in the family, even if not a specifically Hadrami one (Osella and Osella, 2007; Manger, 2010). In Hyderabad, returning Chaush who had 'discovered' their Hadrami roots in the Gulf began opening Yemeni restaurants, a more profitable expression of rediscovered origins perhaps than wearing an *abaya*; the first one opened in 1997 and there are several dozen in the city today (Mohammed, 2020; Mukherjee, 2020).

There are therefore shifts in diasporic orientations. Today, Saudi Arabia has replaced Southeast Asia as the source of Hadrami wealth (Pritzkat, 1999). Remittances from the kingdom are essential to many families in the homeland and the links between the two countries are neatly symbolised by the gleaming four-wheel drives with Saudi licence plates that arrive in the wadi during Ramadan, or the Saudi coat of arms over the lintel of emigrants' houses. They are also manifested in the support for an independent Hadramawt, which would (at least in the imagination of some) remove Hadramis' status as Yemeni citizens and radically transform relationships between Saudi Arabia and Hadramawt (Walker, 2015). Today's equivalent of the Al Kaf family is undoubtedly the Bugshans of Wadi Doan. Abdullah Bugshan's philanthropic activities have funded schools and hospitals across the governorate and, in a (conscious?) echo of the Al Kafs, he has constructed a road from Mukalla to Wadi Doan. More than this, however, Bugshan encourages a sense of diasporic identity among Hadramis in Saudi Arabia, most notably by funding visits to the homeland for his compatriots, and elsewhere, for example, by granting scholarships to Hadrami students, many of whom are in Malaysia where they undoubtedly encounter Malaysians of Hadrami origin. Likewise, students coming to study at the schools of Tarim, particularly at Dar al Mustafa (for men) and Dar al Zahra (for women), encounter students from elsewhere in the diaspora, and although not all these students are of Hadrami origin, many are. Dar al Zahra was particularly novel in that it provided one of the few acceptable ways for *muwalladin* women to visit Hadramawt.[8]

Other activities both at home and in the diaspora unite diasporic Hadramis, allowing for the renewal of old connections or the discovery of unknown ones: The Maulid in Lamu, Kenya, for example, or the pilgrimage to the tomb of Nabi Hud. These events, which are numerous, bring people together (Alatas, 2007). There are advantages to the development of connections, some quite explicitly invoked. The government of Singapore has drawn on the Hadrami identities of some of its more prominent citizens, and the existence of networks, both historical and contemporary, to encourage business and trade with the Arab world, as manifested, for example, in an exhibition on the Hadramis of Southeast Asia at the National Library of Singapore in 2010 and explicitly linked to the Second ASEAN-Gulf Cooperation Council Ministerial meeting (Library Association of Singapore 2010).

Today Hadramis have moved beyond the Indian Ocean and are on every continent; the diaspora continues to reinvent itself, sometimes socially relevant, sometimes important and influential, economically, politically and religiously. It may be envisaged perhaps as a latent network, a plurilocal society, a *mahjar*, as it is called in Arabic, a socially emplaced diaspora (Walker, 2015), most of whose members have other identities; if the Bakhresas and the Balalas of Tanzania and Kenya are Hadramis, they are Tanzanians and Kenyans first in their daily lives and they generally do not see themselves as particularly diasporic. They are, however, like Hadramis across the world, aware of their heritage, and the Hadrami diaspora that they constitute is a very real one.

Notes

1. A *nisba* is a demonym used in Arabic to identify individuals by their place of origin.
2. A school of jurisprudence in Sunni Islam.
3. Girls were occasionally sent back to the homeland, but in such cases they were unlikely to return to East Africa.
4. The exception was citizens of the Yemen Arab Republic, the former North Yemen, who, uniquely, and under the terms of the 1934 Treaty of Taif between the two countries, were permitted to enter and reside in Saudi Arabia almost without restriction.
5. That said, the historic use of the 'al-Hadrami' *nisba* suggests that there has always been a Hadrami identity of some sort.
6. Ingrams served in Zanzibar and Mauritius before being appointed to Aden in 1933 and then to Mukalla as Resident Advisor in 1937, spending a total of ten years in South Arabia.
7. According to some sources, Hud was the father of Qahtan, the ancestor of the 'true' Arabs (including Yemenis and Hadramis), and Qahtan was the father of Hazarmaveth. Hud is therefore the ancestor of all 'true' Hadramis (but not the *sada*).
8. These schools were founded in the late 1990s to provide a more formal religious education, including a diploma, that had not hitherto been available in Tarim, and were particularly aimed at foreigners.

Acknowledgements

I would like to thank Anne Bang and Martin Slama for their comments on a draft of this chapter.

References

Abdul Jaleel, P.K.M. (2015) 'Hadrami Sayyid Diaspora in Kerala and Singapore: a comparative study', PhD thesis, Jawaharlal Nehru University.
Abdurahiman, K.P. (2004) 'Mappila heritage: a study in their social and cultural life', PhD thesis, University of Calicut.
Abushouk, A.I. and Ibrahim, H.A. (2009) *The Hadhrami Diaspora in Southeast Asia: Identity Maintenance or Assimilation?* Leiden: Brill.
Alajmi, A.M. (2017) 'The model immigrant: second generation Hadramis in Kuwait and the legacy of "good reputation"', in Babar, Z. (ed.) *Arab Migrant Communities in the GCC*. London: Hurst & Co., pp. 65–84.
Alatas, I.F. (2007) 'The upsurge of memory in the case of *haul*: a problem of Islamic historiography in Indonesia', *Journal of Indonesian Islam* 1(2), pp. 267–279.
Andaya, L.Y. (2011) 'The Gujarati legacy in southeast Asia', in Varadarajan, L. (ed.) *Gujarat and the Sea*. Vadodara: Darshak Itihas Nidhi, pp. 385–404.
Bang, A. (2003) *Sufis and Scholars of the Sea: Family Networks in East Africa, 1860–1925*. London: Routledge Curzon.
Bang, A. (2014) *Islamic Sufi Networks in the Western Indian Ocean (c. 1880–1940): Ripples of Reform*. Leiden: Brill.
Barbosa, D. (1866) *A Description of the Coasts of East Africa and Malabar in the Beginning of the Sixteenth Century*. London: The Hakluyt Society.

Beckerleg, S. (2009) 'From ocean to lakes: cultural transformations of Yemenis in Kenya and Uganda', *African and Asian Studies*, 8(3), pp. 288–308.

Bent, J.T. (1894) 'Expedition to the Hadramut', *The Geographical Journal*, 4(4), pp. 315–331.

Bezabeh, S.A. (2011) 'Yemeni families in the early history of Addis Ababa, Ethiopia ca.1900–1950: a revisionist approach in diasporic historiography', *Cahiers d'Études africaines*, 51(4), pp. 893–919.

Bezabeh, S.A. (2017) 'Arab diasporas in geopolitical spaces: imperial contestation and the making of colonial subjecthood in the port of Djibouti (1919–1939)', *Cahiers d'Études africaines*, 225, pp. 17–38.

Brehony, N. (ed.) (2017) *Hadhramaut and its Diaspora: Yemeni Politics, Identity and Migration*. London: I.B. Tauris.

Bujra, A.S. (1967) 'Political conflict and stratification in Hadramaut – I', *Middle Eastern Studies*, 3(4), pp. 355–375.

Casson, L. (1989) *The Periplus Maris Erythraei: Text with Introduction, Translation, and Commentary*. Princeton, NJ: Princeton University Press.

Clarence-Smith, W.G. (2004) 'Middle Eastern migrants in the Philippines: entrepreneurs and cultural brokers', *Asian Journal of Social Science*, 32(3), pp. 425–457.

Dale, S.F. (1990) 'Trade, conversion and the growth of the Islamic community of Kerala, South India', *Studia Islamica*, 71, pp. 155–175.

Dale, S.F. (1997) 'The Hadrami diaspora in south-western India: the role of the Sayyids of the Malabar coast', in Freitag, U. and Clarence-Smith. W.G. (eds) *Hadhrami Traders, Scholars and Statesmen in the Indian Ocean, 1750s–1960s*. Leiden: Brill, pp. 175–184.

de Jonge, H. and Kaptein, N. (eds) (2002) *Transcending Borders: Arabs, Politics, Trade and Islam in Southeast Asia*. Leiden: KITLV Press.

El-Zein, A.H. (1974) *Sacred Meadows: A Structural Analysis of Religious Symbolism in an East African Town*. Evanston, IL: Northwestern University Press.

Ewald, J. and Clarence-Smith, W.G. (1997) 'The economic role of the Hadhrami diaspora in the Red Sea and the Gulf of Aden, 1820s to 1930s', in Freitag, U. and Clarence-Smith. W.G. (eds) *Hadhrami Traders, Scholars and Statesmen in the Indian Ocean, 1750s–1960s*. Leiden: Brill, pp. 281–296.

Feener, R.M. (2004) 'Hybridity and the "Hadhrami diaspora" in the Indian Ocean Muslim networks', *Asian Journal of Social Science*, 32(3), pp. 353–372.

Forbes, A.D.W. (1981) 'Southern Arabia and the Islamicisation of the central Indian Ocean archipelagoes', *Archipel*, 21, pp. 55–92.

Freitag, U. (2002) 'Arab merchants in Singapore: attempt at a collective biography', in de Jonge, H. and Kaptein, N. (eds) *Transcending Borders: Arabs, Politics, Trade and Islam in Southeast Asia*. Leiden: KITLV, pp. 109–142.

Freitag, U. (2003) *Indian Ocean Migrants and State Formation in Hadhramaut: Reforming the Homeland*. Leiden: Brill.

Freitag, U. (2020) *A History of Jeddah: The Gate to Mecca in the Nineteenth and Twentieth Centuries*. Cambridge: Cambridge University Press.

Freitag, U. and Clarence-Smith, W.G. (eds) (1997) *Hadhrami Traders, Scholars, and Statesmen in the Indian Ocean, 1750s–1960s*. Leiden: Brill.

Gibson, T. (2007) *Islamic Narrative and Authority in Southeast Asia: from the 16th to the 21st Century*. Basingstoke: Palgrave Macmillan.

Hartwig, F. (1997) 'Expansion, state foundation and reform: the contest for power in Hadhramaut in the nineteenth century', in Freitag, U. and Clarence-Smith, W.G. (eds) *Hadhrami Traders, Scholars, and Statesmen in the Indian Ocean, 1750s–1960s*. Leiden: Brill, pp. 35–50.

Ho, E. (2006) *The Graves of Tarim: Genealogy and Mobility across the Indian Ocean*. Berkeley, CA: University of California Press.

Hourani, G. (1951) *Arab Seafaring in the Indian Ocean in Ancient and Early Medieval Times*. Princeton, NJ: Princeton University Press.

Ingrams, W.H. (1937) *A Report on the Social, Economic and Political Condition of the Hadhramaut*. London: Colonial Office/HMSO.

Ingrams, W.H. (1966) *Arabia and the Isles*, 3rd edn. London: John Murray.

Istiqomah, I. (2020) 'The Hadrami Arabs of Ambon: an ethnographic study of diasporic identity construction in everyday life', PhD thesis. University of Groningen.

Jacob, W.C. (2019) *For God or Empire: Sayyid Fadl and the Indian Ocean World*. Stanford, CA: Stanford University Press.

Karim, W.J. (2009) 'The Hadrami diaspora in the straits of Malacca: economic and political empowerment at the ocean's edge', in Karim, W.J. (ed.) *Straits Muslims: Diasporas of the Northern Passage of the Straits of Malacca*. Georgetown: Ed. Straits G.T., pp. 121–140.

Khalidi, O. (1997) 'The Hadrami role in the politics and society of colonial India, 1750s–1950s', in Freitag, U. and Clarence-Smith. W.G. (eds) *Hadhrami Traders, Scholars and Statesmen in the Indian Ocean, 1750s–1960s*. Leiden: Brill, pp. 67–81.

Khalidi, O. (2004) 'Sayyids of Hadhramaut in early modern India', *Asian Journal of Social Science*, 32(3), pp. 329–352.

Knysh, A. (1999) 'The Sāda in history: a critical essay on Ḥaḍramī historiography', *Journal of the Royal Asiatic Society*, 9(2), pp. 215–222.

Kuzhiyan, M.A. (2016) 'Poetics of piety: genre, self-fashioning, and the Mappila lifescape', *Journal of the Royal Asiatic Society*, 26(3), pp. 423–441.

Le Guennec-Coppens, F. (1991) 'Qui épouse-t-on chez les Hadrami d'Afrique orientale? Les réseaux d'alliances', in Le Guennec-Coppens, F. and Caplan, P. (eds) *Les Swahili entre Afrique et Arabie*. Paris: Karthala, pp. 145–162.

Library Association of Singapore (2010) 'Rihlah: Arabs in Southeast Asia'. Available at: www.las.org.sg/wp/blog/bulletin/from-libraries/rihlah-arabs-in-southeast-asia-exhibition (accessed 20 July 2020).

Mandal, S. (2018) *Becoming Arab: Creole Histories and Modern Identity in the Malay World*. Cambridge: Cambridge University Press.

Manger, L. (2010) *The Hadrami Diaspora: Community-Building on the Indian Ocean Rim*. New York: Berghahn Books.

Martin, B.G. (1974) 'Arab migrations to East Africa in medieval times', *The International Journal of African Historical Studies*, 7(3), pp. 367–390.

Miller, R.E. (1992) *Mappila Muslims of Kerala: A Study in Islamic Trends*. Madras: Orient Longman.

Miran, J. (2012) 'Red Sea translocals: Hadrami migration, entrepreneurship, and strategies of integration in Eritrea, 1840s–1970s', *Northeast African Studies*, 12(1), pp. 129–167.

Mobini-Kesheh, N. (1999) *The Hadrami Awakening: Community and Identity in the Netherlands East Indies, 1900–1942*. Ithaca, NY: Cornell SEAP Publications.

Mohammed, S. (2020) 'Why Hyderabad's Yemeni descendants worry about proving their citizenship,' *The Hindu*, 29 February 2020. Available at: www.thehindu.com/society/why-hyderabads-yemeni-descendants-worry-about-proving-their-citizenship/article30949526.ece (accessed 13 July 2020).

Mukherjee, A. (2020) 'Idea of homeland/s: Hadramis of Barkas in the Persian Gulf', in Gowricharn, R. (ed.) *Shifting Transnational Bonding in Indian Diaspora*. London: Routledge, pp. 197–210.

Osella, F. and Osella, C. (2007) '"I Am Gulf": the production of cosmopolitanism among the Koyas of Kozhikode, Kerala', in Simpson, E. and Kresse, K. (eds) *Struggling with History: Islam and Cosmopolitanism in the Western Indian Ocean*. New York: Columbia University Press, pp. 323–355.

Osella, F. and Osella, C. (2008) 'Islamism and social reform in Kerala, South India', *Modern Asian Studies*, 42(2), pp. 317–346.

Parfitt, T. (2000) *Journey to the Vanished City: The Search for a Lost Tribe of Israel*. New York: Vintage Books.

Pétriat, P. (2016) *Le Négoce des Lieux Saints: Négociants hadramis de Djedda, 1850–1950*. Paris: Publications de la Sorbonne.

Pritzkat, T. (1999) 'The Hadrami community in Saudi Arabia and the rationale of investing in the homeland', in Leveau, R., Mermier, F. and Steinbach, U. (eds) *Le Yémen contemporain*. Paris: Karthala, pp. 399–418.

Schottenhammer, A. (2012) 'The "China Seas" in world history: a general outline of the role of Chinese and East Asian maritime space from its origins to c. 1800', *Journal of Marine and Island Cultures*, 1(2), pp. 63–86.

Serjeant, R.B. (1957) *The Saiyids of Hadramawt: An Inaugural Lecture Delivered on 5 June 1956*. London: SOAS.

Sharifah, Z.S.H. (2004) 'History and the indigenization of the Arabs in Kedah, Malaysia', *Asian Journal of Social Science*, 32(3), pp. 401–424.

Sherman, T.C. (2011) 'Migration, citizenship and belonging in Hyderabad (Deccan), 1946–1956', *Modern Asian Studies*, 45(1), pp. 81–107.

Slama, M. (2011) 'Paths of institutionalization, varying divisions, and contested radicalisms: comparing Hadhrami communities on Java and Sulawesi', *Comparative Studies of South Asia, Africa and the Middle East*, 31(2), pp. 331–342.

Slama, M. (2015) 'Papua as an Islamic Frontier: preaching in "the Jungle" and the multiplicity of spatio-temporal hierarchisations', in Slama, M. and Munro, J. (eds) *From 'Stone-Age' to 'Real-Time': Exploring*

Papuan Temporalities, Mobilities and Religiosities. Canberra: Australian National University Press, pp. 243–270.
Ṭāhā, ʿA.D. (1989) *The Muslim Conquest and Settlement of North Africa and Spain*. London: Routledge.
Tibbetts, G.R. (1957) 'Early Muslim traders in south-east Asia', *Journal of the Malay Branch of the Royal Asiatic Society*, 30(1), pp. 1–45.
van den Berg, L.W.C. (1886) *Le Ḥadhramout et les colonies arabes dans l'archipel Indien*. Batavia: Impr. du gouvernement.
van der Kroef, J.M. (1953) 'The Arabs in Indonesia', *Middle East Journal*, 7(3), pp. 300–323.
von Maltzan, H. (1865) *Meine Wallfahrt nach Mekka: Reise in der Küstengegend und im innern von Hedschas*. Leipzig: Nachdr. der Ausg.
Walker, I. (2008) 'Hadramis, Shimalis and Muwalladin: negotiating cosmopolitan identities between the Swahili coast and southern Yemen', *Journal of Eastern African Studies*, 2(1), pp. 44–59.
Walker, I. (2011) 'Hybridity, belonging, and mobilities: the intercontinental peripatetics of a transnational community', *Population, Space and Place*, 17(2), pp. 167–178.
Walker, I. (2012) 'Comorians and Hadramis in the western Indian Ocean: diasporic practices in a comparative context', *Social Dynamics*, 38(3), pp. 435–453.
Walker, I. (2015) 'Hadrami identities in Saudi Arabia', in Brehony, N. and al Sarhan, S. (eds) *Rebuilding Yemen: Political, Economic and Social Challenges*. Berlin: Gerlach Books, pp. 42–60.

29
HADRAMI CONNECTIONS WITH THE MALAY WORLD
Creole histories, transcultural Islam and racialisation

Sumit K. Mandal

This chapter focuses on an Arab diaspora in Southeast Asia whose transcultural network challenges the bounded understandings of identity that have dominated with the rise of nation-states and regions as units of analysis. The Arabs who migrated to Southeast Asia came almost exclusively from the Hadramaut in Yemen and were part of a larger diaspora that stretched across the Indian Ocean littoral from Africa to Asia (Freitag and Clarence-Smith, 1997; de Jonge and Kaptein, 2002; Ho, 2006). The Hadrami diaspora was not a linear extension of a culturally cohesive network that extended from southern Arabia to the Malay world, the largely Muslim archipelago within Southeast Asia. Rather, Hadramis interacted and intermixed with people across their various diasporic destinations. Connections were maintained across vast distances between these diversely constituted communities through a shared identification with the genealogy of the Prophet Muhammad (Ho, 2006). Men rather than women made the journey and these men married locally. The children from these marriages were creole as they resembled neither their Hadrami fathers nor their Malay, Bugis or Javanese mothers, but a self-standing combination of both. These children were absorbed into the Prophetic lineage and became part of the diaspora in this manner. The Hadrami diaspora was thus a transcultural network that was constituted by an enormous array of people of culturally diverse origin from Africa to Asia.

The chapter turns to the connections forged by the Hadrami diaspora between the Middle East and Southeast Asia to bring to the fore forms of negotiating human interaction and negotiations of difference worthy of closer scrutiny and greater attention. It considers the Hadrami diaspora as a network that allows for the flow not only of people, ideas and goods across vast distances but exemplifies a site of complex cultural interaction in the face of understandings of cultural influence and change that rest on the notion of a one-way flow from a core to a periphery. Such understandings are particularly true in the case of the transmission of Islam.

Hadramis, as Arabs, have been identified with the flow of an orthodox Islam from west to east that has transformed the region from tolerant to intolerant understandings of the faith. Views of this nature, first promulgated by nineteenth-century colonial scholar-bureaucrats, have had a surprisingly long life as they continue to inform contemporary journalists, politicians and activists. In the present time, the connection is believed to have facilitated the introduction of a conservative, if not extremist, Islamic politics, variously labelled 'Salafi' or 'Wahhabi'. It is not uncommon for Indonesians and others in the region concerned about Islamic conservatism in their country to attribute it to 'Arabisation'. Some Muslim organisations and public intellectuals in Indonesia, Malaysia and Singapore describe the growing social conservatism of their co-religionists, often in such performative acts as the adoption of Arab dress, as the outcome of 'Arabisation'. Although Saudi Arabia is not believed to have caused this change, it is said to have provided a lot of support for it through an extensive campaign that has gone beyond outward expressions of conservatism to 'strident campaigns against minority Muslim sects, the consolidation of a highly organized Islamist political party, and the influential alumni roster of a single, small Saudi-funded university' as part of a 'broad vision of combining aid and proselytization' (Varagur, 2020, p. 18).

Hadramis have been viewed by some as among the drivers of 'Arabisation' even though scholars have provided nuanced approaches to understanding the conservative turn and cautioned against the use of the term as a broad brush (Saat, 2018). Indeed, a number of Hadramis have emerged as high profile supporters of conservatism. Habib Rizieq Shihab, for example, is a graduate of the small but influential university mentioned above and furthered his studies in Saudi Arabia (Varagur, 2020, p. 15). He returned to Indonesia in 1998 to establish the *Front Pembela Islam* (Islamic Defenders Front), which made a name for itself by taking vigilante actions against bars and brothels in Jakarta, the country's capital. At the same time, as we shall see in the following pages, many Hadramis have kept with their long history of integrating into the Malay world a combination of Sufism and a celebration of the Prophet that runs contrary to the conservative turn.

This chapter considers Hadrami diasporic connections as they were developed in the premodern era, disrupted in the colonial and national periods and then rediscovered since the 1990s, to offer a better understanding of the continued relevance and significance of these historical linkages. The chapter concludes by examining the case of Habib Syech, a Hadrami religious figure whose transnational circulations as a singing preacher draw on premodern patterns even as he mobilises the mass concert format and latest technologies to project his music to vast audiences. Before proceeding, however, it is helpful to lay out a conceptualisation of the place of the long-term histories and geographical imaginations in relation to recent histories of nation-states.

Conceptualising the diasporic relationship with the Malay world

Hadramis have been present throughout Southeast Asia, but they have been the largest in number and most influential in the Malay world. While the term 'Malay world' is imperfect, as it tends to be associated today with ethnic Malays in Malaysia in particular, it becomes helpful when seen, as Henk Maier (2004, p. 26) suggests, as a more fluid and ambiguous overlap of language, space and people in the archipelagic region. For at least five hundred years, Malay has developed into a lingua franca that interconnects disparate islands, and it is no wonder that it is today the national language of four countries: Indonesia, Malaysia, Singapore and Brunei. In this chapter, the term 'Malay world' serves well as a means of imagining the premodern past when borders and identities were more porous. The chapter rests on a reconsideration of both the spatial and temporal terms of understanding the Hadrami diaspora and its transcultural interactions and identities. Let us first turn to the temporal by drawing together the national and pre-national pasts.

Scholarship is fragmented not only along national and regional lines but also between the national and pre-national pasts. In contemporary nation-states, there is little room or motivation to consider the long and fluid histories of interactions and mobility on a transregional scale. Much contemporary scholarship on identity in the countries that emerged from the Malay world remains largely embedded in the racialised historiography, thinking and language established by colonial states. Does this mean that the fluid histories of interactions and mobility on a transregional scale that characterised the Malay world for millennia are of no consequence? How do we make sense of the older diasporic formations in today's national and racialised contexts?

The chapter takes up the challenge of engaging with and integrating two seemingly incongruous histories, namely the longer histories of Indian Ocean interaction and the shorter histories of nation-states. Hadramis represent the older histories and the possibility of connection across the Indian Ocean and, in this regard, are an important residual presence of the fluid past. This past is neither erased nor irrecoverable but, at the same time, it does not sit comfortably in the racialised contexts of present-day nation-states. Sarah Stein (2016) observes, in her study of Ottoman Jews in Europe, that the vast majority of people did not belong in a legal sense to a state in the early modern world. The growth of the modern passport regime and the consolidation of understandings of citizenship only took place in the late nineteenth and early twentieth centuries. There is palpable evidence of the coexistence of both creole Hadramis, who emerged from the transcultural past, and racialised citizenship in Indonesia, Malaysia and Singapore, which leads to the question of spatiality.

Arabness in the Malay world offers a lens through which to observe the workings of the localisation of Islamic ideas and politics circulating at the national, regional and transregional scales that would otherwise not be obvious. People of Arab descent in Indonesia, Malaysia and Singapore represent, if not embody, transregional ties to the Hadramaut. A simplistic view of this connection is that it works much like a conduit for ideas from Arabic-speaking countries to the Malay world as represented by the term 'Arabisation'.

Rather than a conduit, this chapter takes the position that the connection between people of Arab descent in the Malay world and their distant land of origin is the source of a variety of multiscalar circulations of ideas and politics. My book (Mandal, 2018) asserts that a modern Arab identity was crystallised in early twentieth-century Java under Dutch rule. Forged by Hadramis who claimed descent from the Prophet, this identity was contested from the outset by Muslim modernists who opposed its hierarchical nature. The question of identity turned on different representations of Arabness and their perspectives on hierarchy and leadership within Arab circles but also Muslim colonial subjects as a whole. The position of Arabs as leaders of Muslims – especially if they were *sayyid* or descended from the Prophet – was questioned and debated. This moment under colonial rule inflected the long history of Hadrami interactions with the Malay world by introducing exclusivist and racialised understandings of Arab identity. Although more bounded understandings of identity became dominant, they did not erase multidimensional creole identities altogether.

Arabness has had a complex and changing place in the Malay world, in which exclusivist and inclusionary politics have been in contestation. On the one hand, Hadramis have circulated within the Malay world as outsiders with transregional historical and genealogical connections to the Hadramaut. On the other hand, they are intimately tied to the local context through marriage and acculturation. In this regard, the Hadrami diaspora offers a means of overcoming the spatial barriers imposed by the area studies rubrics of the 'Middle East' and 'Southeast Asia' as well as the temporal divide proposed between a pre-national and a national past. The Hadrami diaspora represents a transcultural connection between the Hadramaut and the Malay world, whose making and unmaking had significant implications for the terms of identity and belonging.

The making and unmaking of transregional connections

Small groups of Hadramis became part of the courts of the Malay world from the seventeenth century onwards, though their presence in Southeast Asia probably goes back several centuries earlier. They arrived armed with experience as traders, diplomats and religious adepts, gained from their sojourns across the Indian Ocean, especially along the western coast of the Indian subcontinent. The archipelago was dotted with numerous coastal polities whose rulers had converted to Islam in the preceding centuries and were eager to be better integrated into the larger and thriving transoceanic Islamic trading and political networks of the time. Besides their knowledge of trade, diplomacy, multiple languages and Islam, these Hadramis were prized for their Prophetic lineage. They came to assume positions of authority in Malay courts and in some instances became part of the ruling elite themselves. They were influential figures in the sultanate of Aceh in the eighteenth century and became part of the ruling elites of Siak, Jambi, Perlis, Kubu, Riau and Sulu, stretching across the Malay world from Sumatra in the west to northern Borneo in the east. Hadrami *sayyids* became intimate outsiders who had close ties with the Malay world and diasporic pathways that connected them to the Hadramaut and other locations in the Indian Ocean. Creole Hadramis thrived as significant figures in Malay courts and as merchants who controlled a considerable amount of inter-island trade and shipping. They were eclipsed only with the establishment of Dutch and British colonial states in the nineteenth century.

The colonial state boundaries drawn in 1824 separated the spheres of Dutch and British control in the Malay world and the respective territories became sites of increasing expansion, control and economic exploitation in the course of the nineteenth and early twentieth centuries, which led to the Dutch East Indies and British Malaya. The fledgling nation-states of Indonesia and Malaysia emerged in the middle of the twentieth century from practically the same colonial boundaries.

The process of colonial racial categorisation began to gather steam by the middle of the nineteenth century and developed in an uneven way across the different colonial states, becoming an important if not singular reference point of governance. The extent of the reach of racialised thinking was substantial as its categories and terms were translated and localised by Asian intellectuals (Khor Manickam, 2009).

Colonial racial categorisation applied the term 'Arab' to Hadramis and reduced the scope of their fluidity and mobility but did not erase them altogether. At the same time, Hadramis responded to the introduction of racialised emplacement and thinking by registering complaints to the colonial authorities about the restrictions on travel and residence imposed on them. To further improve their lot, they developed charitable associations and educational institutions to equip their young with the necessary knowledge and skills to succeed in colonial society. Their schools engaged colonial modernity on their own terms by teaching the subjects taught in colonial European schools alongside an emphasis on the Arabic language and Islamic subjects. Many members of the Hadrami community looked to the Ottoman Empire to advance their vision of Islamic modernity and a few wealthy families sent their children to schools such as the Galatasaray in Istanbul.

In the early twentieth century, Hadramis established themselves as leaders of Arabs and Muslims in the Malay world by building organisations and schools in which the primacy of their Prophetic genealogy and social status was preserved. At the same time, other Hadramis, inspired by the Islamic modernist thinking emerging from Cairo, resisted the idea of genealogical ascendancy. The two sides grew apart over the twentieth century and established rival organisations, schools and periodicals that represented their respective points of view.

The rise of nation-states following the end of colonial rule in the middle of the twentieth century led to ruptures between the Hadramaut and diasporic destinations in the Malay world. Hadramis faced considerable pressure to conform to the norms and bounds of national identity in the newly independent countries. Once citizenship regimes were put in place and enforced in the emerging nation-states, the boundaries between insider and outsider or indigene and foreigner were policed and reinforced. Hadramis tended to suppress their ancestral links to the Hadramaut to conform to the insistence on an allegiance to national identities in the early decades of independence. Compounding these ruptures, travel between the Malay world and the Hadramaut became difficult during the Cold War, when the two areas fell within the orbit of the United States and the Soviet Union, respectively. Citizens of Indonesia, Malaysia and Singapore were cut off from their ancestral homeland as their countries did not have diplomatic relations with the People's Democratic Republic of Yemen, the Marxist government that ruled the Hadramaut.

Cut off from the Hadramaut by the Cold War on the global stage, Hadramis in the Malay world found themselves in nation-states that institutionalised racial difference following independence. Politics in Malaysia and Singapore, and, to a lesser extent, Indonesia, became organised around parties that represented racial groups. Forms of political mobilisation along racially exclusive or xenophobic lines also emerged to a greater or lesser degree in all three states. Besides the racialisation practised by states, as we have already seen, influential individuals and organisations in the Malay world racialise aspects of Islam they find undesirable by deploying the term 'Arabisation'. In their view, the moderate and inclusive tendency that they claim of Islam in the Malay world needs to be protected from the social conservatism and political extremism represented by the term.

The Hadrami-established transregional connections between the Hadramaut and the Malay world in the seventeenth century were unmade with the rise of nation-states and the institutionalisation of racial difference in the second half of the twentieth century. Although long-standing creole communities did not disappear altogether, they tended to suppress their Hadrami ancestry and identify with their respective national identities. Hadrami identity had all but been erased, especially in the public life of the nation-states.

The rediscovery of Hadrami identity

The rediscovery of Hadrami identity in Indonesia, Malaysia and Singapore began in the 1990s and drew on the vestigial histories of the diaspora's long-standing interactions with the Malay world. The Marxist government in Yemen fell in 1990, following the collapse of the Soviet Union, and Hadramis gradually began to recall ties with family members that had faded due to the long period of separation; some also travelled to the Hadramaut. Through the rediscovery of their transregional connections, many began to gradually rejuvenate and express their Hadrami identity in Indonesia, Malaysia and Singapore. Citizens of these countries began to explore their ancestral roots publicly as the pressures to conform to a national identity diminished.

The Arab Association of Singapore was active in discussions about the reconnection and newspapers published stories about the island republic's Hadrami citizens. Academic conferences were held in Indonesia and Malaysia that discussed the role of each country's Hadrami community. The genealogical roots in the Hadramaut of a Malaysian holder of the revolving kingship were published in a national daily. These developments frequently received the backing of governments that were keen on building economic ties with what was now a unified Yemen. Malaysia became a destination for many young Yemenis in search of a university education

(Mandal, 2014). A symbolic but concrete representation of this process of the rediscovery of Hadrami roots was the growing use of the term 'Hadramaut' itself, which had been lost to the region's previous generations, such as in the names of emerging Hadrami-owned restaurants.

Within this context of rediscovery, there were notable individual efforts to engage racialised thinking by drawing on creole Hadrami histories. Syed Imran Alsagoff, a Malaysian former journalist, wrote in his blog about his transregional biography at a racially charged moment in public life when long-established migrants were labelled *pendatang*. The term simply means 'newcomer' in Malay but has become a derogatory reference to migrants. As a counterpoint to this racialised language, Syed Imran wrote:

> For example, I myself am of *pendatang* descent ... My grandparents on my father's side migrated from Mecca to Brunei, then came here, while those on my mother's side came from the Hadhramut [sic], Yemen. We are *pendatang* and 'guests' like practically all the people of [Malaysia].
>
> (Alsagoff, 2008)

The Indonesian poet Zeffry Alkatiri has explored his grandfather's journey from the Hadramaut to Indonesia in poems that evocatively describe the stages of his transregional passage until his death in Jakarta (Alkatiri, 2004). Ben Sohib, the Indonesian author, has written novels about the struggles of a young Hadrami Indonesian protagonist with the weight of age-old *sayyid* tradition that his father expects him to bear (Sohib, 2006; 2008). The connections and tensions of the transregional past are nicely laid out in these creative works.

Besides the above efforts in the arts and public life, Hadrami religious figures from both Yemen and the Malay world have become more active and visible in public life in the past few decades. Of these figures, Habib Syech is one of the most prominent and influential as well as pertinent to this chapter because he manifests a notable and instructive mobility within the Hadrami diaspora today.

Habib Syech and transcultural Islam

Habib Syech Bin Abdul Qadir Assegaf is better known as Habib Syech to millions of people in Southeast Asia and beyond because of his performance of *selawat* (the Malay iteration of the Arabic word for praise songs). He is part of the expanding number of preachers of Hadrami descent who were born in the Malay world but frequently trained in the Hadramaut or elsewhere. The rise of such preachers was noted in Jakarta in the early 2000s with a corresponding growth in their influence in politics and in response to a growing demand for 'public ritual' (Abaza, 2004). Their protégés have become even more popular and authoritative today with the now well-travelled pathway of education in the Hadramaut itself (Syamsul, 2020). The Hadrami figures in question are often descendants of the Prophet. Besides carrying the honorific 'Sayyid', many are referred to as 'Habib' to convey a greater level of intimacy. Habib Syech is one such figure and could be described as a singing preacher with an enormous popular reach through his devotional songs in Arabic, Indonesian and Javanese. He travels from his native Indonesia to Malaysia, Singapore and other countries to perform *selawat* in massive concerts.

Figures such as Habib Syech, as well as those from the Hadramaut, tour cities in the different countries of the Malay world comfortably and are establishing a tradition as they place their Prophetic genealogy and, thereby, a tacit form of their leadership of Muslims, in the public eye. Their public behaviour is infused with Sufi practices and forms of devotion that are conveyed in similarly tacit rather than overt ways. It might be more accurate to describe these acts as the renewal of a tradition, as Hadrami *sayyids* have placed their esteemed genealogy at the centre of the understandings of Islam they disseminated in the region for centuries. Their present efforts differ because they are engaging with the public through sermons and concerts on a massive scale and promoting their efforts via contemporary marketing methods (from billboards to social media). Habib Syech has transformed the *selawat* tradition from its origins as a community-level and intimate practice to massive concerts with video recordings of his music drawing millions of listeners on YouTube.

Far from the reductionist terms of the discourse of 'Arabisation', the transformation of the *selawat* tradition in Indonesia and its transnational passage from Indonesia to Malaysia in the hands of Habib Syech capture the peculiar role played by Arabs in the Malay world in the transmission and localisation of Islamic ideas. The Arabness that Habib Syech and his co-descendants represent rests on the primacy of Prophetic genealogy; the *selawat* genre in itself consists of songs of praise to the Prophet. Given the importance these Hadramis place on genealogy over ethnicity and nationality, they could be seen as a network that transcends and bridges the differences between Indonesia and Malaysia.

Habib Syech's emphasis on Prophetic lineage draws on long-standing histories of the Hadrami diaspora in the Malay world while shoring it up today through an engagement not by strictly formal religious means but rather by cultural politics. Besides the dramatic shift in scale from intimate, community-level singing, Habib Syech's concerts underscore genealogical primacy not by decree, so to speak, but through performance. The absence of overt statements by Habib Syech and his co-descendants highlighting Prophetic genealogy during the concerts is significant. The singing preacher has built an appreciative following through his voice, charisma and command of the audience. He cultivates the primacy of Prophetic genealogy through a performative, rather than overt, politics.

Habib Syech's cultural politics are not easily captured by the terms 'traditionalist', 'Salafi' or 'Wahhabi', which are applied to understandings of the contemporary politics of Muslim societies in the Malay world and beyond. While at first sight, Habib Syech and his co-descendants might seem to represent a certain conservatism, they are not necessarily responsible for the rise in socially conservative practices or exclusivist politics that some in the region describe as 'Arabisation'. Mark Woodward and his co-authors (2012) have argued that Habib Syech represents a politics of peace and the accommodation of religious and ethnic difference, in contrast to other influential Islamic leaders, such as Habib Rizieq Shihab, who rose to prominence by promoting vigilantism.

The rise of Habib Syech can best be understood by viewing him as part of the long-standing Hadrami diaspora in the Indian Ocean. The ability of Hadrami descendants of the Prophet to cultivate genealogical primacy rests on their historical presence, intimacy and renewed relevance within diasporic destinations such as the Malay world. They embody as well as shape a Muslim world that rests on historical connections made between societies that have in common an appreciation of Prophetic genealogy, expressed, for example, through *selawat*.

The Muslim world envisioned by Habib Syech is demarcated not along geographical or political lines but as a transregional cultural geography in which forms of expressing devotion to the Prophet such as *selawat* flourish. The making of this cultural geography rests on claims of difference from other centres of influence, such as Saudi Arabia. It is worth quoting from an Indonesian news report to see how Habib Syech positions Indonesia in relation to other nations through the degree of freedom afforded to *selawat*:

> Let us be thankful for what this nation has. Look, how the governor can sit [with us] with ease. This is not the case in other countries. I was in Singapore, all kinds of

permits were necessary for *selawat*. In Indonesia [we] are supported instead. Everything proceeds smoothly, he said.

(Iqbal, 2018)

Habib Syech asks the Islamic community to be thankful to be in Indonesia. He noted that, permission for a *selawat* event is difficult to obtain in Egypt and, even in Madina, one has to whisper when reading *selawat* out of fear of being ousted by the police.

> "Some time ago I was in Madina to perform *umrah* [minor pilgrimage to Mecca], reading *selawat* in whispers, fearful of being ousted after spotting the police. Over here, it is the police who provide the security instead. This is what we should be thankful for in our nation," he said.

(ibid.)

From the above excerpt, Habib Syech's worldview could quite easily be construed as Indonesia-centred. After all, he has said that 'people should go on the *hajj* to Saudi Arabia but study Islam in Yogyakarta [in Indonesia]' (Woodward et al., 2012, p. 130). However, Hadramis such as Habib Syech represent a transcultural Islam and circulate across national and regional boundaries. He envisions and actively shapes a Muslim world whose reach is marked by the degree to which the expression of devotion to the Prophet is central.

Conclusion

The racialised politics of Indonesia, Malaysia and Singapore loom larger than the transcultural histories of the Hadrami diaspora that this chapter has explored. Racialised thinking structures public life in important ways even though the sense of belonging to multiple places and transregional connections are alive. If nothing else, the Hadrami diaspora and its history continue to point to an alternative vocabulary of belonging and identity. There are inevitable contradictions between the expectations of the racialised present and the long history of transcultural interaction in the contemporary Malay world. Of the many instances of such contradictions, the case of the 2017 presidential elections in Singapore is a particularly good illustration.

Halimah Yacob was elected as the first woman and the second ethnic Malay to the presidency of Singapore but not without controversy. The Singaporean government reserved the position for ethnic Malays as part of its effort to establish representation by the different ethnic groups within its culturally diverse population. A debate arose, however, on whether the finalists for the post were truly 'Malay' and this brought into the picture the question of racial purity. The government resolved this debate by putting together a committee made up of members of the community to certify the candidate's Malay racial status. Halimah Yacob's father was of Indian descent, which is perfectly in tune with the history of Malayness and, as it turns out, acceptable to the community. Significantly, the crisis was created by framing the presidential election along racial lines, while the resolution to the crisis seems to have been found by drawing on a Malay world history in which Indianness, as well as Hadraminess, in many instances was acceptable in a flexible understanding of Malayness. As noted at the outset, the transcultural history of the Hadrami diaspora overlapped with India. Not only did Hadramis arrive in the Malay world with experience of living and working in the subcontinent but they were often the children of Hadrami-Indian marriages.

The Hadrami diaspora offers a way of negotiating the world through a Prophetic genealogy and thereby expands the scope for understanding human interaction beyond racial or national vocabularies. The histories of the diaspora's interactions with the Malay world are creole histories, namely narratives of interconnection and intermixing. These creole histories have frequently been neglected in favour of racialised narratives that arose with colonialism and have been sustained by independent nation-states. Beyond the case of the Malay world, creole Hadrami histories represent a vocabulary and a way of understanding interconnection and intermixing in global history.

Creole histories are repositories of vocabularies of connection that speak for scales beyond nation-states and categories beyond race. They have the potential to prise open notions of identity and belonging and thereby suggest more inclusive futures. It is important, however, to recognise that expansive transregional histories exist in tension with contemporary exclusivist racialised politics. It is necessary, therefore, to draw into the same analytical frame the long and transcultural histories of diasporic interaction and the short and racialised histories of nation-states rather than view them as distinct processes. Much contemporary scholarship on Southeast Asia is focused on racialised categories, thinking and language because these perspectives do help in understanding the workings of Indonesia, Malaysia and Singapore. Racialised logics continue to play an important role, particularly in the governance of these states. However, there is a body of scholarship that has viewed the Malay world as a site of enormous interaction between people and thus an exemplary place to study how difference has been negotiated and outsiders such as Hadramis became insiders (Kahn, 2006; Ho, 2013; Mandal, 2018). This scholarship has explored the cosmopolitan character of the Malay world and its transregional architecture.

At the same time, the scholarship on Southeast Asia has been provoked to consider deep connections with the Middle East through a number of works in the past two decades (Freitag and Clarence-Smith, 1997; Ho, 2006; Tagliacozzo, 2009). Beyond the Hadrami diaspora, explorations of transregional connections, forged, for example, by the pilgrimage to Mecca and training in Islamic studies in Mecca and Cairo, have been gradually brought to the fore in the study of Southeast Asia. As for the Middle East, Engseng Ho in particular has shown how a different idea of the region emerges when the seaward journeys of Hadramis are considered.

The study of the Hadrami diaspora could help to expand, if not render porous, the scope of regions such as the Middle East and Southeast Asia. Understandings of regions have been profoundly shaped not only by the rise of nation-states but conflicts over territory with origins in the twentieth century. These have naturally turned the attention on the region inward; it has been a landward rather than a seaward orientation.

The re-assertion of territorially-bound national identities and citizenships in the early twenty-first century has made the task of exploring diasporic connections more urgent. In 2018, the Israeli parliament passed a law that prioritises the nation-state's Jewish citizens. This has been viewed as a measure to establish Jewish racial exclusivity. In 2019, the parliament of India extended the possibility of citizenship to undocumented migrants from a few neighbouring countries who were Hindu, Sikh, Buddhist, Jain, Parsi and Christian but excluded Muslims. This has been viewed as a means by which the pro-Hindu ruling party declared its antipathy towards Muslims in India, who constitute the country's second-largest faith community. In Israel, India and other countries, such racialising projects are always new, though they claim to be fulfilling or completing the natural trajectory of a biological and cultural entity with a long history. The category of a Jewish and Hindu citizen is being created today in Israel and India respectively. Similar processes are underway whenever race and citizenship are codified by states. Creole histories are repositories that are a counterpoint to racialising projects and can be rediscovered and mobilised as they have been in the Malay world since the 1990s.

The Hadrami diaspora could be conceptualised as a bridging space between the Middle East and Southeast Asia. In this regard, the dissemination of Hadramis serves not only as the bridge but also as a bridging space between the two regions separated by the Indian Ocean. A bridge could easily be thought of as a conduit through which Islamic ideas have passed from west to east in a one-way flow. This has, of course, been a lasting idea that has undergirded explanations of the conversion of the Malay world to Islam as well as racialised representations of Arabs and Islam as negative influences on the Malay world. A bridging space suggests the possibility of a more complex connection through which there have been different scales of circulation and interaction that are not necessarily one-way or predictable. The idea is helpful not only in understanding Arabs in relation to the racialised politics that inform contemporary Indonesia, Malaysia and Singapore. Arabs as a bridging space helps to historicise and draw attention to the changing and multidimensional nature of identities by asking questions about how belonging and identity operate more generally.

Acknowledgements

This chapter draws on a paper presented at the conference 'Claiming and Making Muslim Worlds: Across and Between the Local and Global', organised by the Leibniz-Zentrum Moderner Orient in Berlin in April 2019 and the workshop 'Pop morality in Islamic Indonesia and Malaysia', organised by Monash University Australia, Monash University Malaysia, and Universitas Negeri Malang in Bandar Sunway, Malaysia, in October 2019. It also draws on a paper presented at the Berliner Forum seminar series of the Forum Transregionale Studien, Berlin, April 2019, and the seminar series of the Department of Malay Studies, in conjunction with the Asia Research Institute, of the National University of Singapore in January 2020. I would like to acknowledge the organisers of the above-mentioned meetings and thank their participants for discussions that have helped in developing this chapter. I am grateful to the editors of the present volume for their thoughtful critique and comments on an earlier draft.

References

Abaza, M. (2004) 'Markets of faith: Jakartan da'wa and Islamic gentrification', *Archipel*, 67(1), pp. 173–202.
Alkatiri, Z.J. (2004) *Catatan seorang pejalan dari Hadrami*. Jakarta: Komunitas Bambu.
Alsagoff, S.I. (2008) 'Antara pendatang dan penumpang', 8 September. Available at: http://kudaranggi.blogspot.com/2008/09/antara-pendatang-dan-penumpang.html (accessed 15 September 2020).
Freitag, U. and Clarence-Smith, W.G. (eds) (1997) *Hadrami Traders, Scholars and Statesmen in the Indian Ocean, 1750s–1960s*. Leiden: Brill.
Ho, E. (2006) *Graves of Tarim: Genealogy and Mobility across the Indian Ocean*. Berkeley, CA: University of California Press.
Ho, E. (2013) 'Foreigners and mediators in the constitution of Malay sovereignty', *Indonesia and the Malay World*, 41(120), pp. 146–167.
Iqbal, F. (2018) 'Habib Syech Bin Abdul Qadir Assegaf ingatkan umat Islam cintai Indonesia', *Merdeka*, 18 November. Available at: www.merdeka.com/peristiwa/habib-syech-bin-abdul-qadir-assegaf-ingatkan-umat-islam-cintai-indonesia.html (accessed 10 March 2019).
de Jonge, H. and Kaptein, N. (eds) (2002) *Transcending Borders: Arabs, Politics, Trade and Islam in Southeast Asia*. Leiden: KITLV Press.
Kahn, J.S. (2006) *Other Malays: Nationalism and Cosmopolitanism in the Modern Malay World*. Singapore: NUS Press.
Khor Manickam, S. (2009) 'Common ground: Race and the colonial universe in British Malaya', *Journal of Southeast Asian Studies*, 409(3), pp. 593–612.

Maier, H. (2004) *We Are Playing Relatives: A Survey of Malay Writing*. Leiden: KITLV Press.

Mandal, S.K. (2014) 'Arabs in the urban social landscapes of Malaysia: Historical connections and belonging', *Citizenship Studies*, 18(8), pp. 807–822.

Mandal, S.K. (2018) *Becoming Arab: Creole Histories and Modern Identity in the Malay World*. Cambridge: Cambridge University Press.

Norshahril, S. (2018) 'Competing discourses among Malaysian Muftis: Still a case of Arabization?' in Norshahril, S. (ed.) *Islam in Southeast Asia: Negotiating Modernity*. Singapore: ISEAS – Yusuf Ishak Institute, pp. 35–62.

Syamsul R. (2020) 'Revitalizing Hadhrami authority: New networks, figures and institutions among Habā'ib in Indonesia', *Studia Islamika*, 27(2), pp. 239–272.

Sohib, B. (2006) *The Da Peci Code*. Jakarta: Ufuk Press.

Sohib, B. (2008) *Rosid dan Delia*. Jakarta: Ufuk Press.

Stein, S.A. (2016) *Extraterritorial Dreams: European Citizenship, Sephardi Jews, and the Ottoman Twentieth Century*. Chicago: University of Chicago Press.

Tagliacozzo, E. (ed.) (2009) *Southeast Asia and the Middle East: Islam, Movement, and the* Longue Durée. Singapore: NUS Press.

Varagur, K. (2020) *The Call: Inside the Global Saudi Religious Project*. New York: Columbia University Press.

Woodward, M., Rohmaniyah, I., Amin, A., Ma'arif, S., Coleman, D.M. and Sani Umar, M. (2012) 'Ordering what is right, forbidding what is wrong: Two faces of Hadhrami *dakwah* in contemporary Indonesia', *Review of Indonesian and Malaysian Affairs* 46(2), pp. 105–146.

30
TOWARDS A NEW MODE OF READING MUSLIM DIASPORA WRITING

Muslimness and the homing desire in Abu-Jaber's *Crescent* and Shafak's *The Saint of Incipient Insanities*

Neriman Kuyucu

The issues surrounding Muslim identities – including assumptions about Islamist extremism, the influx of refugees and the incompatibility of Islam with Western democratic principles – have frequently been covered by mass media and investigated in academic circles. However, broader theoretical questions about the formation of Muslim subjectivity and Muslim diasporic literary expression, in particular, remain understudied. This chapter broadens the various ways in which Muslim diasporic subjectivities can be theorised and used as an analytic tool in reading literary texts by writers of Muslim origin. To this end, I draw on diaspora studies to offer an analysis of two novels by writers of Muslim and Middle Eastern origin, Diana Abu-Jaber's *Crescent* (2003) and Elif Shafak's *The Saint of Incipient Insanities* (2004) (henceforth *The Saint*), in which the notions of Muslimness, home and cultural identity are entwined with the theme of diaspora. By examining the intersection of Muslimness and the complex politics of homing desires as depicted in these novels, I seek to forge a new conceptual framework, 'Muslim diaspora space', as a lens for reading Muslim narratives.

The analytical framework of Muslim diaspora space highlights a supra-national space of belonging that escapes the confines of ethnicity, nationality and religiosity. It further registers a profound shift from the polarising discourses on Islam towards the complex processes by which writers of Muslim origin and their Muslim characters create new sites of belonging as Muslims and rightful citizens/residents of the Global North. Focusing on the intimate link between 'arrival' and 'departure,' anthropologist Avtar Brah (1996, pp. 192–193) defines diaspora space as a concept that 'places the discourse of "home" and "dispersion" in creative tension, *inscribing a homing desire while simultaneously critiquing discourses of fixed origins*' (italics in original). Brah's formulation of homing desire, which she argues 'is not the same thing as desire for a "homeland"' (ibid., p. 180), challenges the emphasis placed on the politics of ethno-national origins and strong ties to the native country in diaspora studies. The desire to reconstruct home in diaspora space then transgresses the yearning for a return to the place of origin; it is about 'the desire to feel at home achieved by physically and symbolically reconstituting spaces which provide some kind of ontological security' (Fortier, 2001, p. 409). In this sense, diasporic consciousness is in a constant state of flux within the shifting interstices of uprootedness and attachment. Muslim diaspora space, as a conceptual category, takes its impetus from such liminal spaces and brings to light a literary site in which fixed notions of home, cultural identity and Muslimness can be coded and decoded. In reconceptualising 'Muslim diaspora' through a literary lens, my aim is not to erase religious subjectivity; rather, I caution against the reduction of the Muslim figure to a single ideological element. Muslim diaspora space as a mode of analysis, I suggest, brings to light the ways in which writers of Muslim origin transgress the generic theme of 'East Meets West', emphasising authorial intention to refuse polarisations encrypted in the signs of 'nation', 'Islam' and 'the West.'

Both Abu-Jaber and Shafak's oeuvres are characterised by a preoccupation with questions of belonging, displacement and Muslimness. Several excellent studies have analysed *Crescent*, drawing attention to the deconstruction of dominant narratives about Arab and Arab American identity in Abu-Jaber's writing (see, for example, Fadda-Conrey, 2006; Al-Joulan, 2010). Although Shafak's works, particularly *The Bastard of Istanbul* (2006) and *10 Minutes 38 Seconds in This Strange World* (2019), which was shortlisted for the 2019 Booker Prize, have received critical attention (Simon, 2015; Atayurt-Fenge, 2017; Saeed and Zain, 2018), little has been written on her debut in English, *The Saint of Incipient Insanities*. Re-reading *Crescent* and *The Saint* contrapuntally, through the lens of Muslim diaspora space, I suggest, can offer an even more nuanced understanding of their complex representations of Muslim subjectivities.

As Muslims are subjected to greater media and political scrutiny, the perception of Muslim identities still relies heavily on the assumption that Islam can be defined 'by means of a handful of recklessly general and repeatedly deployed clichés' (Said, 1981, p. 11). Roy (2004) aptly calls the media and policy-induced prejudice against Muslim populations 'the Western Approach', a culturalist approach that prevails on both sides of the Atlantic despite contextual differences. Although Muslims, Arabs and Middle Easterners have already been wary of potential hostility from the larger society since 9/11, the common Western approach popularised by state leaders to 'control' Muslim communities has assumed new dimensions recently under a global rise in neo-nationalism and xenophobic rhetoric across the United States and Europe. In light of growing Islamophobia, Muslims are expected to perform a type of Muslimness that affirms their loyalty to the larger society by defending, explaining or justifying their Muslimness. As a result, Muslimness as a cultural and a spiritual marker is emptied of its ontological depth, and, as Gianni (2016, p. 5) argues, 'the default position of Muslims' subjectivity is being bad, but they can become "good" if proven "good," namely if they are recognised as such by non-Muslims'. The conflation of Muslimness and radical Islam plays a key role in Islamophobic discourses that interpellate Muslim subjects into the good Muslim/bad Muslim framework. This fusion further elides the conflicting patterns of identity reconfiguration, occluding alternative articulations of Muslimness. In other words, Muslimness, as represented and articulated by Muslims themselves, is continually disrupted by their stereotypical representations as violent, radical and oppressed in the mainstream media. Despite the drastic increase in anti-Muslim hostilities in the United States and Europe,[1] the sociopolitical discourse has yet to shift to constructive discussions that highlight the diverse voices of Muslims. Conversely, Muslim identities continue to be homogenised as fundamentally orthodox and threatening.

Diaspora as a particular form of migration can be illuminating in understanding the shifting notions of Muslimness, although little work has approached 'Muslim diaspora' and the positionality of Muslims within it from a pluralistic cultural studies approach. The majority of the existing literature on Islam focuses on Muslim populations in minority contexts in relation to exile and connection to the homeland and/or to a prescriptive and restrictive mode of Islam (Metcalf, 1996; Jenkins, 1999; Landau, 2010; Takim, 2018). Similarly, the small number of studies on the theoretical potentials of the concept have predominantly examined its scope and limitations through a historical, social science perspective. Some scholars emphasise ethno-nationalism as a primordial constituent of diaspora (see, for example, Sheffer, 2006; Wald, 2008); in this sense, the notion of a collective Muslim identity lends itself to a variety of paradoxical questions rather than to reality. For others, the formation of a shared Muslim identity is intimately linked with transnational Islam, operating within the realm of political Islam (Yadlin, 2002; Kundnani, 2014). The overwhelming emphasis on the axis of political Islam and ethno-national clusters eclipses the large number of Muslims – from emerging queer and gay voices to 'lapsed' and agnostic Muslims – who fall between the discursive cracks in current discussions. In this context, I suggest that contemporary fiction by writers of Muslim origin offers critical insights into debates and scholarship on Muslim subjectivities.

The pivotal role artistic forms of expression play in shaping collective perceptions about immigrants and diaspora communities has been studied extensively (White, 1995; Appadurai, 1996; Král, 2009). As Seyhan (2001, p. 7) shows, 'ultimately, every theory of postcolonial, transnational, or diasporic literature and art is most convincingly articulated and performed by works of literature and art themselves'. Nevertheless, neo-orientalist narratives that draw on Orientalist tropes about Islam have gained unprecedented popularity since *The Satanic Verses* controversy and 9/11. Gendered violence and 'radical Islam' underlie these narratives, which are framed and marketed to appeal to the modern Western reader. Though an increasing number of contemporary writers of Muslim origin investigate the multifaceted nature of Muslimness, 'they do not enjoy equal exposure' (Morey, 2018, p. 28). This emerging creative collectivity is reflective of the social trends and patterns within Muslim communities across North America and Europe, with Muslim individuals and communities uniting around 'the urgent contemporary and common concerns and grievances that these diasporic communities experience in relation to "the host countries they now live"' (Moghissi, 2006, p. 5). Writers of Muslim origin in this context constitute a diasporic collectivity, not because of shared ethnicity, practice or commitment but because they participate in overlapping reconfigurations of Muslimness in contemporary literary imaginations.

Ahmed (2015, p. 197) reconceptualises Islam as a phenomenon 'whereby and wherein truth and meaning are constituted and distributed in particular ways and are not adequately captured or apprehended by the concept of religion'. When religion rather than truth or meaning is the primary lens through which we understand Muslimness, he posits, we tend to overlook 'central ways in which Muslims have conceptualised being Muslim' (ibid., p. 201). In this spirit, the literary reimagining of Muslimness reflects a sense of collectivity that incorporates a wide range of relations to Islam – from pious to non-practising – against the backdrop of the inflammatory rhetoric of othering. Abu-Jaber and Shafak provide a case in point for the alternative ways in which diasporic Muslim subjectivity is being reimagined as innately diverse, complex and synchronously Islamic. *Crescent* and *The Saint* present multifaceted Muslim characters making connections across ethnic and racial differences, extending the connection among Muslims into the wider society. In this diaspora space, I argue, the processes by which the characters redefine their Muslimness are closely linked to the characters' desire to feel at home in diaspora.

Focused on immigrant characters from Muslim countries, *The Saint* is concerned with the complexities of diasporic experience, faith and belonging beyond ethnic and national identities. The novel follows the curious trajectory of Ömer Sipahioğlu, who relocates to Boston from Turkey to pursue his doctorate. Ömer's first few days in the United States mirror the realities of a newly arrived international student; he strives to find housing, feels a pang of longing for his friends and family at times and is befuddled with the switch to English. Through its protagonist's trials and tribulations in Turkey and the United States, Shafak masterfully brings together multilayered characters of different backgrounds and origins: two graduate students of Muslim origin, Ömer from Turkey and Abed from Morocco; their roommate Piyu, a devout Catholic Spaniard who dates Alegre, a second-generation Mexican American; and Gail, a quirky, queer Jewish American. Ömer's abrupt marriage to Gail, who reconstructs her identity every couple of years, initiates his long-suppressed meditations on identity and religion.

In her discussion of diaspora space, Brah (1996, p. 193) calls into question the emphasis placed on 'the traumas of separation and dislocation' in studies on diaspora communities. Without a doubt, displacement is an integral part of the diasporic experience, but she adds that diasporas are also 'the sites of hope and new beginnings' (ibid.). For Brah, diasporic consciousness oscillates between the tension of home and dispersion and loss and hope, inscribing a homing desire that emerges within the interstices of 'stability' and 'mobility'. The complexity of affiliation for diasporic subjects is reflected in Ömer's vacillation between excitement and sheer terror during his journey. His ontological struggle is emblematically triggered on the transcontinental flight from Istanbul to Boston. Ömer finds himself wallowing in complexity: 'what was he doing, where was he going, why was he leaving his country, what difference would it make to have a Ph.D. in political science in America' (Shafak, 2004, p. 77). However, his reflection soon gives way to 'a set of uplifting decisions' about being more mindful, studious and confident in Boston, replacing his anxieties with a desire to rebuild himself. This shift in perspective occurs precisely 'somewhere above the Atlantic Ocean' (ibid., p. 77), which serves as a cogent symbol of the realm of the beyond, where the established dichotomies between centrality and peripherality are suspended, eventually to be replaced and recreated within the 'interstitial passage between fixed identifications' which creates 'a cultural hybridity that entertains difference without an assumed or imposed hierarchy' (Bhabha, 1994, p. 5). 'The Atlantic Ocean' as a representation of deterritorialised spaces occupied by immigrants foreshadows the theme of a homing desire that emerges in a transnational juncture throughout the novel. In particular, the lens of Muslim diaspora space brings to focus the ways in which its Muslim protagonists Ömer and Abed recognise not only the importance of a point of origin but also of connections beyond ethnic, national and sectarian identities in the spaces of inhabitance they call 'home'.

At first, Ömer's homing desire does not stipulate a point of origin, as he seeks to erase his Muslimness as well as his Turkishness through 'the privileged pleasure of being a nobody' in a foreign nation (Shafak, 2004, p. 52). Once he settles in Boston, however, he vacillates between affirming and negating his Turkish Muslim diasporic identity. The difficult process of 'arriving' and integrating into a new culture and language, along with the stereotypes against which he and his roommates battle (ibid., p. 111), reminds him of his indelible foreignness as a Muslim and a Middle Easterner. What emerges out of this identity affirming and negating dichotomy is a discernible sense of loss illustrated by Ömer's relation to the umlaut on his name. As he drunkenly tells Abed one night, he will 'put the dots of my name back to their place'; 'Back in Turkey he used to be Ömer Sipahioğlu … here in America he had become an Omar Sipahioglu' (ibid., p. 5), referring to the more common Arab version of his name. As the suggestive title of his dissertation indicates, 'Blood, Brain and Belonging: Nationalism and the Intellectuals in the Middle East' (ibid., p. 218), Ömer's attempts to debunk the paradigm of identity is futile. In a conversation with Abed and Piyu painted with 'this common shade named *The Difficulty of Being a Non-American in America*' (ibid., p. 108, italics in original), he states 'When you are a foreigner, you can't be your humble self anymore. I am my nation, my place of birth. I am everything except me' (ibid., p. 110). Ömer's reflection points to the complex ways in which the tension between home and dispersion inscribes a homing desire that does not necessarily imply a yearning for the homeland. If a homing desire is 'centrally about our political and personal struggles over the regulation of belonging' (Brah, 1996, p. 192), Ömer's relationship to Muslimness and Turkishness in the United States is mediated by his socially, politically and historically specific lived realities. An analysis of this process of homing desire through the lens of Muslim diaspora space reveals how Muslimness becomes intertwined with the theme of displacement and belonging in the novel.

Shafak places Ömer's and Abed's Muslim identification at the heart of their homing desires, as she brings forth interaction among Muslims and interactions between Muslims and the wider society, as illustrated by Ömer's and Abed's friendship and their connection with Piyu, Alegre and Gail. In Brah's formulation, homing desire emerges in a diaspora space where 'the configurations of power that differentiate diasporas internally' also 'situate them in relation to one another' (ibid., p. 209). Inhabited by immigrants, refugees, international students, as well as long-settled populations, a diaspora space that is specifically Muslim shifts the focus from the dichotomies between the majority and the minority, as well as the secular and the religious, towards a contact zone that is marked by diversity, multi-axial locationality and dynamic interaction. Shafak, for instance, draws on the conflict between the secular and the religious that dominates contemporary debates on Muslim subjectivities to highlight its totalising tendencies. The juxtaposition of Ömer, a 'lapsed' Muslim, and Abed, whom Ömer defines as 'a spider-headed Muslim' (Shafak, 2004, p. 13), adds levity to the narrative while allowing Shafak to address the inimical nature of these terms. Ömer explains that spider-headed is 'the Turkish expression for people like you … long-behind-the-times, conservative, old-style, traditionalist' (ibid., p. 13). Befuddled, Abed retorts, 'That means pious in my book. I am a pious Muslim whereas you are a lost one' (ibid., p. 14). Such exchanges between Ömer and Abed – at the beginning – are crucial within the context of Muslim diaspora space, for they provide a springboard through which the text initiates its deconstruction of the static modes of understanding Muslimness.

As the narrative delves deeper into the intersecting diasporic experiences of Ömer and Abed, the drastic shift in the characters' perception of 'conservative' and 'lost' is amplified. Although Ömer remains a 'lapsed' Muslim throughout the novel, he recognises that he is indeed a traditionalist at times (ibid., p. 108). In a similar vein, Abed ceases to assert the hegemony of a pious self as 'true Muslimness' as he does the difficult work of negotiating his accountability to Islamic norms and ideals (ibid., p. 342). Ömer's drinking habits do not render him blasphemous, for he will always remain Abed's 'Muslim brother' (ibid., p. 148); likewise, Abed's decision to sexually experiment does not make him 'not-Muslim-enough' (ibid., p. 348). As Abed tells Ömer when his mother, during her visit, insists on sacrificing a ram in Boston, 'Omar [*sic*], my brother. You should help me. No matter what, you are a Muslim, right?' (ibid., p.198). Despite his agnosticism, Ömer is indeed a Muslim, as the narrator emphasises his Muslim cultural identity with the phrase 'a born Muslim' (ibid., p. 11). Ömer and Abed's subsequent adventures highlight not only the solidarity between the two characters as diasporic Muslims but also foreshadow the ways they redefine the meaning of Muslimness, challenging the mainstream perception of Islam. Ömer's 'nominal' Muslimness, for instance, is heightened in the diaspora, becoming a constitutive part of his identity. As exemplified in the slaughter episode, Ömer and Abed redefine *halal* and *haram* (ibid., p. 199). Such a reconfiguration may challenge traditional formulations of Islam by interaction with realities in diaspora spaces through 'the lived experience of locality' (Brah, 1996, p. 192). Despite the agonising machinations of diasporic experience, the protagonists begin to reconstruct a new sense of being at home within the interstices of uprootedness and attachment, Muslimness as religion and cultural identity. The instability of migratory movement in this context opens up the space, the 'rim of an inbetween reality'

(Bhabha, 1992, p. 148), in which they can redefine Islamic norms as they relate to their homing desires. Muslimness as a living reality rather than a prescriptive belief system inscribes a point of origin which enables Ömer and Abed to 'celebrate a beginning which adds to and fertilises further multiple points of other displacements' (Al Deek, 2016, p. 20). However, it is not until the end when Gail commits suicide in Istanbul that Shafak's characters begin to perceive their displacement(s) as the fertile ground for new modes of being and belonging.

As Yazıcıoğlu (2009, p. 61) argues, Gail's suicidal attitude in the novel 'recalls the eternally displaced Jew'. Perennially locked in the absence of a place of origin and a family, Gail is paradoxically fixed within the paradigm of interstiality. Gail 'free-floats and claims no historical specificity, belonging everywhere by virtue of belonging nowhere' (Al Deek, 2016, p. 21). The last chapter takes us to the Bosporus Bridge in Istanbul located in between 'the East' and 'the West' – a signifier of the liminal spaces in which most migrants find themselves. Gail's desire for 'the inbetween' is emphasised as Gail passes the bridge with her husband Ömer, and she thinks to herself, 'this inbetweendom was the right place, and this very moment was the right time to die' (Shafak, 2004, p. 347). The narrative then shifts to Ömer and their friends to mark the very moment they all simultaneously negotiate uprootedness and attachment. As tragic as it is, Gail's suicide – an attempt to occupy the-in-between-spaces – paradoxically emerges as a celebration of a beginning for Ömer and Abed. During Gail's fall from the bridge, we are offered a glimpse into a new beginning for Abed. For the first time, he breaks away from Islamic ideals as prescribed in religious texts when he returns to be with a love interest at the laundromat, undergoing 'a subtle loosening of the moorings that tied him into his homeland' (ibid., p. 348). The narrator explains, 'Not that he felt less connected to his life in Morocco now. But somehow he felt more connected to his life in the United States' (ibid., p. 348). In this context, the diasporic experience does not inscribe his homing desire through 'a wish to return to a "place of origin"' (Brah, 1996, p. 193) or to a pure form of Islam. Instead, Abed's homing desire is constituted through his acceptance of his multiple positionalities as a Muslim Moroccan man living in Boston; neither his Muslimness nor his Moroccan identity is erased in this process. His identity as Muslim Moroccan thus moves beyond the confines of locality and scripture towards transnational levels of signification within the context of Muslim diaspora space.

Similarly, Ömer's travels between Boston and Turkey become a rite of passage towards self-realisation, serving as a meditation on the complex processes of cultural identity formation. As he watches Gail on the bridge, 'a fleeting consolation crosses [his] mind. She won't die ... People do not commit suicide on other people's soil, and this is not her homeland' (Shafak, 2004, p. 359). 'But did she ever have one?' the narrator interjects, 'Who is the real stranger – the one who lives in a foreign land and knows he belongs elsewhere or the one who lives the life of a foreigner in her native land and has nowhere else to belong' (ibid., pp. 350–351). The traumatic incident that unfolds in his native country reveals to Ömer that the oscillation between multiple identities and conflicting loyalties brings forth a sense of loss, as well as a sense of newness and belonging. Although he feels detached from Turkey occasionally, Ömer recognises his Turkishness and his Muslim heritage as his point of origin, which, as opposed to a free-floating movement registers an orientation, a starting point, 'an identity's history, its gravitating "somewhere," as well as its simultaneous undergoing of transformation, its multiple metamorphoses' (Al Deek, 2016, p. 27). As Ömer and Abed reject fixed definitions of identity, ethnicity and religion in the novel, the diasporic connections they cultivate enable them to celebrate not only their shifting subjectivities but also the 'Eastern ethos' (Shafak, 2004, p. 108) around which they were raised. Ömer's and Abed's deepening connection across their differences forms an essential part of their homing desires, symbolising the vast possibilities that can arise in a diaspora space. In this sense, they are analogous to 'birds of migration' that 'initially detached from their own flocks to migrate to faraway lands', and 'once there, they flocked into detachments' (ibid., p. 81). 'Flock[ing] into detachments' in this context points to 'new sites of belonging' (Friedman, 1998, p. 68) that emphasise the visibility of sameness rather than differences among Muslim communities, and by extension among other diasporic groups as well as local populations.

Abu-Jaber's *Crescent* delves deeper into the in-between-difference spaces occupied by Muslim diasporic characters. Like *The Saint*, 'Muslimness' provides the subtext within which *Crescent* operates its leitmotif: displacement, cross-cultural connections and homing desire. The novel chronicles the intertwined stories of Han, an Iraqi professor of Islamic history and Arabic literature at UCLA, and Sirine, a second-generation Iraqi American chef. Forced to leave Iraq due to his political publications against Saddam Hussein, Han grapples with the irrevocable loss of his home and family. He meets Sirine at Nadia's Café, a Lebanese restaurant in Irangeles, where she starts working after a long career in French, Italian and Los Angeles restaurants. As Han helps Sirine reclaim her Muslim Iraqi heritage and Sirine introduces him to American culture, the notions of Muslimness become linked to the protagonists' homing desires throughout the novel.

Friedman (1998, p. 68) argues that the overemphasis placed on ethno-national and cultural difference in diaspora studies obfuscates 'interactive mediations between difference, the blending as well as clashing that takes place in the contact zones between difference'. She thus shifts the theoretical focus to the spaces in between difference, 'the dialogic between sameness and difference, between mimesis and alterity' (ibid., p. 103). Like Brah, Friedman emphasises contradiction as a crucible to the formation of diasporic subjectivity. Re-reading Han and Sirine's love story through the lens of Muslim diaspora space points to the ways the novel privileges experiences of 'homing diaspora' over an ethnic, national and sectarian kinship. Muslim diaspora space in the novel emerges as a paradoxical space of possibilities, which allows for new expressions of home and Muslimness.

Nadia's Café, the main setting of the novel, serves as a cogent metaphor of such spaces in between difference. As 'a little flavor of home' (Abu-Jaber, 2003, p. 22) for the students and immigrants from the Middle East, the café registers a profound shift from the dominant discourse on extremism, religiosity and nationality towards Muslimness as an episteme that is ambivalent, diverse and cultural. The names of its regulars from Egypt and Kuwait – Schmaal, Jenoob, Shark and Gharb – mean, respectively, North, South, East and West (Fadda-Conrey, 2006, p. 195). This foreshadows its importance as a space of encounter where differences are reconciled, highlighting the multifaceted nature of Middle Eastern identity. The plot unfolds against the backdrop of the Iraqi War, and the novel's references to Islamophobic rhetoric are subtle yet powerful. 'Sometimes Sirine used to scan the room and imagine the word *terrorist*', the narrator states, 'but all that came back to her were words like *lonely*, and *young*' and 'infinitely vulnerable and tender' (Abu-Jaber, 2003, p. 22). While the novel sets forth the cultural and geographical diversity of its Muslim and Middle Eastern characters, its emphasis is on the ways in which they reconcile their ethno-national and religious differences. In this spirit, the café's portrayal evokes a sense of home, with its 'little TV permanently tuned to the all-Arabic station, with news from Qatar … Kuwait, endless Egyptian movies, Bedouin soap operas in Arabic, and American soap operas with Arabic subtitles' (ibid., pp. 22–23); with stacks of textbooks and newspapers 'from home … Algeria, Bethlehem, Baghdad' (ibid., pp. 195–196). Through its occupants of diverse backgrounds – Middle Easterners, Muslims, Christians, the Mexican chef Victor Hernandez and Californians alike – Nadia's Café provides the context that allows Muslim Middle Eastern characters to relate to one another as well as to the larger community.

The novel draws on Muslimness as a cultural and a spiritual signifier, with its characters reclaiming Islam as a powerful symbol of the Middle Eastern cultural ethos. For instance, despite the café's owner Um-Nadia's agnosticism and the large number of Christian customers, there are special menus and celebrations at Nadia's at both Christmas and Ramadan – because 'they all like to eat the traditional foods prepared throughout the Middle East to celebrate the nightly fast-breaking during Ramadan' (ibid., p. 273). The café is resignified as a diaspora space that is highlighted by Muslim and Christian rituals when 'Muslims all over town ... loiter[ing] outside and waiting for tables, Iranians, Saudis, Palestinians, Lebanese, even Malaysians, Pakistanis, and Croatians' (ibid., p. 297) during Ramadan; and the next day, the café is lit with a string of Christmas lights (ibid., p. 280). By highlighting the idea of Islam as a way of identification for both Christians and Muslims (Field, 2006, p. 220), Abu-Jaber calls into question dichotomies that propagate a single, religious vision of Islam. It is against this background that Sirine and Han's subjectivities undergo consistent transformation in the processes of meaning-making, interaction and expression.

Through Han and Sirine's quest for home, Abu-Jaber further maps the intersections of Muslimness, which evoke memories of home and diasporic spaces as they are articulated in terms of a homing desire. Han's agonising distance from home prompts Sirine to revisit her own memories – the absence of her parents, her forgotten ties to Iraq and her Islamic heritage. On one occasion, Han meditates on the difficulty of grasping 'the thought of never returning' (Abu-Jaber, 2003, p. 68). His reflection strikes a chord with Sirine who later tells him, 'I guess I'm always looking for my home, a little bit. Even though I live here, I have this feeling that my real home is somewhere else somehow' (ibid., p. 132). As Han delineates the life he left behind – the vivid streets of Iraq, the picturesque mountains, the chaotic *souk* – Sirine recalls the painful memories of her parents' continuous move around the globe as American Red Cross employees and their death in Africa. Han thus inspires Sirine to explore her familial and cultural ties while she offers Han a multifarious image of American and Arab American culture. Even though Han initially retains a firm connection to his homeland, he soon moves beyond the dream for a homeward journey towards a homing desire.

His longing to feel at home is instantiated as he seeks to bridge the emotional and cultural gap between Sirine and himself, which in turn helps him transgress the barriers between himself and American society on a larger scale. As he tells Sirine on a beach in Los Angeles, 'For a moment, I forgot that this was America. I was on the banks of the Tigris. I haven't forgotten any of it ... Since I've met you – it's starting to return. I'm beginning to feel it and see it' (Abu-Jaber, 2003, pp. 210–211). Han articulates his diasporic existence through absences – of the sight, taste and memory of Iraq – until he meets Sirine. His journey back to Sirine and California at the end of the novel, after his sudden return to Iraq to tend to his sick mother, points at a shift from his perception of home-as-homeland towards a homing desire detached from the spatial concept of location. Han's 'home coming' at the end signifies his reconfiguration of home within 'the motions of journeying between homes, of hailing ghosts from the past, of leaving and staying put, of continual reprocessing of what home is/was/maybe' (Fortier, 2001, p. 402). Since Islam is 'what shaped [his] character and mind and gave [him] hope for the future' (Abu-Jaber, 2003, p. 177), his homing desire also involves a constant transformation of what Muslimness is/was/maybe. Al Deek (2016, p. 58) argues that 'a translated cultural identity is one that does not totally break from the past' but rather is rerouted at the site of intercultural encounter. As Han's cultural identity undergoes a cultural translation, 'Muslimness' emerges as the bind that ties him to his place of origin.

In a key episode, Sirine curiously asks Han about Islam during dinner 'after another glass of wine' (Abu-Jaber, 2003, p. 80). In response, Han elucidates the interior of mosques, recites the *athan* and demonstrates the genuflections as an inebriated Sirine joins him. The contradictory references – two opposite sexes drinking wine, getting intimate and praying – overtly challenge traditional prescriptions of Islam. This scene, however, demonstrates that Han's displacements allow him to articulate new modes of Muslimness as he moves across borders. Every time his 'old way of being' is translated into new contexts, so is the normative way of being a Muslim. 'I haven't prayed in some time', he states, 'I'm out of practice' (ibid., p. 80). Having read a letter sent to Han from Iraq that discussed his strict adherence to Islamic principles, Sirine finds his statement intriguing. When she asks him later whether he believes 'your religion defines who you are', he stresses the complexities of affiliation for a diasporic subject. 'I'm no longer a believer', he says, 'but I still consider myself a Muslim. In some ways, my religion is even more important to me because of that' (ibid., p. 182). Han's emphasis on the importance of Muslimness despite his agnosticism is crucial within the context of Muslim diaspora space, for he offers an alternative vision of Muslimness. He no longer subscribes to any one of the scholastic, philosophical, or theological approaches evoked by the concept of Islam; instead, he engages with a combination of various registers to generate the meaning of his diasporic self through 'unifying contradictions of Islam' (Ahmed, 2015, p. 506). 'The fact of exile', Han stresses, 'is bigger than everything else in my life' (Abu-Jaber, 2003, p. 183). He does so by clicking his prayer beads, which represents his desire to establish a series of connections between his Muslim and diasporic identity. Moreover, Sirine's journey to explore her long-forgotten Muslim identity through her visit to a Sufi dervish meeting (ibid., p. 264) and her participation in a 'Women in Islam' meeting (ibid., p. 186) underscore Muslimness as a process of meaning-making for both characters. Han reconfigures what it means to be a Muslim in a new setting in the absence of Islamic signifiers such as the call to prayer and the sight of minarets, all of which remind him of home. Like Ömer and Abed, Han's homing desire does not imply a geographical return but suggests 'a return to oneself, a return to history, so that we understand what exactly happened, why it happened and who we are' (Said, 2000, p. 22). With the help of Sirine, he reclaims the contradictory and paradoxical nature of his identity that finds its articulation in a diaspora space in which the concepts of Muslimness and Americanness are redefined.

Both novels highlight Muslimness as a discursive process to which the production and accommodation of internal contradiction are fundamental. As Abu-Jaber and Shafak explore the lives of their Muslim migrant protagonists, they present a mode of Muslimness that fluctuates and evolves through intercultural exchange(s) and displacement(s). While these new forms of Muslimness challenge orthodox Islam, they also have the potential to unsettle the established notions of national identities in Europe and North America. According to Hassan (2012), it is often the double-bind in which Muslims find themselves that gives rise to new articulations of Islam. 'Despite the reckless bombast of Islamophobes and Islamists', Hassan (ibid., p. 87) writes, 'the many Islams continue their migrations, moving into the future, giving rise to newness as they combine with other forms of culture'. In this context, where the heterogeneity of Muslim populations is still overlooked, Muslim diaspora space as a conceptual tool *magnifies* how Muslim writers contest traditional categories of not only Islam but also 'Western-ness'. The estrangement of Ömer, Abed, Han and Sirine does not make them turn away from their new countries; on the contrary, through the diasporic connections that they build, they inscribe their Muslimness and 'foreignness' into social, cultural and geographical spaces in the Global North.

Focusing on imagination and self-representation as a key sociocultural force in the context of Muslim Middle Eastern diasporas, this chapter has demonstrated that Shafak and Abu-Jaber create diasporic contexts that allow diverse Muslim characters to interact among themselves and relate to the larger society. An examination of Muslim diasporic cultural and literary expression,

I have suggested, means reimagining the processes of production, consumption and circulation as situated at a point of dynamic encounter where Muslimness is both transculturalised and translocalised through the experiences and practices of those who identify as Muslim. This chapter highlights the urgency in diaspora and literary studies to generate more conversations on the following interlocking questions: What are some of the ways in which Muslim diasporic texts offer alternative visions of Islam and alternative modes of being and belonging? How has the notion of Muslimness informed diasporic literary production? Can new approaches to reading Muslim narratives help migrants and citizens of Muslim origin make sense of the chaos and ongoing shifts that characterise contemporary experience? Given the growing trend of Islamophobia and anti-immigration rhetoric today, such questions about Muslim subjectivities and Muslim diasporic artistic expression have never been more important.

Note

1 Texts such as Nafisi's *Reading Lolita in Tehran* (2003), which implies that Islam provides the source for the Iranian Islamic State's oppression; Hirsi Ali's *The Caged Virgin* (2004) and *Infidel* (Ali, 2006), which discuss Islam as the tyrannical force behind the dehumanisation of Muslim women; and Ahmed's *Disgraced* (2008), which depicts the practice of honor killings as inherently Islamic, all recycle negative representations of Islam.

References

Abu-Jaber, D. (2003) *Crescent*. New York: W.W. Norton & Company.
Ahmed, S. (2008) *Disgraced*. London: Headline.
Ahmed, S. (2015) *What Is Islam? The Importance of Being Islamic*. Princeton, NJ: Princeton University Press. Al Deek, A. (2016) *Writing Displacement*. London: Palgrave Macmillan.
Ali, A.H. (2004) *The Caged Virgin*. New York: Free Press.
Ali, A.H. (2006) *Infidel: My Life*. New York: Free Press.
Al-Joulan, N.A. (2010) 'Diana Abu-Jaber's *Arabian Jazz*: hybridizing Arab-American feminism and literature', *Mosaic*, 43(4), pp. 69–85.
Atayurt-Fenge, Z. (2017) '"This is a world of spectacles": cyclical narratives and circular visionary formations in Elif Shafak's *The Gaze*', *Critique*, 58(3), p. 287.
Appadurai, A. (1996) *Modernity at Large*. Minneapolis, MN: University of Minnesota Press.
Bayrakli, E. and Hafez, F. (2019) 'The state of Islamophobia in Europe in 2018,' *European Islamophobia*. Available at: www.islamophobiaeurope.com/wp-content/uploads/2019/09/EIR_2018.pdf (accessed 12 January 2020).
Bhabha, H. (1992) 'The world and the home', *Social Text*, 31(32), pp. 141–153.
Bhabha, H. (1994) *The Location of Culture*. London: Routledge.
Brah, A. (1996) *Cartographies of Diaspora: Contesting Identities*. New York: Routledge.
Council on American-Islamic Relations (2018) 'CAIR report: anti-Muslim bias incidents, hate crimes spike in second quarter of 2018'. Available at: www.cair.com/press_releases/cair-report-anti-muslim-bias-incidents-hate-crimes-spike-in-second-quarter-of-2018/ (accessed 20 January 2020).
Fadda-Conrey, C. (2006) 'Arab American literature in the ethnic borderland: cultural intersections in Diana Abu-Jaber's *Crescent*', *MELUS*, 31(4), pp. 187–205.
Field, R.E. (2006) 'A prophet in her own town: an interview with Diana Abu-Jaber', *MELUS*, *31*(4), pp. 207–225.
Fortier, A.M. (2001) '"Coming home": queer migrations and multiple evocations of home', *European Journal of Cultural Studies*, 4(4), pp. 405–424.
Friedman, S.S. (1998) *Mappings: Feminism and the Cultural Geographies of Encounter*. Princeton, NJ: Princeton University Press.
Gianni, M. (2016) 'Muslims' integration as a way to defuse the "Muslim Question",' *Critical Research on Religion*, 4(1), pp. 21–36.
Hassan, S.D. (2012) 'Infinite hijra: migrant Islam, Muslim American literature, and the anti-mimesis of the Taqwacores', in *Culture, Diaspora, and Modernity in Muslim Writing*. London: Routledge.

Jenkins, E. Jr (1999) *The Muslim Diaspora: A Comprehensive Chronology of the Spread of Islam in Asia, Africa, Europe and the Americas*. Jefferson, NC: MacFarland & Company.

Král, F. (2009) *Critical Identities in Contemporary Anglophone Diasporic Literature*. London: Palgrave Macmillan.

Kundnani, A. (2014) *The Muslims Are Coming*. New York: Verso.

Landau, J.M. (2010) 'Diaspora nationalism: the Turkish case', in *The Call of the Homeland: Diaspora Nationalisms, Past and Present*. Leiden: Brill.

Metcalf, B.D. (1996) *Making Muslim Space in North America and Europe*. Berkeley, CA: University of California Press.

Moghissi, H. (ed.) (2006) *Muslim Diaspora: Gender, Culture and Identity*. New York: Routledge.

Morey, P. (2018) *Islamophobia and the Novel*. New York: Columbia University Press.

Nafisi, A. (2003) *Reading Lolita in Tehran*. New York: Random House.

Roy, O. (2004) *Globalized Islam*. New York: Columbia University Press.

Saeed, A. and Zain, F. (2018) 'Texts within text: an intertextual study of Elif Shafak's *The Forty Rules of Love*', *NUML Journal of Critical Inquiry*, 16(1), pp. 29–45.

Said, E.W. (1981) *Covering Islam*. New York: Pantheon Books.

Said, E.W. (2000) 'Edward Said talks to Jacqueline Rose, interviewed by Jacqueline Rose', in *Edward Said and the Work of the Critic*. Durham, NC: Duke University Press.

Seyhan, A. (2001) *Writing outside the Nation*. Princeton, NJ: Princeton University Press.

Shafak, E. (2004) *The Saint of Incipient Insanities*. New York: Farrar, Straus and Giroux.

Sheffer, G. (2006) 'Transnationalism and ethnonational diasporism', *Diaspora: A Journal of Transnational Studies*, 15(1), pp. 121–144.

Simon, A. (2015) 'Mythology, taboo and cultural identity in Elif Shafak's *The Bastard of Istanbul*', *Postcolonialist*, 2(2), pp. 111–121.

Takim, L. (2018) 'Shi'ism in the American diaspora: challenges and opportunities', *Journal of Muslim Minority Affairs*, 38(1), pp. 73–86.

Wald, K. (2008). 'Homeland interests, hostland politics: politicized ethnic identity among Middle Eastern heritage groups in the United States', *The International Migration Review*, 42(2), pp. 273–301.

White, P. (1995) 'Geography, literature and migration', in King, R., Connell, J. and White, P. (eds) *Writing across Worlds: Literature and Migration*. London: Routledge, pp. 1–18.

Yadlin, R. (2002) 'The Muslim diaspora in the West', in Moshe, M. and Sheffer, G. (eds) *Middle Eastern Minorities and Diasporas*. Sussex: Sussex Academic Press, pp. 219–230.

Yazıcıoğlu, Ö.Ö. (2009) 'Who is the other? Melting in the pot in Elif Shafak's *The Saint of Incipient Insanities* and *The Bastard of Istanbul*', *Litera*, 22(2), pp. 54–70.

31
THE ARMENIAN MIDDLE EAST
Boundaries, pathways and horizons

Sossie Kasbarian

Armenians and diaspora (studies)

In the last three decades, the concept of diaspora has attracted great interest from scholars across a number of disciplines and a range of area studies. In 1991, the pioneering *Diaspora – A Journal of Transnational Studies* was founded with Khachig Tölölyan at the helm. Tölölyan and other notable pioneers[1] set out a clear intellectual agenda and proceeded to carve out a space for the conceptual and empirical study of diaspora, while mindful of its inherent expansiveness as an idea and practice. Within the terrain that became known as diaspora studies, the Armenian case was considered one of the 'classical' diasporas, for whom living in diaspora was an intrinsic part of their pre-modern identity. For contemporary diaspora theorists, the Armenians met all the criteria of being a diaspora in the original usage, i.e. a forced displacement to multiple sites, and identified as a 'victim diaspora' (Cohen, 1997). The Armenians were conceptualised as a historical 'old' diaspora,[2] enduring and thriving in a global age, revived and reinvested by global trends and developments, the latter simultaneously giving rise to a proliferation of 'new' diasporas, groups that were previously defined as 'immigrant, expatriate, refugee, guest worker, exile community, overseas community, ethnic community' (Tölölyan, 1991, p. 4). The matching and resonance of the term to a post-modern, global age resulted in a remarkable phoenix-like rise of the once 'Other of the nation state' to 'exemplary communities of the transnational moment' (ibid., p. 5).

The connection between the Middle East and diaspora is ancient. The paradigmatic Jewish diaspora is of Middle Eastern origin and two other 'classical' diasporas, the Armenians and Greeks, are closely associated with the region and central to a historical understanding of the term. In the past three decades, a substantial scholarship has developed, founded on the triad of diaspora community, host state and homeland. This basic model has persisted in the social sciences in areas of study, ranging from migration and refugees studies to international relations, taking for granted a clear point of origin and a present site of residence. Arguably, the humanities are less fixated on static sites, recognising fluidity and context as defining features of long-established diasporas. This non-linear approach best allows for the intrinsic dynamism of long-established diasporas to be released and studied from within as well as from without – the emic and the etic (Tölölyan, 2007).

This chapter surveys the Armenian experience of the Middle East not simply through the traditional triadic prism, but by focusing on local Middle Eastern Armenian communities, each with their own particular situations and dynamics. This approach recognises the Armenian experience as an inherent part of societies, and not as temporary guests and immutable Others in a 'host state'. It also allows us to view the Armenians as a transnational people spread throughout the Middle East (and beyond), both rooted at home and routed through multiple orientations and connections. This framing considers the Armenian diaspora in the region through differentiated experiences, rather than in rigorous categories. It recognises the intrinsic fluidity of diaspora both as concept and practice, and the Middle East as a site that is living and vibrant. This research framework is a contribution towards a people-centred political sociology that engages with local, national and regional contexts.[3]

Armenians and the Middle East

Armenians have had a diasporic presence in the Middle East from ancient times, with multiple peaks and dips (Hovannisian, 1974; 1997) but the roots of the contemporary communities predominantly date to the 1915–1916 genocide perpetrated by the Ottoman state (Kevorkian, 2011; Suny, 2015). Today Middle Eastern Armenian communities, both discrete and connected to each other, embody all permutations of the contemporary diasporic experience. At the same time, they are connected to the 'step-homeland' (Kasbarian, 2016), the Republic of Armenia, not an ancestral land of origin but a site of potential migration for diasporans. Middle Eastern Armenians since the Soviet period have migrated to Armenia out of ideological commitment, or because of conflict in their homes in Iraq, Iran, Palestine, Lebanon, and most recently Syria (Pattie, 2004; Laycock, 2016; Kasbarian, 2016). Many of the latter did not ultimately stay in Armenia but emigrated to the West (usually to the United States or Canada) when the opportunity arose.

Within Middle East studies, Armenians have historically been largely absent, or considered outsiders and marginal (see, for example, Hourani, 1947). Studies of Armenians in the region are often framed around the premise that they are foreign to the region and therefore treated with suspicion, caution or exoticism; alternatively, they are subsumed within broader subjects like Christians or minorities of the region, thereby flattening their differentiated experiences and denying them voice. Studies of Armenian communities in the region have been criticised as insular in their approaches and concerns.[4] The Ottoman millet system and its modern-day forms in most Middle Eastern states have been a pivotal factor in perpetuating the idea of 'preserving' distinct, static (potentially reified and essentialist) identities, which has arguably served traditional Armenian religious and political leadership well (Barkey and Gavrilis, 2016). This has undoubtedly contributed to a trend in seeing the Armenians as intrinsically different from their non-Armenian neighbours in the region (Sanjian, 2001; Tchilingirian, 2015), but one could equally argue that this tendency is shared by other groups too. This is a region that has been viewed through the complex but tired lens of sectarianism for decades, often giving rise to self-perpetuating material realities which obscure histories of coexistence and conviviality.[5]

This insularity has shifted in recent years, reflecting the critical and postcolonial turn in the Western academy, and a new engagement with interdisciplinary research and emancipatory politics. The intellectual project to bring once peripheral histories into the mainstream, to excavate and articulate hidden and silenced voices and experiences, has inspired scholars to situate Armenians within mainstream histories of the region. Historians of the First World War, in particular, have been instrumental in repositioning Armenians as central to modern Middle

East history (Laycock, 2015; Rogan, 2015; Watenpaugh, 2015; Robson, 2017; White, 2017) There are also a number of ground-breaking recent studies on the Lebanese Armenian community, stressing their identity and agency as Lebanese citizens (Nucho, 2016; Nalbantian, 2020). Comparative surveys of the Armenians of the Middle East have been relatively rare, but reflect a gradual shift from a sense of existential and internalised threat from genocide survivors to relative security and belonging among their third- and fourth-generation descendants (Hovannissian, 1974; Sanjian, 2001; Tchilingirian, 2015).

Despite great strides, in grounding Armenians within Middle Eastern studies, the narrative of Armenians as outsiders persists. This is underpinned by a political undercurrent that depicts Armenians as interlopers; even in rooted communities like Lebanon, where the Armenians are part of the political fabric, there has been a normalisation of anti-Armenian hate speech in recent years permeating the public sphere, orchestrated and/or mobilised by Turkey extending its power base among certain Islamists affiliated to the Muslim Brotherhood and sympathisers of the AKP (Erdoğan's increasingly authoritarian, conservative Sunni ruling party, in power in Turkey since 2000) (Tashjian, 2020). The current wave of anti-Armenianness has been on display at least since the commemorations of the genocide in 2015 (Kasbarian, 2018) with certain Islamist leaders unironically simultaneously denying the genocide and calling for its resumption/completion while proclaiming solidarity with Turkey. This rhetoric also proliferates in social media, particularly around 24 April, the date when the genocide is commemorated annually (Tashjian, 2016). A recent *cause célèbre* concerned Nishan Der Haroutunian, the host of a popular television programme on Al Jadeed TV who responded strongly on air upon receiving a social media message from a viewer calling him 'a refugee and insidious foreigner'. This opened up the floodgates, resulting in anti-Armenian street protests in West Beirut on 11 June 2020, with Turkish and Lebanese flags on display among the anti-Armenian banners and slogans (Tashjian, 2020). Lebanese Armenians were unequivocally reminded of their vulnerability in the face of Turkish power projection. Such is the neo-Ottoman expansionism of the Turkish state, that Der Haroutunian is to stand trial for 'insulting Turkey' (Haddad, 2020). This suggests that regardless of significant scholarship, entrenched narratives and frameworks of analyses in Middle East studies still only allow a precarious and insecure space for Armenians as a liminal, intersectional, diasporic people.

This chapter is a brief survey of the Armenian diaspora in the Middle East context, situated at the intersection of Armenian studies, Middle East studies and diaspora studies. In this chapter, I draw on extensive field research in Lebanon, Turkey, Egypt and Armenia conducted from 2003–2017, as well as secondary sources and wider studies. My analysis situates the Armenian experience within studies of Middle East diasporas as set out by the research agenda of the last decade (Gorman and Kasbarian, 2015; Rowe, 2019), examining local contexts and situating them within wider trends and developments.

Foundations and framing

While there has been an Armenian presence in the Middle East since ancient times, the roots of contemporary Armenian communities predominantly date to the 1915 genocide perpetrated by the Young Turks. The mandate authorities estimated that by 1923, over 200,000 Armenian genocide survivors had passed through Aleppo (Watenpaugh, 2006, p. 281). Sanjian (2001, p. 154) writes that 'by the mid-1920s there were about 100,000 Armenian refugees and orphans settled in Syria, over 40,000 in Lebanon, some 10,000 in Iraq, a similar number in Palestine and Transjordan, and another 25,000 in Egypt.' Refugee camps were set up, eventually becoming Armenian neighbourhoods; Ottoman Armenia was 'reconstructed' in Syria and

Lebanon (Migliorino, 2008). Historians have written vividly about the survival, resilience and renaissance of these communities (ibid.; Payaslian, 2007). In the Syrian case, the Armenian community is described as having undergone a 'transformation from abject poverty into an urban proto-middle class' (Watenpaugh, 2006, p. 280). Crucially, at the same time, as noted by Panossian (2006, p. 29), modern Armenian diasporic identity was actively constructed: 'Under the leadership of competing organisations, a heterogeneous group of people ... were moulded into a relatively coherent community with a collective consciousness as a diasporic nation.' In this respect, it is important to acknowledge that modern Armenian diasporic identity is also a Middle Eastern identity, which was coalesced in post-Ottoman Arab state systems. Diaspora leaders and groups (re)emerged in this period of recuperation and recovery and continued to mould and lead the communities that grew out of them.

As the genocide is the foundation of the contemporary Armenian diaspora, it is important in any survey of the region to acknowledge the remnant Armenians in modern-day Turkey. The Armenians of Turkey are the descendants of this once significant 'loyal' Ottoman millet (*millet i sadika*) who stayed in their ancestral homeland as it violently transitioned from an empire to a republic that continues to consider them enemies and traitors. As such, they represent a unique community within the Armenian diaspora, one that has been under continuous existential threat. The community, currently estimated at around 50,000 Armenians, is one of the minorities of the Turkish state, occupying a precarious space founded on political and social pragmatism (Tchilingirian, 2016). Underlying the contemporary situation of the Armenians is the rupture of the 1915 genocide, a violence that is repeated in its 'symbolic' form in the language of denial and the militant and exclusionary nationalism permeating every layer of the state. This is a community that is in a permanent state of negotiation of its continuing coexistence in wider society and within a state that denies its history (Kasbarian, 2016).

Dating from medieval Islamic times (Dadoyan, 2011–2014), the Armenians have a long and distinguished history in Egypt that belies their small numbers. The modern community is composed of Armenians who trace their ancestry to distinct waves of arrivals – those who fled the massacres in Anatolia in the late nineteenth century, survivors of the 1915 genocide, more recent arrivals from neighbouring Arab countries, and arrivals from Armenia – all of whom joined older, established Armenian communities in Cairo and Alexandria, dating back centuries. For the Armenian diaspora, Egypt has historic importance, culturally, socially and politically. In the nineteenth century, Egypt was the Armenian epicentre in the Middle East and the site of prolific cultural production and intellectual activity. Venerable diaspora institutions were founded there, such as the Armenian General Benevolent Union (AGBU) in 1906 (by the son of Nubar Pasha – the Armenian first Prime Minister of Egypt, appointed in 1876) (Adalian, 1980; Al-Imam, 2003). At the same time, Armenians were part of the cosmopolitan urban landscape and active players in Egyptian cultural, economic, political and social life. After the revolution of 1952 and Nasser's nationalisation policies, the Armenians (and the other 'foreign communities') in Egypt started to mass migrate, most notably to the United States, Australia and Canada but also to (then Soviet) Armenia. The present-day community, which is thought to number less than 5,000, is considered to be a community in decline. As such, it is often evoked in the same resigned tone as previously vibrant and important communities that have faded away, like the Armenian communities in India or Ethiopia. Nonetheless, there is also reason to be hopeful that a community in its advanced 'golden years', which has considerable wealth and resources, can nurture new trajectories and communities in the region.

In contrast, the continuing importance of Lebanon for the Armenian diaspora cannot be over-stated (Nalbantian, 2020). Post-genocide Beirut became the undisputed 'centre' of the

Armenian diaspora, both due to the size of the community (peaking before the Civil War at 180,000), and its being recognised and actively engaged as an integral part of the burgeoning Lebanese state. Before the civil war, Beirut was the headquarters of the diaspora leadership, with the Catholicosate of Cilicia in Antelias and the three main political parties and institutions' nuclei based there, administering their satellites throughout the diaspora (Schahgaldian, 1979). It was also the hub of cultural production and intellectual life, producing priests, teachers, artists and intellectuals that, as diasporic agents, served the diaspora communities in the West. These gatekeepers of diasporic identity, as examples of governance, defined, shaped, led and maintained Armenian communities worldwide for decades (Migliorino, 2008). Indeed, Beirut as the heart of the diaspora flowed vitality and vigour into its transnational communities until the long civil war, which weakened the economy and led to the mass emigration (of all Lebanese) which continues today. The present-day community is vastly reduced and its structures are in decline. It is perhaps most useful to view the Lebanese community as one with enduring influence and significance, despite mass emigration and general decline, and one that has contributed to the planting and growing of new communities throughout the world. In that sense, it is an exemplary diaspora community, one that reproduces itself and grows in other environments, adapts and is strengthened by their new situation.

While having a shared history with the Lebanese case, the Syrian Armenian community has been decimated by the civil war which has been raging since 2011. The modern Syrian state was shaped by complex historical processes and dynamics between the French Mandate, the League of Nations, international humanitarian agencies, the Syrian nation (as envisioned by Syrian Arab nationalists) and refugee settlement. White (2017, p. 145) makes the point that Syria's refugees in the inter-war period (Armenians and other Christians, as well as Kurds and Assyrians) were 'a site for the articulation of the national and international (a sphere which was itself in construction in the period).' The newcomer Armenians were at first seen as a threat to the Syrian nation by Arab nationalists and a source of resentment, gradually becoming an important element in state-building. While treated as refugees, the Armenians were granted Syrian citizenship by the French authorities after 1925. Syrian Arab attitudes towards the Armenians changed over time and they were held as a positive example of a Syrian community (ibid., pp. 170–174); Syria became home. The Armenian population was around 125,000 in 1946, when Syria gained independence from the French Mandate, and perhaps as high as 150,000 in the 1960s (Migliorino, 2008, pp. 32–34, 89, 148). Tchilingirian's research (2015, p. 11) suggests the Syrian Armenian community peaked at 150,000 in 1975 and had reduced to 70,000 by 2008.[6] Many in the western Armenian diaspora consider the Syrian-Armenian community their 'mother community' from where they emigrated to the United States, Canada and South America, and have maintained both emotional and material links to Syria.[7]

The once strong and vibrant communities in Aleppo, Damascus, and smaller towns, have been ravaged by a seemingly endless war that has resulted in the worst humanitarian crisis of this century. The Syrian Armenians are among the 6.6 million citizens (UNCHR, n.d.) who have fled the country and sought refuge elsewhere. A significant number have done so in Armenia, either temporarily or with a view to staying. The Syrian Armenians in Armenia are the latest significant wave of diasporan Armenians seeking refuge from troubled homes in the Middle East. While it is unclear how many of these refugees will stay in Armenia in the long term, this case encapsulates many of the struggles and challenges faced by the Armenian diaspora in the Middle East. It is a useful lens to reflect on the concepts and realities that underpin a diaspora – questions of home, homeland, return, nostalgic longing and belonging – as well as the states and societies that they span.

Tradition and trends

As previously discussed, the post-Ottoman nation-states that emerged through the colonial and postcolonial periods each have retained elements of the Ottoman state. This is particularly pertinent to the millet system, whose legacy continues in modern form in these states. This translates to minorities within each state being defined by their religious identity, and their relationship to the state as citizens mediated through that community and their religious leaders (and other community institutions) (Barkey and Gavrilis, 2016). This accounts for the continuing eminence of the Armenian Apostolic Orthodox Church in particular in the region, the Catholicos of Antelias (Lebanon) and the Patriarchs of Turkey and Lebanon.

The quasi-millet organisation of Christian minorities within the post-Ottoman states has allowed for the operations of community schools, social clubs and associations and social and cultural production, usually affiliated (at least historically) to a quasi-political party/ association: the Armenian Revolutionary Federation (Dashnak Party), founded in Tbilisi in 1889; the Democratic Liberal Party (Ramgavar Party), founded in Istanbul in 1921; the Social Democratic Party (Hunchakian Party), founded in Geneva in 1887; and the AGBU, 'the world's largest non-profit organization devoted to upholding the Armenian heritage through educational, cultural and humanitarian programs' (AGBU, n.d.), established in Cairo in 1906. This community organisation has led to a formulaic and familiar infrastructure throughout the Middle East, and a model that has been transported and transplanted by Middle Eastern emigrants to Armenian communities in the West. Armenian diasporic life has traditionally been structured (and sometimes divided) around this community model, with these institutions and their leaders at the helm, privileging patriarchal and conservative norms and institutions. It has also enforced a 'religious' state-decreed identity on citizens of Armenian origins, regardless of their beliefs and their relationship with the Armenian community they are officially bound to.

Though Armenian life has traditionally been defined and arbitrated by community institutions and religious leaders, in practice, this has become less relevant to younger generations who claim their national citizenship more actively and boldly. This can be seen throughout the region, where young activists coalesce with fellow non-Armenian citizens around issues that unite them as Egyptians, Lebanese, and so on. For some young people I interviewed, the church and traditional institutions and narratives have done them a disservice in keeping them at a distance from the state and from active belonging, claiming rights and exercising agency as full and equal citizens. Armenians in Turkey who have grown up in a climate of fear and silencing, to some extent, have moved from hiding and docility to negotiation and coexistence. Influential intellectuals and advocates, notably the newspaper *Agos*, have contributed to new voices in the public sphere, paying a heavy price – the murder of its chief editor and founder Hrant Dink on 19 January 2007. Dink's funeral procession on the streets of Istanbul was a turning point for many Armenians, who 'were no longer afraid to speak out' (interview extract, June 2013) as well as a poignant and unprecedented event in the history of contemporary Turkey that few can forget. The youth movement *Nor Zartonk* (New Renaissance) carries this torch with clear principles and missions to demand equality and justice for Turkey's Armenian citizens. However, these views now operate in a climate of increasing repression in Erdoğan's Turkey. While the period 2005–2013 seemed to represent some sort of democratic breakthrough in Turkey, at least at the level of civil society (Kasbarian, 2016), this has been put to a definitive end by the escalating authoritarianism of the regime – the ongoing war against the Kurds, the continuing purges of all elements deemed to be a threat to the state, as well as Erdoğan's aggression against Turkey's neighbours, Greece, Cyprus and Armenia.[8]

Lebanon is a weak state (despite its endurance),⁹ with strong communities (defined by religious identity) vying for power. The consociational system, which protects differences and promotes power-sharing along communal lines, has guaranteed the Armenian role in the Lebanese state. The system, while safeguarding communities and Lebanon's diversity, also inevitably perpetuates sectarianism and vulnerability to external powers' influence. This has privileged the traditional communitarian institutions of Lebanon for decades and organised all aspects of life along sectarian lines, directly contributing to Lebanon's economic and political crises and endemic corruption. Younger generations who are more critical of the sectarian foundation of the state and society are challenging these strongholds and actively constructing counter-narratives and inclusive egalitarian movements that strive for an overarching Lebanese identity and common civic culture. An active civil society movement galvanised around specific issues, such as #YouStink from the summer of 2015 (Taylor, 2015), has been a huge element in this and Armenians along with other communities have played an active role. This exemplifies the move from 'integration', the traditional discourse of community leadership, to being active Lebanese, while also crucially making the Armenian dimension an indivisible part of being Lebanese, not as outsiders and others, but as integral to the Lebanese nation. It reflects a shift from making the state work for the good of the community to 'shaping' and moulding the nation as active political agents (Nalbantian, 2020).

Traditional institutions and leaders in Egypt are also taking the initiative to adapt to changing circumstances and reaching out to their flock on their terms. There is the recognition that as the community is in decline in terms of numbers, openness and adaptability are key to survival. The development of the Armenian Catholic community in Egypt is reflected in the changes in the language used during church services. Whereas originally it had been Armenian and Turkish (with the Ottoman arrivals), it became Armenian and French (during the colonial period) and most recently French and Arabic. Today Armenian Catholics who speak Armenian are in the minority – most of them being Francophone and Arabophone.¹⁰ The Armenian Catholic Church in Cairo, therefore, conducts services in Arabic and French. They also hold Armenian language classes in the church for Armenians who never learned the language (not having been to Armenian schools) and non-Armenian spouses. 'The marriage of two Armenians is now the exception' (interview extract, July 2017) and marrying Muslims is no longer taboo. Indeed, the traditional pillars of Armenian diaspora identity in the Middle East – language, religion, endogamy and community – have all been challenged and reinterpreted for the particular context and locality.

Narrating the community, negotiating the nation

Diaspora communities have always been subjected to narratives imposed on them by states and majority populations. As such, they have had to confront or respond to versions of their experience articulated by others who are usually in a position of power over them. Being a minority carries with it not just numerical disadvantage but also the tendency to be considered peripheral to the national story. National(ist) narratives of the region have tended to exclude the Armenians or view them in a problematic or anachronistic way. This is clear from national history textbooks at state schools, in mainstream histories and in popular media. This is, of course, most pronounced in Turkey, where the paranoid state views the Armenians as a potential fifth column, which utterly belies their tiny numbers and their subaltern status (Suciyan, 2016; Tchilingirian, 2016). Nonetheless, community leaders and activists have been challenging these prevailing ideas, stereotypes and discourses by articulating their own narratives and exercising agency as citizens who speak for themselves (Papazian, 2017). These reflect the struggles faced by the communities internally but are also designed to challenge state narratives, i.e. for external consumption.

In Egypt, the community has in recent years made a concerted effort to open up to the wider Egyptian public and have more of a presence in the Egyptian public sphere. This involves high profile cultural events, media coverage and a greater presence in the arts and cultural scene. These events are generally well attended as there is interest in Egypt among a certain class and nostalgia for what is interpreted as a different Egypt and a bygone age. In an interview with His Excellency the Armenian Ambassador to Egypt, Dr Armen Melkonian, in July 2017 in Cairo, he shared that the 'Cultural Days of Armenia' cultural exchanges between Armenia and Egypt are popular, as are locally produced cultural events like the nation-wide screening of the 2016 documentary *We Are Egyptian Armenians*.[11] First screened at the Cairo International Film Festival in 2016 and described by the director as 'a forgotten part of our history, and an unseen part of our present' (Nasr, 2016), the documentary garnered international attention and acclaim.[12] The embassy was also responsible for helping to establish a centre for Armenian Studies at Cairo University in 2007 (relaunched in 2014) which would be 'responsible for all the studies which are historically and culturally related to Armenians, in addition to its role in the field of boosting the cultural relations between Egypt and Armenia' (Cairo University, 2014). The Centre held an international conference on 'Armenian Studies in the Arab World' in October 2016.

Politically too, the community has become more vocal. The *Hai Tad* (Armenian Cause, affiliated to the ARF Party) office, for example, has been increasingly active since 2006, its leader shared with me that a vision to 'get the community out of its ghetto' motivated him and his colleagues to 'open up the community to Egypt and Egyptians'. Armenian community leaders and groups have sought and cultivated relationships with Egyptian journalists, artists, intellectuals and research centres, which have taken on a life of their own, resulting in a higher media profile (e.g. Meuse, 2012), and important cultural productions like the first Egyptian documentary (in Arabic, 2015) *Who Killed the Armenians?*[13] One of the community leaders I met in Heliopolis in the summer of 2017 told me that the office has also been concentrating its efforts to lobby parliament, 'publicising Armenians and Armenia' to the media. This proliferation of activities was most evident in the run-up to the genocide centenary in 2015, with a special committee set up, resulting in Egyptian media covering it extensively, as well as regular features about the local community and its history (e.g. Abdel-Massih, 2015). These initiatives and policies serve a two-fold purpose – on the one hand, they curate and construct an Armenian Egyptian image in the public domain; on the other hand, they act as a form of validation and self-representation that construct a master narrative for internal community consumption.

Part of this conscious endeavour to curate or contribute to the narratives lies in the latent insecurities among the community. Soon after they arrived in 1919, refugees were subjected to attack, apparently in retaliation for their (and Greeks and other foreigners') lack of support for the nationalist movement, seeing it to be tied to their persecution under the Ottomans from which they had fled. Armenians, Greeks and other foreigners in this period faced violence, damage to businesses and properties, and looting (Soliman, 2015, pp. 33–34). More recent in collective memory are the measures during the Nasser nationalisation era, which weakened all 'foreign communities'. It is possible to discern an underlying fear that their properties could be confiscated, that the community schools could be interfered with, that their freedom in the community clubs might be curtailed – all of which are the everyday experiences by the community in Turkey. Here, community schools and social spaces are tightly controlled and watched over (in the schools' case literally by a state vice principal-government agent) and churches are vandalised regularly (see, for example, International Christian Concern, 2020). In the case of Egypt, the frequent attacks on the Coptic minority are the backdrop to the precarious situation that a tiny minority like the Armenians has to navigate with caution. Therefore, it is essential to perform loyalty to the government in public and official settings, regardless of personal feelings. In my interviews in 2017, it was apparent that these lines of caution are being crossed by the younger generation, who are speaking out *as Egyptians* about political matters, particularly in the realm of social media.

Diaspora community narratives for external audiences overwhelmingly stress and perform their belonging and commitment to the nation. This can be from a position of subalternity and fear, as in Turkey, from latent insecurity and protectionism, as in Egypt, or from confidence and endurance, as in Lebanon. Unlike newer diasporic communities in the Gulf States, these Armenian communities are all state-recognised as minorities and their members as citizens, and are all communities of longevity. However, they are not likely to be permanent or even 'sedentary' (Tölölyan, 2007) communities. In all three cases, there is steady migration from the whole population and the Armenians are no exception. In a 2019 survey, Armenians in Lebanon were asked about the likelihood of their 'moving out of Lebanon in the coming 5 years'. Nearly six in 10 (58 per cent) said, it is 'Very likely/likely' that they would (Tchilingirian, 2019), a figure in keeping with the trend in the region as a whole, although higher than the average Lebanese (Arab Barometer, 2019). In Egypt and Lebanon, the harsh economic conditions are a major factor informing these decisions. Lebanon's protracted political crisis is also a significant contributory factor in emigration. Turkey has been a country of economic emigration for decades even though its economy until recently was robust. In Egypt and Turkey, the increasingly repressive illiberal regimes are forcing many to leave if they can.

For minorities like the Armenians, controlling the narrative is even more important in times of crisis. The official line of belonging and commitment seeks to safeguard the community and protect its present and future, downplaying internal struggles to adapt to changing economic, social and political landscapes. The possibility of leaving is omnipresent, but its discussion is restricted.

Homes and homelands

'Homeland' is a key concept for diasporas, and acts as an orientation and unifying tool. In the Armenian case, 'homeland' is particularly complex (Kasbarian, 2015). Due to the absence of a feasible direct link to the ancestral Ottoman homelands, the Republic of Armenia, with whom the western Armenian diaspora (descendants of Ottoman Armenians) has no historical physical connection, serves as a substitute for a modern-day homeland. Diasporans, therefore, have to negotiate the gap between a mythical lost homeland and an actual modern-day 'step-homeland' in the shape of the contemporary Armenian state.[14] As part of its nation-building project, Armenia encouraged diasporan migrations to Armenia during the Soviet period in organised drives (Pattie, 2004; Laycock, 2016), and since the collapse of the Soviet Union, has been rebranding itself as a homeland for diasporans (Panossian, 1998). It has served as a site of refuge (temporary or permanent) for Armenians fleeing war and difficulties in their home states from the Middle East, Palestine, Lebanon, Iraq, Syria and Iran, as well as Armenians from Azerbaijan in the late 1980s and early 1990s, many of whom still live in poverty in the outskirts of Yerevan. The Syrian Armenians are the latest wave of diasporan Armenians seeking refuge from troubled homes.

The ongoing Syrian civil war has created Syrian refugees now numbering over 5.6 million.[15] Of these, an estimated 24,000 Syrians of Armenian origin have arrived in the Republic of

Armenia since 2011. UNHCR estimates that, for 2016, those who have stayed number around 15,000. In 2016, the departures from Armenia of Syrians exceeded the new arrivals. However, the continual arrival of Syrians in Armenia indicates that this is a fluid situation. This suggests that Syrian Armenians' encounter with Armenia is a process of negotiation – Armenia is simultaneously a site of refuge, a historic or potential homeland, and a temporary transit zone in which to recover, recuperate and regroup (Kasbarian, 2020). The peculiarity of the Syrian Armenian case means that they are not classed as refugees, as the government grants and facilitates their citizenship or residence permits. As explained to me by Christoph Bierwirth, UNHCR Representative in Armenia, in an interview in November 2016, this refugee wave has 'become and remained an Armenian issue'.

Armenia as the remnant site of eastern Armenia can lay claim to western Armenians from the former Ottoman lands,[16] with Ottoman Armenian life now relegated to memory, archive and dedicated cultural projects, such as houshamadyan.com, a project and website aiming to reconstruct and preserve the memory of Armenian life in the Ottoman Empire through research. Eastern and western Armenia, the former influenced by Ottoman (and later Arab) culture, the latter by Russian and Persian, were differentiated by language and culture more broadly.[17] As such, the Syrian Armenians' encounter with Armenia is a meeting between western and eastern Armenia, to put it crudely. Obviously, the past three decades have meant that these two 'representations' have met many times, and in many contexts, and their differences are more familiar than foreign. Nonetheless, for many Syrian Armenians, being in Armenia is not a comfortable position, as they are caught between the home of attachment (Syria) and the new potential home of 'emplacement'(ibid.). In fact, some Syrians have gone back to Syria, where they at least have physical homes and businesses (if they haven't been destroyed). Many have emigrated further afield, most notably to Canada.[18] In these cases, Armenia has served as a transit home. Others have found jobs in the Arab Gulf States and have stationed their families in Armenia while they send remittances and go back and forth. In these cases, Armenia serves as a safe and secure base and allows families to reconfigure their collective lives.

For recent Syrian Armenian arrivals, Armenia is neither home nor a foreign place, and being there is challenging. On the one hand, the official welcoming line of the government, the historical and nationalist connections, and cultural similarities make Armenia an obvious choice. On the other hand, the latter can in fact make Armenia more complicated and alienating as a site of refuge for Syrians who might never have even visited and have lived for generations in Syria. Armenia is best conceived as playing different overlapping roles at different junctures – as a land of refuge, a transit site, a step-homeland and a national motherland. Syria is still very much home, and the destruction of Syrian Armenian life is a source of great sorrow, for both this community and the diaspora at large.

Broadening horizons and shifting boundaries: Armenians and/of the Middle East

For Armenians, it is useful to have a broader conceptualisation of the Middle East as a transnational terrain that includes the Republic of Armenia and is a vibrant site of diasporan life. The deterritorialisation of national and ethnic identities in recent years has contributed to conceptualising nations (and by extension, regions) as unbound, extending far beyond their geographic boundaries, particularly evident in the domain of culture. Arguably, the frontiers of the Middle East in the Armenian case extend to North America, where Middle Eastern Armenians have settled en masse since the 1970s, making up vibrant and multi-generational communities, most notably in California, Boston and New York. The ease and proliferation of travel and communication (particularly through social media) have meant that these different Armenian communities are connected as never before, creating as much continuity as there is contrast as one moves from one site to another. For previous generations, emigrating to the United States or Armenia from Lebanon, for example, would have meant a rupture, and maintaining connections to Lebanon would have required a challenging commitment to transnationalism. As these trajectories have become increasingly common, movement has become more circular rather than linear or teleological. For many individuals and families, whether one is in Lebanon, Los Angeles or Yerevan, there is an integrity and cohesion of identity, purpose and interests that allow for a broader sense of being Armenian. In these journeys, categories of home and host are subverted, each of the sites can be both. As living in diaspora has become more established it is easier to be more comfortably Armenian in diaspora, without feeling the pressures of previous generations who were confronted with exclusion, assimilation or integration policies and narratives of nationalist states. As more people are at ease with several identities (one or more of which might be national), being diasporan – i.e. having a sense of being simultaneously at home and 'out of place' (Said 1999) meaningfully connected to those near and far, performing cultural practices and following norms that are both shared and contested – has become common.

This is well demonstrated by the ease with which young Armenians participate online and in person in social, protest and revolutionary movements spanning Armenia, the Middle East states and North America. My observation of young activists online between 2017–2020 suggests that disparate global sites converge through their activism and their ideals, such that one can simultaneously be active in the revolution in Lebanon, and in Armenia, and participate in the appeal to social welfare in the United States.[19] For these young cosmopolitans, whose identities are relatively unproblematically multi-layered, seamlessly moving from one (physical or online) milieu to another with relative ease and confidence is the essence of being diasporan, and the only way of being Armenian they have experienced. Similarly, moving away from the Middle East community (whether Beirut or Cairo) is only a physical (and often temporary) act because one remains meaningfully and actively connected and because one meets people of the same background and sensibilities in the new site in Yerevan or Paris or Los Angeles, for example. So, it is perfectly possible to simultaneously be and act as a Lebanese (Armenian) in Paris, French (Armenian) in Yerevan, and American (Armenian) in the United States, crucially because each of these identities have rooted articulation and histories, and active communities that define and navigate them. To use an analogy from more material culture, the proliferation of Levantine restaurants and eateries in Armenia (opened by Lebanese and Syrian Armenians) in recent years is a notable contribution to the 'diasporising'[20] of the 'homeland' – bringing diaspora cuisine and culture into the mainstream and creating a broader Armenian culture and identity, one that encompasses Armenia, the Middle East and Western states. These restaurants are also sites of this 'diasporising' – spaces where locals and diasporans partake in and perform a more inclusive and expansive Armenian identity (Kasbarian, 2020).

Robin Cohen, in his seminal book, *Global Diasporas* (1997), uses a gardening metaphor to illustrate how diasporas are transplanted and spread. In the case of Egypt, Lebanon and Syria, it is clear that these communities are contributing to the rise of Armenian communities elsewhere, whether within the Middle East, in the Arab Gulf States, or further afield in the Western diaspora. This trajectory can be reinterpreted as resurgence rather than decline. Old diasporas such as the Armenians are replete with examples of the rise and fall of communities and the ebb and flow of endings, beginnings and changes. Diaspora is never static, composed of different waves in tandem, some waxing and some waning at different points. In the case of historical communities, as in Egypt, the Armenian presence will endure through its impressive range of material heritage, at once testifying to vibrant local pasts and hinting at a continuing diasporisation that carries with it its Egyptian culture and legacies. Furthermore, these new diaspora communities are composed of nascent dual diasporans. Egyptian or Syrian Armenians are also part of the burgeoning Egyptian or Syrian diaspora and are becoming Gulf Egyptian Armenians, Canadian Egyptian Armenians, and so on.[21]

This overview of the Armenian diaspora suggests that it is perhaps most fruitful to view the Middle East with the familiarity and intimacy of a domestic home – characterised by farewells and reunions, departures and arrivals, dilapidations and renovations. It is a site of permanence as well as fluidity, where Armenian communities are rooted and invested, as well as unsettled and routed elsewhere. One part of their routing is towards Armenia, as an orientation that unifies and lends coherence to a complex and heterogeneous diaspora, or indeed, as a potential homeland. That contradictory tendencies coexist within the region and within each state and community merely reinforces the ingenuity of diaspora – grappling with internal and external pressures and influences, situated within the opportunities and constraints of nationalism and transnationalism.

Notes

1 Including but not limited to Gabriel Sheffer (1986), Stuart Hall (1990), William Safran (1991), Yossi Shain (1991), James Clifford (1994), Avtar Brah (1997), Robin Cohen (1997), Basch, Glick Schiller and Szanton Blanc (1994).
2 The term 'historical diasporas' was applied to the Jews, the Greeks and Armenians (Armstrong, 1976).
3 This chapter draws on Kasbarian (forthcoming) *The Armenian Middle East: Armenian Remnants, Resilience and Reconfigurations*.
4 The historical isolationism of Armenian studies has been challenged by a new generation of Armenian studies scholars engaged in global and 'connected histories' history, notably Sebouh David Aslanian (2011), Houri Berberian (2019), Bedross der Matossian (2014) among many others.
5 Ussama Makdisi (2019, p. 4) grapples with the complexities captured and constructed by 'sectarianism', among which he notes that sectarianism 'can denote a way that members of long marginalised communities make political, cultural, and economic claims to resources and privileges in any given nation'.
6 Tchilingirian (2015, p. 11) makes the important point:

> Precise number of Armenians in the Middle East – and in the Diaspora for that matter – are virtually non-existent. There are no official census figures nor methodologically accurate statistics. However, the figures presented here are based on estimates given by various church representatives and publications over the last few decades.

7 This is evident in the narratives and orientation of community organisations in diaspora (personal observation and research), as well as in recent findings by the Armenian Diaspora Survey (Tchilingirian, 2019).
8 This chapter was written before the Winter 2020 war waged against Armenia by Azerbaijan, with Turkey's support and involvement.
9 This chapter was written before the explosion that devastated Beirut in August 2020, and the escalating crisis of state, governance and the economy.
10 Interview with Armenian Catholic Archbishop, Kricor-Okosdine Coussa, Church details, 2 August 2017. The Armenian Catholics have a church in Alexandria, one in Heliopolis in Cairo and the Patriarchate in downtown Cairo.
11 The team behind the production is Waheed Sobhi, Hannan Ezzat and Eva Dadrian. www.reelhouse.org/docufilm/we-are-egyptian-armenians
12 Interview with Eva Dadrian, Cairo, January 2017.
13 Made by Egyptian satellite TV anchor Myriam Zaki and filmmaker Mohamed Hanafi. https://armenianweekly.com/2015/12/04/who-killed-film/
14 My concept of a 'step-homeland' encapsulates a situation in which two entities that are not related are forced into a familial relationship by external forces, i.e. it is not a naturally occurring relationship but

one that is forged through circumstance. The sense of 'step'-ness also carries with it connotations of difficulty and a need for adjustment by both parties. Most diasporans today, while recognising the 'step' quality of their relationship to the Republic, accept it as the closest entity to a modern homeland and therefore identify with it, however loosely, and support it in varying ways (Kasbarian, 2015).

15 As of July 2019. There are also 6.6 million internally displaced (UNHCR, n.d.).
16 Historically Armenians were divided between the Ottoman and Russian empires. The Ottoman Armenians were exterminated and/or forced to leave and their descendants make up the western diaspora (Middle East, Europe, United States and Canada). The Russian Armenians mostly ended up in what became Soviet Armenia, and they are considered eastern Armenians (also includes Russia and former Soviet Union). Eastern and western therefore refers to distinct cultural differences and historical experiences, but also the two different versions of the Armenian language.
17 Eastern Armenian is the language spoken in Armenia and Iran. The language of the western diaspora is western Armenian (considered an endangered language by UNESCO).
18 Over 40,000 Syrian refugees were resettled in Canada since the start of the war, with 25,000 between November 2015 and March 2016 (Government of Canada, n.d.). As Canada has been a destination country for Armenian refugees from Iraq, Iran and Lebanon since the 1970s, many families already had ties there. Armenian Canadian voluntary organisations helped to facilitate the refugees' applications and arrival, with many of the arrivals being privately sponsored (Halajian, 2015).
19 See for example, the Facebook page 'Armenians for Bernie Sanders', which is 'liked' and 'followed' by a number of non-US-based Armenians.
20 This is my term, which I employ to mean making something more like the diaspora, or more diaspora-like, i.e. it has both material and conceptual applications.
21 Egyptian Armenians are double diasporas abroad as they form associations based on their homeland – Egypt– for example, in Canada. www.facebook.com/Association-of-Egyptians-in-Montreal-AEM-156281527776311/

References

Abdel-Massih (2015) 'Egypt's Armenians', *Watani International*, 22 April. Available at: https://en.watani net.com/features/egypts-armenians/13602/ (accessed 17 September 2021).
Adalian, R. (1980) 'The Armenian colony of Egypt during the reign of Muhammed Ali (1805–1848)', *The Armenian Review*, 33(2), pp. 115–143.
AGBU (n.d.) 'Our Mission'. Available at: https://agbu.org/about/ (accessed 17 September 2021).
Al-Imam, M.R. (2003) *Al-arman fi masr: 1896–1961* [The Armenians in Egypt: 1896–1961]. Cairo: Nubar Printing House.
Arab Barometer (2019) 'Who desires to migrate from MENA?' Available at: www.arabbarometer.org/2019/12/who-desires-to-migrate-from-mena/ (accessed 17 September 2021).
Armstrong, J. (1976) 'Mobilized and proletarian diasporas', *American Political Science Review*, 70(2), pp. 393–408, doi:10.2307/1959646.
Aslanian, S. (2011) *From the Indian Ocean to the Mediterranean: The Global Trade Networks of Armenian Merchants from New Julfa*. Berkeley, CA: University of California Press.
Barkey, K. and Gavrilis, G. (2016) 'The Ottoman millet system: non-territorial autonomy and its contemporary legacy', *Ethnopolitics*, 15(1), pp. 24–42.
Basch, L., Glick Schiller, N. and Szanton Blanc, C. (1994) *Nations Unbound: Transnational Projects, Postcolonial Predicaments and Deterritorialized Nation-States*. Amsterdam: Gordon and Breach.
Berberian, H. (2019) *Roving Revolutionaries: Armenians and the Connected Revolutions in the Russian, Iranian, and Ottoman Worlds*. Berkeley, CA: University of California Press.
Brah, A. (1997) *Cartographies of Diaspora: Contesting Identities*. London: Routledge.
Cairo University (2014) 'Cairo University establishes a Center for Armenian Studies'. Available at: https://cu.edu.eg/Cairo-University-News-9336.html (accessed 17 September 2021).
Clifford, J. (1994) 'Diasporas – further inflections: toward ethnographies of the future', *Cultural Anthropology*, 9(3), pp. 302–338.
Cohen, R. (1997) *Global Diasporas: An Introduction*. London: UCL Press.
Dadoyan, S. (2011–14) *The Armenians in the Medieval Islamic World*. 3 vols. New Brunswick, NJ: Transaction.
Gorman, A. and Kasbarian, S. (2015) *Diasporas of the Modern Middle East: Contextualising Community*. Edinburgh: Edinburgh University Press.

Der Matossian, Bedross. (2014) *Shattered Dreams of Revolution: From Liberty to Violence in the Late Ottoman Empire*. Stanford, CA: Stanford University Press.

Government of Canada (n.d.) 'Syrian Refugee Resettlement Initiative: looking to the future'. Available at: www.canada.ca/en/immigration-refugees-citizenship/services/refugees/welcome-syrian-refugees/looking-future.html (accessed 17 September 2021).

Haddad, N. (2020) 'Outrageous: Lebanese TV host will stand trial in Lebanon for insulting Turkish president', *The 961*, 14 July. Available at: www.the961.com/neshan-trial-insulting-turkish-president/ (accessed 17 September 2021).

Halajian, D. (2015) 'Toronto Armenian community resettles Syrian refugees', *The Armenian Weekly*, 25 December. Available at https://armenianweekly.com/2015/12/25/toronto-syrian-refugees/ (accessed 17 September 2021).

Hall, S. (1990) 'Cultural identity and diaspora', in Williams, P. and Chrisman, L. (eds) *Colonial Discourse and Post-Colonial Theory: A Reader*. New York: Columbia University Press, pp. 392–403.

Hourani, A. (1947) *Minorities in the Arab World*. London: Oxford University Press.

Hovannisian, R.G. (1974) 'The ebb and flow of the Armenian minority in the Arab Middle East', *Middle East Journal*, 28, pp. 19–32.

Hovannisian, R.G. (1997) *The Armenian People: From Ancient to Modern Times*, vol. 1. New York: St Martin's Press.

International Christian Concern (2020) 'Armenian church defaced in Turkey', 28 May. Available at: www.persecution.org/2020/05/28/armenian-church-defaced-turkey/ (accessed 17 September 2021).

Kasbarian, S. (2015) 'The myth and reality of "return" – diaspora in the homeland', *Diaspora: A Journal of Transnational Studies*, 18(3), pp. 358–381.

Kasbarian, S. (2016) 'The Istanbul Armenians: negotiating co-existence', in Bryant, R. (ed.) *Shared Spaces and their Dissolution: Practices of Coexistence in Cyprus and Elsewhere*. Oxford: Berghahn Books, pp. 281–325.

Kasbarian, S. (2018) 'The politics of memory and activism: Armenian diasporic reflections on 2015', *Nationalities Papers: The Journal of Nationalism and Ethnicity*, 46(1), pp. 123–143.

Kasbarian, S. (2020) 'Humanitarian homelands: Syrian Armenians in Armenia since 2011', in Piana, F. and Laycock, J. (eds) *Aid to Armenia*. Manchester: Manchester University Press, pp. 164–179.

Kasbarian, S. (forthcoming) *Diasporizing the Modern Middle East – Armenian Remnants, Resilience and Reconfigurations*.

Kevorkian, R. (2011) *The Armenian Genocide: A Complete History*. London: I.B. Tauris.

Laycock, J. (2015) 'Beyond national narratives? Centenary histories, the First World War and the Armenian genocide', *Revolutionary Russia*, 28(2), pp. 93–117.

Laycock, J. (2016) 'Survivor or Soviet stories? Repatriate narratives in Armenian histories, memories and identities', *History and Memory*, 28(2), pp. 123–151.

Makdisi, U. (2019) *Age of Coexistence: The Ecumenical Frame and the Making of the Modern Arab World*. Berkeley, CA: University of California Press.

Meuse, A.T. (2012) 'Communities: Armenians in Egypt recount rich history', *Egypt Independent*, 27 June. Available at: www.egyptindependent.com/communities-armenians-egypt-recount-rich-history/ (accessed 17 September 2021).

Migliorino, N. (2008) *(Re)Constructing Armenia in Lebanon and Syria*. Oxford: Berghahn Books.

Nalbantian, T. (2020) *Armenians Beyond Diaspora: Making Lebanon Their Own*. Edinburgh: Edinburgh University Press.

Nasr, N. (2016) 'INTERVIEW: "We Are Egyptian Armenians", a film about the history of the Armenian community', ahramonline, 15 December. Available at: https://english.ahram.org.eg/NewsPrint/252048.aspx (accessed 17 September 2021).

Nucho, J.R. (2016) *Everyday Sectarianism in Urban Lebanon*. Princeton, NJ: Princeton University Press.

Panossian, R. (1998) 'Between ambivalence and intrusion: politics and identity in Armenia-diaspora relations', *Diaspora – A Journal of Transnational Studies*, 7(2), pp. 149–196.

Panossian, R. (2006) *The Armenians: From Kings and Priests to Merchants and Commissars*. London: Hurst.

Papazian, H. (2017) 'Between Gezi Park and Kamp Armen: the intersectional activism of leftist Armenian youths in Istanbul', *Turkish Studies*, 18(1), pp. 56–76.

Pattie, S. (2004) 'From the centres to the periphery: "repatriation" to an Armenian homeland in the twentieth century', in Markowitz, F. and Stefansson, A.H. (eds) *Homecomings: Unsettling Paths of Return*. Oxford: Lexington Books, pp. 109–124.

Payaslian, S. (2007) 'Diasporan subalternities: the Armenian community in Syria', *Diaspora* 16(1–2), pp. 92–132.

Robson, L. (2017) *States of Separation*. Berkeley, CA: University of California Press.

Rogan, E. (2015) *The Fall of the Ottomans – The Great War in the Middle East, 1914–20*. London: Allen Lane.

Rowe, P.S. (ed.) (2019) *Routledge Handbook of Minorities in the Middle East*. London: Routledge.

Safran, W. (1991) 'Diasporas in modern societies: myths of homeland and return', *Diaspora* 1(1), pp. 83–99.

Said, E. (1999) *Out of Place: A Memoir*. New York: Vintage.

Sanjian, A. (2001) 'Torn between the "obligation" of preserving a distinct identity and the "advantages" of assimilation: the Armenian experience in the modern Arab World', *Bulletin of the Royal Institute for Inter-Faith Studies*, 3(1), pp. 149–179.

Schahgaldian, N.B. (1979) 'The political integration of an immigrant community into a composite society: the Armenians in Lebanon, 1920–1974'. PhD dissertation, Columbia University.

Shain, Y. (ed.) (1991) *Governments-in-Exile in Contemporary World Politics*. New York: Routledge.

Sheffer, G. (ed.) (1986) *Modern Diasporas in International Politics*. London: Croom Helm.

Soliman, A. (2015) 'The rise of Egyptian nationalism and the perception of foreigners in Egypt 1914–1923', in Fraser, T.G. (ed.) *The First World War and Its Aftermath: The Shaping of the Middle East*. Berkeley, CA: Gingko, pp. 19–39.

Suciyan, T. (2016) *The Armenians in Modern Turkey: Post-Genocide Society, Politics and History*. London: I.B. Tauris.

Suny, R.G. (2015) *They Can Live in the Desert But Nowhere Else: A History of the Armenian Genocide*. Princeton, NJ: Princeton University Press.

Tashjian, Y. (2016) 'The Armenian genocide: solidarity vs. denial', *New Eastern Politics*, 26 April. Available at: www.neweasternpolitics.com/the-armenian-genocide-solidarity-vs-denial-yeghia-tashjian/ (accessed 17 September 2021).

Tashjian, Y. (2020) 'The neo-Ottomans are back: how should Lebanese Armenians respond?' *The Armenian Weekly*, 24 June. Available at: https://armenianweekly.com/2020/06/24/the-neo-ottomans-are-back-how-should-lebanese-armenians-respond/ (accessed 17 September 2021).

Taylor, A. (2015) 'Lebanon's #YouStink anti-government protests', *The Atlantic*, 24 August. Available at: www.theatlantic.com/photo/2015/08/lebanons-youstink-anti-government-protests/402163/ (accessed 17 September 2021).

Tchilingirian, H. (2015) 'Armenian communities in the Middle East between imposed and uncertain future', *Analytical Journal*, 7, Yerevan State University, Centre for Civilisation and Cultural Studies, pp. 217–248 [in Armenian]. [Հրաչ Չիլինգիրյան (2015) «Միջին Արեվելքի Հայկական Համայնքները Պարտադրված և Անորոշ Ապագայի Միջեվ»,*Վերլուծական տեղեկագիր*, հ. 7. Երեվանի Պետական Համալսարան, Քաղաքակրթական և Մշակույթային հետազոտությունների Կենտրոն, Էջ], 217–248 .

Tchilingirian, H. (2016) 'The "other" citizens: Armenians in Turkey between isolation and (dis)integration', *Journal of the Society for Armenian Studies*, 25, pp. 123–155.

Tchilingirian, H. (ed.) (2019) *Armenian Diaspora Survey*. London: Armenia Institute. Available at: www.armeniandiasporasurvey.com/2019-survey (accessed 17 September 2021).

Tölölyan, K. (1991) 'The nation-state and its others', *Diaspora: A Journal of Transnational Studies*, 1(1), pp. 3–7.

Tölölyan, K. (2007) 'The contemporary discourse of diaspora studies', *Comparative Studies of South Asia, Africa and the Middle East*, 27(3), pp. 647–651.

UNHCR (n.d.) 'Refugee population statistics database'. Available at: www.unhcr.org/refugee-statistics/ (accessed 21 March 2021).

Watenpaugh, K.D. (2006) *Being Modern in the Middle East*. Princeton, NJ: Princeton University Press.

Watenpaugh, K.D. (2015) *Bread from Stones: The Middle East and the Making of Modern Humanitarianism*. Berkeley, CA: University of California Press.White, B.T. (2017) 'Refugees and the definition of Syria, 1920–1939', *Past & Present*, 235(1), pp. 141–178. https://doi.org/10.1093/pastj/gtw048.

32
NEGOTIATING PLACEMAKING
Public-private spaces and Hinduism in Oman

Sandhya Rao Mehta

Introduction

A popular tale among the Hindu Gujarati trading community in Northern Oman is the story of their commercial success at the time of the Yaarubi dynasty, which ruled coastal Oman in the seventeenth century. Shared by many members of the community even now, it is said that, in recognition of their contribution to the economic prosperity of the ruling Sultans, they were allowed to build a temple in the port of Muscat in 1650. An idol of Govindraj (Lord Krishna) was brought from Basra (present-day Iraq) and placed in this new temple. Adorned with traditional Hindu costumes, this idol was then also given an Omani dagger or *khanjar*, creating a syncretic Hindu temple deity adorned with the symbolism of the Hindu faith as well as the Omani Sultanate. This gesture is interpreted by the descendants of that Hindu community today as representing the historical relationship between Hindu merchants in Oman and the ruling Omani Sultan, and appreciation of the freedoms given to them to practise their religious rituals. The story forms an integral part of all oral conversations with the Hindu Gujaratis today, reflecting pride in their historic ties to the city of Muscat and to the Islamic rulers who made their presence and prosperity possible. It also draws our attention to the strategies used by the Hindu community to access cultural and religious concessions in a conservative Muslim kingdom, a challenge that continues today.

This chapter highlights the multiple ways in which Hindus[1] in Oman, and to a lesser extent across the Gulf Cooperation Council (GCC) region, negotiate, retain and reinterpret their religious identity. Based on fieldwork, personal observations and interviews with members of the Hindu community, I outline the historical and contemporary role that Hindus have had and continue to play in Oman. In an Islamic kingdom, which is officially predicated on a homogeneous Muslim (Ibadi) identity, Hindus in Oman have been able to leverage their historical relations, maximise the scope of state-sanctioned practices, and create new ways of making private spaces into public spaces to practise a highly communal and participatory faith. The creative use of existing physical spaces helps religious communities to work within state-sanctioned limitations while creating and sustaining not only a vibrant Hindu community but also their involvement in transnational organisations. Different transnational Hindu movements, such as the International Society for Krishna Consciousness (ISKON), the *Sathya Sai* movement and the Art of Living organisation are further popularised and practised in 'public-private spaces', such as apartments and gated communities. The increased use of technology and social media also ensures wider participation in transnational networks while often providing alternatives to an overreliance on physical temples, which are few in number and often tied to necessary government licences. In many ways, religious prayers, rituals and ceremonies have now been transplanted to the digital sphere, allowing for transnational gatherings of Hindus to commemorate and practise specific versions of their faith.

Thus, while Hindus have been considered to be a religious minority and outliers in the Arabian Gulf, their historical and present survival suggests that religious belonging and identity should be studied beyond reducing these terms to minoritism, persecution and tolerance, to an interest in the complex ways that these practices are sustained. Vertovec's (2000) notion of super-diversity, often associated with the cultures of cosmopolitan world cities, has some relevance to the case of Hindus and Hinduism in Oman. Taking its cue from Cohen and Fischer's (2019) notion of 'complexifying complex diasporas', Vertovec notes that 'super-diversity' helps us to understand the complexity of the conditions, variety and scope of mobilities, creating new methodologies and ways of understanding emerging issues in diaspora and transnationalism (Vertovec, 2020). Accordingly, no two religious diasporas are similar and each could benefit from a closer study of the particular circumstances and strategies that make them unique. In contextualising the role of the Hindu community in Oman, we find constant re-invention, new and emerging strategies to retain and pass on its heritage, as well as new ways to keep up with national (Indian) and transnational Hindu movements. While some strategies indicate global trends, others are particular to the unique historical connection that the Hindu community has in Oman.

The Hindu diaspora

Indian diaspora movements are often divided into three major stages: (1) the period of indenture in the nineteenth century; (2) the post-partition movement following Indian independence in 1947; and (3) the migration of technocrats from India after 1980, largely to the United States of America (Jayaram, 2004; Hegde and Sahoo, 2017). With Hindus comprising more than 80% per cent of India's population (Census India, 2001), much of its migrant population is also Hindu, except those who left India for Pakistan in 1947. Vertovec (2000) referred to the presence of a 'Hindu diaspora', acknowledging, after Parekh (1994), that Hinduism was central to the self-identification of most Hindus around the world and played a significant role in the notion of Indian ethnicity. The majority of work on the Hindu diaspora focuses on the white-collar European or North American examples (Jaffrelot and Therwath, 2007; Raj, 2012). More recently, the Caribbean and other islands associated with indentured labour have benefitted from attention (Lal, 1996; Pande, 2020; Vertovec, 2000). In all such accounts, the Indian communities around the Indian Ocean, along the coasts of Yemen, the Gulf of Oman, and the eastern coast of Africa have been less explored, even though they have a historically rich tradition of travel, migration and cultural interconnections. Hindus have 400 years of continuous presence in and around the Arabian Peninsula, and ties that go back millennia. Hindu communities of the Arabian Sea have shared economic and cultural ties with the ports along its shores while establishing themselves as a well-defined group of people with considerable economic and commercial clout (Peterson, 2004; Onley, 2009; 2014; Goswami, 2016). Today, they share transnational ties with extended families across the world and perform versions of Hinduism that are closely tied to their places of origin in the various states of India.

While Indians form a minority diaspora community within the GCC countries, they have been able to establish themselves as active social groups with shared political and religious interests through transnational and translocal participation. Hinduism's contribution to establishing religious nationalism or *Hindutva* and its role in propelling a Hindu majority national government to power in India has been well documented (Sud, 2008; Thobani, 2019). Specific studies in the GCC countries (Ilias, 2015; Oommen, 2015) also show that Hindus are actively engaged in affecting change in India, primarily through informal religious networks and involvement in financing and supporting political parties and politicians.

The religious life of the Indian diaspora[2] in the Arabian Gulf has been explored for its influence on Indian politics as well as its participation in transnational organisations (Oommen, 2015). For example, in his work on the Malayali community in Kuwait, Oommen suggests that:

> religion has become a site for various identity-based community-centred networks among these immigrants. Groups inclined towards taking fundamentalist positions, such as Pentecostal and Evangelical Christian denominations, but also some Muslim organizations with strong Wahabi traditions such as the Jamaat-e-Islami, and Hindu groups like the Rashtriya Swayamsevak Sangh (RSS) and followers of Mata Amritanandamayi Devi (AMMA), all have made inroads into the lives of Keralite migrants in the GCC countries.
>
> *(2015, p. 2)*

The Hindu community in Oman shares many of the uncertainties of other diasporic and migrant groups in the Gulf region who have no opportunity for political participation and, in many cases, lack religious freedoms. As migrant workers, and therefore non-citizens, Hindus have no political rights in the Gulf, and their religious freedoms are curtailed, if not denied outright, as in Saudi Arabia. Perceiving themselves as homogeneous Islamic societies, all the countries of the Arabian Gulf base their political identity on various forms of Islam, with few rights given to religious minorities (Pew Forum, 2009; Khashan 2016). In Oman, the negotiation of Hindu religious identity is uniquely noteworthy in the context of the Arabian Peninsula, owing to the community's historical importance in the Sultanate.

The historical presence of Hindus in Oman

The earliest reference to a Hindu presence in the Persian Gulf can be found in the work of the Arab historian Abu Zayd Hasan in 916 AD, in which mention is made of a hundred Hindu merchants in the southern port of Siraf (Onley, 2014). With the rise and fall of adjoining ports, this community may have moved to Kish, Hormuz and Bandar Abbas along the Iranian coast, and then to Muscat: 'The oldest community in the Gulf today, also Hindu like that in Siraf, is the one in Muscat, which dates to at least the fifteenth century' (ibid., p. 232). Numerous sources indicate the historical presence of Hindu trader communities in Bahrain and Oman. Allen Jr (1981), Bose (2009), Onley (2014) and Potter (2017) suggest that the cities along the coast of present-day Oman, including Sur, Sohar, Muttrah and Muscat, saw Hindu traders bring their wives and children, attesting to the comparatively peaceful living conditions there. One of the earliest recorded pieces of evidence is the incident of the Hindu trader Naruttim who, in 1650, took umbrage at the Portuguese commander asking to marry his daughter. In anger, Naruttim instead helped Sultan Sayf Al-Yaarubi to defeat the Portuguese, after which the Sultan showed his gratitude by giving the Hindu merchants further trading rights and exemption from the *jizyah* tax levied on non-Muslims (Allen Jr, 1981; Peterson, 2004). Not only does this history record the contribution of Hindus to Omani resistance to the Portuguese invaders, but it also underlines the presence of Hindu families in Muscat as far back as the seventeenth century. Of course, Potter (2017) cautions that the continued presence of any community cannot be read as the absence of strife or persecution. Speaking of the Hindu traders, he says: 'They were easily identified by distinctive garb and were to some extent self-contained communities who could provide financial backing to merchants, dhow captains, and ruling families. Their financial success, however, could make them targets of attack' (ibid., p. 17).

Physical evidence of Hindus in Oman can be found in the ruins of an ancient temple in Qalhat, a fragment of which is in the National Museum in Muscat. The carved slab in the shape of a lotus flower, significant in Hindu mythology, is traced to the tenth century and is said to have remained intact until the end of the thirteenth century (Al Moosawi, 2019). The early documented evidence of temples in Muscat can be traced back to the mid-seventeenth century when Gujaratis helped the Yaarubis defeat the Portuguese. They were able to live with most of the customs and rituals of the community intact, including having a cowshed, a cremation ground and a temple. During the rule of Ahmad Bin Said in the eighteenth century, the Banians (Gujarati traders) are said to have had a total of four temples, only one of which survives today (Allen Jr, 1981). In January 1765, 1,200 Hindus were accounted for by the Danish traveller Neibuhr, who visited Muscat and recorded that:

> In no other Mahometan city are the Indians so numerous as in Maskat; their number in this city amounts to no fewer than 1200. They are permitted to live agreeable to their own laws, to bring wives hither, to set up idols in their chambers, and to burn their dead.
>
> *(ibid., p. 41)*

Hindu merchants were indispensable to the network of circulatory trade, which brought much-needed food and other items to the inland desert inhabitants. The success of the traders meant that they could gain concessions from the Muslim rulers and these concessions often involved religious permissions like retaining customary clothing, owning cowsheds for milk and digging wells for use by their community. Commercial success was directly linked to religious freedoms in early Gulf trade and continues until today (Allen Jr, 1981; Goswami, 2016). Over time, these Hindu merchants were successful in trading along the Indian Ocean routes and saw much success in the early twentieth century when they traded in dates and guns with Europe and the United States, often supporting the Omani rulers who gave them customs and excise benefits, enabling the merchants to trade profitably (ibid.). Some of these merchants were subsequently appointed as customs officials and were under the British protectorate, giving them recourse to British law concerning non-payment of loans and other trade issues, but this brought no additional religious freedoms.

By 1970, when the Sultanate of Oman was founded, Hindu merchants were commercially successful enough to lay claim on governance, potentially asking for a stake in the new nation through administrative positions. However, Oman defined itself as an Islamic nation and established a government and civil service consisting of Omani (Muslim) citizens. Although they were the single most commercially successful group of residents, with historical links and successful businesses, the Hindu community was effectively sidelined as Oman established itself as an independent Sultanate, even calling its own diaspora in Zanzibar and other Gulf States back to develop the nation. Some of the Hindu merchant families, however, retained their economic clout and were able to leverage it for economic concessions as well as religious freedoms for the community. Some families were eventually given Omani citizenship but many more still rely on resident or investor visas that must be periodically renewed. According to some members within the Hindu, Gujarati community that I have spoken to, in 1970, over 120

Hindu families could prove their continuous presence in Oman since 1900 and would have been entitled to citizenship.

Within an Omani context, Hindus have a reputation for being productive and cooperative, but also sufficiently distanced from local politics – an approach that has helped them maintain their relevance and status. The community also had the advantage of being viewed largely as self-sufficient, with no tendencies toward proselytising or posing any political threat to the state. This enabled Hindus to continue practising their faith, leveraging their historical and commercial contributions, as well as using a variety of creative strategies such as the use of public-private spaces, at times in conjunction with the government, but also through engagement with transnational Hindu movements, which I discuss later in the chapter. Before doing so I first turn to the condition, role and position of Hindus and Hinduism in Oman today.

Hinduism in contemporary Oman

As an officially Islamic kingdom, Oman frames itself as a homogeneous Ibadi country, an identity central to its nation-building exercise in 1970 when the erstwhile kingdoms of Uman and Muscat were brought together, along with Dhofar in the south. Oman has a Basic Statute, established in 1996 and its Ministry of Justice and Legal Affairs website describes the country as 'An Arab, Islamic, Independent State' (article 1) and states that 'The religion of the State is Islam and Islamic Sharia is the basis for legislation' (Ministry of Justice and Legal Affairs, 1996, Article 2). There is no mention of multiculturalism, diversity or the possibility of other religions or sects being integral to the state. In fact, such a proposition would be contrary to the nationalist project.

Nothing in the physical spaces of Muscat, not to speak of the country's interior and smaller cities, exudes anything but Islamic architecture, with all residential and commercial areas dotted with spires of the old, new and ever-growing number of mosques. Simultaneously, the subsuming of religious institutions into the structure of the state has ensured that even Islamic religious events are closely monitored to prevent radicalisation among citizens and residents. According to Al Salimi, an Omani scholar of theology, '[t]his has permitted Oman to modernise and engage with a global society in an amicable, non-sectarian, manner' (2011, p. 147). With its focus on heritage and encouragement of a homogeneous Omani identity, it is clear that other religions and faiths will remain marginal, tolerated and accepted as long as they make no demands on the state and limit their role to commerce.

The place for other religious communities in this scenario appears to be very limited. Oman maintains strict rules on public congregations and the public performance of religious ceremonies across all faiths. It does not allow organised public festivities on pavements, public parks, beaches or any space of common use. In fact, the only publicly visible festive occasions are the Iftar offerings in the month of Ramadan, either outside a mosque or even a public space like shops or malls. Social and religious events have to go through official channels and permissions, which also entail visa regulations if the event involves participants from outside the country. As such, the space for religious expression and public ritual is restrictive and minimal. Yet, a combination of strategies involving both the state and the Hindu community makes possible the presence of a vibrant Hindu community which, with the cooperation of the relevant branches of government, has creatively redefined 'public-private' spaces for ritual gatherings and celebrations.

In the public performance of Hindu rituals, formal and informal practices coalesce, allowing for the presence of 'official' sites of prayer, such as temples, as well as privately created spaces that act as temples, without being designated as such by the authorities. That such informal spaces are allowed to exist along with the official temples in Oman testifies to the blurring of lines between formal and informal spaces as well as modes of worship, creating syncretic religious practices. The presence of the two Hindu temples in Muscat is often cited by official Omani sources as a sign of the country's religious tolerance. As mentioned above, there have been historical references to Hindu temples in Oman, and these are mentioned in official sources, such as the National Museum, which showcases the papers of the land granted to the Krishna temple, ostensibly as a public sign of official tolerance. One of the temples that exists today is the historic Shiva temple in Muttrah, originally built in 1870. This Motishwar Mahadev temple is located near the Al Alam Palace and consists of three deities, Motishwar Mahadev, Adi Motishwar Mahadev Temple and Hanuman. The powerful Banyan merchant families, who have considerable business clout and managed to become Omani citizens, acquired land for the construction of the second temple, the Krishna temple in Darsait, which was built on land granted by Sultan Qaboos. According to the Hindu Temple Management webpage, more than 3,000 people visit the temples on weekends, with almost 7,000 visiting on religious occasions (Hindu Temple Management, 2020). Both temples are zealously managed by the Hindu Mahajan, an organisation made up of the old Gujarati merchant community. The website also adds this interesting caveat:

> As per directives from Ministry of Endowments and Religious Affairs all the religious festivals and functions are organized/celebrated in the Temple premises/Hall. All the Government authorities are very cooperative in permitting/helping in the organizing of the various religious functions.

This official declaration is significant in the way that it legitimises the existence of the temple in an Islamic city while declaring that its operation is within the laws of the land. Such declarations are common in all congregations, most of which begin with a customary reference to the ruling Sultan.

The official acceptance of temples, in a sense 'Omanising' Hindus as part of the official state discourse, allows for a tacit political acceptance of this historical community, albeit one that is limited. The existence and regulation of a small number of temples are perhaps as far as the state could go, but in practice, the two temples are insufficient to cater to the large number of Hindus who live in various pockets of labour camps and other distant spaces, such as oil rigs and construction sites like dockyards. The Shiva and Krishna temples are, in fact, both located close to each other and rather inaccessible to many other Hindus across the country, who are not able to participate in the religious rituals observed there. Most workers, for example, have no access to public transport to come to these temples and often, no permission to leave their places of work. This has resulted in a large number of Hindus performing their religious rituals in informal settings, often with the support of the supervisor, or others who are in charge of residential arrangements for these workers. The vacuum created by the absence of temples is filled by other spaces, a room in a labour camp, an unfinished residential building on the outskirts of the city, or even an abandoned farmhouse, allowing Hindus to congregate in more accessible locations across the country. Over time, such spaces have become recognised, unofficially, as temples and have even been marked as such on digital maps.

Thus, this blurring of public and private space, as well as the use of informal spaces for formal, religious occasions points to a variety of strategies that the Hindu community makes use of to perform their religion. It also indicates that religious diasporas often negotiate through official systems to create informal rituals and practices to make up for the absence of formal religious spaces. A private hall or room could thus be given sacred status just by temporarily placing a deity there.

In a similar vein, Vásquez and Knott (2014, p. 329) observe that in the Malaysian city of Kuala Lumpur, the absence of formal public religious places has created informal spaces of worship in neighbourhoods across the city, often without government involvement. Similarly in Oman, while there is an official reference to only two temples in the country, a cursory look at digital maps of cities like Sohar and Salalah indicates locations of 'temples' like ISKON, Shiva temple and 'Mukti Dham'. On closer inspection, however, it is clear that these are private properties, usually large farmhouses with a dedicated villa for prayer that is designated as a temple. At times, they are hastily put up in spaces inside labour camps. These places are allowed to exist under state laws as long as they are registered as an organisation or a centre. These 'temples' act not only as places of worship, but also as community centres for socialisation, particularly for single men and women like domestic workers who congregate there with friends and use it as a social occasion. Single men usually work in the construction and infrastructure sectors and rarely have enough resources to meet at a restaurant or a friend's house. The temples thus play a dual role as social and religious spaces.

The reality for most Hindus in Oman is that Hindu festivals are just another day in the work calendar, especially for blue-collar workers and domestic workers who are not able to take a day off to observe the rituals and prayers of these occasions. Thus, religious festivals like Diwali, Holi or Ganesh puja, all public celebrations in India, have to become private events to be celebrated by oneself, or, if possible, in a makeshift community centre 'temple' (if it is physically accessible), after work hours and with far more reserve than in their home states in India. It is clear that these places of worship exist with the knowledge of the authorities but are allowed only as long as they are not perceived to be a 'threat', either because they are seen as being too noisy and thus discernible, or to be seen as forms of proselytising. In other words, these practices are tolerated as long as they remain largely invisible and do not become public beyond the confines of the informal spaces themselves or the Hindu participants.

Vásquez and Knott (ibid., p. 326) suggest that many states 'manage the migrants' presence and visibility or invisibility within these urban spaces'. By allowing the establishment of religious spaces that are situated away from residential localities and having companies ferry workers to and from these temples, the state can, at once, create opportunities for religious involvement of its expatriate populations but also do so in ways that do not disturb the perceived peace or allow a more robust involvement of the community.

Within the temple halls

While public processions are not allowed by the law, festivals and religious observances are still observed by Hindus, almost always with the tacit support of Omani officials, yet another example of the impact that the older merchant families have had on the local government. The official temples and other places of worship have large compounds in which performative events, which are an inextricable part of Hinduism, are enacted. *Holi*, the festival of colour, *Jaganath Rath Yatra* (the procession of Lord Jaganath), *Janmashtami* (the festival of the birth of Lord Krishna), *Durga Puja* and many other such festivities are all held within the compounds of the temple premises, often with multiple notices not to litter or take celebrations outside the compound. The ritual bonfire, playing with coloured water, participating in dances like the *dandia* and public chanting during ritual weddings of gods and goddesses (*Kalyanam*) are all observed and celebrated strictly within the temple halls. At times, religious events like the *Rath Yatra* are even done symbolically inside the temple itself, if particular permissions are not available on time. Thus, it is important that rituals be conducted, although the nature and size of the ritual could vary, depending on circumstances.

The cooperation between the state and the Hindu community is best represented during the *Navratri* and *Shivaratri* celebrations. The *Navratri*, a nine-day festival important to the Gujarati community, includes the *dandiya raas*, a series of public dance events involving the whole community. This is now a very popular pan-India event, packaged and commercialised with professional DJs and live bands lending music and song, framed in a religious context. In Muscat city, two or three specific places are allocated where these events can take place. Most of them are sponsored by the Gujarati families who hold much clout in commercial circles, along with the support of relevant administrative units like the local municipality. Thousands of Hindu residents attend these events, which take place in a large compound with ample parking inside the grounds. The event is coordinated by the local police who station some security around and inside the event, primarily for easy mobility rather than in anticipation of any law and order issues. Similarly, the old Shiva temple sees thousands of visitors on *Shivaratri*, a day sacred to devotees. Situated in the middle of historic Muscat, the temple is surrounded by houses mainly inhabited by local Muslim Omanis. On this auspicious day for Hindus, the locality is filled with cars and devotees carrying offerings of milk and fruits well into the night. To offset the inconvenience caused to the local populace, over time, the temple organisers have been able to make elaborate arrangements to bus devotees from a central location to which they could drive, thus avoiding traffic snarls in the narrow alleys leading to the historic temple. While this would be seen as just another festive occasion in India, in Muscat, it has become an event to be controlled and managed by the authorities. This involves detailed planning and coordination with the local police and the municipality, with the temple authorities increasingly using its social media pages to inform the public about these arrangements. Thus, while ostensibly offering controlled religious freedoms, it is done so within the ambit of established rules of containment. The Hindu community thus creates innovative ways to incorporate the public nature of its religious ceremonies while adhering to the laws of the land.

Diasporic ritual practices and homemaking

As is well known, Hinduism bases itself on community participation and performance (Kurien, 2015). The absence of public spaces in which festivals like *Diwali*, when firecrackers are lit, or *Ganesh Chathurti*, when idols of Lord Ganesh are paraded and finally immersed in rivers or lakes, necessitate the imaginative conversion of public spaces such as apartment corridors and the gardens of gated communities into extended private ones, with decorations, catering and even idols of worship being placed in such spaces. These practices are not limited to Hindus in Oman. Blunt and Varley's (2004) work on geographies of home among migrant communities refers to the work of Renate Dohmen, who worked on the *kolam* designs outside homes in Tamil Nadu, India, and suggests 'that the designs create a space of belonging not only for individual women and their families, but also for the community at large' (ibid., p. 4). While these spaces are not public in the sense of being parks, beaches or the street, their use can be maximised to create an atmosphere of festivity and prayer while still staying within the law. During such occasions, apartment buildings are transformed into quasi-public community spaces of celebration.

Similarly, in their work on the creation of religious spaces among Hindus in California, Mazumdar and Mazumdar (2009) suggest that the Hindu community found ways of working within local American laws to establish and observe Hindu rituals like lighting a holy fire or making the milk boil over as a housewarming tradition, both of which would set off fire alarms.

They suggest that '[m]odifications are made in diaspora (e.g. muting of the sounds, smells, and sights of religion, such as muffled chanting or music, limited use of fire) so as not to arouse suspicion, panic, and hostility of neighbors' (ibid., p. 259). They also note that Hindus retain religious markers outside their homes in the form of decorative panels at the threshold and make 'rangoli' (intricate drawings) at the front door on festive occasions. Such a creative use of public space, such as the corridor of an apartment building, to establish religious identity points to an imaginative strategy of asserting Hinduism in the diaspora. While very common among Hindu homes in India, such a colourful display of art and artefacts outside India would immediately mark the space as uniquely Hindu. Similarly, in their work on cultural geography and belonging in the city of Muscat, Mehta and Onley (2015) have identified specific geographical areas that are dominated by white-collar Indian professionals as well as the blue-collar workers who are mainly accommodated in 'bachelor' camps, provided by the companies for which they work. Al Khuwair is one such example of an area inhabited by professionals. Residential buildings here are all six-storeyed, with seven to ten apartments on each floor. As Mehta and Onley explain about this community:

> They decorate their houses with auspicious religious symbols. Hindus commonly place mango leaves over their front door and a basil (*tulsi*) plant and images of Lord Ganesha inside the entrance. During festivals such as *Diwali*, they decorate the corridors outside their apartments with *kolam* patterns, indicating good luck, and light the corridor with earthen lamps or candles while exchanging sweets with their neighbours. On such occasions, the apartment building becomes a public space of celebration, one that is shared with Christians and Muslims.
>
> *(ibid., p. 177).*

Such use of space allows communities to regularly gather for religious activities, lining shoes outside, in the traditional Hindu custom, using the corridor as extended space for catering of a religious event, and even creating extended seating space in the event of lecture sessions like a discourse from the Gita or singing of *bhajans* (prayers) by participants and invited guests. Such events tend to be noisy with the use of cymbals and drums, and the aromas of the 'prasad' (food given as an offering, later to be distributed among the devotees). The communal use of private spaces thus replicates homemaking strategies of the diaspora, recreating the rituals of traditional festivities with an imaginative breaking of the public/private space dichotomy, making it publicly Hindu for that time. Some of the most common occasions being hosted from these spaces are the increasingly popular talks and chanting sessions by organisations such as ISKON, Sathya Sai Baba and Art of Living, all of which engage in regular communal activities where even the corridors of apartment buildings would not suffice. Entire private buildings or hotel halls are then engaged for these bigger events, usually with the patronage of businesses or funding by the members of the groups themselves.

Transnational religious engagement

The meteoric rise of pan-Indian Hindu religious movements, such as the Sathya Sai Baba, the Art of Living and ISKON, has often been viewed as facilitating the transition from diaspora to transnationalism, as frequent travel and access to digital sources ensure that contact with 'home' is never fully lost. Sahoo, (2013, p. 23) suggests that '[t]he expansion of international migration and the revolution in information and communication technology have transformed the nature of religious movements, which now attract followers from all parts of the world'.

As Hindus across various Indian communities around the world congregate and partake of religious discourses and new forms of prayer become accessible through frequent contact via the internet, new diasporic Hindu identities are formed. Kurien (2015) shows how religious gatherings called *satsangs* are important for religious minorities to create a sense of community and ensure that religious practices are being handed down to the younger generation. While some of these activities, such as prayers, would be taught to children by the extended family in India, for the diaspora, there is an increased urgency to teach Hindu values to children through participation in more formal organisations. These are organisations that substitute traditional religious rituals and practices in native languages, including Sanskrit, and engage in discussions, chanting and prayers in commonly used Indian languages like Hindi, or even English. The rise of 'ecumenical Hinduism' (Williams, 1998) suggested the bringing together of the diverse sects, languages and regions of Hindu India into uniform symbols and traditions, almost always under one guiding spiritual guru. These groups combine traditional religious scriptures (usually the Bhagavad Gita), adapting them to modern life. The gurus tend to be innovative, approachable and savvy in their use of traditional and social media. In fact, 'global gurus are some of the most vibrant innovators in the field of Hindu religiosity' (Lucia, 2014). At its core, trends in transnational Hinduism point to its adaptability and essential connection with the land in a way that encourages bodily health with judicious use of the environment (through, for example, Ayurveda and yoga) (Bauman and Sanders, 2009). Such re-inventions make Hinduism remain relevant to the Indian diaspora as they offer them accessible ways to connect with their heritage and culture. The increased popularity of such religious movements is also due to their ability to engage in social causes, which impact the educational, health and environmental concerns of younger devotees who could pick and choose from a range of different religious movements. To a large extent, these organisations also reflect the current popularity of Hinduism, both in India and its diaspora, with donations made in these forums for religious activities back home, including the construction of temples.

It is also clear in Oman that institutional patronage allows for specific Hindu messages to be conveyed in private forums while the humanitarian projects of these popular movements lend them credence and recognition. A range of such religious groups gather in smaller, private congregations in individual homes but usually operate under a larger umbrella with state sanction. For example, members of the Sathya Sai International Organization not only meet regularly in private homes (including in labour camps) but they also host an array of public events promoting health and moral education, often in conjunction with the Ministry of Health and the Ministry of Education, organising health checkups and blood donation camps, as well as essay writing competitions on the theme of human values, targeting all schools, not only Indian schools. Similarly, ISKON events are regularly held in private neighbourhoods while large events take place in banquet halls to accommodate the increasing number of devotees who participate. Local nationals are invited at times, giving official sanction to these events while also being an opportunity for official narratives of tolerance, especially as they are wrapped in the secular discourse of ethics and morality rather than a particular religious belief system. ISKON events often involve children in drawing and storytelling sessions, imparting the religious values and narratives of Hindu mythology, which are traditionally given by family in the homeland. Gurus and representatives of these organisations are regular visitors to Muscat where they are hosted by individual families, with religious lectures being given at that time.

The Art of Living, viewed as a less ritualistic organisation with its focus on meditation and yoga, tends to be more visible in public spaces and English language newspapers in Oman, with even a kindergarten in its name in the city. The patronage of some of the commercially successful families in the Art of Living is reflected in its popularity, and more importantly, in its public presence across all media. Promoted as an 'educational and humanitarian movement', the Art of Living has a large transnational following across all faiths but its roots in meditation, yoga and the use of Ayurveda reflect its firmly Hindu origin. The scale of the organisation and international funding accounts for its visibility and engagement across other religious communities as is its ability to connect in English and Hindi, rather than other Indian languages, indicating a pan-Indian clientele. The Art of Living also hosts various lectures and workshops internationally and active participants often visit such events in different parts of the world, thus emphasising the transnational connections created within the Indian diaspora.

Conclusion

In his work on super-diversity, Vertovec suggests that it should be considered 'a concept and approach about new migration patterns' (2019, p. 126), rather than a fully formulated theory that offers answers to questions of why specific migratory phenomena occur. Using this framework, this study suggests that the Hindu diaspora in Oman can be problematised as being more than just a minority community with few religious freedoms in a conservative Muslim nation. Hinduism has been practised in Oman for hundreds of years, and this has given the community a unique position and role in the country, one it has been able to leverage to its advantage in the formal, public sphere. In addition, while the community may not be able to practice its religion publicly, it has been able to wrest sufficient agency to retain religious identity through everyday practices and tactical use of public-private spaces, as well as engagement in transnational religious networks.

The negotiations of religious performance and identity within the Hindu community in Oman are diverse and use a wide range of strategies, from established institutional support to creatively using public-private spaces as well as transnational engagement. Yet, these freedoms exist under the watchful eyes of the authorities who ensure law and order by stopping public manifestations of religious ceremonies. Despite such restrictions, Hindus have been able to engage in the various ritualistic observances of their particular sects, establishing and creatively using private and semi-private spaces. Given the historical ties between Oman and India, as well as the commercial importance of the Hindu community to Oman in the past and even in the present, Hindus occupy a unique position in this Muslim country. Religious diasporas are always being redefined and recreated. In Oman, the Hindu community, while remaining a tiny minority of the population, is still able to leverage its historical, commercial and cultural connections to retain and even redefine itself within the country as well as within a transnational network. In attempts to de-essentialise the Hindu diaspora, its role in the Arabian Gulf adds an additional layer, underlining the complex relationships which exist between historical communities and their changed status in the contemporary context. Blurring the lines between formal and informal, private and public, and state and individual modes of religious practice reveals the complex relationships that are possible within diasporic communities and, in doing so, a new account of Hinduism in Oman is made possible, perhaps a sort of 'Omani Hinduism', unique in its history and contemporary practice.

Notes

1 The Hindu community in Oman is no more homogeneous than it is anywhere in India, or in the diaspora. Hinduism is a large umbrella term that includes different denominations and devotion to different deities. This study uses the term 'Hindu' in a generic manner to refer to anybody who self-identifies as Hindu in the broadest way possible.

2 Although the Hindu (in fact, the Indian) community in the Arabian Gulf is regarded as migrant, rather than diasporic, this study emphasises the historical, multi-generational nature of the Hindu community in Oman and terms it, in this sense, as diasporic.

References

Allen Jr, C.H. (1981) 'The Indian merchant community of Masqaṭ', *Bulletin of the School of Oriental and African Studies, University of London*, 44(1), pp. 39–53.

Al Moosawi, J. (2019) 'Oman, the Gulf region and India', talk given at the Indian Council of World Affairs. Available at: www.youtube.com/watch?v=_SJv7efv05U (accessed 30 October 2020).

Al Salimi, A. (2011) 'The transformation of religious learning in Oman: tradition and modernity', *Journal of the Royal Asiatic Society*, 21(2), pp. 147–157. doi: 10.1017/S1356186310000696

Bauman, C. and Saunders, J.B. (2009) 'Out of India: immigrant Hindus and South Asian Hinduism in the USA', *Religion Compass*, 3(1), pp. 116–135.

Blunt, A. and Varley, A. (2004) 'Introduction: geographies of home', *Cultural Geographies*, 11, pp. 2–6.

Bose, S. (2009) *A Hundred Horizons: The Indian Ocean in the Age of Global Empire*. Cambridge, MA: Harvard University Press.

Census India (2001) 'Census'. Available at: https://censusindia.gov.in/Census_Data_2001/Census_data_finder/C_Series/Population_by_religious_communities.htm (accessed 23 October 2020).

Cohen, R. and Fischer, C. (eds) (2019) *Routledge Handbook of Diaspora Studies*. London: Routledge.

Goswami, C. (2016). *Globalization Before Its Time: The Gujarati Merchants from Kachchh*. Delhi: Penguin Books India.

Hegde, R.S. and Sahoo, A.K. (eds) (2017) *Routledge Handbook of the Indian Diaspora*. London: Routledge.

Hindu Temple Management (2020) Available at: http://hindutemplesom.com (accessed 6 November 2020).

Ilias, M.H. (2015) 'Malayalee migrants and translocal Kerala politics in the Gulf: re-conceptualising the "political"', in Gorman, A. and Kasbarian, S. (eds) *Diasporas of the Modern Middle East*, Edinburgh: Edinburgh University Press, pp. 303–337.

Jaffrelot, C. and Therwath, I. (2007) 'The Sangh Parivar and the Hindu diaspora in the west: what kind of "long-distance nationalism"?' *International Political Sociology*, 1(3), pp. 278–295.

Jayaram, N. (ed.) (2004) *The Indian Diaspora: Dynamics of Migration*. Delhi: Sage Publications India.

Khashan, H. (2016) 'Religious intolerance in the Gulf states', *Middle East Quarterly*, 23(3). Available at: www.meforum.org/6044/religious-intolerance-in-the-gulf-states

Kurien, P. (2015) 'Hinduism in the United States', in Hatcher, B.A. (ed.) *Hinduism in the Modern World*, London: Routledge, pp. 143–157.

Lal, B.V. (1996) 'The Odyssey of indenture: fragmentation and reconstitution in the Indian diaspora', *Diaspora: A Journal of Transnational Studies*, 5(2), pp. 167–188.

Lucia, A. (2014) 'Innovative gurus: tradition and change in contemporary Hinduism', *International Journal of Hindu Studies*, 18(2), pp. 221–263. doi: 10.1007/s11407-014-9159-5

Mazumdar, S. and Mazumdar, S. (2009) 'Religion, immigration, and home making in diaspora: Hindu space in Southern California', *Journal of Environmental Psychology*, 29(2), pp. 256–266.

Mehta, S.R. and Onley, J. (2015) 'The Hindu community in Muscat: creating homes in the diaspora', *Journal of Arabian Studies*, 5(2), pp. 156–183.

Ministry of Justice and Legal Affairs (1996) 'Royal decree (101/96)'. Available at www.mola.gov.om/eng/basicstatute.aspx (accessed 2 November 2020).

Onley, J. (2009) *The Arabian Frontier of the British Raj: Merchants, Rulers, and the British in the Nineteenth Century Gulf*. Oxford: Oxford University Press.

Onley, J. (2014) 'Indian communities in the Persian Gulf, c. 1500–1947', in Potter, L. (ed.) *The Persian Gulf in Modern Times: People, Ports, and History*. New York: Palgrave Macmillan. pp. 231–266.

Oommen, G.Z. (2015) 'Transnational religious dynamics of Syrian Christians from Kerala in Kuwait: blurring the boundaries of belief', *South Asia Research*, 35(1), pp. 1–20.

Pande, A. (ed.) (2020) *Indentured and Post-Indentured Indian Women: Changing Paradigms and Shifting Discourses*. Singapore: Springer.

Parekh, B. (1994) 'Some reflections on the Hindu diaspora', *Journal of Ethnic and Migration Studies*, 20(4), pp. 603–620.

Peterson, J.E. (2004) 'Oman's diverse society: northern Oman', *The Middle East Journal*, 58(1), pp. 32–51.

Pew Research Center (2009) *Global Restrictions on Religion*. Washington, DC: Pew Research Center.

Potter, L.G. (2017) 'Society in the Persian Gulf: before and after oil', *CIRS Occasional Papers*, 18. Qatar: Georgetown University.

Raj, A. (2012) 'The Indian diaspora in North America: the role of networks and associations', *Diaspora Studies*, 5(2), pp. 107–123.

Sahoo, A.K. (2013) 'Reconstructing religious and cultural identity of Indians in the diaspora: the role of Sri Sathya Sai Baba movement', *Sociological Bulletin*, 62(1), pp. 23–39.

Sud, N. (2008) 'Tracing the links between Hindu nationalism and the Indian diaspora', *St Antony's International Review*, 3(2), pp. 50–65.

Thobani, S. (2019) 'Alt-right with the Hindu-right: long-distance nationalism and the perfection of Hindutva', *Ethnic and Racial Studies*, 42(5), pp. 745–762.

Vásquez, M.A. and Knott, K. (2014) 'Three dimensions of religious place making in diaspora', *Global Networks*, 14(3), pp. 326–347.

Vertovec, S. (2000) *The Hindu Diaspora: Comparative Patterns*. London: Routledge.

Vertovec, S. (2019) 'Talking around super-diversity', *Ethnic and Racial Studies*, 42(1), pp. 125–139, doi: 10.1080/01419870.2017.1406128

Vertovec, S. (2020) 'Complexifying complex diaspora' [video], talk at Migration, Diasporas and Sustainable Development: Perspectives, Policies, Opportunities and Challenges, 2–5 November 2020. Global Research Forum for Diaspora and Transnationalism. Available at: www.youtube.com/watch?v=716QD90xE88 (accessed 3 November 2020).

Williams, R. (1998) *Religions of Immigrants from India and Pakistan: New Threads in the American Tapestry*. Cambridge: Cambridge University Press.

INDEX

Adib, August 119–21
Afewerki, Isaias 78
Africa 58, 182, 193, 254, 377, 383, 401; East Africa 15, 79, 368–70, 373, 421; North Africa 9, 91, 93–5, 104–15, 203
agency 8, 32, 78, 83, 101, 115, 152, 217–18, 304, 352–3, 355–8, 360, 362, 407, 410–11, 430
Ahmadinejad, Mahmoud 66, 188
Ahmed, Shahab 396, 402
Al Houda (newspaper) 123
Al Irshad (association) 373
Aleppo 24, 200, 279, 281, 290, 293, 407, 409
Alevi 7, 40, 42, 44–5, 48, 53, 159–60, 162–7; Euro-Alevi 164, 167
Alexandria 52, 120, 359, 408
Algeria 91, 94, 104–5, 107, 109–10, 114, 400
alienation 2, 80, 110, 174–5, 213–14, 323
Alkatiri, Zeffry 388
Allawi', Iyad 321
Al–Houwayek, Patriarch Elias 125
al-Muhajir, Ahmed bin Isa 368, 376
Al-Nakba 329–30, 332
al-Sadr, Musa 143
Alsagoff, Syed Imran 388
al-Sawda, Yousef 118–23
al-Zayn, 'Abdul Mun'am 143, 150
Amazigh activism 9, 92–101
ambivalence 5, 14, 42, 215, 230, 336, 338, 344, 376
American Coptic Association (ACA) 59–60, 62
Amman 205, 278, 317
anti-Semitism 238, 246
Aoun, Michel 151
Appadurai, Arjun 197
Appropriate Behavior 10, 171–2, 175, 177, 179
Arab nation 125, 127, 151; Arab nationalist 126, 307, 409; Arab nationalism 57–8, 321; Arab kingdom 123–4

Arabic newspaper 23, 27, 29–30, 32–6
Arabisation 15, 91, 105, 110–11, 114, 384–5, 387, 389
Arabness 5, 15, 182–4, 188, 197–8, 203–6, 221–2, 224, 227, 385, 389
Argentina 25, 27–8, 30, 305, 309–12
Armenian genocide 40–4, 46–7, 407
Art of Living 420, 428–30
artistic expression 10, 193, 403
assimilation 3, 54, 93, 110, 172, 175, 182, 210, 223, 252, 256, 257, 259, 308, 318–19, 415
Assyrian 1, 7, 42, 305, 316, 341, 409
authoritarianism 1, 13, 133, 166, 283, 354, 410; authoritarian 83, 85–6, 132, 162, 316, 326, 351, 407; anti-authoritarian 97

Ba Alawi (Alawiyyah Sufi order) 368, 371
Ba'th 316–17
Bahrain 252, 258, 368, 422
Bangladesh 250, 253, 256, 334
Beirut 24, 118, 120, 124, 143, 146, 153, 199–200, 288–9, 305, 307, 309–10, 407–9, 415
Berlin 41–2, 44, 162, 166, 200, 205, 238–9, 242–4, 392
Bhabha, Homi 4, 193
biographical availability 92, 96; autobiographical 175–6, 178, 303, 305–6
Boston 121, 212, 239, 243, 307, 312, 396–9, 414
Bourdieu, Pierre 114, 117–19
Brah, Avtar, 394, 397–8, 400
Brazil 25, 28–30, 184, 304, 309, 312
Britishness 14, 324–5
broker: community 230; trade 265; cultural 267–9, 271, 318
Brubaker, Rogers 2, 30–1, 131, 143–4, 161, 260, 263, 329
Bush, George W. 69, 72, 322

Index

businesses 12, 30, 55, 58, 136, 145, 149, 212, 256, 259, 264, 269, 277–80, 283, 292, 310, 373, 375, 412, 414, 423, 428

Cairo 7, 52, 55, 61–2, 82, 120, 124, 199–200, 205, 354, 359, 369, 386, 391, 408, 410–12, 415
Canadian Coptic Association (CCA) 59–60
careers 92, 212, 221, 227, 230–2, 247, 351; activist careers 96, 100; career-making 11, 221
Catalonia 9, 94–6
Chalabi, Ahmed 321
Christian 26, 28, 54–62, 80, 238, 325, 334, 369, 374, 391, 400–1, 406, 409–10, 422, 428; Lebanese 24, 118–20, 122, 144, 146–53, 216, 310; Orthodox 25
citizenship rights 32, 39, 41
clandestine political movements 84, 86
classical diasporas 405
Clifford, James 4, 8, 105–6, 182, 318–19
coexistence 57, 144, 256, 385, 406, 408, 410
Cohen, Robin 4, 8, 96, 329, 356, 415, 423
collective action 8, 31, 68–9, 71, 73, 75, 101, 131, 134, 140, 161, 355
collective identity 2, 69, 131, 141, 150, 160–2, 164, 352–4, 356–7, 362, 373
colonialism 1, 108–10, 120, 182, 188, 190, 391; French 146, 148, 152; homocolonialism 183, 187, 190–1
communal trust 274, 283
community arts 222, 229, 231
community centres 83–4, 86, 426
Congrès Mondial Amazigh (CMA) 104, 107, 109
connectivity 14, 348–9
co-optation 83–5
Coptic Orthodox Church 53, 59, 61–2
corruption 29, 209, 218, 411
cosmopolitan 10, 53, 55, 57, 60, 62, 73–5, 49, 174–5, 177, 217, 219, 224, 238, 391, 408, 421; cosmopolitanism 178, 256; cosmopolitans 224, 415
countercultural 198
creative industries 11, 221, 227, 229, 231, 244
creative labour 223
creative migrants 239, 247
creative migration, broader relevance of 238, 241
creole (histories) 15, 383, 385–8, 391–2
Crescent 396, 400–402
critical events 53–4, 61, 63, 97
cultural capital 120, 217, 221, 238, 246, 267, 271
cultural politics 5, 305, 389
cultural production 4–5, 181, 317, 320, 408–10, 412
cultural workers 221

Damascus 199, 306, 311, 317, 320, 323, 409
de-mobilisation 132, 137, 139
democratic transition 93, 130–2, 137

demographic imbalance 253
deportation 8, 82, 311–12, 323
de-Turkification 164–5
diaspora activism 7, 9, 91–3, 97, 101, 109, 112, 130
diaspora associations 100, 105, 112, 130–2, 134–5, 138–140
diaspora consciousness 5, 10, 181–2, 187, 221
diaspora diplomacy 108
diaspora engagement 39–42, 44–5, 48
diaspora organisations 331; Tunisian 44–5, 131, 134–5, 137; Syrian 291–6; Coptic 60; Amazigh 92, 101
diaspora space 11, 252, 394, 397–8, 400–1; Muslim diaspora space 15, 394–5, 397–400, 402
diaspora studies 2, 4, 69, 85, 171, 173, 238, 246–7, 250, 318, 394, 400, 405, 407
diaspora tax 8, 79, 81, 83–5
diaspora tourism 329, 331
diasporic activists: Coptic 52–4, 60–2; Amazigh 93
diasporic communities 10, 12, 14, 139, 144, 172, 179, 231, 237, 251–2, 256–9, 283, 318, 349, 396, 413, 430; Turkish 40, 42, 45, 160, 341–3, 347; Iranian 173, 178; Lebanese 214, 218–19, 223; Arab 228; Israeli 246; Indian 252; Hui 263, 270–1; Iraqi 13, 317, 320, 326; Hadrami 368, 370; Coptic 59; Eritrean 83
diasporic critical spaces 219
diasporic identity 53, 58, 67–9, 73–4, 153, 175, 179, 193, 229, 263, 378, 397, 402, 408–9
diasporic political field 117–18, 122, 127
diplomatic missions 79, 81, 83–4, 322
Dirlik, Arif 219
discrimination 3, 13, 29, 56, 59, 62, 67, 69–70, 72, 74, 96, 150, 182, 213–14, 254, 257, 276–7, 279, 308, 337
displacement 3–5, 7, 181, 200–1, 215, 219, 286, 304, 316, 334, 355–6, 362, 395, 397–400, 402, 405
documentary (film) 329, 412
domestic workers 79, 81, 82, 253, 426
dress 58, 111, 184, 187, 189, 199, 214–15, 378, 384
Dubai 12, 250–60, 289

Education in their own Language and Culture (OETC) 98
electronic dance music (EDM) 197–206
Emiratis 253, 255
entrepreneurship 11, 225, 238–9, 244, 246, 282
Eritrea 8, 78–86, 369
Eritrean national service 78–9, 83, 85
Eritrean People's Liberation Front (EPLF) 80–1, 84
Eritreans 1, 8, 78–86

Ethiopia 78–81, 83, 86, 253, 369–70, 374, 408
European Union 162–3
Euro-Turk 10, 160–6
exclusion 7–8, 10–2, 24, 67–9, 73–4, 78, 80, 110, 127, 144, 152, 182, 194, 212–14, 217–19, 224, 231, 256, 336, 375, 415; exclusionary 7, 36, 42, 69, 161–2, 165, 167, 232, 251, 254, 408
exploitation 86, 370, 386

Facebook 66, 68, 70, 73, 138, 166, 281, 377
faith 54, 223, 323–5, 391, 396, 420–1, 424
Florida, Richard 238–42, 246
forced displacement 7, 356, 405
forced exile 351–3, 356, 359, 362
forced labour 79, 81–2
forced migration 316, 320
French West Africa 145
Friedman, Susan, 400

gay community 188, 215, 219
Gay International 190–1
General Gouraud 124
generational differences 96–7, 101, 138, 140, 317, 319, 326, 332
genocide 40–8, 406–8, 412
Ghanem, Shukri 123, 126
Gibran, Gibran Khalil 121–2, 125
Gilroy, Paul 5, 182, 342
global discourses 9, 93
global inequalities 237
global narratives 5–6, 210, 217
Global North 79, 186–8, 252–3, 259, 304, 394, 402
global politics 66–8, 75
global trade 12, 270–1
globalisation 1, 6, 172, 190, 218–19, 317
government services 79, 81, 287
Greater Syria 7, 24, 26, 31, 122–6, 144, 304–5
Green Movement 4, 8, 66
grief 73, 201, 329, 333–4, 337–8
guest worker 40–1, 92, 97, 162, 166, 405
Gulf Cooperation Council (GCC) 78–86, 250–2, 254, 258–9, 378, 420–2
Gulf States 12, 78–81, 83–4, 86, 251, 253–4, 256, 260, 295, 367, 375, 378, 413–15, 423
Gurbet 341–2, 344, 346–9

Habib Syech Bin Abdul Qadir Assegaf (Habib Syech) 384, 388–90
Hadramaut 15, 383, 385–8
Hadramis 15, 367–79, 383–7, 389–92
Halimah Yacob 390
Hall, Stuart 5, 106, 108, 131, 140, 318
hierarchies 11, 14, 55–6, 58, 147, 160, 218, 222, 251, 253–6, 318, 352–5, 357–62, 385, 397
Hill Collins, Patricia 215
Hizbullah 143, 150–1, 153

homecoming 14, 325–6, 329, 333, 336
homeland authorities 86
homemaking 8–9, 428
homing desire 394, 397–8, 401
homocolonialism: 181, 183–4, 187, 190–1
homonationalism: 181, 189, 190–1, 194
homophobia 182, 184, 188, 190, 230
host society 2, 4, 10, 13, 59, 78, 84, 92, 99, 143–4, 149, 166, 212–13, 215–16, 219, 251, 267, 268–9, 275–6
hostland 67–9, 210, 250, 263; *see also* host society
humanitarian aid 13, 286–8, 290, 295–6
humanitarian crisis 409
Hussein, Saddam 316–17, 319–24, 326, 400
Hybridity 13, 105, 110, 193, 229, 252, 304, 218, 319–20, 323, 326, 397
Hyderabad 372, 376, 378

Ibadhi 368
identity formation 111, 153, 164, 193, 362, 399
ideology 80, 144, 151, 160, 163, 312, 325, 351–3, 355–6
imagined communities 130, 141, 167, 262
Imazighen 1, 3, 91–2, 95, 98, 100, 104, 106–9, 112, 114
immigration 24, 32, 53, 55–6, 58, 72, 78, 94, 97–100, 105, 114, 131, 139, 143–7, 153, 212, 259, 303, 305, 307, 309, 312–13, 341, 343–4, 347
independence 55, 78–81, 83, 100, 105, 107, 118, 120, 124–7, 130, 143–6, 148–52, 211, 307–8, 329, 372–3, 375, 377, 387, 409, 421
Indian Ocean 15, 367–8, 374, 378, 383, 385–6, 389, 392, 421, 423
indigeneity 9, 93, 105–8, 111–12, 114–15
Indigenous 3, 8–9, 91, 98, 104–15, 147, 194, 222, 226
Indonesia 15, 253, 372–5, 377, 284–92
integration 3, 13, 39, 43, 45, 54, 70, 95, 97–101, 147–50, 152, 172, 175, 238, 246–7, 250, 257, 304, 308–10, 318, 330–1, 353–5, 374, 399, 411, 415
intimidation 60, 63, 80, 332, 361
invention of tradition 121
Iranian Americans 8, 10, 66–74, 171, 173, 175, 178
Iranian election 68, 70, 72–4
Iranianness 171–75, 178
Iraq National Congress (INC) 321–2
Iraqi Communist Party 321
Iraqi Jews 316
Iraqis 13, 201, 316–17, 319–20, 322–3, 325–6
Iraqis of "Iranian origin" (*taba'iyya*) 323
Islam, 394–5, 398, 401–2; African Islam 147
Islamic education in China 262–6, 270
Islamophobia 42, 54, 115, 226, 230, 247, 336, 395, 403

Israel 2, 9, 12, 14, 24, 45, 56–7, 144, 151, 238–47, 316, 328–33, 336, 391

jaaliya 29, 31–3, 36
Jeddah 82–5, 374
Jews 1, 15, 23–4, 44, 46, 55–7, 238, 243–4, 305, 311, 316, 331–2, 385, 391, 397, 399, 405

Kafala system 81–2, 85, 375
Kamel, Mustafa 120
Kerala 371–2
Khairallah, Khairallah 121–3
Kurdish movement 47, 163–5, 317
Kurdishness 163–5, 325
Kuwait 201, 254, 319, 320, 375, 400, 422

labour and residence laws 78
Law on Education in Allochthonous Languages (OALT) 99–100
Le Temps (newspaper) 123–4
League of Liberation of Syria and Lebanon 125
League of Nations 23, 34, 124, 127, 307, 309–10, 409
Légion d'Orient 126
long–distance nationalism 47–8, 58, 117–18, 306, 317, 320
loyalty 42, 47–8, 67, 84–6, 231, 245, 344, 347, 354, 361, 395, 413

Madrid 9, 93–4, 96
mahbere-koms 79, 84–5
mahjar 6, 13–15, 31, 34–6, 52–3, 61–3, 303–12, 379
Malay world 15, 383–92
Malaysia 15, 267, 357, 362, 374, 378, 384–92, 401, 426
Maldives 370–1
Mandate 31, 309–10; British 7, 23–5, 30, 34, 36, 305, 311, 334; French 9, 23, 30, 123, 125, 127, 144–5, 307, 310–12, 407, 409
marginalisation 2, 8, 12, 80, 86, 93, 172–3, 210, 212, 216–17, 219, 224, 268, 323, 330, 342
Maronite 120, 125, 151, 225, 306
masculinities 11, 222, 224, 229, 231, 282, 307
materiality 255, 333
Melbourne 222
memory 2, 68, 110–11, 114, 201, 250–1, 329, 332–5, 355, 401, 412, 414
methodological nationalism (critique of) 6, 10, 105, 160, 167, 237
middlemen 150, 267–8, 367
millet system 15, 406, 408, 410
minority 40, 54, 58, 81, 93, 100, 109, 148–8, 151–3, 165, 193, 213, 222, 243, 270, 287, 338, 368, 384, 395, 398, 411–13, 421, 430
mobilisation 4, 8, 47, 53–4, 58, 70–1, 80, 83, 101, 126–7, 140, 162, 352, 361, 387

Montreal 54, 56–8, 60–1, 198–205, 209–11
Morocco 6, 91–4, 97–101, 104, 262, 270, 397, 399
Moukarzel, Noam 123, 125–6
Mount Lebanon Mutasarrifate 118
mourning 201–2
Mousavi, Mir–Hossein 66
mukhabarat 280–1
multicultural 5, 57, 244, 255–6, 259; multiculturalism 99, 210, 218, 223, 227, 304, 424; policies 211; multiculturalist 98, 221–2, 230
Muslim British subjectivity 325
Muslim diaspora, 263, 395–396
Muslimness, 15, 394–403

Naimy, Mikhail 122, 125
narrative: nationalist 411, 415; diasporic 3, 5, 24, 108, 119, 179, 209, 341, 413; historical 54, 119–21, 153; global 5–6, 210, 217
national identity 42, 44, 46, 48, 61, 67, 117, 121, 123–4, 141, 152, 159, 164–6, 188, 375, 387; ethno–national identity 117, 144; transnational identity 226
National Union of Eritrean Women (NUEW) 85
nation–state 5, 7, 9–10, 13, 41–2, 96, 105, 117–19, 123, 127, 152, 159, 161, 255, 263, 318–19, 375
naturalisation 8, 79, 309
The Netherlands 92–3, 97–101, 240
New York City 66–7, 70, 73–4, 125, 212–13, 244, 308, 312
9/11 15, 67, 71–2, 74, 395–6; *see also* September 11
nostalgia 10, 114, 172–3, 175, 177, 201, 206, 225, 252, 279, 306, 317–18, 329, 335–6, 342, 412
Noujaym, Boulous 118–21, 123

occupation 1; Israeli occupation 332; Ethiopian occupation 80; Algerian occupation 110; Ottoman occupation 306; British occupation 316; US occupation 320
Oriental music 202–4
Orientalism 67, 172, 175, 184, 188; self–Orientalism 183, 227
otherness 1, 173, 222, 229, 321; othering 5, 11, 173, 188, 217, 396
Ottoman: Empire 23–5, 43–4, 119, 123, 145, 159–60, 286, 304, 306, 309, 312, 386, 414; neo–Ottoman 407; subjects 24, 308, 311

Palestinian citizenship 7, 23–4, 31–3, 35–6, 335
pan-Arabism 147–8, 197, 317
Paris 44, 95, 104, 107, 110–12, 120, 122–6, 133–4, 143, 209–10, 212, 216–17, 224, 415

Index

passport 32–3, 79, 81, 84, 86, 149, 245, 254–5, 303, 309, 310, 312, 329, 331, 376–7, 385
patriarchal norms 211–12, 214, 221, 231, 410
Peace Conference in Paris 120, 122–3, 125, 307, 309
peacebuilding 117, 290, 294–5
People's Front for Democracy and Justice (PFDJ) 78, 81, 84
persecution 1–2, 7, 54, 55, 58–9, 80, 151, 192, 316–17, 320, 354–5, 357, 412, 421
Persian 68, 70–1, 74, 174–5, 178–9, 262–70, 323, 371, 414
Peru 23, 27–8, 31–2
philanthropy 13, 219, 286, 289–96, 312, 378
Phoenician 119–22, 144
Picot, Georges 124
pilgrimage 82, 323, 326, 329, 333, 376, 378, 390–1
plurilocality 6, 14–16
political engagement 4, 39, 80, 118, 126, 132, 135, 137, 173, 321, 337, 342
political opportunity 67, 69–70, 73, 93, 98, 130, 140, 161, 354
political oppression 8, 78, 81
political organisation 4, 30, 59, 63, 84, 113, 223
politics of belonging 198, 355
Pope Shenouda III 52, 61–2
postcolonial: era/period 91, 199–200, 258, 410; turn 406; theory 396, 193; context 105, 114; nation 182, 184; subject 194
Prince Faisal bin Al–Hussein 123–5
privilege 160, 211, 217, 238, 245, 247, 257–8, 260, 276
professionals 55–7, 59–60, 62, 70, 223, 226, 238–9, 241, 244–5, 247, 252–3, 257–9, 268, 294, 303, 306, 428
prophetic genealogy 386, 388–9, 391
proselytisation 369, 374
protest 8, 34, 41, 44, 46, 53, 60, 109, 151, 153, 241, 286, 331, 354, 407, 415; Gezi 162, 166; anti–imperialist 58; Iran 66–7, 69–71, 73–4

Qatar 256, 357, 362, 400
queer: -ness 171–2, 177, 188–9, 191, 193, 198, 206; -topia 172, 179

race 11, 15, 42, 110, 131, 146, 150, 152, 171–2, 184, 193, 232, 237, 308, 391
racialization 172–4, 188, 193, 223, 226, 231, 304, 387
racism 149, 173, 182, 188, 227, 229–31, 254, 308
Refugees (Geneva Convention on) 79–80
religion 15–16, 35, 44, 46–8, 54, 105, 121, 144, 146–7, 151–3, 166, 183, 219, 224, 252, 265–6, 268, 270, 319, 335, 342, 356, 396–9, 402, 411, 422, 424–5, 428
religious leaders 59, 62, 367, 369, 371–4, 410

religious minority 15–16, 40, 421–2, 429
remittances 7, 35, 53, 58, 97, 117, 132–4, 139, 143, 148, 162, 290, 309, 321, 376–8, 414; political 122–3, 125, 127; private 85; symbolic 118, 120; social 295; philanthropic 13, 290
Renan, Ernest 119
renewal 8, 14, 63, 81, 352, 361–2, 377–9
repatriation 13, 113, 271, 303–5, 307–12, 319, 329; politics of: 308–11; of conflict 377
repression 67–8, 83–5, 97, 101, 106, 108, 132–3, 184, 186, 274, 351–8, 360–2, 410
residency fees 82, 86
returned migrants 263–4, 266
revolution 415, 428; Tunisian 9, 130–41; Ottoman/Young Turk 30, 144, 306, 308; Iranian 66, 69, 71, 150, 173; Egyptian (2011) 359; Egyptian (Free Officers 1952) 55, 408
Rif 9, 92–5, 99, 101, 110; Riffian 95, 99, 105, 108, 110
Rihani, Amin/Ameen 125, 306
rituals 131, 331; religious 16, 144, 153, 324, 401, 420–1, 423–9

sada 368–74, 376–7; see also sayyid
Sadat, Anwar 52, 58–62
Safran, William 2, 4
Said, Edward 4, 172, 319; see also orientalism
Salafi 374, 377, 384, 389; Salafism 15, 138
saltanah 200
Samneh, George 121, 123
Saudi Arabia 8, 78–86, 266, 270, 374–5, 378, 384, 389, 422
sayyid 368, 371, 373, 376, 385–6, 388–9; see also sada
second-generation: Tunisian 133, 137; Lebanese-Australian 228; Turkish 345; Iranian-American 8, 66–74
sectarianism 143, 151, 287, 406, 411; sectarian violence 7, 52, 60, 323
secularism 71, 152
segmented diasporas 238
selfhood 161, 184, 320, 323, 325–6
September 11 67, 182, 213, 323; see also 9/11
sexualities 176–7, 183, 190, 198
Shafi'i 368–371
Shari'a 52, 60, 279, 424
Shi'i Islam 10, 144, 323
skilled migration 238–40; skilled migrants 243, 245; unskilled migrants 132, 258
social accountability 293–4, 296
social class 150, 152–3, 198
social responsibility 281
societal militarisation 81, 84
soft boundaries 238, 246
soundscape 197–8, 201
South Africa 46, 244
South Asian diaspora 251, 320

Southeast Asia 15, 368, 372–4, 376–8, 383–6, 388, 391–2
South–South Migration 153
Spain 9, 92–8, 368
sponsorship system 250, 252; *see also kafāla*
Sri Lanka 253, 370
stateless 7, 108
statelessness 330
state-owned enterprise (SOE) 263–4
step-homeland 406, 414
subaltern 112, 198, 411; subalternity 413
subjectivity 13, 167, 182, 184, 189, 318–19, 323–6, 348; indigenous 108, 114; subjectivities 2, 5, 14, 106, 115, 161, 190, 252, 257, 316–17, 352. 362, 394–6, 398–401; gendered 106, 111
Sudan 5, 79–83, 86, 361
surveillance 8, 69, 81, 85–6, 133, 147, 304, 309
Sweden 48, 159, 162–3, 166–7, 341–7
Syrian Central Assembly 123–5

Tabet, Ayoub 125
Tabet, Jack 119, 121
Tamazgha 91, 104–5, 108, 110, 114
Tamazight 94–6, 100, 105–6, 111–12
temporariness 3, 12, 250–1, 254, 259
Tölölyan, Khachig 4, 405
transculturalism 15, 192, 383–5, 388–91, 403
translation 5, 98–9, 160, 231, 268, 401
transnationalism 10, 40, 144, 152–3, 251–2, 258, 263, 270, 317–19, 415–16, 421, 428; transnational activism 7, 321, 353; transnational connections 10, 12, 144, 218, 258–9, 262, 319–20, 326, 430; transnational networks 16, 31, 108, 130, 252, 254, 258, 421, 430; transnational control 80; transnational Hinduism 420–1, 424, 429; transnational oppression 281; transnational organisations 80, 83, 420, 422; transnational relations 95, 117; transnational spaces 2, 4, 58, 84, 163, 262

transregional connections 385–91
Tunisia 9, 91, 104–5, 130–41, 199, 203
Turkishness 7, 10, 40, 42, 159–61, 163–6, 347, 397–9
Tyan, Ferdinand 119–20

UNHCR 81–2, 414
Union of Kurdistan (PUK) 321
United Arab Emirates (UAE) 252–6, 289, 375
unskilled labourers 79, 93, 132, 254, 258
US invasion of Iraq (2003) 224, 319, 322–3

Vertovec, Stephen 356, 421, 430
village visits 331–3
vulnerability 73, 252, 260, 287, 342–3, 347, 349, 407, 411

Wadi Doan 369, 374, 378
Wahhabi 384, 389
war: Lebanon-Israel War 9, 144, 146, 150–2, 239, 241; Second World War 55 Israeli-Arab War 56, 239; Eritrea-Ethiopia War 78; Algerian War 114; Lebanese Civil War 143, 146, 209, 216, 223, 329–30; Syrian Civil War, 153, 286–7, 291, 413; Cold War 172, 387; Iran-Iraq War 201; Afghanistan War 223; Iraq War 223; Gulf War 319–20; First World War 7, 25, 30, 44, 58, 118, 120–1, 123, 125, 145, 304–6, 309, 406
West Africa 143–8, 152–3
Wilson, Woodrow 124–6
womanhood 218, 225–7
working class migrants 132, 221–2, 252, 254, 258

Yemen 81, 316, 367–9, 371–2, 375, 377–8, 383, 387–8, 421
Yiwu 262–4, 266, 268–70
Yuval-Davis, Nina 218

Zanzibar 370, 374, 423
Zionist 23, 31, 34, 57, 245